The European Right

The European Right

A Historical Profile

Hans Rogger and Eugen Weber

EDITORS

University of California Press

Berkeley and Los Angeles

University of California Press
Berkeley and Los Angeles, California
First Paper-bound Edition, 1966
Second Printing, 1974
© 1965 by The Regents of the University of California
ISBN: 0-520-01080-9
Library of Congress Catalog Card Number: 65-18562
Printed in the United States of America

Contributors

ISTVÁN DEÁK, Assistant Professor of History at Columbia University, is a native of Hungary. He has studied at the Sorbonne and at Columbia University.

J. R. JONES, who received his doctorate from Cambridge in 1953, is Senior Lecturer at the University of East Anglia. He is currently engaged in a study of conservative back-bench politics in the period before 1914. His book, *The Whigs*, was published in 1961.

ERNST NOLTE received his doctorate in philosophy at the University of Freiburg (Breisgau) in 1952. He is Professor of Modern History at the University of Marburg. Several of his studies on the problems of fascism and right-wing movements have appeared in German historical journals. His book, *Der Faschismus in seiner Epoche* (1963), has been translated into English under the title *Three Faces of Fascism*.

STANLEY PAYNE is Associate Professor of History at the University of California, Los Angeles. He is the author of *Falange* (1961), *A History of the Western World in Modern Times* (with S. B. Clough and Otto Pflanze, 1964), and *The Military in Modern Spain* (1966).

MARVIN RINTALA, who holds a doctorate in political science from the Fletcher School of Law and Diplomacy, has taught at Tufts and Brown Universities. He is now Associate Professor at

Boston College. His book, *Three Generations: The Extreme Right in Finnish Politics,* was published in 1962.

HANS ROGGER is Professor of History at the University of California, Los Angeles, and Director of its Russian and East European Studies Center. He has written *National Consciousness in 18th Century Russia* (1960), the Russian section of *The European Impact of the American Civil War* (1966), and a number of articles on topics of Russian and Soviet history.

SALVATORE SALADINO, who received his doctorate at Columbia University in 1955, is Associate Professor of History at Queens College, The City University, New York.

JEAN STENGERS is Professor of Contemporary History at the University of Brussels and editor of the *Revue Belge de Philologie et d'Histoire.* He has devoted several books to the Congo (notably *Combien le Congo a-t-il coûté à la Belgique?* and *Belgique et Congo: L'Elaboration de la Charte Coloniale*), and is now Chairman of the Commission of History of the Belgian Académie Royale des Sciences d'Outre-Mer. On Belgian history he has written numerous articles and a book, *Une Expérience d'enquête électorale,* published in 1959.

EUGEN WEBER is Professor of Modern European History at the University of California, Los Angeles, and Chairman of the Department of History. Among his books: *The Nationalist Revival in France* (1959), *Action Française* (1962), and *Varieties of Fascism* (1964).

ANDREW G. WHITESIDE, who received his doctorate at Harvard University, is Associate Professor of History at Queens College, The City University, New York. He is the author of *Austrian National Socialism before 1918.*

Contents

Introduction   EUGEN WEBER   1

England   J. R. JONES   29

France   EUGEN WEBER   71

Belgium   JEAN STENGERS   128

Spain   STANLEY PAYNE   168

Italy   SALVATORE SALADINO   208

Germany   ERNST NOLTE   261

Austria   ANDREW WHITESIDE   308

Hungary   ISTVÁN DEÁK   364

Finland   MARVIN RINTALA   408

Russia   HANS ROGGER   443

Romania   EUGEN WEBER   501

Afterthoughts   HANS ROGGER   575

The Right
An Introduction[*]

EUGEN WEBER

Left and Right: Which is which? Who belongs to which? It is a question, here, of categories, definitions, and classifications so commonplace that we scarcely give it a thought. Walter Theimer's *Encyclopedia of World Politics* tells us that right-wing parties are the conservative and nationalist parties whose representatives customarily sit on the right-hand side when viewed from the president's chair. The *Petit Larousse* explains that "the Right includes the least advanced parties," and "the most advanced parties sit at the extreme left." But what, after all, is an "advanced" party? "They accuse us of belonging to the extreme Right," an ex-Algerian settler was to tell an interviewer of *France-Observateur* (April 18, 1963). "We are on the right because the proletariat is now on the right. As soon as one of our members does well for himself and earns a good living, he reads the left-wing papers. . . ." So the position has become more ambiguous since the days of the French National Assembly in which "the progressives sat on the left, the moderates in the center, and the conservatives on the right." Moderates may still sit in the center, but on the wings the situation is nebulous and the distribution of the political spectrum increasingly uncertain.

[*] I wish to express my thanks to the American Council of Learned Societies and the John Simon Guggenheim Memorial Foundation whose fellowships, in 1962 and 1963–64 respectively, facilitated the preparation of my essays in this book, and to the Research Grants Committee of the University of California, Los Angeles, for its constant and helpful generosity.

Did Peron belong to the Right because he was a dictator, or to the Left because much of his power rested on the unions? Is a nationalistic dictator like Nasser on the Right, or does his radicalism, his reformism, place him on the Left? Does dictatorship automatically classify a man, a party, a regime, as being of the Right, and, if so, what do we do about Stalin or Tito? Does radicalism or revolution provide an automatic definition of the Left or does it allow for Kemal Ataturk and Nasser? We see there can be revolutions of the Left and Right, dictatorships of the Left and Right, planned economies of the Left and Right and, obviously, totalitarianism of the Left and Right. Can we find the criterion of the Left in its popular appeal, its reliance on universal suffrage? But the most reactionary demagogues rely on popular appeal; and plebiscitarian dictatorships like that of Napoleon III, like that of Hitler, rest on universal suffrage, as many conservative regimes have done. We know at least, or think we know, that the Left tends toward change, and the Right to conserve: this puts Ataturk on the left, with Hitler and Porfirio Diaz; and Franco, Baldwin, Salazar, Poincaré, and Churchill in the same right-wing basket.

It would seem, in effect, that the label is cracking. We continue to use it but no longer know, cannot possibly know for sure, quite what it covers, quite what we mean. Even more than big and small or good and bad, Left and Right have become a matter of opinion not of fact, a matter of taste not definition. Unlike "big and small," however, scale serves only to confuse the issue, for, whereas the bigger is more obviously big, more obviously different from the small, the extreme Right is less obviously different from the extreme Left. In politics, the two extremes have much in common, and since, in talking of Right and Left, we often think of extreme examples as being supposed to embody the most significant characteristics, it follows that, by referring to the areas where these features are most confused, we make confusion worse confounded.

Over the past hundred years a great deal of attention has been directed to political movements and ideologies of the Left, but relatively little to their opposite numbers of the Right.[1] Identified

---

[1] A note on spelling might be appropriate at this point. We have *tried* to use capitals for specific political phenomena, lower case for political topography or

either with unthinking reaction or with stupid conservatism, the latter has appeared largely as a negative force with little interest for the political analyst. The major exceptions to this rule were furnished by Fascism and National Socialism, but even these are only just beginning to be studied without prejudice. Usually, Fascism and Nazism have been viewed as forms of antidoctrinaire activism or opportunistic power politics masquerading behind a nonsense cult of blood and race, strange phenomena exploding into maleficent being outside historical context. Good studies of either remain to be written, and most other political expressions of the extreme Right still await a chronicler.

The general public has barely begun to differentiate between conservative and radical phenomena, of either Left or Right. The distinction is rendered more difficult by the generalized use of such terms as nationalism, socialism, revolution, action, order, and freedom, without much effort to clarify their meaning. On the other hand, as we have just seen, apparently antagonistic doctrines and parties have more in common than their open opposition may lead one to suppose. We might understand certain political phenomena better by identifying them as radical or moderate, theoretical or spontaneous, than by trying to fit them into categories experience is rendering out of date.

This is a conclusion that several of the contributors to this volume seem to have reached and which I have tried to argue in an essay, "New Wine in Old Bottles," printed in the *French Historical Studies* of 1959. But the categories survive the criticism and persist in the language, hence in the reality, of political thought and action. Since we cannot analyze Right and Left away, it seems worthwhile to try to understand them. And since so much attention has been devoted to the Left, an introduction to its necessary counterpart seems in order. By bringing together a number of essays on right-wing movements and their origins we hope to throw some

---

attitudes. Thus we write of the Conservative, Liberal, or Radical parties, but of conservative, liberal, or radical tendencies; we speak of the Right as a specific body whose sympathizers are on the right, and of nationalism or fascism as doctrines sometimes expressed in National(ist) or Fascist movements and parties. This practice, which the nature of the subject makes necessary, can be confusing at times, a fact for which we apologize from the outset,

light on the sources, the nature, and the ideology of these little-known phenomena. Because of this interest in the original pattern, we have on the whole avoided discussion of right-wing regimes that reached power. Besides, when it becomes successful, the extreme Right tends to turn into something else, which it is not our object to examine here.

We did not try to be exhaustive. Contributors were asked to approach the subject in general, synthetic terms, dispensing with the usual scholarly apparatus of references and notes; but, for those who may want to read further, a brief list of suggested readings follows each essay. Nor did we attempt to cover all the wide field of the European Right, but contented ourselves instead with what seemed a fairly representative sample of the variety of movements and conditions that historians may encounter. There are essays on Western Europe—France, Belgium, England, and Spain; on Central Europe—Germany, Austria, and Italy; and on Eastern Europe—Russia, Hungary, Romania, and Finland. They discuss the movements of the extreme Right, its relations with conservative or moderate supporters of the established order, and also with its left-wing critics. They indicate that, although frequently anti-intellectual in their statements, the movements of the Right, more numerous and influential than we are sometimes told, developed definite and suggestive doctrines of their own which both reflected and affected the world in which they lived. They also show more clearly than has been done so far the differences between moderate and radical Right, and also between different kinds of right-wing radicalism.

It is possible to recognize certain constants: the love-hate relationship between old and new Right and also between the extremes of Left and Right; the organic doctrines of society—and hence of nationalism—and the part these play in right-wing thought; and the mythological component of extreme Right appeals—manifest destiny, national revival and revivalism, chosen people complex, and so forth. But before we turn to these, a word should be said about the major question that arises from a reading of these essays, that of defining not only the Right but the differences between and the relations of its various components. It was in the hope of such an answer that we undertook this study. But we are little nearer an answer now than we were when we started, if only because so many different answers have been offered, with almost as many interpretations as there are situations outlined in the essays that follow. The more we have inspected the image of the Right, the less sure we have become of what it is. So, what this book suggests is rather further questions than an answer, questions based on the variety of facts and interpretations here presented, and on the inconclusive tone we have of necessity adopted.

It seems that, even more than the Left, a given Right must be defined in terms of its particular situation. What may appear progressive or even revolutionary under certain conditions is part of the established order under others. Factors of comparison in certain circumstances do not exist in others. Some rightists regard representative institutions as leading to aristocracy, others to ochlocracy, others again cherish them as stabilizing factors. British, French, and Italian conservatives accept the parliamentary mode. German or Hungarian conservatives tend to be authoritarian. Nationalism, so often connected with the Right, shed its revolutionary associations only during the last third of the nineteenth century, and then only partly. British, Belgian, and Austrian conservatives do not appreciate nationalism; nor does the patriotism of French or Finnish moderates stretch to the immoderate lengths advocated by a more nationalistic Right.

Professor Saladino, for instance, contrasts the old Italian Right —moderate social conservatives, parliamentary, and liberal—with the new nationalistic Right that rose in the 1890's—a movement rather than a party, contemptuous of the parliamentary system, activistic, and radical. The former were "moderate in methods and conservative in outlook." The latter favored change for its own sake, but also change away from democracy: radical change in all existing institutions, to increase the power of the state which they set out to capture. The old Right envisaged the order it cared for in constitutional and parliamentary terms; the new wanted power, not to maintain the existing order, but to impose its own authoritarian new one. Where conservatives accepted the need for limits and concessions, a system of checks and balances appropriate to the pendulum swings of popular choice, the radicals' conception of political effectiveness was totalitarian.

What applies to Italy holds good with some variation for almost every country where any form of bourgeois liberalism had come to power: for Britain, France, and Belgium, where parliamentary and constitutional rule was well established by the end of the nineteenth century; for Finland, where such rule came with independence after 1917; even for Hungary, where parliament served the interests of a ruling coalition of landed and money interests. Finland's president, P. E. Svinhufvud, believed, Professor Rintala tells us, "in the rule of law." In 1932, to defend the law, this conservative nationalist scotched the nationalist revolt of the radical Lapua Movement. The People's Patriotic Movement (PPM) he then helped to set up was meant to provide a legal bourgeois front against both Socialism and Communism, and to be a Finnish counterpart of France's Croix de Feu, providing an alternative to more extreme nonparty movements of the Right which threatened the law, the peace, the order of the land.

Unlike the Croix de Feu, however, the Finnish PPM soon became more radical than its respectable founders had hoped, rejecting any connection with reaction, conservatism, or capital. The PPM declared itself closer to the Communists who were its foremost enemies than to existing parties: it wanted to provide "a creative radical alternative" to Communism. And in this also it was typical of its kind: Degrelle, the Belgian Rexist, has written that his stoutest troops came from Marxist ranks, and Szalasi, in Hungary, showed more sympathy for workers and peasants than for the effete and corrupt gentry and bourgeoisie. Everywhere the radical Right looks to the people, to the proletariat, and attacks capital and bourgeoisie. It can do this the better because of the phenomenon of transformism, which Saladino describes as the "obliteration of clear distinctions between Right and Left for the sake of securing a parliamentary majority. . . ."

In effect, in most countries, as Saladino tells of Italy, the coming to power of professed left-wing groups has meant not radical reforms but the moderation of the Left and the disappearance of former distinctions between the historical Right and historical Left.

This is the process that can be seen confusing French political issues, among others. True, while the historical Left became governmental and moderate, its place in the van of reform was taken by syndicalism and Marxism. But theirs were doctrines of class war; and their divisive radicalism did not have a general appeal, not even among the working classes. In the circumstances, right-wing radicalism seems to have served a multiple function: it replaced the edulcorated radicalism of the historical Left, offered a radical alternative to Marxism, and preached an apocalyptic myth that claimed to be unifying rather than divisive. In Italy, Corradini opposed "national socialism" to mere class socialism, transferring the concept of necessary war from the internal to the external plane. In Austria and Bohemia, National Socialist parties catered to the two dominant yearnings of modern radical democracy, proposing revolutionary changes both in socioeconomic and in national conditions.

But this is just what Ernst Nolte seems to have in mind when he describes the extreme Right as a mirror image of the radical Left. Radical Nationalists took over the Marxist argument that contemporary institutions, morality, and laws reflected the values and desires of the ruling group. Instead of concluding that the proletariat should oppose its own exclusive interest to that of the ruling bourgeoisie, they simply proclaimed the need for a total national good and national will to be imposed upon all. Their nationalistic appeal, however, was different from that of an earlier day. The revolutionary nationalism of the nineteenth century had been humanitarian, as all revolutionary doctrines grounded in the Enlightenment had been. Even the doctrine of class war had been sparked by humanitarian indignation. The nationalist revolutionaries of the twentieth century considered only mankind in the mass: "the sand of humanity," as Nietzsche said, "all very equal, very small, very round." Disillusioned, particularist, and pragmatic, they transferred the concept of class war onto a tribal plane, and their exclusivism discarded the liberal and universalistic implications of earlier nationalism.

For the new Right, social Darwinism was translated into national and racial terms, the dialectic of history worked itself out in the manifest destiny of nations. This reference to destiny, so common in nationalist and Fascist vocabulary, is typical of our times, when, as Malraux points out, the sense of destiny has taken over from the sense of freedom. Humanity's destiny, as the nineteenth century envisaged it, had been to advance toward ever greater freedom and self-realization. But where, once upon a time, destiny was the justification of conquest, today it serves more often to explain defeat. Far from being the captain of his soul, the master of his fate, contemporary man is conditioned; free at most to admit a fate that has been laid down for him in history or in the stars, living, as Pobedonostsev had it, in a world "where everything returns toward the primitive chaos and we in all this ferment feel ourselves impotent."

Whatever else it be, this modern destiny seems above all finite. For Spengler, the destiny of the West is death; and the equation of destiny with death appears after World War I in Paul Valéry's reminder that our civilization, too, is mortal, in Drieu La Rochelle's suicidal sense of doom, and in Karl Jasper's affirmation of a twilight of civilizations. "A man who is both active and pessimistic is a Fascist or will be one," writes André Malraux in *Man's Hope* (1937). Certainly, even when its language is optimistic, the underlying mood of the Right, particularly the extreme Right, is pessimistic and especially appropriate to a threatened or declining society, to men or social groups that feel disillusioned or resentful. "What is Fascism," asks Daniel Guérin in his *Fascisme et Grand Capital* (1945), "if not the direct product of Socialist failure?" For Max Ascoli and Arthur Feiler, in *Fascism for Whom?* (1938), "Fascism was the product of democratic decay." Thierry Maulnier, a disciple of Maurras, agrees: "The reason why 'fascisms' come into being is the political and social failure of liberal democracy. . . ." Whoever fails, some failure is the cause alleged: in Italy the extreme Right rises out of the disillusion following unification, in France out of disgust with Republican corruption, in England as in Russia or in Germany out of the shortcomings of the state, the debilities of empire.

In every instance, the growing power and significance of radical movements, whether Left or Right, is attributed to the unsatisfactory character of the available means of political expression; and this, in turn, is because of changes in the social and economic structures that had generated the classic political alignments and to which current political language and practice still clung. Recent studies of Asia and Africa suggest that the decay of traditional social and economic structures has played an important part in the development of their nationalistic movements. The same is true of European countries, where the last sixty or seventy years have seen a serious socioeconomic revolution and the growth of new classes not catered to by preëxisting political arrangements. More noted by sociologists than by historians, the gradual integration of the "outs," of the economically underprivileged, does much to explain the rightward drift of Western politics in our time. However, the lower-middle groups it helped to produce or grow were, quantitatively, a new social phenomenon made up of working people on their way up the socioeconomic ladder and bourgeois on their way down (even if only relatively so). For these people, the class-conscious arguments of the classic Left had no more appeal than the contented self-congratulations of conservatism. They were not satisfied with things as they were, but shunned the prospect of proletarian revolution.

Unable to fit into existing political divisions which did not reflect their needs or aspirations, they rejected both status quo and class war. Ideologically speaking, they tried to find some place above the inessential struggle of factions which, meaningless to them, were considered ipso facto harmful to the nation, that is to society as a whole with which, in true Marxist fashion, they identified their interests. Here we have the roots of what, eventually, would be labeled fascism and what, as a rule, provides the nationalist appeal. The new slogan that met their needs was a call for unity, above and beyond parties. Mussolini wrote as much when he explained the doctrine of Fascism in 1932, but fifty years before that the statutes of the *Ligue des Patriotes* had expressed the same idea: "Republican, Bonapartist, Legitimist, Orleanist, these are merely forenames. The family name is patriot."

The nationalist ideology, in other words, although it has many affinities with that of the historic Right (which is why when the former wanes or fails its troops generally go to swell the numbers of the latter), is neither Left nor Right. It is part of the attempt to cut out new political avenues, to forge doctrines fitted to the changing realities of the last three score years. Its apparent confusions are owing to the fact that the vast and growing group to which it can appeal, the displaced persons of twentieth century politics, are not a united whole, but divided into those who are clawing their way upward and those making desperate efforts not to slip down.

There is still one other thing to bear in mind. After World War I, in northwestern and most of Central Europe, the advocates of change had to struggle no longer against the traditional aristocracy or oligarchy of birth and privilege, but against the damned compact liberal majority of replete republicans and sometimes-radicals. In Eastern Europe, however, the sociopolitical structure was more reminiscent of nineteenth- than of twentieth-century conditions, bearing strong similarities to the revolutionary situation of 1848. The power struggle was waged between representatives of vested interests, and the irruption of new contenders for power into this restricted and antiquated arena had a peculiarly savage quality, reminiscent less of modern industrial society than of the chiliastic peasant and worker revolts of an earlier age. The concomitant on the doctrinal plane was an ideological simplicity, a yearning for purity and salvation, as absent from the restricted and dingy politics of the ruling local "elite" as from those of our more skeptical industrial society.

Much has been made of the fact that, as Seymour Lipset puts it in his essay on *Political Man* (1963), extremist movements presently "appeal to the disgruntled and the psychologically homeless, to the personal failures, the economically insecure, the uneducated, unsophisticated and authoritarian persons at every level of society." But, although social adjustment is usually a good thing, there are societies in which maladjustment seems desirable and refusal to adjust a positive virtue. In societies where economic development, educational attainment, and public morality are low, the honest and hard-working man may find himself disgruntled and psychologically homeless; strength of character may spell personal failure, enterprise and integrity may make for economic insecurity. Where illiteracy is rife and sophistication equivalent to cynical corruption, the judgments implied in Lipset's definition become questionable.

Societies fitting this description are not exceptional; their critics perform a useful function, and it is sometimes a toss-up whether such critics will swing toward extreme Right or Left. In circumstances, however, where the radical Left is crushed or otherwise eliminated from effective political activity, as was true in Hungary and Romania; or where nationalism appears to be a necessary political stance, as in the new nations struggling to free themselves from economic and political bonds that independence has not removed, the extremist of the Right may be a necessary, perhaps healthy, antibody reacting against stagnation or decay in the only way circumstances make possible: that is, by some form of violence.

In the industrially developed countries of Europe where some form of conservative moderation prevailed, the pendulum of ideological reference swung between temperate liberal reform and wistful traditionalistic reaction. Except in times of grave social and economic crisis or collapse, radical reaction was left to small bands of intellectuals and to isolated, uninfluential political mavericks. In the underdeveloped countries of Eastern Europe, however, the social basis of such middle-class conservatism was lacking. The good life was something close to the traditional ways of the land-owning gentry, the economy was geared to serve a code of conspicuous consumption amidst widespread scarcity. Dissent, reaction against such conditions, quashed in their liberal or leftist forms, could express themselves only in nationalistic terms: that is, on the radical Right.

The revolutionary potential of the peasantry, too, was a constant reality in Eastern Europe. Where peasant parties, tamed by middle-class leaders and a deferential mentality, failed to express the aspirations of the peasantry, national-socialist leagues appeared to exploit the mass of wretched small landowners and laborers, with their debts and frustrations, their hope for land or more land, their resentment of the new ways of financial or industrial enterprise and of the bureaucratic state. It is possible to see such leagues exploiting the pool of rural and just-up-from-the-land resentments and frustrations. It is equally true to say that these leagues answered a need that other political movements tried to stifle or ignore. Moderate reform provided no answer to the problems of these people. Only drastic economic changes could improve their lot, only drastic social and moral changes could eliminate the corrupt and cynical tone of an Establishment for which laissez faire, laissez passer was less an economic doctrine than a license to forage and plunder.

In circumstances such as these, status politics, even in the broadest sense of the term, were far less significant than breadbasket politics. The frustrations to which the agitator addressed himself were less emotional than material, and the role he could play in his country's politics more concrete and positive than that of his Western counterparts.

North American experience may here be misleading. As described in *The Radical Right* (edited by Daniel Bell, 1964) or in Edward Shils' *Torments of Secrecy* (1956), circumstances and problems in North America are radically different from those in the rest of the world. A highly mobile society stresses stability. A prosperous society insists on status. The call for domestic conformity, predominant in the United States, is only an incidental part of more positive European platforms which stress the dynamic potential of national unity rather than the mollifying aspects of conformist security.

We must beware of limiting the spirit of the Right to a simple protest against the fact that society is changing and/or against the direction of change. While this view, common to most of the contributors to Daniel Bell's suggestive symposium, also fits several movements of the European Right, other movements are best described as protests against the fact that society was not changing fast enough, and as demands for change—in whatever direction. This may be an exaggerated picture of the insistent, often aimless activism of the *fascios* or of Rex, of intellectuals *qui n'aiment que les trains qui partent,* of Balkan bully-boys marching for marching's sake. But, certainly, insistence on change and opposition to the existing order were more—and more often—in evidence than the Poujadism that comparisons with American attitudes tend to evoke.

One of the most stimulating contributions to the definition and classification of right-wing tendencies is to be found in Seymour Lipset's *Political Man*. In Chapter V of that work Lipset suggests three categories into which extremist ideologies and groups may be divided. The first is the *Center*, which includes the classic fascist movements; is statist and antiliberal, opposed to big business, trade unions, and socialism; and which appeals to the middle classes, "especially small businessmen, white-collar workers and the anticlerical sections of the professional classes." The second is the *Left*, which, like Communism at the opposite end of the political spectrum, appeals to the lower as against the middle and upper classes. The major difference between extremists of this category and Communists is the nationalism of the former. Their leaders are often army officers who want "to create a more vital society by destroying the corrupt privileged strata which they believe have kept the masses in poverty, the economy underdeveloped, and the army demoralized and underpaid." To Peron, whom Lipset cites as typical of this group, we might add figures such as that of Nasser in Egypt and perhaps even Szalasi in Hungary. Lipset's third category, that of the *Right*, is represented by such movements as those of Horthy, Dollfuss, Salazar, and Maurras. These "are conservative, not revolutionary," and "seek to change political institutions in order to preserve or restore cultural and economic ones, while extremists of the center and left seek to use political means for cultural and social revolution." Their followers tend to be wealthier, more traditionalistic, more religious, and monarchistic rather than totalitarian.

In some ways, Lipset's broad categories neatly solve the problem of differentiation. In other ways they are less satisfactory for, as with so many broad categories, some phenomena do not quite fit into the slots destined for them. Yet one can learn even from the shortcomings, which no speculative structure dealing with human activities can hope to avoid.

The *Right*, for instance, is supposed to include "movements" like those of Horthy in Hungary or Salazar in Portugal—which, however, never really existed as such, because, unlike Maurras, Horthy and Salazar had no movement of their own. Significantly, the policies of such men were not policies of movement at all, but were rather holding operations organized as a rule in alliance with, or with the approval of, moderate conservative forces. Like Antonescu, Franco, and Pétain, Horthy, Dollfuss, and Salazar rule or ruled over simili-monarchies devoted to what we may call the party of Resistance. Thus, Lipset's third category is useful largely to help us compare and contrast true extremist movements with those sometimes labeled so because of temporary alliances and superficial similarities.

If we turn to the middle-class fascists of the *Center*, we find a mentality characterized by frustrated resentment against modernization, rationalization, and reform, which is closer to the politics of Poujade than to those of Hitler. Indeed, for Lipset, Poujadism is a form of postliberal centrist authoritarianism similar to Nazism at least in its appeal and in its social roots. Yet neither National Socialists nor Fascists rejected the developing industrial order as the followers of Pierre Poujade have done, and Lipset's Poujadist small businessmen would surely be happier with Franco or Salazar than under the rule of a "classic fascist movement." In France, when they had the choice, they showed their true colors by preferring the Croix de Feu to rowdier leagues, and, later on, Pétain to Déat or Doriot.

As for the middle-class support enjoyed by the Nazis, this has to be placed in the historical context of the depression years. The same middle classes that voted heavily for the National Socialist German Workers' party preferred a conservative (*Right*) authoritarianism until faced with ruin and complete socioeconomic displacement. Only when the storm engulfed them did any port seem good. The public of Poujade is threatened by less urgent disasters. More important, the wrecks of these small businessmen are isolated events, private tragedies in a prosperous and booming economy. They appear to others neither the reflection of a common predicament nor a portent of things to come. It is, indeed, because the economy moves forward that they founder. These are not conditions propitious to a coherent or effective movement of dissent, let alone revolt. Nor do they recall the attitudes and preconditions of the National Socialists' triumph in Germany.

The most interesting of Lipset's categories, and the one I find most useful, is the second, that of the *Left*. If we count the peasantry among their number, the "unorganized working classes who are suffering from the tensions inherent in rapid industrialization" furnish the major social base of extremist movements hard to classify as either Right or Left. This is clearest in Asia, Africa, and Latin America. But fascism "of the Left" as described by Lipset in connection with the movements and policies of Juan Peron and Getulio Vargas is strongly reminiscent of Hungary and especially of Romania where socioeconomic conditions were similar to those of postcolonial nations, and also reminiscent of the predicament and activities of certain "displaced masses" in the advanced economies, such as the Breton peasants. Evidently, societies in the throes of urbanization and industrialization, dominated by foreign powers, exploited by foreign capital, germinate movements of protest and reform which all, whether labeled Communist or Fascist, Right or Left, appeal to the urban and rural disinherited, the poorer classes, and certain intellectual, idealistic, or authoritarian reformers in ways that make existing categories particularly confusing.

On the other hand, whether valid or not, reference to Left and Right is a reality in countries where, as in France, these have become essential terms of political definition, vocabulary, and thought. In this sense, the presence of a Left–Right dichotomy may itself provide a signpost of political analysis, suggesting a tradition of public political debate, a politicized and relatively literate public, and the kind of socioeconomic evolution we associate with the industrial development and structure of Western societies. This is the background that makes Left and Right meaningful terms. Professor Whiteside tells us that in Austria the Left–Right division was far less clear than in the West. There, as in Hungary and Romania, it represented alien categories superimposed on native realities of a different order; different because the country's economic and social evolution was different from that of the West, even if the imported political language hides the fact.

For my part, I am inclined to define the major components of the Right in terms of the three R's: Reaction against the tendencies of the present; Resistance to change; and Radicalism, which has radical change in mind. The first looks back to a golden age it would like to recapture by abolishing not only the present but the intervening period: back to the old regime with Maurras, back to a small-owners' and small-business world with Poujade. The second is essentially conservative, resisting proposed changes, defending instituted ones which have become part of the established order. *Natura,* they like to say, *non facit saltum.* English conservatism is the touchstone of this group which does not deny all change but resists it for a time with the argument that reforms must conform to the habits and traditions society has evolved. Satisfied reformers join it once they have achieved their ends, and thus the conservative or moderate supporters of Resistance are the most numerous section of the Right. Least numerous, perhaps, the Radicals are also the most active. They are the revolutionaries of the Right, sometimes confused with the party of reaction and often themselves confused. They do have in common with reactionaries a desire for radical change, a heartfelt rejection of the existing order, and a strong leaning to violence. And some conservatives may take up radical positions when an important cause or interest is threatened. But the most explicit aim of radicals is total power. Otherwise their program tends to vagueness. It was best expressed by Mussolini's words in the *Popolo d'Italia* of October 4, 1922: "The democrats of *Il Mondo* want to know our program? It is to break the bones of the democrats of *Il Mondo.* And the sooner the better."

Seen in this light, Bismarck appears as a radical; for, as Nolte shows us, he cared little for the form but much for the substance of power. Bismarck's vaunted conservatism was hardly conservative where the structure of institutions or politics both inside and outside Germany was concerned. It was antiliberal, antidemocratic, and devoted to enlarging the power of the state and of its rulers albeit by the most radical changes. But Bismarck belonged to an older generation and, although he made his debut on the very extreme of the Right, his policy was authoritarian but not totalitarian, and his statism comparable to that of pre-1917 Russia. Like the Russian state, that of Bismarck could be revolutionary at times. The state provides the great revolutionary force before the age of mass democracy. But it is hard to define it as of the Right or Left, as in a truly authoritarian system such categories have little relevance. They only become significant when freedom of thought and speech creates the opportunity for political action and debate. When Nolte tells us that "the origin of the Right always lies in the challenge of the Left," he indicates the impossibility of Right or Left existing in a totalitarian system when control is so complete that the party in power has no alternative against which to define itself. And this suggests that in the old-fashioned authoritarian world where the Right was almost everything, the square pegs of political decisions did not have to fit the round holes of a different political structure.

Once the aristocratic authoritarian system of the old regime had been replaced by one in which political decisions were left—at least in principle—to universal suffrage, the radical authoritarian approach of Bismarck was out of date. At the very least, it had to learn how to operate in new conditions; and conditions changed so rapidly as to outrun the change in formal institutions. The liberal politics of the nineteenth century were representative and parliamentary. But the representative system of which parliament is the symbol functioned adequately only in a deferential society, where distinction of achievement and wealth had replaced distinction of birth, but where the concept of distinction as such survived and the elector, who respected his representative, trusted him to serve his interests. The parliamentary representative system had been worked out by and for an elitist society not much more inclusive than the aristocratic society it replaced. In the mass society that took over at the end of the nineteenth century, with its democratic structure and its egalitarian ideology, parliament either did not, or was no longer felt to, work properly. Its shortcomings stood out, the bargains of everyday give-and-take became evidence of corruption, and compromise acquired a pejorative meaning, for mass society spoke in high-flown generalities and could not allow anything less than their integral fulfillment.

The mass electorate might have been more tolerant had it felt better represented. But the petite bourgeoisie on one hand, the newly significant industrial workers on the other, did not recognize either the pattern or the language of parliamentary politics as their own. The latter reflected the psychology of nineteenth-century elitist politics, which had been rationalistic and utilitarian: liberalism and marxism both argued that, in the end, men will understand their interests and act in consequence. But the psychology of a mass electorate, as John Stuart Mill discovered before Gustave LeBon, is irrationalistic, and politicians learned to appeal not to mind but to emotion, seeking less to persuade than to manipulate.

This development suited the Right, for, ever since it had been challenged by the rationalistic heirs of the Enlightenment, the Right had tended to depreciate reason as artificial and misleading, too far removed from personal experience and from the instinctive sources of reality. The peasant, it was argued, knows his land better than any agronomist, the slave-driver understands slaves better than any starry-eyed liberal, and no *déraciné*, no rootless intellectual, could ever feel the national reality, cultural or political, as one who was rooted in its blood and soil—*la terre et les morts*. All this was well enough but for the awkward fact that the established order most West European conservatives defended was itself founded on reforms, revolutions, constitutions inspired by reason, reasoning, and, often, by the liberal and enlightened tradition of the eighteenth century. The apparent contradiction could be resolved only by interpreting reason as the province of skepticism, cynicism, and pessimism; which resulted in a "clear-sighted" vision of decay or catastrophe, which in turn implied the authoritarian and elitist manipulation of the masses by grimly unidealistic power groups. The Machiavellian activities of this undeceived elite would find a necessary counterpart in the activistic and idealistic elitism of a would-be new aristocracy, the imitators of a nobility for whom, as Drieu La Rochelle put it, "thinking came down to giving and taking blows."

"Nothing is ever accomplished without bloodshed," Drieu would write in the same vein, in *Le Jeune européen* (1927). "I look forward to a bloodbath like an old man about to die." The sacrificial note and the expectation of resurgency deserve attention here. So does the reference to age and death by a man in his thirties. Here is a typical voice of the Right, the expression of a society on the downgrade. Its moderates were the optimistic liberals of yore, asking only to enjoy the fruits of past enterprise—and, after them, the deluge. Its extremists wanted to bring everything crashing down now, either because they thought they had lost all, or because they thought they had everything to gain. To them the only remedy lies in catastrophe, the only hope in catastrophic regeneration. It is a relevant fact that, in our time, the much used word "Apocalypse" stands not for the "revelation" of its old, true meaning, but for a catastrophic end. Apocalypse and Götterdämmerung are one. That is what revelation reveals!

It is on this ground that reconciliation proves possible between radicals of Right and Left and also between the three R's of the Right. The former can join in a *politique du pire* to bring the existing order down; and many a rapprochement between Nationalists and Syndicalists, between Fascists and Communists, can be explained only by the temporary conjunction of their hatreds. The antibourgeois, anticapitalist militant who leaves Communist for Fascist ranks, and sometimes vice versa, is a familiar figure; and d'Annunzio, whom Professor Saladino mentions crossing from extreme Right to extreme Left for the sake of "life and eloquence," presumably crossed back again for much the same reason. The fact is that, whatever their ultimate intentions, activists of any ilk find themselves involved in similar campaigns, similar organizational and didactic problems, so that the sociopolitical dynamism of their enterprise is stronger than the verbal differences between them. Thus the ideological options they may choose make little difference to the behavior of their agents as long as they remain in the realm of action. Hence the coincidences between extreme Right and Left.

On the other hand, the nationalism which is so much a part of the ideology of the radical Right prevented its attacks on the established order from being also attacks on the state itself. They wanted to capture the state, not destroy it, and found it hard to preach revolution and certainly to practise it as long as conservative nationalists were holding the levers of power. Thus there was little in radical appeals that posed a serious immediate threat to the more moderate Right, the party of Resistance, as long as the latter felt secure in their positions, political and social. When they felt threatened, on the other hand, the extreme Right's favorite slogans of national unity, patriotism, and order had a familiar sound, more reassuring than those that came from left-wing enemies of the regime. Thus, the British Military Attaché in Berlin could not "help feeling the most decent Britons, were they Germans of today [1931], would be Stahlhelmers," supporting "a sane patriotism with the idea of consolidating the orderly elements of society against Bolshevik ideas." [2]

In a crisis, the troops of both radicalism and reaction were seen as reinforcements for a party of resistance which hoped, sooner or later, to integrate them in the ruling system. And what applied to relatively moderate movements like the Stahlhelm or the Croix de Feu, applied equally to the Brown Shirts, the Green Shirts, or the Falange. Such was the thinking of conservatives in Italy and Germany, where their plans failed, and in Finland and Spain, where they succeeded. And just as on the national plane the violence and brutality of the radical Right became acceptable to conservatives who viewed them as defenders against the threat of a radical Left, so on the international plane the violence and brutality of Fascist powers would be accepted for similar reasons by the conservative leaders of countries like Britain and France, in the belief of an identity of anti-Communist aims. Even before World War I ended, the real danger for the chief of Britain's General Staff was not the Boche but Bolshevism. By the 1930's, as Lord Halifax told Hitler, he and other British ministers "were fully aware that the Fuhrer had not only achieved a great deal inside Germany herself, but that, by destroying Communism in his country, he had barred its road to Western Europe and that Germany therefore could rightly be regarded as a bulwark of the West against Bolshevism." This was the Nazi Germany of ruthless tyranny and concentration camps, the representative of a revolution of nihilism against which the West was constantly being warned. But, in conservative eyes, a much worse revolution threatened, against which any ally would do. It all comes down to saying, as Sir William Hayter bluntly put it,

---

[2] This and the quotations in the following paragraph are from Lionel Kochan, *The Struggle for Germany* (Edinburgh: 1963), pp. 11, 103–104, 116.

that "the non-Fascist Right in England and Germany thought that Fascism would do their dirty work for them."

Nietzsche had insisted that the mass of mankind deserves attention only as an obstacle or as an instrument: "For the rest, may the devil and statistics take them." His curse was remarkably accurate. In Nietzsche's footsteps, the twentieth century set out to use both devils and statistics to destroy the obstacles and manipulate the instruments. Of the two, however, the devils have prevailed. In a society divided by social and economic issues, only a common dream or a common nightmare could provide a unifying force. In the waking world of everyday reality, dreams (or nightmares) can only be taken on faith—hence the insistence on faith in those "realities" which are incapable of rational explanation. "Fascism is a religious conception," Mussolini affirmed—like Karelianism, like Hungarism, or Codreanu's Legion of the Archangel Michael. "Nothing great can be accomplished except in a state of amorous passion, of religious mysticism," Il Duce insisted in a speech of October 5, 1922. A School of Fascist Mystique consequently opened in Milan, and the Ballila Credo affirmed straightforwardly: "I believe in our Holy Father, Facism." Hitler, too, in his Nuremberg speech of September 13, 1935, told his followers that it was *faith* and the believing heart that secured his triumph against the counsel of reason.

It might be argued that in societies where individualistic thought and attitudes were generalized, the creation of collective thought presented a problem to be solved only by invention and manipulation. Older societies had shared a common language of symbol and myth. In modern societies these are lacking or not generally recognized; they have to be rediscovered, reinvented, reasserted. Hence, perhaps, the importance of history, which has become the theology of our time, a reservoir in which one delves to find the particular traditions that might suit one's ends—for even myths must have some root in reality. Hence, above all, a certain kind of modern myth which differs from that of the ancients in that it is not the expression of a truth, otherwise too profound for mass comprehension, but a manipulative device. The myth or symbol of an earlier day had been a parable, describing some reality considered too profound, too complex, too abstruse. The myth of our time very often goes counter to existing reality, ignores or distorts it in order to change it. In other words, from being the reflection of a truth, this sort of myth now becomes a deliberate lie, exploiting the power of symbols for ulterior purposes.

We find this first in the politics of modern nationalism and then of fascism. But we find it above all in the work of Georges Sorel, characteristic of the conjunction of extremes which marks the radicalism of our time: a Marxist who rewrites Marx *ad usum delphini,* for the benefit of both syndicalists and fascists. His revision abandons Marx's old-fashioned belief in the conjunction of interest and understanding for an opportunistic didacticism of more modern stamp. Adam Smith and Ricardo have been left behind for good; the new prophets would be Machiavelli and Nietzsche. To Sorel, myths were energizing, unifying, propagandistic devices. He agreed with Renan that men never admit truth for good reasons, and therefore have to be given the bad reasons they will accept. This is why he proposed to offer them what he called myths—compounds or constructs that move and operate on a plane where they will not encounter logical, discursive thought. Sorel claimed that his myth was supraintellectual, which actually means that it is not intellectual, that it is an attempt to evoke and harness certain dynamic images which will produce, as he puts it, "an entirely epic state of mind, and at the same time bend all the energies of the mind" for a great common effort.

This in itself was nothing new. At the end of the eighteenth century, the Jacobins had realized the unifying and dynamic uses of a great dream articulated, so to speak, in cult and ritual. Since that time a number of utopian reformers, like Saint-Simon and Auguste Comte, had provided the systems and societies they devised with exemplary religions. But all these earlier myths had sought to express or celebrate what they conceived to be a reality, be it Virtue, the Fatherland, or the upward march of Humanity. They enshrined what their inventors saw as an universal truth. Sorel, however, did not know what truth was! In his *Reflexions on Violence,* which, since its publication in 1906, has remained the great seminal work of this point of view, he explains that he wants to operate like the science of his day, which "makes no claim to know the true nature of things, and which confines itself to discovering relations that can be used for practical ends." His myth would be purely pragmatic, something that, he tells us, "must be judged as a means of acting on the present"—a *means*, as in politics, not a reflection of an *end*, as in religion; not real as the myths and rituals of believers are real because they express and are part of a higher order of reality; not apocalyptic but simply instrumental.

Here was the true political thought of a relativistic age, which did not believe in ultimate principles because it had seen them run, but did believe in energy, in force, in unthinking passions, because these are the constants that men and movements tap for action. Such vital forces were what the new politics and politicians also tried to tap with whatever instruments were likely to serve them. They did this quite deliberately, by inventing the myth of the general strike, by appealing to the pride and to the hatreds of groups great and small, by reviving the memories of bygone rights and bygone greatness, whether true or false, by marshaling all sorts of resentments and directing them against evil alien forces supposed to threaten society, either from outside or from within. Sorel did not remain alone. His almost exact contemporary in Italy, Wilfredo Pareto, produced a similar analysis of politics and social forces; in France, Maurice Barrès was well aware of the importance of symbolic forces; Fritz Stern's *Politics of Cultural Despair* (1962) shows much the same development in Germany as mirrored in the thought of Langbehn and Lagarde; even the English, though less inclined to theory, reflected similar attitudes in men like Rhodes, Kipling, and Joseph Chamberlain. The thing to remember, however, is that all of them looked on their manipulatory inventions as means to a higher end, which was in every instance the purification and revival of a class, a nation, or a "race" that had a task to perform, a white man's burden to carry, or a destiny to fulfill.

We are thus faced with the fascinating paradox that the revival of myth in the West took place in the service of certain higher myths which, for their part, seem to have been quasi-religious beliefs—beliefs, and not inventions! The Nation (or the Class, the

Party, the Race) was seen as a reality very similar to the God of the Old Testament: not a philosophical notion, an abstract concept, a moral allegory, but a real, terrible power which manifests itself most obviously in its anger, in violent catastrophic acts like wars and strikes and revolutions. The numinous nature of the Nation is something quite different from the mere collection of voters slouching off to the polls: it is a *mystery*. And before the mystery of the Nation, as before that of God, man is nothing, nothing but a creature—the very creature of the superior entity in function of which he exists. The Nation is the depositary of the fundamental force from which its members draw their life, a force reminiscent of the Melanesian's mana. This mana must be invoked for Society's sake, it must be conjured up from those depths where, forgotten, it has been lying dormant while Society, cut off from its roots, from its source of life energy, weakens and decays. The nationalist usually couples this impersonal mana with the animistic vision of something primitive societies also know very well: *la terre et les morts*—a world animated and dynamized by ancestral spirits and traditions. Out of this conjunction he produces a new religion, celebrating both mana and ancestors as sources of social energy for national revival, reform, and self-assertion.

In a world where identity and common purpose seem lacking, where old habits and certainties disintegrate, the appeal to ancestral sources is a natural reaction, a childish turning to parental authority for reassurance. But the nationalist's reaction is less childish than religious. In the great midden heap of ancestral traditions, says the nationalist, is the profound, lasting reality: the Sacred Ultimate compared to which worldly contingencies are unreal. Nationalists always contrast the *pays légal*—the existing institutional and constitutional set-up—with the *pays réel*—the true, profound entity, the Platonic idea to which they want to make society conform. And the very notion of a "national" or "nationalist" revival is interesting, because it suggests magic rather than the reality of the everyday political world. In effect, the nationalist is a revivalist, in that ancient sense in which a sick, corrupted body may be brought back to perfection and rightness by being set right with the world and with its own true nature.

The priests and witches of primitive societies set out to heal a sick man by making him die and be reborn, purified and strong; and primitive societies themselves go through the same ritual at intervals for much the same purpose. In the eyes of nationalists, the nation, too, is a living organism; and if it is ill it cannot be patched up as one might an engine; it has to be magically healed and revived by an appeal to the depths, to the roots, not just of existing society, but of life itself. The frequent references to Energy in nationalist vocabulary may be regarded as incantations, invocations of the life-force whose revival alone can heal wounds and solve problems too serious for empirical approach.

Now, if the Nationalist is actually a sort of witch doctor, then we might expect him to act like one. In his studies in the comparative history of religions, Mircea Eliade has told us that the shaman, the priest-witch of many societies, uses certain special methods designed to abolish the actual human condition, that of fallen man, and to reintegrate the condition of primordial man, unfallen and pure. The shaman's techniques vary, but they always include calling on auxiliary spirits, using drums or dancing to prepare a mystic voyage to the cosmic realm, and inducing a trance, either feigned or real, all with the aim of fulfilling his mission as healer or leader of souls. Eliade, of course, is talking about primitive religions. But one cannot help being struck by the coincidence between the techniques of the shaman and those of the great popular leaders of the past century, especially the Fascist leaders of the last few decades. They also call on auxiliary spirits of the soil and the dead, they also use a *stimmungsmusik* of drums and marches, they also work themselves and their hearers into a trance, either feigned or real, they also delight in being the healers and leaders of souls. There are verbatim references to this last in the writings of Barrès and Degrelle, not to mention Hitler, who was often described as possessed or in a trance and who never doubted his own mediumistic powers. Nor can it be a coincidence that if we go into the etymology of the word *fascism* we find that the Latin *fascinum*—charm, witchcraft —is related to *fascia*—bundle, cluster. Indeed, the symbol of binding is frequent in witchcraft and religion, entering even into the etymology of the last, with the Latin *ligare*—to bind, to charm.

Professor Eliade tells us that, when the shaman has got into an ecstatic state, the resistance of things disappears and unsurmountable difficulties give way, which is not surprising as even the Apostle Paul knew that enough faith could move mountains. But he adds, and this becomes more interesting, that feelings of guilt and social conflict also disappear, that extraordinary hopes and desires are fulfilled, and the exalted human being comes close to God in power —practically becomes a god. To the extent that he believes in the reality of his experience, the man possessed feels himself endowed with superhuman powers. This, one would suggest, is very close to a certain fascist magic which, of course, does not always work, any more than does that of the shamans, but which is *meant* to work in this way and sometimes does by persuading a man, or a group of men, or even a whole society for a while, that the magic *is* working in the way it is supposed to,[3] making them bigger and stronger, rendering them invulnerable, exorcising social conflicts and guilt, placing them, as it were, "beyond good and evil," so that nothing they do can sully or defile them—from which it follows, among other things, that all outrages and excesses are permissible.

One could even argue that the uniforms which seem an integral part of every fascist movement are so important because they play a magic role; because, just as the masks of gods or demons in certain religious rituals turn their wearers into gods or demons, so, in a sense, does the uniform, which is the mask of the Knight, the Man of War, the Man of Honor and Power, which is also the sign that its wearer is not subject to the laws of civil society, but answers to a higher law and a higher calling. The man who wears a uniform, like the man who wears the mask or the sign of the god, is irresponsible in a special sense, and the medieval cleric, like the soldier of today, could not be tried in a civil court—but only because he

---

[3] See Ascoli and Feiler, *Fascism For Whom?* (New York: 1938), p. 63: "In a way they were against the economic order because it was an order which could nail individuals and families to their status with little or no hope of redemption —short of revolution. They were against the economic order because it was economic, based on the hard reality of the productive process. By denying this reality they set themselves free." And on page 84: "Fascism, at least in its Italian conception, is an attempt to escape from the compelling forces of economics. . . ."

is responsible in another court, to another and higher power. In this sense, the uniform is also a highly egalitarian device, because, apart from their own hierarchy, its wearers are equal among themselves as against the noninitiates. Once you put on the uniform, the "artificial," "superficial" social, economic, and sartorial differences of the outside world are abolished. But if it is an egalitarian symbol, the uniform is also a highly elitist one, because it sets apart the initiated from the uninitiated.

We need not insist on analogies that may be simply coincidental. It does not seem exaggerated, however, to regard uniforms, like other nationalist or fascist paraphernalia, as serving a compensatory function which is at least partly mythological and magic, in societies where collective experience of every sort had been decaying and had to be restored. Fascist and Nazi ceremonies appear as vast revivalist and energizing sacraments or rites, much like the black masses which we know underwent a striking revival in the late nineteenth century, and for similar reasons: when the white magic of the traditional religion, which satisfied profound psychological needs, decayed, black magic rose to take some of its place. Deliberately or not, magic and myth were mobilized to fill the gap left by the unsatisfactory performance of traditional ritual and its rationalistic substitutes. The intriguing thing is that even when Mussolini tells us that his attitude was purely opportunistic, even when Hitler extols the propagandistic lie, it is hard to tell whether the myth was their servant or their master. An imperial or a racial myth which may have been developed as a weapon in the struggle for power can very well take over; the leader and the party may find themselves prisoners of their myths, led into actions and directions that are far from opportune in order to fulfill their mystic destiny, play out the role assigned to them, in a strange doom that becomes more important than immediate worldly ends or interests, even when it leads to Götterdämmerung!

In this sense the radical leader, not the fascist alone, is very much the possessed servant of the myth he handles at his peril, as all witches do. He is also a poet in the old Greek sense, where poetry is quite literally make-believe and carries ominous overtones: "For the craft of the poet," Plato tells us, "is light and winged and holy, and he is not capable of poetry until he is inspired and out of his mind, and there is no reason in him. Until he gets into this state, any man is powerless to produce poetry and to prophesy."

But it is worth remembering that from Plato's *Republic* such poets were excluded. They were tricksters and, in the end, their influence must prove socially subversive: "Strip what the poet has to say of its poetical coloring, and I think you must have seen what it comes to in plain prose. It is like a face which was never really handsome, when it has lost the fresh bloom of youth."

England

J. R. JONES

In England, because of the strength of conservative forces, the term *Right* applies largely to groups within the Tory party. Those groups that broke away from the party, or were organized separately, although ideologically interesting because of their similarity to movements in other countries, had little practical or immediate influence. In England the continuity of institutions, the gradual and peaceful evolution of society, and the absence of sudden economic catastrophe or defeat by foreign enemies, means that extremist ideas and movements have received comparatively minor attention and support. The task of the Right has not been to formulate new principles or develop new political systems, but to try to ensure that the Tory party followed and practiced those it had inherited from the past, but which its leaders tended to neglect or evade.

The continuity of English conservatism has, however, often been exaggerated. This has resulted in an erroneous equation of the English Right with simple reaction, masking the existence of a radical Right, which, although owing little to contemporary European movements, possessed considerable and even decisive importance at times, especially in the revolutionary situations of the years before 1914 and the year of the general strike, 1926. The apparently massive strength and predominant influence of conservatism in the last seventy-five years have led historians to miss the fact that, during long periods of this time, many conservatives felt that they were irretrievably on the defensive, faced not with just electoral defeat but also doomed to become a permanent and shrinking minority, exercising a dwindling influence on the mind and life of the nation. In such a situation reactionaries could suggest no positive solution; it was left to radical conservatives to argue that what was needed was not an obstinate adherence to old principles, but their reinvigoration, restatement, extension, and adaptation to the new circumstances that faced nation and party. The Right saw itself as the realist section of the party, living in the present, not in the past, and looking to the future. Its members laid emphasis on the need for long-term, positive, and constructive policies in the interests of the nation. But it also embodied the old characteristic Tory militancy in politics; the Right believed in waging a continuous and aggressive offensive against the forces of radicalism and socialism. This kind of opinion was widely voiced at the turn of the century, especially in the years after 1903 when there was increasing dissatisfaction at the failure of Tory leaders to make any energetic or systematic effort to reassert and restate conservative principles, or to realize them in practical and constructive policies. This movement of dissatisfaction is the starting point for the present study of the English Right.

Conservative principles, originally formulated by Bolingbroke and Burke, were restated in the nineteenth century by Sir Robert Peel and Benjamin Disraeli. But neither of these leaders commanded the complete support of his party, either in his lifetime or in retrospect. It can be said that they bequeathed divergent political traditions, indeed it can be argued that in each generation (provided that the talent is available) the Tory party must always choose between a Peel and a Disraeli. The Peelite tradition, with its passion for justice and right, laid primary emphasis on sound administration, on responsibility (which governed their attitude while in opposition as well as when in office), and on a readiness to accept constructive reforms, if and when the case for them had been made out. Those who disliked the Peelite position represented it as reflecting an attitude of impracticable high-mindedness, an aversion to the crude and rough business of everyday politics, and a timidity that resulted in successive surrenders to pressure involving the betrayal of conservative principles as well as the interests of the party. Disraeli, in contrast to Peel, was, above all, the party leader, with a zest for political infighting; he was the embodiment of political courage and endurance who relentlessly carried the fight into his enemies' camp. He was, in addition, the Tory of political imagination who could, by his reinterpretation of principles, and by his constructive policies, capture the minds of a generation, and also mobilize mass support for the immediate advantage of the party. Unlike Peel, he knew that he had first to become the leader of the party before he could become a statesman. On the other side, many conservatives (notably the Cecils) distrusted him as having been primarily an intriguer, an unscrupulous tactician and opportunist who tried to cover his political immorality and sterility by grandiose but empty phrase-making about empire, constitution, and the condition of the people.

Admittedly the divisions in the Tory ranks were never so weakening as those among their opponents, but in the years after 1900 it seemed to many Conservatives that they were suffering from the defects and weaknesses of both the Peelite and the Disraelian traditions without enjoying any of their advantages. Under Balfour, their leaders, by their pessimism and remoteness from the party, approached the worst defeatism of Peel. They lacked imaginative or constructive statesmanship, they were lethargic, inefficient, and slow, out of touch with the nation and with their own rank and file. They lacked fighting spirit and initiative, they disregarded (but, nevertheless, resented) any form of criticism. Arthur James Balfour and his principal associates seemed to acknowledge that they were conducting a rearguard action, not merely against their parliamentary opponents, but also against the rising forces of subversive radicalism and socialism.

These Tory leaders were not sufficiently farsighted, energetic, or combative to grasp the initiative and reverse the trend; they had no strategy, but only a futile reliance on short-term tactics. Yet these men—"mandarins" was a contemporary term—would not make way for others; they represented a tenacious, exclusive group that resented intruders, whether they were pushy individuals or members of new social classes. They had been brought up in the ap-

parently permanent and impregnable circumstances of upper-class
Victorian England; they lived in an insulated section of society,
unaware that the very bases of English life—stability, prosperity,
and security—were being threatened by developments at home and
abroad. Balfour, nephew of the previous prime minister, the third
Marquess of Salisbury, was something of a dilettante, who prided
himself on his detachment; he was a philosopher, not a partisan,
and, although a skilled parliamentarian, he had little understanding
of, or sympathy with, the people and the Tory rank and file. He
was prime minister for two main reasons: his birth, and to keep
Joseph Chamberlain out, or at least to prevent the dissensions that
would have arisen if Chamberlain had become prime minister.

By contrast, members of the English Right regarded themselves
as realists. They saw, rightly, that Balfour was leading the party to
electoral disaster, but they represented even more forcefully their
dismay that he was neglecting the new dangers that faced the nation, as well as the Conservative party. Before 1905 they urged
the leaders of the party to use their power to tackle these problems.
After the Liberal victory in 1906 they contended that power must
be recovered, for the sake of the nation as well as the party, as, in
their view, the Liberal government was following an antinational
policy that would destroy the empire. Old leaders and traditionalists
might be content to play the party game, observing its conventions
and treating the Liberal government as if it were respectable and
responsible, but for the Right it must be destroyed before it destroyed the nation.

The Right prided itself on having a clear view of the issues that
faced the nation, and contended that the appropriate solutions,
which it advocated, constituted a coherent, comprehensive, and
constructive policy. In contrast, the traditionalists were accused of
having no general understanding of these measures' necessity, and
of lacking the necessary decisiveness to bring about their prompt
implementation. Members of the Right, including an important
section of younger businessmen, could see that the economy was
in relative decline with massive and chronic unemployment, industrial stagnation, and the loss of markets. Unless this could be
remedied there could be no progress toward the solution of the

many appalling social problems of poverty, ill-health, squalid environments, a depressed countryside, and constant emigration, all factors that sapped the strength and virility of the "race." The self-governing colonies, despite their services in the South African war, were drifting away from Britain; unless this trend could be reversed the empire would soon disintegrate, and such disintegration would have catastrophic effects—as, after a century of security, the nation was threatened by the development of German might, specifically by her sea power. Defense, military as well as naval, must therefore receive more attention than it had needed in the past, but from mental laziness and complacency most Englishmen could not be brought to realize that now the existence and independence of the nation was at stake.

At home the enemy was more familiar—but also more formidable than in the recent past; it was the "separatist" elements whom the Right denounced as antinational. There were the radicals (as well as the socialists) who preached the class war for political advantage; the Irish Nationalists and their accomplices, backed by American money, who aimed at the disintegration of the United Kingdom; and the allegedly influential alien plutocrats and their allies, the self-interested professional politicians, who were accused of bringing unprecedented corruption into politics. Right-wing observers cited the growth of cynicism and disrespect for religion, the rigid mentality and restrictive attitudes of the majority of both employers and trade unionists, the hysteria of the suffragettes, and the apathy and ostentatious self-indulgence of a spectacular section of the upper classes as testifying to a deep-seated national malaise. What was even more alarming was the lack of response to the warnings of experience as well as to those of journalists and speakers. Most people ignored the evidence—military incompetence in South Africa, the naval challenge from Germany, the loss of export markets to both Germany and the United States; and they did not seem to appreciate the damage inflicted on the economy by strikes.

In developing the policies to meet national problems, and in order to reinvigorate the nation, the Right was inspired by politicians rather than by political philosophers or ideologists; it was to Joseph Chamberlain and Alfred, Lord Milner, that it looked for guidance as well as leadership. Chamberlain and Milner were on the surface dissimilar but their roles were complementary. Chamberlain, formerly a manufacturer, mayor of Birmingham, and a Unitarian, had transformed at least the face of English politics during his period as an advanced radical. Credited with the creation of the Radical political machine in the 1870's and 1880's, he had advocated sweeping policies of social reform before he broke with the Liberals over Irish Home Rule. As leader of the Liberal Unionists he had supported the Tories, and as Colonial Secretary from 1895 had initiated a new departure in imperial policy, particularly in West and South Africa. Milner belonged to another group from which the English ruling class has always recruited strength, the intellectual aristocracy. The son of a poor Irish doctor who emigrated to Germany, he had risen by outstanding academic ability. Educated at Balliol College, Oxford, then the great forcing house of talent, he had served as an administrator in Egypt and in the home civil service, and as High Commissioner during the crisis years in South Africa before, during, and after the Boer war. Both Milner and Chamberlain were men of intense but narrow vision. Milner, throughout his life, was entirely occupied with his idea of imperialism. Chamberlain, it is true, took up and developed several main lines—but always one at a time, and once he had moved on to a new subject he largely lost interest in what he had been dealing with in the past. So he campaigned at first for civic enterprise and urban improvement, then for party organization, social reform, and the satisfaction of nonconformist grievances. When he opposed Home Rule these earlier causes were largely forgotten, and during his work at the Colonial Office he even allowed the Liberal Unionist organization to fall into decay. Finally, in the last phase of his active career, he became absorbed by the campaign for Imperial Preference and Tariff Reform.

Chamberlain's and Milner's beliefs were for the most part arrived at in response to current, concrete issues rather than in accordance with general, theoretical principles. Like almost all English politicians, members of the Right were empiricists and pragmatists. Some were fully aware of developments in Europe, especially in France, and a few read the works of contemporary ideologists such as Maurras, Barrès, and Enrico Corradini, but the vast majority of even the most knowledgeable and intelligent were determinedly insular. The Right was guided and inspired by Chamberlain and Milner, whose speeches were fully reported in the press, and discussed at length by the extremely influential weekly and monthly journals. The purposes of the Right were practical and immediate, they were formulated by active politicians, working journalists, and administrators, not by intellectuals or philosophers. The Right wanted, first, the conversion of the Tory party, and then of the nation. Its members were encouraged by the hope of early success and stimulated by the fear that the crisis was deepening, and that current opportunities would not recur. As the struggle intensified, and the prospects of victory receded, so the vigor and vehemence of the Right increased. By 1914, when the situation reached the point of greatest tension, the Right possessed more coherence and strength than ever before—or since—in the most acute political crisis of modern English history.

Joseph Chamberlain's name is associated with his campaigns for Imperial Preference and Tariff Reform, Milner's with Imperialism, particularly in South Africa. It would, however, be arbitrary to make any sharp distinction between them. The men and their causes were directly, avowedly, and inextricably connected; significantly and symbolically it was in a discussion with Milner in Johannesburg that Chamberlain first explicitly expressed the need for Imperial Preference as the means by which imperial unity could be achieved. Both men believed that all the policies they advocated were interdependent, that the political, economic, social, and defense aspects were all part of a realizable whole.

The meaning of the word *imperialism* has changed so much since Milner's time that it needs careful definition if his principles and intentions are to be understood. So far as Milner himself is concerned, a more accurate term would be *nationalism,* a main characteristic of the Right in Europe, but a term that is difficult at first sight to apply to English politics. Imperialism for Milner and the Right certainly did not mean policies of aggression, of painting the map red (an English color in those days); "limited expansion, but unlimited tenacity" was Milner's own phrase. Furthermore, the imperialism of the Right did not, as is often stated now, concern itself primarily with the newly acquired tropical colonies, or Egypt and India. Milner's chief emphasis was on the development and self-fulfillment of the English "race," a word he interpreted in a broad sense. He did not mean race in the ethnic sense, and he generously included the other inhabitants of the British Isles in his definition of English. He did not talk of blood or soil; what he prized were those characteristics of the English which fitted them for their special mission. These included the language, the spiritual heritage, the traditions of liberality, tolerance, respect for personal freedom and individuality, the power of peaceful assimilation, the sense of service, and the spirit of sacrifice. In parentheses it can be seen how far removed these characteristics were from the German or Prussian tradition with which Milner was, and is, often associated. Above all Milner spoke of the mission of the English race. He wrote, "It is a question of preserving the unity of a great race, of enabling it, by maintaining that unity, to develop freely on its own lines, and to continue its distinctive mission in the world."

This mission was the building, consolidation, and development of an empire, and for this task the English were the best equipped. Anything that assisted the nation, from army reform to housing reform to improve the people's health, he regarded as part of his policy of imperialism. Anything or anybody—such as Paul Kruger and his calculated affronts to English subjects in the Transvaal— that obstructed imperial development was an enemy. Originally a Liberal, Milner had, after Gladstone's introduction of the Home Rule bill, come to realize that he could work usefully only with the Tories. At worst they might be stupid, mentally torpid, and prejudiced, but they were essentially patriotic, stressing the idea of service to the community, and they were empirical, not doctrinaire or dogmatic, in their politics.

In Milner's view two major dangers to the empire existed at home. The first was liberal dogmatism, the consequences of which he had feared during his years in Egypt and South Africa. Liberal theoreticians propounded policies without knowing anything about actual conditions, and without foreseeing the consequences of their proposals. Most of these men he despised as sentimentalists, congenitally incapable of facing realities, and the task of educating them politically ran up against their obstinate refusal to admit that they had ever been in error. Liberal doctrinaires could always be relied upon to sacrifice friends in the attempt to propitiate enemies —an assertion echoed by the Right down to the recent controversies over Katanga and Central Africa.

The second danger was even more damaging because it stemmed from a fundamental weakness of the constitution. The system of politics that Milner called the party game filled him with despair. The emphasis on immediate and electoral considerations, the narrow horizons of the average politician and his tendency to compromise, his fear or envy of great men and his desire to restrict their activities, his distrust of the expert, the concern of parliament with minor and local questions—all these things made Milner wonder how the empire had ever come into existence. He doubted whether it could continue to survive under such a system in an increasingly menacing world. He believed that none of the major problems facing England could be solved by means of the party system, but no politician would admit that these should be placed above party considerations. Milner felt himself profoundly out of sympathy with party politics, and after his return from South Africa virtually turned his back on them. He wrote, "I realise I can't swim against a maelstrom of rotten opinion, and I am not going to try." He was not a politician, and had no intention of becoming one.

Only one field existed in which Milner was both eager and determined to act—the field of imperial politics as a whole. His remedy for the defects of the party system, for the narrowness of what he called "this rotten assembly in Westminster," was imperial union. In his earlier years he favored a gradual advance, but later he advocated the early and complete establishment of an imperial constitution, with an executive council to deal with "world business," that is, foreign policy, defense, communications, and trade. Only such a course would enable these vital issues to be elevated above mere party considerations; there must be "permanent organic union" or there would be disintegration. One aspect of Milner's ideal deserves elaboration. It is fashionable to equate imperialism with the *raj*, or rule over India and the colonial dependencies—the "white man's burden." Certainly this was a major concern of Milner's, as can be seen in his classic study, *England in Egypt*, but it was not true that he ignored the self-governing colonies, or that the Right generally disliked them because their governments pursued radical economic and social policies.[1] Quite the reverse. Milner underestimated the difficulties, but he believed that he could build imperial union on the basis of a wider imperial patriotism. He did not think that this was visionary or unattainable; had not the last generation of Canadians created a nation after confederation? Even more relevant was the establishment of the Commonwealth of Australia in 1900. A wide imperial patriotism could be fostered, but these developments showed that there was no time to be lost; if the colonials were continually slighted, and their interests persistently neglected, then they might come to think that their developing local nationalism would conflict with a wider imperial patriotism. Milner, and the Right generally, never fully appreciated the reluctance of colonial governments (especially the Canadian) to become involved in imperial policies and commitments. Members of the Right applauded the Canadian government for offering reciprocity, without fully understanding the conditions. Again, the Right admired aspects of Australian politics, particularly the introduction of compulsory military training.

Milner also underestimated the difficulty of creating a sentiment of imperial patriotism in England, and he never really showed how this was to be done. By placing himself outside party politics he was, in effect, abdicating leadership and direct influence. He wrote, during the worst crisis in South Africa, about how great a thing it was to be, even for a short time, "the leader of a people, possessing their unbounded confidence," but by refusing persistent invitations to enter active party politics he was consciously discarding the only

[1] See, for instance, A. P. Thornton, *The Imperial Idea and its Enemies* (1959), p. 46. A survey of Right Tory speeches in *Hansard*, and of articles in such journals as the *National Review* (particularly at the time of colonial prime ministers' conferences), will disprove his assertion that "the true imperialist took more pride in the possession of India, in the pace of the British march in Africa . . . than ever he could summon up in respect of the rather hum-drum glories of colonial self-government."

instrument by which he could further his purposes. This distaste
for party he also transmitted to his pupils, who were to regard
themselves either as administrators, not politicians, or as influential
advisers behind the political scene. Only in a crisis would Milner
emerge from his semiretirement: in 1914, when he became active
in the Ulster Defence League as Edward Carson's understudy, and
after 1916, as a member of the War Cabinet.

Joseph Chamberlain was almost the only politician Milner exempted from his generalization that the party system produced
only mediocrities. Unlike Milner, Chamberlain was a politician to
his fingertips. He dominated and overshadowed colleagues and opponents alike, so that it now demands an effort of imagination to
appreciate his eminence and influence at the turn of the century.
Chamberlain had courage, experience, and energy. When once he
had made up his mind he pursued his objectives with determination
and industry. If necessary, and it often was, he could be totally
unscrupulous in his methods, but although an expert, professional
politician, he also had a wide political vision.

Chamberlain possessed almost all the qualities needed in a leader,
but they were dangerous endowments as they not only provoked
the frenzied hatred of enemies (perpetuated in the hostility of most
liberal historians), but they also perturbed many of his nominal
colleagues. Traditionalists feared the practical consequences of his
restless energy, the complications and difficulties his dynamic policies must entail. They never overcame their suspicion that Chamberlain remained at heart the radical agitator from the past. Many
resented him as "pushful Joe," a social as well as political climber.
A natural, human resentment filled many colleagues who had to
live in his shadow—such as the Whig, Spencer Compton, eighth
Duke of Devonshire, Sir Michael Hicks-Beach, and even the detached Balfour, who was not exempt from this feeling.

In one important respect Chamberlain was defective. Salisbury
had once said that "no one loved Joe," and he was right. Chamberlain had a hard, impermeable arrogance. His superb self-assurance
was combined with self-centeredness, a lack of real interest in other
people and their opinions and feelings, including unfortunately the
young and as yet obscure. On the platform, as a speaker, he ap-

peared as an attractive figure, but in private his hard personality tended to repel. As a consequence his appeal to the younger generation was intellectual rather than personal, but for that reason it was to be long-lived, and he succeeded in inspiring a group of disciples that was to continue his campaign after a stroke forced him out of active politics. This was an exceedingly varied group. Leopold Stennett Amery, whose attractively presented and forcefully argued memoirs may well lead historians to overemphasize his contemporary influence and importance, undoubtedly damaged his career by his single-minded and passionate advocacy of imperial union. Such men as James Louis Garvin, the great editor of the *Observer,* who probably possessed more influence than any other journalist in English history; Sir Halford Mackinder, the pioneer geopolitician who was converted from Liberalism; and Leopold James Maxse, who, as editor of the *National Review,* provided the Right with its most effective forum during these years, were all numbered among Chamberlain's followers. His influence was also considerable on such different, and differing, characters as Stanley Baldwin, the future prime minister, and Max Aitken, later Lord Beaverbrook, who came to England from Canada after the collapse of Chamberlain's health, and was still fighting for Chamberlain's policies in 1963.

Chamberlain's campaign for Imperial Preference and Tariff Reform really did deserve those much over-used phrases, "an act of political courage," "a challenge to the nation," and it remains an almost unique example of political initiative in modern English history. It is difficult today to realize the audacity of his onslaught on some of the most firmly held and universally accepted economic and political ideas and theories. The odds were heavily against him as he defied long-established views and prejudices. The onus of proof was on him, there had been little preparation, no predisposition to believe him. Chamberlain infringed what Milner described as the fundamental maxim of English politics, that it was easier to do nothing than to try to do something. He staked his career on the campaign, exposing himself to misrepresentation, especially by fellow ministers. Apart from personal considerations, and these mattered, traditionalist conservatives despised Chamberlain's proposals as "materialistic," condemning them as crude bait intended to secure the support of interested sections. There was some truth in this suggestion. Chamberlain intended his campaign to appeal directly to the business community, but even more to the working class by holding out the prospect of a permanent reduction in unemployment.

Chamberlain's opponents were quick to detect the fallacies in his arguments, but, although there was much that was careless and unconvincing in his use of economics and history, his purpose was clear. Behind the material considerations there lay a great and inspiring ideal, which would give to politics a sense of purpose and direction. He and the Right supporters whom he inspired saw in Imperial Preference and Tariff Reform the practical means for bringing about imperial union and national revival. Great benefits would follow, such as an effective defense system, a new expansion of the economy, and the means to finance constructive policies of social welfare at home. If the policy were rejected, they believed that the result would be a slow but continual decline of the power, prosperity, and morale of the nation, until the Empire disintegrated from its own weaknesses, or was overwhelmed by a rival power.

When Chamberlain was removed from active politics, his cause was continued by the Right, the men he had inspired and who regarded themselves as constructive conservatives. To them, as to Chamberlain, negative policies of resistance, for example against Home Rule, were not enough. To them Imperial Preference (rather than Tariff Reform) was, par excellence, the national policy for which they had been waiting. It rose above local issues and trivialities. In their view it was national precisely because it was not a class issue. Many younger Tories had for some time been disturbed by the growth of class consciousness, and by the eagerness of radicals (as well as socialists) to intensify and exploit it. Their honesty compelled them to admit that social and economic conditions were such as to make the working class discontented (the rate of emigration proved this); therefore, reforms became an urgent and imperative necessity. The Right contended that old political attitudes, whether the traditionalist emphasis on sound administration or the doctrine of laissez-faire (of which free trade was the logical fulfillment), could provide no real solution.

This was the basic distinction between the Right and those Tories earlier described as traditionalists. The latter implicitly accepted laissez-faire assumptions, whereas the Right would accept state action, within certain limits, and this still continues as an important distinction within the present-day Tory party.[2] The tariff was the clearest and most relevant example; by its means the state could protect and further particular economic interests and those of the community as a whole. Another example, and a major concern of the Right in the years before 1914, was compulsory military training; the interests of the individual were not always considered paramount, and sometimes he must be reminded that he had obligations as well as rights. But, unlike Sir Oswald Mosley and the fascists later, the Right emphasized that limits did exist on state action. Few at this time believed that the state was organic, having a primacy over the individual in all circumstances. Most members of the Right would have agreed with one of their leaders, Richard Greville, nineteenth Lord Willoughby de Broke, when he wrote, "Liberty must pervade all Social Progress, and without it no Social Reform is worth having," and when he went on to quote Bolingbroke to the effect that "the good of the people is the ultimate and true end of government."

The stroke that forced Chamberlain into retirement, and the aversion to active politics which Milner never overcame, left the Right without a single acknowledged leader. For this reason it had to accept Balfour's uninspiring, unsympathetic, and unsuccessful leadership of the party, and this was why, in 1910, it had to turn to the extremely reactionary Earl of Halsbury, who at least had the merit of being a fighter, in the best tradition of Tory pugnacity.

---

[2] The strength of laissez-faire elements has been repeatedly recruited from outside the Tory party—as in 1886, 1918–1922, and 1931. On each occasion the party leaders welcomed this accession of strength, even though it might mean watering down Tory policy; hence the dislike of the Right for these "coalitionist" tendencies. Today the laissez-faire tendency is chiefly represented by the so-called progressive Bow Group.

Bonar Law, too, was a fighter but he could never give the party the same kind of lead on wider issues as Chamberlain had provided. It remained for a group of younger men, many of whom were later to achieve prominence, to continue Chamberlain's mission and propagate his message. They continued to work for imperial union and Imperial Preference, but they also became absorbed by the critical struggle that developed after 1909. They tried to keep the wider issues before the public, but their main immediate task was defensive: to save the nation and the constitution from what they denounced as the deliberately destructive policies of the Liberal government.

The behavior of the Tories generally and of the Right particularly during this crisis, needs careful examination to be understood. Most historians of the period have found the policies so disastrously wrong as to be incredible. They have found it difficult, or impossible, to explain what the Tories had in mind.[3] Not surprisingly they have, in many instances, produced misleading interpretations, such as that the party was divided into two sections, the stupid diehards and the sane moderates, and they have failed to see that the former consisted of members of the Right as well as reactionaries. The latter, led by Halsbury, resisted any kind of change or reform, but the Right had positive, even constructive, reasons for their opposition, and their conduct was consistent with their earlier advocacy of Imperial Preference and their later resistance to Home Rule.

Among the underestimated and misunderstood leaders of the pre-1914 Right was Lord Willoughby de Broke. The leading historian of the period calls him "a young man better known in hunting circles than in politics"; another describes him as "the fox-hunting Willoughby [without] much mental prowess." [4] In 1910 he was forty-one, and his articles and speeches reveal him as a forceful, thoughtful, and intelligent writer, an excellent parliamentarian,

---

[3] R. C. K. Ensor's *England, 1870–1914* (1936) is still the most influential and authoritative study, and deservedly so. Excellently written and organized, its outstanding merits have tended to conceal the fact that it is the work of a partisan who participated in the events of the years, 1902–1914. Despite his efforts to be fair-minded, a bias in favor of the Asquith government colors his picture of the years 1910–1914.

[4] Ensor, *op. cit.*, p. 428, and Roy Jenkins, *Mr. Balfour's Poodle* (1954), p. 162.

and a useful organizer. He thought for himself, and he was one of the few Right advocates of votes for women. He led the fight against the Parliament Act and organized the Ulster Defence League against Home Rule, but he also argued and worked for constructive policies. He realized that the Tory party could no longer gain and retain power through the mistakes of its opponents and by exploiting their divisions. He admitted that in the past conservatism had been associated with class privilege, and that only by following a truly national policy and showing willingness and ability to improve the condition of the people could this reputation be effaced.

Although he acted with the reactionary Halsbury as a leader of the "die-hard" peers who fought the Parliament Act, Willoughby was ready to accept sweeping reform of the House of Lords. He conceded that the principle of a hereditary peerage was anomalous, and he was willing to abandon it in order to enable the upper house to play the part of an effective second chamber. This was the crucial point—the powers, not the composition, of the Lords. The preservation of the constitution demanded a strong upper house, and tradition must not stand in the way. Lord Willoughby contended that Toryism, if it was to survive, must justify its existence. The upper classes, instead of leaving politics to demagogues, must resume the duty of giving a lead to the nation. He analyzed the fundamental principles of what he called "National Toryism"— national and imperial consciousness, race regeneration (a vague phrase, which was not elaborated in detail, but did not mean racialism in the fascist sense of the word), the subordination of party and sectional to national interests, and especially the fostering of national unity in place of class consciousness, and the general improvement of the environment, spiritual and intellectual as well as material. The principles of justice, unity, freedom, duty, responsibility, and patriotism must, he felt, be systematically inculcated. In his view the Tory party did not need a specific program, but it did need an intelligible policy and the vigor and spirit to convince the people that it would be carried out.

In the attempt to implement these proposals, Lord Willoughby founded a "ginger" group, the National Reveille movement, and also played an active part in the National Service League. Groups such as these flourished in both Tory and Liberal parties in the years before 1914. They had as their object the promotion of some particular cause or interest, and, although on occasion they might criticize and embarrass the official leadership of the party, there was no question of disciplining their members. In contrast, the Labour party even then, and still more later, was always more suspicious of groups within the party, fearing that they might prove subversive and divisive of party unity and discipline—hence the hostility to Sir Oswald Mosley in 1930–1931, and to Aneurin Bevan in both the 1930's and the 1950's. With the Tories this fear that groups within the party—Winston Churchill's associates in the 1930's, the "Suez rebels" in 1956–1957—are really or potentially antiparty is a comparatively recent development, partly the result of press publicity and speculation. There is another difference now. Before 1914 such groups, in which journalists always took an active part, used the press to further their political purposes; since 1945 the politicians have more often served as a facade for commercially organized and purposeful pressure groups.

Like Lord Willoughby, the other leaders of the Right regarded themselves as constructive Tories, as practical exponents of Chamberlain's imperial and economic policies—a point that distinguished them from the mere adventurers or frondeurs. The Right tried to further these policies by pamphleteering, by campaigns of public speeches, and by journalism. The Compatriots' Club, originally a dining and discussion group, acted as the main organization for these activities. But while the Liberals held office there was little in the way of long-term policy that the Right could achieve, although its members (and especially Amery) were careful to maintain links with colonial opinion, and to reassure colonial statesmen that the views of the government (and the hesitations of official Tory leaders) did not truly represent public opinion. The first essential task of the Right was the conversion of the Tory party, if possible by persuasion. But in the face of intransigent free-trade opinion some of its enthusiastic adherents tried to use pressure. A group known as the Confederates (including Amery and Henry Page Croft) tried to force Tory free traders out of constituencies where they had been, or might be, adopted as candidates, an activity that stretched official tolerance to its limits, and that did not in fact achieve much—largely because of local resentment against any outside interference with constituency affairs.

The Right naturally (and properly) thought that the official leadership was insufficiently assiduous and combative. But until 1909 the differences between the Right and the traditionalists, despite constant disputes over tariff policy, were not vitally important or irreparable. Balfour's reliance on the old tactic, depending on the incompetence and weakness of the Liberals, seemed to be justified by its results—a long series of by-election victories, which apparently indicated a Liberal defeat at the next elections. When David Lloyd George launched his shrewd counteroffensive with the so-called people's budget, the Right was as wrong as any other section of the party in thinking that the budget would be just one among many issues, and that it would not enable the Liberals to check the decline in their support. However, after the two general elections of 1910, fought and won by the Liberals on the issues of the budget and the veto of the Lords, the Tory party found itself in an impasse; it was then that the Right began to develop its own policy, and to increase its strength and influence.

The crisis over the Parliament Act, and the conduct of the Right and the reactionaries in trying to defeat it in the Lords, so compelling the king to create sufficient peers to force its passage, has seemed to many historians to defy rational explanation. Reactionaries like Halsbury simply thought that the bill was morally wrong and must be resisted whatever the consequences; the motives of the Right were more subtle. In the first place, its members feared that a compromise over the Lords would have enervating moral consequences; there had been too many compromises already and the prospect of another would weaken the morale and resolution of the Tory rank and file. On the other hand, a fighting stand would stiffen opinion; a display of courage was needed. In the second place, if the Lords surrendered their powers it would be extremely difficult to restore them at some future date. But if the Lords went down fighting, then the Tories could pledge that powers of which they had been deprived by force would be restored. Reactionaries and traditionalists expressed horror at the idea of tampering with hereditary rights, but the Right cared little for such things. They wanted an effective second chamber, one that could force matters back to the electorate as well as to the Commons. An elective system would be acceptable in place of the hereditary principle. Therefore, the members of the Right argued that nothing would be lost by provoking the government into securing the mass creation of peers, even as many as three or five hundred. The more the better. Such a wholesale change in the character of the Lords would enforce sweeping and fundamental reform of the house. Anticipating what was in fact to happen, they saw that a reduction in the powers of the Lords would mean single-chamber government, and a probable danger to the constitution.

Historians have described this attitude as suicidal, arguing that after the mass creation of peers there would be nothing to prevent the Liberal government from passing any measure it wanted— Home Rule especially. At the time, the Right discounted this argument. Herbert Henry Asquith and his colleagues, so the Right asserted endlessly, did not *want* Home Rule. They had no option in the matter, because they depended on Irish support in the Commons, but few Liberals, and fewer of the rank and file (among whom Protestant feeling was strong), showed any enthusiasm. Once ennobled, many of the new Liberal peers would vote against Home Rule in sufficient numbers to ensure its defeat. Or they would insist on amendments that the Irish Nationalists could never accept, because of Sinn Fein and O'Brienite pressure at home. Would Asquith dare to go to the country? Could he persuade the king to create more peers without another election? Tories had no doubt that they would win a smashing victory in any elections fought on the Home Rule issue.

A good deal of attention has been paid to the difficulties of the Tory position after 1910. Certainly there were many—for example, there could not be an early dissolution after the two elections of 1910, they could delay but not defeat Home Rule by constitutional means, and they were in process of changing leaders. Traditionalists were despondent, but the Right militants were confidently aggressive. In their opinion the far greater and more numerous difficulties of Asquith's government cried out for ruthless exploitation, and if this were done the Liberals might be broken for a generation, as after 1886. But there must be no question of any compromise, conciliation, or conferences. The two parties were on a collision course. Whichever flinched from the impact and turned aside would be shattered. The Right believed, from experience, that apart from Lloyd George and Churchill the Liberals had the weaker nerves. The risks were high, both of defeat or of civil disturbance, but they were preferable to a weak compromise, which would be in fact a concealed surrender, as in 1910.

The Right justified this fighting policy, which could well have resulted in permanent damage to the constitution, by strategic, long-term, as well as opportunist or tactical, considerations. Its members sincerely hated the Liberal government as antinational. All Tories agreed on opposition to Home Rule, all were alarmed by the development of socialism, although the Right was much more aware of the menace of syndicalism. But on the identity of the principal enemy the Right and the traditionalists differed. For the latter the struggle was parliamentary, against the orthodox Liberals, their opposite numbers on the other side of the house. The Right saw the real issue in politics as something far more serious and fundamental, interpreting the crisis of 1914 not as an abnormal or surprising development, but as the logical and inevitable outcome of the pernicious, antinational principles of subversive radicalism, the principles of Cobdenism.

Cobdenism, "a comprehensive doctrine of political destructiveness," was the enemy. Its most obvious manifestation, an obstinate attachment to free trade, was significant because of its dogmatic basis. Cobdenites were doctrinaires, impervious to argument, blind to the changes in economic conditions. Of course, usually this blindness was from mental inertia, but there was another aspect of Cobdenism that was intrinsically more vicious, and all the more dangerous because it was so prevalent among the younger generation. The essence of Cobdenism, in the view of the Right, was its narrow appeal to purely sectional interests, elevating these above the national interest. Although the Right did not, at this time, put the interests of the state above those of the individual under all circum-

stances, they condemned Cobdenism for sacrificing the interests of
the state and nation to those of sectional groups that supported the
Liberal party. In apparent confirmation of this thesis, the Liberal
government after 1906 put forward an aggregate of policies with
narrowly sectional appeal: education bills intended not to advance
education but to gratify the sectarian prejudices of the nonconformists; licensing bills to satisfy the temperance movements (and
the mainly Liberal licensed grocers); Welsh church disestablish-
ment; land bills purporting to help the landless but intended primarily to stir up feeling against landowners; and the supreme example of Home Rule, which had had the effect of capturing the
Irish vote in England for the Liberals.

In the view of the Right there was a logical connection between
this emphasis on sectional interests and the corruption that, it was
alleged, now reached unprecedented proportions. This charge provided the Right with one of its main propaganda lines, citing massive jobbery and nepotism, an expanded traffic in honors, the voting
of salaries for M.P.'s, the crude inducements used to win support
for the Insurance Act, and the prospect held out to Welsh Liberals
of looting church endowments. The Right compared corruption
under the Liberals to the state of politics in the Third Republic
and, like French supporters of Boulanger, hoped to exploit public
disgust in order to bring down the government, whereas many of
the Tory leaders were reluctant to wash dirty clothes in public.
The principal and most odious scandal concerned the Marconi contracts, which Maxse compared to the Panama scandal, but there
were many others also—over Persian Gulf oil contracts, speculation
allegedly based on inside knowledge of the decision to move the
capital of India to Delhi, the Archer-Shee case, Lord Charles Beresford's attacks on Admiral Sir John Fisher's naval policies and appointments, and the Indian silver transactions.

This corruption was linked by the Right with the activities and
influence of what Garvin in the *Observer* termed the "plunder-
bund." This term he applied to the group of financiers and businessmen, mostly of German-Jewish origin (for instance, Alfred Moritz
Mond, Sir Edgar Speyer, and Sir John Tomlinson Brunner) who
were active in the radical wing of the Liberal party. The Right,

as in Continental countries, denounced these men as aliens—worse, as traitors serving the interests of the national enemy, Germany. Maxse noted that these alien radicals were all opponents of a big navy and jumped to the wild conclusion that this was part of a systematic plan to enable Germany to achieve parity in battleships. He also accused the alien radicals of using their control and influence in the press to distort and slant news, and especially to paint a false picture of European affairs and German policies. Even wilder accusations were made that certain ministers were literally in the pockets of some of these financiers. This abuse had unpleasant undertones. Right speakers and writers (apart from the separate Chesterton-Belloc group) disclaimed anti-Semitic feelings, not very convincingly, but went on to assert that anti-Semitism was being generated by the antinational and corrupt activities of a few wealthy Jews, as well as by the economic competition created by destitute refugees from Russia who were crowding into the East End of London—with explosive effects twenty-five years later.

The Right used the word "traitor" rather freely. It was based on a justified dislike of the "little Englander" sentiments common among radicals, but at times the attacks on ministers mounted to the point of hysteria. Churchill was the main target for attacks; he was "half an alien, and wholly undesirable," with Maxse suggesting that even if his policies ruined England Churchill would be unaffected, as he would emigrate to North America and fit naturally into the role of a Tammany politician. When Churchill was at the Admiralty, Right disapproval of his naval administration led to his being quite seriously described as "the Kaiser's *homme de confiance* in the Cabinet." Lloyd George was also the subject of vicious attacks, mainly on account of his associates, and Asquith was charged with failing to exercise control over his antinational colleagues.

Almost all these attacks were vicious rubbish, but the Right was on sounder ground when its writers and speakers tried to awaken a complacent nation to the deepening dangers of the international situation. The Right led the demand for army reform during the last years of the Balfour administration. It supported Lord Roberts in his tireless campaign for compulsory military training. From a very early stage the Right (almost alone) detected and publicized the challenge of the new German navy and agitated for accelerated naval building. The Imperial Maritime League, a breakaway from the Navy League, was an organ of the Right, or perhaps it would be more accurate to reverse this relation; the Right, with some exceptions like Garvin, allowed itself to be sidetracked into the vendetta waged by Lord Charles Beresford against Admiral Fisher and his naval reform policies. These policies—concerning the concentration of the fleet in home waters, the ruthless scrapping of obsolescent warships, the proposal of a new system of cadet education, the design and building of Dreadnoughts and battle cruisers —were all deeply controversial within the Royal Navy as well as in political circles. Partly to overcome stubborn and massive resistance (and partly because of defects of temperament), Fisher would promote only those upon whom he could rely. His alleged favoritism divided the navy, so, in consequence, Fisher tried to secure his position and power by canvassing support in the press, at Buckingham Palace, and in Whitehall, as well as in parliament. Naturally, his many naval enemies, led by Beresford, were quick to use the same weapons against him.

The Right also launched into a total condemnation of Richard Burdon Haldane's Territoral Army as a sham, useless in the event of war. One (irrelevant) reason for this was Haldane's well-publicized pro-German sympathies—which were exploited viciously and continuously—but another was based on the thesis that in a Continental war the decision would be reached in the first few weeks by mass armies. A partly trained force, like the Territorials, would be unserviceable; only conscription would make England prepared.

The Right enjoyed strong support in the press, especially in the *Times, Observer,* and *Daily Mail,* which warned an apathetic and ill-informed public that war was probable, indeed inevitable unless the Germans could be deterred by large-scale preparations. These papers wanted to convert the ententes into alliances. Most Englishmen believed, as also in more recent times, that France was a decadent, corrupt, and unreliable country; the Right (interestingly, its members were largely Dreyfusard) pointed to the revival of French national spirit and to the natural tendency of Frenchmen to unite in an emergency. Russia was defended against incessant radical and socialist attacks, and in 1911, as fellow imperialists, the Right championed Italy's campaign in Tripolitania, fearing that the unfavorable attitude of the government and most of the press would drive the Italians back into the arms of Germany and Austria. Throughout the period after 1900 the Right hammered away at this theme, that the independence of the nation was at stake, and that Germany was a deliberately aggressive power that would deal with her opponents piecemeal unless they united, as she had done with Denmark in 1864, Austria in 1866, and France in 1870.

During this same period, as A. J. P. Taylor has pointed out, radicals and socialists were consistently pro-German, anti-Russian, and (rightly) suspicious that France hoped and intended to involve England in a European war. The Right compared these attitudes with earlier radical sympathy for Russia and France, seeing in this change another proof of the old Cobdenite maxim of friendship with England's enemies and enmity to her friends. Radical pro-Boer speeches were recalled, propaganda made out of the antimilitary and antinaval speeches of radicals like Byles and King. The radicals, and the ministers, were charged with ignoring national interests and neglecting defense. Above all they betrayed their traditional "little Englander" principles, deliberately dividing the nation by the policies they pursued, at the very time when unity was more needed than ever.

The main attack by the Right on Asquith's government centered on the government's determination to pass the Home Rule bill. Why did Asquith persist with it when it had not been a major issue at the last elections? The Right answered that the ministers would do anything to hold their offices—allegedly for the sake of their salaries and the corrupt use they could make of their patronage. More seriously, it could be seen that the ministers feared not just electoral defeat if they dissolved parliament, but the breakup of the party. The Right concluded that this meant putting party before nation; the Liberals had entered into a "corrupt bargain" with the Irish Nationalists, and were content to hold onto office at the price of disrupting the United Kingdom and sacrificing all Irish loyalists. All Tories opposed Home Rule, but the Right gave particular emphasis to the Ulster question, whose importance had first been appreciated by the original self-styled Tory radical, Lord Randolph Churchill.

To the Right the Ulster Volunteer movement was an example, model or exemplar, of what they hoped to achieve in the British Isles as a whole. Here was a movement of all classes, uniting great landlords, industrialists, the professional classes, and the clergy with humble tenant farmers and the big industrial working-class population of Belfast and the smaller towns. A highly developed sense of community, based on militant Protestantism, a fervent patriotism, and a dour determination, made a striking impression on Tory visitors from England. The Right always claimed to be, par excellence, the "national" movement (just as the Left always claimed to represent the "people"); in Ulster such a movement already existed, disciplined, determined, energetic, and effective. In Ireland almost everyone was commited, and active in support of his cause. The population was sharply and irrevocably divided into two camps, Protestant and Catholic, Volunteer and Nationalist. Leaders spoke in earnest, and if some Ulstermen still harbored suspicions of Edward Carson, their chief, as a lawyer and a Dubliner, there could be no doubt that James Craig (the Ulsterman who was to be Prime Minister of Northern Ireland from 1921 until his death in 1940) would fight and die for his cause. All this was, the Right thought, a refreshing contrast to the politics of procrastination, the persistent tendency to seek compromises, the cross-bench mentality of Westminster politics.

Asquith and his colleagues believed that the Volunteer movement was a bluff, an error perpetuated by many historians. Nothing could be further from the truth. Ulstermen, leaders and rank and file, were in grim earnest. So, too, was the Right in England. Andrew Bonar Law went as far as (or perhaps rather further than) the official leader of the Opposition could go, and was severely criticized for doing so. Some Tories were ready for a compromise, some of the most vociferous (like F. E. Smith, as his future record was to show) would have run for cover when the crisis came. But the real Right in England, Willoughby de Broke, Milner, Page Croft, Amery, and Colonel John Gretton, would have fought side by side with Carson and Craig. Unlike the traditionalist Tories the Right was not interested in finding a formula that would permit a compromise; it followed the old maxim of the first Earl of Shaftesbury, that things must be worse before they could be better. In other words, intensify the crisis, take the offensive, try to drive a wedge between Liberals and Nationalists, paralyze government by refusing to pass the Annual Army Act except under conditions that would prevent the use of force in Ulster, or, alternatively, encourage and exploit the natural reservations of the army officers. Logically, if at first sight strangely, the Right welcomed the formation of the Nationalist Volunteers; once two unofficial armies faced each other, the issue was out of the hands of the government —and a limit existed to temporizing and prevarication. The Right believed that Asquith was now in their hands. He might pass, but he could not enforce, the Home Rule Bill. Yet he must persist with this now unrealizable measure, because the withdrawal of Nationalist support would lead to the collapse of his majority.

The international crisis suddenly cut across the Home Rule crisis, and no one can now say what would have happened otherwise. Never again has a domestic crisis of such difficulty and intensity developed, except momentarily in 1926, and as a consequence the Right has never since acquired such determination, cohesion, and support. In the interwar years there were many single issues—Ireland again, socialism, syndicalism, relations with Russia, India, international affairs—on which Right opinion was focused, but these questions did not coincide in time, or combine together, as in 1910–1914.

On the Left, as well as the Right, there was considerable discontent in these years before 1914 at the failure of orthodox Liberal politicians to apply themselves to the real problems that faced the nation. Most of this discontent found expression in syndicalism and the breakaway socialist groups, but two sections eventually reached conclusions and views that closely resembled those of the French Right. One group, originating in radical Liberalism, centered around Hilaire Belloc and the Chestertons, Gilbert and Cecil. The other, based in the Labour movement, reflected the views of Robert Blatchford.

The resemblances to the French Right can be partly explained by personal factors. Belloc was half French, and his friends were all Francophile and violently anti-Prussian. They had, or later found, a common ground in their militant Catholicism, and for them the universality of the Church provided the same wider focus for loyalty that imperialism gave the Tory Right. From the time of the Boer war, Belloc and the Chestertons were, in fact, violently and specifically anti-imperialist, and linked imperialism with the alien plutocracy they denounced for its growing influence in England. Influenced by their faith they looked back to an imaginary England of religion, order, stability, and common prosperity which they supposed to have existed in medieval times. This nostalgia combined with a hostility to industrialism, and its social consequences, which they derived from one of the main streams of early nineteenth-century radicalism.

Belloc and the Chestertons differed in one crucial respect from all other groups (including the Tory Right) except the extreme Left. They did not regard property as sacred. Indeed, they argued that the existing system of property ownership was the source of all the most serious evils that weakened the nation. A fundamental reform in this system was essential if any reforms were to prove effective. In his book, *The Servile State,* Belloc contended that the vast majority of the people, as never before, were economically dependent on a few landowners and capitalists, that in place of the old distinction between those with votes and those without there was now a much wider gap between those who were economically free and those who were not. In his view, the present state of society was unstable and could not endure; it must end in one of three ways. The first possibility, socialism or collectivism, was no real solution in Belloc's view because it merely substituted state control for capitalist control. The second possibility was that of the establishment, through the extension of existing trends, of the "servile state." The masses would be assured of subsistence, but would have inferior status; control would rest in the hands of capitalists, especially those connected with the new trusts and combines, not the state. The third possibility, which was Belloc's own solution, he termed "distributism"—a return to the wider and more equal distribution of property ownership, such as had existed in medieval times. This was to be achieved by heavy taxation of the rich, group ownership of land, councils of trades and professions (resembling Mussolini's later fascist corporations), and local regional councils equipped with powers by charter. Parliament was so far gone in decay that it was to have no real place in this system, one of whose main and most desirable characteristics was to be the absence of opportunities for parties and party politics.

Belloc sat as a radical Liberal M.P. from 1906 to 1910, and so had personal experience to justify his view that no major reforms could be carried through parliament or the party system. Representative government, which had been intended as the organ of democracy, had been turned by systematic corruption into the engine of an oligarchy. *The Party System,* published in 1911, contained the thesis that the parties' need for political funds had given the wealthy the means to control politics, and quoted, as one of the grossest and most blatant examples, the sale of honors by both parties. Cecil Chesterton, in *Eye Witness* (later *New Witness*), led the attack on what he shrilly denounced as the corrupt and self-seeking plutocracy. These papers made up for their small circulation by fearless, if often exaggerated, attacks on grievances; because of their precarious financial position they were not intimidated by threats of actions for libel. They appealed to the same sense of curiosity and scandal among the educated that made *John Bull* the most popular of all publications for the masses.

Belloc was shrewdly compared at the time with Déroulède, and in their attacks on the largely alien Liberal plutocrats, on the "Randlords" from South Africa, on what he termed the "modern Anglo-Judaic plutocracy," he and Chesterton were following the same lines of denunciation as the contemporary French Right. Belloc also dismissed party politics as shadow-fighting; politicians played the game of ins and outs, but the real decisions on all major issues were taken by the combined front benches, which were recruited from a small, exclusive, and interrelated social class. He had bitter personal experience of the impotence of the individual or independent M.P., and of the way in which all issues were treated from an exclusively party angle. He saw no real exceptions to this rule; he described both the two great decisions in recent English history, Gladstone on Home Rule and Chamberlain on Imperial Preference, as merely the decisions of "an intriguer of prominence, for some purpose of his own, to break the rules."

Belloc's blatant anti-Semitism, his open contempt for party politics, and his refusal to consider compromise, discredited him in parliament. It was as a journalist that he achieved influence, but influence of an entirely negative sort. Distributism was never fully worked out in detail until Mosley took it up, via Italy. The *New Witness* had a sensational but short-lived influence, its main function being to intervene in individual cases of injustice in the administration of what Belloc condemned as oppressive, servile, laws —for instance, the Mental Deficiency act.

Blatchford, too, was important primarily as a journalist, as editor of the *Clarion*. He was the first really successful popularizer of socialist ideas, but some of his principal characteristics eventually separated him from the orthodox Labour movement. He was a hedonist and a militant atheist, enough in themselves to cause suspicion among the serious and largely nonconformist Labour leaders of the first generation. A former regular soldier, he was a fervent patriot, an enemy of Cobdenite internationalism, a supporter of the Boer war, and later one of the first to draw attention to the German menace. Similarly he was an economic nationalist, supporting tariffs—although he suspected Chamberlain's motives. He disliked Labour subservience to the Liberals, and gradually extended this feeling into opposition to parliamentarianism—instead he favored the referendum—and the party system. His unusual combination of jingo patriotism with socialism resulted, under English conditions, in his isolation. In France or Germany, by contrast, he would have been incorporated in the mainstream organizations of the Right.

Whereas the Right constituted an easily identifiable and extremely formidable factor in English politics in the years before

1914, it mattered far less after 1918, and in the interwar years generally. It has often been claimed that this virtual elimination of political extremism, on the Right as well as on the Left, and the reëstablishment of constitutional politics, was the great achievement of Baldwin. There is some truth in this explanation, but the chief reason for the relative insignificance and impotence of the Right, at least, was the breakup of the combination that had existed before 1914. Some of the imperialists of the old Right—such as Amery and George Lloyd—held office under Baldwin without being able to influence his major policy decisions. Their former colleagues remained as an isolated group on the back-benches. The adventurers and frondeurs, who had naturally gravitated to Lloyd George's side, formed a separate and discredited group for some time after the breakup of the Coalition. Furthermore, the reactions of members of the prewar Right now varied with every major issue—tariffs and especially the so-called food taxes, defense, French policy in Germany, the League of Nations, India, trade-union rights and the law, retrenchment, and expenditure on social services. Men who were bitterly hostile on one issue united on another. Page Croft and Roundell Cecil Palmer, Viscount Wolmer, confirmed protectionists and imperialists, combined with their old enemy Churchill over India. The Indian issue split the ranks and reduced the effectiveness of the minority who pressed, during the 1930's, for rearmament and vigilance against Germany. Churchill's own reputation for inconsistency and opportunism was in itself a disadvantage and led many to disregard his warnings on foreign affairs. In particular his opposition to tariffs alienated determined protectionists, his hankering for a new alliance with Lloyd George alarmed all those who had helped to break up the Coalition, and his joining with the diehards in obstructing the Government of India bill led moderate Tories to distrust his judgment. The "Round Table" group of Milner's pupils, who disagreed with the diehards and Churchill over India, were the inspirers of the policies of appeasement which the former supported, but the latter resisted. These examples of division could be multiplied almost indefinitely on other less important issues.

It would, therefore, be arbitrary to pick out a "Right" in interwar politics; with two exceptions no formed Right group or leader existed for any length of time as a major influence. The first exception is Lord Beaverbrook, a politician of a type relatively new in English politics. The second, entirely separate from the first, consists of the authoritarian Right in the Union Movement of Sir Oswald Mosley. Otherwise, the old prewar Right revived on only two crucial occasions, in 1922 in the decision not to continue the Coalition, and at the time of the general strike in 1926. The most significant division within the interwar Tory party was not so much between Right and Left, traditionalist and progressive, imperialist and isolationist, as between those who stood for long-term policies and those whose attitude was largely governed by short-term considerations, who thought primarily of the immediate advantage of the party and themselves. And it was because he proved himself successful in this latter, short-term sense that Baldwin survived and flourished. The times when he was in greatest danger were periods of difficulty for the party, not the nation, as in 1923–1924, when electoral defeat led to the formation of the first Labour government, and in 1929 and 1930, when the party's performance in the elections and in opposition seemed to be faltering. When he succeeded electorally, as in 1924, 1931, and 1935, most Tories were satisfied. They thought primarily in terms of a parliamentary majority. In the electoral victories of 1931 and 1935, Baldwin satisfied them on that score; whether and how he subsequently dealt with the issues of unemployment and rearmament was less important. As Amery commented after the 1935 elections, "If majorities, as such, are an end in themselves regardless of what can be done with them, or of the intellectual and moral paralysis one is prepared to accept as the price of securing them, he has been more than justified now, as in 1924 and 1931."

The political career of Lord Beaverbrook provides perhaps the clearest example of Right politics in the interwar years. He has been too easily dismissed as a press lord, lumped together with his Fleet Street rivals Northcliffe and Rothermere as a new and undesirable type in politics. This is a distorting oversimplification. Northcliffe was a journalist, not a serious politician, who tried, crudely and unsuccessfully, to exploit his influence over public opinion for undefined purposes. He knew clearly only what he disliked; as a self-made man he remained envious of what he termed the Old Gang, the patrician Tories and the professional machine politicians like Sir George Younger. But otherwise all he had to offer were stunts and publicity campaigns, not serious policies. As a consequence, despite his ownership of the *Times* and the *Daily Mail*, the latter the first mass circulation paper in England, his influence rapidly subsided after 1918. Beaverbrook's *Daily Express*, although much smaller in circulation, rapidly surpassed its rival in political and popular influence. As a politician, Northcliffe rates in the same class as Horatio Bottomley of *John Bull*. Rothermere had a better understanding of the nature of politics and power, but no very clear idea of what he himself wanted to achieve. His interventions were often ill-timed and he was guilty of repeated major errors of judgment; for instance, his incredibly inept attempts to dictate the composition of the Cabinet in 1923 and 1930, his flirtation with Fascism in 1934, and his quixotic support of Hungarian revisionism.

Beaverbrook, in contrast, has throughout his career tried to follow a consistent policy, with constant objectives. The famous judgment passed on him by Baldwin, that he and Rothermere were exercising the prerogative of the harlot, power without responsibility, together with the mistaken tactics he has often adopted, have tended to obscure this fact. But Beaverbrook can be seen as the direct continuator (rather than descendant) of the pre-1914 Right. In the first place, as a Canadian who made his way without connections or influence, he has always stood as a popular Tory, jealous of oligarchical or aristocratic control of the party. As a purveyor of news to the masses, he could claim to know more about the mentality, opinions, and prejudices of the people than the party leaders did. What he forgot was that Baldwin's strength rested on his unexcelled skill and knowledge as a parliamentarian; Beaverbrook has never succeeded at Westminster, and has never shared in the politicians' veneration for parliamentary forms and traditions. As the proprietor who built up a newspaper empire, Beaverbrook had succeeded in selling the public what it wanted, and he thought he knew what policies, as well as news, it wanted.

Many of these were short-term appeals: retrenchment in the 1920's; isolation, no European entanglements, no war in the 1930's.

But these were not just stunts; a consistent attitude lay behind them. Beaverbrook has always been an imperialist in the nationalist sense, concentrating his attention on the empire, and particularly on the self-governing dominions, urging its maximum development, and pressing the government and the nation to turn its back on Europe. This attitude, which led him into consistent and at first almost unique opposition to the Common Market in 1960–1963, in the 1920's made him launch an "Empire Crusade" for imperial free trade. However, there were complicating factors which obscured this objective at the time. Beaverbrook, who had played such an important part in securing the party leadership for Bonar Law in 1911, and in removing Asquith in 1916, and had continued as Bonar Law's confidant, resented Baldwin's neglect of the press generally and of himself particularly. He denied that he pursued a vendetta against Baldwin, but there is no doubt that his ally, Rothermere, did, and that much of his support came from anti-Baldwin politicians including survivors of the Coalition. On the other side, there can be no doubt that a large section of Baldwin's supporters hated the popular press and openly pursued a vendetta against Beaverbrook which went back to his activities in 1911 and 1916. They misrepresented his campaign as mere mischief making, and attacked him as just an inveterate intriguer and political fixer.

Politics, like war, are an option of difficulties, and Beaverbrook was trapped in a genuine political dilemma. He wanted things done, especially in imperial politics, but could they be achieved by orthodox methods? A strong protectionist organization, the Empire Industries Association, already existed, with a membership of over two hundred M.P.'s. Should he satisfy himself by supporting a constitutional course of action within the party conventions? This was a safe course, but was it likely to produce early or tangible results, however strong its case and enthusiasm? After all, protectionists like William Clive Bridgeman and Amery had been advocating imperial protection for years, without result. The conservative Central Office bureaucrats and the leaders in the Lords were hostile. Again, Beaverbrook wanted a working agreement with the dynamic Lloyd George, who was producing a spate of proposals to deal with unemployment and other major problems, and who could be won for tariffs. But the party men, remembering 1918–1922, would have nothing to do with him.

Beaverbrook, despairing of action by the Tory leaders, formed the United Empire party, unwisely in association with Rothermere, whose erratic behavior proved a liability. This met at first with widespread, spontaneous support, and one smashing by-election victory (at West Fulham) showed what might be achieved. But once it became obvious that this would be a breakaway movement, that its activities would have to be directed against Tory candidates, the support evaporated. Beaverbrook recognized the difficulties of his position. He did not want to smash the Tory party. Sincerely and seriously he attempted to come to terms with Baldwin, but whether he reached an agreement or whether he fought on, the brutal fact remained that power, and the achievement of his policies, lay beyond his grasp. Loyalty to the party has always been the first principle of the orthodox Tory. By appealing to this loyalty, Baldwin, despite his lack of success at the time as leader of the opposition, was able to consolidate his position as leader in June and again in October, 1930, and to fight off another challenge, by Churchill, early in 1931. It was not until the crisis of the war, in 1940, that Beaverbrook joined Churchill in power, but attention must be drawn to the less appreciated fact that this partnership was continued in the first months of peace. Churchill and Beaverbrook were the Tory principals in the disastrous general elections of 1945. Their total defeat led to the eclipse of the Right; for the last eighteen years control has been in the hands of the orthodox, the liberal Tories, and the professionals.

In writing of the 1930's, historians, especially those who were adults at the time, have concentrated on foreign policy and its effects so much that they have tended to treat purely domestic politics as either directly connected with, or subordinate to, foreign affairs. Sir Oswald Mosley and the fascists have usually been regarded as an imitative movement, interesting mainly because they show the influence in England of political developments in Europe. They are still described, in the jargon and following the propaganda of the time, as a German or Italian Fifth Column. This emphasis can, of course, be exaggerated. Mosley and his followers were, at least in their own eyes, the response from the Right to primarily domestic issues; they were the reincarnation of the pre-1914 Right, just as the Communists could regard themselves as the descendants of the prewar syndicalists. It is significant that Mosley broke away from the Labour party in March, 1931, and founded the British Union of Fascists in October, 1932—that is, before Hitler's seizure of power and the beginning of international tension—and that similarly it was at this time that the Communists began to attract young intellectuals in large numbers. The reasons for this expansion of the political extremes were primarily domestic; foreign-policy considerations were to come later.

Mosley and the fascists had the same reasons for dissatisfaction with the kind of leadership offered by the main parties, and politicians, as the young men who had hailed Chamberlain's challenge to the old men and the old conceptions in 1903. They had even more reason for alarm at the state of the nation, for the same problems remained as in 1903, but in aggravated form. Politicians, intellectuals, economists, businessmen, and trade unionists mostly adhered to outmoded concepts, drifted with the course of events, oblivious to the forces that were changing the world. The nation was apathetic, passive, and inert. Chronic mass unemployment was accepted with resignation, whole sectors of the economy had become obsolete. Pacifism, cynical disillusionment, or hedonism had largely submerged the patriotism that the Right cherished. The response to unrest in India and Egypt seemed to show, as administrators in those countries complained, that a "will to rule" no longer existed. The slogans with which politicians appealed to the public were "Safety First," "Business as Usual," "Repose and Retrenchment."

The challenge was similar to that of thirty years before, but the response was different. The fact that the prewar Right had still not achieved any of its principal objectives showed that there must be a clean break with the past, specifically with the party system.

The Tory party must be replaced, as unfitted for constructive purposes. From experience, Mosley also castigated the Labour party for ineffectiveness as well as for antinational tendencies. Like Milner, Mosley rejected the party system, but in the fascist system of Benito Mussolini he now had an alternative with which to replace it. Admittedly this was of foreign origin, but Mosley claimed that fascism was relevant because it was modern, in accordance with the spirit and needs of the age, and because it alone could save the nation from the imminent and total catastrophe he predicted and still predicts today. Unlike leaders of the earliest British fascist movements, Mosley did not see himself as the auxiliary of the Tories; rather he would take over from them as the crisis intensified and the decisive clash began.

The earlier movements (the British Fascists, founded in 1923, the Fascist League, the British National Fascists, and about ten more splinter groups—such was the tendency to split and break away) were theatrical rather than practical. They adopted fascist salutes, uniforms, terms, and other externals without any real understanding of fascist ideas and theories. They appealed to reactionary, rather than radical, elements of the Tory party, and were almost entirely upper class in composition, relying heavily on families with a service or overseas civil service background. The one exception was the rabidly anti-Semitic Imperial Fascist League of Arnold Leese, which he founded in 1929 and which can be more accurately described as Nazi than fascist.

Mosley's stated objectives were traditional to the Right. He claimed to be a nationalist and an imperialist, emphasizing the need for imperial unity and development, and strenuously repudiated the charge that he would sell out English interests to foreign powers. He insisted, and this was perhaps his main attraction, that things must be done, decisions must be made on all the major problems; Mosley made frequent use of words like *dynamic, action, decision.* The fascists also demanded social reforms, promised a major attack on unemployment, poverty, and bad housing; they proposed a health service, and planned big public works programs. Rather more vaguely they spoke of the revival of the national spirit, of patriotism, of dedication and discipline, and of the leadership principle or, as it was sometimes phrased in a gesture to an English characteristic not so often found among Italians, team spirit. Not surprisingly, many Englishmen, especially conservatives and old members of the Right, were attracted by these high-sounding words. Mosley also appealed specifically to the young, although the initial response came from the young middle-aged—that is, from men who had fought in the last stages of the war, or had been just too young to do so. But though many were attracted, only those recruited from the extreme Left (mainly the Independent Labour party) or the extreme Right (the old fascist leagues) stayed in any numbers.

It is easy now to understand why so many should have turned to Mosley, but even easier to understand why others were so quickly repelled.[5] Many fundamental fascist principles repelled would-be followers. Mosley was too autocratic and tended to select and promote as lieutenants only those prepared to follow him without hesitation or reservation. Fascist violence did not at first exceed what was acceptable at that time, but it became something of a cult, and when it was applied systematically and ruthlessly—as at the great rallies in 1934 and 1935—and provocatively—as in the London marches of 1936 and 1937—it earned almost universal disapproval. Much more damaging was the anti-Semitism, which, after 1934, became a characteristic—in the eyes of the public the chief characteristic—of fascism. Mosley always spoke of the English *race*, and of the need for its regeneration. Like Mussolini, he was not at first anti-Semitic, although from the beginning he denounced "alien influences" and cosmopolitanism; but he attracted many who were strongly anti-Semitic, especially in the East End of London, the only area in which he ever gained mass support. His thus-enhanced anti-Semitism became a particularly fatal liability because it led to his being associated with Hitler, and Hitler's brand of anti-Semitism was something even the warmest advocates of an understanding with Germany could not stomach. Three of these, the seventh Marquess of Londonderry, Sir Philip Gibbs, and Victor Cazalet, frankly warned German officials of the fatal

---

[5] This tendency had already been foreshadowed in the rapid breakup of the New Party in 1930–1931.

damage done by Nazi anti-Semitism. Only eccentrics like Admiral Sir Barry Domvile and Captain Archibald Henry Maule Ramsay, who had swallowed the *Protocols of the Elders of Zion* and other propaganda, publicly and avowedly expressed strongly anti-Semitic views.

There was one more fundamental obstacle to the acceptance of fascism by even conservatives of the Right. They were attracted to it by their own dislike of what Mosley denounced—the stagnation attributable to the party system, the slump in national morale, the failure to check the spread of subversive ideas and movements at home or abroad. So far as they understood them, they rejected the "liberal" conceptions of natural rights and popular sovereignty which derived from Voltaire, Rousseau, and the French Revolution. But this did not mean that they would accept an organic, all-powerful state, to which the individual must be permanently subordinated. They suspected the abstract idea of "liberty" and its political implications, but instead they postulated the old English concept of "liberties," and these were specific rights belonging to the individual; they were not conferred on him by a government or the state. It followed that few would accept the institutional system that the fascists proposed. They disliked the party system, but they did not want to introduce the corporative state with all its authoritarian trappings. Mosley proposed that the government should be responsible to the people through quinquennial plebiscites. Parliament, elected on an occupational franchise, would have only minor functions; the Commons, meeting for only short periods, would merely scrutinize legislation, the upper house would be purely advisory. A Grand Council of Fascists would advise the king on the choice of a successor to the prime minister. Local government would also be based on an occupational franchise, but much greater importance would be attached to the twenty-four corporations and the National Council of Corporations, which were to control the economic life of the nation and would be composed of representatives of the government, the workers, and the employers.

Many Tories took an interest in the fascist movement, particularly in the early stages. A few ex-officers played a more or less active part. Most fascist militants were working class or lower-middle class; the Tories would never have accepted William Joyce or the proletarian East End leaders, such as Mick Clarke, Moir, and Goulding, in any position of prominence. Joyce acted as a Tory steward in the 1920's, but it is doubtful whether he would have advanced further. He is also an interesting example of a type common in the European Right but rare in England—the refugee who had suffered for the national cause. A significantly large proportion of the fascist rank and file came over from the extreme Left, some from the Communists, but more from the Independent Labour party. John Beckett, W. J. Leaper, Raven Thomson, and John Scanlon were among the most prominent examples.

Imitating communist techniques, the fascists formed front organizations, some of which were also assisted by the German Embassy. It was these bodies, such as the January Club (a forum for debate and discussion in which fascist ideas could be expounded and propagated), that attracted conservatives, but most of them were moribund by 1936, before the real controversy over Anglo-German relations began. This is a point that needs emphasis and elaboration. For understandable reasons, and with great effect in 1945, left-wing publicists tried to convict those Tories who had ever taken an interest in fascism of a general sympathy for it, and for the policy of appeasement which they depicted as antinational in intention and consequences. Yet there was no real connection between fascism at home and appeasement of Germany. Of those Tories who expressed an interest in fascism, only one, Lord Lloyd, was of any real moment, and he proved himself to be one of the strongest and most persistent enemies of appeasement. Appeasement was the policy of the orthodox Tories, of those who were "progressive" or "liberal" on domestic matters but who were not really interested in foreign affairs. When the issue was joined in 1938, the resulting division cut across existing lines. Most of those who had followed the Churchill policy concerning India now deserted him. Most of the "social imperialists" of the Round Table group helped to formulate and execute the appeasement policy; a few bitterly opposed it. The Left, too, was divided, with the pacifist wing and the *New Statesman* denouncing the idea of war for the Sudetenland. And if we are to find a prominent figure who pinned his hopes of political power on appeasement, it is to the Left that we must look for a kind of Pétain, to Lloyd George. Excluded from power by those whom he despised as mediocrities, exasperated by their failures at home and abroad, he was profoundly impressed (and flattered) by Hitler. During periods of crisis—at the time of the general strike, and again in 1938–1940—Lloyd George was consistently pessimistic and defeatist, both in parliament and in his syndicated articles in the American press. As early as 1936 he advocated the return to Germany of the former German colonies, he championed the Sudeten Germans in 1938–1939, and in October, 1939, he came out for negotiations with Hitler, after the German victory in Poland.

The Right in England has achieved a temporary influence only at times of crisis, when vital issues mattered, and major decisions had to be made. But in normal times, and this has meant the whole period covered by this study (except for the years 1910–1914), politics have been able to follow their normal course and political differences have been kept within the agreed conventions. The restricted influence of the Right within the Tory party, and its complete failure as a separate organization, is directly linked with the similar failure of the radical Left. The failure of the minority movement, a communist campaign to seize control of union leadership, restricted the influence of the most militant Right enemies of the trade unions. The collapse of the efforts of Sir Stafford Cripps (whose weird performance as an irresponsible and reckless demagogue in the 1930's has yet to be evaluated) to form a popular front, deprived the fascists of the one argument that might have brought them considerable support. When fascists and communists rioted in London the *Times* could, with a touch of complacency, condemn them as a nuisance, not as a danger.

Loyalty to two main parties has continued to be the principal characteristic of English politics, and party considerations have generally taken precedence over policies and principles. Broadly speaking, each party has drawn its support from clearly defined social groups and classes. In the past the working-class vote tended to go to the Liberals, now most of it goes to Labour, although the Tories have always received significant working-class support in some regions, notably Lancashire and the industrial Midlands. Again, although many intellectuals and younger voters among the middle class vote Labour, the vast majority steadily vote Tory. Extremists have failed to make an impact largely because of the lack of support from any significant social class or group. The extreme Left gained a mass following only in the slum areas of London and Glasgow; its appeal has been to the disgruntled among all classes. Similarly, the Right cannot be correlated with any social category. Before 1914, because of the political crisis, it consisted of the more combative, and in some ways the more constructive, Tories. Since 1918 it has attracted support mainly from the more impatient and aggressive of the upper class, particularly the military, the driftwood of the middle class, and the most deprived elements of the working class—before 1939 in the East End of London, since 1945 in such areas as Notting Hill. Thus, as might be expected, there is a connection between political stability and the class stratification of English society. Englishmen are proud of their immunity from political convulsions, but whether the means by which this has been achieved, and the conditions which have encouraged it, will prove beneficent in the long run, only time will tell.

SUGGESTED READING

AMERY, LEOPOLD, C. M. S. *My Political Life*. London: 1953–1955. 3 vols.

BEAVERBROOK, LORD WILLIAM, M. A. *Men and Power*. London: 1956.
———. *Politicians and the War*. London: 1928–1932. 2 vols.

BELLOC, HILAIRE. *The Servile State*. London: 1912.

BELLOC, HILAIRE, and CECIL CHESTERTON. *The Party System*. London: 1911.

BLAKE, ROBERT. *The Unknown Prime Minister*. London: 1955.

BLATCHFORD, ROBERT. *My Eighty Years*. London: 1931.

CECIL, LORD HUGH R. *Conservatism*. London: 1912.

CHESTERTON, CECIL E. *Party and People*. London: 1910.

CHESTERTON, GILBERT KEITH. "The Patriotic Idea," in Lucian Oldershaw, ed., *England: A Nation*. London: 1904.

COLIN, G. F. ADAM. *The Life of Lord Lloyd*. London: 1948.

CRANKSHAW, EDWARD. *The Forsaken Idea*. London: 1952.

CROSS, COLIN. *The Fascists in Britain*. London: 1961.

ENSOR, ROBERT CHARLES. *England, 1870–1914*. Oxford: 1936.

GOLDMAN, SYDNEY. *The Empire and the Century*. London: 1905.

JEBB, RICHARD. *Studies in Colonial Nationalism*. London: 1905.

JENKINS, ROY. *Mr. Balfour's Poodle*. London: 1954.

MCDOWELL, ROBERT B. *British Conservatism, 1832–1914*. London: 1914.

MCKENZIE, ROBERT T. *British Political Parties*. Melbourne: 1955.

MACKINDER, HALFORD J. *The Modern British State*. London: 1914.

MILNER, LORD ALFRED. *England in Egypt*. London: 1892.

———. *The Nation and the Empire*. London, New York: 1913.

MOSLEY, SIR OSWALD. *The Greater Britain*. London: 1932.

———. *Mosley—Right or Wrong?* London: 1961.

———. Articles in the *National Review* (ed. L. J. Maxse).

RAYMOND, JOHN, ED. *The Baldwin Age*. London: 1960.

ROWSE, ALFRED L. *All Souls and Appeasement*. London, New York: 1961.

SCHUMPETER, JOSEPH A. *Imperialism and Social Classes*. New York: 1951.

SEMMEL, BERNARD B. *Imperialism and Social Reform*. Cambridge, Mass.: 1960.

THORNTON, ARCHIBALD P. *The Imperial Idea and its Enemies*. London, New York: 1959.

TYLER, JOHN E. *The Struggle for Imperial Unity*. London, New York: 1938.

WILKINSON, J. L. *The Great Alternative*. London: 1902.

———. *War and Policy*. London: 1910.

WRENCH, SIR J. EVELYN. *Alfred, Lord Milner*. London: 1958.

France

EUGEN WEBER

"For the last hundred years," writes René Rémond in his indispensable study of the Right in France, "no political force can avoid the question which scans our political life: Right or Left? Sooner or later, all movements are forced to enter the framework of this space with only two known dimensions: Right and Left."

History has placed the birth of this curious and arbitrary division in September, 1789, when the doctrinal differences of the National Assembly were first translated into topographical terms. Having taken their stand to the right of the President's chair, the upper clergy and the great nobles set out to obstruct and oppose the reformers of the "patriot" majority to the left of the podium. The two great political categories of modern times—the one exasperated, the other rationalistic, both verbose—seem to spring fully armed from this historical occasion. The kaleidoscopic changes of the next few years were to provide not only the slogans of centuries to come, but an object lesson in the speed with which Left becomes Right, showing how satisfied reformers, having achieved their ends, turn to defend them against those who ask for more, or for different, changes.

Nevertheless, in the perspective of things to come, historians have been chary of using terms like Left and Right for the periods of the Revolution and the Empire. Things move too fast. Although the leftward progression from Feuillants to Girondins to Jacobins seems clear enough, it is more difficult to decide between the claims of Danton and Robespierre when a recent student presents the latter as a precursor of "totalitarian democracy" or to tell whether Directory or Empire was the more reactionary phenomenon. Hence, it is with the restoration of a prince "who had learnt nothing and forgotten nothing," and particularly with the *Chambre introuvable* of 1815—unmatchable for its unconditional royalism—that the historian of the Right in France comes into his own.

Although the restored monarchy might have been willing to take things up from where they had gone wrong a quarter of a century before, ignoring the unpleasantness in between, the historian can scarcely do so. Nor could most men of the time. For they defined themselves and justified their policies largely in terms of the Revolution they had survived. And the politics of the new regime reflected the different mentalities, the different approaches, that would be those of "the French Right" in the century to come: on one hand, the conservatives, concerned largely with the present and trying to make the best of it, rejecting the principle of revolution but also that of counterrevolution just as unsettling, just as violent; on the other hand the Ultras, as they were known from their ultraroyalism—be it even against the king.

Characteristically, the Ultras were identified by a label and a point of view, vague perhaps but not indefinite. Not so the conservatives, who carried no particular title, no capital C, and were opportunistic, ready to work with beneficiaries of previous regimes, republican or imperial. They recognized experience, they respected success, above all they appreciated stability; for its sake, although any revolution in the making was anathema, a revolution once made might well be accepted for fear of further changes. In or out of power, we have here the prototype of what Rémond describes as Orleanism, less a party than a state of mind found in all the regimes that followed that of Bonaparte.

The Ultras, too, exhibited already the constant characteristics of what we call the extreme Right. The long exile of emigration, the isolation of provincial life, gave them little political experience. Considering honesty and loyalty above expediency, their intransigeance made them shun the politically possible for the absolute.

Revolution was evil, and there could be no compromise with evil or with those who treat with it. Opposed to the Reds, the Ultras were equally opposed to the beneficiaries of the existing order: the great nobles and upper bourgeoisie, who set their interests above the country's good. And they expressed these views (last but not least of their enduring characteristics) in very forceful ways. If the potential Orleanist was a moderate, a man of government and interests par excellence, the Ultra was an extremist, the man of a simple faith and faithfulness which experience in no way affects. Time and failure seemed merely to enhance the bright intransigeance of his dream, the romantic dream of a time when Victor Hugo could write an ode to Quiberon, and Lamartine sing the coronation of King Charles X. The Ultras were romantics, with Chateaubriand, as they would be a hundred years later with Montherlant or Drieu La Rochelle, slaking their thirst for action and enthusiasm in the fast-flowing waters of some political torrent.

Men of affairs, the Orleanists were also men of peace. Ultras were violent and combative by nature, at least in word and gesture: among them were La Bourdonnaye, so extreme that his own friends called him the White Jacobin; Jules de Polignac, whose Catholic faith would not bow even to the royal Charter; and Chateaubriand, who preferred to scuttle his very successful review, *Le Conservateur*, rather than submit its articles to any press censorship, even that of his king. They recognized this trait in themselves and took a rueful pride in it. As the most faithful of royalist resistance leaders, the Chouan, Cadoudal, said to a comrade in 1800: "If ever the King recovers his throne, he would do well to have us shot. We shall never be, you and I, anything but conspirators." Old Bolsheviks and old Chouans present much the same problem, or so it seems.

Already, we notice certain constant traits: Catholicism, stubbornness, independence, interest in conspiracy, and a rapprochement with the diametrically opposed extreme of the detested Jacobins which was suggestive of the future. Nor was this last so out of place, for the extreme Right always inclined to a kind of aristocratic populism, relying on the traditional forces and uncorrupted loyalties of "the people" against the bourgeoisie they both detested. It was the Marquis de Villèle, long the prime minister of Charles X, who advised his friends, if they wanted the upper class elected, to "reach down as far as you can and thus annul the middle class which is the only one you have to fear." And the Ultras did envisage a much broader electoral appeal than the more conservative right would countenance. Later, in opposition under Louis-Philippe, we find the Legitimists unreconciled to his rule appealing to the workers, distributing tracts in working-class quarters, bewailing the fate of the Lyon proletariat shelled on the new king's orders. On several occasions, Legitimists came forward to pay the heavy fines inflicted on left-wing Republican publications. Republicans and Legitimists met and became friends in prison; there was even an attempt (patronized by Chateaubriand) to found a joint publication prophetically titled *La Nation*. Later, shortly before 1914, followers of Georges Sorel and Charles Maurras were to plan a similar enterprise, and the monthly *L'Indépendance* would briefly group syndicalists, nationalists, and royalists in similar opposition to the existing system.

It is easy to explain such doings by a *politique du pire* (a leaning toward the worst rather than a lesser evil) which made the unreconciled Right prefer the enemies of regimes other than their own to moderates who came to terms with the prevailing system. But the *politique du pire* is merely the logical rejection of a corrupt and corrupting system, essentially Orleanist in nature, even before 1830, even after 1848, than which system nothing could be worse. On the political plane, the revolutionaries, republican or syndicalist, who really intended to change the existing order, were closer to the Ultras than were their own moderate cousins and in-laws who merely intended to improve it. After 1830, common hostility to the existing order did provide a logical ground on which radical revolutionaries and radical reactionaries could meet, just as identical solicitude for the existing order provided the common ground of conservatives both of the Left and Right.

Actually, under the July Monarchy (1830–1848), the extreme right in its first and Legitimist guise played only the slightest role. Conservatives sat in the seats of power, moderate in everything but the conservation of their control, and Ultras once more left public affairs for internal emigration. If we connect political and economic developments, as we tend to do, accounts of this period explain the collapse of Restoration aristocracy by the rise of economic forces that those who replaced the Bourbons in 1830 seem to represent. But finance capital did not replace landed property in the space of a few weeks or months around 1830. The sudden eclipse of a politically significant class whose economic and social positions remained largely unshaken cannot be ascribed to economic changes that were far from sudden. So we must look not exactly elsewhere, but further. It was partly the Legitimists' vanity that suggested their abstentionist tactics after the July Revolution, but it was also the confidence they placed in the strength of their socioeconomic position. We know that, as things turned out, retaliation turned to abdication, and the internal emigration designed to isolate the upstart Orléans, isolated the Legitimists instead. This happened because the Right as a whole was divided, its most active representatives leaning toward a liberalism that the Ultras most abhorred and that Orleanism embodied.

Liberalism was one of the branches of the revolutionary tradition, and an essential factor of nineteenth-century political confusion—because we find it both on the Left and on the Right. In each instance, however, it is there because of a coincidence. Standing for individual freedom and free enterprise, liberalism appears at different times connected with different political groups, its political interests varying with its social and economic success. Its first appearance on the political scene was made on behalf of eighteenth-century Enlightenment and of a more rational distribution of social power. In the society of the Old Regime, economic resources were distributed or redistributed according to the views and interests of a ruling group whose position was based on birth. Rights were not determined by present merit and labor, but by something that had been done in the past. Social permanence was founded in the hereditary permanence of social authority and the institutionalized permanence of moral authority. In every field, hierarchy was founded not on experience, performance, or need, but on tradition, on the arbitrary reflection of past circumstances.

Whenever economic conditions evolve faster than the social

order, some kind of upheaval becomes necessary to adapt one to the other. In this particular instance, an important section of the possessing classes wanted to change the existing order radically. It was encouraged to do that by the enlightened ideas of reason, liberty, and progress, according to which the past has no rights for its own sake, and reason alone can justify the actions and order of the present. Everything, said the advocates of reason against mere tradition, should be explained and justified before the court of reason. The chief protagonists of this view, which stressed the individual's liberty to use his reason and apply it in his free enterprise, were the economically dynamic classes—business, industry, finance. These were the engineers of social change and, as they judged, of social progress. Did not reasonable observation of the past show change and progress to be identical? Desiring freedom from the old restrictions, restrictions for anachronistic freedoms, the party of movement (as it came to be known) was a party of change which acknowledged traditions only to criticize them.

Here we have the first term of the revolutionary trinity. But to liberalism of this kind political liberty is simply the guarantee of an economic determinism which cannot be improved upon by human interference. This means that liberty must remain largely liberty *from*, the field free from restrictions, where competence and enterprise assert themselves to form or join the ruling elite. This view of society, however, was not only opposed to the indolent privileges of birth, but to an important component of the Revolutionary tradition: Jacobin egalitarianism. The liberal followed the rationalist tradition of Condorcet, limiting political activity to property-owners in the belief that propertyless men lack a motive for supporting the state. The Jacobin stood in the tradition of Rousseau, his egalitarianism profoundly subversive of both traditionalist hierarchy and liberal enterprise. The Jacobin did not reject property as he rejected birth, but claimed his share of it, thus denying the ultimate virtue of private enterprise and violating the sanctity of private property in the name of abstract justice, concrete need, and a rationalism of his own which pitted the last two terms of the revolutionary trinity against the first.

Liberty, Equality, and Fraternity do not necessarily hang together. And Fraternity (adopted only later, as an afterthought) was rightly seen as necessary to temper the rigors of Liberty or make Equality endurable. In effect, the enterprising proponents of Liberty did not believe in Equality, and the hungry devotees of the latter cared little enough for Liberty. This is why we find liberals on the Left when calling for liberty, and on the Right when defending their conception of liberty against egalitarians. It is also why, in 1830, the upper-class descendants of this Enlightenment tradition—the imperial aristocracy (Soult, Moret, Sébastiani), the families of the old magisterial nobility (Molé, Pasquier), the liberal aristocracy, like the Broglies—sided not so much with the son of Philippe-Egalité as with his party. For the Orleanists appeared (at least to themselves) as the party of competence, intelligence, and reason: a party of professors like Guizot, and of publicists like Thiers, which marshaled the resources not only of the banks but also of the University, the Académie, the Institut.

This alliance between the liveliest elements of the aristocracy and what Beau de Loménie calls the great bourgeois dynasties produced a regime that was politically liberal and socially conservative, after the manner of the English whom the Orleanists admired. Its existence, however, depended on the extent to which it satisfied its beneficiaries. The Orleanists had to be numerous enough to hold their own, active enough to recruit, convert, impress. A rationalist elite, recruiting only very selectively by coöption, was not likely to fulfill these conditions. Fortunately, the typical Orleanist, more concerned with private enterprise than with public affairs, cared little for the name of a regime provided its institutions suited his needs. Hence, the moderate Right (as I shall call it now) adjusted itself well enough to the political revolution of the Second Republic and even to the social revolution of the Second Empire. And the adjustments reflected what they considered fundamental: their economic interests. In 1848 the liberal and the Jacobin revolutions clashed, and even a Bonaparte could prove acceptable if he would hold the Jacobin revolution at bay.

More authoritarian than Orleanists would like, more nationalistic than Legitimists would care for, trailing the revolutionary overtones that must forever cling to Napoleon as to his nephew, Bonapartism entered the scene in 1848, and with it appeared a new category of the French Right. Antiparliamentary, egalitarian, and popular, it stood against the other currents and tendencies of the Right: it was undignified, amoral, illiberal, indifferent to conservatism and to all traditions but the one it incorporated. This makes all the more remarkable the way in which President Louis-Napoleon, then Emperor Napoleon III, was accepted by a moderate Right whose leaders he first bamboozled and then imprisoned. Two explanations for this have been suggested: one, the middle-class fear of working-class revolution, which made it welcome any port in a storm; the other, the middle-class greed for gain which persuaded it, well-served by a period and policy of great material expansion, to sacrifice political principle to economic expediency.

Both these explanations are valid up to a point. But one must add that Napoleon III symbolized the Revolution and guaranteed its gains in a way no other figure "of the Right" could do. He thus represented a special kind of conservatism, particularly that of the peasants who remained faithful to him to the very end; and the support of interests vested in the legitimacy of revolution gave his rightism a very different hue from any other. Even his attitude toward labor lacked the clarity that liberals would have liked: the revolutionaries, crushed in June, 1848, had referred to a Jacobin version of the property argument. Where the Girondists, like Condorcet, like the *monarchie censitaire,* had argued that a man without property was a man with no stake in the country— hence not to be entrusted with a vote, for economic irresponsibility implied political irresponsibility—others turned the argument around to reach nationalist and collectivistic conclusions. The nation was one, and so was its welfare. If political and economic responsibilities were related, so were political and economic rights. The common interest had to be opposed to the private selfishness of the liberals, and the general will to their individualistic rationalism. This is the basis of a Jacobinism of both the Left and Right, which would be reflected in due course in the doctrine of nationalists like Maurice Barrès and, also, to some extent, in that of the Communists. For the moment, it was the essence of the threat from which Napoleon III was supposed to save the property-owning classes.

But the new ruler remembered the nationalist implications of his own tradition, and the authoritarian claim that he served not a class, but all society. The Second Empire was the reign of movement, of enterprise, of action often for action's sake, above all of organization—the great idea of the Saint-Simonians who played such an important part in its economy. It offered tremendous opportunities for individual financial enterprise, but it abandoned liberalism for interventionism (there would have been fewer opportunities without it), and this meant also concern for the lot of the workers—not only as individual candidates for bourgeois status, but as members of a class that wanted to organize and to improve its lot *as such*. Some of the workers remembered this, and in July, 1878, the striking miners of Anzin, led by a Bonapartist, tried to bring out their fellow miners at Denain with cries of "Long live Napoleon IV!" They were unsuccessful, as it happens, for the velleities of the proletariat had been crushed in 1871 by an old Orleanist. "The ground is strewn with corpses," Thiers had remarked upon reëntering Paris after the Commune had been put down. "This dreadful sight shall serve as a lesson."

The Third Republic, founded under the aegis of Adolphe Thiers, sometime minister of Louis-Philippe, expressed well enough a point of view Thiers had voiced earlier, before the plebiscitary menace of the Empire: "True republicans fear the masses, the vile masses which have caused the downfall of all republics." Evidently, the republicans Thiers had in mind were patrician republicans, and this was the kind of Republic he sought to found: Daniel Halévy's *République des Notables,* an Orleanist regime without an Orléans.

In this connection, it is worth remembering that the monarchist and reactionary National Assembly of 1871–1872 was as ready to vote an income tax as it had been to establish universal military service, and that only Thiers and his supporters thwarted these trends, proposing instead to rely on discriminatory long-term service for the army, on tariffs and loans for the treasury. Conservatism had made new recruits, and Thiers' position reflected the profound tendencies of peasantry and middle classes: individualism, protectionism, discrimination, and deep attachment to privileges— provided these were their own.

The heyday of the Notables was brief. The upper-middle-class conservatism of the seventies had to give way to another middle class, republican on principle and strongly politicized. It was the revenge of lawyers and teachers over the industrialists and economists who served the Empire of the man who has been called a Saint-Simon on horseback. Technicians were replaced by "intellectuals"—middle-class intellectuals, no longer appealing to the old elite of birth and talent, but to a vast, undifferentiated public, mainly of the middle and lower-middle class.

The historical connection between Revolution and Republic, the antiaristocratic and anticlerical appeals of Republican politicians, even the objective socioeconomic tendency of their measures, was to give the last third of the nineteenth century a leftist coloring. Nevertheless, one need not be surprised to see the progressives of one day becoming the moderates of the morrow, for politicians merely reflect the public to which they appeal. What better potential conservatives could one wish for than these petit bourgeois Republicans, these little people, *petits propriétaires*, who read the *Petit journal*, cheered the *petit soldat*, ran their *petit commerce*, and sipped their *petit vin blanc*, while aspiring to become *petits rentiers*?

The years from the 1870's to 1914 were for France the high point of a democratic capitalism that drained the savings of these small investors into the enterprises of the great money powers. "The bourgeoisie must come to include all the population," a Saint Simonian, Michel Chevalier, had declared under the Empire. But it was under the Third Republic that this worthy purpose came nearest to fulfillment. In 1867, joint stock companies had been freed of all governmental interference. Their extension would go far to realize Chevalier's wish, and to establish first the economic solidarity of the high and the small bourgeoisie, then the involvement of the security-minded small investor in the state— because the state, the biggest enterprise of all, seemed to offer the safest and stablest opportunities for investment. What the Orleanist elite had failed to do, the capitalist enterprise of the late nineteenth and early twentieth centuries achieved, thus defusing an important section of society.

This increasingly stable and comprehensive bourgeois society was increasingly engaged in unproductive occupations. The number of persons dealing exclusively in goods produced by others doubled between 1866 and 1906, that of their employees tripled, while the country's population increased 3 per cent. Not surprisingly, the new society was also highly class conscious. The practical elimination of higher estates merely meant a recategorization within the dominant class. Already under the Second Empire, when the new prosperity was causing serious social confusion, when the newly founded department stores (Bon Marché, 1852; Louvre, 1855; Printemps, 1865; Samaritaine, 1869) offered everything to everybody who could pay for it, *haute couture* had appeared to provide sartorial distinction and help differentiate between rich and poor by the cut and quality of their apparel. At the same time, Baron Haussman's urban policies defined and regrouped working-class quarters, just as in the comfortable new buildings of the bourgeois districts unheated, unlighted *chambres de bonne* were designed to fill the awkward angles underneath the roof.

But where the mid-nineteenth-century bourgeoisie set itself off by sumptuary distinctions and other material tricks fit for parvenus, the Third Republic preferred to emphasize educational differences essential to social promotion under the new, neo-Orleanist regime. The elite of the Republic was to be one of "intellect and capacity," trained, selected, and distinguished mostly in the schools. The founding of the Ecole Libre des Sciences Politiques in 1872, "to give a head to the masses" and to provide "political mechanics, technicians, and specialists" for the new France, symbolized this elitist effort. Between 1900 and 1937, 116 out of 120 *Conseillers d'Etat*, 209 out of 218 *Inspecteurs des Finances*, 83 out of 94 *Conseillers à la Cour des Comptes*, and 249 out of 284 members of the diplomatic corps, had passed through this nursery of the Republican elite.

The masses would be given leadership, but the classes carefully kept their hands on the levers of power. In 1882, the Republic's famed educational reforms separated elementary and higher education, ignoring the egalitarian principles they claimed to advance and making quite sure that the elite of the future would be siphoned through the bottlenecks they set up. The country's managers, its teachers, and its rulers, were recruited from the university and the *grandes écoles*, which could be entered only through *lycée* or *collège*. Even a progressive-minded Republican anticlerical, mayor of a village in the west of France, strongly objected to higher education for lower-class children. He was all for schools and schooling, writes Roger Thabault in *Mon Village* (Paris: 1944), "but he felt very strongly the anxiety of the bourgeois before the rising tide of unemployed graduates."

The opposition forces of the Third Republic, the scum of the dissatisfied, the adventurous, the angry, the bitter, and the hopeful on both Left and Right, would be recruited from the ranks of these unemployed. In cafés, in down-at-heel salons, in bare editorial rooms, the unemployed bachelors plotted their conquest of fame and fortune and never quite made it. Some of them sought compensation or revenge by taking up the cause of social revolution: anarchism, syndicalism, or socialism. Others, in the same mood, gravitated to the other extreme, attacking the regime from the far Right, decrying the democracy they scorned because it scorned them, the egalitarian system that had served them ill, the authorities who had failed to discern their worth. We cannot ignore their constant role in the annals of the Right, but the authoritarian nationalism to which they chose to hitch their pallid stars is not thereby explained. For these men were its creatures, not its creators.

We shall not grasp the ideological roots of the new nationalist Right, either, or of the Third Republic unless we understand the intentions and the principles of the Republic's education policy which was always, as intended by its authors, as national as it was republican. To the men of the Left, but of the moderate, opportunistic, Orleanistic Left, who came to power after 1879, the Republic's only hope of success—that is, of survival—lay in education, an education that would form citizens, republicans, and electors—a stable basis for the new democracy. But the democracy they envisaged, although enlightened in the eighteenth-century sense of the term, was of a very limited kind. And the education they envisaged would inculcate above all a sense of patriotism and of social order, with the teacher and the officer as the twin pillars of the fatherland.

After the cascade of regimes and revolutions that followed on each other's heels from 1789, after the humiliations of 1870, patriotism and stability were the chief concerns of the new educators. Above all, they had to settle the Republic itself on firm foundations; for French unity, once based on the alliance of altar and throne, had to be reconstructed now on another basis—that of patriotic *duty*, which would be the corollary of republican liberty. This duty was not primarily demonstrated or reasoned, although it was that, too: essentially, patriotism was a revelation. It was taught, it was imposed as an indisputable verity. Others might try to prove the commandment that man must love his fatherland; true Republicans knew it as an article of faith. And this held good for other aspects of the system; for dogmatic patriotism also justified the stability of the regime and the social and moral values of the classes identified with it. "The revolutions which were necessary in the past are not necessary today," wrote Ernest Lavisse in the elementary text of history almost every French schoolboy read. "French society is ruled by just laws because it is a democratic society. All the French are equal in their rights; but there are between us inequalities which come from nature or from wealth. These inequalities cannot disappear."

It was the business of the schools to train citizens as electors, not as competitors, in a deferential society and a practical, productive one, aiming, as Lavisse put it, to "mettre tout Français en culture pour qu'il rende son maximum." Patriotism, yes; social utility, yes; social promotion, eventually, perhaps. National education did indeed turn out republican patriots; but when the Republic, which had been a great mystique, became first a compromise and then an excuse, and when the fatherland seemed to be sinking into weakness and corruption, these very ideals turned against their moderate promoters, providing dangerous slogans which were to shake the Republic itself and the republican institutions that had once justified it.

The beginning of this process appeared in the late 1880's, with the Boulangist crisis in which a popular general gathered around him an unusual coalition of all the discontented: radicals, reactionaries, and patriots. The Republic was settling down all right, but lower and lower in the mire. Abroad, it seemed to shun the forceful policy which alone could recover the provinces lost in 1871; at home, its anticlericalism antagonized the Catholics and its scandals shocked the respectable. The moderate Right, which approved a cautious foreign policy, objected more strongly to anticlericalism; the Jacobin Left, enthusiastically anticlerical, was disappointed by the waning of revanchism, disillusioned by the loss of republican purity. The rallying cry of all Boulangists would soon be "Down with the thieves!"—a cry to be heard again at regular intervals in the Republic's annals. And Maurice Barrès, a deputy at the age of twenty-seven, noted that the basis of Boulangism was "an appeal to honesty." On this vague, loose platform, Jacobins, Bonapartists, Royalists, and Blanquist Socialists could agree, with no other doctrine in common and with a leader who provided none—nor leadership, either.

True Boulangists, like Barrès, were authoritarians with strong nationalist and socialist leanings. But they were swamped by the mass following of the extreme Left *and* Right, which expressed a temperament and a dissatisfaction rather than a doctrine, and they were ignored by a leader who was not even dynamic enough to follow his troops. However, Boulangism, even in its failure, had a profound effect on French politics and political problems. In the decade after 1879 the new Republic had tended to the Left—moderately, but clearly enough—its insecurity and newness leading moderate Republicans to rely on fellow Republicans of more radical hue for the preservation of the regime. But in the crisis of Boulangism, the Radicals had proved untrustworthy. Fascinated by the General's nationalist and popular appeal, they had revealed themselves more Jacobin than Republican. Frightened by this narrow escape, the moderate Republicans now turned to their fellow moderates on the Right, seeking to conciliate them, toning down the more radical implications of their republicanism and particularly the anticlericalism that had cemented the alliance with the

Left. This led the Radicals to turn even more fiercely against moderates of every hue, against a parliament dominated by moderates and discredited by the unsavory bargains struck in its corrupt corridors. Forged in such fires and dissensions, verified by the great Panama scandal in 1893, antiparliamentarism bred the nationalism and the nationalist frame of mind that was to play such a singular part in the affairs of the Third Republic.

A major aspect of the Boulangist appeal had been the rehabilitation of the army humiliated by Prussian defeat, the restoration of the nation's pride in its army and of the army's pride in itself, and the renewed evocation of the lost provinces—Alsace and Lorraine. Boulanger had been "Général Revanche." After his fall, this idea, heretofore so dear to the Left, became more and more a prerogative of the Right. One of the greatest promoters of revanche had been Paul Déroulède, who had founded the Ligue des Patriotes in 1882 to work for the recovery of Alsace and Lorraine. At that time, Déroulède and his league stood close to Jules Ferry, Paul Bert, and the other Republican founders of the secular and patriotic educational system. But Déroulède became one of General Boulanger's warmest supporters and, after the General's defeat, his league shifted toward the Right, taking its chauvinism with it at the very time when, on the extreme left, Marxist propaganda was beginning to wear down the traditional popular patriotism of the working classes. In the late eighties, the Russian alliance would speed this trend, the Left suspecting and the Right rejoicing over closer relations with the most reactionary regime in Europe. Finally, a decade later, the whirlpool of the Dreyfus Affair put the finishing touches to an evolution by which the cult of revanche, fiery patriotism, and the militarism associated with them, were to pass from the Left to the Right.

Schooled in the popular agitation of the eighties, the Ligue des Patriotes was the first of many movements organized not for electoral and parliamentary action, but for the mobilization and manipulation of crowds outside the established structure of parties and parliament, indeed, even against them. Here we have the source and prototype of the nationalism that, according to René Rémond, is simply a reincarnation of Bonapartism. As Rémond writes, "Taste for authority, prestige of force, attraction of adventure and glory, cult of the leader, anti-parliamentarism, appeal to the masses, all the characteristics of Bonapartism meet again in Nationalism." In some ways, we might go further back than that and recognize certain aspects of the restoration Ultras: turbulent, intransigent, more concerned with persons than with doctrine, the nationalists seem to prolong a certain activist and combative tradition peculiar to all extremes.

The activist nature of fin-de-siècle nationalism conformed to a widespread contemporary mood, which we encounter in the works of such men as Nietzsche, Kipling, and Gabriele d'Annunzio. Its most representative figure, Maurice Barrès, had sought and found in it "something to nourish my imagination, my sensibility, my soul," had taken exquisite pleasure in "molding the souls" of his followers while reviving his own failing sensibility by the "political gymnastics" that first Boulangism, then nationalism, afforded. As another bellwether of this mood, Major Marchand, expressed it, he preferred the risk of French society exploding from too much violence to seeing it sink into a cowardly and mortal sleep. "We had absolutely to get going," Marchand, just back from Fachoda, wrote his friend Léon Daudet, "even at the risk of a bad fall, in order to catch up the other societies which had left us remarkably far behind these last thirty years. I do not pretend that we have taken the right way. But I do think we shall make it, all the same." The important thing was to start; the direction was secondary.

Impulsive, passionate, untheoretical, the nationalists emphasized energy and action as against intellect and words. Militaristic, violent, vulgar, populist, they were in effect very far from the old Right, and different even in certain respects from the Bonapartists, so much of whose strength lay in the countryside. For the nationalists were a peculiarly urban phenomenon, and their agitation scarcely touched the masses of the peasantry. One might say with little exaggeration that nationalism was a Parisian movement, its major successes gained among the people of Paris whose democracy consisted largely of hating the rich and despising the poor, its influence carried through France by Paris papers, like Rochefort's

L'Intransigeant and Drumont's *La Libre Parole,* which expressed this sort of petit-bourgeois radicalism.

Pierre Gaxotte once likened the French elector to an Edam cheese, red outside and white inside, revolutionary to obtain a pension and conservative to preserve it. With all its injustice, this sally goes a long way to explain the rightward shift—or drift—of an apparently left-wing electorate. And the crux of the explanation seems to lie in the makeup and orientation of those middle classes in which, as early as 1791, the Girondins had seen the fulcrum of power. During the nineteenth century, this vast and complex group (largely self-defined) was alternately seen as guardian of the established order against what François Guizot called the mad pretensions of levelers and anarchists, or as the ally, or potential ally, of the working class in the struggle for social revolution. We have seen how this had come to be, and how, in practice, it actually played both these parts.

Yet the classic interpretation of recent French history as a long leftward trend appears to be based only on the latter role—on a period of history in which the middle classes (to use the most general terms) were in favor of change, be it even revolutionary change. Even then the reforms they sought were political, not economic or social. Social and particularly economic reforms were subordinated to the political and to the middle-class concern for property, security, and order. As long as the chief bones of contention were of a "political" nature—legal, organizational, constitutional —the concern for order and security did not prevent an important segment of the middle class from ranging itself on the Left. Even the prospect of a revolution did not frighten them away, partly because revolution had entered national tradition, partly because it remained more talk than reality, partly, too, because it could be expected to improve their position. But it had to be the right kind of revolution: February, not June, in 1848; the republican September 4, 1870, not the Social Revolutionary Commune of March 18, 1871. And it had to limit itself to political, not social, changes.

On these terms, the middle-class groups usually continued to be in favor of change—until the elections of 1877, the resignation of the royalist Marshal MacMahon in 1879, and the election of a sound republican to the presidency. After 1879, their major aims attained, the political gains that could still interest moderate-minded republicans were few. Their continuance on the Left was owing to the need, first real, then only apparent, to defend their gains. It was owing also to the inevitable inertia of minds already made up within an established tradition. It was justified by making the most of a number of surviving issues. But these, in effect, were only two—free secular education and anticlericalism—neither of which could endanger property or the middle-class order. It was on this common platform, in which defense of republican institutions was a sine qua non, that the alliance of republicans and Radicals, and Radicals and Socialists, could be forged and maintained for some time. But we have seen that the Boulangist crisis raised grave doubts about the radical public's allegiance to the status quo and, early in the nineties, the *ralliement* of Catholic conservatives to the Republic marked a fairly general acceptance of the regime at just about the time when the educational reforms of Jules Ferry had become part and parcel of its structure. Republic and school no longer served as subjects of dispute, and this placed a severe strain on the unity of a Left now running short of common issues, a strain that would soon be translated into new political alignments. At the same time that growing numbers of right-wing moderates accepted the established order, a new idea rising on the Left, the idea of collectivism, threatened the notion of property and furnished a common basis of interest and principle for a major reversal of alliances in the politics of the Republic.

During most of the nineteenth century, the bourgeois dynasties in power had defended their places and their interests by straightforward and brutal repression, legalized by their control of the legislative and executive structure. Now the institutions of the Republic, the political formulas that sanctioned them, the rise of the lesser middle classes—the *nouvelles couches sociales*—that Gambetta hailed, all these established a political democracy that made earlier methods inapplicable and called for the kind of political organization that a more brutal system could dispense with. Since middle-class democracy could no longer stifle hostile political activity, it had to organize to meet its challenge. The development of work-ing-class organization and ideology in the 1890's, rejecting the established system and arraying themselves against it, called for an answer that the ordinary moderate citizen was not equipped to furnish but that nationalist leagues were eager to provide: a coun-tersocialism, emphasizing pragmatic reform against the utopian col-lectivism of labor, and stressing the common cause of lower bour-geoisie and workers in opposition to big money, big industry, big business, and the corrupt, oppressive machinery of parliament and state.

Far from being a representative institution, parliament was a symbol of factionalism and a divisive force. In the service of sinis-ter, un-French ends, political parties conducted a kind of endless civil war, perpetuating anarchy and chaos, suggesting and creating social divisions no less noxious for being artificial. The common interest of Frenchmen was that their country should be powerful and prosperous. This could not be while France was torn by fac-tional dissensions and selfish strife, whose most acute form was the class warfare initiated by Socialist threats to property and order. Classes and class divisions were false and evil myths devised by foreigners to weaken France, whose social improvement could stem only from social harmony. National unity had to be asserted both against the country's foreign foes and against the representa-tives of internal disintegration and anarchy. The principle of na-tional unity suggested the arguments of national populism: the revolutionary workers were not bad, merely misguided, deluded by alien doctrines and by leaders who were either foreign or sold to foreign gold.

The nationalist defined himself, by counterdefinition, as being against the foreign and the foreigner, whether the hereditary enemy of the moment, the alien, or the Protestant. Inevitably, he discovered the Jew as alien-in-residence, ubiquitous exploiter, cor-rupter, and debaucher of good citizens. Little known in France, anti-Semitism had been largely a facet of working class anticapi-talism until Drumont popularized it as part of an appeal to the economic fears and resentments of the middle classes. The Jew of Drumont, like that of Proudhon, was the symbol of that money power which small shopkeepers, artisans, and businessmen detested as much as the workers did, of that new order which all the tenants of the old decried, of those changes which so many sections of a France otherwise divided joined in suspecting. Furthermore, anti-Semitism provided an excellent diversion, often unaware, for social protests which could otherwise endanger non-Jewish interests.

True conservatives showed only the faintest sympathy for an anti-Semitism whose excesses they deemed vulgar and whose attacks on Jewish property or enterprise threatened their own, at least by implication. They were not far wrong, for anti-Semitism carried socioeconomic overtones, and when Drumont, for instance, ran successfully as anti-Semitic candidate in Algiers (1898), it was in connection with a vaster operation directed against two of the greatest representatives of big business interests, neither of them Jewish: Thomson, deputy of Constantine, and Etienne, deputy of Oran.

The danger might be distant, but conservatives had much to lose; nor were they convinced by the violent rigmaroles of anti-Semitic demagogues. Middle and lower-middle class, however, were influenced more easily. Their minds were less critical, their sense of menace greater, their understanding of the economic forces affecting them far less. One of the great figures of fin-de-siècle anti-Semitism, Max Régis, a hoodlum who reigned for several years as mayor of Algiers, used to lead the crowds in a "Marseillaise anti-juive," with this refrain:

> Y a trop longtemps qu'nous sommes dans la misère
> Chassons l'Etranger / Ça f'ra travailler.
> Ce qu'il nous faut c'est un meilleur salaire,
> Chassons du pays / Tout'cette bande de Youddis!

The memoirs of contemporary anti-Semites like Raphael Viau are one long witness to the petty economic resentments that led men into anti-Semitism.

If economic and social resentments on the one hand, and doctrinal needs on the other, were dominant in the development of nationalist anti-Semitism, a third factor must not be forgotten: religion. I have said little about the part played by religious questions in the fortunes of the Right, because the subject is immense and obscure. As different individuals' interpretations of religious commandments could lead them to either Right or Left, the student of politics is reduced to viewing the religious issue as a political one. From this perspective, the coincidence between the positions of the Catholic Church and those of the Right is almost constant. But which Right? In circumstances where the revolutionary tradition of the Left establishes a presumption of irreligion or, at least, anticlericalism, the most extreme antirevolutionaries would logically be the strongest supporters of religion. But the defenders of religion are not necessarily at one with the Church, and the hierarchy often feels more at home with moderate conservatives, even if they be skeptics, than with wild reactionaries inclined to Gallicanism or, at any rate, to rocking the boat.

This has generally been true, and, although coincidences may occasionally bring Church and extremists together, the basis of the Right's regard for the Church is that the latter represents order, hierarchy, and discipline. Paul Bourget, for instance, a writer of repute in the late nineteenth century and a representative figure of republican reaction, would come to feel that, in the midst of the ambiant anarchy of the nineties, no stronger discipline could be found than that of a Church that for centuries had managed to maintain an orderly cohesion between so many human beings. For Bourget, as for many other converts to Catholicism, the social value of the Church was a major argument in its favor.

Nationalists and anti-Semites, on the other hand, although occasionally congratulating Rome for triumphing over its Jewish origins, were not as deeply concerned with social order, or discipline of a conservative sort. They were seldom clerical, often agnostic, sometimes even anticlerical. Hence, this particular aspect of religion or religious politics affected them little. It is rather the negative side of religion's nineteenth-century fortunes that may have affected nationalist mentality and the nationalist appeal. The second half of the nineteenth century was notoriously a period of religious decay, so much so that in 1882 Nietzsche found it appropriate to announce the death of God. A new religion of science had succeeded the Voltairian skepticism of a more enlightened age.

Church-going faltered, along with religious faith. And this crisis of belief led to a flare-up of compensatory superstitions, sciences in the fashionable vein of the time, but occult sciences.

Besides, whether church-going or not, the minds of the nineteenth century were essentially religious in their tendency to believe in superhuman controlling powers of one sort or another. Mentalities familiar with the supernatural, whether "scientific" or "religious," inclined to seek the hidden factors and meanings of all events in some area beyond that of evident causes. Awareness of analogies was not reserved for Baudelaire—or Freud. It prevailed widely in a time when, as in the Middle Ages, everything could be taken as a sign; especially by intelligences trained in the scholastic tradition of the Catholic Church or the symbolic paraphernalia of Freemasonry. Here we may find a partial explanation of Catholic anti-Semitism and anti-Masonism, which went to extraordinary lengths, and of the readiness of a vast public to accept theories of hidden enemies and sinister plots—Jewish or Masonic for the Catholic public, Jesuit for anticlericals.

The masses, moreover, had been strongly affected by the popular and miracle-minded Catholic revival of the 1870's, the great pilgrimages to Lourdes and La Salette, the mystical pietism and pugnacity of the Assumptionist Fathers who left their mark on this age and their newspaper, *La Croix,* to ours. God had long before this become a personality of the Right. Now, the satanic, the symbolic, the supernatural were pressed into service against His enemies. The addiction of the great figures of popular nationalism to spiritualism and magic is a remarkable and intriguing fact. Drumont was extremely superstitious; his city editor, Gaston Méry, founded a periodical devoted to magic—*L'Echo du Merveilleux*; Léon Daudet and Charles Maurras of the Action Française were fascinated by graphology, palmistry, and clairvoyance; mediums and sorcerers were an integral part of the mysterious and conspiratorial world in which nationalists and anti-Semites moved. Often indifferent to God, their minds found little difficulty believing in the devil, and the devil theory of history was an important part of their appeal for a public that could find little other explanation for its difficulties and its misadventures.

Chauvinism, dissatisfaction, the promise of action, the reflection of diverse resentments and fears—nationalism embodied all of these in a vague invertebrate way and in a multitude of movements, most of them Parisian, most of them founded in the nineties, before and during the Dreyfus conflict. Among the better known of these movements were Déroulède's Ligue des Patriotes, Jules Guérin's Ligue Antisémitique and his Grand Occident (counterpart of the Masons' Grand Orient), Drumont's Jeunesse Antisémite, and the Ligue de la Patrie Française which briefly included the flower of the Academy and of fashionable right-wing society. These and a dozen more competed for subventions from much the same quarters, resented their fellows who poached on the same preserves, distrusted their rivals, and conspired to get rid of each other.

In the 1890's as in the 1930's the leagues could never agree on a common aim. For a brief while this may have proved an advantage, for it allowed the nationalists to adjust their appeals to the interests and the resentments of a varied electorate: Socialists in the poorer areas, to whom they represented themselves as "patriot" or "antigovernmental" socialists; radicals in the more prosperous areas, whom they attracted by championing the interests of the nation and of the little man; conservatives of the richer quarters, to whom they appealed as defenders of order. The success of this protean policy may be seen from the fact that the majority of the Paris municipal council members has been in the hands of the Right since 1900.

But their success was an imperfect one, and the nationalists gained little from either conservatives satisfied with their right-wing representatives, or workers who had been organized by Socialists and Syndicalists. A recent essay by D. R. Watson (in *The Right in France 1890–1919*, edited by David Shapiro [London: 1962]) argues that the nationalism of 1900, appealing to Center and Right, was not a reincarnation of Boulangism, which had rather rallied the two extremes against the Center. By 1900, however, the development of Socialist organization prevented a union of the discontented of the Left and Right, such as Boulanger had briefly headed. This time, the function of the nationalists was different. They built an ideological bridge over which sections of the middle class, lower-middle class, and unorganized workers could cross to a republican Right which no longer threatened the existing order, but promised to defend it against collectivism and its own corruption.

Once the troops had crossed, however, once Paris had been "clearly divided on social and economic lines," the bridge was no longer needed, and nationalism faded away, its representatives becoming indistinguishable from the rest of the Right—but of a new Right (as François Goguel tells us), "republican at least in name, socially conservative, opposed to the anticlericalism and antimilitarism of the Left." Indeed, the very anticlericalism and antimilitarism that served to unite Radicals and Socialists at the turn of the century was to help to disunite them when those radicals who remained adamant to nationalist siren songs in 1900 succumbed later to very similar appeals, but from significantly different quarters.

The point is that after 1905, when the last great dispute was settled, though hardly laid to rest by the separation of Church and state, the only remaining issues were socioeconomic. When the Socialists stressed this by calling on their Radical neighbors to move on to economic reforms, they met a very cold reception. The moderate republicans, who had put up with revolution when it had been political, and the Radical middle class, who had accepted change provided it was legal and constitutional, would have no part of reforms that might threaten their interests and, above all, their property.

Yet changes in apparent orientation are sometimes less easy to make than changes in real orientation. The Radicals before World War I were still counted, and counted themselves, as a party of movement; and they might have been embarrassed by the difficulty of reconciling ethos and interest if, at this juncture, they too (and *as Radicals*) had not found a bridge over which they could approach the party of order. This extremely important bridge was provided by the patriotic issues of the prewar years, in particular those following the Agadir crisis of 1911. The concern for social defense was thus complemented by the more meritorious claims of national defense. A moderate and patriotic majority emerged, including not only Radicals but also Independent Socialists like Millerand and Viviani. They elected Raymond Poincaré President of the Republic, they prepared for war, and they did their best to eschew an income tax.

The "sacred union" of the wartime years consecrated this evolution, and the "national" election of 1919 marked less a victory of the Right than a further broadening of a Center now including many Radicals and Independent Socialists. Of the forty-three cabinets that ruled the country between the victory of 1918 and the defeat of 1940, nineteen were pretty clearly of the Right, nine recognizably of the Left, and fourteen of the Center. Most of the last category, however, leaned away from the Left. The Center was nothing if not moderate, conservative even in the ritual repetition of traditional Left-sounding formulas. And certainly, by the twenties, few could doubt that (whatever their formulas and whatever their pretexts) this was where the Radicals belonged. Radicals participated in practically every cabinet after 1924, and led sixteen of them, but their attitude was seldom less than moderate. Their evolution reflected a change in the orientation of a section of the middle classes crucial in affecting the balance of political power, and it strengthened not the extremes, as one might have expected from the party label or from its Jacobin tradition, but the forces of conservatism.

Meanwhile, what of the leagues? While the middle classes gradually moved into the realm of respectability or, at least, of conservatism, what were the extremists to do who, in moments of crisis, voiced the resentments and embodied the wilder fantasies and aspirations of this class? Representing a mood rather than an idea, a reaction rather than a program, the leagues withered and vanished when the crisis that brought them forth was past, their public temporarily reassured, one set of problems apparently solved. During such periods, their public—generally apolitical anyway—finds that moderate political parties suffice to their needs. By 1904 or 1905, all the leagues that had flourished and flaunted and strutted a few years before had vanished. Only one league survived and would survive for many years: the Action Française, founded in 1899 by a few young intellectuals of the Patrie Française who were determined to think through the problems and factors of France's situation, work out a doctrine and a pattern for the salvation and regeneration of the country, and preach it to all who would hear.

The Action Française, in other words, set out to provide what the modern French Right always lacked: a doctrine; and it survived by virtue of this doctrine which gave it a cohesion, a continuity, a *personality*, which other movements of the extreme Right never had. Under the influence of a young royalist, Charles Maurras, the Action Française developed its doctrine, the philosophy of integral nationalism. And the accident of one man's stubborn will created not only the most important doctrinaire movement of the French Right, but recreated a monarchism most Frenchmen had believed was dead.

To save his country from the decay and disorder of the present, Maurras sought out the sources of French welfare, prosperity, and glory in the permanencies of the past, in those institutions that had proved their worth in the hard trials of historical experience. He concluded that only hereditary monarchy could provide the unity, stability, and authority without which the nation was bound to rattle itself to pieces. The violent break of the Revolution had to be mended not by integrating its debilitating principles into the French tradition, but by cutting them out, by eliminating the doings of a century of individualistic anarchy, wiping the slate clean, and starting out again where things had gone awry in 1789.

However, it was not Maurras's royalist demonstrations that won him the attention of a broader conservative public, but his insistence on order as "the first condition of the country's regeneration and salvation." Order, discipline, hierarchy were now doctrinally marshaled to oppose the false and subversive ideas of liberty for the individual at the expense of the social good, of equality contrary to natural law, of a doctrinaire factionalism that divided and weakened the nation for the benefit of particular interests. The nation, Maurras explained (as had been explained before, but many had forgotten)—the nation is an organic whole, no member, no part of which can assert himself or itself unduly without hurting the general interest; and between contending natural interests an arbiter is needed, the monarchical authority of a single power, of a single man, committed not to this side or to that but to the whole. Maurras was less a royalist than a monarchist, ready to break with the king if he did not fulfill his role as written, ready to welcome the monarchy of a Pétain who seemed to fill the bill. And Vichy in its first period was a Maurrassian monarchy, "a social hierarchy," as Pétain phrased it in his message of October 11, 1940, "rejecting the false idea of the natural equality of men" and putting into practice—or, at least, into law—many ideas of Maurras.

But before this tragic fulfillment of his teachings and his dreams, Maurras was to make the Action Française the great didactic center of the Right, the school from which a variety of more radical heresies arose, source and authority also for a conservative mass otherwise devoid of doctrine. The moderate, whether elector or politician, is no doctrinaire and generally relies on what he describes as common sense. Every now and then, however, a challenge faces him in which "enormous perils" seem to "call for simple ideas and vigorous acts." At moments like these, the moderate welcomes an ideology and, above all, the troops his mild, pacific nature cannot furnish but which, failing the army and police, the leagues supply. This is when the demands of moderates coincide with the offer of extreme rightists, when the moderate caught in a power struggle recognizes the possibilities of a radical Right, which in turn needs his money, his manpower, and his respectable endorsement. On this basis, and also by unceasing and didactic propaganda, the Action Française spread its influence and its ideas in moderate and republican circles far removed from personal contact. In an unstable world it suggested stability—of a kind; in a feeble world it showed determination; above all, it offered certainty—not so much in its doctrine, which few really grasped, as in the authority of a doctrinaire whom so many respected. For half a century Maurras was the Marx of the Right, as much quoted, as little read, as often misinterpreted as the greater, nobler, no less cantankerous, prophet of the Left.

To the young men of the pre-1914 generation, avid for a positive creed, for a doctrine of action, Maurras offered the certainty they sought. Agathon's *Les Jeunes gens d'aujourd'hui* (1912),

Romain Rolland's *Jean Cristophe* (especially Vol. X, 1912), Roger Martin du Gard's *Jean Barois* (1913), and many other contemporary documents bear witness to his hold on a narrow but important group of students and intellectuals. Before, during, and after World War I many felt his breath: Proust, Gide, Bernanos, Montherlant, Malraux, Drieu La Rochelle, and Maritain. The influence of his newspaper, the *Action Française*, appearing daily between 1908 and 1944, went far afield; even, between the wars, beyond the country's borders. But by that time the Action Française movement was no longer on the extreme Right. After 1919 the extreme Right would be something else, more radical and more extreme than a movement that stood for order could properly countenance or possibly match.

The difference between Action Française and its largely contemporary successors became evident in a dispute that arose in its own ranks between two contributors to the royalist newspaper, René Jouhandeau and Georges Valois. In 1924, the former had published an *Eloge du bourgeois français* that analyzed and synthesized the virtues of the bourgeoisie, expressing the hope that these could be applied in the governance of the state. To this, Valois answered the same year in the preface to another book, *La Révolution nationale*, that although it would be fine to run the state's administration or its treasury like that of a business enterprise, it would be disastrous to apply the same mentality to its general policy, its justice, or its army. France, said Valois, is not and must not be a bourgeois state, the preserve of a class and of a spirit foreign to the men who fought and won the war not for a party, not for a class, but for the French fatherland and for its greatness. The veteran, said Valois, notes that though he made the victory, the bourgeois—conservative, liberal, or Radical—made the profits. No veteran would lift a finger to defend bourgeois interests or restore bourgeois order. The state's only hope lay in the heroic spirit that had won the war, asserting the rights of the organic whole over selfish mercantile and money interests; a spirit incarnated in a self-designated leader who would impose his will and his design on the national revolution and on the new national state.

Valois had to wait sixteen years for the realization of this vision; but the organic, revolutionary, and heroic arguments he had advanced suggested the pattern of the interwar leagues, fascist or national-socialist variants of earlier nationalism. His own *Faisceau* was among the first of these groupings whose main characteristic was movement and whose distinctive sign, as Plumyène and Lassiera remark in their little book on French fascisms, would be a tendency to bracket Joan of Arc and the Paris Commune: the heroic traditions of the Right and Left.

"The value of the world lies in its extremes, its endurance in its mean. Its merit lies only in its ultras, its lasting power in its moderates." Thus wrote Paul Valéry. For most of the nineteenth and the twentieth century France has been ruled by moderates, but by moderates who were not always moderate. "No one wishing to be of the Right, or reactionary, or even conservative," *Le Temps* of January 7, 1934, complained, "these opinions, condemned to anonymity, have adopted the neighboring name of moderate. There is in our country a moderation which includes an extremity." These two quotations summarize the paradox of French politics: the inspiration of the Ultras, the domination of the moderates, the fact that the inspiration of the dominant moderates is naturally and necessarily of the Right.

There is a certain ambiguity about terms like Left and Right, conservative or moderate, but these terms cannot be avoided, they are part of the language, part of the political spectrum, and easier to place in practice than they are to define in theory. When the issue is not philosophical but arises out of a political situation, conservatism (let us call it, but moderation does as well) defines itself not in theoretical terms but in terms of the problems it has to face. Hence, the well-known tendency of radicals to become conservatives, of revolutionaries who have achieved their ends to defend their new order. This is commonplace. But while the attitudes of men and parties change and their politics change, too, doctrines evolve more slowly. And this leaves us the apparent paradox of conservative Liberals, conservative Radicals, conservative

Social Democrats, even conservative Communists in places where their doctrines (or at least their representatives) have found satisfaction and power.

In such circumstances, reactionary movements and parties may turn out to be the only truly revolutionary ones, and may thereby attract that section of the public that inclines as much toward actively revolutionary parties as it does toward traditionally revolutionary parties, and for the same reasons—of which doctrine is the least important—and to whom change, the prospect of a radical transformation, counts more than the precise direction of the change.

And yet the revolutionary character of so many right-wing radicals seems less important to their moderate neighbors than the violent campaigns they conduct against the revolutionaries of the Left. This must be largely because most conservatives, too, would like to see great changes made, but are afraid of even little ones, would like to see current disorders settled, but without unsettling anything. The only label that they understand, because it means exactly what they make it mean, is *National,* the symbol of a nation that has a confused notion of what it does not want but no idea of what it does. Both the entente and the misunderstanding between moderates and radicals of the Right is based on this term, *National,* which covers a multitude of sins and a multitude of confusions, forgotten during temporary alliances, apparent during moments of success when the more numerous moderates wish only to *enjoy* their new-won power while the radicals want to *use* it.

The nationalist rallying cry may also briefly hide profound temperamental differences between the sections of the Right, a difference that affects not only their ends but even their attitude toward the means needed to gain some coincidental goal. Radicals, as their name implies, are willing to be radical. But moderates cannot face the necessity of many acts their wishes call for. They countenance only gestures and parades. Now gestures are also the joy of radicals, and the more ineffective their political action the more ostentatious the gesture is likely to be. Then, when it passes from the striking to the shocking, this kind of romantic extremism, which may disquiet moderates, is sometimes counterbalanced by the romanticism of moderates who endow their extremists with the glamor they themselves lack.

Moderate conservatives are spoiled romantics who see in right-wing extremism the image of a dream, the counterpart also of a constant nightmare: Babbitt's dream of knighthood, Monsieur Prudhomme's nightmare of disorder. Therefore, while they reconcile themselves to extremism on utilitarian grounds, their rationalizations are grounded in velleitarian fantasies. We see this very well in Abel Bonnard's 1936 discussion of moderatism, the classical treatment of the subject, when the author comes to the delicate issues of Fascism and dictatorship. Dictators, one gathers, are unpleasant but necessary, and so, although disapproving of them, Bonnard nevertheless justifies them as "the painful remedy of a profound evil, the rudimentary expression of order when it is opposed to chaos, justified especially by what they prevent."

The romantic fertility of the moderate mind manifests itself largely in the evils it manages to fancy; and this stultified romanticism then endows the dictators who have been accepted for utilitarian reasons with a glamor that will match all the horrors they avert. Where democratic politicians are sordidly unheroic, the dictator appears "a tragic character" (Bonnard *dixit*), painted in Byronic terms: "Eclairé par une lumière livide qui le montre entouré d'abîmes, offert à la foudre encore plus qu'à la gloire." What Bonnard feels about dictators, quite perceptively as it happens, his fellow moderates feel, at least some of the time, about the dictators' humbler followers. A glamor surrounds them, the reflection of brandished torches, the echo of martial sounds, a magnified memory, too, of boy scout ideals—"This fine ideal of valliance, of generosity, of optimism, characteristic of the new chivalry," as a *roman scout* of the 1920's put it, unconsciously prefiguring the principles of Darnand's Militia of 1943.

The similarities between scoutism and the interwar leagues deserve to be studied: the common emphasis on patriotism, on youth, on service, on the virtues of a chivalry closer to Walter Scott than to the Middle Ages, and, also, more surprisingly, the common opposition to Big Capital and to the Reds (see, for example, Pierre Delsuc's *La Rude nuit de Kervizel* [Paris: 1928]). Oddly, certain moods, certain turns of phrase, reveal a conservative image of the leagues as movements not very different from the scouts. "Nothing more legitimate, nothing more necessary," writes Bonnard about the leagues, "since they marked the revival in the nation of a virile love of order, outside of a political system so vitiated that [clean sentiments] could not express themselves within it."

Thus the conservatives, although they have little liking for the violence of right-wing extremists, appreciate their healthy, virile principles while resolutely ignoring their true nature. They blame their excesses, they profess not to take them seriously (pranks to work off an excess of animal spirits), but tacitly they rely on them. One more paradox, of course, is that conservatives so sensitive to the dangers on their left should be so astigmatic about the perils on their right.

And yet the irony of this Red Menace, which played such an important part in the destinies of France, the irony of the career of the Socialist and Communist Left, is that it began exactly at the time when the possibility of a class policy was beginning to wane. We shall see below how, in a society where class distinctions and class doctrines existed before Marx's time, the class whose turn it was to dominate the others and whose victory the theoreticians continued to predict or fear, found itself on the defensive at precisely the moment when its leaders wanted to take the offensive.

The chief weakness of French Socialism after World War I was a poverty of political thought, which seems to have prevented the renewal of theories and doctrines on the basis of fresh analyses of the situation. It may be that the international orientation peculiar to socialism, far from encouraging a comparative analysis, merely furnished facile arguments to demonstrate the inevitability of a process which, apparent elsewhere, could also be expected with confidence at home. This was hardly so certain, however, for the economic and social situation of France, and hence her political perspectives were not the same as those of Germany or England. The great mistake of the French was to believe that the experience of another century and of different political and industrial organizations could apply to their particular circumstances. It was the kind of mistake that soldiers make when they prepare the coming war on the lessons learned in past ones.

In France, the condition of the working class at the beginning of the century lent itself quite readily to a Marxist analysis. But, as Sorel perceived, the economic trend on which Marxist theory was based had already altered and the impoverishment of the proletariat was giving way to its social advance. Workers were still exploited, but they were less and less ground down. The revolutionary proletariat was being drained into the petite bourgeoisie, just when the Socialists were taking the lead of the forces of the Left. The familiar dialectic of revolution worked badly or not at all: the revolution had been stabilized at a liberal or Girondin stage and, while the Marxist went on hoping for a Jacobin revolution to follow, the pressures that might be described as Jacobin no longer operated in a radical sense but in a reactionary one. When the new-style Jacobins opposed the liberal state most conservatives had ended by accepting, it was not in the hope of a fresh social advance, but to drag it back or make it let go. The old opposition between republicans "who favor radical reforms" and republicans "who favor opportune reforms"—between radicals and opportunists—was reviving. But the new opportunists included the majority of what, a generation before, had been the revolutionary class; and the Socialists, as long as they persisted in their radicalism, were isolated in a society where their old bourgeois allies had passed to conservatism and the troops of popular Jacobinism revealed disquieting sympathies for nationalism, Bonapartism, and other varieties of reaction and mayhem.

The novelty after 1920 was to be provided by the founding and the rise of the Communist Party, which both complicated and simplified the political situation. By reconstituting a truly revolutionary party of the Left, Communism was going to push all other parties toward the Right. It divided the Left even further, making quite impossible any lasting majority or any united action that would be both coherent and effective. Last but not least, it justified more than ever the activity of an extreme Right which, in the absence of Communism, would have found it much more difficult to gain the sympathy and support of the respectable public. After Communism had refreshed a socialism that time had moderated, the Right, even the conservative Right in power, could not react against its own extremists as it did against those of the enemy camp. This attitude and this reaction gained ground during the thirties, especially after the shock of the Popular Front victory of 1936. The proliferation of leagues of fascist inspiration reflected the social pressures of a period of social and economic crisis protracted by the incapacity of all parties to see either the situation or their own position very clearly.

The circumstances in which fascist-inspired leagues first appeared in France are significant enough. At the end of World War I, the only nationalist league of any importance was the royalist Action Française. Its leaders—Charles Maurras, Léon Daudet, the historian Jacques Bainville—had great intellectual influence (Daudet was a founder-member of the Académie Goncourt, and the other two were elected to the Académie Française); its newspaper had the highest sale of all the "opinion" dailies (as opposed to the popular press with its mass sales); and the success of its patriotic campaigns and the heroism of its members had further increased its prestige. The first book in French on the new Italian movement—Le Fascisme, by Pietro Gorgolini—was published in 1922 by the Nouvelle Librarie Nationale of the Action Française. Two years later, a left-wing paper, Le Quotidien, of February 11, 1924, still affirmed that "Fascism has merely taken over the doctrine of integral nationalism." Thus, to begin with, we find interest in Fascism, sympathy for it, but hardly Fascism itself; only the native, integral nationalism of Charles Maurras.

The change that followed can be dated with precision. It began on Sunday, November 23, 1924, when the transfer of the ashes of Jean Jaurès to the Pantheon provided the occasion for a vast, orderly, and impressive Socialist and Communist parade very frightening to the moderates. The recently elected left-wing coalition seemed incapable of defending the middle class against the social menace represented by the hundreds of red banners, the thousands of cloth caps which flowed slowly along the boulevards and past the reviewing stand. For Gustave Hervé, a former left-wing Socialist now converted to national-socialist views, "the forest of red flags" was following "the funeral of the bourgeoisie." Many Parisians agreed with foreboding. "This is when the revolutionary menace became clear to everybody," the *Action Française* noted, "and the alarm it caused led to the constitution, in Paris as in the provinces, of numerous groups of national and social defense."

In a few days, "patriotic movements" sprang up suddenly and everywhere. Veterans' organizations which had rubbed along from hand to mouth—Ligue des chefs de section, *Légions*—leaped into activity, and new leagues were founded: the Ligue Républicaine Nationale of Aléxandre Millerand, only recently President of the Republic, who had been forced to resign by the leftist coalition; the Jeunesses Patriotes of Pierre Taittinger, which carried on Déroulède's tradition and that of the Ligue des Patriotes in a Bonapartist vein; the Faisceau of Georges Valois. In the provinces, "defense committees" were set up, recruiting hundreds and even thousands of members in a week or two. Nevertheless, as in 1900, the leagues would remain largely a Parisian phenomenon, and it was the Action Française whose recruitment benefited most from the alert. Other movements, more properly fascist, like the Faisceau, lasted only as long as the governments of the left-wing coalition and the concomitant fall in the value of the franc. In July, 1926, Raymond Poincaré became prime minister, stabilized the franc, and reassured property owners. The danger of an active Left once past, the fears of the bourgeoisie temporarily allayed, their support of the leagues diminished to vanishing point. Soon the left-wing press could rejoice that "Fascism and reaction" had been crushed. It was, on the contrary, *because* reaction was doing well that Fascism was doing badly. Nor would it revive until the early thirties, when the economic crisis soon turned into a political crisis, the failure of liberal capitalism being interpreted as the failure of liberal and parliamentary politics.

During 1932 and 1933 the most active of the leagues was still the Action Française, whose shock troops, the so-called *camelots du roi*, dominated the Latin Quarter and the faculties. As there is a tendency to underestimate the numbers of the leagues, it is worth noting that in 1934 the Action Française counted some 60,000 or

70,000 members, including 1,000 or 1,500 *camelots* in Paris. Comparing these figures to those of the Communists, who had about 40,000 militants, or even with the 130,000 members of the Socialist Party (SFIO), we find that the militants of the extreme Right were in no way inferior in number to those of the extreme Left.

Meanwhile, another organization was rising which would reach impressive proportions in the later thirties. Founded in 1927 as a select gathering of veterans decorated under fire, the Croix de Feu only began to develop at the end of the twenties under the brisk leadership of a retired soldier, Colonel François de La Rocque. Opening its ranks first to all veterans, then to their families, finally to sympathizers of every sort, drawing subsidies from every quarter (including, it was alleged, the government's secret funds), La Rocque was able to claim several hundred thousand dues-paying members in 1935, between one and two million in 1938. By then, his league, dissolved in 1936, had been reformed as a political party —the Parti Social Français. But Croix de Feu or PSF, La Rocque's movement was far from fascist ("We are not Fascist!" its periodical, *Le Flambeau,* insisted on November 1, 1929) and its slogans sounded a familiar note: "The cult of the fatherland and the love of French order." "Order and discipline freely accepted, yes," *Le Flambeau* explained; "but not brutal repression, not force in the service of private interests, opinion stifled, regimentation, militarism. . . ." It was La Rocque who launched a slogan with a future, "Travail, Famille, Patrie," which reflected the common conservatism of the Croix de Feu and of the Vichy regime that later adopted it. As a real Fascist, Maurice Bardèche, has recently remarked, nothing could be more emasculating: Labor means submission to the rich, Family means submission to morality, Fatherland means submission to the gendarme. Everything is a question of submission, of obedience, of toeing the line. In this respect, the PSF had more in common with Charles de Gaulle's postwar RPF (Rassemblement du Peuple Français) than with any fascist league. It shared with the former a fundamental conservatism and a veneer of discipline, a superficial violence expressed in displays of motorized derring-do, attacks on offices and meetings of political opponents, a great deal of talk, and even some leaders. As a trade union leader told Alexander Werth, French correspondent of the *Manchester Guardian,* in 1936, "The people who now call themselves Croix de Feu are just the old reactionaries who have always been our enemies. They are not really Fascists, you know."

So the major leagues of the 1930's were still far from Fascism. Their masters were either elderly or conservative or both; respectable men with good social and official connections, hardly likely to appeal to idealistic, rebelly-minded youth in search of an ideal, an inspiration, an answer *now* to present problems. To such as these, the moralistic appeals of older nationalists sounded like cauteries for wooden legs. Communism challenged them because it suggested a transition from exploitative liberal capitalism to an equitable industrial society. To this Fascism proposed an alternative, just as violent, just as revolutionary, but one that preserved national unity and spared patriotic sensibilities. The middle classes could not admit a doctrine of class war that threatened their good conscience when it suggested that their interest did not necessarily coincide with that of the whole nation. Middle-class intellectuals could not accept a class division that excluded them from the modern world of struggle and progress, and from the dialectically chosen people of toilers. They reacted to the challenge of Communism by taking up many of its externals; they spoke up for human dignity and for a classless society hierarchized according to capability, talent, and function in a way that old Bolsheviks would not have found unfamiliar, and, beyond their national self-affirmation, some even thrilled at the possibilities of internationalism.

The old Jacobin leitmotif was heard again with Drieu La Rochelle, as it had been in 1900, as it would be in 1956 with Pierre Poujade, calling for battle against the two great, stifling, anonymous monsters of Big Business and the Red International, but especially against the former—"the exploitation of man by money and for it." The reference to hierarchy was refurbished by Bertrand de Jouvenel, scion of an eminent republican family and a great admirer of Fascist and Nazi dynamism, who advertised Doriot's promise of "a just inequality. . . . Hierarchy, yes! Hierarchy based on ancestors' services, no! Hierarchy based on services rendered now!" Another familiar note was sounded by Neo-Socialist Marcel Déat in 1934: "Is one a Fascist," the Socialist turncoat asked rhetorically, "because one wants the indispensable authority needed to reëstablish order in the social chaos? Is one a Fascist because one wants to limit certain anarchic and dangerous liberties, impose certain social disciplines, the better to guarantee the necessary freedoms of the individual? I do not think so . . ." (*1934*, June 13, 1934). Others clearly did.

Yet if these movements were to provide a valid alternative to Communism, a countercommunism with any hope at all, they had to go beyond mere repudiation of economic liberalism. Communism is more than social discipline or anticapitalism: it is a comradeship, a crusade, a great inspiring adventure, and this was the particular realm where French Fascists sought its counterpart. As it was put by Robert Brasillach, who was the poet of this mood before he became its martyr for being shot after the Liberation: "We have long since seen Fascism as a poem, the very poetry of the twentieth century (with Communism, of course). I know perfectly well that Communism has its greatness too, just as exalting." Elsewhere, he would remember that "Fascism was for us no political or economic doctrine. It was not the imitation of foreign models. . . . But Fascism is a mood, an anticonformist spirit, antibourgeois in the first place and irreverent. It is a spirit opposed to prejudices, class prejudices and others. It is the very spirit of friendship that we wanted to see rising to the level of a national comradeship."

The contradictions are irrelevant here, the spirit is all. A poem, a prank, a comradeship—these young literary Fascists (Drieu, Brasillach, Bardèche, Rebatet) sound like one of the young men of the pre-1914 generation painted by Romain Rolland: "He was truly French; he had a rebellious temper and an innate love of order. He needed a leader, yet was incapable of bearing any." "Youth looks for action," asserted a young man in a pamphlet of 1935, *Les Jeunes face au monde politicien*. "That is why it joins the leagues, Right or Left." But, as to the merits of the Left or Right, "grands dieux, si on savait comme ils s'en foutent!" The previous year had seen the production of a play, by Drieu La Rochelle, entitled *The Leader*, whose hero ends a fiery tirade by proclaiming, "We don't know what is to be done, but we shall do it!" The young sampled one faction after another, appreciating any movement for movement's sake, and ending in an absurd activism. "Struggle without faith," wrote Henri de Montherlant in *Le Solstice de Juin,* a few years later, "is necessarily the formula to which we come in the end."

Tired of Maurras, disappointed in La Rocque, what did these young men have to choose from among the other leagues? The Francistes of Marcel Bucard, the Solidarité Française of Jean Renaud, were the only two leagues that deliberately imitated foreign models, even to the uniforms they wore. Public opinion found their doctrine rather thin, their heads rather thick, their methods particularly brutal. Very tough, very active, not very numerous, they recruited mostly employees, small shopkeepers, unskilled laborers, and ex-servicemen attracted by their straightforward anti-capitalism. They did not appeal to bright young men. There were also peasant leagues, taxpayers' leagues, and pressure-cum-study groups for members of a higher social level. Most successful, however, in attracting both workers and intellectuals, was the Parti Populaire Français of Jacques Doriot, founded in 1936 by the ex-Communist mayor of the industrial suburb of St. Denis.

Drawing heavily on the local branch of the Communist Party, the PPF also recruited a remarkable constellation in the world of letters: Alexis Carrel, Drieu La Rochelle, Alfred Fabre-Luce, Georges Suarez, Ramon Fernandez, Bertrand de Jouvenel, and Marcel Jouhandeau. By March, 1937, the party boasted a membership of 130,000, and its paper, *L'Emancipation nationale,* printed 200,000 copies a day. Sixty-five per cent of the membership, it was claimed, was of working-class origin. Five years later, under the German occupation, the crowd at a Doriotist meeting in the great rotunda of the Paris *Vel d'Hiv* still numbered about twenty thousand, "a clearly proletarian crowd: little people, artisans, housewives."

Doriot brought them the reassurance and the certainty such crowds have always sought. "The men of the PPF," writes Drieu, "have a firm, straightforward look because they have found the solution. . . ." What the solution was, beyond the mixture as before but more forcefully delivered, he does not tell us. Where certainty sufficed, details would be out of place. The answer may be found in another remark of Drieu's, part of some jottings he published in 1934, before falling under Doriot's spell, in a collection of essays entitled *Socialisme Fasciste*. "These people," he writes, "in what do they believe? They have been taught to believe in themselves; that is stupid. They must be given a god. Since there is no more god in heaven, let us give them a god on earth. Gods are born on earth; then they rise to heaven." Drieu was not alone in thinking in this way; unfortunately (or fortunately), like many Frenchmen, he was a born agnostic. Like Romain Rolland's young hero, he wanted authority, he wanted a god, but could not accept one for long: "Son ironie impitoyable les perçait tous à jour."

Paradoxically, the great role of these para-Fascist movements and of their publications (which were numerous and widely read) was to inspire anti-Fascism and to act as the political catalysts of the divided Left. The Popular Front, which won the elections of 1936, had been deliberately invented (it was first called the Common Front) by a young Radical, Gaston Bergery, to steal the Facists' thunder and appeal to the same "politically invertebrate mass" in a situation where "the first to find simple formulas, colorful slogans, will be the masters of the herd" (*1934*, March 28, 1934). Surprisingly enough, the first lap of such a contest was won by the Left, at least in electoral terms, in the spring of 1936. But victory, accompanied by vast and frightening strikes, so intimidated its moderate members as to disintegrate the Popular Front itself and drive the parliamentary majority into increasingly authoritarian measures designed less to face the growing foreign danger than to crush the red specter at home. Equally important, fear of Communism persuaded many patriotic Frenchmen to prefer the firmly anti-Communist rulers of Germany and Italy to the highly suspicious rulers of France itself. Even those who did not prefer the rule of Hitler to that of Léon Blum found it hard to reconcile their patriotism and their anti-Communism, their interest in the defeat of France's German enemy with their interest in the preservation of the Soviets' German foe.

Such scruples played a major part in the political incoherence of the Munich years, in the refusal to "fight for Jews" or for "democracy." The extraordinary and triumphal reception that awaited Premier Daladier on his return from Munich, the flags, the tears, the half-million or more who blessed and cheered him on the way in from the airfield, this pathetic celebration reflected widespread popular relief. But there was more to it than that. An influential minority agreed when a recognized spokesman of the Right pointed out the French dilemma: either defeat and occupation, or victory and "the collapse of those authoritarian systems which constitute the main rampart against Communist revolution." A French victory, declared Thierry Maulnier, then of the *Action française*, today of the *Figaro*, "would have been less a victory of France than a victory of principles rightly considered as leading straight to the ruin of France and of civilization."

The problems of war and peace confused the party divisions to a degree that went far beyond the issues of mere foreign policy. There were anti-Fascist pacifists, there were enemies of Germany who, for that reason, wanted an alliance with Italy, there were intellectuals who refused to fight for democracy, and good democrats to whom Prague seemed very far indeed. Marcel Deat's refusal to die for Danzig was quite understandable when taken in itself, had it not implied the subtler affirmation of sympathy for those who coveted the city. It is not surprising that many felt confused—especially as Right-Left relations were complicated by the fact that the majority of the Left, which had been pacifist, internationalist, and Germanophile, became increasingly warlike and anti-German after 1933. What with traditionalist rightists who continued to fix their eyes on the blue line of the Vosges, more traditionalist traditionalists like Montherlant's great uncle, "qui ne manquait jamais, lorsqu'il faisait pipi, de se tourner du coté de l'Angleterre," and those Socialists or ex-Socialists who put either pacifism or anti-Communism before anti-Fascism, by the time of Munich, says Jacques Debu-Bridel, "it had become impossible to speak of parties; only factions were left."

Nevertheless, whatever the confusion and whatever its motives, the fact remains that a majority of Frenchmen continued to look left with fear and with suspicion, and considered the extreme Left a source of social revolution or of war, a greater threat than the Right. A glance at electoral results shows that Right and Center won a majority of votes cast in all elections between 1893 and 1924. In 1928, for the first time, they seemed to get a minority of votes, even though superior discipline brought them a majority of seats in the Chamber. This, however, leaves out of account the ever more moderate character of the Radical party, which, as has been indicated, should in actuality be situated in the center rather than on the left. If we credit the Center with the Radical votes of the 1920's, the domination of the French electoral and parliamentary scene by Right and Center continues without interruption until 1936. Even then the break is brief and, as shown by Georges Dupeux in his study of the 1936 elections, it is more apparent than real.

So, what begins by looking like a trend to the left, appears on further examination to reflect not a leftward trend in the country's political orientation, but a rightward trend within the parties that came to power. In other words, a party "of the Left" became what the French call governmental before entering the government, and moderate once it had done so. One thinks of Laval's advice to the young Debu-Bridel, the future Gaullist senator, who had started his political career in 1932 as a candidate of the Right: "One must never start out on the Right," said Laval, who had started way out on the Left himself. "It is bad. You should start from the Left . . . as far left as possible . . . and then keep coming back, coming back . . . not too fast. One must begin by inspiring fear. It is a condition of success." Provided, of course, one knows how to reassure thereafter. This is the way in which the moderate Right was made.

It is ironic that the most rabid representatives of French patriotism should find their mitigated triumph in a tragic national defeat. At least, as Maurras wrote in the *Action française* of January 15, 1942, "our worst defeat had the fortunate result of ridding us of democracy." In its moments of crisis, modern France traditionally turns toward old men, *patres patriae,* whom habit has endowed with the authority the nation yearns to abdicate. Thiers had been seventy-four in 1871, Clemenceau seventy-six in 1917, Poincaré sixty-six in 1926, Doumergue seventy-one in 1934, and de Gaulle would be sixty-eight in 1958. Marshal Pétain, who had been sixty at Verdun, was eighty-four in 1940. Just as the eddying masses of 1936 had carried with them the bourgeois and petit bourgeois leaders of the so-called Left, the swirling tides of June, 1940, brought in flaccid old men to fill the nation's need. In each crisis, mountains seem to labor to bring forth only anticlimax, with an incongruity reminiscent of those spring floods which, over the devastated landscape, amid housetops and lopsided telegraph poles, carry along now a chamber pot, now a bowler hat, and now a Louis XV *bidet*.

The particular incongruity, and also the interest of the 1940–1944 period, was that it provided a kaleidoscope of all the right-wing tendencies we have found so far, as well as some that space and synthesis have forced us to ignore. Pétain's Vichy, in its first phase, was the monarchy of Maurras, anachronistic, appealing to the primeval sources of the nation's strength, and, above all, to the soil. In the *Figaro* of July 3, 1940, François Mauriac described Pétain's voice as calling "from the depths of our history." A year later, Daniel Halévy (*Les Trois Epreuves*) heard the same voice sounding "from the depth of time, reflection of a heroic and generous past." In August, 1940, we hear Pétain himself declare that France "will become once more . . . an essentially agricultural nation." Without a Morgenthau to impose it, and quite apart from any plans the Nazi conquerors had for them, we find the French, these French at any rate, deciding to go back, to pull down their industrial superstructures and to resign from the discomforts of the modern age.

In its second phase, Vichy seems to have sought to reconcile the deals and compromises typical of moderate opportunism—an orientation represented with brio by Laval—with the conservative and patriotic moralism of national regeneration through clean living and high thinking—youth camps and Catholicism—and a technocratic, managerial trend that put efficiency above political allegiance. Meanwhile, in occupied Paris, the heirs of the extremist leagues urged collaboration with the Nazis, social revolution, and a changing of the guard to promote youth over the dinosaur survivors of another age.

As in 1938, Right and extreme Right had split on the question of resistance to the enemy. So had the Left. Representatives of every political conviction could be found in every camp and in every section of every camp. Here, however, we are concerned with continuities; and in this sense the Right continues true to its own nature, deeply divided, feuding and fussing, more utopian, whether in Paris or Vichy, than the utopian leftists whom it had pursued with sarcasms in its attempts to build a Jeffersonian golden age in the rump of France, or convert Frenchmen into adherents of Hitler's new order in Europe. Having sown the wind for fifteen years and more, they were going to reap the whirlwind at the Liberation. When *L'Humanité* (January 11, 1945) averred that "our hatred is a French hatred," the phrase was more just than they knew. Robert Aron in his *Histoire de la Libération de la France* (1959) estimates the number of summary executions at between thirty and forty thousand.

The Liberation had been largely a revolution against the Right, extreme or conservative; and after it one would have thought the Right down for the count, out for a generation. Yet, within two years, the postliberation coalition of the Left had again dissolved and the great drift toward the center had resumed its course. The votes cast in 1946 marked the beginning of an electoral trend in favor of the Right which has not, so far, been reversed. By 1951 it had become obvious to all. True, many still felt obliged to use the jargon of the Left, but the ensuing verbal confusion did not hamper the Right's advance, which was evidenced by the Pinay cabinet of 1952 and the election of a moderate, René Coty, to the presidency in 1954. By Christmas, 1954, a right-wing leader could boast without fear of contradiction that the Independents (i.e., conservatives) constituted the most powerful parliamentary group. And if, of late, this leading position has been taken over by the new Gaullist UNR (Union pour la nouvelle République), the essence of the situation has changed but little.

Indeed, it does not seem to have changed too much over the last sixty or seventy years. There is still an intransigent, or seem-

ingly intransigent, extreme Left that preaches economic change
and social revolution. There is still a Left, so called, which success
has watered down to moderation and whose activities must be
termed "counterrevolutionary" because, as David Thomson puts
it, they "[blunt] some consequences of the Revolution by accepting and turning against them some of its other consequences and
implications." There is still an extreme Right, unreconciled to the
existing order, both threatening it and tolerated by it because of
its intransigent nationalism. There is still a majority Right, determined to maintain or recover its advantages, its property, its social
position, if need be by violent means. The revolution of May 13,
1958, preliminary of a Fifth Republic, was not the work of Fascists, though Fascists participated in it. It was a violently defensive movement whose leaders and supporters had two not uncon-
nected aims: to defend their property and to restore order in the
state. These men were mainly middle-class property-owners, far
more serious about their business than the bright young *camelots*
of yore, more numerous and determined than any Fascist *ligueurs*.
They were the same men who had reacted violently when scared
in 1848, in 1871, and again in the 1920's and 1930's—the real
conservatives, ready to go to any lengths to preserve the middle
way.

All this must not be contemplated in its political aspect only,
however, for political developments themselves are more than reflections of plots hatched in parliamentary lobbies or tactical moves
of opportunistic politicians. They are the tardy and hesitant reflection of fundamental social and economic changes, ultimately responsible for the displacement of the center of gravity as we have
traced it above. To say this begs the question; for, obviously, it is
as difficult to explain the changes that occurred in the country's
social complexion as it is to explain those we have traced in its
political expression. It may be, however, that a shift in perspective
will help reveal more clearly, if not the answers, at least the circumstances and factors of the problem.

The process I have outlined is the product of two interdependent
factors: fear of a revolutionary peril on the Left, whether Republi-

can or Radical or Socialist or Communist; and the great demographic and social revolution which is only beginning to be studied.
It seems evident that opposition to left-wing pressures often reconciled old enemies, as in 1848, in 1871, and pretty steadily since that
time. In 1919, to take only more recent instances, many Radicals
moved toward moderatism and joined the National coalition of the
Right less by electoral cunning than from suspicion of an intransigent and Moscow-connected Socialism. Even in 1924, the reconciliation of Radicals and Socialists in the famous Cartel des gauches
was itself a consequence of the setting up of a French Communist
Party, which, after 1920, rejected the Socialists to their Right. The
coalition that triumphed in 1924 was that of a very mitigated Left,
amputated of its more radical wing, and it represented a common
mistrust of the revolutionary party. This mistrust permitted the
sometime partisans of revolution to join in a common antagonism
not only toward the traditional enemy on the Right but also, sometimes especially, toward the disquieting neighbor on the Left.

In the Côte d'Or, for instance, many "men of the Left" passed to
the Right and were elected with moderate votes, but also with the
votes of Radicals who followed them in this evolution. The apparent disappearance of a classic Right in such circumstances often
meant its victory in practice. As Raymond Long explains in his
study of Les Elections législatives en Côte d'Or (1958), the main
thing was to join together in opposing the Communist peril. "But
in the process the center of political gravity had shifted: from
Center-Left where the majority stood before 1914, it had passed to
Center-Right."

This hatred of the moderate Left for Communism (a hatred that
the Communists returned with interest) was suspended at intervals,
but it would never quite abate, persisting even in the Popular
Front itself. Many Radical dignitaries resigned rather than work
with Reds. Others stood on their principles, ignoring the political
truce. It was a Radical-Socialist candidate at Evreux who, in 1936,
attacked the Front to which his own party belonged: "It was set
up by the Communists who remain its guiding spirits and who, in
case of victory, will reap its benefits. In the near future they will
install a Soviet dictatorship in France as they have done in Russia."

By 1937, Charles Maurras could comment, in the *Action fran-çaise* of November 28, that "nothing separates Radicals from Right-Republicans. . . . Certainly 'the Right' is excluded from the political union. But radicalism shares the ideas of the Right."

While the Radicals moved toward the right, the Socialists were shifting into *their* place; and when, in his study of the 1936 elections, Georges Dupeux refers to the "radicalization of the Socialist party," he does not mean that it became more radical, but less so, more like the Radicals, more inclined to opportunistic coöperation with moderates than with Communists. In 1928, the historian Charles Seignobos had described the Socialist position as "a formal opposition without true hostility." In 1936, Socialists in power deliberately avoided a socialist policy, preferring one so moderate that it may be considered of the Center.

How was it that parties "of movement," parties in whose vocabulary the revolutionary tradition loomed so large, reacted against the Communist temptation and that their troops, far from welcoming the Communist appeal, distrusted and feared it to the point of alliance—open or not—with their old enemies? Who were these Socialists, these Radicals, so little socialist, so far from radical? Why, in an industrialized society, did the official Left not only shun or evade revolutionary appeals, but try to crush the partisans of revolution?

These questions bring us to an aspect of social history which remains rather obscure in spite of much discussion. It is not enough to say that at a certain moment the satisfied middle classes passed from the party of movement to that of established order. We must try to understand why the party of movement could not replace its losses and why its new recruits did not suffice, especially after World War I, to recreate a reform majority as dynamic as that of preceding generations.

Having been the party of political reform based on the middle classes in the nineteenth century, the Socialist or Communist Left of the twentieth century became the party of economic and social reforms based on the working classes and, particularly, on the industrial proletariat. The pressure of Socialism at the end of the nineteenth and the beginning of the twentieth century was based on the rapid expansion and organization of working-class population, itself created by the rapid expansion of French industry in the two decades preceding 1914. This evolution, both technical and human, slowed down after the war. The level of industrial production in 1938 was little different from what it had been in 1913. The number of men employed in industry and transport was roughly the same in 1936, year of the great triumph of the Left, as at the beginning of the century. In his *Bilan de l'économie française, 1919–1946* (Paris: 1947), Charles Bettelheim shows that they were 7,225,000 in 1906, 8,464,000 in 1931 (including 329,000 unemployed), and 7,415,000 in 1936. Between 1866 and 1906 the industrial population had grown by 2,758,000; in the thirty years that followed it grew by 190,000. Thus, apart from certain sectors, like the automobile or the steel industries, the expansion of French industry slowed or stopped after the war: so did that of the working class. And if, statistically at least, the production level remained stable enough, it fell off in relation to other countries, despite the accession of new industry in the recovered territories of Alsace and Lorraine. Between 1913 and 1937, French production fell by 27 per cent on the world scale and by 37 per cent on the European scale (including Russia). As a result, says Bettelheim, "France tended increasingly to cut herself off from the world. This turning-in on oneself may be found in most countries on the morrow of the War and even more during the economic crisis of 1929 and after, but it is particularly striking in France."

While in Germany the same difficulties, the same original retreat into a national shell, were to lead rather quickly to an autarchic and expansionist policy, in France the passing years merely emphasized the isolation. Political and economic regression followed industrial stagnation. In 1931, explaining the mentality of the average Frenchman, André Siegfried defined him as a social reactionary, tending altogether toward conservation and resistance to change, a man who fears revolution—not Socialist or Communist, but "the revolution of American productivity which forces people to be productive." This social and economic conservatism, this concern for order and stability rather than renewal or conquest, this desire to protect things as they are rather than produce more, expressed itself in an ideological archaism and found fulfillment with Pétain in the return to the soil, the glorification of old artisan traditions, the reductio ad absurdum of the wish for security so widespread in previous years.

It would be hard to exaggerate the part played by *rentes* and *retraites* in this development that turned so many Frenchmen and the country itself from movement to stagnation. The financial developments of the late nineteenth century had given middle-class Frenchmen what they dreamed of—liberty and property both. The establishment of pensions gave them a vested interest in stability. The word *retraite* is used to describe both retirement and the retirement pension; it also means retreat, refuge, shelter, hiding-place, shrinking, contraction. To France and to Frenchmen, especially between the two wars, all these meanings applied. And the same social conservatism, even more apparent in the countryside, kept French agriculture in its old inefficient rut, its prices higher than the world average, its techniques well below the standards of the West. Unenterprising, technically backward, with poor yields and high production costs, agriculture, Bettelheim tells us, "presented in the already sluggish economy of France a factor of obsolescence that must on no account be underestimated."

The industrial working class was expanding more slowly than we might expect, industry and agriculture were conservative and inefficient; add to this the progress of the middle class—a middle class taken in the broadest sense, but bourgeois enough to be either conservative or reactionary because it feared for its acquired rights: property, pensions, savings, and a way of life. In his remarkable study of French society (*Histoire des populations françaises et de leurs attitudes devant la vie* [Paris: 1948]), Philippe Aries points out that, in most cities,

. . . for a thousand inhabitants there are eighty-five more workers in 1931 than in 1866, but also eighty-five more bourgeois [trade, administration, liberal professions]. The bourgeois world has grown in the same proportion as the working-class world. And if the graphic curve of working-class increase is a regular one between 1866 and 1931, that of the bourgeoisie rises steeply after 1906. After that time, the bourgeoisie grows faster than the proletariat.

Statistics of small businesses are very revealing about a sector of the middle class particularly inclined to defend the existing order or to change it in a direction other than that of the classic Left. From 1,864,000 in 1906, the number of tradesmen rose to 2,343,-000 in 1936. Their proportion of the active population rose from 9 per cent in 1906 to 11.5 per cent in 1936, while their sales rose so little and their profits were so minimal that Bettelheim denounces *le petit commerce* as modern camouflage for unemployment, an uncomfortable harbor for capital and men who find no use in a stagnant industry. We have here a class whose frustrations match its stunted hopes, excellent material for the critic of democracy, of the republican and parliamentary regime, for the bard of a popular demonology attributing the problems of small business to political corruption and waste, explaining the bankruptcy of marginal enterprises by the deep-laid plots of sinister conspirators.

The difficulties and the obsolescence of the commercial sector appear very clearly in the statistics of national revenue. In 1913, private revenues were rising by five billion a year and the rhythm of growth of public and private wealth was rapid. Between 1900 and 1913 national revenue increased by 37 per cent. In 1936 private revenues had fallen by about one-fifth in twenty-three years, the rhythm of growth had vanished, and public spending was going up.

Who had been most affected by these developments, either directly or indirectly? First of all, the small investors for whom the collapse of foreign bonds followed by the slow depreciation of state bonds meant poverty, or, at least, serious financial difficulties. Then the owners and shareholders of certain industrial enterprises slow to adapt (paper, foodstuffs, leather goods), hit by the depression (glassware, crystals, luxury goods), or threatened by the competition of larger enterprises (agricultural equipment). Their economic position was not always weaker or their productivity less, and their retrogression was only relative, but they felt themselves threatened by forces they did not always understand but which they readily identified: a Judeo-Masonic or Bolshevik conspiracy, the encroaching plutocracy always in cahoots with forces of evil determined to destroy all that was good and fine in France, beginning with themselves.

The same was often true of other provincial notables overwhelmed by metropolitan pressures and encroachments, menaced in their property and prestige by the industrial and financial powers of the modern age. Paradoxically, some of the difficulties affecting provincial notables sometimes actually strengthened their local position. Before 1914 provincial towns had benefited from the rural exodus. After the war this exodus began to drain them, too, in the direction of Paris. In the rather static atmosphere the loss of their best blood created, local social aspirations turned more than ever toward the representatives of the out-of-date: the priest, the old families, good Catholic (or, in some places, Protestant) society, the municipal or departmental archivist generally trained in the reactionary stronghold of the Ecole des Chartes, the doctor or the druggist who had often been *camelots du roi*, the small industrialist or businessman worried by Bolshevism, monopolies and state interference—these set the intellectual and political tone. And this society, more or less reactionary in the strict sense of the term, became the more important, the more influential, in the absence of the young and enterprising whom Paris attracted. The young, the adventurous, the aspiring, made for Paris; and meanwhile the old returned home to retire, thus further intensifying the conservative atmosphere of the country towns.

But age did not affect only provincial towns that had once been the nurseries of radicalism. The whole country was aging. France was slipping back in a world 1.97 per cent of whose total population it furnished in 1938 as against 2.3 per cent in 1913. It retreated also in terms of energy and age. The fight against death was more successful than it had been in the nineteenth century and fewer people died; but, while the old were learning to live longer, the young learned not to procreate. The control of death went along with the control of births. At the beginning of the nineteenth century, for ten thousand inhabitants France had known each year an excess of sixty-six births. This excess fell to thirty-three for the years from 1861 to 1865, to eleven between 1906 and

1910, to eight between 1931 and 1935. Beginning in 1936, every year would see more people dying than being born. Throughout the decade of the thirties, as Bettelheim put it, France had become the country "where there are fewest young people and the most old people." It was the old who ruled, their lasting power stifling the first enthusiasms of the young, so that a comparison between China and France seems justified on other grounds than merely gastronomic.

This gerontocracy encouraged the natural conservatism of property-owners in search of security and order, of those in quest of artificial paradises not in the utopian future but in the royalist or traditionalist past. It represented the dead weight of age in power whose psychological effect was to diminish even further the scanty initiative that industry and business showed. Who denounced all these things? Who so much as pointed them out? Not the classic Socialists, the moderate Radicals, the conservatives camouflaged under a variety of labels, all led by chiefs of ripe maturity. One might ask whether certain political adventures, often starting on the Left but ending on the Right (Bergery, Déat, Doriot) did not stem from the need to escape the sloth, the narrows of a *cursus honorum* whose prizes went to the longest-lived. In any event, it was the extremists of Left and Right, enemies of the regime, fugitives from the old political formations who, alone, seemed to notice the bottlenecks and to blame the ruling group and the order that enshrined them.

Not surprisingly, then, the dynamic and minoritarian parties were and are on the extremes. But what do they represent? What do they ask? Briefly, the extreme Right speaks of patriotism and order, sacrifice and regeneration, the destiny of France and of the franc. The extreme Left calls for economic reforms, social changes, and, later, anti-Fascism. Both are sentimental. But the appeal of the former (especially as it concerns more attitudes than actions) can be heard with sympathy by a varied public; that of the latter aims chiefly at a particular class which, we have seen, is not increasing much and hardly feels its oats. It is heard in the countryside as well, but that is not where it reaps the best results between the wars, and when it does it will be by becoming much more moderate, both in tactics and in tone. Outside the urban milieu, the Communists gain ground by trying to look like Radicals; and this "radicalization" means a more heterogeneous following and a more personalized, old-fashioned approach.

But while the extreme Left is generally quite limited to urban and industrial areas, the extreme Right is not. True, it draws its stoutest troops from the urban petite bourgeoisie, especially that of Paris. But it is not afraid to use national and socialist doctrines when approaching an electorate which is also that of the classic Left. Neo-Socialists, PSF, PPF, are national-socialist movements or would like to be, just as a certain section of the Gaullist RPF and UNR has aspired to be since the war. All, like Jean-Jacques Susini, one of the leaders of the Algerian OAS, want "to reconcile the movement of social emancipation that is rocking the world and the national fact . . . to gather in a general synthesis these two currents that have shaken the twentieth century." All, like the leaders of a new movement allergic to traditional categorizations, try to reconcile "Patrie et Progrès." All reject the conservatism of privilege, the values of the bourgeois order, the selfishness and stultification of the old on every side and especially at the top.

Yet, despite the subversive tumult which they raise, the leagues of the extreme Right are not like the Communists at the other extreme, condemned, opposed by their more moderate neighbors. Though they do shock the conservatives, though they too are sometimes disowned for the sake of some moderate combination, nonetheless the Nationalists, Royalists, proto-Fascists of all sorts, have more friends on their side. They find more listeners who, although they do not approve their violence, are affected by their doctrines, or who, although they do not accept their doctrines, are influenced by their ideas, or who, although they do not care for their ideas, are impressed by their violence. This was particularly true of the Action Française, a movement with no political power but of tremendous influence; and it seems equally true in the last few years.

It may be that all these people are less disturbing from the electoral point of view for moderate politicians who fear the Communists. But it is above all that they speak a language the respectable Right can recognize as its own, when the violence has been discounted: order, hierarchy, authority, nation, are acceptable ideas which a right-thinking man can sincerely approve. The Communists also speak a language that Socialists and sometimes Radicals recognize, but with a shudder, for their slogans are those that the reformed leftist has no desire to perpetuate, let alone realize. Besides, while Communist ideas have nothing to attract the new rising classes, the technicians, the managers, the small people often more bourgeois by aspiration than by economic and social position, the activists of the Right could and still can hope to fish, like Jacques Doriot, in the troubled waters of a proletariat disgusted with the regime and looking for a slogan or an authority. As much as possible, the conservatives will keep these extremists away from the levers of power. But they will collaborate with them in need with less hesitation than left-wing conservatives have shown so far about working with the Communists. They will also be more influenced by their ideology. While Socialists find Communism forbidding, and Socialism repels the Radicals, the extreme right doctrines drawn from Maurras, from Sorel, from Valois, attract and inspire many conservatives—which brings us back to André Siegfried's conviction that no policy of the Center can exist, that there is no such thing as a Center, and that a politician must in the end, when the chips are down, rely either on the Socialists and Communists or on the Catholics and Royalists.

If this be so, however, why is there a Center, after all; and why this vast moderate plain that rolls over the past century and a half incorporating one after another so many movements and so many spokesmen of change, rocking them into moderation, soothing them into conservatism, turning in the hollow of its convictions the most radical expostulations into safe commonplaces? The answer is, of course, that if no Center policy exists, policies are improvised as they are needed; if there is no continuity of doctrine there is continuity itself, the very principle of continuity, protean, malleable, and opportunistic; if the slogans have been borrowed now from the Left and now from the Right, the manipulative techniques are sure and, behind them, lies the determination to last and to preserve. There is no stronger factor of endurance, and this is the essence of the center, the essence of the moderate Right: it is essentially conservative, embodying the great adaptable Orleanist tradition, ever changing, always the same.

The extremes are different and the extreme Right is peculiar to itself. Ultra, Nationalist, proto-Fascist, it provides the cheerleaders, the adventurous, romantic battle cries to which people lend an ear at times of crisis when heroic remedies appeal even to the unheroic. When there is peace, this radicalism seems incongruous, anachronistic, or awkwardly doctrinaire. When it has a doctrine, it is too intransigent to be politic. Soon it becomes anachronistic, too anachronistic (as with the Ultras or the Action Française) to attract recruits. When it has no doctrine, as the Fascists have none, it has no continuity. A spirit of movement, reaction, or crisis can have no continuity: not just in terms of time which alters cases, but of adherents, too. Such radicalism, offering no historical interpretation, no key to current experience, no means of adjustment to the changing world, remains a movement for the young, the socially and economically uncommitted who have not yet invested in a worldly calling or career, who are still available in every sense of the term. Some men live on like this, perpetually rolling stones in a flurry of movement; but most men change. They win that which they sought, they marry and have children, they grow up, they turn their minds and energies elsewhere, and they become conservative: they join the Center. Proto-Fascists may do this more easily, since no principle, no firm doctrine will deter them and the opportunism life demands is intrinsic to their pragmatic creed. No class, no constantly recruited group exists, persists to furnish them a stable clientèle. They are wandering minstrels, troubadours of a sterner, plainer world, or leaders into battle, the bright, terrible lunatic fringe of the dull and prudent, the damned compact liberal majority.

But occasions for heroic action are rare. And few of those committed to things as they are will long countenance heroics once the crisis has been resolved, preferably by some sort of unheroic compromise. Only prolonged crisis could provide the circumstances in which the extreme Right prospered. But in France's balanced economy, slackness went along with stability; men feared for the established order and men disordered it, but there was no collapse.

No vast class of economically dispossessed, of socially displaced persons provided the troops of a radical experiment. There were always too many people who had too much to lose for extremist gambles to stand a serious chance. Recurrent crises were resolved by surrenders, mutual surrenders, for no one wished to rock the boat too hard, least of all the great mass of conservatives. And, while moderation prospered, the radicals, stranded by such unsuitable conditions, were left to sing and shout and strut on a little promontory of their own.

SUGGESTED READING

BARDÈCHE, MAURICE. *Qu'est-ce que le fascisme?* Paris: 1961.

BARRÈS, MAURICE. *Scènes et doctrines du nationalisme.* Paris: 1925. 2 vols.

BEAU DE LOMÉNIE, E. *Les Responsabilités des dynasties bourgeoises.* Paris: 1943–1963. 4 vols.

BERNANOS, GEORGES. *La Grande peur des bien-pensants.* Paris: 1931.

————. *Les Grands cimetières sous la lune.* Paris: 1938.

BONNARD, ABEL. *Les Modérés.* Paris: 1936.

BRASILLACH, ROBERT. *Notre avant-guerre.* Paris: 1941.

BYRNES, ROBERT F. *Antisemitism in Modern France.* New Brunswick, N. J.: 1950.

CLÉMENT, MARCEL. *Enquête sur le Nationalisme.* Paris: 1957.

CURTIS, MICHAEL. *Three Against the Third Republic.* Princeton: 1959.

DANSETTE, ADRIEN. *Le Boulangisme.* Paris: 1946.

DRIEU LA ROCHELLE, PIERRE. *Avec Doriot.* Paris: 1937.

————. *Socialisme fasciste.* Paris: 1934.

DRUMONT, EDOUARD. *La France juive.* Paris: 1887.

GIRARDET, RAOUL. "Notes sur l'esprit d'un fascisme français," *Revue Française de science politique.* September, 1955.

HERVET, ROBERT. *Les Chantiers de la jeunesse.* Paris: 1962.

HOFFMANN, STANLEY. *Le Mouvement Poujade.* Paris: 1956.

LA ROCQUE, EDITH and GILES DE. *La Rocque tel qu'il était.* Paris: 1962.

LA ROCQUE, FRANÇOIS DE. *Service Public.* Paris: 1934.

LEMAÎTRE, HENRI. *Les Fascismes dans l'histoire.* Paris: 1959.

LHOMME, JEAN. *La Grande bourgeoisie au pouvoir.* Paris: 1960.

MAURRAS, CHARLES. *Au Signe de Flore.* Paris: 1933.

————. *Mes idées politiques.* Paris: 1937.

MAXENCE, JEAN-PIERRE. *Histoire de dix ans, 1927–1937.* Paris: 1937.

MOHLER, ARMIN. *Die französische Rechte.* Munich: 1958.

NORA, PIERRE. "Ernest Lavisse: son rôle dans la formation du sentiment national," *Revue Historique.* July-September, 1962.

OSGOOD, SAMUEL M. *French Royalism under the Third and Fourth Republics.* The Hague: 1960.

PLUMYÈNE, JEAN, and RAYMOND LASIERA. *Les Fascismes français, 1923–1963.* Paris: 1963.

REBATET, LUCIEN. *Les Décombres.* Paris: 1942.

RÉMOND, RENÉ. *La Droite en France.* Paris: 1954.

SÉRANT, PAUL. *Le Romantisme fasciste.* Paris: 1960.

SOREL, GEORGES. *Réflexions sur la violence.* Paris: 1906.

VALLAT, XAVIER. *La Croix, les lys et la peine des hommes.* Paris: 1960.

———. *Le Nez de Cléopatre.* Paris: 1957.

VANDROMME, POL. *La Droite buisonnière.* Paris: 1960.

VARENNES, CLAUDE. *Le Destin de Marcel Déat.* Paris: 1948.

WEBER, EUGEN. *Action Française.* Stanford: 1962.

———. *The Nationalist Revival in France, 1905–1914.* Berkeley and Los Angeles: 1959.

Belgium

JEAN STENGERS

To align the subject of this chapter with that of the other contributions, I am compelled to describe under the name *Right* some Belgian realities that conform to our definition of the word but that were not known by that name in their own time.

In Belgium, in contrast to France, the word *Right* never applied to political tendencies hostile to the existing system. It is, in our history, the traditional name of a party that has always adhered strictly to the pattern of Belgian institutions—as, for example, the Catholic party. This requires a short study of our political vocabulary.

The Belgian constitution of 1831 established two houses of parliament: a Chamber of Representatives and a Senate. From the beginning, the Chamber sat in a semicircle; the Senate did the same after a few years. Quite soon, the Catholics in the Chamber took to sitting to the right of the president, and the liberals to the left, and so the *droite* and *gauche* of our history were born.

The interest of that phenomenon is that it took place at a time when, apparently, Catholics and liberals were not directly opposed in parliament. Until 1847, all the governments had declared themselves as "unionist"; they meant to be above parties and described their policy as one of permanent compromise. Most cabinets were *cabinets mixtes:* coalitions composed of both Catholics and liberals. In Parliament, their policy was nearly always supported by a joint majority of Catholic and liberal moderates, and opposed by a kind of "party of movement," of very fluid composition, which also included Catholics as well as liberals. This means that, in parliament during the unionist period, Catholics never opposed liberals as such.

In the country at large, however, and in political thinking, there was a fundamental division of opinions and loyalties between Catholics and liberals. It did not then or at any time coincide completely with a religious division. A great majority of liberals, in the middle of the nineteenth century, were regular churchgoers (and, apart from a tiny Protestant minority, Belgium is a Roman Catholic country). But the liberal ideal of a lay state with a sharp distinction between civil and religious affairs, and the Catholic ideal of a society where the influence of religion would be used to the general good, clashed permanently throughout the country. It was according to these two fundamental schools of thinking that, after a time, deputies began to choose their seats in the Chamber. Ten years after the beginning of Belgian independence this had become an established habit and, quite naturally, the political vocabulary adapted itself to the situation in the semicircle: *gauche* and *droite* became synonymous with *liberal* and *Catholic*. As early as 1841 the two words were being used in debates; in a few years they became quite common. Needless to say, their quick success was aided by the fact that the Belgian public, which took a great interest in French affairs, had been for long accustomed to the various shades of meaning of *droite, centre,* and *gauche* in French political life.

Throughout the nineteenth century, Right and Left remained mainly connected with parliamentary activities. They served to designate Catholics or liberals as a whole, but were used mainly in respect to the two parliamentary groups. In the newspapers, for instance, a "meeting of the Right" (*réunion de la droite*) meant a meeting of the Catholic members of the Chamber. The great Catholic leader Charles Woeste described his party as having three pillars: *"la droite, les associations, et la presse"* (i.e., the parliamentary group, the political associations, and the Catholic news-papers).

In parliament, both Catholics and liberals had their internal divisions, but only among the liberals were these strong enough to lead to a special grouping of seats. In the 1880's, the Radicals, headed by Paul Janson, who struggled for an enlarged franchise, rallied to the extreme Left and became known as such. This lasted for only a short time, as in 1894 all seats of the extreme left were taken over by the Socialists, who entered parliament as a result of the constitutional reform of 1893, which established universal male suffrage. Among the Catholics, different shades of opinion gave birth to different labels. Just before World War I, for instance, there was the "Old Right," that is, the conservatives led by Charles Woeste, as opposed to the "Young Right," those with more ad-vanced social ideas; later there was the conservative Right (*droite conservatrice*) as distinguished from the Christian Democrats; but this never led to a choice of different seats and even less to a formal break in the unity of the Right.

The appearance of the Socialists brought some complication into the political vocabulary. There were now two parties on the left side of the assembly, two *gauche*s. They were called the Liberal Left (*gauche libérale*) and the Socialist Left (*gauche socialiste*), but the singular Left (*la gauche*) remained in common use to cover Socialists *and* Liberals as well as Communists later on. This meant that in spite of the enormous differences between these parties, they had a common characteristic inherited from the traditional Left of the earlier nineteenth century: they were anticlerical parties and wanted a lay society with lay schools. The Catholics, as champions of the Catholic schools, were on the other side of the fence.

Until quite recent times, in a country where the dividing lines between political opinions, creeds, languages, and social ideas very rarely coincide—which makes the picture of Belgian society a very complicated one indeed—the two groups with the strongest affini-ties, in which a Belgian had to be placed first if one wished to un-derstand him, were those of the *hommes de gauche* and the *hommes de droite*. These people had generally attended different schools—lay or Catholic—and had in many respects quite distinct political sentiments. For the latter, religious values were part of the social order and to question them was to endanger that order; for the former, religion was a concept like any other and, like any other, open to discussion. This antagonism still exists, but in order of psychological importance it is now superseded by that between the Flemish-speaking and French-speaking Belgians.

In the interwar period, but much more after World War II, some Socialist and other writers tended, when speaking of Right and Left, to stress social attitudes rather than the old distinction between Catholics and anticlericals. They would consider the Liberals, because of their rather conservative program, as belonging to the Right. They would put the Liberals and the Catholics (or only a part of the Catholics) together and brand them as a "reactionary Right." But these new uses of Right—and also, naturally, of Left —have always been very fluid ones,[1] and never resulted in a really fixed vocabulary.

In any event, neither this recent use of "Right," nor the traditional one, can form a basis for this contribution; it would then have too little in common with the other chapters of the present book.

It is also impossible to keep to what would have been called, in our history, the "extreme Right." This phrase, in fact, never found its way into our political vocabulary. It did not originate in parliament, as no party ever agreed to being seated to the right of the traditional Right. In 1936, Rexists went so far as to use physical force in order to avoid sitting there and were finally and paradoxically accommodated in the center. (These incidents took place in several provincial councils; in parliament things went more smoothly.) "Extreme Right" was sometimes used in political

---

[1] In their books, *Les Elections belges. Explication de la répartition géographique des suffrages* (Brussels: 1956), and *Atlas des élections belges, 1919–1954* (Brussels: 1958), which are the best analyses of twentieth-century electoral results, R. De Smet and R. Evalenko oscillate between two different *gauches*. One *gauche*, in their first book, comprises only the Socialists and Communists, and a second one, in the *Atlas*, covers the Liberals, Socialists, and Communists. This shows that they are not quite sure of the first one. See my comments on the two books in the *Revue de l'Université de Bruxelles* (January-March 1958), and in the *Revue Belge de Philologie et d'Histoire*, XL (1962), 423 ff.

propaganda and as a term of abuse, but with so little stability of meaning that the words cannot serve as a guide.

This being so, what will be my own definition? I shall consider as belonging to the Right all movements aiming at a change of the political regime when that change would strengthen the authority of the executive.

A first remark must be that such movements very rarely envisaged a complete change of institutions. Insofar as they recognized the existence of Belgium itself—and all did so, with the exception of a few Flemish movements—all movements of the Right allowed for the retention of at least one element of the regime: the monarchy.

In Belgian history the monarchy nearly always enjoyed immunity from the criticism leveled at other institutions. The only attacks it ever suffered came from the Socialists. Until the end of the reign of Leopold II (1909), the Socialists displayed strong republican convictions. They spared neither the monarchical system nor the King himself, who was violently abused in their publications. When Leopold was succeeded by Albert I, whose personality did not offer such a good target for attacks, the republicanism of the Socialists became more theoretical. It died out altogether in 1914 when the King became the hero of his people with the result that, after World War I, the monarchy was no longer a problem in Belgian political life. Even during the major crisis of the so-called royal question (1945–1950) the monarchical system was not questioned. It was only an individual occupant of the throne, such as King Leopold III, who was rejected by a large part of the country. Even a leading Socialist could declare without a hint of contradiction that "Belgium needed monarchy as much as bread."

All leaders of the Right—with the exception, noted above, of some Flemish rightists—always declared themselves loyal subjects of the king. This, it may be observed, proved something of a handicap to their movements. It was even a double handicap. First, they could not attack the regime as a whole, which is the simplest and most effective method for any radical opposition. Unlike the members of Action Française, they had no integral figure to detest, no *gueuse* to destroy. They were forced to distinguish between what they wished to keep and what they wished to change. The Flemish Nationalists, in that respect, had a better hand to play, as they rejected the whole system and in fact the Belgian state itself: *Weg met België* ("Down with Belgium") was quite simple, and simple slogans are often the most forceful.

A second handicap was that to ask for a "strong man" to take the affairs of the country in hand might easily appear an indirect offense to the head of the state. This was particularly true during the reign of Albert I (1909–1934), and the King's immense prestige certainly silenced more than one voice that would otherwise have appealed for a "strong man." Léon Degrelle, the Rexist leader, who presented himself as strong man and savior, came at the beginning of a new reign, and Leopold III, still a young sovereign, had not his father's moral stature. It may be doubted whether, with King Albert still on the throne, so many thousand Belgians would have shouted their enthusiasm for Degrelle with such good conscience.

True, the movements of the Right could demand more effective powers for the King himself, so as to make him truly the country's ruler. This was in fact proposed by more than one right-wing program, but roused little enthusiasm and had little chance of success since King Albert, himself a model of constitutional discretion, was likely to be the first opponent of any such reform. Interestingly enough, while pleading for greater powers for the crown, many advocates of such a measure avoided mentioning the King's name, Albert I; they seem to have felt instinctively that it would make their arguments appear ridiculous.

The Right, as it has been defined above, developed in Belgium only during the interwar period. It had no significance whatever before World War I and lost most of its significance after World War II.

This does not mean that before 1914 all Belgian institutions were so admired by all citizens that no change of the principles of the constitution was ever envisaged. But the changes envisaged or asked for were quite foreign to the concerns of the Right. Criticism sometimes came from great parliamentarians, like Woeste, or the Liberal, Paul Hymans. In his *Crise du parlementarisme*—written, it is true, in 1897, shortly *before* he entered parliament—Hymans deplored the violence of debates, and the poor quality of the legislation they produced. It is also a fact that violence increased in the Assembly after the appearance of the Socialists, who began by being very turbulent indeed, and that lawmaking in such a feverish atmosphere met with serious difficulties, among them the plague of endless amendments, each of which had to be discussed at considerable length. At any rate, if parliament was criticized (and many a critic discovered symptoms of a crisis in its functioning long before 1914), those who wished to reform it looked in most instances to a better representative system, such as might be achieved by a representation of professional or corporative interests.[2] They never considered, as the Right would later, the possibility of reducing the power of Parliament itself.

The only movement that could, at first sight, be called a nineteenth-century ancestor of the Right, was the Ultramontanism of the years 1852–1880, which boasted a content and meaning peculiar to Belgium that was distinct from the general sense of ultramontanism common to the whole Catholic world. As a school of thought that rejected some of the most important principles of the constitution, it opposed what it considered "the liberty of evil": that is, a constitutional protection extended alike to the enemies of God and to his servants. In doing this, Ultramontanists hearkened to the great voice of Pius IX, heard from time to time in Latin, but even more perhaps to the powerful notes of the Parisian journalist Louis Veuillot, whom they could read every day in French.

---

[2] The champion of the system of representation of interests was Adolphe Prins, Professor of Law at the University of Brussels (1845–1919). "Interest groups," he argued (industry, commerce, agriculture, etc.), would be electoral bodies with a better understanding of the country's needs than anonymous groups of citizens inhabiting the same district. This naturally implied that these groups should have a minimum of organization, but Prins did not insist on any corporatist organization; he simply wanted a new representative system. It is interesting to note that a step in that direction was made in 1895 when the law concerning the election of communal councils was revised; in large boroughs, the law provided for a small minority of councilors being elected by employers and workers respectively. This limited reform proved so disappointing that the provision was abandoned in 1921.

They were, at any rate, profoundly convinced Catholics who wished the state to conform to the religious dictates of the Church. As soon as possible, therefore, all "nefarious liberties" that comforted and sheltered the enemies of the Church—such as liberty of the press, for instance—had to be stricken from the constitution.

This point of view, however, was held by only a minority. All Catholic deputies proclaimed themselves faithful to the constitution and to its liberties. No declared Ultramontanist even won a seat in the Chamber. But many of them gained influence in Catholic newspapers and, in the 1870's, a large part of the Catholic press spoke lightly of the constitution, reserving its praise for the Pope's *Syllabus of Errors* (1864) and its condemnation of liberalism.

Such was briefly the Ultramontanist position, which caused great damage to Catholics in public opinion, and which ended shortly after the death of Pio Nono (1878), when Pope Leo XIII, considering that damage, quietly ordered the leaders of the movement to cease attacking the Belgian constitution. Was that Ultramontanism a first manifestation of the Right? Not according to our definition, for what the Ultramontanists attacked in the constitution were the "liberties," which in their eyes contradicted the privileges truth must enjoy. About the political regime itself, they had little to say; they had no great objection to it.

In 1875, one of the main Belgian Ultramontanists, Charles Périn, professor of political economy at the University of Louvain, devoted a lengthy book to *Les Lois de la société chrétienne* ("The Laws of Christian Society"). In his chapters on civil government, he denounced the parliamentary system as a "liberal hypocrisy" and made an apology for the *ancien régime*. It is curious to note how little echo these views found in the Catholic newspapers which were the mouthpiece of the Ultramontanist campaign. This indicates that the Ultramontanists cared little about the structure of political power as such and were ready enough to accept the existing regime. Their true preoccupations were elsewhere, where they believed the rights of God and his Church had to be reëstablished.

Thus, the appearance of the Right after World War I was definitely a new phenomenon in Belgian political life.

Before World War I, the Belgian people as a whole did not feel that their political institutions presented any real problem. There were, it is true, important political questions at stake. The winning of power was one. Catholics had held an absolute majority since 1884, while Liberals and Socialists struggled energetically to displace them. Another big question was the franchise. The universal suffrage established in 1893 was "tempered" by plural votes allotted to certain categories of citizens. The Socialists demanded universal suffrage, and they had launched two general strikes to get it. The suffrage and the elections to be won were the great political preoccupations of most Belgians. To the nature of the political regime itself they devoted little thought, taking it for granted. As indicated before, parliament was criticized, and reforms that might improve it were in the air. But criticism never turned into rejection, and the proposed reforms came from political scientists rather than from political movements; they had no impact whatsoever on the masses.

The change after the war was threefold. First, the working of the regime came under increasingly severe fire from large sectors of the press and public opinion. There was growing disappointment and disgust over what was called the incompetence and inefficiency of Parliament, the arrogance of the parties to which authority was said to submit, their petty rivalries, and the impotence of government as illustrated by too many ministerial crises. Some national newspapers like the *Nation Belge* (conservative nationalist) or the *Vingtième Siècle* (conservative Catholic) often had very harsh things to say about all that went wrong in the political institutions of the country.

From this there arose—and this was a second novelty—a real concern about the reform of these institutions. "Réforme de l'Etat" became a watchword, in the thirties still more than in the twenties.[3]

---

[3] See, for instance, the important works of Herbert Speyer (*La Réforme de l'état en Belgique*, 1927; *Corporatisme ou parlementarisme réformé*, 1935). A collective effort by some of the best political scientists of the country was that, in 1936–1938, of the Centre d'Etudes pour la Réforme de l'Etat. Two reports, under the title *La Réforme de l'état*, were published in 1937 and 1938. Suggestions were made, for example, that parliament, in its law-making activity, should often restrict itself to establishing general principles and then leave the govern-

Most of those who thought about such a reform wanted a better and stronger executive. Many believed that this could be achieved without any fundamental change of the institutional pattern, merely by adjustments. Others, however, deprecated such a small-scale policy; in their eyes the evil was so great that only a major change could cure it. They formed the Right.

The Right was the third new phenomenon.

How many Belgians did it attract? It is practically impossible to tell. Neither electoral results nor official membership figures can offer any precise data. There were, to put it briefly, two kinds of movements of the Right. One of these derived most of its glamor from the fact that its program and organization bore the distinct mark of the Right. But these movements (either because they felt too weak, or for reasons of principle) never took part in electoral contests; on the other hand their numbers, when known, do not always give an accurate idea of their importance and influence, for they had sympathizers as well as members. The Verdinaso, for instance, the most distinctly Fascist organization of the thirties, had a very small membership of a few thousand, but it also had a halo—an area of effectiveness, more or less intense, going well beyond the hard kernel of militant supporters.

Other movements, particularly the Flemish National League (VNV) and the Rexist party, fought the elections. But they belonged to the second category of movements; in them the ideas and ideals of the Right were eclipsed by other and more powerful factors, and it is these that in fact mainly accounted for their success. It is impossible to determine how many of their supporters really wanted the *Right* to succeed.

All figures would therefore be misleading. But this much may be ascertained:

1) The Right always remained a marginal force. In the twenties even the Socialists, who were often apt to exaggerate its danger, regarded it as rather contemptible. "Much ado about nothing," said the Socialist leader Emile Vandervelde in 1924. In the thirties, the rightist trend gathered strength, but it remained rather small

---

ment free to apply them, and that both government and parliament should be helped by advisory councils specializing in certain fields.

compared with the democratic political formations. The latter never lost their immense majority nor—more important—their morale. A crisis like that of May 13, 1958, in France, where there were democrats enough but few ready to fight for democracy, was never to be feared in Belgium. Any attempt at a coup de force would have been opposed and crushed.

2) If figures are impossible to give, it is not because a part of the Right lay hidden. All movements of the Right worked in the open. There was no equivalent of the French Cagoule in Belgium.

3) The marginal character of the Right was in part owing to the fact that it found recruits only in certain social strata. The working class remained practically untouched. The peasantry was little affected. Most adherents came from the small bourgeoisie of the towns (employees, craftsmen, shopkeepers, small industrialists), with a sprinkling of intellectuals (doctors, lawyers, students). Big industry and the banks, as a whole, kept aloof.

This last remark means that, except for a few months when Rexism was at its height—and was helped by some generous donors —the movements of the Right usually drifted, financially, in rather difficult or even very difficult waters. The financial help of Mussolini to Degrelle, and of Hitler's Germany to the VNV, was most welcome as national resources were lacking.

Before we come to the movements themselves, however, it is imperative to understand the factors that contributed to their birth and development.

We have already mentioned, as one main factor, dissatisfaction with the functioning of political institutions. This dissatisfaction stemmed in part from objective defects of these institutions, but still more, perhaps, from the faults ascribed to them when the country passed through difficult times. Difficulties there were aplenty in the Belgium of the interwar years. Trouble came mainly from the postwar financial crisis, then from the Flemish question, then from the great depression of 1930. All these furnished occasions to brand parliament as incapable and government as lacking authority. As a matter of fact, there were instances in which neither government nor parliament cut a very good figure. There were objective and inescapable signs of crisis in the affairs of the country and the way they were handled. The most striking sign of all, perhaps, was that the government had to ask repeatedly for special powers (*lois de pouvoirs spéciaux*) enabling it to legislate by executive fiat; the normal legislative power, parliament, did not seem fit to meet urgent needs.

But if parliament was a favorite target for attacks, political parties were denounced as a still greater evil. Part of the explanation lies in the fact that, after the war, all three parties (Catholics, Liberals, and Socialists) now took part in the government. From 1884 to 1914 the Catholic party had governed alone, without any interruption. There were few Belgians, at that time, who did not think that their first and most exciting duty was either to keep the Catholics in saddle, or to unsaddle them. World War I brought this exciting game to an end. Between 1914 and 1918, for national reasons, the Belgian government had become tripartite (with ministers from three parties). It remained so after the victory. In 1919 the Catholics lost their absolute majority in parliament and did not recover it until 1950. Coalitions, therefore, were imperative. They were of different kinds; tripartite, Catholic-Socialist (1925–1926), and Catholic-Liberal, the latter being the most frequent. Having shared in the government, at one time or another, all parties now seemed to bear a common responsibility. It was thus their fault if things did not go well. Much more than parliament, it was the "regime of parties" that excited hostility.

Apart from these very general motivations, many other more specific factors played their part in the development of a right-wing psychology.

One, disillusioned nationalism, resulted directly from the war. Belgian nationalism (as distinct from Belgian national feeling) was mainly a by-product of the war. It grew mostly, and in many respects almost exclusively, in the French-speaking section of the population—which, by the way, extended to Flanders, where the upper classes were still largely French-speaking. Nationalism was a mixture of various dreams: the dream of a greater Belgium, recovering the Grand Duchy of Luxembourg and Dutch Limburg, lost in 1839; the dream of a patriotic Belgium, doing away once and forever with all separatist movements, especially Flemish ones;

the dream of a victorious country keeping Germany down and making her pay. Needless to say, all these dreams were disappointed. The ensuing disillusion turned some people against the political system, which they held responsible for the failure. War veterans or retired officers would henceforth provide typical followers of the right-wing movements. It is characteristic that the two chief movements of this kind in the twenties, the Action Nationale of Pierre Nothomb and the Légion Nationale, both started as nationalist movements before turning definitely to the Right; and, as we shall see below, Pierre Nothomb himself headed the campaign for the recovery of Luxemburg and Limburg.

The great depression of 1930 and the following years came as an unprecedented shock, but, curiously enough, its political consequences were rather limited. In the 1932 elections economic preoccupations were not in the foreground. The Catholics succeeded —and this was really a masterpiece of political propaganda—in concentrating on traditional and convenient themes, such as "saving our children's beautiful souls" (by the help given to Catholic schools). In the 1936 elections the triumph of the Rexist party was only partly related, as we shall see later, to the economic difficulties of the time. The Communists benefited from the depression much more than did the Right (winning one seat out of 187 in 1929, three out of 187 in 1932, and nine out of 202 in 1936). Only one party of the Right really sprang from the crisis. It was the party of the *réalistes,* founded by a demagogue named Janssens, who proposed political as well as economic panaceas: the abolition of parliament, the establishment of a dictatorship, and the doubling of everybody's salary. Janssens registered a startling 18 per cent of the votes cast in a Brussels by-election in 1935—in which many of the voters seem, however, to have expressed a rather twisted sense of humor. After that his party collapsed completely.

The war and the great depression were striking events. But silently, almost unnoticed, other developments were taking place which would turn to the benefit of the Right. One was the dwindling role played by the Notables on the political scene. Before 1893, when suffrage was still limited to about 2 per cent of the population, the squire, the doctor, the notary, the solicitor, and all the other gentlemen to whom the common people looked as figures of authority and prestige, had been in many ways the masters of the political game. Everyone courted them, and their vote could be of vital importance. When the question of an enlarged franchise was discussed, one of the fears expressed by the opponents of universal suffrage was that it would lead to the triumph of the political "machine" and of the professional politician. American examples were quoted. As a matter of fact, neither "rings" nor "bosses" ever invaded Belgium, but with the coming of universal suffrage in 1893, though it was tempered by plural votes until 1919, politics became more and more a profession, two of the main requisites of success being the efficient handling of the party machinery and of larger masses of electors. For the Notables this marked a very perceptible decline. A man of fortune, or social status, or both, but without a place in a political machine, who was too shy to address large audiences and could not write popular articles, would often feel helpless in politics. Resentful of the contrast between his importance in society and his political insignificance, such a man was ready to turn against the "regime of parties."

A second fundamental evolution was the widening gulf between the poor or nonexistent organization of the middle classes and the better organization of other classes. The middle classes in Belgium have never been able to take a common stand in strong, substantial organizations of their own. Individualism, lack of a sense of discipline, and political antagonism have always resulted in a variety of professional organizations with no common link. In contrast to this, the workers' unions were growing, and they had two strong federations, one Socialist and one Catholic. By 1914 their total membership stood around 250,000. Ten years later it had grown to 700,000, and twenty years later to 875,000. Organized labor had become a major factor in politics as well as in economic life. So, in another sector, had the Boerenbond (the Flemish peasants' league), which operated as a highly efficient representative of rural interests. The influence of the great bankers, too, never excited more comment than during the interwar period; an all-powerful man like Emile Francqui, of the Société Générale, appeared in that respect as a symbol. Organization was evidently not lacking in that sector either. Facing the determined organization of the unions, Boerenbond, and banks, the middle classes often had the unhappy feeling of being but a collection of lightweights squeezed between heavyweights. This helps to explain the attraction of "corporatist" ideas, which were treasured by nearly all movements of the Right. In a corporatist organization of society, men of the middle classes thought, they would regain influence and perhaps even leadership. It is a quite characteristic fact that, in most movements, these corporatist dreams generally went along with a declared hostility toward trade unions and strong denunciations of the sinister influence of banks.

These corporatist ideas, however, cannot be fully understood unless they are seen as part of general contemporary currents of thought, which crossed political as they did national frontiers. This brings us to another momentous factor, that of foreign intellectual influences. One name here is of outstanding importance: Charles Maurras, who, in the middle twenties, was a hero of young Catholic intellectuals. "Our young men read Maurras with enthusiasm," wrote Abbé Jacques Leclercq in 1925. Maurras' influence was strongest among the students of Catholic Louvain University—especially those from the French section—and among the Catholic students of Liège, a state university. The *Action française* sold hundreds of copies in Louvain daily. When, in 1925, the *Cahiers de la Jeunesse Catholique* asked their readers to answer the question, "Among the writers of the last twenty-five years, whom do you consider as your masters?," Maurras' name headed the poll, far ahead of more conventional Catholic figures. Although it was later revealed that the so-called poll had been a hoax,[4] Maurras' success was a true reflection of his immense prestige among young

---

[4] It is practically certain that some friends of the *Cahiers* concocted answers in the name of quite imaginary readers. They did not suspect that their innocent joke would have enormous consequences. The results of the poll caused great anger and indignation in some Catholic circles which could not tolerate that an atheist like Maurras should become the mentor of Belgian youth. Controversies on the subject raged in Belgian newspapers for a time. They were the direct origin of the moves taken by Rome to condemn the Action Française and Maurras. A few dozen faked votes had made history.

Catholics. To them Maurras appeared, in the words of a sympathetic priest, as a "great oak on a devastated plain." In the turmoil of the time only he seemed to offer a solid, well-established doctrine, and a personality sufficiently forceful to master that turmoil. The psychology of youth is also an important factor here. Young men often need a revolutionary faith, which fades when they mature. Action Française proposed the notion of a right-wing revolution, which attracted young Catholics, just as Communism attracted other young men who would afterward become moderate Socialists or even Liberals. In either instance, the brief revolutionary spell often reflected no more than a *crise de jeunesse*.

It came as a shock when, at the end of 1926, Maurras and the Action Française were condemned by Rome. With most of Maurras' followers, Catholic discipline prevailed. Only in Liège did some students maintain allegiance to their old master, and the bishop of Liège had to condemn the paper they continued to publish. At Louvain, practically all the students submitted. They were guided into submission by some priests, like Mgr. Picard, who had a strong influence on youth and who fully accepted the orders of Rome. But abandonment of Maurras did not mean abandonment of the authoritarian ideas for which he stood. In all student publications, throughout the twenties, even though Maurras was dropped, "authority" remained the watchword. Though no longer a hero, Maurras still loomed in the background. Léon Degrelle, a student at Louvain in 1926–1927, was one of those who readily submitted to the condemnation, but ten years later when he founded a Rexist daily paper he named it *Pays Réel*, a title drawn directly from Maurrassian terminology.

Some of the young Catholics whose hearts had responded to "authority" during their student years at Liège or Louvain later rallied to Rexism or other movements of the Right, which shall be mentioned shortly. Most of them, however, and the best of them as regards intellectual capacity, did not. Against the menace of dictatorship—external and internal—they stood up for democracy. This was true, for instance, with Abbé Jacques Leclercq, one of the most influential minds of the period, who had flirted with Maurrassism around 1925, but whose publication *La Cité chrétienne* became in the thirties one of the most lucid defenders of social and political democracy. It is striking to note how many ex-Maurrassians supported the *Cité chrétienne*. Their *crise de jeunesse* was over.

At Louvain, and among Catholic students, the intellectual atmosphere largely changed in the thirties. A new influence progressively took the lead, that of the French periodical *Esprit* and of Emmanuel Mounier. With their social and individual preoccupations, they provided an almost complete antidote to Maurras.

Generally speaking, the *Action française* was no longer much read in Belgium in the thirties, as it had been around 1925. But other French publications of the Right now captured a large public, especially *Gringoire* and *Candide*, less for strictly ideological reasons than because they made such good reading. Young and old alike enjoyed them, with significant effects on their political outlook. The rabid denunciations of the scandals of French democracy which *Candide* and *Gringoire* provided in such vivid terms led many of their Belgian readers to associate democracy with scandals, whether consciously or not. This proved a great psychological boost for Rexist propaganda. The success of Rexism is not understandable without knowing of the Stavisky affair, *Gringoire*, and *Candide*.

All these came from France. But there was also Italy. Mussolini inspired great sympathy in the Belgian bourgeoisie. He was generally regarded as having saved Italy from chaos. Nobody, or practically nobody, thought that Fascism as such could be imported from Italy. Even Mussolini's staunchest admirers—and there were some who bestowed the highest praise on him—stressed the difference between Italy and Belgium. Mussolini's Italy never really served as a model. But it helped, and helped considerably, to create a climate favorable to regimes of "order" and "authority." A Belgian bourgeois, Catholic or not, would come back from Italy repeating after others, and with equal admiration, that "trains were now running on time" and that the workers knew their place. These were good marks for "order" and "authority."

Such a climate was never fostered by Hitler's Germany. Hitler meant—any other disquieting characteristics of his dictatorship apart—a renewal of the German threat to Belgium. This nobody could like, except some Flemish nationalists so hostile to Belgian unity that, to destroy it, they could not help looking even to Germany as a possible ally. Some VNV circles were the only ones in which sympathy for Hitler's Germany could be felt. A few individuals also admired Hitler as a man. But they were not many. Degrelle was one of them.

If we may now glance briefly at the various movements of the Right, a first category would include those who did not try to mass "troops" in the streets, but relied on the diffusion of their ideals and theories. We might call them the intellectual movements.

The Pour l'Autorité group, which in 1927 shortened its name to L'Autorité, was named for a periodical published from 1924 to 1932 by young Catholics who had, in most instances, just graduated from the University of Louvain. Among them were some of the most brilliant young men of their generation, strongly influenced by Maurras. Pour L'Autorité rejoiced, in 1925, in the results of the poll of the *Cahiers de la Jeunesse Catholique*. It advocated no revolt against the Catholic party; on the contrary, it wanted to be a laboratory of ideas where the doctrines of the party were elaborated. There was no effort to work outside an aristocracy of young intellectuals; at banquets of the group, full evening dress was compulsory. As regards ideas, did they really belong to the Right? They were at least on the fringe. They called for a stronger executive, and for a curbing of the exaggerated power of the legislative. The reforms proposed, such as cutting the number of deputies in parliament, shortening its sessions, and limiting its powers, tend to adapt rather than to change the system of institutions. But the general climate of the movement, with its basic and repeated plea for more "authority," has many characteristics of the Right.

The Réaction group was the Right in its most ferocious form. It consisted of a tiny group of men of letters (especially Robert Poulet, a very talented journalist, who was to play a great role in the collaborationist press during World War II), war veterans, corporatist theoreticians, and so on. The group was established in 1932, and their organ for two years (1933–1935) was the *Revue*

Réactionnaire, with only three to four hundred subscribers. It tried to foster a "powerful current of opinion against parliament and democracy"; it felt that the old parties must disappear and "abdicate their sovereignty into the hands of the king." The king, who would govern with the help of a corporatist system, would be given the most extensive powers, including legislative power. In 1935 the *Revue Réactionnaire* was succeeded by the *Revue de l'Ordre Corporatif* (1935–1940), which continued the struggle for a "corporate monarchy."

The *Nation Belge* was founded in 1918 by a brilliant journalist, Fernand Neuray. True to its title, Neuray made it the mouthpiece of Belgian nationalism. Much appreciated in the army, it was often called the "journal des officiers" and opened its columns to many French writers of the Action Française. Very critical of parliament and political parties, its position in that regard remained for many years mainly a negative one. This changed around 1933, and still more after Neuray's death in 1934. A positive program was then defended by new collaborators, among whom were Robert Poulet and other members of the Réaction group (Réaction in a way invading the *Nation Belge*). The parliamentary regime was dying; it should be replaced by a corporatist state, with a strong executive power around the king. These ideas, however, were much more diluted than in the *Revue Réactionnaire*—the *Nation Belge* being a daily paper of general interest—and were presented in a much less offensive way. The new team certainly felt that by taking too strong a stand it would shock many of the paper's traditional readers. Degrelle and Rex often received sympathetic treatment, but the *Nation Belge* never adhered to Rexism.

The authoritarian democracy of Henri De Man was rather an isolated instance but is important because De Man himself was an important personality. De Man (1885–1953) had won a worldwide reputation as a Socialist theoretician (*Au delà du marxisme,* 1927). He was author of the *Plan du travail* (1933), which Belgian Socialists acclaimed as the best way of fighting the economic crisis, and he held ministerial posts from 1935 to 1938. In 1939 he succeeded Emile Vandervelde as president of the Socialist party. By that time, however, as he himself confessed, he had "lost faith" in classical parliamentary democracy, which he thought incapable of curbing the great money-powers that had to be brought to heel if fundamental economic reforms were to succeed. Only an "authoritarian" democracy could serve as an appropriate tool for Socialist reforms. In 1939 De Man expressed his views in several articles published in the Flemish periodical *Leiding*. He wanted governments set up for four years, during which time parliament would not be permitted to overthrow them; budgets voted for four years; and one chamber instead of the bicameral system. At the same time, he renewed his earlier proposals for a corporatist system that would have its say in economic questions. World War II came before these views could be discussed by the Socialist party itself. In the country they found very little echo. But after the German victory of May and June, 1940, De Man's loss of faith in democracy had a direct result. As president of the Socialist party, he then issued a manifesto celebrating the collapse of "decrepit" democracies as a "liberation" for the working class. A short spell of collaboration with the Germans ensued; but De Man did not find much more comfort there. He ended his life an exile in Switzerland. He had no disciples.

A second category of movements were those that could boast organized troops.

The Action Nationale was founded by Pierre Nothomb, a profuse writer and orator, and perhaps the most active figure of Belgian nationalism after 1918. Nothomb (born in 1887) made his debut in the field of foreign policy, in which he found widespread support. His Comité de Politique Nationale, founded in 1919, included generals, businessmen, lawyers, men of letters, and politicians (even a few Socialist politicians at the beginning), and exercised some influence. But enthusiasm for grand schemes such as the annexation of Limburg and Luxemburg, which came to nothing, soon subsided, and Nothomb turned more and more to problems of Belgian internal policy, with determined rightist views. In this new form his nationalism lost the majority of its early supporters (the military element was the most faithful), but it tried to compensate for its loss of influence by increasingly violent language. Mouthpiece of this second phase was the weekly paper

L'Action Nationale (1924–1930), characterized by strong hostility against parliamentary democracy. "A democratic regime must necessarily ruin our civilization" (1925). The archenemy was Marxism, founded by a "Juif boche," Karl Marx; the movement was above all antisocialist, and demonstrated admiration for Mussolini in its most effusive form. Belgium, it said, must seek the alliance of the only "real force surviving in the West: that is Rome" (1926). The Italian corporatist system was much admired. The corporatist theoretician Corradini, wrote Nothomb, is "our *maître à penser,*" perhaps even more than Maurras (Maurras being quite characteristically the yardstick). The positive program of the Action Nationale included a strong government responsible to the king rather than to parliament, and the creation of corporatist organs with legislative responsibility. All in all it was a rather sketchy ideology. Its carrier would be an organization founded in 1925, the Jeunesses Nationales (1925–1932), with some two to three thousand members, mainly pupils of Catholic colleges from the ages of about sixteen to nineteen. They wore no uniforms, but badges. These young men were in attendance at meetings of the Action Nationale, sold the paper in the streets, paraded at patriotic ceremonies, brawled with young socialist "guards" and with Flemish nationalists (whom their movement hated as much as it did the Socialists), and rioted against theaters showing Soviet films. Their most celebrated exploit was the sack of a Soviet exhibition in Brussels in 1928. The Socialists denounced Nothomb as a "fascist leader," but as a leader he never gained any real prestige; a liberal newspaper called him a "Napoleon of the teenagers" (*Napoléon de la marmaille*). Rather strangely, this declared enemy of the parliamentary system regularly attempted to enter parliament; in 1925 and 1929 he was on the Catholic list, but with no success. This proved a source of confusion for many of his supporters and one of the main reasons for the end of his movement. In 1936, M. Nothomb became a Catholic senator.

The Légion Nationale was established in 1922. At first it was a very small movement of disillusioned officers and ex-servicemen of the Great War, disgusted by political parties and hoping for the day when Belgium would be rid of all its enemies—the Germanophiles, communists, and politicians. Strong nationalism was the keynote. There was great gusto for order, authority, Maurras, and Mussolini. After 1927 the movement gained fresh impetus from its new leader, Paul Hoornaert. Hoornaert, a lawyer from Liège (Liège had been from the beginning and would remain the real center of the Légion), had been a brilliant officer in the Great War. A staunch patriot, he was a leader of the Resistance during World War II and died in a German concentration camp. Under his command, the Légion developed into a paramilitary organization; it boasted mobile troops in uniform, with helmets and sticks. In the thirties, uniformed Légionnaires may have numbered between two and four thousand. The movement maintained "houses" in the main Belgian towns, but especially in the Walloon part of the country, for, though it had some Flemish recruits and a paper in Flemish, the Légion was predominantly French-speaking. Young men joined it, some of them from the Jeunesses Nationales. The aim of this military organization was not to stage a coup de force, but to form a nucleus of power for the day when Belgium, converted to the ideas of the Légion, would be ripe for "national revolution." Meanwhile, the Légionnaires were needed to defend the country against any revolutionary attempt from the Left. In fact, they had some severe street fights with Socialist militants. In July, 1934, a law was passed forbidding all private militias. It was aimed at both the Légion Nationale and the Verdinaso. But it was easily dodged and had little effect.

Hoornaert's ideal of a "national revolution" was to wipe out everything connected with the existing political regime, the king excepted. The new order would have nothing to do with parliamentary democracy or political parties. Its basis would be a corporatist system, with legislative power vested in corporatist chambers. About the executive, the program was less detailed. Hoornaert disclaimed the idea of a dictatorship, but naturally wanted the government to be "strong." Future developments were left to take care of themselves, but the Légion was quite definite in its determination never to compromise with parliamentary democracy. Rexism was condemned because it took the form of a political party sitting in parliament.

Nevertheless, the Légion Nationale and Rexism offer many striking analogies. They had a common hatred for Marxism, and associated it with the Jews; *judéo-marxisme* was for both movements the archenemy. In contrast to Degrelle, however, the leaders of the Légion, true to the anti-German tradition of Belgian nationalism, showed no sympathy for Germany or Hitler.

The Verdinaso was, like the Légion Nationale, a moderate-size body of trained men, yet it was much more important than the Légion for it had an influence and attraction the Légion never possessed. The Légion had recruits but few admirers. The Verdinaso had both. This was owing mainly to the powerful personality of its founder and leader, Joris Van Severen.

Van Severen (1894–1940), the son of a notary in West Flanders, was studying law at Ghent when the 1914 war broke out. In the Belgian army, he took a leading part in the secret organization that upheld the rights of the Flemish soldiers and the Flemish language against the French-speaking army command. This "movement of the front" (*frontbeweging*) developed after the war into a political movement, the *frontpartij*, with Flemish nationalist views. Van Severen was one of its deputies in the Chamber from 1921 to 1929. During that time he never failed to denounce the Belgian state as the irreconcilable enemy of the Flemish. In 1928, notably, he delivered in the Chamber the fiercest anti-Belgian speech that assembly had ever heard. In 1929, as a result of a mischievous trick of his Catholic opponents, he was not reëlected.[5] Two years later, he founded an organization of his own, the Verbond van Dietsche Nationaalsolidaristen (League of the Dutch-speaking partisans of national solidarity) or Verdinaso. Its members were called *dinasos*.

From 1931 to 1940 Van Severen succeeded in creating and maintaining a real fervor among his followers, while leading them along surprisingly changing paths. At first, the Verdinaso was dedicated to the realization of *Dietschland,* that is, a state where the whole *dietsche* (Dutch-speaking) nation, artificially divided between Hol-

---

[5] Van Severen gained more votes than in the previous elections of 1925. But the Catholics arranged their electoral alliances in such a way that, owing to the very complicated Belgian electoral system, these votes helped to elect not Van Severen himself, but one of his fellow candidates in another district.

land and Belgium, would find itself reunited. This would mean the end of Belgium (as Flanders alone, naturally, was to join *Dietschland*), but the end of an old enemy could only be rejoiced at. Then Van Severen turned suddenly from *Dietschland* to the *Dietsche Rijk:* a political union between Holland, Belgium, and Luxemburg, whereby the glorious *Pays-Bas* of the sixteenth century would be revived. In this new vision, Belgium was saved and even exalted. By 1937, the *dinasos* were exhibiting the Belgian flag and singing the Belgian national anthem. They finally became ardent Belgian nationalists.

That such strange evolutions cost Van Severen only a few adherents shows that the main attraction lay elsewhere than in *Dietschland* and the *Dietsche Rijk*. It lay rather in the style Van Severen had given his movement. Here young men who, in the turmoil and disorder of the times, felt the need of a mental stability, could find order and discipline. In the militias of the *Verdinaso* they could not only wear a military uniform, take part in maneuvers, camps, and parades, salute with arm uplifted, and so forth, but they could also be elated by Van Severen's assurance that their strict discipline made them the aristocrats of the day. They obeyed a leader who looked to the future with steellike assurance; a leader, too, who spoke to their sense of idealism. With him, they would build a new society.

It would be an authoritarian society. Van Severen had long drunk at the fount of the Action Française and of Maurras, whom he hailed as his master. For Mussolini, too, he had great admiration. He despised democracy. "No intelligent man still believes in democracy," he wrote in 1933. The "national solidarity" he preached was a "new order" based upon a corporatist system. But he did not conceal that the Verdinaso meant first to "seize power"; in that respect the fascist character of his movement was quite obvious.

The Verdinaso's center of gravity was the region of West Flanders, where Van Severen had been elected during the years from 1921 to 1929. But adherents were gained in the whole Flemish part of the country, notably among the university students of Ghent and Louvain. The movement also had a branch in Holland

and, after Van Severen's conversion to the *Dietsche Rijk,* it had a small branch even in the Walloon part of the country. From 1936, along with its papers and pamphlets in Flemish, it published a monthly in French (whose 1939 title was *Pays-Bas belgiques!*).

Van Severen met with a tragic end in May, 1940, when, as a political prisoner, he was murdered by French soldiers in northern France. Many *dinasos,* during the German occupation, tried to remain faithful to the style of life they had learned from him. This led them, however, in two quite opposite directions: some *dinasos* took a leading part in the Resistance, others collaborated with the Germans. What Van Severen's own attitude would have been will ever remain a matter for speculation.

We finally come, in the general description of the Right, to its only two mass movements: Rex and the VNV. Both were, as noted before, special cases: they clearly belonged to the Right but their appeal and their success were owing to factors that had in the main little to do with the Right.[6] They are, from that point of view, rather complicated cases.

The VNV—Vlaamsch Nationaal Verbond (Flemish National League)—was a political party, established in 1933 as a means of uniting the various Flemish nationalist organizations.

These organizations had, until that time, been united only by their common hatred of Belgian unity, considered as the source of all Flemish miseries; by their common Flemish national feeling; and by a common aim—to destroy the unitary Belgian state. But whether strong, like the *frontpartij* of the twenties, or weak, they generally worked apart, each in its region or sector. No common political program had ever been elaborated.

After 1932, unity seemed imperative for two reasons: to surmount the defeat Flemish nationalism had suffered in the 1932 elections, and to meet the Verdinaso's competition.

Flemish nationalists had won four seats in the Chamber in 1921,

---

[6] The same can be said of the *réalistes* of 1935–1936 (see above, p. 140); the explanation of their brief success lay mainly in their wild demagogy as regards economic "reforms" and only slightly in their call for a dictatorship.

six in 1925, and eleven in 1929; in 1932 the upward trend was reversed and they fell back to nine. The head of their parliamentary group was not reëlected. This setback was the more disquieting as Van Severen's dynamism and attraction appeared a serious menace for the future. A common stand was clearly necessary. In 1933 the VNV was founded under the chairmanship of Staf De Clercq (1884–1942), a former schoolmaster and Flemish nationalist deputy (1919–1932) who had won a wide popularity in the rural part of the Brussels district. The program of the new party insisted, as expected, on the "liberation" of the Flemish people from the clutches of the Belgian state. But it also mentioned the reform of institutions—and here a real, in some ways unexpected, change occurred in the direction taken by Flemish nationalism.

Authoritarian interests had so far been in a minority within the Flemish movement and Flemish nationalists were generally considered good democrats. This explains why, in Antwerp for instance, there was a degree of friendship between some leaders of the *frontpartij* and Socialist politicians like Camille Huysmans. The main paper of Flemish nationalism, *De Schelde*, published in Antwerp, looked upon fascism with mistrust. Fascism in Belgium, it explained, would be supported by the officer corps and the high bourgeoisie—that is, by the most anti-Flemish elements in the country, to be guarded against.

In 1933, however, the problem for the founders of the VNV was a double one. They had to secure the adherence of all nationalist groups; but one of these groups, in West Flanders, which bore the brunt of Van Severen's competition, had met the challenge by outdoing the Verdinaso in political extremism, and now it strongly insisted on an authoritarian program. A second problem was to make the VNV platform look as attractive as possible, to make it a source of inspiration for its members. Was parliamentary democracy inspiring? Nobody could say so in the atmosphere of the year 1933, and the success of Van Severen's propaganda seemed to point to the contrary. For these reasons, the VNV, echoing the Verdinaso slogan, chose to extol a system of national "solidarity" to take the place of decrepit democracy. The new order was to be a corporate one, doing away with the nefarious dictatorship of political parties—all in all, an authoritarian regime.

In the same spirit of competition with the Verdinaso, the VNV declared for the reunification of the *dietsche* people, of the Flemish and their Dutch brothers.

As we have seen, Van Severen's line of policy underwent a drastic change (and Flemish nationalists derided it by speaking of Belginaso instead of Verdinaso); but the VNV line, from 1933 to 1940, remained unchanged. Party papers like *Volk en Staat* (the new name taken by *De Schelde* in 1936) and speakers at political rallies went on singing the praise of the *dietsche* state of the future, criticizing disorderly democracy and stressing the advantages a new corporate order would ensure. More strikingly, perhaps, the party's authoritarian character appeared in the role devoted to its chief. Staf De Clercq was the *leider* (Dutch equivalent of the German *Führer*) and, although not much more than a shrewd politician, he tried to give himself some of the airs of his German colleague. Uniforms, outstretched-arm salutes, and great shouts of collective enthusiasm became a part of VNV pageantry.

But all this remained rather superficial. The real appeal was directed toward Flemish nationalism and not to the *dietsche* ideal. Union with the Dutch brothers (who were brothers by their language but whom few really liked) was regarded as an aim for the remote future. When it came to practical politics, the common goal was the autonomy of Flanders. The movement's official flag might be adorned with a *delta* showing the unity of the *dietsche* people of the Rhine, Meuse, and Scheldt delta, but the only flag popular with the rank and file remained the yellow banner with the black lion of Flanders.

Similarly, the propaganda for a "new order" was never very vociferous except in a few limited circles. Some Flemish nationalists of democratic convictions, such as Herman Vos, who, until 1932, headed the parliamentary group and later passed over to the Socialists, refused to adhere to the VNV. But others, including several deputies, did adhere because they felt that the antiparliamentary part of the program was of only secondary importance. Their position was a rather uneasy one, but they tried—not unsuccessfully, in some instances—to tone down the party's antidemocratic utterances. At any rate, the "new order" was never defined in detail; it remained a sketchy outline, filled with corporatist clichés, and never became the core of the party's ideology.

What really mattered to the bulk of Flemish electors who voted for the VNV was the lion of Flanders, as opposed to the Belgian flag. Belgian unity, in their eyes, necessarily meant iniquitous treatment of their native language, the domination of Flanders by Walloon interest and French influence, and a perpetual sacrifice of true Flemish interests. They wanted Flanders to become the mistress of her own destiny.

Such was the main significance of the 168,000 votes registered by Flemish nationalists in 1936, and of their 185,000 votes in 1939. They elected 16 deputies in 1936, and 17 in 1939 (out of 202 for the whole Chamber). Regional percentages were as follows: For the four Flemish provinces and the Flemish cantons of the province of Brabant taken together, 13 per cent of the votes in 1936, and 15 per cent in 1939; for the Flemish districts (*arrondissements*) in 1936, from 5 per cent to 25 per cent. The five districts with peak results of above 20 per cent were those of Turnhout (in the province of Antwerp), Veurne (Furnes), and Ypres (in West Flanders), as well as the two districts of the province of Limburg.

These were predominantly rural areas. The figures clearly reveal that Flemish nationalism, especially in the thirties, was particularly strong in the countryside and in the small towns. The big towns yielded much lower results.

In some rural cantons, the Flemish nationalists' percentages in 1936 and 1939 went as high as 35 or 40 per cent. This meant a mass movement in every sense of the word, and one not limited by the usual dividing line, in Belgian politics, between Catholics and parties of the Left. True, nearly all the VNV leaders had a militant Catholic ideal, but it would be wrong to think the same of their troops—to think, in other words, that, if they had not been nationalist, all the VNV electors would have cast their votes for Catholics. In fact, after World War II, when the VNV was dissolved, a significant section of its former electorate went over to the Socialist or the Liberal party. The VNV, as a nationalist movement, had carried along people of diverse political opinions.

A last remark about the VNV is that some of its leaders and journalists—as a legacy, no doubt, of the collaboration between German and Flemish extremism during World War I—showed great sympathy for Germany and even for the Nazi regime. *Volk en Staat* received subsidies from Berlin. Just before World War II, this inclination toward Germany contrasted all the more strikingly with the attitude of strict neutrality adopted by Van Severen, who never received any money from Germany. This sympathy for Germany was the preface, in fact, to the decision to collaborate with Hitler which the VNV (though not all its followers) would take during the second German occupation.

On May 24, 1936, the Rex party, completely new and entering the electoral contest for the first time, conquered 21 seats (out of 202) in the Chamber. One Belgian in nine, one French-speaking Belgian in six, had voted for the Rexists and for their leader Léon Degrelle. This is undoubtedly the most striking event in the history of the Right.

Two fundamental interpretations of this emergence of Rex have found their way into history books. As both are fundamental delusions, they must be disposed of first of all.

1) It is often believed that the success of Rex stemmed largely, perhaps chiefly, from the great economic depression. It is the classical story, one thinks, of anger and despair, caused by an economic crisis, turning into political extremism. This interpretation is contradicted by the simple chronology of the facts. The twelve months preceding the 1936 elections were a period of swift and marked economic recovery. Unemployment had fallen sharply, as had the number of bankruptcies. The dominant feeling was one of relief and hope in the future. True, there were still many victims of the crisis, especially in the middle classes, and those who had not yet reaped the fruits of the recovery were the more bitter for it—and the more ready, as a consequence, to listen to extremist propaganda. But on the whole, Rex did not derive much benefit from the economic situation; the roots of its success lay elsewhere.

2) Approximately 270,000 male Belgian electors supported Degrelle's party. Many a commentator has since shuddered at the thought that Belgium in 1936 contained 270,000 fascists (not counting their wives, enfranchised only in 1948). This is also a gross misinterpretation of the facts. The great majority of Rexist electors were ordinary citizens who had no fascist dictatorship in mind, nor even any type of right-wing regime, but believed that Rexism would rejuvenate and purify the political atmosphere. That was all. Let us consider Luxemburg, for instance, Degrelle's native province, where Rex polled highest: 29 per cent of the votes. In some purely rural districts of the province, there was more than one Rexist in every three electors. In the district of Laroche-en-Ardenne, the proportion was nearly 1 in 2: 48 per cent. Would it not be ludicrous to imagine that the decent peasants of the villages around Laroche had become fascists? They were no more than naïve enthusiasts.[7]

True, those who did not see, in 1936, that Degrelle was drifting into fascist waters showed little political acumen. But their lack of perspicacity must not be exaggerated. Degrelle had not yet fully revealed his aims before the general election. Officially, Rex repudiated any fascist ambition, and Degrelle was clever enough to stay away from declared authoritarians; he would not associate, for instance, with the Légion Nationale.

It was not fascism or a fascist program that accounts for the Rexist votes of 1936, but deception. Let us turn then to the master deceiver, Léon Degrelle.

Degrelle was born in Bouillon, a small town in the south of Luxemburg, in 1906. His father, a brewer, was an active member of the Catholic party. As a student in Louvain (where he studied Law, but never took his degree), Léon Degrelle became closely associated with the Action Catholique de la Jeunesse Belge (ACJB), a religious movement that was gaining ground among the bour-

---

[7] Generally speaking, it is obvious that very few of the rural electors who voted for either Rex or the VNV (see above, p. 155) shared in any right-wing ideology. Hence our general assessment of p. 138, where we wrote that "the peasantry was little affected" by the Right in its proper sense.

geoisie at the same time as the Jeunesse Ouvrière Chrétienne (JOC) was making headway among the working classes.[8] A protégé of Mgr. Picard, the great organizer of the ACJB, Degrelle was given the direction of the publishing department of the movement, which evolved in 1931 into an autonomous publishing house, also called Rex. All this pointed to a religious crusade—Rex paid homage to the kingship of Christ, *Christus Rex*—and young Degrelle appeared at first as an intrepid crusader. Dynamism, and an extraordinary dynamism indeed, seemed the keynote of his personality, but he combined this with an unusual sense of the dramatic; in everything he wrote, and later in his public speeches, he seized his readers or his audience by the throat and left them panting. His self-confidence was unlimited, and so were his ambitions. As a director of Rex he displayed such megalomania and launched such a number of periodicals (religious, literary, for family life, and so on) that the enterprise came close to bankruptcy. The aim of all his actions, he repeatedly asserted, was the triumph of the Catholic faith, the triumph of Christ, but under this religious label his propaganda became progressively more and more political: Communism, Freemasonry, high finance, all came under fire, and Catholic politicians and the Catholic party were censured for their incompetence and stupid passivity. As early as 1934–1935, Degrelle made no secret about what he wanted, which was, he told his friends, to "govern his country."

The turning point came on November 2, 1935. At a sitting, held that day, of the main organization of the Catholic party, the Fédération des Cercles, Degrelle ascended the tribune by force and cast violent abuse at a number of the party's leaders, whom he branded as rotten politicians. Complete rupture with the Catholic party rapidly followed. A major adventure now lay ahead: within six months the young man, still in his twenties (he would be thirty in June, 1936), was to build up the biggest party Belgium had ever known outside the three "traditional" ones (Catholics, Liberals, and Socialists). He did not start from scratch. His passionate

---

[8] The JOC, for a time, was officially affiliated with the ACJB, but in fact the two organizations always worked quite apart from each other.

writing and his passionate words had already rallied around him a number of young Catholics, mainly from the ACJB, and these groups already had some kind of loose organization throughout the country. But from the original hundreds to 270,000 electors, the distance was very, very great. It was covered in six months. This exploit was above all one of oratory. Degrelle stormed the country with a torrent of inflammatory speeches. The former champion of Christ no longer appealed to the religious feelings of his audiences. Rexism, as a party, would find support among all Belgians, irrespective of their religion or lack of it. Degrelle's appeal to his countrymen was to their sense of purity. He denounced with incredible violence the corruptness of politicians and the collusion between finance and Parliament. The gang of *pourris* ("the corrupt") had to be swept out. The word *pourris* applied to every kind of politician, and the brooms that Rexist militants brandished to show what must be done were the clearest symbols of the campaign.

To prove his case, Degrelle made much of several recent scandals that had revealed some political figures in a far from flattering light. But how justified were his generalizations? Did he come at a moment when there was a real crisis in parliamentary morality, or rather at a time of greater public sensitivity to such scandals as there were? The question is not easy to answer, but probably the phenomenon was chiefly one of greater awareness. Political life, as a whole, has always been rather clean in Belgium. No evidence suggests marked changes in that respect during the interwar period. But financial crashes during the great depression had publicized, as never before, the part some politicians played in financial institutions, their manipulations and their deals. That made a deplorable impression, as did the Stavisky affair and the French scandals. Degrelle's demagogy appeared at a propitious moment.

The results of the elections of May, 1936, deserve a short analysis. The Rexists' percentage of votes for the whole country was 11.50 per cent. The four Walloon provinces voted for them as follows: Luxemburg, 29 per cent; Namur, 20 per cent; Liège, 19 per cent; Hainaut, 8 per cent. The eight urban cantons of Brussels ranged from 13 to 24 per cent. In the four Flemish provinces and

the Flemish cantons of Brabant, the average was 7 per cent. Rex
had published a paper in Flemish and had some very ardent Flemish-
speaking supporters, but the response to Degrelle's propaganda, in
the north of Belgium, was particularly marked among the French-
speaking upper classes, the so-called *fransquillons*.

The great majority of Rexist electors were deserters from the
Catholic party. For the Catholics, the elections were in fact a disaster; they lost 16 seats. But the Liberals and even the Socialists
also suffered from Degrelle's attraction. In the urban cantons of
Brussels, particularly, it seems certain that more than 40 per cent
of Rexist votes came from former Liberals or Socialists. Elsewhere,
however, the proportion was much lower. Rexism, at any rate, was
not just a defection from the Catholic party; like the VNV in
Flanders, it had swept across the traditional dividing line of Belgian
political life.

The movement was predominantly middle-class, from lawyers
and professors down to shopkeepers and employees. A number of
intellectuals—nearly all Catholics—had fallen under Degrelle's
spell and had abandoned reason for enthusiasm. Rural areas yielded
many recruits. The working class, on the contrary, yielded very
few. In Hainaut, and especially in the industrial cantons of the
province, Rexists were least successful.

The psychology of Rexist electors has sometimes been compared
to that of the French Poujadists of 1956. The outcry against politicians of every description—all of them *pourris*—was in fact
reëchoed by the *sortir les sortants* of Poujade. That was in both
instances the negative element. But the positive hope Degrelle had
awakened was a very strong one, too; those who believed in him
also believed that vigorous use of the broom would make for a
better and more beautiful Belgium. They were disgusted, but hopeful.

The elections of May, 1936, startled governing circles. But they
had no disintegrating effect. Instead, in the following months the
weaknesses of the Rexist movement came to light quite clearly.
These weaknesses were the inability of Rex to elaborate a political
program as appealing as its electoral propaganda had been; the in-
experience of most of Degrelle's staff; the lack of organized social

support for the party; and, last, the party's powerlessness in Flanders.

What Degrelle, during the weeks of his hectic electoral campaign, had called his program, hardly deserved that name. It was rather electoral propaganda consisting of a violent denunciation of the politicians, parties, and, naturally, of parliament (a body of incompetent profiteers which should not sit for more than two months a year, he said); of a moving, if not very precise, description of the wonderful renewal Rex would bring the country; and, in the best tradition of all new parties, of a lot of generous promises made to all social classes, especially the middle ones. About his positive plans for the reform of institutions, Degrelle remained very vague. The elaboration of a real program came only after the elections. But it proved rather disappointing for many, or at least not very exciting. The party, in fact, had no political thinkers. All Degrelle did, and could do, was fall back on the old formulas of corporatism: the solidarity of all social classes would be secured by a corporate order, legislative competence would be given to corporate bodies, and so on. This was familiar ground for a number of his followers—those who had really right-wing views—and they liked it. But such a program could not rouse popular enthusiasm. It never made a hit.

For any clear-sighted observer, moreover, it became more and more obvious that these corporatist theories, in themselves a serious menace to democracy, were only a cover for still more dangerous ambitions. What Degrelle evidently aimed at was a single-party system, as a support for his personal dictatorship. Degrelle himself emphatically denied this, but his denials carried little weight when compared with the general trend of the Rexist movement. Rex would not be called a political party. It claimed to be a conquering movement, marching toward victory—*Rex vaincra* ("Rex will vanquish") was its war cry—which, at the time of victory, would crush the old, decrepit, obnoxious parties. Such an increasingly fascist smell cost Degrelle many of his early admirers.

Another of Degrelle's handicaps was that political talent, around him, was as scarce as political thinking. Rexist candidates for the election, especially, had been recruited very quickly and almost at random. In parliament, Rexist deputies and senators cut a very poor figure. Degrelle himself had not stood for election—a decision he certainly regretted—and all he could do was encourage his men from the visitors' gallery. Most of them were failures. In other sectors of the party's life, the lack of experienced staff was also acute.

Throughout its brief history, Rexism remained essentially a one-man show. Everything centered upon the *chef de Rex,* his sayings, his portraits, his articles in the *Pays Réel* (the party's official paper), his leadership. Personal adulation for the *chef* ran higher than in any other movement. In some women it took the form of hysteria. But hysterical women were no substitute for able political collaborators.

Nor were enthusiastic audiences—and enthusiasm, at Degrelle's meetings, did not flag for a good while—any substitute for the organized social support a party needs in the long run. The Catholic and the Socialist parties were built largely on the solid rock of Catholic or Socialist unions, mutual insurance societies, coöperatives, and so forth. Rex tried to found its own unions, but these never got anywhere. A lot of money flowed in from the upper classes, but it came only from individuals who were either sincerely converted to Rex or, as was often true, were taking insurance against the future. Thus, in September, 1936, one of the country's main industrialists sent in a two-months' subscription—which was not renewed—for over one hundred thousand copies of the *Pays Réel.* On the whole, employers' syndicates, industrial or banking interests, gave no backing. Rex could never rest on any organized group.

What Degrelle certainly hoped for was that a popular wave, aroused by his eloquence, would sweep away the regime and bring him to power. The black spot, however, in this wonderful vision—which remained only a vision, for no Rexist coup d'etat was ever seriously prepared—was undoubtedly Flanders. There, in the event of a popular uprising or any similar phenomenon, Rex would be no match for the VNV. In the northern half of Belgium, Degrelle's chances were minimal. There, his only opportunity was to negotiate with the VNV. In October, 1936, he entered into an agreement with Staf De Clercq which provided that the two parts of the country should be given a large degree of autonomy. This pact implied that Rex was abandoning Flanders to the VNV. Although the agreement never had any practical results, and although it was officially denounced less than one year later, it caused a great uproar and did much harm to Rexism. Degrelle pleaded that he had brought the other party to better feelings toward Belgium. The bare fact, in the public's eyes, was that he had come to terms with Belgium's enemies.

Such were the inner weaknesses of Rex. But they were counterbalanced for a time by the extraordinary power of Degrelle's oratory. Throughout 1936 and the beginning of 1937, rallies addressed by the *chef de Rex* kept firing large crowds with enthusiasm and fervor. In January, 1937, Degrelle held meetings in the largest hall of Brussels for six consecutive nights; the house was full every night. *Rex vaincra,* his followers cried endlessly. But for victory, some concrete step was necessary. Degrelle resorted to the most popular one among aspirants to supreme power: the plebiscite. A national plebiscite was not possible under constitutional terms, so Degrelle sought one in the capital of Belgium. In March, 1937, he ordered one of the Rexist deputies elected by the Brussels district to resign, together with all his elected replacements, thus making a by-election compulsory. Degrelle himself would be a candidate.

Democratic parties felt that the hour had come for a trial of strength. Their division might prove fatal. Catholics, Liberals, and Socialists agreed to present a single candidate: the Prime Minister, M. Paul Van Zeeland. The Prime Minister versus Degrelle; the vote would be thus for or against the existing regime.

The stakes were so high that no one could remain neutral. *Le Soir,* the major Belgian paper, left its ordinary pedestal of neutrality to defend democracy. The fascist peril also prodded the Church into action. On the eve of the by-election, the Cardinal-Archbishop of Malines published a statement condemning Rex as "a danger for the country and for the Church" and forbidding his flock to vote for it.

The results of the poll of April 11, 1937, were: Van Zeeland, 275,000 votes, or 80 per cent of the total; Degrelle, 69,000, or 20 per cent. The VNV had asked its electors—nearly 6 per cent of the electorate—to vote for Degrelle. That left Rex, properly speaking, with little more than 14 per cent of the votes—a percentage inferior to that of May, 1936. Power, for Degrelle, was now out of reach.

November 2, 1935, had been the first turning point in his career. April 11, 1937, was the second. After that date, the story of Rex is that of progressive decay. Two years later, at the general elections of April, 1939, Rexist votes dropped to 4 per cent. Instead of the former twenty-one, four Rexists, including this time Degrelle himself, were returned to the Chamber.

By that date, Rex had lost not only two-thirds of its former electors, but also most of its financial resources. It was now very poor. For long, Degrelle had received large subsidies from Mussolini, and Germany had furnished cheap newsprint for his *Pays Réel*. In January, 1940, he also asked for German money to publish a new paper in support of Belgium's policy of neutrality, but that plan did not materialize. Degrelle undoubtedly had great admiration for Hitler and a strong inclination toward the Nazi regime, but there is no evidence to show that before the invasion of Belgium he was in any way a German agent.

The Belgian Right, as was said at the beginning of this essay, always remained a rather marginal phenomenon. The description of the various movements that composed it may have made this more understandable. All these movements, which opposed the political regime, constantly toyed with political ideas. But their authoritarian ideology was not accompanied by any forceful economic or social program, was not capable of attracting particular social groups, or of arousing their enthusiasm (like De Man's *Plan du Travail*, which was rapturously acclaimed by hundreds of thousands of Socialist workers). All movements could win at least some political converts. None could, by its social action and program, win the permanent support of any section of Belgian society. Corporatism, it may be conceded, had some appeal for members of the unorganized or ill-organized middle classes; but for the middle classes as a whole it never became an inspiration.

The VNV enjoyed a particular position. It was supported by a powerful passion, that of Flemish nationalism. For that reason, it bore in some respects more resemblance to the "traditional" parties than to other movements of the Right.

For the "traditional" parties, and for the VNV as well, good leadership was an important factor of success, but not the main one. They could, for a time at least, have done without competent leaders. Yet for most movements of the Right, which had no permanent hold on a large sector of society or opinion, the leader's talent was the main measure of success. The story of Rex is that of Léon Degrelle, the story of the Verdinaso is that of Van Severen. It is quite conceivable, and even probable, that, had Degrelle not existed, no phenomenon like Rexism would have occurred, although truly fascist movements like the Légion Nationale would probably have been somewhat stronger. Flemish nationalism, on the other hand—and so the VNV—were, as it seems, inevitable developments in the evolution of the country.

The Right would have been stronger if its forces had been united. But the story we have told is one of division. The main factor of division was the attitude to Belgium. Patriotic movements like the Action Nationale or the Légion Nationale—all movements, in fact, with "national" in their titles—could not be reconciled with Flemish movements that aimed at the destruction of Belgian unity. Even Degrelle's effort to work hand in hand with the VNV was short-lived. Tactical opposition was also strong. Pierre Nothomb's yearning for a parliamentary seat was condemned by the Légion Nationale as high treason. The Légion Nationale itself could not possibly have been an ally for Degrelle as long as he sought to hide his dictatorial ambitions. Everyone, in fact, remained entrenched in his own camp.

A few words about the end of the story:

From 1940 to 1944 Belgium was occupied by Germany. The VNV leaders and some of their troops collaborated with the Germans wholeheartedly and from the very beginning. After some delay, Degrelle did the same. At the beginning of January, 1941, he too would shout, "Heil Hitler!" From July, 1941, until the end of the war, he wore the German uniform, fighting on the Eastern front in a Walloon brigade incorporated in the German army.[9] A great number of prewar Rexists dissociated themselves from him—some even entering Resistance movements—but Rex itself became an organ of civil as well as military collaboration with the occupying power.

This attitude earned both the VNV and Rex the detestation of a vast majority, the immense majority, of the Belgian population. Allied victory destroyed them both. With them went down the Right, which was now definitely associated with the crimes of Nazi Germany.

The Right has not revived in Belgium since then, except in tiny and insignificant groups. The new form of Flemish nationalism, for instance, which emerged after the war—in which some former members of the VNV, who were pardoned, take an active part—is now fully dedicated to democracy. A handful of old Maurrassians have not disarmed, but they are no more than relics.

The Right is no longer. The horrors of the 1940–1944 period have brought it down. They keep it down still.

SUGGESTED READING

General background:

BAUDHUIN, F. Histoire économique de la Belgique, 1914–1939. Brussels: 1944. 2 vols.

HÖJER, C.-H. Le Régime parlementaire belge de 1918 à 1940. Uppsala: 1946.

KALKEN, F. VAN. Entre deux guerres. Esquisse de la vie politique en Belgique de 1918 à 1940. Brussels: 1944.

Of general interest on the Belgian Right:

GÉORIS-REITSHOF, M. L'Extrême-droite et le néo-fascisme en Belgique. Brussels: 1962.

VANDERVEKEN, G. Le Fascisme en Europe. Brussels: 1930. (Chapter on Belgium.)

WEBER, EUGEN. Action Française. Stanford: 1962.

---

[9] Since 1945, Léon Degrelle has lived in exile, for the most part in Spain. He has been condemned to death by Belgian tribunals.

WILLEMSEN, A. W. *Het Vlaams-Nationalisme, 1914–1940.* Groningen: 1958.
WULLUS-RUDIGER, J. *En Marge de la politique belge, 1914–1956.* Paris: 1957.

For particular movements:

BRUYNE, A. DE. *Joris Van Severen. Droom en daad.* Zulte: 1961.
DAYE, P. *Léon Degrelle et le rexisme.* Paris: 1937.
DEGRELLE, LÉON. *La Cohue de 1940.* Lausanne: 1949.
DE MAN, H. *Après coup. Mémoires.* Brussels: 1941.
———. *Cavalier seul. Quarante-cinq années de socialisme européen.* Geneva: 1948.
HOYOIS, G. *Aux Origines de l'Action Catholique. Monseigneur Picard.* Brussels: 1960. (Essential for Rex.)
NARVAEZ, LOUISE. *Degrelle m'a dit.* . . . Paris: 1961.
SERRUYS, J. W. *Sous le signe de l'autorité.* Brussels: 1935.
VROYLANDE, R. DE. *Quand Rex était petit.* Louvain: 1936.

Spain

STANLEY PAYNE

International opinion has probably more closely identified reactionary tendencies with modern Spain than with any other West European country. The most reactionary political movement of the nineteenth century, Carlism, flourished there between 1830 and 1880. For the next fifty years, however, until the 1930's, the country was dominated by moderate forces of conservatism and liberalism. It was not until after the challenge of the progressivist Republic appeared in 1931 that modern right-wing forces clearly emerged in Spain.

The same factors that sustained Carlism vigorously for half a century discouraged the subsequent development of a modern, radical rightist movement. Social, economic, and cultural changes in Spain have been so slow and hesitant that the country has never been exposed to the full effects of modern, nineteenth-century liberalism, and hence there was proportionately less incentive to combat this through the formation of radical right-wing groups. The generally low level of education and the slow rate of urbanization, which long hampered growth of a strong leftist movement, also made almost impossible the early genesis of a Spanish Right that could appeal to mass public opinion, manipulate the demogogic potential of modern communications, or propound new forms of political and economic organization.

Though the Spanish people were traditionally monarchist and

Catholic, lingering economic and cultural backwardness made it very difficult to weld the entire land into an interconnected whole. Spain has never been a fully united country, but throughout most of the modern period has been a unique kind of regional federation ruled by a hereditary monarch. The three centuries from 1480 to 1780 nonetheless witnessed a fairly continuous effort by the Spanish kings to make their rule centralized and absolute. The regional Cortes (legislative) system had been largely eliminated by the mid-seventeenth century, and considerable administrative unity was achieved under the new Bourbon dynasty of the eighteenth century. During the reign of Charles III (1759–1788) the nation probably achieved the greatest degree of unity it has ever known. These were years of enlightened despotism in the better sense of the term, reforming administration and carrying out cultural and economic projects that raised Spain to the highest level of prosperity that she had known.

After the Middle Ages, the centralizing efforts of Castilian and Aragonese kings had provoked violent reactions from the upper nobility. From the mid-seventeenth to the mid-eighteenth century, the frondeur spirit had been dormant, save for the civil struggle of the War of the Spanish Succession, but the innovations of Charles III did more than had the actions of his immediate predecessors to arouse the ire of the privileged elements. Centralization of power in the hands of royal ministers, mild economic reforms, sumptuary laws, all offered reasons for grievance among the nobility or established powers in the provinces. Likewise, the anticlerical policy of enlightened despotism created strong resentment among that minority of the nobility that remained intensely pious. The riot provoked against Charles III's finance minister, Esquilache, in 1774, followed a pattern created centuries earlier and destined to survive for at least a century more. Aristocratic opponents of the government took advantage of certain popular grievances—in this instance, clothing regulations against the traditional Spanish cape —to encourage a riot of the lower classes against a royal minister, bringing his dismissal.

Charles III was sufficiently discreet and strong-willed to maintain the equilibrium of his government. His son, Charles IV

(1788–1808), entirely lacked his father's qualities and was never able to maintain control of his own regime. The effort of Charles IV's favorite, Godoy, to continue a variant of enlightened despotism, plus the outbreak of the French revolution, which caused both emulation and apprehension in Spain, made it almost impossible to hold the government's course. The reign of Charles IV thus saw, on the one hand, a sudden growth in the number of liberals and even would-be revolutionaries in Spain, and, on the other hand, a sharp antagonism on the part of the Church, much of the aristocracy, and other influential elements. The intermittent Godoy ministries attempted to repress liberalism while sustaining a policy of authoritarian reform. They did not in any way appease the foes of enlightened despotism in Spain, who engineered the famous Aranjuez riot of the spring of 1808, leading to the abdication of Charles IV and the accession of his supposedly less despotic son, Ferdinand VII.

The French invasion, which followed a few months later, completely altered the domestic political and institutional balance in Spain. The eighteenth-century Bourbon system was swept away, and the whole nation rose up in a blind popular reaction against the invader. Liberal elements, especially from the southern towns, dominated the Cortes which eventually met at Cadiz in 1812, whereas the forces of traditionalism remained disunited, in some areas leading guerrilla bands against the French, in others simply remaining confused and awaiting the better day.

It seems accurate to trace the origins of the traditionalistic reaction to the anticonstitutional minority, called the *serviles*, in the Cadiz Cortes. The actual following enjoyed by the *servil* attitude cannot be calculated precisely, but it should be remembered that the Cadiz Cortes were themselves rather unrepresentative, resting upon a narrow electoral basis. The basic position of the *serviles* was that Spain did not need a new liberal written constitution—which would only make for selfishness and disunity—because she possessed a historical constitution composed of custom, royal laws, and *fueros* (legal rights or privileges) for the various regions. All that was needed was to reactivate the historic, traditional constitution of Spain. The royal power could not be limited by the abstract "national sovereignty" claimed by the constitution, for the power given to the king by God and people was absolute. This did not mean that there was serious danger of royal despotism, for the king was limited by the fear of God, the traditional *fueros,* and the possibility of censure of properly constituted Cortes. Further, to diminish the power and prerogatives of the Church was treason, for the historic structure of Spanish government had been imbued with Catholicism and Church power, and the working relationship of Church and state guaranteed the sanctity and adequacy of the latter.

This, in a nutshell, was what came to be known as Carlism. The first complete editing of the traditionalist program was presented in the 1814 *Manifiesto de los Persas.* The title *Persians,* adopted by the absolutists, was a reference to the custom of the ancient Persians of enduring a month of anarchy before the crowning of each king, in order to appreciate better the blessings of a proper monarchy. The *Persas* recited a long list of historical arguments for their point of view, and called upon Ferdinand, on his return to Spain, to resume full royal rule, overturning the liberal constitution. This agreed perfectly with Ferdinand's desires. The return of despotism in 1814 aroused scant reaction, for incipient Spanish liberalism was the doctrine of only a tiny middle-class and aristocratic elite, largely out of contact with the lower-middle class or the great mass of the people. Royalism was the only attitude that had any meaning for the lower classes in 1814, for personal identification was possible with a monarch, but not with a written piece of paper. Hence in 1814 the Madrid rabble greeted the return of absolutism with cries of "Down with the constitution!," "Death to Liberty!," and "Long live chains!" The idea was zealously propagated that concepts such as constitutionalism were, after all, foreign French ideas.

Ferdinand, however, was by no means a traditionalist absolutist. The latter were true reactionaries who saw the need for sweeping reforms in order to realize their ideology. They were led by provincial nobility and, to some extent, clerics, who had no desire to see the return of ministerial despotism in Madrid. By contrast, Ferdinand was only interested in personal despotism, being anxious to restore the authority enjoyed by his grandfather, Charles III. He never quite understood the traditionalist absolutists and clericals, who stood for monarchism as a return to an earlier decentralized authoritarian structure.

Nonetheless, when a small group of Army officers took advantage of the weakness and confusion of Ferdinand's government to force acceptance of the constitution, in 1820, the traditionalist absolutists stood loyally behind the monarch's prerogatives. Within a year they had resorted to violence, forming guerrilla bands in northeastern Spain to fight against the liberals just as ten years earlier they had been decimating the French invader. Internal political conflict was now so sharp that the French intervention of 1823 was received with joy by the traditional absolutists and with general approval, or at least acquiescence, by most of the lower classes.

Within two years, the rejoicing of the clerical and traditionalist absolutists over Ferdinand's "liberation" had turned to bitter disillusion. It was now fully clear that the King had no intention of respecting the old *fueros* of the various regions, the rights of the aristocracy, or the independent power of the Church; he even refused, for example, to reëstablish the Inquisition. By 1826 he was surrounded by a purely personal camarilla and also with proponents of a new version of enlightened despotism, ex-liberals who believed in strongly centralized government. If Ferdinand had dissolved the constitutional Cortes, he had no intention of restoring any traditional, pre-seventeenth-century body.

After fifteen years of unswerving support for Ferdinand, the traditionalist absolutists began to turn against him. In 1822 they had established an absolutist regency at Seo de Urgel in Catalonia to protect the royal prerogatives; in 1826 they began to look for another king to uphold these same principles. Their candidate was Ferdinand's younger brother, D. Carlos, who was known not so much for his political talent as for his overriding sense of honor, tradition, and devotion to the Church. Though Ferdinand was only in middle age, his health was failing and he had no children. The traditionalist absolutists were thus becoming Carlists, and saw no reason why a faithless monarch should not abdicate the throne to a more honorable heir.

In December, 1826, there was issued the manifesto of the *Realistas puros* ("Pure Royalists"), as some of the traditionalist absolutists on this occasion chose to call themselves. To assure the restoration of the Inquisition and respect for *fueros*, they were now asking for the accession of D. Carlos. The first months of 1827 saw once more the formation of guerrilla bands in the mountains of northern Catalonia, this time under the aegis of a junta containing a disproportionate number of Churchmen. Ferdinand's army quelled the rebellion within a short time and shot the lay members of the Junta, although the clergy were spared.

The last five years of Ferdinand's reign accentuated the rift between the royalist centralism of the Court and the traditionalist absolutists, or Carlists. The birth of two daughters to Ferdinand's fourth queen, after 1830, made it dynastically feasible for Ferdinand's followers to continue the centralized monarchy after the king's death. Since there was a strong question as to whether or not the Spanish Bourbons had brought the Salic Law with them to Spain, Ferdinand prepared a pragmatic sanction leaving the throne to his elder daughter, Isabel. Don Carlos insisted on the illegality of any such dispensation, and stubbornly maintained what he called his right to the throne.

When Ferdinand died early in 1833, the succession of Isabel was obtained by the quick, effective work of several small groups of royalist centralists and moderate liberals within and just outside of the government. The Carlists, excluded from all positions of power, reacted as had their predecessors in 1808, 1821, and 1827. They raised the guerrilla flag and formed irregular bands to fight for the Pretender.

The first Carlist war lasted seven years, until 1840. Such long duration was not so much owing to the undeniable military prowess of the Carlists as to the weakness of the centralized monarchy and the popularity of the traditionalist cause among the peasantry, especially in the north. The remaining proponents of enlightened despotism constituted an extremely small minority.

The liberals, in turn, saw their influence restricted to the larger cities and sectors of the middle and upper classes. On the other hand, there seems to have been a definite tendency among the peasants to regard urban leaders, merchants, and politicians as untrustworthy. Political and cultural ideas from Paris or Madrid were meaningless. The rural population preferred the more tangible rights of local custom to the abstract liberty of modern constitutionalism. Religion, the king, and the old laws—this was the only political ideology that made much sense to the peasants of northern Spain.

Carlism was particularly strong in the northeast, in the Basque Provinces, Navarre, Catalonia, and parts of Aragon, Old Castile, and the Levant. This was, roughly, the region of the petty landowning peasantry, where the structure of rural life remained cohesive and the social hierarchy was more natural and solidly structured than in other parts of Spain. Here the lower classes were more devout; neither great latifundia nor urban commercialization had made inroads on their psychology and style of life. In the Basque world and in parts of Catalonia, especially, regional differences encouraged a strong sense of alienation from the central government. For all these reasons—tradition, religious fervor, and regional rights—the reactionary, decentralized monarchism of D. Carlos exerted strong appeal. Carlism was indeed a popular cause.

Carlism was, however, violent and bloody in the extreme. It was the first major reactionary movement in nineteenth-century Europe, and none exceeded it in physical furore. The murderous quality of Carlist tactics was in part owing to the religious or crusading quality the cause had acquired for many of its followers. It took on the character of a new inquisition. Political enemies were also the "enemies of God," as a common Carlist phrase had it, and scant quarter was given to the infidels. On the other hand, a second cause for the barbarous violence of the Carlist campaigns was owing to a directly opposite reason: that, in this guerrilla war, all kinds of bandits and plunderers joined the movement so that they could loot and murder under a peculiar kind of moral sanction.

Politically, D. Carlos had been surrounded by a coterie of aristo-cratic counselors, most of whom lacked any particular insight and helped to keep the movement within a narrow, sterile circle. Seven years of exhausting struggle began to wear down the faithful peasants of the northeast. By 1839 there was a strong desire to return to the villages. The war was brought to a close by a com-promise agreement, the "abrazo de Vergara," which promised re-spect for Basque regional *fueros* and also promised to incorporate all the regular Carlist officers into the national Spanish army. The Carlist movement temporarily fell apart in suspicion and bitter mutual recrimination among various leaders and subfactions: If the cause had not triumphed despite its righteousness, then there must have been betrayal or hidden evil among some of its members. Carlism in defeat was strongly addicted to the witch-hunt, and a number of minor Carlist leaders were executed by their superiors.

From 1840 to 1868 the country was dominated by a pseudo-liberal oligarchy, and government alternated between years of greater relaxation and greater reassertion of control. The famous "reactionaries" of the latter phases, such as the army leader Nar-váez and the civilian Bravo Murillo, were in fact constitutional liberals *sui generis,* determined though they were to restrict the suffrage to less than 2 per cent of the population. Despite the manifold shortcomings of Spain's oligarchical liberalism, it did manage to maintain stable government for these three decades. The only significant criticism of the situation from the Right still came from Carlism, but the next major rebellion, or Second Carlist War (1847–1849), was kept well under control by the Madrid govern-ment.

A basic weakness of the Carlist Right throughout the century was that it exerted scant appeal on leaders of the Spanish army. Thrust into the role of national leaders by the country's institu-tional fragility, military officers were predominantly drawn to liberal causes. The great majority of the nineteenth-century army revolts, or pronunciamientos, were aimed either at liberalizing the government or restoring the constitutional monarchy to a more solid base. The military commonly regarded Carlism as a factious, antinational movement. Only a very small minority of the officers

were Carlist, and the only major Carlist effort at an army pronunciamiento, in 1860, was a complete failure.

The most important ideological spokesman for reaction during
the reign of Isabel was a handsome, eloquent nobleman, Juan
Donoso Cortés (1809–1853). For some of his logic, Cortés drew
on Bonald and de Maistre, but he broadened the framework somewhat beyond traditionalist reaction and so might be considered, as
in the study of Carl Schmitt, a precursor of the twentieth-century
Right. By the 1840's, Cortés laid stress on socialism as the principal
form of subversion that would have to be combated in the future.
To avert the danger, he said that authoritarian control would be
necessary. In this, as in his rejection of the royal dynastic issue and
his apprehension of Russia as one of the major long-range threats
to the European status quo, he achieved a cosmopolitanism beyond
the Carlists. The pillars of Donoso Cortés' system were the Church,
the tradition of social hierarchy, and an hierarchically organized
authoritarian government. During the 1850's, however, his speeches
and writings had little effect on his contemporaries.

The eventual revival of Carlism in the 1870's was owing less to
the movement's own impetus than to the breakdown of the shaky
structure of Spanish liberalism. The contradictions and inadequacies of Isabel's reign that had become unendurable for the active
minority of the population (1868), the instability of the subsequent constitutional monarchy for which an Italian prince had to
be imported (1870–1873), the anarchy and excess marking the
Republic which followed (1873–1874)—all this helped to revive
in the minds of some the Carlist argument that only their branch
of the dynasty could provide stable rule for Spain.

The Carlism of the third war (1872–1877) was a trifle different
from that of the 1830's. Carlism continued in large measure to be
a matter of family and regional tradition. It was still centered in
the northeast, especially in Navarre and the Basque provinces,
though now within a smaller radius. However, it had begun to
assume a more organized and sophisticated political aspect. A number of conservative Catholic intellectuals, who before 1868 had
supported the central government, now joined Carlism and helped
to formulate its political ideology more precisely. The outstanding

Carlist ideologue of this decade was Antonio Aparisi Guijarro, who did much to publicize the basic Carlist program concerning the king's ruling as well as reigning, the traditionalist corporative Cortes, decentralization, and the overriding influence of Catholicism. Aparisi, however, did not ignore the fact that the traditionalist institutions, such as the Cortes and the Inquisition, would have to be adjusted to modern needs. Furthermore, there was now discernible among some Carlists a more "modern" approach, one not so much interested in the "old laws" and the "traditional constitution" as in an effective modern authoritarian state, more centralist than the original Carlist attitude might have permitted.

The current pretender, D. Carlos "VII," had more political personality than his grandfather. He did not find the varieties of neo-Carlists and the elderly men who constituted the senior council of his faction overly congenial, but he cultivated his personal authority and initiative at their expense. At the height of the fighting, in 1874, D. Carlos tried to win over some of the liberals by stressing the nondespotic aspects of the Carlist program. He officially renounced any desire to reëstablish the old Inquisition, and stressed that it was not the function of the monarchy to impose a royal dictatorship on the nation. Rather, he said, the governmental institutions of the new Spain would be created by a new Cortes elected in the proper traditional fashion. The principal effect of these ploys was not, however, to win over the liberals but to provoke recriminations within Carlist ranks between theocrats and pretotalitarians on the one hand and those royalists who accepted D. Carlos' dicta on the other.

The resources at the disposal of the central power in the 1870's were greater than they had been in the 1830's. After the restoration of the regular constitutional monarchy (1875), these forces could be effectively concentrated, and the Carlists were put down within a year or so. The last months of the third Carlist war paralleled those of the first, full of internecine conflict and bitter recrimination. The government victory of 1876–1877 was more complete than that of 1840, and the local Basque privileges, fiscal and otherwise, were eliminated almost altogether.

The constitutional monarchy of 1876 through 1923 was more

stable than its predecessor, although it was similarly based on a restricted suffrage and strong central power. A high premium was placed upon making the regime viable in the short run, and conciliation was given considerable emphasis. Leaders of the new regime succeeded in winning over a minority of both chastened ex-liberals and disenchanted members of the Carlist Right, for the experiences of the past decade had tended to discourage extremism.

At first, all the regular Carlist leaders stood firm against the new liberal monarchy: it was constitutional, centralized, and ruled by the "usurping" line; worst of all, it was not ultra-Catholic, in the Carlist sense. The new regime recognized the Catholic Church as the official religion, granted it special financial privileges, and mildly harassed other churches and philosophies, but it made no attempt to proscribe the latter and in its official dealings kept a certain distance from the Church. For the Carlist Right, the religious issue began to take on more importance than ever as the hopes built on the dynastic principle faded. Don Carlos "VII" might never be king, but the real issue now was true religion. A government and society thoroughly Catholic, a virtual theocracy, was the only way to avoid the evil of the century.

Just as a strong sector of Carlism was settling into this ultra-intransigent mold, much of the hierarchy of the Spanish Church began to move in the opposite direction. For four decades the Church had been largely Carlist. Now the hierarchy had wearied of attaching Catholic interests too closely to what gave every indication of being a lost cause. The new Spanish regime was liberal, but discreetly so. It provided strong guarantees for the Church which would in turn save the latter's financial position. By 1880 the Spanish Church was making its peace with the liberal state. The most compromising Carlists recognized the inevitable, and, after being expelled by the Carlists, joined the dominant "Liberal-Conservative Party" in 1883.

From 1879 to 1885 the representative of D. Carlos in Spain was D. Cándido Nocedal. In 1875 the latter's son, Ramón, had founded a Carlist newspaper, El Siglo Futuro, in Madrid, and it became the prototype of a number of provincial organs advocating a sort of pretotalitarian theocracy. Together, they launched violent attacks on "collaborationists" and on Catholics associated with "liberalism." The fact that a majority of the Spanish hierarchy, with the evident blessing of Rome, was supporting collaboration, only increased the shrillness of the theocrats. For Ramón Nocedal and his peers, the whole issue of Carlist Traditionalism was now transcended by the question of the dominance of Catholic authoritarianism.

Largely because of this attitude, D. Ramón failed to be appointed Carlist chief in Spain on the death of his father in 1885. Don Carlos did not want to be represented by someone who subordinated more and more all Carlist politics to a single issue, and who consumed his energy in violent attacks on less intransigent Catholics. Finally, in 1887, D. Carlos published a statement in which he insisted that internecine quarreling between Carlists on definitions of the Catholic state must cease, repeating that all problems of political organization were to be decided by a properly elected Cortes after the eventual establishment of a Carlist regime. Furthermore, D. Carlos insisted on absolute obedience to his will in this, saying that it was up to him to decide which of his erstwhile Catholic subjects were tainted by liberal heresy in public matters. After protests from several Traditionalist newspapers, D. Carlos went so far as to suspend them.

The result was the secession of the Nocedal group from Carlism in mid-1888. They rejected current Carlism as having degenerated into Fernandine despotism politically and having compromised with liberalism on religious issues. D. Ramón set up a new organization of his own, the Integrists, to propagate true and pure Traditionalism. In differentiating Integrism or "pure Traditionalism" from contemporary Carlism, Nocedal emphasized two things. The first was super-Catholicism, "the rule of Jesus Christ," as he termed it, "in society; Jesus Christ ruling in the laws and customs, in public and private institutions, in all education, in all propaganda, written and spoken, in king and in subjects as well. . . ." The second was the denial, contrary even to Aparisi or D. Carlos himself, that any significant change need be made in reimposing the political, judicial, and cultural institutions of late medieval Spain, which, he said, could and should be restored exactly as they had been in 1517 or 1700.

There was nothing really new about such notions in themselves, but the degree to which Nocedal wished to apply them would have been without precedent in either medieval or Habsburg Spain. Hardly anyone in the fifteenth and sixteenth centuries would have pretended to such a pure theocracy. Nocedal's ideology was in large part a reaction to the lagging liberal transformation of a basically traditional society. As such, it exaggerated out of all proportion the theocratic tendencies of an earlier period.

Nocedal was very careful in his explanation of the Carlist principle of the Divine Right of Kings, for such authority was vested in God alone and was only vouchsafed to kings as His temporary vicars. The king's duty was to God first and to the people second. Even in purely secular policy he had to be bound by the Church. A king who failed in his duty to God or people had forfeited the authority granted by God, and could be deposed. Similarly, God's authority might be given to any form of government that exalted Catholicism. Monarchism was a historic system, but Nocedal later developed a pragmatic, accidentalist theory of political forms and explicitly stated that several kinds of governmental structure, even a corporative republic, would be acceptable if suffused with authoritarian Catholicism.

Integrism did not precisely constitute a political movement, for it did not engage in political activities, properly speaking. It was rather an ideological diatribe, resting on an attitude of political mysticism. Those most ardently berated by Integrists were not really the Liberals and leftists, but Catholic moderates who repudiated the hate-filled world of Integrist intransigence. Though the Integrists at first had the support of a large percentage of Carlists, the passage of a decade saw many of the latter return to the strict monarchist fold. The first Carlist youth organization had been founded in 1886, and by the turn of the century it had won back almost all the younger followers of Nocedal. Integrism per se did not long survive D. Ramón's death in 1906. Nocedal's last months had been embittered by the desertion of some of his erstwhile strongest clerical supporters, such as a faction of ultrareactionary

Jesuits which had long supported the extreme clerical position in politics but now wanted to adopt a more pragmatic attitude. Nonetheless, the spirit and influence of Integrism lingered, and was easily revived in certain religious and cultural circles during periods of stress.

The four decades from 1876 to 1917 formed the most constructive era in the history of Spanish liberalism. For the time being, traditionalist reaction seemed to have been buried by the waves of historical evolution. The shock of the loss of the remainder of the empire in 1898 did serve to reëmphasize how weak modern Spain was, but the Carlist conspiracy of 1898–1900 that tried to take advantage of the disaster never came to a head. The only prominent spokesman for Carlism during these years was the Cortes deputy Juan Vázquez de Mella, an orator and publicist. More practical than Nocedal, Mella paid somewhat more attention to social problems, and emphasized the corporate state as the only sound solution. He was in correspondence with Albert de Mun and with Catholic and monarchist corporatists in several countries. To the apparent success of Spanish liberalism in the early twentieth century, Mella opposed a theory of catastrophe, according to which an enormous disaster would have to be provoked before Spanish leaders would come to their senses.

In a changing social and political atmosphere, the old regional protest of the traditionalist reactionaries against political centralism sometimes took sharply different forms. At least in their early years, the two movements of "regional nationalism," in Catalonia and the Basque country, were in part expressions of a new kind of post-Carlist protest. Given the cantonalist spirit of Spaniards, it was not surprising that, in the fashion of Integrism, some Carlist followers should lose sight of the dynastic issue and emphasize traditionalist principles purely within their local context. This was the burden of *La Tradició Catalana* (1892) by the Bishop of Vich, Torras y Bages. According to him, Catalonia was especially significant because it maintained pious tradition more faithfully than did the rest of Spain.

Catalan nationalism was, however, liberal and even democratic almost from the very beginning, and reactionary Catalan traditionalism was not the major force in its development. Basque nationalism was more specifically post-Carlist. It arose following the example and failure of Carlism, under the incentive of modern nationalist movements (especially that of Catalonia) and of the industrial development of Vizcaya and Guipuzcoa at the turn of the century. Sabino Arana Goiri, the creator of Basque ideology, came from a Carlist family and was himself a Carlist in his early years. The motto he had formulated by 1893, "God and our old laws," reflected a traditionalist ideology reduced to the regionalist level and shorn of the dynastic issue. For obvious reasons, Basque nationalism scored its first political success in 1898. Growing slowly but steadily during the next three decades, it evoked the strongest response from the surrounding Carlist population and at first specifically eschewed any appeal to liberals or republicans, applying to them the old epithet, "enemies of God." During its formative years, Basque nationalism was sometimes discreetly encouraged from Madrid as an antidote to Carlism. Since the two movements competed for the same support, brawls between their followers were not infrequent after 1904.

The second decade of the twentieth century was a period of great political flux in Spain, revealing the ultimate failure of oligarchical liberalism to lead the country. After the famous "Bloody Week" of 1909, in which three days of rioting at Barcelona provided excuse for the execution of the anarchist philosopher Ferrer, all liberal and leftist forces combined to veto formation of any future cabinet by the leader of the once dominant "Liberal-Conservative Party," Antonio Maura. The ostracism of Maura during these years very nearly pushed Spain's leading conservative statesman into the role of champion of a new rightist reform movement. Maura's austerity, rectitude, eloquence, and intelligence, his championing of what he called a "revolution from above," strengthening national institutions while partially decentralizing local government, all designated him as the man to head a middle-class reaction against the nation's growing political fractionalization. The Maurist movement, which began to grow quickly in 1914, was, however, more the work of Maura's followers than of Maura himself. Despite his utter disdain for parliamentary factions and leftists, D. Antonio was a sincere, convinced constitutionalist.

Though the "Maurists" were sometimes eager to make of "Maurism" a kind of antiparliamentary nationalist authoritarian reform movement, Maura himself could not encourage this. His extraparliamentary action was limited to occasional speeches before large crowds in several major cities. He denounced the divisive forces in the Cortes, but not the principle of a democratically elected Cortes itself. For him, "Maurism" was a personal style rather than an ideology or anything approaching a movement. The outbreak of World War I retarded rather than encouraged the Maurists, for it brought a frenetic round of economic activity and social change, at least in the north, and tended momentarily to polarize political interest around the problem of Spanish neutrality. Maurism thus completely failed to develop into a real political movement; its significance, like that of Integrism, lay in the psychological climate it encouraged, which would begin to flourish within a few more years.

Much more important than Maurism during these years was the return of the military to the center of the political stage. Despite the great political importance of the Spanish army during the century before, the military had never had any distinct political philosophy of its own. In Spain there was no real ideology of militarism such as existed in most other continental countries, and the army had been predominantly liberal during the earlier century. For four decades after the establishment of a successful liberal monarchy in 1876, the army had largely kept out of politics.

During the first part of the new century, a fundamental change in political orientation took place. Certain obvious causes can be cited: the intensification of the class struggle, which made the army an indispensable guarantor of domestic order; the growth of regionalism, which infuriated the patriotic spirit of the military; the nation's political and diplomatic stagnation, which made it impossible to support bellicose enterprises; and, perhaps most fundamental, the aftermath of the defeat in 1898, in which the army was somewhat unfairly made the scapegoat for an entire nation's irresponsibility. Because of the weakness of Spanish institutions, the army now found itself called upon to preserve the nation's order, unity, and prestige, yet at the same time was in the lamentable state of an inflated bureaucracy lacking proper equipment or training. The haggling politicians seemed unconcerned, while the burgeoning Left denigrated the army as an instrument of tyranny. The life of recruits was so wretched that Spaniards emigrated by the thousands to avoid the draft. Junior officers were so miserably paid that marriage was officially prohibited for infantry lieutenants without private income until they were promoted. The questions of command and promotion were open to unbridled favoritism, so that the minority of active officers volunteered for service in Morocco, where corruption was most rife and military exploits could earn the quickest promotions. This in turn provoked an intensely hostile reaction from the majority who remained in the peninsula. Sensitive and petulant, the army came to look on itself as the only bulwark of patriotism and unity in a land riven by division, but a bulwark essentially ignored by the people and government alike.

World War I precipitated this dissatisfaction. Economic opportunity brought sudden prosperity to part of Spain, but rapid inflation cast the bureaucratic sectors of the petty bourgeoisie (among which, economically, the army would have to be included) into desperate straits. All the while, special promotions for the *africanista* officers continued, increasing the already intense resentment. In 1916, officers in the peninsula decided to do something about it, and organized Juntas de Defensa to protect their professional interests. They were encouraged by the examples of the burgeoning working-class movement and, more particularly, the aristocratic Artillery Corps, which had guarded itself from special favoritism for several generations by adhering to strict seniority promotion under the auspices of a special junta of senior officers.

By the spring of 1917 juntas had been organized in nearly all the important garrisons of Spain. They specifically disavowed any political goals, but their actions belied their words, for they talked persistently of the need to purify and revitalize the nation, and of doing something about the parliamentary chaos—though what was never made clear. The juntas were, of course, extralegal formations, and by the end of May, 1917, the government was sufficiently worried to try to bring them under discipline. Though the major junta leaders in Barcelona were arrested for a few days, their companions stood firm and the government lost its courage. The king, Alfonso XIII, though worried about the insubordination of the juntas, soon decided to try to fish in troubled waters and sought by private communications with the *junteros* to bolster his personal power in the army.

The junta leaders were therefore released, and their pressure provoked the fall of the government, the third time since 1895 that the army had indirectly accomplished such a feat. The juntas emphasized honesty, unity, and some vague form of reorganization. They were more or less antiparliamentary, but they did not really propose that the constitutional system be overturned. Their political goals were limited instead to some sort of realignment of forces and an improvement in the position of the army, providing it with greater power, respect, and emoluments.

The paucity of the *junteros'* political culture could not have been greater. They had no explicit concept of political organization at all, and there was such a diversity of political views among their thousands of members that about the only things they were agreed on was the need for greater personal rewards and some kind of political influence. Insofar as they possessed a higher ideology, it was tied to patriotism, but it would be an exaggeration to call them a prefascist movement. In the long run, they were much more conservative than radical, and stood behind the government to defeat the general strike of 1917. Several months later, when the government was once more reorganized, the influence of the juntas was officially recognized by the government's appointing their leaders to posts in the Ministry of War. During 1918 a minor military reform was carried out, raising salaries all along the line. These measures mollified the juntas, but did not encourage them to disband. Finally, in 1919, the Minister of War tried to incorporate and subordinate them within the government structure by officially converting them into "Investigative Commissions" of the army in each part of Spain.

Although the juntas had not tried seriously either to change or to usurp the existing political system, the example of their indiscipline and the pressure they exerted further diminished the prestige and unity of constitutional government. They had also made it clear that the new political ambitions of the army were no longer liberal or parliamentarian. At the same time, their activity was perhaps more harmful to the army than to the parliament, for the last vestiges of military unity were now being lost amid political and professional confusion.

By the early 1920's the Spanish state was no longer menaced by any specific extreme of Left or Right but by an extraordinary situation of internal disunity and irresponsibility that was easily capable of degenerating into political anarchy. Although the parliamentary government might have limped along for years, no national consensus supported it. In the famous term of Ortega y Gasset, the nation was civically "invertebrate."

The army attempted to supply the backbone, not because the army was united or had a clear political ideology, but because it enjoyed a monopoly of force. Even then, the only thing that crystallized the apprehension of the king and the military hierarchy was the general demand for punishment for the disastrous defeats suffered in Morocco in 1921. Fifty years of halting civic education had had some effect, for the idea of rebellion still seems never seriously to have entered the minds of most generals. The coup of September, 1923, temporarily ending constitutional government in Spain, was carried out by only a handful of conspirators around General Miguel Primo de Rivera, aided by the benevolence of the King.

The popular reaction to this coup indicated general approval of some kind of authoritarian nationalist reform, taken in a broad and popular sense. This feeling extended from wealthy Catalan bourgeois, fearful of eventual social revolution, to Galician peasants, tired of the exactions of corrupt local political bosses. Primo de Rivera believed himself to be the faithful interpreter of such sentiment. In his highly personalistic way, Primo liked to consider himself a constitutionalist and something of a liberal. During the first months of the dictatorship he was even more emphatic than the usual Hispanic military usurper in insisting that he had come only to straighten things out, that he would probably be in power for less than a year, and that the constitution of 1876 was still the basic law of the land.

On the other hand, Primo exalted the axiom that parties and politicians were not to be trusted. Though he said that he did not intend to imitate Mussolini, he admitted within a few days of his coup that he had been "inspired" by aspects of the Fascist example. The best thing, according to Primo, was a purely military regime run by a directory of generals who would clean things up and then perhaps give the politicians another opportunity to try their hand.

The dictatorship quelled internal disorder and, with French aid, brought the Moroccan fighting to an end after four years. In 1926 the dictatorship reached its height. The nation was prosperous, politically quiet, and in its most solid international position of nearly half a century. If Primo really had no plans for a new kind of rightist authoritarian nationalist regime, the time had logically come to return to legality.

The dictator finally began to aver that he thought an authoritarian system should be continued for a longer time, but he could never decide what to do about the nominal authority of the king, nor did he prepare a new institutional charter to take the place of the constitution. As Primo had often emphasized, he was a man of impulse and intuition. Since the military directory had proved incompetent, he replaced it with a civilian cabinet which was bolstered by a political front, the "Patriotic Union," composed of civilian followers without a clear ideology. The structure of the regime was bolstered by a special appointive assembly, a massive public works program, and a nationwide series of labor arbitration committees. All this followed no plan or ideology, for each major step taken by the regime was based on an ad hoc decision. Few people went so far as to label the dictatorship fascist, though Primo was obviously groping toward much more than another nineteenth-century government on the Narváez pattern.

Primo's coup had originally been supported by much popular feeling, but it had never enjoyed an organized political following. Since the regime was seemingly incapable of creating a consistent ideology, each new development helped to give it more and more the appearance of an inharmonious collage. One reason for its political and ideological flimsiness was the complete lack of elements of the extreme right on which it might have built. The pre-1923 conservatives had nearly all been constitutionalists who grew restive under a military dictatorship. Amid the traditional Spanish cultural isolation, no group of intellectuals or activists had been notably inspired either by Italian Fascism or by the Action Française. The dictatorship thus limped out its life amid the residues of nineteenth-century liberalism. As Curzio Malaparte then observed, the only feasible person to compare with Primo was Pilsudski. The dictator was powerless to resolve his own contradictions, and the flimsiness of his political structure was such that it did not even sustain the loyalty of the Army.

As his temporary triumphs began to turn to ashes under the heat of economic and political pressure, Primo was gravely hurt and surprised to find that he had almost no positive supporters at all. His collapse also carried along with it the constitutional monarchy, for Spanish conservatives had been so discouraged by uncoordinated authoritarian rule that scant serious effort was made to avoid the coming of the Republic one year later, in 1931. Most of the conservative or authoritarian-minded elements in Spain were left temporarily leaderless and disorganized.

The installation of a Republican regime, bringing an anticlerical constitution, the first real democracy in Spanish history, and the threat of further violence from the Left, soon provoked a reaction. In 1931 most middle-class conservatives preferred to support a legal, constitutionalist conservative party, but extremists were developing other ideas. During the previous year there had already been an abortive attempt to create a Spanish Nationalist Party in support of the monarchy. Replete with street gangs, this was the first genuine expression of the twentieth-century radical Right in Spain, though it had little program other than reactionary patriotism, the principle of authority, and a large army.

The reactionary simplism of the Spanish Nationalist Party limited it to only a few hundred members. A more radical effort was the founding of the weekly, *La Conquista del Estado,* in Madrid, during March, 1931. Ramiro Ledesma Ramos, founder of the journal, was a postal clerk and former essayist on philosophical themes who had been overwhelmingly impressed by Nazism and Italian Fascism. Combing his hair over his forehead, Hitler fashion, he threw himself into the task of creating some kind of Spanish nationalist and revolutionary fascist-type movement. Ledesma could most succinctly be defined as a variant of National Bolshevik, though he does not seem to have been acquainted with Ernst Niekisch. In 1931 he had no following at all.

At the same time another small group was being organized in the old Castillian capital of Valladolid. Its founder, Onésimo Redondo Ortega, was a lawyer from the lowest level of the petty bourgeoisie. He was hyper-Catholic, and had studied and taught in a Catholic college in Germany, where he had been exposed to Nazism and other elements of German radicalism. Unlike Ledesma, Redondo did not want to imitate secular fascism, but instead to encourage a Spanish nationalist reaction, linked strongly to Catholicism, against all modern liberalism. The social base to which he appealed was the provincial petit bourgeois of northern Spain. His demagogy was rural, devoted to the traditionalistic, hyper-Catholic, post-Carlist, often apolitical lower-middle classes of the small towns, now menaced by the economic domination of big cities and the urban revolutionary movements. Unlike Ledesma, he did not insist on the "revolutionary" quality of radical nationalism, but, more mildly, called his Juntas Castellanas de Acción Hispánica (organized in July, 1931) the "extreme Right," opposed to the triumphant liberalism of the Republic and the Catalan movement.

In October, 1931, Ledesma and Redondo managed to surmount the differences between them to create a new group called the Juntas de Ofensiva Nacional Sindicalista (JONS), but their forces, together with those of the abortive Spanish Nationalist Party, could scarcely have totaled more than one thousand members in all of Spain. During this time most of the Spanish middle class was more than willing to leave the nation's future up to the evolving moderate liberal Republic.

Quite apart from these tiny, isolated nuclei of fascistic nationalism, Spanish monarchists also were slowly organizing their own reaction to the Republic. During 1930 handfuls of ultramonarchists had formed little groups with such names as Civic Reaction, Aristocratic Action, and Monarchist Action, all of which adopted a stronger line than the official monarchist front supporting D. Alfonso in the last days of his reign. A few weeks after the advent of the Republic these elements began to regroup, and, during 1931, their representatives held several meetings with D. Alfonso in France. Contributions were collected from wealthy supporters, and funds were made available to ultramonarchist generals to attempt to organize a military revolt in the spring and summer of 1931. These efforts came to naught.

Meanwhile, the impact of the Republic and its anticlerical laws was helping to revive Carlism. Militia squads of *requetés,* as the Carlist volunteers were called, once more drilled among the peasant population of the Navarrese hills, while Integrists and orthodox Carlists began to forget their past differences. Don Jaime, the current pretender, died in the autumn of 1931 and was succeeded by his childless uncle, the eighty-two-year-old D. Alfonso Carlos, a veteran of the third Carlist war. Whereas D. Jaime had been resolutely anti-Integrist, the attitude of D. Alfonso Carlos was much more benevolent; the succession of D. Alfonso Carlos* therefore helped to reunite all the clerical ultra-Right. A new organization, the Comunión Tradicionalista, was formed as the political representation of Carlism, and former Integrists occupied leading positions in the new group. As religious and political tensions mounted, more and more sons and grandsons of Carlism returned to the old flag, so that by 1934 the "Comunión Tradicionalista" claimed to number over six hundred thousand.

The coming of the Republic had so infuriated Carlist leaders that they were even willing to drop part of their intransigent iso-

---

* Since D. Alfonso Carlos was the last living member of the direct male line of the Carlist dynasty, the line was obviously near extinction. This occasioned a growing crisis, for, since Carlism was more doctrinal than dynastic, its followers could not renounce the political movement for lack of an heir, but, on the other hand, one of its basic principles had been that of the sole right of male succession. During the next five years, at least five alternative candidates of collateral branches were suggested as eventual successors to D. Alfonso Carlos, but no conclusion could be reached. Former Integrists were less disturbed than orthodox Carlists, as they would actually view the disappearance of the dynastic issue as something of a blessing.

lationism in favor of limited coöperation with *alfonsino* monarchists. By 1932 perhaps the majority of Spanish monarchists had renounced liberalism, for regular parliamentary government was inadequate to sustain monarchism in Spain. Even the supporters of D. Alfonso were coming to accept a variant of the Traditionalist program of authoritarian king and corporate Cortes, bolstering their ideas with examples drawn from fascist and corporatist ideologues in France, Italy, and Austria. On the other hand, monarchist feeling had shrunk so desperately under Alfonso XIII that it was now doubtful if the *alfonsinos* had as many followers as had the Carlists, though there was much more wealth behind them. Twice in 1931–1932 efforts were made to reach dynastic agreements between the opposing branches, but neither tentative accord could be put into practice.

At this time a major share of the burden of monarchist propaganda was carried by the new review *Acción Española*, founded at the end of 1931. This journal was written on a relatively high intellectual plane and carried the work of such writers and ideologues as Ramiro de Maeztu, Victor Pradera, and Eugenio Vegas Latapié. It was strongly influenced by *Action Française*, whence the title. The political program advanced was monarchist, nationalist, corporative, and clerical. The last principle constituted the main difference between *Acción Española* and *maurrasisme*, for the former was super-Catholic. Much of Carlism was accepted, save for the dynastic issue, and several of the leading contributors, such as Pradera, were Carlist or at least Integrist.

During 1932 Carlists and Alfonsine monarchists worked together to prepare a coup against the Republican government. Secret caches of arms were stored in Navarre and the Basque provinces, but the main goal of the conspirators was to win the support of the army generals, which was indispensable for an effective coup. A few of the officers were monarchists, but most of them, chastened by Primo's example, had accepted the Republic and were reluctant to rebel against it. The clumsiness and vengefulness of Republican politicians nonetheless quickly managed to alienate most of the military. The successful effort to halve the officer corps, the reduction of the military budget, the conspicuous attention given the lower ranks, and the government's obvious delight in humbling the military hierarchy—all these helped create considerable discontent by mid-1932. Furthermore, the steps taken that summer to grant autonomy to Catalonia increased a sense of injured patriotism among the military, and, while monarchists intrigued, a circle of conservative Republicans was pressuring key military figures to make a coup that would moderate, but not overthrow, the present regime.

The military pronunciamiento that was attempted in August, 1932, by General Jose Sanjurjo and a handful of other conspirators was a confused affair. It drew little concrete support, for the plotters themselves were disunited regarding their final goal and the effort disintegrated almost as soon as it began. Sanjurjo himself was an uncertain tool of intriguers and never fully understood the nature of the movement he was supposedly leading. Together with several hundred others, he was trapped by Republican police and sent to prison.

Despite this fiasco, monarchist conspirators continued to plot through the winter of 1932–1933. A new organization, Renovación Española, was founded to serve as a political front for clandestine activity. During the campaign for the second Republican Cortes elections of October, 1933, Carlists and *alfonsinos* united in a coalition labeled TYRE (Tradicionalistas y Renovación Española), which formed part of the united Right front of all the middle-class conservative groups. With the Left completely disunited, moderates and conservatives were able to score a general electoral victory. Only a modest share of the rewards, however, went to the monarchists, who won less than 10 per cent of the seats in the new chamber. Conservative Republicans were now in control of the government, and extremist groups seemed superfluous to the bulk of the middle classes.

During 1934 the monarchist Right went through a new organizational phase. It found a leader in José Calvo Sotelo, former finance minister under Primo de Rivera. During three years in Parisian exile, Calvo had been strongly influenced by Maurras and his followers. Returning to Spain, he cast aside all lingering traces of his semiconstitutionalist Maurist youth and propagated an explicit doctrine of authoritarian corporatism as the basis for the "installation," rather than the "restoration," of a viable monarchy. Since the climate of Spanish conservatism was not now propitious for monarchism per se, he worked to weld together a new rightist coalition which would stress corporative nationalism and an authoritarian state more than the royalist issue. The resulting National Bloc, organized in December, 1934, was based on the *alfonsino* monarchists, but also included Carlists and certain other extremely conservative elements, the Carlists lending support only in return for guarantees of their autonomy. In its opening manifesto, the adjective "totalitarian" was given a prominent place.

The potential role of a Spanish fascist party had, however, already been preëmpted by a small formation called Falange Española, organized a few days before the 1933 elections. The fascistic nuclei formed by Ledesma and Redondo had made no impression at all during their first two years of existence, but a number of people formerly of Patriotic Union background felt that the hour was somehow favorable in 1933 for a new authoritarian nationalist movement in Spain, a real party of Spanish fascism. The central figure of this effort, José Antonio Primo de Rivera, was the eldest son of the late dictator. An intellectual young man of rather aristocratic manner and liberal temperament, he felt impelled to take some initiative to continue the political labors of his father in a more sophisticated, dynamic form. The Falange began with considerable financial and personal support from Patriotic Union circles and was able to swallow up the JONS in February, 1934, when the two movements merged. The ideological content of Spanish fascism remained very vague, however. Some thought it would be a literal transcription of Mussolini's ideas, a few looked to it for Nazism, and many assumed it was just a revitalization of the Patriotic Union. In any event, on the whole it looked much too radical to interest the Spanish Right, which could generate little interest in new ideological interpretations, especially since the Left had already been roundly defeated in the last elections.

Precisely because of such defeat, however, the parliamentary Left now rejected moderation and vetoed the participation of clerical conservatives in the government. Though the main conservative coalition, the CEDA (Spanish Confederation of Autonomous Rightist Groups), was Republican and did not propose to overturn the regime, the Left nevertheless insisted it would never tolerate a step back. Even the hitherto cautious Socialists spoke openly of revolution.

In this atmosphere political unrest began to grow once more among the military. The scars of the reform of 1931–1932 still hurt, and the threats of the increasingly radical Left roused the army spirit. During the spring of 1934 a group of officers, none higher than the rank of colonel, organized a clandestine Unión Militar Española (UME), which soon had juntas and cells in almost every garrison. Unlike the juntas of 1917, these had no animus against the generals, for this organization was not the result of intraservice rivalry, but of a direct political malaise aroused by the Left. The aims of the UME nonetheless were not entirely clear. The original Junta Central adopted a program according to which its only goal was to sustain the authority of the state and avert revolution. Concerning military intervention to prevent subversion, UME leaders vowed to hold power for only the briefest possible period before returning the government to popular sovereignty. It soon became clear, however, that many influential members were not in accord with these principles, for there grew a feeling that, in order to overcome political disunity, some kind of regular military dictatorship would be necessary.

The expected leftist rebellion occurred in October, 1934. UME propaganda was possibly of some effect in stiffening junior officers for the repression of the rebels. Beyond that, the UME soon seemed superfluous, for the Left was totally defeated, and the moderates were more firmly in control than ever. The most radical UME affiliates grew increasingly dissatisfied, saying that the danger of subversion would always exist so long as the Republican moderates were not replaced by an authoritarian state. Conversations were therefore held in November, 1934, between UME leaders and José Antonio Primo de Rivera, now National Chief of the Falange. Primo de Rivera agreed to support a military coup, recognizing that the insignificant Falange, with only a few thousand members, could pretend to very little on its own.

The result of these developments was that by the beginning of 1935 the three major elements of the Spanish Right—monarchist corporatism, Falangism, and military authoritarianism—had begun to assume clear form. Relations between these groups were still weak and uncertain, and no one of them possessed significant independent strength. Calvo Sotelo was consequently anxious to include the Falange in his National Bloc, but Falangist leaders were now more eager than ever to avoid identification with the Right and to develop an authentically revolutionary movement. Such a firm attitude was owing to several factors. For example, monarchist intriguers had just been foiled in efforts to take over the Falange, and had been expelled from the party. Moreover, José Antonio Primo de Rivera had begun to clarify his own position and in so doing moved nearer the revolutionary notions of Ledesma. To differentiate Falangism from monarchist authoritarianism, an official program was edited in January, 1935, and stood as the classic definition of Spanish fascist doctrine. Among the twenty-seven points listed, the following ideas were particularly emphasized:

1) political unity of Spain and elimination of regional separatism;
2) abolition of political parties;
3) establishment of a nationalist dictatorship led by the Falange;
4) efficacy of violence in regenerating Spain;
5) development of Spanish imperial power;
6) expansion and strengthening of the armed forces;
7) recognition and support of Catholicism as the official religion of Spain but rejection of any clerical influence in government;
8) sweeping economic reform referred to as a "revolution," which emphasized the following points:
    (a) establishment of a complete system of national syndicates, embracing employers and employees, to organize, coördinate, and represent all of Spain's economic activity;
    (b) establishment of a great agrarian reform, reclaiming waste land, improving techniques, concentrating scattered holdings, and reorganizing the great latifundia;
    (c) stimulation of industrial expansion;
    (d) respect for private property, but nationalization of credit facilities by the state to eliminate capitalist usury.*

---

* The full Falangist economic program was not specifically stated in the Twenty-Seven Points of January, 1935, but was elaborated by José Antonio Primo de Rivera and other Falangist statesmen later during that year.

In this way the Falange defined its "revolutionary" position as against the "reactionary" attitude of the National Bloc, which was vigorously denounced by Falangists. This was, indeed, the first genuinely revolutionary program to appear among Spanish movements of the extreme Right. In its social and economic goals, and in its concept of dictatorship, Falangism had become clearly a radical, not a reactionary, movement. Falangist leaders, in fact, denied that the movement belonged to the Right at all. Radicalization of the Falange's social and economic platform did not, however, enable it to win any significant following, for the class spirit of the workers was too militantly organized. It has accurately been said that the history of the second Republic until 1936 could be written without having to make reference to the Falange.

The National Bloc was only a little stronger, though it had both more appeal for the extreme right-wing element of the middle classes, and ample financial backing. In March, 1934, monarchist representatives had worked out an assistance pact with the Italian government in the event they were able to initiate a coup, but throughout 1935 Spanish politics were dominated by the CEDA and other equally moderate conservatives. As both Falangists and monarchists clearly understood, the opportunity to overthrow the Republic could come only through the army.

The leading generals, however, were not at all interested in tampering with what, at least for a few months, seemed a stable political situation. Military conspiracy during 1935 was therefore a function mainly of the junior officers composing the UME, among whom the radical faction was now gaining the upper hand. In June, 1935, a UME representative carried on unsuccessful negotiations with business elements in Paris for a one-million-dollar loan to finance a military coup; the monarchist General Fanjul, Under Secretary of War in the second half of 1935 and a principal UME leader, insisted that military rebellion was the only solution for Spain's political problems.

After the moderate conservatives had become completely paralyzed by their own parliamentary maneuvers, new elections were scheduled for February, 1936. The Comunión Tradicionalista now formally affiliated with the National Bloc, which in turn joined with the CEDA and smaller conservative groups to form a National Front to face the Popular Front of the Left. The only elements remaining outside the National Front were the Basque Nationalists, rapidly evolving toward liberalism as they realized they stood very little chance of winning local autonomy from a rightist government, and the Falange, too weak and radical to merit much attention, too independent and revolutionary to subordinate itself to conservatives.

The rightist alliance lost the election by a narrow margin. Although Cedists later attempted halfheartedly to reorganize the Right-Center, the result of the Popular Front victory was to disorient moderate conservatism in Spain. Within twenty-four hours of the elections, strong efforts were made both by Calvo Sotelo and the CEDA's Gil Robles to get the Army to take over. General Fanjul was ready and willing, but General Francisco Franco, the Chief of Staff, and other leading figures would not make such a move on their own authority. The great majority of the officers were by no means partisans of the Right. Though many of the young ones, especially, believed in the need for military control, most of the key commanders would not budge unless there was a direct danger of the Left overthrowing the state.

The only nonleftist group which seemed to benefit from the Popular Front victory was the Falange. The triumph of Left-liberalism and the confident prophecies of revolution voiced by Socialists and Anarchists finally began to stir up the middle classes and impel them toward a more radical position. The National Bloc seemed inadequate, too closely associated with the past. Monarchism stirred fewer and fewer people, and the only new idea available was Falangism. The process of semifascistization undergone by the Spanish middle classes during 1936 was an almost purely negative reaction. The idea of national-syndicalist revolution as a creative process never took hold, but the notion of nationalist authoritarianism on a radical twentieth-century Falangist line became very attractive. The monarchists now began to give much of their financial support to the Falangists, who were soon doing all they could to contribute to the climate of disorder in Spain during the spring of 1936. In mid-March the Falange was therefore outlawed and broken up as an organized party.

Meanwhile, in clerical and ultrareactionary circles, Carlism regained vogue. As always during a time of crisis, there was a reawakened yearning toward the old dogmas. The Carlist paramilitary organization was expanded, and a military committee was set up across the French border in St. Jean de Luz. Several plans were made for a Carlist rebellion, but these had to be shelved for lack of support among army officers.

By the middle of spring the political organizations of the extreme Right had exhausted all their own resources and were helpless to apply significant civic pressure against the regime. Any lingering doubt regarding the absolute necessity of relying on the military had vanished, although time had not in any way resolved the disunity and political confusion among the officers. Various UME groups were conspiring actively in separate parts of Spain, but internal coördination or coöperation with civilian elements was almost nil.

Many potential rebels looked for inspiration to General Sanjurjo, the nominal leader of the 1932 revolt. Sanjurjo, however, feared he would be left in the lurch once more and, from his exile in Portugal, showed no interest in active leadership. At the end of May he delegated his personal authority to General Emilio Mola, former police chief for the monarchy and recently ousted from his post as head of the army in Morocco. Mola had had to deal with secret organizations in the past, and enjoyed relative freedom as military commander in the Carlist territory of Navarre. Politically, he could only with some difficulty be classed as a representative of the Right, for he was not a member of the UME and not basically monarchist. He disdained Carlism and Traditionalist clericalism, but believed that the country did need an authoritarian regime for a short time and agreed that this could only be provided by the army. During May, June, and early July he wrote several outlines of the political form the new dictatorship should take, emphasizing retention of most recent social reforms, freedom of religion, and separation of church and state (still relatively radical ideas in Spain), with eventual devolution of authority to a parliament of the conservative parties. Suffrage was, however, to be limited.

The conspiracy took shape during the month of June. Mola received the pledges of most UME leaders, and by July political contact had been made with Calvo Sotelo and Gil Robles. Mola was anxious to avoid being compromised with rightist politicians, and discussions were limited to exchange of information and occasional provision of funds by civilians.

A major problem was to obtain unity among the minority of officers actively supporting the rebellion, and to gain the adherence of certain key generals with national prestige. The most important of the latter was General Franco, whose eminence as Chief of Staff and past reputation as a field commander in Morocco had given him unusual prestige among the indispensable Moroccan veterans. Heretofore Franco had sedulously avoided identification with the Right. He had not been compromised in the 1932 rebellion and, through family ties, had been identified with the moderate conservatives. Cold, prudent, calculating, and ambitious, his very coldness and self-control had helped to bolster his prestige. The last thing Franco wanted was to ruin his career through involvement in a half-baked military rebellion. As late as the end of June, though maintaining contact with the conspirators, he had not pledged his adherence.

Worried over the flimsiness of his conspiracy, Mola grew more and more concerned about auxiliary support. The militia of the Navarrese Carlists were anxious to join the rebellion, yet their leaders refused to permit participation in a cause not directed toward establishment of a Traditionalist monarchy. For his part, Mola would make no political compromises, saying only that the movement was devoted to the restoration of order, and that the future of a new regime could not be prejudiced by prior sectarian agreements. The matter was then referred to Sanjurjo, who was slated to become eventual head of the new military government. Reluctantly, after a few token concessions from Sanjurjo, on July 12 the Carlist leaders gave in—after it had become clear that their own followers could scarcely be restrained. The Falangists, similarly, had no choice but to support the army conspiracy. Though José Antonio Primo de Rivera still distrusted the political reliability of the officers, he recognized the impotence of Falangism and issued careful instructions to limit the Falangist support.

On July 13, Calvo Sotelo was murdered in Madrid. Within forty-eight hours the last details of the conspiracy were set, and the rebellion began on July 17. The coup failed completely in most of the major population centers, leading Spain into civil war, an eventuality for which the rebel leaders had not been prepared either politically or militarily.

The sudden death of Sanjurjo in an airplane accident on leaving Lisbon left the rebellion without even a nominal chief. The movement had no very exact political character, and in fact had officially begun under the Republican flag, because of the quasi liberalism or lack of political identification of thousands of the officers. As it turned out, the first civilian politicians on the spot at military headquarters in northern Spain were *alfonsino* monarchists, who provided financial credit and diplomatic contacts for the military Junta established at Burgos on July 22. Their influence remained only marginal, for the army leaders were determined to keep power in military hands.

A strong campaign was then waged by a handful of influential rebel leaders to have Franco, who had joined the rising at the eleventh hour, named Commander-in-Chief of the military effort. This was a logical choice, in one sense, for no one else, not even Mola, had the influence and reputation of Franco. His supporters did not, however, stop here. After it had been agreed at the end of September to name Franco *Generalissimo,* an executive coup de main transformed the office into that of Chief of State, or full dictator. The elements most concerned with elevating Franco to absolute personal authority were the monarchist generals (themselves a definite minority) and leaders of the Moroccan army, the military elite. The monarchists seem to have felt that, given the impossibility of an immediate restoration, the best substitute was temporary single-ruler dictatorship—technically imposed only for the duration of hostilities—which would make a later transition to authoritarian monarchy easier.

The result, as it turned out, was complete military dictatorship, lacking ideology or institutional substance. Slowly, in 1937–1938, the framework of an authoritarian nationalist state was worked out, in large part with the aid of Franco's brother-in-law, Serrano Súñer. The consequence was a syncretistic hodgepodge of all elements of Spanish conservatism and the radical right. Since Franco had few political ideas of his own, he was not averse to using those of others. The fusion of Falangists and Carlists in April, 1937, was an ideological monstrosity most easily accomplished by an unintellectual leader to whom all ideas and programs are suspect. Franco and Serrano Súñer were pointing toward such a broad synthesis that the very possibility of a rightist opposition would become a contradiction in terms. In theory, most of the Falangist program was adopted by the state, but reactionary Traditionalism was also incorporated through the new clerical laws, which granted the Spanish Catholic Church support and power such as it had not enjoyed since the eighteenth century. The monarchists were assuaged with key positions and promises that, when the right time came, Franco would certainly restore the main branch of the dynasty. The new regime was neither Falangist, Traditionalist, nor monarchist, but a mixture of all three, with the support of big business, under a fundamentally military dictatorship.

The polarization of political energies brought by the Civil War was so extreme that Franco largely succeeded in welding this strange coalition together. The Spanish Right had been swallowed up. Certain key leaders resisted, but they were easily eliminated. Manuel Hedilla, the last independent leader of the Falange, who insisted on the original Falangist principles, was shipped off to confinement in the Canary Islands. Fal Conde, the Carlist leader, who would not participate in the Falangist-Carlist fusion, was sometimes kept under house arrest. The rank and file, however, forgot all these difficulties and accepted the National Front of *franquismo* as the most adequate compromise for the time being. Yet the success of Franco's agglomeration would have been unthinkable save for the fact of Civil War.

Uncomfortable with ideology at the beginning, Franco avoided it more and more as the years passed. He liked to pose as the arbiter of all patriotic elements. So long as the Civil War could be kept alive for the next thirty years or so, there would be no danger of any burgeoning of an independent Right, nor would moderate conservatives have the courage to rebel. There was much murmuring and even some conspiracy inside the movement, but no real rightist opposition.

As for the Carlists, they opposed liberal monarchism much more than they opposed *franquismo*. They were therefore flattered and favored by the regime, which offered them much more than had any previous government. It could even be argued that *franquismo* was as close as one could ever get to Carlism in twentieth-century terms. After the farce of the 1947 action converting the dictatorship into a self-styled Regency, Franco nominally represented the prelude to monarchy. As an "arbiter" of the movement, he reflected the old Traditionalist desire for an unfettered authority which would nonetheless be respectful of the various divergent sectors of conservative interest. The Cortes installed in 1943 was undemocratic and corporative, thereby approximating to a considerable degree the century-old Carlist demand for a "traditional" Cortes. The author of the original Cortes decree was a Falangist who came from a Carlist family, and the Cortes president was himself a Carlist. As for clericalism, the 1938 culture and education laws, and the whole structure of Church-state relations, culminating in the 1951 Concordat, granted most Traditionalist demands in the religious sphere. Franco might even be termed an uncrowned Carlist king.

There is a definite historical logic to this situation, as the classic expression of reactionary extremism in Spain has obviously been Carlist Traditionalism. The fact that Traditionalism, as formulated in the first half of the nineteenth century, was in part a falsification of Spanish historical tradition is irrelevant in this connection. A reactionary program for modern Spain had inevitably had to create certain new ideas, even while imputing them to the evolution of the medieval past. The extreme slowness of social, economic, and cultural change in Spain, together with the fact that liberal ideas and political forms were introduced before such change had neared completion, created a problem with which Spanish society could not cope and made possible the extraordinary strength and staying power of the Carlist spirit. Even as the country was transformed, the rhythm was so halting and the new challenges so difficult that the bedrock of Carlism was solidified after each effort to dissolve it. In the meager, drowsy atmosphere of *franquismo*, the rank and file following of Carlism once more declined. The apoliticization toward which the regime aimed wilted enthusiasm, and after 1939 the lack of a truly authentic Carlist candidate for the throne splintered the movement altogether. Nonetheless, the importance of Carlism as a conditioning factor in the reactions of Spanish conservatives under stress is clearly much greater than the actual numerical following of Carlism in the twentieth century would indicate.

On the other hand, as is evidenced by failure of Falangism to win genuine dominance, it is clear that the more dynamic, or revolutionary, expression of the twentieth-century Right, usually termed fascism, has enjoyed less success. The same factors that, for long, perpetuated Carlism, Integrism, and conservative oligarchy and hindered the development of true liberalism also impeded the growth of a vigorous fascism. The timidity of the Spanish middle classes, and their aversion to any forceful confrontation with modern problems, helped make a genuine national revolution impossible. The Falangists did make one major attempt, in 1956, to reorganize the structure of the Spanish state, their goal being to institutionalize the dominance of a Falangist oligarchy. This failed completely, because of the opposition of the army and Church hierarchy, and the disinclination of Franco himself.

The only new expression of the Right to appear in Spain during the years of the Franco regime has been the secret Catholic secular institute, Opus Dei. First organized by an Aragonese priest in 1939, Opus Dei began to achieve prominence only after the Civil War. It is not a regular clerical order, for most of its members have careers in the secular world, and some are married. The institute defines itself as an "association of exclusively religious character," and claims to have no specific political orientation whatever beyond general conformity to Catholic theological criteria. In practice, however, the goal of Opus seems to be the dominance of

Catholicism in secular as well as religious affairs, with special attention to economic life, education, and politics. By the 1950's, the order had attracted a highly influential elite membership that controlled several aspects of Spanish economic affairs, was achieving remarkable power over university teaching positions, and after 1957 held several seats in Franco's cabinet.

Judging by the publications of its most articulate members, the political philosophy of Opus Dei tends to be elitist and reactionary. The institute's Spanish university, the Estudio General de Navarra, is located in Pamplona, the geographical center of Carlist clericalism. However, the political techniques in which it shows interest are often modern and sophisticated. Ideally, Opus theorists propose a corporative monarchy with limited oligarchical representation. The leading Opus intellectuals do not condemn all democracies or representative constitutional governments in the abstract, but hold that such forms are only desirable in nations with an extremely strong institutional structure, capable of guaranteeing order and stability, together with the dominance of "natural elites" of religious and social leadership. In practice, the Opus chiefs show a certain bent for technocracy, emphasizing as they do the control of money and intellect.

Opus Dei is not per se a political movement, but a religious and social organization. As such, it cannot be simply compared with either Carlism or Falangism. The organizational tools with which it would hope to see state and society maintained draw on aspects of both prior political movements but also add new ingredients. Opus accepts the theocratic bent and the stress on oligarchic corporative monarchy that is reminiscent of Carlism, but it also accepts some of the more limited aspects of the Falangist social program, such as the notion of a structure of national syndicalism. However, the attempt to organize and use the existing major capitalist interests, together with the strong emphasis on education and intellectual influence, are unique. Because of the hybrid nature of Opus Dei, and the relatively recent date of its rise, no very definite conclusions about it can be reached. It would seem unlikely, however, that Opus, which disapproves of the opportunism and incompleteness of the Franco regime, will become more than an influential pressure group, though it may have considerable voice in the evolution of the Right.

The fundamental tendency of rightist forces in nineteenth- and twentieth-century Spain has been reactionary. The violence with which the Traditionalist idea was wielded and the exaggeration of its expression might be termed "radical" and were, in a sense, novelties, although this refers more to the degree to which such principles were exploited than to their basic substance.

It has been seen that Falangism, however, contained genuine elements of nationalist revolution and so aspired to a different dimension of extremism. Three of the radical rightist aspects of the Falange's program were adopted by the Franco regime: emphasis on centralized dictatorship; demagogic employment of modern propaganda techniques, especially with regard to nationalism and national institutions; and the idea of corporatist-syndicalist social reform. Only the first of these was thoroughly implemented, however, and the third has been largely slighted. Since Franco's military dictatorship soon became a fundamentally bureaucratic system, indifference to ideology was built into it, making the subordination of revolutionary Falangism almost unavoidable. Just as the regime eventually renounced any genuine aspiration to totalitarianism, so it rejected total identification with any radical programmatic ideology. The goal, instead, became a compromise blending the modern Right, clerical reaction, and potentially progressive features of a bureaucratic pseudo technocracy.

SUGGESTED READING

The conflict of political extremes at the end of the eighteenth century has been studied in CARLOS CORONA's *Revolución y reacción en el reinado de Carlos IV* (Madrid: 1958). FEDERICO SUÁREZ VERDAGUER has provided the clearest explanation of the origin of the Carlist position in *La Crisis política del antigno régimen en Espana* (Madrid: 1950), although his account is somewhat biased. The same interpretation is made even more precise in SUÁREZ' *Conservadores, innovadores y restauradores en las postrimerías del antiguo régimen* (Pamplona: 1955).

The massive thirty-volume *Historia del Tradicionalismo español* (Seville: 1941–1958), MELCHOR FERRER, ed., is not a history of Carlism but rather an enormous anthology of pro-Carlist accounts of episodes in that movement's history. ROMAN OYARZUN, *Historia del Carlismo* (Madrid: 1939), gives the nearest approximation to a history of Carlism, though it is quite one sided. FERRER'S *Breve historia del legitismo español* (Madrid: 1958) is but a chronological synopsis. On the other hand, VINCENTE MARRERO'S *El Tradicionalismo español del siglo XIX* (Madrid: 1955) is a useful collection of speeches and writings.

Donoso Cortés, his ideology and influence, have been studied by EDMUND SCHRAMM (Hamburg: 1935), CARL SCHMITT (Hamburg: 1940), and DIETMAR WESTERMEYER (Munster: 1940). MELCHOR FERRER, ed., *Los Escritos políticos de Carlos VII* (Madrid: 1957), explains the position of the Carlist pretender of the last third of the nineteenth century. There is a biography by the CONDE DE RODEZNO: *Carlos VII, duque de Madrid* (Madrid: 1932). JOHN N. SCHUMACHER, S.J., "Integrism," in *The Catholic Historical Review*, XLVIII (Oct., 1962), 343–364, is an excellent essay. Also, the *Obras completas* of JUAN VAZQUEZ DE MELLA Y FANJUL have recently been republished (Madrid: 1961).

For the background and development of the regionalist movements, see JAIME VICENS VIVES' superb general study, *Cataluña en el siglo XIX* (Madrid: 1961), and the compilations by MAXIMIANO GARCIA VENERO, *Historia del nacionalismo catalan* (Madrid: 1944) and *Historia del nacionalismo vasco* (Madrid: 1945).

There is no adequate study of Antonio Maura. The least unsatisfactory biography is DIEGO SEVILLA ANDRÉS' *Antonio Maura* (Barcelona: 1954). Maura's speeches and essays are collected in *Trienta y cinco anos de vida pública* (Madrid: 1953). The "Maurist Youth" have scarcely been investigated at all, but JOSE GUTIÉRREZ RAVÉ'S *Yo fui un joven maurista* (Madrid: 1946) is the account of a participant.

The dearth of published material on the Spanish Army and its affairs is almost absolute, but the problems of 1917 are somewhat clarified by the CONDE DE ROMANONES, *El Ejército y la política* (Madrid: 1920), and JOSÉ MARIA CAPO, *Las Juntas Militares de Defensa* (Havana: 1922).

The regime of General Miguel Primo de Rivera has received scant study. GABRIEL MAURA GAMAZO'S two-volume *Bosquejo histórico de la dictadura* (Madrid: 1930) remains the best general account. JULIÁN PERMARTÍN'S *Los Valores históricos de la Dictadura* (Madrid: 1929) is the principal apologium. DILLWYN F. RATCLIFF'S *Prelude to Franco* (New York: 1957) is a not completely satisfactory effort to study political aspects of the regime. The dictator himself is best revealed in JACINTO CAPELLA'S *La Verdad de Primo de Rivera* (Madrid: 1933).

SANTIAGO GALINDO HERRERO'S *Los Partidos monárquicos bajo la Segunda Republica* (Madrid: 1956) is very useful concerning the monarchist reaction after 1931. On *Acción Española*, there is an anthology by EUGENIO VEGAS LATAPIÉ (Madrid: 1940), as well as his *Escritos políticos* (Madrid: 1940). Vegas has also written *Las Ideas políticas de Calvo Sotelo* (Madrid: 1942).

The political doctrines of the founders of Falangism may be found in ONÉSIMO REDONDO ORTEGA, *Obras completas* (Valladolid: 1939), RAMIRO LEDESMA RAMOS, *¿Fascismo en España?* (Madrid: 1935) and *Discurso a las* *juventudes de España* (Madrid: 1935), and JOSÉ ANTONIO PRIMO DE RIVERA, *Obras completas* (Madrid: 1952). The movement as a whole has been studied in STANLEY G. PAYNE, *Falange* (Stanford: 1961). On the role of Carlism in the 1930's, see LUIS REDONDO and JUAN DE ZAVALA, *El Requeté* (Barcelona: 1957). General Franco's pronouncements during the formative period of his regime have been collected in *Palabras del Caudillo, 19 abril 1937–9 diciembre 1942* (Madrid: 1943).

The self-image of the leaders of Opus Dei may be found in two essays published in booklet form, FLORENTINO PÉREZ EMBID, *Mons. José María Escrivá de Balaguer y Albas* (Barcelona: 1961), and JULIÁN HERRANZ, *El Opus Dei* (Pamplona: 1962). More critical evaluations are given by MANUEL ORTUÑO, in *Cuadernos Americanos* (Jan.-Feb., 1963), and WILLIAM G. EBENSTEIN, *Church and State in Franco Spain* (Princeton: 1960).

Italy

SALVATORE SALADINO

The contrast between the old or "historical" Italian Right of the years of national unification and the new or Nationalist Right of the early twentieth century is seen most vividly in the personalities of some of the protagonists. The former was a parliamentary bloc best represented first by Cavour and later by Quintino Sella and Marco Minghetti, all devoted in varying degrees to political and economic liberalism as well as to moderate social conservatism; the latter, although ready to exploit the avenue to power offered by the parliamentary system, was contemptuous of it, and while it called itself a party it described itself as a movement, and personi-fied its ideology in the radical nationalist Enrico Corradini or the political sensualist Gabriele d'Annunzio. The political line which connects Corradini and d'Annunzio with fascism is not straight but it is nonetheless unmistakable. Only a gross distortion of the facts can make for a connection between the Old Right of Cavour and the New Right whose men and ideology eventually found a welcome place in the National Fascist party.

It has been contended that the new Italian Right, which achieved its early successes in the Libyan War and World War I and its greatest success with the advent of Fascism, was a reaction to the liberalization of Italy's political and social life. This is quite cor-rect and, although not the whole truth of the matter, it is a truth which establishes a key distinction between the Old Right and the

New. For, as hostile as a follower of the Cavourian Right may have been to the advanced liberalism of Italy's governments during the decade preceding World War I, his hostility did not easily move him to dispense with parliamentary government, advocate the abrogation of statutory rights, affirm the permanent and complete priority of the state over the individual—or, perhaps, even suggest a still higher priority of an elite class over the state itself.

The moderate conservatives of the Old Right were moderate in method and conservative in outlook. Cavour's political heirs revealed their moderation by accepting as pragmatically desirable the basic approach of early nineteenth-century liberalism, with its emphasis on individual rights and limitation of the power of the state. Their moderation was further evidenced by exclusion from their ranks—or, at best, unwilling toleration—of historically shipwrecked groups, such as supporters of royal absolutism and defenders of an inflexible social order. But, although not opposed to change—preferably the cautious and unhurried variety—the men of the Old Right were genuinely conservative in their reluctance to democratize the country's political institutions and in the jealous defense of their economically privileged position. Their moderation, which we have identified as a characteristic of their political practices, is thus seen as inseparable from their conservatism, for it was feared that socioeconomic privilege along class lines could not long survive a politically democratic state.

The position of the New Right reveals a similar practical inseparability of methods and outlook, but the similarity ends there. Such men as Corradini and d'Annunzio appeared to favor change for its own sake, as a function of their doctrine of "action," but also because change would mean moving away from the democratic institutions being erected by the governments of their own day. This hostility toward democracy would seem to establish a point of contact between the Old Right and the New. But the contact has no binding effect because the New Right was neither moderate nor conservative: not moderate because it had no effective scruples about the rights of the individual, the authority of the state, or moral limitations on political practices; not conservative because it was prepared to change all the basic institutions of the state in order to increase its power—which, in fact, meant the power of those who would wield the state's authority.

Power and its exercise were, then, the goals of the New Right; because, as some genuinely believed, power in their hands alone could redeem the nation from the depths into which individualistic liberalism was supposed to have plunged it, or because "action" is impossible without power, or because the exercise of power is the sole justification necessary for its possession. However acquired and however justified, the men of the New Right conceived the power they would exercise as enveloping the whole nation and the totality of each individual's existence. Those among them who felt the need to justify an exercise of such total power reasoned that the very totality of its application excluded it as a function of a party or a part of the nation; it had to be the expression of a movement which rose above all party distinctions, annulled them, and thus became one with the nation. This genuinely totalitarian conception of itself as a movement and not a party further distinguishes the New Right from its earlier namesake and establishes another fundamental difference between the two. The Old Right, although it sought to serve the entire nation, understood itself realistically as a party and as the expression of the views and interests of only part of the nation. Hence it was forced to conclude—and accepted the conclusion—that its exercise of the power of the state had necessarily to be limited, both in scope and in time. Limitation of the scope of its power while the party was in office made mandatory the acceptance of a fundamental statute; limitation of time obliged it to accept the principle of a periodic mandate and the consequent practice of periodic elections. Thus, the moderate Right was constitutionalist and parliamentarian in its commitment, while the New (or radical) Right, with its totalitarian conception of political power, would happily do without both effective fundamental statutes and parliamentary institutions.

Not bound by political traditions—although appeal to tradition as such was one of the many attractions it offered—the radical Right was supremely flexible in the methods it employed to reach a maximum audience. It made of opportunism not just a political convenience but the essential principle of its ideology; absolutely pragmatic in its approach, the whole of its ideology was identical with the sum of all the political expedients necessary for its acquisition of power in the nation and the expansion of the nation's power in the world. Hence, the radical Right found no difficulty in using all those devices and techniques of domestic politics developed by the parties of the democratic and socialist Left. Universal suffrage, mass organization, directing cadres of professional party functionaries, periodic congresses and popular assemblies with all the choreographic trappings necessary for the rousing of enthusiasm—these and other devices were employed by the radical Right in a fashion deemed unseemly and unnecessary by the men of the Old Right, whose somewhat aristocratic view of politics and their role in it prevented them from being more than a parliamentary bloc which, if not indifferent to mass support, was unwilling to adopt the techniques necessary to acquire it.

Further, although the Old Right was prepared, when necessary, to engage in political transactions with its opponents, it viewed these transactions as expedients of the moment to be abandoned at the earliest occasion. But the New Right was ready to accept support from any quarter, it had no qualms about adopting the views of groups as varied as unreconstructed royalists and revolutionary syndicalists and, in fact, would compromise on any point except its asserted mission to lead Italy from her state of international submissiveness to one of international primacy.

The question of precisely where Italy's destiny and greatness lay —in fruitful action promoting domestic order and prosperity or in venturesome activity leading to international preëminence—is the last major point to separate the Old Right from the new manifestation which claimed the word nationalist as exclusively its own, as if the party with which Cavour had led Italy to national unity had no rightful claim to it at all. True, the Right which we have variously defined as new, radical, or nationalist did not deny that Cavour's followers, as well as his opponents to the Left, had all played a worthy role in national unification. But the men of the new Right viewed their predecessors' achievement as only the first, if indispensable, step toward a greater nationalism which they accused the governments of the post-Cavourian period of either neglecting or positively obstructing. To this neglect or obstruction the New Right attributed the fact, almost universally admitted, that Italian political life between unification and the end of the nineteenth century was afflicted with a sense of disillusionment, anxiety, and even despair. Admitted with nearly equal unanimity is the other fact that the appearance of the New Right was in large part the consequence of a reaction against the prevalent disillusionment. In order, then, to understand how it happened that the New Right came to political prominence in Italy during the first two decades of the twentieth century, it is necessary to examine a number of developments during the preceding forty years, not with the intention of summarizing *all* the significant aspects of Italian life of the period, but only those that help in the examination of the growth of the malaise for which the New Right hoped to offer what it considered the only effective remedies: total unity within the nation and imperial greatness in the outside world.

With the completion of unification in 1870, it was said by persons high and low that the heroic phase of Italy's history had come to an end and that after the poetry of the Risorgimento there had come the prose of everyday existence. Benedetto Croce has remarked how vain it would have been to point out that the new prose could well be poetry, different from the former but no less beautiful. Whence, therefore, the almost immediate pessimism at the very moment of the much-longed-for success? It came in part from the fact that unification, so long sought, had come with unexpected speed, and this very speed left unreasoning doubts about its permanence or even its reality. It came in part because the final success had been accompanied by not always glorious military experiences—as at Custoza and Lissa during the war of 1866—by a veritable civil war in the south, and by humiliating public wrangles between the proponents of bold action and the ever present advocates of caution. It came, finally, because unification, once achieved, had broken the link that held together all the disparate forces and men of the Risorgimento. And this common bond—uniting in goal if not in means the Right and the Left, Cavour and Garibaldi, Ricasoli and Crispi—broke just when, unification completed, it was no longer feasible to deny that the kingdom's current domestic problems were fully as great as those already surmounted. As long as it had been possible to rally against a common external enemy, Austria, it had also been possible to focus all attention on matters of foreign policy and away from economic, social, and administrative problems. These were problems requiring a heroism and a concerted effort certainly as elevated and intense as that demonstrated against the traditional external enemy. But the internal enemy was not so readily identified and was even less readily attacked. For dealing with such problems as fiscal stability, relations with the Church, administrative reorganization of the previously separate states, and defense of the authority of the unitary state there was no traditional approach. Divided as they had been on *how* to unify Italy, the Right and its opponent, the Left, had been united at least in the common goal. They were far less united on other problems, not only on the means to be employed but also on the very nature of the problems facing them.

To the degree that any of the immediate postunification questions were met adequately, the merit belongs to Cavour's political heirs of the moderate or "historical" Right, who were in power with minor interruptions from 1861 to 1876. The solutions the moderate Right imposed on the young nation were so burdensome and severe in terms of taxation, tariffs, military service, and administrative rigidity, that many Italians, especially in the ill-favored southern regions, wondered whether unification had been achieved only to serve the demands of tax gatherers, customs officers, military policemen, and inflexible magistrates.

Certainly, unification was not the millenarian delivery the less sophisticated had expected it to be. Besides, there appeared little of the heroic or poetic or even necessary in the person of Quintino Sella, three times Finance Minister from 1862 to 1873, and reputed to be the most hated minister of his period. The hatred is understandable, if not justifiable. The almost obsessive quest for a balanced budget, which he deemed indispensable not only to fiscal stability but also to the moral and international respectability of the new and fragile state, led Sella to practice "ferocious" taxation and "economy to the bone." The picture of a tax accountant as the chief person of the state did not make for political popularity and Sella's lack of it, affecting the whole of the party to which he belonged, was one of the factors that led to the parliamentary and electoral defeat of the Right in 1876. Thereupon the deputies of the Left moved from the opposition to the ministerial benches. An era had ended, a new one was beginning—or so it was thought, both by those who viewed the change as a calamity and by those who saw in it either the delayed and final episode of Italy's Risorgimento or simply the installation of a milder and less vexing authority.

What was this Left that came into power in 1876? It was less of a party than the Right had been, even more lacking than the Right in cadres and nationwide political organization, and without a distinctive character other than a pronouncedly democratic or popular orientation. Its ranks included remnants of the "historical" Left—that democratic party that opposed Cavour's "historical" Right in the preunification Piedmontese parliament but did not challenge the institution of monarchy. The Left of 1876 included also those of Mazzini's followers who had never reconciled themselves to monarchy, as well as others who had abandoned their master in his republican intransigence but remained attached to his democratic principles. Garibaldi and his followers could find no place on the Right, which they considered too timid in foreign policy and too conservative in domestic policy, and so also chose the Left. Finally, political groups that had particular grievances against the policies of the Right—opponents of highly centralized administration, southern regionalists hostile to northern economic interests, and even some supporters of the ousted Bourbons—all sought refuge in the Left as the only effective political expression of their varied discontents. Clearly, the Left was even more heterogeneous than the Right, whence the despair on the part of many that the so-called "parliamentary revolution" of 1876 meant the further muddying of the country's political waters rather than the "clarity" to which all ostensibly aspired.

Certainly, the advent of the Left in 1876 did not produce political clarity. It could not be otherwise, if by clarity was meant two distinct political formations, one in power and the other in opposition, each the champion of a distinct party program. It has been asserted, and admitted, to the point of banality that after the completion of unification in 1870 the fundamental distinction between the historical Right and Left ceased to exist, and that what remained were two political groupings bearing the old labels, each kept together by traditional personal attachments and common antagonisms, but no longer divided one from the other by a real difference on how to achieve unification. True, our characterization of the old Right as moderate and conservative and of the Left as democratic would seem to suggest that such differences remained even after 1870; but these characterizations are generalizations, truer of the personal disposition of the men in the two respective parliamentary blocs than of their policies in power. One might suppose that after 1876 the governments of the Left would translate their democratic and even republican traditions into concrete acts, with vigorous opposition from the Right. This occurred only partially, and for a complex of reasons. First, once in power, the Left realized the intrinsic difficulty of radically reforming the nation's basic institutions without revolutionary commotions; second, many leaders of the Left found their earlier radicalism, convenient and easy while in opposition, much attenuated by the responsibilities of office; and, finally, the heterogeneous nature of the Left forced its leaders into all sorts of compromises, both with their own followers and even with members of the nominal opposition. The result was a moderation that brought the Left closer to the Right and that rendered less clear than ever the differences between the two parliamentary blocs. In fact, a noted spokesman for the Right, Silvio Spaventa, described the early governments of the Left as being the same of those of the Right, only worse. Another critic wrote: "The Right acted, the Left incited to action. There is the whole difference." The latter judgment is correct in the suggestion of a certain activist extravagance on the part of the Left but not correct if its author meant to imply that the Left was without accomplishment.

Modest and much slower paced than pleased those of its followers who were still attached to the revolutionary traditions of the Risorgimento, the governments of the Left did achieve a num-

ber of important reforms, such as compulsory elementary education, the abolition of the hated grist tax, a more democratic
electoral law, accident insurance for workers, and a uniform penal
code. These achievements were the work of moderates from both
camps and were made possible by a parliamentary phenomenon
known as transformism, which meant literally a transformation of
old parties into something new, but meant practically the obliteration of clear distinctions between the Right and the Left for the
sake of securing a parliamentary majority to support this or that
ministry. The success of the phenomenon was facilitated by the
realization, after 1876, that neither of the "historical" parties was
homogeneous enough to play its role in the classical conception of
parliamentary government. One party in power and another in
vigorous opposition may, in the abstract, be the ideal parliamentary
condition, but it was not practical for Italy in the nineteenth
century. The man who understood the reality of Italy's parliamentary situation was Agostino Depretis, who assumed the leadership of the Left in 1873 and carried it to electoral and parliamentary victory in 1876 with a "program of hope." Between 1876
and 1887 Depretis led eight governments for a total tenure of
nearly nine years; for the balance of those eleven years Italy was
led by Benedetto Cairoli, another man of the Left not in sympathy
with Depretis' rather too flexible or transformist views.

The practice of transformism came out into the open during the
electoral campaign of 1882 when Marco Minghetti, whose ministry
of the Right had been turned out of office in the "parliamentary
revolution" of 1876, announced his support of the moderate program presented by Depretis, the man who had replaced him in office. As a consequence, five leaders of the Left abandoned Depretis
and formed a "pentarchy" to lead the opposition against their
former colleague. There began a violent campaign against Depretis'
parliamentary practices, which were characterized as unscrupulous
and immoral, leading to the degeneration of parliamentary institutions, and vitiating the country's public and private life. Spokesmen from all sectors of the political spectrum joined in the campaign. The radical democrat Felice Cavallotti spoke of acrobatic
politics, of petty transactions and petty transformations, and of a

parliamentarism reduced to living by the day. Francesco Crispi, one of the pentarchs and formerly a republican, Mazzinian, and Garibaldian, as well as, in 1877, Depretis' Minister of the Interior, accused Depretis of making a "lie" of the parliamentary system because "for the despotism of a king there is substituted the despotism of a Minister." And some spokesmen of the "untransformed" Right wrote gravely of the need to restore to the king those prerogatives of which he had been deprived by a parliamentary oligarchy. The whole parliamentary system was subjected to an indictment that ranged from the carefully reasoned and highly intellectual work of Gaetano Mosca to the most atrocious libels of the scandalmongering press. One of the results of the campaign against real and alleged parliamentary corruption was the confirmation and dissemination of that sense of disillusionment which had seized the country during the first decade of unification and which the "parliamentary revolution" of 1876 had hardly dispelled.

Italy's failures, or marked lack of any great success, in foreign ventures further aggravated the sense of national weakness to which the parliamentary situation contributed. Political corruption and the absence of genuine political alternatives might be tolerable, argued the critics of transformism, if at least the governments of the period had achieved successes in foreign affairs. But what could be expected, said the same critics, when foreign policy was conducted by governments that, by preventing the formation of distinct and well-organized political parties, stunted the growth of an enlightened public opinion which could be a source of strength in negotiations with foreign powers? Besides, political leaders forever enmeshed in parliamentary manipulations were not given to bold and farsighted foreign policies. In truth, Italy's experience in foreign affairs had not been happy. An irreconcilable Papacy, which would not accept the guarantees offered it by the law of 1871 in compensation for the loss of its temporal domains, was a source of weakness in foreign as well as domestic affairs. This double weakness was a factor in Cairoli's policy of "clean hands" which prevented Italy from extracting any territorial gains in the Adriatic at the Congress of Berlin in 1878. Lack of adequate diplomatic and military preparation prevented Cairoli, again in power in 1881, from obstructing France's occupation of Tunisia, where the population of Italian origin far outnumbered the French. His government did not long survive this setback; it was accused of incompetence for having allowed the Adriatic to become an Austrian sea, and the Sicilian sea to become a French lake.

Italy's isolation, as proved by its failure at the Congress of Berlin and during the crisis with France over Tunisia, induced Cairoli's successor, Depretis, to enter into an alliance with Austria and Germany in 1882. But this Triple Alliance was viewed as an offense by all those Italians in whom anti-Austrian sentiments were strong as well as by those who saw the alliance with the two empires as a buttress for domestic conservatism. Although the Triple Alliance proved later to be an embarrassment for Italy, it did, at the time of its inception, end the country's international isolation and permit it to seek colonial consolation elsewhere for the loss of Tunisia. But, once again, fortune was unkind. Italy's search for a colonial future in areas adjacent to the Red Sea led to conflict with Ethiopia and resulted in the extermination of an Italian column of over five hundred men at Dogali in 1887. Depretis' government, brought down by news of this defeat, met the same fate as that of Cairoli in 1881 when France occupied Tunisia; and although Depretis was reconfirmed in office after a prolonged crisis, death brought an end to his career in July 1887. The way was now open for Francesco Crispi, who formed a new government, keeping the Interior and Foreign Ministries for himself. The prosaic age of Sella, Depretis, and Cairoli was over; a decade of action, if not of poetry, was about to begin and, once again, a new Italy seemed to emerge. But its future was not clear.

The growing sense of dissatisfaction with uninspired domestic policies and lackluster foreign ventures made many feel and some even say: Did we and our fathers fight and suffer so much for unity and independence that Italy might come to this? Where lies the cure for our ills?

Toward the end of the century, two men with distinct and opposing remedies appeared—Francesco Crispi and Giovanni Giolitti; and although their specifics proved ineffective at first, both men set precedents that helped determine Italy's history until the advent of fascism. The contrast between Crispi and Giolitti could not have been more marked, despite the fact that both were men of the Left. When Crispi formed his first ministry in 1887 he was sixty-eight years old and had had more than forty years of political activity which included a distinguished role in the unification of the country. His earlier fierce republicanism had given way to an ardent attachment to the monarchy; the radical democracy of his youth now revealed a strong authoritarian bent; and although he had been a revolutionary conspirator while a follower of Mazzini and Garibaldi, the responsibility of power convinced him that martial law was the most effective way of dealing with radical movements of social protest. His parliamentary manner was abrupt, his speeches fiery, and his personal relations with political colleagues rarely easy.

If boldness best characterized Crispi's political and private life, caution, patience, sobriety, and meticulous attention to detail are the terms most frequently used to describe Giolitti. The latter had no revolutionary past, had played no role in Italy's unification, and had risen to political prominence along the administrative ladder. Although he sat at Left-Center when he entered parliament in 1882 as one of Depretis' supporters, Giolitti's ties with men of the moderate Right had been close and personal. The paths of the Sicilian Crispi and the Piedmontese Giolitti were to cross in a few years, when, having discredited Crispi's Finance and Treasury Minister, Giolitti took his place at the Treasury in 1889. The personal animosity that developed from the circumstances of his rise to office accentuated the fundamental and radical divergence between the two men's points of view. Crispi's adventurous foreign policies and authoritarian methods, although a failure, were to become a source of inspiration for the Nationalist Right, which was always to claim him as its great precursor; Giolitti's insistence on socioeconomic improvement, on political compromise designed to domesticate political radicals, and on caution in foreign as in financial affairs earned him the opposition of irreconcilable extremists from both the Right and the Left. And where Giolitti's approach was the one that triumphed during the decade preceding World War I, Crispi's

self-proclaimed political heirs had their victory during the war and
the four years that followed.

What were Crispi's policies or what national needs did he attempt to meet during the nine years, between 1887 and 1896,
when he towered over Italy's political life? An opposition speech
of 1885 in parliament synthesized his major views and expressed
the source of his appeal:

Italy is a young kingdom, a young state. The seven peoples which remained
divided until a few years ago were old, decrepit, corrupted by priest and
policeman, and you, Left and Right, have not known how to educate them
in twenty-five years. . . . To the old vices and corruptions you have added
new ones which frequently are inherent in the false practice of constitutional government.

The remedy? "Place there [on the ministerial bench] an energetic
man . . . a man with a clear program . . . and then, gentlemen,
you may be able to hope that these seven peoples, decrepit and
corrupted by despotism, may become serious and virtuous peoples."

Crispi was not indifferent to the charges of authoritarianism
and megalomania frequently occasioned by this speech and others
like it. He defended himself by explaining that for him liberty
meant "respect for individual rights in harmony with the rights
of the nation"; and that, although in extraordinary circumstances
arbitrary power might be entrusted to one man, this power could
be exercised with one aim only—to return as quickly as possible to
normal circumstances. The essence of Crispi's political thought and
the tragedy of his political life are all there: his willingness to assume arbitrary power, his realization that such power could be
justified only by extraordinary circumstances and on condition that
it end as quickly as possible, and his practical inability to determine
the circumstances for its proper assumption and its speedy re-
linquishment.

The extraordinary circumstances that developed during his ten-
ures of office (1887–1891 and 1894–1896) were largely of his own
making. Early in 1888 Crispi's deep-rooted antipathy for France
and preference for Bismarck's Germany became a factor in a four

years' tariff war with France which proved economically disastrous for Italy. Relations with France were made even worse by competing interests in Tunisia and the Red Sea area, leading to new charges, most commonly from the Right, that Crispi's megalomania was injuring the country's real interests. The accusation touched Crispi in a tender spot, as he revealed in a speech of October, 1889, in defense of his expansionist foreign policy. He argued that his was not a personal megalomania but one on behalf of the nation: "The nation, just as an individual's body, needs air in which to breathe." But Crispi's appeal to imperialism as a nationally unifying force was not enough to disarm his opponents, of either Left or Right. And, in fact, it was the Right, stung by Crispi's accusation that it had followed a "servile" foreign policy while in power, that brought about Crispi's fall in 1891, after three and a half years in office.

Crispi's strong manner had failed to redeem Italy; it was now the turn of less adventurous men. The first of these was the Marquis Antonio di Rudinì who, as leader of the Right, was designated by parliamentary practice to assume office. Di Rudinì chose Baron Giovanni Nicotera, an old radical of the Left, as his leading colleague at the Ministry of the Interior, and this choice confirmed the fact that transformism was not a peculiarity that afflicted only governments of the Left but a necessity dictated by parliamentary realities. Indeed, it can be said that di Rudinì's ministry, by its acceptance of transformism, formally recognized that by 1891 all that existed in parliament were transient formations divided more by the personality of their leaders than by genuine programmatic differences. But what was true of parliament was no longer true of the country at large. Outside parliament a new political consciousness was developing, a consciousness that found expression in two directions: one, socialism, that looked toward a radical social transformation as the only way to solve basic domestic problems; the other, expansionist nationalism, that aimed at an equally radical transformation by transposing the solution of domestic problems to the international plane. Crispi misunderstood socialist agitation as being merely an act of conspirators against the authority of the state rather than what it actually was, an exasperated re-action to grave social inequities; he understood better the desire for national pride and self-assertion.

Di Rudinì's ministry appeared to understand neither phenome-non and so, although it did attempt to spare the country's economy and relieve social distress by withdrawing from Crispi's adventur-ous position in foreign affairs, it could offer only Nicotera's repres-sive methods against continuing social unrest. This failure by the ministry to understand the nature of the country's real sentiments did not escape parliament which, charging weakness, dismissed di Rudinì within little more than a year of his assumption of office. The time had come for a second anti-Crispian, Giovanni Giolitti, to try his hand at putting order into the affairs of state.

The program with which Giolitti presented his government to the Chamber revealed that he had made his choice in favor of domestic social progress and against international greatness. This helps to explain the hostile judgment Crispi gave when asked by King Umberto I for his opinion of Giolitti. In 1892, however, Giolitti proved unable to develop his program, which was funda-mentally the one he carried out during the decade before 1914 when he became undisputed master of Italy. The program of 1892 was the rudimentary expression of the view that, before Italy's political life could be transformed into more orderly processes, there had to come a progressive transformation of social and eco-nomic institutions. Giolitti reasoned that if this transformation were not facilitated and encouraged along peaceful lines by the positive action of the governing classes, it would come by means of social revolution. Consequently, adventures in foreign policy were to be avoided at all costs because Italy had not the material and moral resources to be prosperous and stable at home as well as great abroad. It was, as the nationalists were later to say in derision, the concept of a "little Italy," petit bourgeois, and "stay-at-home" in foreign affairs, the very concept Crispi attributed to the Old Right when he accused its representatives of servility. For Crispi, no na-tion could aspire to greatness unless it transcended its material limitations by an act of heroic will, unless it achieved by boldness

what it would never be given. Thus thought Crispi, as did the men
of the New Right who were to lionize him and despise Giolitti.

Giolitti failed to realize his program during his first ministry
because of conservative displeasure with his refusal to engage in
"blind repression" of the violent agitation of peasants' and workers'
leagues in Sicily, and because of grave accusations leveled against
him in 1893 for his alleged responsibility and involvement in a
massive bank scandal. King and country once again turned to
Crispi, who now gave himself over to the execution of those two
policies the New Right was soon to make its own: the elimination
by force of all divisive elements in the nation, and the raising of
the nation to international greatness by daring colonial ventures.
The most divisive of all the elements in the country was deemed to
be the Socialists, precisely because of their international, antinational Marxist creed. By the time of Crispi's second period in power,
1893–1896, socialism in Italy had moved far ahead in both numbers and influence from the days when it had first been introduced
to the country in the 1860's, largely through the efforts of the
Russian anarchist, Michael Bakunin. Bakunin's struggles with Marx
and Mazzini's hostility toward both of them delayed the development of a cohesive socialist movement until the early 1890's. By
then all the economic and social problems left unresolved by unification—which was preëminently a political achievement—were
aggravated by new ones resulting from rapid industrialization and
urbanization. Socialism offered a solution to all these problems, and
when a Marxist Socialist party was formed, in 1892, it soon proclaimed as its program the collectivization of economic life by
means of the class struggle and revolution.

The depth and extent of socialism's appeal in Italy at the end of
the century have been described by Benedetto Croce—himself attracted to Marxism in his youth but, not long after, one of its
most acute critics—as winning over "all, or almost all, the flower
of the younger generation . . . to remain uninfluenced by and
indifferent to it, or to assume, as some did, an attitude of unreasoning hostility toward it, was a sure sign of inferiority." Croce's
judgment on the early effects of socialism was that it raised Italy

"from the depths into which she had sunk after the exhaustion of the spiritual force of the Risorgimento." But this spiritual force was still strong in Crispi, who was not of the new generation and was not only unsympathetic to socialism but appeared not even to understand the reasons for its existence and the sources of its growing strength. Crispi did not realize that socialism was succeeding where Mazzini and Garibaldi had failed—in rousing popular enthusiasm and then channeling it as a propulsive force by means of well-directed mass organization. The facts of Italy's changing economic and social life taught the Socialists a lesson that had escaped Crispi's generation, the Left as well as the Right; but it was a lesson the New Right would learn well, not only from the successful example offered by the Socialists but also from the New Right's realization that in order to fight socialism as an antinational force it would have to adopt its opponent's methods.

Crispi's methods of fighting socialism and the other parties of the extreme Left revealed that he mistook a symptom for the disease. The real disease was the grave economic dislocation occasioned by an agricultural crisis in the south and rapid industrialization in the north. Socialist agitation was largely an effect of, or reaction to, the dislocation and not its principal cause. Determined to treat the symptom, Crispi used repressive measures, including martial law and mass arrests—not only of Socialists and Anarchists, but of less radical opponents as well. Supported in parliament by a strong majority whose election he assured in 1895 by adept manipulations reminiscent of his old opponent Depretis, Crispi proceeded to embark on a great colonial venture in Ethiopia, partly to distract public opinion from domestic problems and partly in pursuit of his fixed policy of imperial greatness. The venture came to a disastrous end at the battle of Adowa in March, 1896, a defeat far greater in national humiliation than in the actual losses of about eight thousand men. Four days later Crispi fell from office, never to return; and for a decade and a half little was heard of colonial expansion from the ministerial bench in the Chamber. But while parliament was for once nearly unanimous in its condemnation of Crispi, and from the country there rose the cry "Away from Africa," one man, Enrico Corradini, stood in Crispi's defense and, from the experience of personal shame at Italy's humiliation, was able to extract the spiritual energy that led to the beginning of the Nationalist movement.

Determined to convert the shame of Adowa into a source of pride, Corradini put aside Crispi's failure at imperial greatness and, in a speech on March 1, 1914, commemorating the anniversary of the defeat at Adowa, emphasized what to him had been the far more important fact even eighteen years earlier, that at least Crispi had tried: "He had against him all parties, the one whence he came as well as those he had always fought; all the Italy of little men rose against the hero, the only true Italian, who was the personification of the whole country and its aggrandizement."

Corradini was correct in his recollection of the general hostility to Crispi in 1896 but the lapse of eighteen years had much attenuated the spiritual disorientation he had sensed then. Another contributor to Nationalist thought, Scipio Sighele, expressed more directly the sense of disillusionment and self-deprecation that afflicted Italy in the 1890's. From the fact of Italy's defeat in Africa, Spain's defeat in its war with the United States, and France's agonizing crisis during the Dreyfus affair, Sighele and others constructed a theory of old races and new ones, placing Italy and the other Latin peoples among the former. Sighele later abandoned this theory, which he himself described as simplistic, but he never abandoned his hostility toward parliamentary institutions and representative government in general. Sighele's work, *Contro il parlamentarismo*, was published in 1895, two years after Ruggero Bonghi's article, "The Office of the Prince in a Free State," in which the notable spokesman of the Old Right insisted that the prince, in his office of moral superintendence, need not heed the wishes of parliament's majority in the choice of ministers. Two years after Sighele's work, Sidney Sonnino, a moderate conservative, wrote his famous article, "Torniamo allo Statuto" ("Let us return to the Constitution"), in which he repeated substantially Bonghi's position, arguing that the only way to end the misery of the political transactions occasioned by ministerial dependence on parliamentary majorities was to make the government responsible to the king alone.

It would appear that the crisis of the 1890's, manifested in various scandals, in military defeat, and in grave domestic unrest, not only shook the nation's confidence in itself and its form of government but also led to a significant political realignment. The nature of this realignment became clear during the four years after Crispi's fall in 1896. Right and Left agreed on the need to liquidate the African venture, the former largely because of the fiscal burden of colonial enterprises and the latter because of democratic sentiment, domestic social concerns, or preoccupation with the unredeemed (irredent) Italian-speaking provinces still in the Austrian empire.

There was far less agreement on the solution of pressing social questions. Giolitti's program included not only fiscal economies but also extensive social reforms, such as progressive income tax, governmental neutrality in conflicts between labor and employers, and wide latitude in the enjoyment of civil liberties. But the ministries that governed Italy between Crispi's fall and 1900 appeared incapable of avoiding Crispi's error of employing repressive methods in the face of mounting popular agitation. These ministries, led by Di Rudinì between 1896 to 1898 and by General Luigi Pelloux from 1898 to 1900, were predominantly of the Right and seemed, by their methods, to confirm the charge of authoritarianism which the liberal Left as well as the Radicals, Socialists, and Republicans of the extreme Left leveled against them. Di Rudinì's Ministry did not long survive the excesses of its repressive measures, and when the new government was entrusted to General Pelloux, who had a liberal past—he sat at the Left on entering parliament in 1880—it seemed that an effort would be made to follow a policy of reconciliation with the parties representing the discontented masses of the country. But in 1899 Pelloux reorganized his ministry in a decidedly conservative direction and, allegedly under the influence of Sonnino, "the grey eminence," Pelloux appeared about to alter the basic institutions of parliament. Unsure of parliamentary support, he proposed to restrict freedom of the press, association, and public assembly by means of a royal decree. Acceptance of this practice, especially if it acquired the force of a constitutional precedent, could have meant the beginning of the end of parliamentary government.

The first to respond actively against the decree law was the extreme Left, the *Estrema*, which engaged in systematic parliamentary obstructionism. The government retaliated by proroguing parliament for three months and arresting some of its more outspoken opponents. It could (or chose) not to retaliate against a judgment of the High Court of Cassation which annulled the decree law, and was thereby forced to present its restrictive measures to parliament for approval. The extreme Left resumed its obstructionism, comforted by the support of poet-novelist-dramatist Gabriele d'Annunzio, who had entered parliament in 1897 in order to "persuade the world that I am able in all things." In a dramatic gesture d'Annunzio had risen from the benches of the extreme Right where he had previously sat and walked across the Chamber to the extreme Left. Several days before he had said in a private gathering: "I know that on one side there are many dead men who shout and on the other side a few who are alive and eloquent. As a man of intellect I choose life."

The extreme Left received more adequate support from the moderate Left whose leaders, Giolitti and Zanardelli, aroused by the high-handedness of the Speaker in curbing obstructionism, declared the proceedings null and void and abandoned the Chamber, as did the *Estrema*. There were shouts of "Down with the king" and "Long live the Constituent Assembly," the latter an echo of the extreme Left's long-standing demand for a special convocation to alter the *Statuto* of 1848 and perhaps abolish the monarchy. Had Pelloux and Sonnino been as reactionary and authoritarian as their opponents charged, the absence of the opposition from the Chamber should have prompted them to carry out a bold stroke; instead, they decided to put the issue to the voters. The electorate rebuffed the government by doubling the Socialist deputation (from sixteen to thirty-two) and by raising the total opposition strength to over two hundred. Pelloux still had a majority but it was so slender that, after an unsuccessful attempt at compromise with the opposition, he chose to resign in June, 1900.

Thus came to an end what many have interpreted as the gravest constitutional crisis of the Italian state before Fascism. Pelloux's and Sonnino's apparent attempt to restore to the crown the prerogatives reserved to it in the *Statuto,* prerogatives that half a century of parliamentary tradition had greatly weakened, produced a number of consequences. The behavior of the Right was stigmatized as authoritarian and unconstitutional, a characterization not completely warranted because, as Croce has maintained, Pelloux's supporters were not true but "degenerate heirs" of the Old Right, and because they did not, after all, make a determined effort to undo the country's liberal institutions. Appealing to the electorate instead of carrying out a coup d'etat may have been a grave error of judgment, but it does suggest that Pelloux and Sonnino recoiled from an obviously authoritarian course. Criticized by their enemies on the Left for having tried to alter traditional parliamentary practices and by the true authoritarians for having failed in their effort out of timidity, the leaders of the Old Right began the twentieth century with a reputation that, although not completely deserved, worked against their return to power until the outbreak of World War I.

The decline in the Right's prestige involved the monarchy as well. As a soldier, General Pelloux was felt to be especially susceptible to royal pressure, because of the soldier's oath to the king and the army's traditional attachment to the dynasty. The monarchy's involvement in the crisis was heightened by the fact that Sonnino was an outspoken champion of the restoration of royal prerogatives in the choice of ministers, the dissolution of parliament, and the issuance of decrees while parliament was not in session. Had it not been for Umberto I's assassination in 1900, soon after the fall of Pelloux, Italy might have experienced a revival of republicanism as a reaction to Umberto's conservatism and to the efforts Sonnino and others had made to revitalize royal power. The accession of Victor Emmanuel III, who showed a preference for the moderate Left, relieved the monarchy of the burden of the former king's associations. Victor Emmanuel's turn to the Left may have been dictated less by personal conviction than political necessity, and the political situation after 1900 pointed to a revival of the fortunes of the groups on the Left.

This revival had become evident during the last few months of Pelloux's ministry, when the moderate or liberal Left rallied with the Radicals, Republicans, and Socialists of the *Estrema* to obstruct Pelloux's revision of parliamentary practices. With all the parties at the left of the Chamber thus joined in opposition to a ministry dominated by men of the Right, it seemed for a moment as if the much desired political clarity of a two-party system had at last been achieved in a fundamental debate concerning the country's institutions. The clarity was brief, partly because much of the Right had no heart for the antiliberal role with which the Pelloux ministry seemed to have burdened it and partly because the future was destined to be with Giolitti who, as a sophisticated practitioner of transformism, meant to avoid the peril of a political polarization into irreconcilable extremes.

Giolitti's return to power as Minister of the Interior in Giuseppe Zanardelli's government of 1901–1903 marked the beginning of his sway over Italian politics until 1914; it also marked the abandonment of Crispi's colonial imperialism, as well as his policy of domestic repression, which Di Rudinì and Pelloux had continued. Giolittian Italy was not to be great, but it was to be more prosperous, more egalitarian, and freer. All those who still yearned for greatness and were prepared to sacrifice liberty for the sake of totalitarian unity as an avenue to greatness saw in Giolitti's Italy the antithesis of their desires. Out of their disaffection were to arise the first coherent manifestations of the New Right.

Disoriented by their experiences during the Pelloux period, the heirs of the Old Right either engaged in ineffectual opposition to Giolitti or, as did Sonnino in 1903, came around to accepting Giolitti's judgment that the most effective way of preserving the essence of liberal institutions was to convince the masses that the state was not their enemy but "the impartial guardian of all classes of citizens." This conversion of part of the Old Right to the views of a man of the moderate Left was not without precedent in the nineteenth century but it did mean that a programmatic or ideological opposition from the Old Right to Giolitti's views was no longer politically meaningful. Most of Italy now seemed to have moved to the Left, and into the vacuum that resulted on the Right there moved a new formation, with Enrico Corradini as its principal spokesman.

Corradini had become politically conscious during the days of Italy's defeat in 1896, an event which shocked him out of his individualistic theories of art and esthetics into a concern for the greater human entity, the nation. He had experienced the influence of d'Annunzio, then the leading representative in Italy of art for art's sake, and the champion of the artist's prerogative to unrestricted freedom; but after Adowa Corradini moved away from the d'Annunzian preoccupation with physical and intellectual sensuality and converted the latter's literary elitism into a political position. This conversion was best expressed by Corradini in his drama, *Giulio Cesare* (1902), where he glorified Caesar as the veritable personification of the genius of the Roman empire. This identification of national greatness with one man—an empire builder—became a fixed point in Corradini's thought and helps explain his admiration for Crispi, a would-be empire builder. It also helps explain Corradini's hostility toward Giolitti, who replaced Zanardelli as prime minister in 1903, the same year Corradini founded the periodical *Il Regno,* in which most of the basic doctrines of the Nationalist movement were first expressed.

The coincidence of the two events is far from accidental. Corradini's explanation of why he founded *Il Regno* was that he and his collaborators wished to be "a voice among all those who are grieved and indignant with the baseness of the present national situation. And above all against [the baseness of] ignoble socialism . . . and to vituperate those who seem to be determined to be beaten: to vituperate the Italian bourgeoisie which directs and governs the country." Corradini's reference was unmistakably to Giolitti's policy of promoting the cause of the lower classes and of inducing the Socialists to collaborate with the government in the furthering of this cause. Giolitti's success with the Socialists was measured by the fact that in 1901 and 1902 they supported Zanardelli's ministry precisely because its domestic policy, shaped by Giolitti as

Minister of the Interior, was intended to facilitate the peaceful expansion of the labor-union movement. Socialist support of a bourgeois ministry aroused the ire not only of Corradini, who viewed it as a sign of bourgeois weakness, but also of the intransigents or militants in the socialist movement, who feared a weakening of revolutionary ardor. This was exactly what Giolitti intended, and he could draw comfort from the fact that at the Socialist party congress of 1902 the evolutionary, reformist, or moderate wing of the party triumphed over the extremists. Thus Giolitti was faced with opposition from the extremists in both camps: from Corradini and his followers because Giolitti's policies were interpreted as a betrayal, out of weakness, of the interests of the bourgeoisie; from the revolutionary Socialists because his success in "domesticating" their moderate colleagues was viewed as leading to a betrayal of the essence of socialism. Out of this common hostility to the Giolittian program of class reconciliation by mutual concessions there emerged the first signs of what in the future would become a link or passageway that would unite the extreme Right and extreme Left in a common front against the moderates in the two classes of Italian society. This linkage or union of the two extremes became evident on the eve of Italy's intervention in World War I and after the war it was a determining factor in Fascism's advent to power. But in 1903 it was still only a possibility and not a likelihood because, as Corradini publicly recognized in a work of 1914, the Nationalist doctrines of *Il Regno* were in a state of "indecision and confusion." In 1903 Nationalism had the appearance of an exasperated bourgeois reaction against both the growing power of the socialist movement and the apparent complicity of "bourgeois" governments in its growth. But the germs of most of Nationalism's future doctrines are easily found in the issues of *Il Regno* during its less than three years of existence, and these make amply clear that Nationalism was something more than a passing variant of bourgeois conservatism.

Corradini's principal associates at *Il Regno* were the twenty-two-year-old Giovanni Papini, editor-in-chief, and the even younger Giuseppe Prezzolini. Prezzolini explained *Il Regno's* short life as owing to the contrast in temperament and ideas between Corradini and his young collaborators. The former was still d'Annunzian in his "heroic" and esthetic preoccupations, full of "noisy recollections of imperial Rome" and of "vague conceptions of the strength of the 'race,' of 'destiny,' of 'Latinity' "; the latter were more concerned with the practical, economic, and social aspects of Nationalism. *Il Regno* was not only antisocialist but antidemocratic as well; it was systematically antiparliamentarian, which gave it a sense of affinity with revolutionary Socialists and Syndicalists. It asserted the moral value of social struggle, of war, and of imperial conquest. *Il Regno*'s articles emphasized the importance of foreign over domestic affairs; in the latter sphere they exalted the growing industrial and commercial expansion of Italy as a source of national pride and pointed to large-scale emigration as a drain on the nation's human and spiritual resources. Above all other men in Italy's recent past they glorified Crispi: "The last great statesman Italy has had . . . a statesman in the heroic sense of the word." In short, the formative Nationalism of the *Il Regno* period was a denunciation of all the qualities characteristic of "bourgeois" society in the pejorative sense of the word: pacifist, unheroic, cautious, and practical, which were precisely the qualities held up to scorn by the d'Annunzian vogue of heroic daring and heroic pleasure.

The influence exercised by d'Annunzianism—generally characterized as a manifestation of the end-of-the-century dissatisfaction with bourgeois or prosaic society—was especially great on the younger generation, particularly that part of it not attracted to socialism. As long as socialism had the heroic character of a movement of a few noble elect struggling against conservative forces and institutions, it possessed a fascination much of the youth of Italy did not resist. But during the first decade of the twentieth century socialism appeared to be on the way to success. It moderated its earlier revolutionary program, became parliamentarian, and acquired a mass following and an organizational bureaucracy, thus losing its appeal to more adventurous spirits, who abandoned it either for revolutionary syndicalism or an equally revolutionary nationalism.

Several articles by the youthful Prezzolini in *Il Regno* of 1903–

1904, acknowledging the influence of Gaetano Mosca and Vilfredo Pareto, referred to the Socialist leadership of the day as an "aristocracy of brigands" composed of "human refuse," and to socialism itself as "an industry, with its careers, bureaucracy, and salaries." Nor was Prezzolini more charitable to much of the bourgeoisie. He divided Italy into two parts, one that acted and worked, and another that chattered and idled; and in the latter category the most noxious portion was the "governmental [parliamentary] bourgeoisie, which is the falsest of aristocracies because it is the most useless." Only the industrial bourgeoisie earned the admiration of both Prezzolini and Papini, the latter explaining that, in spite of governmental obstacles and the threat of strikes, it was in the process of converting Italy into a great industrial state, having understood that "the surest way to save itself from socialism is to augment the wealth." To Papini this forward-looking economic expansion was the essence of Italy's "new nationalism," far superior to the poetic and philosophical nationalism of the Risorgimento, which looked to the past for greatness. His reference to "literary and ideological nationalism, made of words and memories," was an implied criticism of Corradini. Papini then addressed himself to d'Annunzio in a fashion obliquely critical also of the poet: "And may heaven grant, O poet, that the fatherland we love become great once again not only with the plow and the prow but also with the thought which creates empires of dreams and with the sword which brings forth empires on earth."

By early 1905 the differences between Corradini and his young collaborators on the precise nature of the "new nationalism" led to a final break. Prezzolini especially was critical of the literary bombast of Il Regno's founder, and the latter did not take kindly to Prezzolini's suggestion that in the future "the fetish of parliamentarianism" might well be replaced by a new form of government composed of syndicates of workers. Not that Corradini was a defender of parliamentary government; he simply had not yet come to the point, reached between 1908 and 1910, when he began to formulate the concept of Italy as a proletarian nation. This concept made possible a rapprochement between Corradini's wing in the

Nationalist movement and the revolutionary Syndicalists, on the ground that Italy's imperial expansion would in fact be a form of proletarian imperialism.

The evolution of Corradini's thought between 1905, when his association with *Il Regno* ended, and 1910, when he helped form the Nationalist party, is not clear in its details although it is precise enough in general outline. A number of factors helped form the trend of his thought. First, there was the criticism to which he and his followers were subjected by the contributors to a new periodical, *La Voce*—founded in 1908 by Prezzolini—among whom were Papini, Croce, Gaetano Salvemini, Giovanni Amendola, and Prezzolini himself. The list reads like a galaxy of some of Italy's brightest intellectual stars and *La Voce* is generally judged to have been a major force in the shaping of Italy's prewar intellectual climate. The associations to which Prezzolini and Papini were exposed at *La Voce*, particularly with Croce, led them to "a profound ideological transformation" and to the position that ethical and spiritual values were far more important than "the brutal success of force," domestic improvement far more urgent than foreign conquest, and socialism and democracy more significant historically than they had formerly thought. *La Voce*'s assertion of this position brought it into violent contrast with Corradini's followers. Undoubtedly, Corradini's Nationalists profited from their dialogue with *La Voce* in being forced to express and defend their position with greater clarity.

As late as 1908, Corradini's thought was still preoccupied with socialism as the great antagonist. He then asserted that, although human existence was indisputably collectivist in nature, it was not collectivist in a socialist sense. Socialism made the individual the measure of all things while real life—that is, nationalist collectivism—wanted to transcend the individual to produce greater organisms or greater essential forms. Nationalism was therefore "the doctrine of those who view the nation as the greatest unit of collective life, as a truly and literally greater individual being." Corradini was aware that such a doctrine exposed him to the argument of the internationalists that a community of nations would logically constitute an even greater organism. He defended himself by arguing that "struggle is life," and if nations came into existence to end struggle within, they could continue to live only by engaging in struggle without: "internal peace for the sake of external war." It followed for Corradini that nationalism had necessarily to be imperialistic, for imperialism was the recognition of "the useful function of war." He denied the doctrine of the inviolability of human life on the ground that such a doctrine was a form of "individual egoism" that lived parasitically on the altruism of the collectivity. "Rationally speaking, the individual has no more importance than a drop of water with respect to the sea," and although war would be incomprehensible for the sake of the individual, it was a necessity for nations. "All the world is imperialistic," asserted Corradini, "either internally or externally; and today there is a proletarian imperialism which goes by the name of socialism."

With this assertion Corradini revealed that as early as 1908 he had taken the first tentative step toward the identification of revolutionary socialism as the domestic imperialism of the proletarian class. He was not yet prepared to offer an alliance to this class on the terms that if it would end its divisive imperialism at home it could join the Nationalists in their imperialism abroad. That offer was to be extended shortly before World War I when Corradini definitively adopted the doctrine of Italy as a proletarian nation, thereby asking the revolutionary Socialists to convert their class struggle at home into an imperialistic struggle on behalf of their proletarian nation. But as early as 1908 Nationalists and revolutionary Socialists already had at least one attitude in common, and that was the hostility they shared toward the prevailing regime or ruling class: "In the midst of these herds of sheep and clever little men who constitute in Italy the so-called ruling classes, give me one hundred men who are ready to die and Italy is renewed." This call for a hundred heroes to dispatch the "greedy and inept clienteles we have on our necks," was made by Corradini; it could just as easily have come from some of the more individualistic revolutionary socialists.

Corradini's Nationalists had also in common with the revolutionary Socialists the criticism to which both were subjected by the contributors to La Voce and like-minded writers. This criticism had the effect of compelling the Nationalists to impose on themselves a greater intellectual discipline but it also led to so sharp a depletion of their ranks that the movement ran the risk of becoming an ineffectual fringe phenomenon. It escaped this fate after 1908 because of two developments, one international and the other domestic. The international event was Austria-Hungary's annexation of Bosnia-Herzegovina; the domestic one was the rapprochement between the Nationalists and the Syndicalists, who constituted the revolutionary wing of the Italian labor movement.

News of the annexation of Bosnia-Herzegovina brought expectations that Italy would receive adequate compensation for Austria-Hungary's alteration of the status quo, as provided for in Article VII of the treaty of the Triple Alliance. When it became obvious that no such compensation was forthcoming, the government, led by Giolitti, had to face severe criticism from all sectors of parliament. It is generally agreed that the widespread dissatisfaction with the government's failure to gain concessions from Austria in 1908 saved the Nationalists from what would otherwise have been a rapid decline. The Nationalist writer Scipio Sighele expressed a sentiment that went far beyond the limits of his small group when he wrote of how much "an able diplomacy could have claimed and obtained from Austria at this troubled moment in international affairs." The reference was unmistakably to the hope that Austria could have been persuaded to grant linguistic and administrative autonomy to unredeemed Italian-speaking provinces in the south Tyrol, Julian Venetia (Venezia Giulia), and Dalmatia. The dashing of this hope worked in favor of the Nationalists, attracting to their movement not only many Italians who had lost confidence in the government but particularly the Irredentists. This latter group, small in number but strong in the sentimental support of nearly all Italians, had been led before 1908 by men whose Mazzinian and Garibaldian traditions placed them on the Left and therefore quite distant from the Nationalists, who were vociferous critics of the Left. After 1908 both movements, Nationalism and Irredentism, deëmphasized the traditions that divided them in order to reach more easily the one objective they had in common. Differences did remain: the Irredentists were concerned exclusively with the acquisition of the Italian-speaking provinces still in the Austrian empire while the Nationalists had imperialistic ambitions that went far beyond the Irredenta.

Encouraged by the influx into their movement of not only Irredentists but also of those Republicans, Socialists, Syndicalists, and Liberals who were discontented with Italy's position in the world, the Nationalists called a congress in Florence in December, 1910. The congress discussed every significant aspect of Italy's internal and international situation, including relations with other political groups, the problem of emigration, military preparation, Irredentism, and foreign policy in general. Corradini was a leading speaker, concerning himself particularly with emigration, the southern question, and the proletarian nature of Italian imperialism. The three topics were intimately related in Corradini's mind: mass emigration, especially from the south, was a necessity so long as Italy had no colonial empire to which it could send its sons and both still retain their allegiance and profit from their labor. Without colonies Italy's emigrants were doomed to exploitation for others' benefit, playing the role toward the host countries which the Socialists said the proletariat played vis-à-vis the bourgeoisie: their work was everything and they were nothing. Corradini reasoned that Italy was materially and morally a have-not or "proletarian nation," and that the role of Nationalists was to do for all of Italy what the Socialists had done for the proletariat. He asserted that what he preached was a "national socialism" in contrast to proletarian socialism—"our teacher and adversary"—that told the workers that their solidarity should be not with the Italian nation but with the workers of the world. He explained: "It is necessary to nail into the brain of the workers the fact that it is to their greater interest to be in solidarity *with their employers* and *above all* with their nation, and to the devil with solidarity with their comrades in Paraguay and Cochin-China." Corradini thus expressed clearly and openly his developing concept of a "national egoism" that transcended the egoism of a class and would alter the internal struggle of classes into an international struggle between proletarian and affluent nations.

A month after the congress of December, 1910, Corradini,

aware of the attraction the concept of Italy as a proletarian nation could have for Italian Socialists, continued to develop it in a long speech he repeated in a number of important Italian cities. Having decided at the congress to convert the Nationalist movement into a party, it became necessary to engage in active proselytizing, seeking converts in all quarters. After some hesitation the Republicans had been made welcome at the congress and in the party by eliminating an earlier reference to defense of established institutions. Corradini's speech of January, 1911, openly courted the Socialists by repeating that "Nationalism wishes to be for the whole nation that which socialism was for the proletariat alone . . . [that is] an attempt at redemption. . . ." Such a redemption could come only through the creation of a national consciousness from which the individual citizen would derive a sense of duty and discipline that would render the nation able to perform its role. The nation's role was identified as expansionist and, inasmuch as "nations do not acquire, they conquer," this role meant war, and war meant necessarily the subordination of the individual to the national interest.

This insistence on war as the supreme national act and on the consequent need to subordinate the individual to the nation did not have the approval of all the Nationalists at the Florence congress. Liberal and democratic elements attracted to nationalism because of patriotism and irredentist feelings apparently did not share Corradini's views on expansionist imperialism and totalitarian government. This was attested to by the composition of the managing board of the *Idea Nazionale,* a weekly that began publication on March 1, 1911. Included on the board were Corradini, Luigi Federzoni, Francesco Coppola, Roberto Forges Davanzati, and Maurizio Maraviglia. Federzoni had acquired some renown as a journalist, especially for a series of articles he had written in 1909 against the Germanization of the Lake Garda region. At the Florence congress he spoke against the "pavid servility" of Italy's foreign policy, attributing it to the weakness and improvidence of the government and to the ignorance and impulsiveness of public opinion. Federzoni, with his doctrine of an "egoistic" foreign policy, was clearly in Corradini's camp, as was Maraviglia, with his diatribe against individualistic liberalism and socialism, and as also were Coppola and Forges Davanzati. Sighele was not included on the managing board apparently because, as he said at the congress, his Irredentism was "the purest flower of nationalism," and not "desire of conquest." The liberal Nationalist Giovanni Borelli also was excluded, and there was no place for a Republican representative.

The program with which the *Idea Nazionale* began publication on March 1—a date deliberately chosen to commemorate the Italian defeat at Adowa in 1896—made clear that the weekly was determined to channel the Nationalist movement in an illiberal, antidemocratic, and imperialistic direction. It proposed to recapture the genius and greatness of imperial Rome; to reinvigorate the authority of the state against the dissolving action of parties and classes; to fight against the corruption of parliamentarianism and Masonic democracy as well as against socialism, the one bourgeois and the other proletarian, but both antinational; to promote class solidarity in order to achieve greater collective well-being by political and economic competition with other nations; and to defend both the monarchy and the Church as traditional institutions making for national solidarity.

The whole program was a triumph for Corradini, for it confirmed the adoption of his views, which were not only totalitarian but authoritarian as well. They were totalitarian in the insistence that the power of the state should not be limited by any consideration, not even that of the welfare of the individual, who was no more important than "a drop of water with respect to the sea"; and more specifically totalitarian in the claim that the power of the state should be total not only in the sense of its being unlimited but also in its extension to all phases of the life of the individual. It followed pragmatically that such totalitarian power could be exercised most effectively by an authoritarian government, or else individual interest, as expressed through democratic practices, would prevail over what the Nationalists considered the superior interests of the nation. The point of meeting or confluence of authoritarianism and totalitarianism was precisely in the identical view both approaches had of the role or significance of the individual. For the Nationalists who followed Corradini the individual was a subordinate entity in terms of his relation to the whole (the nation) and to the ruling authority. Total power demanded total authority.

For the sake of the superior interests of the nation, the Nationalists were prepared to recognize and respect the historical utility of such traditional institutions as the Church and monarchy; but, individual exceptions aside, the Nationalists did not mean thereby to be irrevocably committed to any one national institution, for that would render the whole of the nation subservient to a part and would be a denial of their major pragmatic premise that the parts of the nation justified themselves only in their service to the whole.

These views were generally accepted by the group of Nationalists who rallied around Corradini and the *Idea Nazionale,* and it was this group that triumphed at the two subsequent party congresses, at Rome in December, 1912, and at Milan in May, 1914.

Between the first congress of 1910 and that of 1912 came the Italo-Turkish or Libyan War. At first it appeared to be a major success for the Nationalists, then it led to some internal disorientation, and finally it became a source of greater strength. The Libyan War began in September, 1911, and ended in October, 1912, with Turkish recognition of Italian sovereignty over Tripolitania and Cyrenaica. Most Italians at first acclaimed the war, and Croce's analysis of its popularity and perhaps its historical necessity is generally accepted, subject only to minor modifications. According to Croce, Italy's economic and social progress during the first decade of the twentieth century was an aspect of growing national strength which, in his words, "could not lack a corresponding manifestation in foreign policy." Ironically, the statesman who drew this conclusion was none other than the "stay-at-home" Giolitti, under whose political leadership the war was waged and won. Not that Giolitti had become Corradini's convert, nor that he, the man who abhorred rhetoric, had fallen under the sway of the poetic d'Annunzian glorification of war. It was simply that Giolitti had concluded that Libya could not be allowed to fall under the control of other powers and that, diplomatic and military preparation being complete in 1911, the time for war had come. Certainly, Nationalist agitation for imperial greatness served Giolitti well but the Nationalists' subsequent claim that the acquisition of Libya was their exclusive achievement is not warranted by the facts.

The Libyan war should have been the occasion for an immediate and sustained rise in the stock of the Nationalist party, but this did not happen—for two reasons: first, as nearly everyone had become imperialist, including Giolitti, many argued that there was no longer any need for a Nationalist party that made agitation for imperialistic expansion its chief reason for existence. Second, the Nationalists had represented the Libyan War as a "stroll in the sun" toward "the promised land." When the stroll slowed down to the standstill of a long and costly campaign of gradual conquest and the promised land proved to be a delusion, popular reaction turned against the party that had fostered expectations impossible to realize. At that point the Nationalists once again ran the risk of political extinction, from which they were saved by developments in the Republican and Socialist parties. Both political groups had a minority that supported the Libyan War as a national necessity in spite of the Republicans' abhorrence for any royally supported enterprise and the doctrinaire opposition of the Socialists to imperialistic wars. The consequence was that both minorities were expelled from their respective parties in 1912 and, especially important, the Socialist congress of July, 1912, led to the triumph of the revolutionary intransigents led by Benito Mussolini. This triumph not only secured Mussolini a place on the party's Directorate but also led to his editorship of the party's principal newspaper, *Avanti;* from its pages he inveighed for two years against the evils of the Giolittian parliamentary regime and against those members of his own party who had collaborated with the great "domesticator" in dampening the revolutionary fervor of the working classes.

The Nationalists could not expect any immediate and direct gain from the victory of the extremists, especially in the Socialist party; but the long-range consequences were in their favor. Divided as they were in ideological positions, the extremists of Right and Left were united in their common hostility to the Giolittian system and in their common preference for violence, internal or external. This preference had already moved a number of Syndicalists to recognize how much they had in common with the Nationalists. Angelo Olivetti, a theorist of syndicalism, supported the Libyan War as a desirable experience in violence and as a concrete expression of his ideas: "Syndicalism abhors the pallid conventual equality of which collectivism dreams, and serves instead as a prelude to the formation of combative and conquering elites, unleashed in the assault toward wealth and life." From a common root in the elitist doctrines of Mosca and Pareto there had evolved the antithetical concepts of proletarian and national elites, and it was Corradini's signal achievement to have effected an explicit synthesis of the two in his doctrine of Italy as a proletarian nation obstructed in its development by the "plutocracies" of the world.

An article written by Corradini in November, 1912, a month before the second Nationalist congress, referred to the Libyan and Balkan wars as a struggle by proletarian nations against a common enemy, "European plutocracy." And for Corradini the most plutocratic of European nations was democratic and Masonic France. This article was but a prelude to the campaign he and his followers unleashed at the party's congress in December, 1912, against democracy and Freemasonry, which they condemned as egalitarian, pacifist, and internationalist. This condemnation, though reducing the party's ranks because of the withdrawal of those who could not accept it, rendered it more homogeneous, as Corradini and Federzoni had wished. The latter, in addition, achieved in this way a personal success in his long campaign against the Masons. There were other gains from the action of the congress: it eliminated at least one barrier in securing support from conservative Catholics, to whom Freemasonry was an outrage, and it brought the Nationalists still closer to the revolutionary Socialists who, under Mussolini's guidance, had openly insisted on the expulsion of Masons from the party as early as 1910. Mussolini's hostility to Freemasonry was based essentially on the same arguments the Nationalists employed. Both nationalism and revolutionary socialism were in agreement in demanding the exclusive allegiance of all their followers and could not tolerate any sharing of loyalties, particularly with an organization that was too pacifist and democratic or too bourgeois.

The Nationalists, if not the Socialists, showed an immediate gain from their anti-Masonic stand. In the general elections of November, 1913, Federzoni and Luigi Medici del Vascello were elected deputies from Rome, the city where the Masonic issue was most intensely fought and whose mayor, Ernesto Nathan, grand master of Italian Freemasonry, resigned as a consequence of the defeat of the candidates he had supported. Six Nationalists entered parliament in 1913, and this success persuaded the party of the wisdom of its tactic in progressively disassociating itself from other political formations.

Having broken definitively with the democratic parties at the congresses of 1910 and 1912, the Nationalists moved toward the completion of their self-imposed political isolation by turning against the liberal or moderate groups in the country. Corradini prepared the way with a speech he delivered in a number of important cities in December, 1913. He analyzed the results of the general elections of the preceding month and concluded that they confirmed the decadence of the liberal parties, especially as led by Giolitti. This decadence was revealed by liberalism's failure to perform its historic role, which was to promote class solidarity at home and international greatness abroad. Consequently, reasoned Corradini, it was the duty of the Nationalists to do what the liberals had failed to do. In order to carry out their self-appointed role as sole redeemers of Italy on both the national and international scene, the Nationalists, assembled at the Milan congress of May, 1914, adopted a resolution obliging all members of the party to end their association with other parties, specifically the Liberals. The future official theorist of Fascism, Alfredo Rocco, registered a personal triumph by having the congress accept his views on the incompatibility of nationalism and liberalism in both political and economic doctrines, and the congress openly came out in favor of economic protectionism.

With their last prewar congress, the Nationalists completed the formulation of their basic doctrines that revealed how radically the movement differed from liberalism of the Right as well as of the Left and how much it had in common with the positions of the extreme Left. The successes of the extreme Left during the elections of 1913, and the victory of Mussolini's revolutionary wing at the Socialist congress of April, 1914, suggested that the country was moving away from Giolitti's moderate course and that his program of domesticating the extremists into constructive political forces had met with a serious setback. This reversal need not have been permanent; but Giolitti's absence from office at the time of the outbreak of war in 1914 and his subsequent adoption of a neutralist position made possible a coalition of all those opposed not only to his neutralist stand but to his domestic program as well. For many Italians, and particularly the extremists of Right and Left, intervention in the war was desirable not only for territorial gain but also and especially because it would mean the end of the Giolittian regime. During the ten months between August, 1914, and May, 1915, when Italy finally entered the war, a political and spiritual reorientation occurred in the country which led to the first major victory of political extremism since unification. Out of this victory over Giolittian moderation was forged a permanent link between the extremes, at first for the sake of external war and later for internal revolution. The eventual meeting and fusion of the extreme Right and extreme Left in Fascism was also to mean the end of Italy's constitutional and parliamentary regime.

The tragic aspect of Italy's intervention in World War I was that it took place after ten months of neutrality, and under a government that never commanded the genuine support of parliament's Giolittian majority. This double fact led to an irreconcilable split between neutralists and interventionists and the conviction on the part of the latter that war could come and be won only over the dead body of parliamentary institutions. For the Nationalists the war was therefore the supreme fulfillment of their doctrines, which looked toward the achievement of an international and domestic revolution. Ironically, they were abetted in this by the collaboration of elements from the moderate Right and Left as well as from the extreme Left, all of whom had particular and conflicting reasons for desiring war but held one common view: if Giolitti and the parliamentary majority still loyal to him insisted on neutrality, then war would have to come against his will and that of parliament. Thus, even parties preëminently parliamentarian and constitutional in nature came to adopt a revolutionary or subversive position which shook the foundations of Italy's basic institutions during the war and from which the country did not recover in the postwar period.

The tragedy began with a political accident. Disturbed by the results of the general elections of 1913, which had shaken his parliamentary majority, Giolitti resigned in March, 1914, in the belief that a brief absence from power would give him time to reassess the political situation. The new government was entrusted to Antonio Salandra, a man of the Right who had served under Di Rudinì and General Pelloux and who had been an intimate collaborator of Sonnino. The general expectation in the country was that Salandra would remain in power only so long as Giolitti wished it and that the latter would and could return to office whenever he chose. But the outbreak of war altered the situation. Giolitti could not turn Salandra out of office during an international crisis. Besides, Salandra's declaration of Italy's neutrality early in August was a decision that had the almost unanimous backing of the country, including Giolitti, who was thereby persuaded that he had in Salandra a reliable lieutenant. But toward the end of 1914 Salandra and Sonnino—who became Foreign Minister in November, 1914—became convinced that Italy's territorial aspirations made intervention on the side of the Entente necessary. There was no real possibility of joining the war on the side of Austria and Germany: the Triple Alliance did not oblige Italy to support its allies if war came of their own initiative; the unredeemed provinces could not easily be gained by a war against the Entente; and the country would not accept a war on the side of Austria. In fact, only the Nationalists had seriously suggested intervention on behalf of Austria and Germany; but when, after the declaration of neutrality, this course became most unlikely, the Nationalists quickly changed their position and began to agitate for war against Italy's allies. They explained that they wanted war not to fight against German imperialism which, they reasoned, was as legitimate as Italian imperialism, nor to favor French "radical-socialist democracy," which they considered in cancerous decadence and opposed to Italian aims. The Nationalists wanted war against Austria in order to complete Italy's unification and to assert Italy's predominance in the Balkans, the Adriatic, and the entire Mediterranean. This position was radically at odds with that of the democratic interventionists, who wanted war precisely in the name of democracy as symbolized by France and against the autocratic Central Powers. The democratic interventionists were not indifferent to the call of irredentism, but they responded to it in the spirit of national self-determination and not in that of imperial conquest.

The interventionists were clearly divided in their motives but they were united in their hostility to Giolitti, who became increasingly convinced that Italy should stay neutral because he saw the war as long and costly and because he felt that it was possible to extract territorial concessions from Austria as the price of Italy's continued neutrality. Giolitti's position was shared by parliament's majority and by the bulk of the Catholic and Socialist political organizations, both professedly pacifistic. But a minority of Socialists—principally from the revolutionary wing—underwent a conversion best represented by Mussolini who, by November, 1914, abandoned his earlier unqualified neutralism in favor of a war which he interpreted as the beginning of a great and revolutionary transformation of society.

Italy's government, convinced of the futility of its efforts to extract territorial concessions from Austria as the price of Italy's continued neutrality, fearful that the war might be concluded without Italy's participation, and spurred on by the interventionist press—which included the influential *Corriere della Sera*—committed the country and the king to the Entente in the Treaty of London in April, 1915. Giolitti made an effort to void this commitment by marshaling his parliamentary majority against the government. But the effective power of the country was no longer in his hands. He had against him the king, who was reported to prefer abdication to breaking his commitment, and he had to face the risk of a civil war, since Mussolini's *fasci di azione rivoluzionaria* and the Nationalists both threatened "either war or revolution." The struggle was uneven. Enveloped by the orgiastic oratory of d'Annunzio, who had returned from self-imposed French exile to preach the virtues of war, and faced with massive street demonstrations which Salandra's government had no intention of curbing, parliament and country submitted to the will of a minority. In May 1915—"the radiant days of May" of interventionist oratory—Italy entered the war from which so much was expected and from which so many calamities resulted, not the least of these being the realization that a determined minority could override the wishes of the majority of the nation and its elected representatives. The lesson was not lost on the Fascists and all others who, in the postwar period, repeatedly appealed to their "radiant days" of glory in 1915.

That extremists of Right and Left should cherish their triumph over parliament is an easily fathomed phenomenon; but that such moderate Liberals as the interests and supporters behind the *Corriere della Sera* and the democratic Socialists led by Leonida Bissolati should have seconded the subversion of parliamentary institutions on the ground that they, a minority, and not the parliamentary majority were the genuine representatives of the nation's will, meant acceptance on their part of the elitist views championed by the Nationalists. In time the moderate liberal and democratic interventionists were to regret their subversive role during 1915 and the war years, but their repentance could not erase the damage done to the country's parliamentary institutions and traditions. Salandra and Sonnino, in particular, discovered early that it was difficult to ride the tiger of rabid interventionism. Their task was made difficult by two factors: The first was that, contrary to their expectation, Italy's entry into the war did not immediately decide the conflict in favor of the Allies. The resulting disappointment helped revive the debate over the wisdom of intervention, the neutralists insisting that their opposition to war had been vindicated, and the war parties replying that their opponents were unpatriotic and that parliament, the center of neutralist power, had to be excluded from the conduct of the war. The second factor was a consequence of Italy having declared war against only Austria and not Germany as well. This strange circumstance was an expression of the government's view that Italy had its "own war" to fight, which was against Austria and not Germany. The democratic interventionists could not accept this interpretation, which only the Nationalists shared with the government; as a consequence Salandra was forced to resign in June, 1916, and war was finally declared on Germany in August of that year. But Sonnino remained at the Foreign Ministry and his permanence in that office, until June, 1919, became a source of discontent for the democratic interventionists, who rejected Sonnino's narrow conception of "Italy's war" as enshrined in the territorial concessions promised by the Entente in the Treaty of London.

In 1917 the division among the war parties over the nature and aims of the war almost led to a return of the neutralists to power. The fury of the uncompromising interventionists knew no bounds in the face of this prospect. They called for a military dictatorship and sent urgent appeals to General Luigi Cadorna, the Chief of Staff and commander of all ground forces. Cadorna may have been receptive to the spirit of these appeals although he was reluctant to act upon them. But Italy's military disaster at Caporetto toward the end of 1917 eliminated him from the scene while, at the same time, it rallied even the neutralists to a more active participation in the war effort. In spite of their openly patriotic stand at the time of Caporetto, the neutralists still remained suspect, and to block their return to power the interventionists formed a Fascio di difesa nazionale to keep the government in the hands of the war parties. The Fascio—its adherents were usually called *fascisti*—disintegrated during the last year of war because there simply could be no agreement between Sonnino's and the Nationalists' war aims of territorial aggrandizement and those of the democratic interventionists, who accepted the Wilsonian view of the war and of the peace treaties to follow. Neither of these two views had much in common with the stand of those revolutionaries from the extreme Left who had welcomed the war as the first and necessary step in the total rearrangement of the national and world scene.

As a consequence, Italy at the end of the war was divided as probably never before in its history as a united nation.

This division, which persisted and became aggravated during the first three years of the postwar period, was an essential element in the complex of events that led Mussolini and Fascism to power in 1922. Although it is not the purpose of this study to enter into the whole story of the advent of Fascism and even less to examine the policies the Fascist regime followed after 1922, it is necessary to trace briefly the end of the Nationalist movement by its absorption into Fascism. The first point of concrete contact between the two movements became apparent during the ten months of Italian neutrality when Mussolini and his revolutionary interventionists acquired a common goal with the Nationalists in their desire for war. Implicit in the doctrines of the two movements was an even earlier area of agreement in their common hostility toward the moderate prewar program of the Giolittian era, and most explicit was the desire of both to achieve power after the end of the war. This last element could and did prove to be a source of rivalry, rooted more in personal competition than in any grave doctrinal dispute. Once Mussolini decided to adopt the Nationalist program and, even more important, agreed to share some of his power with the Nationalists, all signs of dispute vanished although some personal rivalry remained.

The end of the war found Mussolini and the Nationalists in some disarray. Final victory appeared to justify the interventionists, but the country had paid too dearly for the uncertain benefits gained from the war. As soon as hostilities had ended, it became clear that the neutralists—they were still called by this name during the war and even after—would attempt to exploit politically the stand they had taken against war in the light of the sacrifices the nation had had to make. The war parties had to prove that the war had been justified either, as did the Nationalists, by insisting on considerable territorial gains or, as did the democratic interventionists, by emphasizing the need for a just peace and a new and equitable international order. Mussolini tried to exploit both approaches. The program adopted by him and the approximately one hundred others who met in Milan in March, 1919, to found

the Fasci di combattimento, included support for the League of
Nations as well as a demand for Fiume and Dalmatia. Both Mussolini and the Nationalists insisted on Fiume in spite of the fact
that Italy had made no claim to the city in the Treaty of London.
The program of the *Fasci* also made mention of such radical proposals as progressive income taxes, expropriatory taxes on war
profits, nationalization of the munitions industries, a minimum
wage, and workers' participation in the management of industry.
The Nationalists could not be pleased with the first four proposals
but the last one was not too dissimilar from Rocco's program, presented to the Nationalist party congress of March, 1919, in which
he advocated a corporative organization of industry based on co-
operating workers' syndicates and employer organizations which
were eventually to replace existing political institutions as the directing organs of the state. It was the corporative state in rough
form or, as Rocco called it, "integral syndicalism."

Nationalists and Fascists had another meeting of minds when,
after the Italian delegation abandoned the Paris peace conference
late in April to protest their allies' refusal to grant Italy Fiume,
the *Idea Nazionale* and Mussolini's *Popolo d'Italia* both insisted
that the Italian government seize Fiume and present the allies with
a fait accompli. D'Annunzio came to Rome and made the same
demand in a speech which evoked the "radiant days of May."
Within five months the poet, who had acquired a distinguished
combat record as an aviator during the war, moved from words
to deeds and seized Fiume with a group of volunteer legionnaires,
among whom the *Arditi* predominated. The *Arditi,* shock troops
organized during the war, wore black shirts; d'Annunzio made
frequent speeches from balconies to which his audience responded
with chants later to be adopted by the Fascists; and the poet-
turned-statesman even granted his captive city a constitution with
corporatist provisions. More significant than the obvious similarities
between d'Annunzio's theatrics and later Fascist practices was the
precedent the Fiume episode set. Soldiers on active duty had defied
an Italian government that was either too weak or too much an
accomplice to move against them; a private army had come into
existence outside the authority of the state; military officers and

private individuals had supported the Fiume venture with money, men, and arms in clear violation of the law; and the discipline as well as the nonpolitical tradition of the armed forces had been seriously shaken. True, all that proved necessary to end the Fiume episode in 1920 was a cannon shot by regular Italian forces; but this shot required some courage on the part of the government, then led by Giolitti, who had returned to power in June, 1920. The government that Mussolini toppled with his march on Rome in 1922 was to lack this courage, and thereby doomed the parliamentary regime.

In fact, the condition of the regime, much undermined by wartime experiences, was made more precarious by the postwar crisis in which the extremism of the war years came to full fruition. The Socialists, enormously strengthened by the elections of November, 1919, in which they won 156 seats out of a total of 535, were led by intransigents who looked to Russia for inspiration and guidance. The Catholic Popular party, contesting its first election with a program of advanced social reform, won a hundred seats, thus giving the two mass parties of the old neutralist coalition a virtual veto power over any government not to their liking. Although they would not likely agree on a common program, their combined opposition meant the end for any government; and for three years after 1919 no government was able to avoid for long the hostility of these two mass parties. A virtual paralysis of the parliamentary system resulted, for which the leaders of the prewar liberal Right and Left could find no remedy.

Francesco Saverio Nitti, a leader of the radical Left but not a Socialist, attempted to attract the support of both the Socialists and the Popular party in order to cope with staggering economic problems during his year in office from June, 1919, to June, 1920. He failed in his endeavor and when he left office Italy appeared on the brink of revolution, with the Socialist party in the hands of men calling for a Soviet regime, Fascist and Nationalist squads fighting street battles with the "Reds," and d'Annunzio still in Fiume threatening to march on Italy.

Where Nitti had failed it was hoped that Giolitti would succeed. He did succeed completely in exploding the myth of the revolutionary spirit of the Italian proletariat when he refused to move against the workers who had seized the factories in the north in September, 1920, reasoning, with remarkable clarity, that as soon as the workers realized they could not operate the factories by themselves, they would go home. They did, and thus a genuine revolution, which could have occurred had Giolitti used force, was avoided. He also rid Fiume of d'Annunzio, in December, 1920, after signing the Treaty of Rapallo with Yugoslavia by which Italy abandoned its claims to Dalmatia and agreed to make Fiume an independent state. The Nationalists were furious but Mussolini chose to accept the Treaty and accused the Nationalists of "being hypnotized by the sight of a few islands and beaches in the Adriatic." The failure of the seizure of the factories had apparently persuaded Mussolini that it was time to moderate his policies and go with the tide. He abandoned his earlier republicanism, broke with d'Annunzio, and became increasingly violent against the Socialists, thus earning the support of northern industrial and agrarian interests. Giolitti had found a new recruit; he rewarded him by including his Fascist party in the progovernment electoral list in May, 1921. In this way, the Fascists, who had failed to elect a single candidate in the elections of 1919, now acquired thirty-five seats, easily outdistancing the Nationalists, who proved to be less flexible than Mussolini and his followers.

Giolitti has always been criticized for being the man principally responsible for Fascism's first electoral victory. The most plausible explanation offered for his action is that he wished to domesticate the Fascists by turning them away from irresponsible action in the streets to the responsibilities of parliamentary participation, and to use their parliamentary and popular strength to reduce that of the Catholic Popular and Socialist parties whose opposition was causing him the same difficulties that they had Nitti. If this explanation is accurate, Giolitti certainly miscalculated. Although the Socialists lost some seats, the Popular party gained seven, and Mussolini proved himself a fickle convert to Giolitti's transformism by promptly joining the opposition and continuing his terrorism in the streets.

Unable to secure parliament's approval for emergency powers

to meet an ever mounting fiscal crisis, Giolitti was forced to resign in July, 1921, and for the next fifteen months Italy floundered under three different and ineffective governments. The Socialists continued to topple governments with their opposition and alarmed propertied interests with their strikes and revolutionary threats. The Popular party vacillated between a turn to the right or to the left; the moderates of the Left were irreconcilably divided in their personal hostility toward Nitti or Giolitti; and Salandra and the Nationalists prepared for a revival of the Right with overtures to the Fascists. Meanwhile, street violence reached the point of intermittent civil war, shaking confidence in public authority and inducing political and military officials to make private arrangements regarding the public welfare and their own personal future.

The only men with a clear vision of their goal and no scruples as to how to reach it were the Fascists, who, in flexibility and sheer opportunism, quickly outplayed the Nationalists. And it was to the sometime revolutionary republican leader of the Fascists rather than to the ever loyal monarchist Nationalists that the King entrusted the formation of a new government in October, 1922, as the only escape from an impossible situation. Thus a party with only 35 seats in a parliament of 535 was given power it did not relinquish for two decades. Its numerical weakness in parliament was more than compensated by the disarray of opponents who could offer no viable alternatives. It was strong in the threat of a march on the capital by its private army, in the support of persons of property fearing the phantom of social revolution in spite of its unreality, and in the encouragement of friends at the court who made the King fear for civil war and the loss of his crown should he order the army to move against the Fascist squads. With bitterness and irony Giolitti remarked in November, 1922, that, in Mussolini, parliament had found the government it deserved.

What sort of government did the Fascist regime represent? It was certainly not wholly of the Right, in spite of Mussolini's early preference for seats at the extreme Right of the Chamber. His hostility toward his former Socialist colleagues, who had expelled him from the party in 1914 because of his interventionist agitation, gave him something in common with the conservatives; but it was indicative of his desire to avoid proximity to the Socialists that he chose a seat not in the moderate Center but one at the extreme Right. It was this same hostility to the Socialists, but not necessarily to the whole of socialist thought—which Corradini called "our teacher and adversary"—that led the Nationalists also to sit at the extreme Right. Fascism, and to a lesser extent Nationalism, never wholly abandoned the socialist traditions of their early years, and it was always possible to return to original positions. It is true that Fascism was helped to power by support from industrial and agrarian interests and that this aid was rewarded handsomely by the Fascists after October, 1922. Within two weeks of its rise to power the Fascist government abolished one of Giolitti's most important 1920 reforms, which obliged all holders of bearer-bonds to register these securities in their name, thus subjecting the holders to income and inheritance taxes. In August, 1923, the Fascists largely annulled another 1920 Giolittian reform which taxed progressively all direct inheritance and confiscated that of distant heirs. After 1922 there was no longer any serious talk of earlier proposals to expropriate unexploited private lands and to give workers a share in the management of industry—all of which easily explains the charge leveled as early as 1923 that Fascism was in fact a bourgeois dictatorship. But there is some truth in Corradini's rebuttal of February, 1923, that Fascism was not "the dictatorship of one man, or of a few, or of many," but rather "the dictatorship of a supreme necessity, that of the nation."

Corradini's defense of Fascism as a national dictatorship may in part be explained by the fact that within a month of his defense the Fascist and Nationalist parties concluded a pact which fused the two groups and admitted the Nationalists Federzoni and Maraviglia as permanent members in the Fascist Grand Council. This pact ended most of the personal rivalries that had divided the two parties; and, while Fascism, with its greater numbers, absorbed the smaller Nationalist party, it in turn absorbed the latter's doctrines into its official ideology. In 1925 Mussolini made this acceptance formal by endorsing the contents of a speech delivered by Alfredo Rocco, his Minister of Justice, and a leader of the former

Nationalist party. Rocco's statement of the "Political Doctrine of Fascism" recognized Fascism's debt to socialism as well as to Nationalism, thus echoing Corradini's assertion of June, 1923, that Mussolini was "the Socialist who had become the builder and leader of Fascist nationalism."

If Fascism was at all a movement of the Right, it was so not in its ideology but only in its willingness, between 1922 and 1924, to pursue economic and social policies acceptable to the conservatives. These policies were expedients designed to assure the regime the support of the conservative classes who, by accepting the regime, turned their backs on the political liberalism that had been characteristic of the Old Right. In securing conservative support, Fascism did not itself become conservative; rather, it obliged the men of the Old Right who joined Fascism to give actual or feigned approval to a political order which in its extremist practices had little in common with traditional conservatism. The Nationalists had been doctrinally explicit in their renunciation of liberalism, with its defense of individual rights, and of popular sovereignty, as enshrined in parliamentary democracy. Fascism adopted the doctrines of the Nationalists and, to the degree that it proved possible and convenient, put them into practice. The repressive dictatorship and one-party rule Fascism established after 1925 made it preëminently authoritarian, permanently disassociating it from the political position of the Old Right. It is true that the Old Right had a strong concern for the authority of the state, but it reasoned that, to defend the rights of the individual, the state's authority had to be rendered responsible by means of a constitution and a representative assembly, and this was a politically liberal position even if it did not always meet the demands of popular democracy. Excluding its extremist or revolutionary wing, the Left was not indifferent to the state's authority but was clearly less concerned with it than the Right, emphasizing instead, in varying degrees, the free political initiative of all the people, from the bottom, rather than the initiative of a select few from the top. Nationalist doctrine and Fascist practice were, on the other hand, consciously authoritarian. They broke both with liberalism, in their emphasis on power not responsible to anyone, and with democracy, whose notion of operative popular sovereignty they rejected. Nationalism and Fascism were totalitarian as well, insisting that the totality of national and individual existence be brought under the purview of the state's power, to which there were to be no limits, whether statutory, traditional, or humanitarian. It was the concept of the Moloch or Leviathan state, repugnant to moderate conservatives and progressive liberals alike.

Fascist practice did not always successfully approach the ideal of unchecked—irresponsible—and total power. An attempt was made to create a coerced conformity with an official state ideology by means of a party monopoly of all political instruments and by a total control of all media of information and education for purposes of indoctrination. But, as Rocco foresaw in his speech of 1925, the older generations' attachment to traditional institutions and ideologies made necessary some compromises with men and ideas of Italy's pre-Fascist past. Its quest for eventual unlimited power led Fascism to seek expedient alliances with all groups willing to accept a subordinate position. It was, therefore, out of opportunism that the Fascist State reached an accommodation with the Church in the Lateran Treaty of 1929, achieving what the predominantly anticlerical men of the moderate Right and Left had been unwilling or unable to bring to pass. Not that most leading Fascists, any more than the Nationalists, were genuinely religious or proclerical. It was simply that they found it useful to secure the support of the Church and thus put an end to a source of division in Italy's public life, so promoting greater national power through greater uniformity. The same preoccupation with totalitarian unity explains much in Fascism's domestic and foreign policies, all of which were in marked contrast to the policies followed by the Old Right. The corporative state, with its theory of political representation according to economic categories rather than along geographical and party lines, owed much to syndicalism but nothing to political liberalism. Its ultimate aim was the political regimentation of the nation, while the aim of the planned economy inaugurated after 1925, which was closer to state socialism than to economic liberalism, was economic regimentation.

Although the ultimate aims of both the corporative state and a planned economy were ideologically alien to the views of much of the older generation, the Fascists were sufficiently flexible in domestic political and economic practices to secure the collaboration of men who had no genuine commitment to Fascist ideology or who did not take it seriously. Fascist foreign policy revealed a similar flexibility in acquiring the support of varied other men and means to serve the regime's ultimate ends. Imperialism was justified ideologically by the Nationalists' argument that Italy was a "have-not" or "proletarian" nation and by the doctrine that "expansion is life." The moderates of the Right and Left in the pre-Fascist period had sought no such justification for their unadventurous foreign policies, preferring to be guided by traditional concerns with balance of power and strategic boundaries. But until Italy's commitment to the Axis, Fascism was able to obtain much support from moderate public opinion not by its ideological arguments but by its appeal to a sense of national pride and patriotic duty. What mattered was that the support be there, that it render the regime strong, and that the men in power suffer the least limitation possible on how they chose to lead the nation.

Fascism's ideology as well as its practices make it difficult to classify it as a movement of the traditional Right. This difficulty becomes even greater when one considers that Fascism never wholly abandoned its left-wing revolutionary heritage. The force of this heritage was revealed during the crisis that enveloped Italy and Fascism with the beginning of World War II. That faction in the party most loyal to Fascism's socialist and syndicalist past saw in German National Socialism a kindred spirit, and therefore advocated complete solidarity with Germany. A less radical faction, influenced by whatever there still remained in the party of old-style conservatism and fearful of the consequences of war, sought to detach Italy from its Axis commitment and to lead the country toward a less arbitrary and repressive regime. Mussolini's decision for war in 1940 was a victory for the left wing of the party and when, in September, 1943, that part of Italy still under Fascist and Nazi control was reconstituted into the Italian Social Republic, the triumph of the left wing was complete, if ephemeral. The Republic of Salò, as it was called from the name of the town near

Lake Garda where Mussolini established his headquarters, was republican both as a reaction to the King's "betrayal" of Fascism in July, 1943, and as an expression of the early antimonarchist sentiment which had never vanished in the party. It was "social" because of the socialist tendencies of its leaders, who proclaimed, but never implemented, the nationalization or socialization of all major economic units—partly to punish the "cowardly" bourgeoisie for lack of enthusiasm for the war. The fortunes of war doomed the Social Republic to be stillborn, and the postwar period has not so far been favorable to the Italian Social Movement which is a nostalgic echo of Italy's Fascist past.

The phenomena of Fascism, as well as of Nationalism—its officially acknowledged "precursor" and doctrinal mentor—are too near in time and in emotional associations with Italy's tragic past to make possible an objective historical judgment. But a brief doctrinal analysis has been possible and from this analysis it becomes clear that Nationalism and Fascism cannot be considered either essentially of the Right or of the Left. That the two movements attracted adherents from the extremes of the Right and the Left suggests the need for a new terminology which emphasizes essential qualities. Authoritarian and totalitarian appear to be more appropriate descriptive terms. This assertion of a need for a new terminology is intended as a justification for the terms "new" or "radical" Right frequently employed in this study; for, although Nationalism and Fascism have, following tradition, been classified as movements of the Right, it appeared necessary to explain how inadequate the traditional terminology has become in the light of new and novel political manifestations.

SUGGESTED READING

ANSALDO, GIOVANNI. *Il ministro della buona vita: Giolitti e i suoi tempi.* Milan: 1950.

ARCARI, PAOLA MARIA. *Le elaborazioni della dottrina politica nazionale fra l'unità e l'intervento, 1870–1914.* Florence: 1934–1939. 3 vols.

BINCHY, DANIEL A. *Church and State in Fascist Italy.* New York: 1941.

BONOMI, IVANOE. *From Socialism to Fascism.* London: 1924.

————. *La politica italiana da Porta Pia a Vittorio Veneto, 1870–1918.* Turin: 1946.

————. *La politica italiana dopo Vittorio Veneto.* Turin: 1953.

CHABOD, FEDERICO. *A History of Italian Fascism.* London: 1963.

————. *L'Italia contemporanea, 1918–1948.* Turin: 1961.

————. *Storia della politica estera italiana dal 1870 al 1896.* Vol. I, *Le premesse.* Bari: 1951.

CORRADINI, ENRICO. *Diario postbellico.* Rome: 1924.

————. *Discorsi nazionali.* Rome: 1917.

————. *Discorsi politici, 1902–1923.* Florence: 1923.

————. *Fascismo, vita d'Italia.* Florence: 1925.

————. *Il nazionalismo italiano.* Milan: 1914.

————. *L'ora di Tripoli.* Milan: 1912.

————. *Sopra le vie del nuovo impero.* Milan: 1912.

————. *Il volere d'Italia.* Naples: 1911.

CROCE, BENEDETTO. *Storia d'Italia dal 1871 al 1915.* 9th ed. Bari: 1947

DEAKIN, FREDERICK W. *The Brutal Friendship: Mussolini, Hitler, and the Fall of Italian Fascism.* New York: 1962.

FEDERZONI, LUIGI. *Paradossi di ieri.* Milan: 1926.

————. *Presagi alla nazione.* Milan: 1924.

FINER, HERMAN. *Mussolini's Italy.* New York: 1935.

GALIZZI, VINCENZO. *Giolitti e Salandra.* Bari: 1949.

GERMINO, DANTE L. *The Italian Fascist Party in Power.* Minneapolis: 1960.

GIOLITTI, GIOVANNI. *Memorie della mia vita.* Milan: 1922. 2 vols.

GIURIATI, GIOVANNI. *Con d'Annunzio e Millo in difesa dell'Adriatico.* Florence: 1954.

HAUTECOEUR, LOUIS. *L'Italie sous le ministère Orlando, 1917–1919.* Paris: 1919.

HENTZE, MARGOT. *Pre-fascist Italy: The Rise and Fall of the Parliamentary Régime.* London: 1939.

HILTON-YOUNG, WAYLAND. *The Italian Left: A Short History of Political Socialism in Italy.* New York: 1949.

LÉMONON, ERNEST. *L'Italie d'après-guerre, 1914–1921.* Paris: 1922.

MACARTNEY, MAXWELL H. H., and PAUL CREMONA. *Italy's Foreign and Colonial Policy, 1914–1937.* New York: 1938.

MEGARO, GAUDENS. *Mussolini in the Making.* Boston: 1938.

MICHELS, ROBERTO. *L'imperialismo italiano.* Milan: 1914.

MOSCA, GAETANO. *Sulla teoria dei governi e sul governo parlamentare.* Turin: 1884.

NATALE, GAETANO. *Giolitti e gli italiani.* Milan: 1949.

OCCHINI, PIER LUDOVICO. *Enrico Corradini e la nuova coscienza nazionale.* Florence: 1924.

PAPINI, GIOVANNI, and GIUSEPPE PREZZOLINI. *Vecchio e nuovo nazionalismo.* Milan: 1914.

PERTICONE, GIACOMO. *Gruppi e partiti politici nella vita pubblica italiana.* Modena-Rome: 1946.

————. *La politica italiana nell'ultimo trentennio.* Rome: 1945. 2 vols.

ROCCO, ALFREDO. *The Political Doctrine of Fascism*. International Conciliation Pamphlet No. 223. Worcester, Mass.: 1926.

———. *Scritti e discorsi politici*. Milan: 1938. 3 vols.

ROSSI, A. *The Rise of Italian Fascism, 1918–1922*. London: 1938.

SALADINO, SALVATORE. "Italy, 1917: The Political Consequences of Military Defeat," *The Historian*, XXIV (Nov., 1961), 44–67.

SALANDRA, ANTONIO. *L'intervento, 1915*. Milan: 1930.

———. *La neutralità italiana, 1914*. Milan: 1928.

SALOMONE, A. WILLIAM. *Italian Democracy in the Making*. Philadelphia: 1945.

SALVATORELLI, LUIGI. *Irrealtà nazionalista*. Milan: 1925.

———. *Nazionalfascismo*. Turin: 1923.

———. "Tre colpi di stato," *Il Ponte*, VI (April, 1950).

SALVATORELLI, LUIGI, and GIOVANNI MIRA. *Storia d'Italia nel periodo fascista*. Turin: 1957.

SALVEMINI, GAETANO. *The Fascist Dictatorship in Italy*. New York: 1927.

———. *Il ministro della mala vita*. Rome: 1919.

———. *Under the Axe of Fascism*. New York: 1936.

SIGHELE, SCIPIO. *Il nazionalismo e i partiti politici*. Milan: 1911.

———. *Pagine nazionaliste*. Milan: 1910.

———. *Ultime pagine nazionaliste*. Milan: 1912.

STURZO, LUIGI. *Italy and Fascismo*. New York: 1926.

VALERI, NINO. *Da Giolitti a Mussolini*. Florence: 1956.

———. *La lotta politica in Italia dall'unità al 1925*. Florence: 1958.

WEBSTER, RICHARD A. *The Cross and the Fasces: Christian Democracy and Fascism in Italy*. Stanford: 1960.

WELK, WILLIAM G. *Fascist Economic Policy*. Cambridge, Mass.: 1938.

Germany

ERNST NOLTE

Though a precise definition of the Right presents great difficulties
and can be the result only of extensive research, some commonly
accepted points of departure exist which make preliminary definition possible. The Right is commonly considered to be the political expression of conservatism. There are and were conservative
trends in theology, science, and art, but as a rule one does not
speak about a Right or Left in these areas. Conservative thinking
can be the property of an individual (an early example would be
Justus Möser), but *Right* always designates a group that sets out
to play a direct political role. In the broadest sense of the word
all states and indeed all political structures are intrinsically conservative insofar as they try to maintain their identity. And although such attempts do not necessarily imply an unvarying rigidity, they do reflect the determination of the ruling class to
preserve itself and the rules, attitudes, and traditions it represents.
But a government in full harmony with the nation or exercising
unchallenged rule over compliant subjects could not be called
rightist. The concept becomes meaningful only if the ruling class
has to defend itself in the broader competitive framework of society against an attack based at least in part on principle, or if it
tries to recover political power by using as a springboard the economic or intellectual positions it has retained. It follows that the
origin of the Right always lies in the challenge of the Left and

that both are possible only in a society that provides at least the rudiments of civil liberty—freedom of thought and speech. Since such freedom is anything but natural, it must in its essence be considered as of the Left. But as the contrast with the existing order becomes apparent only by confronting present and past with the prospect of a brighter future, early liberal society tends necessarily not only to demand freedom of thought but also to use this freedom to attack the preliberal state (the old order) in some or all of its aspects. This feudal, prebourgeois state had everywhere in Europe been shaped through the interaction—now friendly, now hostile—of the military nobility and the Christian clergy. Only when the supporters of the feudal order, challenged by the protagonists of the new society, find it necessary to defend themselves or counterattack, can one speak of the existence of a Right.

A definition of the term which limits it to parliamentary groups only would be inaccurate. Before 1848, and even before 1867, no genuine—that is, central—parliament existed in Germany, but as early as the eighteenth century those political alignments emerged which later found parliamentary expression. Contemporaries spoke about the struggle between the party of movement and that of stability, or about the conflict between the monarchical principle and that of popular sovereignty. To disregard this older contest would leave out of account the background against which the parliamentary struggle acquires perspective.

It would be equally misleading to try to solve the difficult task of definition by an uncritical use of fixed sociological categories. It is, of course, true that in the last centuries the middle class has overcome the precapitalist feudal-clerical social structure. Yet this truth is so general that it contributes little to the understanding of the real historical process—for the most striking characteristic of history is that it fulfills itself in ever new syntheses and constant changes of front. Thus, there were aristocrats who were among the outstanding champions of bourgeois society and there were burghers who defended the cause of Church and nobility with conviction and passion. There is little reason to assume that any one trend had exclusive possession of historical truth. That is why the Right proved so resilient and vital, and that is why it is

also meaningful to speak of a "potential Right." In the middle of
the last century, in Prussia, liberals of all shadings were regarded
as revolutionaries and Reds; twenty years later they had, with few
exceptions, become Bismarck's government party. On the other
hand, after the first attacks on their Church in the 1830's, Catholics in Prussia were no more than potential allies of the government; in practice, because of their demand for freedom of press
and assembly, they stood with the Liberals.

Still less can a proper limitation of the subject be achieved by
isolating the Right. One must at least allude to the "thrust" of
revolution which was in each instance the most important impulse
for the development of the Right. But delimitation is unavoidable.
For in its full extent, the history of the German Right is almost
identical with German history of the past hundred years. In Germany the goals of the Left were attained only when circumstances
constrained the Right to make them its own. Therefore, attention
will be focused on three points:

1) The phenomenon of the extreme Right, especially in its anti-
government and antistate forms. This phenomenon is as paradoxical
as it is characteristic, for the "government" position seems to be
the most natural for the Right and, in fact, until 1918 the German
Conservative party (Deutsch-Konservative Partei), at least in
Prussia, was little more than an arm of government and its source
of personnel. On the other hand, the concept of the Right also
implies a certain distance from government and, indeed, the very
first grouping of the Right in Prussia and Germany, the Christlich-
teutsche Tischgesellschaft ("Christian-German Round Table"),
founded in 1810 by Achim von Arnim and Adam Müller, was
antigovernmental. It was about that time that the term Ultras
came into use to describe an extreme tendency within the Right.

2) The elaboration and examination of the hypothesis that, in
general, the Right developed by adopting elements of the Left's
program and tactics; that the extreme Right did so emphatically
and at an early stage, thus acquiring the greatest number of leftist
features while, at the same time, displaying most clearly the essential character of the Right.

3) The question of the continuity of the Right, which is also

the question of its unity (or diversity), for it is far from self-evident that such very different personalities as Ludwig von Gerlach and Adolf Hitler are aspects of the "same" political phenomenon.

It was the French Revolution that drew a sharp line of demarcation between the inherited legacy of feudal culture and bourgeois society, that gave birth to modern politics, and that, for a century and a half, defined political positions and trends. But at the same time the Revolution, in its course, underwent such fundamental changes—from the Proclamation of the Rights of Man and the Citizen to the Jacobin terror and Napoleonic imperialism—that its adherents, too, became divided into antagonistic groups. As a result, it was the friends of individual freedom who began to suspect that, if its intrinsic radical tendencies were not overcome, the bourgeois revolution could lead to the denial of bourgeois society. It is obvious what the emergence of the extreme Jacobin Left meant for the development of the Right. But the Revolution could not have given rise to such differences of opinion had it not stemmed from concrete social and economic conflicts. Its significance lies precisely in the fact that it caused division among adherents of the Enlightenment, that its excesses supplied weapons to its enemies, and that its legacy came to be questioned.

Kant had understood the Enlightenment as man's emergence from self-imposed tutelage; Hegel, looking back to it in old age, thought that never before in his long history had man been guided purely by his reason and built reality after a model fashioned by his mind. For both thinkers the Age of Enlightenment was an unprecedented, universal occurrence in which man made reason the measure of all things and the destroyer of a past characterized by heteronomy and unreason. In these circumstances, certain questions imposed themselves and Kant's further philosophical evolution represents an attempt to supply an answer. Can "man"—that abstraction dear to the Enlightenment—freeing himself from tutelage, be the same as individual man in his uniqueness? Does maturity mean the creative acceptance of preëstablished reason or unconditional negation of the past? Is there not more to man than his reason? In which sense of the word can man be called his own creation? It was in answer to these and other questions that the philosophy of German idealism was developed, a philosophy that is in certain respects but a continuation and transformation of the Enlightenment based on the experience of the French Revolution. It would have been strange, indeed, if so universal a movement had not very soon revealed its political implications for Germany, and if such questions had not been asked even before the sobering experience of the Terror.

In fact, long before 1789, there were radically minded political publicists in Germany whose periodicals and pamphlets attacked the political police, the slavishness of German subjects, the misery of peasants and teachers. On a more intellectual plane, scholars like August Ludwig von Schlözer and Friedrich Karl von Moser seconded the publicists, and the activities of secret societies roused fears not devoid of political undertones. In Bavaria, the Illuminati were prosecuted as early as 1784. The terms of the debate were primarily theological, but this is hardly surprising in view of the close relationship between theology and politics in the feudal state and the fact that theological rationalism was the very beginning of Enlightenment. It is therefore understandable that the most decisive counterattack came from clerical quarters, and to this day European political controversies have retained much of their early religious and ideological character.

Of all the great feudal institutions, the Catholic Church was the one to be attacked first and most directly. More than others it felt itself threatened by the activities of the secret societies and it soon placed Freemasonry under its ban. In Germany, one of the severest defeats of the Church—the dissolution of the Jesuit order —gave rise to novel tactics of counterattack. For it was the ex-Jesuits of Augsburg, who, as involuntary members of secular society from the beginning of the 1780's, worked with such great energy to mobilize believers that religious and political intentions became indistinguishable. Their theory of a worldwide conspiracy against the Church found many adherents and an anonymous pamphlet of 1785 described in detail how the enemy's idea of tolerance would ultimately lead by way of incessant subversion to the "ghastly fires of war."

On the Protestant side, the fight of orthodoxy against the rationalists had long since begun. But although a recognition of the possible political implications of philosophical rationalism was not totally lacking, debate remained for a long time confined within the framework of theology. The situation was different for the pietistic Emkendorf Circle that Count Friedrich Reventlow gathered around him during 1790 on his Holstein estate and that had the unmistakably political goal of winning over the rural population to the cause of conservatism.

An entirely different kind of antirationalist force were the Rosicrucians. They were a product of the Enlightenment but, like Rousseau, they were convinced of the inadequacies of commonsense reason. It was a Rosicrucian, the Prussian minister J. C. Wöllner, whose edict on religion, promulgated at the height of enlightened absolutism, anticipated the Restoration alliance of throne and altar.

The governments of the German states were not alone in their hostility to the French Revolution. Leading German intellectuals abandoned their initial enthusiasm for the Revolution only after much soul-searching, but a Right group for the first time adopted the enemy's method and founded, in 1794, the antirevolutionary secret society Eudaemonia. Its journal of the same name remained until 1798 the central organ of German antirevolutionaries. That this was an unofficial enterprise is shown by the fact that governments hampered and finally stopped its activities.

The German governments saw no need to ally themselves with unofficial and independent counterrevolutionary forces because German revolutionaries were few and weak. Even the Rhenish Club members and Jacobins—prominent among them the young Joseph Görres, the future defender of hierarchy and tradition—played a role during the French protectorate only, and never became popular. The war the German states fought against France was only briefly a war of principle; with the withdrawal of Prussia from the anti-French coalition after the separate Peace of Basel (1795) the defeat of the oft-divided Reich became only a question of time. Yet defeat so little disturbed social stability that, driven by their

greed for booty and compensation, the governments themselves
were able to introduce many of the essential principles of the Revolution. The bigger states devoured the smaller, the secular states
the ecclesiastical, and, as the checkered map of Germany became
less colorful, the principle of legitimacy was dealt a blow from
which it never recovered. Unlike France, the lightning bolts of
revolution in Germany were wielded by the sovereigns and did
not strike the ruling class as a whole, but only its weakest links.
In the states of the Confederation of the Rhine, revolution from
above was pursued most consistently and logically; here an absolutist will created uniform and (under Napoleon's protectorate)
sovereign formations out of feudal variety and against silent resistance. But it was in Prussia that the revolution from above was
most effective.

The Stein-Hardenberg reforms (1807–1808) put an end to
the privileges the nobility enjoyed as landowners: serfdom was
abolished, land could be sold and bought freely, there was no more
domestic service at the manor house, no longer any legal sanction
for interference in such matters as emigration, marriage, and inheritance of peasants who could now begin to enjoy the rights of
a newly created general citizenship. The rudiments of a rational
tax system were introduced and the Jews were emancipated. These
measures severely affected the feudal order and hence the role of
the landed aristocracy. But Stein wanted to go further, to abolish
patrimonial jurisdiction and the tax immunity of manorial estates.
He even planned a national representative body, though it was
still to be based on the old system of estates (Stände). His plans
met with the approval of the leaders of the reorganized army.
General von Gneisenau, for example, wished to base Prussia's future greatness on the threefold excellence of her arms, her constitution, and her learning. A country so fundamentally changed
would, obviously, have become something quite different from
what it had been before.

It is hardly to be wondered at that the work of the reformers
was sharply opposed by many of the old established nobility. One
of its spokesmen, Ludwig von der Marwitz, complained that aliens
wanted to transform old Prussia into a "newfangled Jew-state." In

this leveling process, he said, the lands of Prussia were to be reduced to a dull uniformity; their diversity and individuality had already been disregarded when the Prussian Code of 1794 (*Allgemeines Landrecht*) had tried in vain to make Prussia a unitary state. Marwitz called Stein a troublemaker with lots of brain and much ambition, while Yorck von Wartenburg considered his comrade-in-arms Gneisenau as much of a Jacobin as he did Hardenberg. This resistance of the nobility to the revolution from above achieved its goals by the usual means—petitions, obstruction, and direct pressure on the ruler.

But, although traditional means proved adequate, the nobility did not rely on them exclusively. It was therefore the great significance of the Christlich-teutsche Tischgesellschaft that it could represent the interests of the nobility in a way that went beyond the limited goals of its beginnings. For the "Defense of the Nobility," which Adam Müller had undertaken upon the advice of his friend Friedrich Gentz as well as on his own initiative, was much more than a skillful apology. What had for centuries been unchallenged and self-evident truths, what generations of middle-class intellectuals had regarded as a "confused aggregate of privileges counter to all . . . reason" (Hegel), became for this burgher's son a beautiful structure of the eternal verities of human relations expressed in the romantically tinged language of transcendental philosophy. In Müller we find analyses of the "dead" world of bourgeois property which foreshadow Marx, eulogies of war, reminders of nature's power, and proud visions of a Germanic nobility destined for world rule which seem to anticipate Hitler. It is true that the Tischgesellschaft was in no way a political party, but the many prominent men among its members (Brentano, Savigny, Voss, Clausewitz, Pfuel) gave it an unusual complexion, as did its statutes refusing admission to "Jews, Philistines, and Frenchmen." Above all, it had in Heinrich von Kleist's *Berliner Abendblätter* a publication of high quality—which soon got into serious trouble with the authorities. Thus it is possible to see in the Tischgesellschaft an early form of the German Right, especially since the enlightened circles of the Prussian capital soon engaged in a bitter polemic against it.

Common hatred of Napoleon, which the poet Kleist represented in a much more violent and nationalistic fashion than Baron vom Stein, served to mute antagonism for the party of reform. Hatred of the foreign tyrant also provided the basis for a precarious alliance with a group that worked for the political and social unity of the nation and that may therefore be called a national democratic party. The emphatic Teutonism of Friedrich Ludwig Jahn, the teacher of gymnastics and patriotism, the speeches of Görres against the neglect of Germanism, the invective of Ernst Moritz Arndt against the rootless "Jewishness of cosmopolitanism," should not make one forget that by the word *nation* these men meant something else than Adam Müller and Clemens von Brentano. At least in general tendency, men like Görres were on the side of popular sovereignty, whereas for Adam Müller the authority of Christian-German monarchy is nonderivative. The distance travelled by Johann Gottlieb Fichte from the radical liberalism of his demand for the "Restoration of Freedom of Thought" to the nationalistic-sounding "Addresses to the German Nation" was not as great as later interpretations would have it, and not without reason did Prince Wrede, in an 1814 letter to Metternich, call Görres, the editor of the *Rheinischer Merkur*, a "modern Aristarchus" full of subversive ideas. And, indeed, after the victory over Napoleon, the trends represented by Müller, Stein, and Jahn, split beyond hope of reconciliation.

The dominant personality of the post-Napoleonic period does not, however, belong to any party. Metternich not only distrusted the Prussian romanticists of the *Ständestaat*, he relentlessly persecuted Fichte, Jahn, and Görres as "demagogues" and suspected even Stein himself of being the "spiritual author" of demagoguery. Kleist, as well as Görres and Stein, had first and foremost been an enemy of Napoleon; in fighting him all three had unwittingly adopted certain revolutionary principles. Metternich, however, was an enemy of revolution alone. As a young man he had seen his tutor, an enlightened enthusiast of freedom, turn into a bloody revolutionary; the armies of the Revolution had driven him out of Strasbourg, Mainz, and Brussels; his family had lost all its estates on the left bank of the Rhine and, almost like a beggar, the Rhenish aristocrat had had to seek the favor of the emperor. Fifteen years later when he had taken over the direction of Austrian policy and, by his skillful diplomacy, had, more than anyone, contributed to the defeat of Napoleon, he became not an Austrian but the master of postrevolutionary Europe which, with the help of his "system," he wanted to free from the virus of revolution. If "legitimacy" is conceived in a purely juridical sense as the inviolability of an existing legal order, then Metternich would have had to concede that all the European states had doubtful titles of legitimacy and that he himself had agreed to and even committed acts that were in conflict with this principle. But the revolution against which he fought in the name of legitimacy was for him more than the sum of accidental misdeeds. It was the essence of all that threatened destruction of his world. His system was the last and only deliberate attempt to save the world of the old European nobility, a world fashioned by long tradition, sanctioned by the Church, and that never questioned its right to rule. No matter whether it appeared as a demand for national self-determination, civil liberties, or social equality, the revolution seemed to him to be one. One demand would in the long run always call up the others, the smallest outpost surrendered would bring the invested fortress close to capitulation. Thus, there could be only one tactic of defense: the unbreakable solidarity of all conservative interests.

Firmly convinced that this was a contest of principles, Metternich exerted his influence in even the smallest German states on behalf of the monarchical principle and tried to stop subversion in the remotest corner of Europe. It would be doing him an injustice to overlook that he defended not merely interests but a world and an ethos. When in March, 1848, shortly before his fall, excited crowds were pushing through the streets of Vienna, he said to Anton von Schmerling, who had drawn his attention to the fact that the better classes supported the movement: "My friend, even if you or my son were among people who behave like that, they would still be a mob." But there can be no mistaking the hopelessness and futility of this intransigent attempt at a defense that denounced all basic changes of the social structure as "poisonous" and "fatal," while believing at the same time that they were nothing more than the activities of a few demagogues. When German national feeling was stirred by the question of Schleswig-Holstein in the 1840's, Metternich said with a petulance that clearly reflected what the poet Grillparzer called his antediluvian character: "Is it the business of the University of Heidelberg, the magistrates of German cities . . . of clubs, teachers' and singing societies, to concern themselves with the solution of this problem?"

It may be asked what role could have been played in the development of a German Right by a man who used his high office to fight the emergence of a modern society, which is after all the only kind of society in which a Right can grow. But he who fights against something thereby acknowledges its existence. And Metternich was not content with repressive measures, such as the Karlsbad Decrees (1819) and the more severe Six Articles (1832). In Friedrich Gentz he had found a publicist of international reputation, who knew not only how to suppress newspapers but also how to guide them. In this, Metternich and his adherents were different from those German governments of the Napoleonic period which had no awareness that the struggle was one between conflicting social principles; different also from Bismarck who had to reckon with a parliament: they were the first German example of an authoritarian Right in power; the second example was to be National Socialism. The vast difference between the personalities and practices of Metternich and Hitler is not diminished by the fact that both their systems have a common structural element.

In Prussia also there developed a party in the spirit of Metternich and of the Holy Alliance which, although it was not without influence, did not actually govern even after 1840. But it provided a continuity of persons and ideas from the origins of the Christlich-teutsche Tischgesellschaft to the beginnings of Bismarck's importance in politics. This was the so-called Crown Prince's Circle, and its best known members were Joseph Maria von Radowitz and the brothers Leopold and Ernst Ludwig von Gerlach. As a very young officer, Leopold von Gerlach had been a member of the Tischgesellschaft; for some time after the Wars of Liberation he and Clemens von Brentano had dabbled in "patriotic-romantic-inspired-Christian poetry," but soon the brothers Gerlach had turned to a sterner Protestantism and absorbed the counterrevolutionary teachings of Carl Ludwig von Haller. From these they derived a new justification for their belief in the unrestricted rights of the sovereign and in the inviolability of the rights of the subject—weapons against the sovereignty of the people as well as against the absolutistic inclinations of bureaucracy. From the very beginning, the Crown Prince was one of the gifted young men involved in this two-front war. As they drew closer together, he and his companions confirmed each other in their love for the "medieval" institution of the estates, which still survived at the time. As a consequence of the French July Revolution, the *Berliner Politisches Wochenblatt* ("Berlin Political Weekly") was founded in 1831 to give expression to their ideas. The main aim of the weekly was to coördinate the antirevolutionary activities of Catholics and Protestants. This aim was characteristic of a Germany that, with the exception of Austria, was divided along confessional lines; it proved so important and has so often been ignored that a closer look at its earliest organ may be worthwhile.

The paper carried as its motto de Maistre's famous dictum: "Nous ne voulons pas la contre-révolution, mais *le contraire de la révolution.*" The demand for popular sovereignty was considered the essence of revolution, and popular sovereignty would be realized (as Gentz had made clear) by the introduction of representative institutions. Only the "organic estates of the Christian-German monarchy" would guarantee the freedom of the individual against the revolutionary terror exercised in the name of public welfare and against an equally revolutionary absolutist despotism. This argument reflects the nobility's struggle for the retention of its class privileges, but it is at the same time the origin of conservative opposition to any kind of totalitarianism. The journal's polemics against the *Gazette de France* and against its dangerous tendency to borrow the idea of national will from the revolution are characteristic of the German *Vormärz* (the period before the revolutions of March, 1848) and of the differences in the position of the German and French Right.

The close attention with which the *Weekly* followed the social-ist movement in its early stages and almost deliberately exag-gerated its importance was less a reaction to the real threat of socialism than an attempt to rob the middle class movement of self-confidence by conjuring up this horrible spectre. But it is precisely as a result of this argument that these resolute aristocrats hit upon the idea of a possible alliance with the educated middle class, an alliance which would be based not upon the principle of popular sovereignty but upon their common fear of the mob—which the revolution would rouse against them both. The periodi-cal conveys a sense of intellectual resourcefulness, and of confi-dence that these aristocrats would be able to maintain their leading role in such an alliance. In spite of its monotonously antirevolu-tionary tenor it often combines intellectual sophistication with firmness in matters of principle and a mastery of concrete socio-logical analysis, which, paradoxically, seems to anticipate historical materialism. The man who was first to try to arrange this alliance between nobility and educated middle class, Joseph Maria von Radowitz, was one of the *Weekly*'s founders; the one who finally managed to bring it about, Bismarck, was for a while close to its other founders. True, the periodical failed long before Bismarck met the Gerlachs and before Radowitz became the King's chief adviser. It failed because it proved impossible to achieve its aim of reconciling Catholics and Protestants. National consciousness had not been able to overcome religious differences.

At the same time, a phenomenon uniquely German became im-portant: the phenomenon of a particularist Right. Under Ludwig I, Bavaria had turned from Enlightenment to Catholicism without being able to suppress the liberal opposition altogether. And it was from Munich, where he was Professor of History, that Joseph Görres, in 1837, flung against the Prussian government one of the most passionate and reckless pamphlets ever written, his *Athana-sius*. In this fashion a party that was in one German state the Right, became in another the Left. The *Historisch-politische Blätter*, which Jarcke and Görres's son Guido founded in 1838 as a political organ of German Catholicism, was soon suppressed in Prussia. These papers were at one and the same time cause and consequence of the basic fact that in a Christian Germany a unified Christian Right was impossible. It was natural that the *Historisch-politische Blätter* should demand freedom of the press above all else, but the paper never forgot to present Catholicism as the most solid bastion against the threatening revolution. The publishers were the first to point proudly to a phenomenon that both confirmed and weakened the predictions of the revolutionaries: for pilgrimages to the "Holy Cloak" at Trier (Trèves), the Church had been able to mobilize masses of people in numbers beyond the wildest dreams of democrats, let alone Socialists.

In this way, the most important foundations for the German Right had been laid, and the outlines of future political constellations could be discerned when the years of the *Vormärz*, which Ranke called the halcyon years and Marx the years of misery, came to an end and Europe, vaguely expectant, drifted toward revolution.

When Frederick William IV summoned the United Prussian Diet in 1847, Metternich saw in this a herald of the coming revolution. Full of concern, Metternich asked his envoy in Berlin what the sitting order would be: "Will the separate corporations of the provincial estates sit separately or will the individuals of whom they are composed be allowed to mingle? In the latter case, the elective affinities which divide the assembly into Right, Left, and Center will play a role." It was a decisive question and it touched upon the fundamental difference between representation by estates or by parties. In the Prussian diet the question was decided against Metternich and, hence, in favor of forming a Right that would have to contest its position against the Left outside of parliament as well as in it and that might be able to reach an understanding with the parliamentary center. The word *might* indicates the inevitable cleavage of the Right into a moderate and extreme wing, and in the United Diet there were already references to "ultraconservatives." The extreme Right soon called attention to itself by such strange parliamentary methods as shuffling of feet and noisy disturbances. One of its number, the young deputy Otto von Bismarck-Schönhausen, made himself conspicuous by such a provocative defense of anachronistic feudal privileges that even the moderate liberals were indignant and thought they saw the "narrow spirit of the middle ages" embodied before them on the rostrum of the House.

Not one of the Prussian ultraconservatives was elected to the National Assembly at Frankfurt which had been chosen after the March Revolution on the basis of the most modern franchise yet devised by a people that had only yesterday been ruled by an authoritarian regime. The Right at Frankfurt was dominated by men like Radowitz who had long been convinced that conservatives should cease to fight the yearning for national unity and ally with it instead. Even this Right was not the expression of a solid or organized party. Like all the other fractions of the Assembly, it was called by the name of its meeting place—Café Milani—and included Catholics and Protestants, advocates of a Greater Germany which included Austria, and their "kleindeutsch" opponents, nobles and burghers, and, for this reason, did not always remain united in the great battles of the coming years. But it stood consistently for the rights of the individual states and princes against the centralism of the Left. The Right thus became the advocate of constitutional compromise against the claim that the Assembly was the sole source of constitutional law. Even without the many uprisings of radical democrats, the liberals would, in all likelihood, have moved closer to the Right. Immediately after the first successes of the March Revolution a leading liberal had written: "Now we are all becoming defenders of the government." Thus the constitution of the Reich grew out of a compromise inside the Assembly, and with the formation of a "right Center" the outlines of a new Right became visible. On this basis a compromise might have been achieved between the reality of the individual states and the ideal of national unity, between the aristocratic past and the bourgeois future, between the defensive nature of the German Confederation and the power claims of the projected Reich, claims most decisively supported by the Left. But the refusal of Frederick William IV to become the emperor of such a Reich, because he wanted neither to bear a "democratic" crown offered him by a popularly elected assembly, nor to preside over a rump-Germany without Austria, frustrated the work of the National Assembly and led eventually to its demise. With this, the weight of events was once again shifted from the moderate to the extreme Right, from Frankfurt to Berlin, from Radowitz to Bismarck.

None of the German rulers had been so deeply humiliated and driven into such an ambivalent position as the King of Prussia. As late as March 10, 1848, he still wanted to mass troops "in order to speak to the German revolution with a bass voice"; on March 18, the rebellious Berliners were victorious over the hitherto unbeaten forces of the proudest army in the world; on the next day the King bared his head in tribute to two hundred victims of the fighting. Nevertheless, it was his own decision to ride through Berlin wearing the revolutionary colors; it was he himself, in his own language, who gave the promise that "from now on Prussia will be merged in Germany." Frederick William was more German than Prussian, more thinker than soldier, more dreamer than *Realpolitiker*. The ultraconservatives had every reason for resenting the King. Bismarck intended to lead the Schönhausen peasants against Berlin; he tried to induce the Princess Augusta to contrive a coup d'etat and the Potsdam officers to liberate the "prisoner" King in Berlin. But the King did not feel a prisoner, and the Prussian extreme Right therefore had to save Prussia and the kingdom *against* the King of Prussia.

As early as the end of March the brothers Gerlach had tried to form a shadow cabinet in order to influence government and king against making further concessions; in April, Bismarck and von Thadden-Trieglaff were the only deputies of the second United Diet who rejected the address in favor of a constitution; in July, Ludwig von Gerlach succeeded in providing a press organ for the emerging Conservative party, the *Neue Preussische Zeitung,* also called *Kreuzzeitung* after the iron cross on its masthead. In August the newly founded League for the Protection of Landed Interests and for the Promotion of the Welfare of all Classes met in Berlin. People derisively called it the Junker Parliament. After the dissolution of the Prussian National Assembly in December, 1848, the Kreuzzeitungspartei formed a special committee (to which

Bismarck belonged) within the central election committee of the Conservative party to repulse elements of "the unprincipled Right" that had become suspect because of their dealings with the Revolution. A process of extraordinary importance was taking place: the deliberate constitution of an extreme and nongovernmental Right which would operate in the full light of publicity and would also know how to operate behind the scenes. As a matter of fact, by participating in public life the extreme Right partook of the Left, if only in the most formal sense of that term. But it proved itself left in a more concrete sense when the *Kreuzzeitung*, under its editor Hermann Wagener, spoke in the rude and vulgar tones that had until then been associated with only radical publications. Thus, at its very beginnings we find the radical Right adopting features of the Left.

By the end of 1848 the scales were tipping in favor of the extreme Right. But since the King was not really one of theirs, it had to fight a last hard battle after his refusal of the imperial crown, tendered by the Frankfurt Assembly. For Frederick William now let his friend Radowitz go ahead with a Prussian scheme for a confederation, which was to be attained with the consent of the other German governments and would also be loosely associated with Austria. In the Erfurt Parliament, summoned in 1850 to discuss these proposals, the Ultras again clearly distinguished themselves from the moderate Right, fighting Radowitz and indirectly their king in public as mercilessly as the camarilla of reactionary generals and officials did in secret. They feared a weakening of Prussia and of the royal power within the framework of a confederation; they hated the remaining liberal features of the proposed constitution; they wanted association with conservative Austria; and they were anxious for the favor of the Czar, the champion of their cause. Bismarck did not hide where he stood: "German unity is something that everybody wants . . . who speaks German, but I do not want it through this constitution." Together with Austria he carried his point. The threat of German unity was removed, Radowitz retired, Frederick William gave up his plans and concluded the agreement of Olmütz. It was Bismarck's conduct that led the liberal deputy Bassermann to voice a significant though debatable insight into the character of the extreme Right: since it, too, maintained that monarchy and nation were incompatible, it was a mirror image of the radical Left.

Rarely has a party gained such an unexpected, complete, and unhoped for victory. Though the influence of the camarilla over king and government was not complete, and the various conservative factions in the Prussian House of Representatives were disunited, the basic policies of the pre-1848 period seemed to be more firmly restored in Prussia than anywhere else. Yet the preconditions of this policy no longer existed: in Austria, Schwarzenberg's *Realpolitik* had taken the place of Metternich's *Prinzipienpolitik*, and the Holy Alliance was but a shadow of its former self by the time it was finally buried in the Crimean War. In Prussia itself a vocal liberalizing tendency appeared, represented by the influential Wochenblattpartei which clamored for a powerful and prestigious Prussia and strenuously opposed an alliance with Austria and Russia. Even at the height of their success the leaders of the extreme Right in Prussia sounded a pessimistic note. Ludwig von Gerlach prophesied at the end of 1851:

Having done its work of corrosion . . . money alone will survive to grind into the dust our lands, our corporate social order and, long before that, the life of our cities. By means of laws which will dissolve and disintegrate all that is firm and substantial, money will subvert marriage and school, the family and the Sabbath, State and Church . . . the pillars and the fundamentals of our fatherland, and finally the army and the throne. . . . Only mechanical forms of government and justice will remain possible . . . until the cultured peoples, ripe for their downfall, give way to new barbarians as they did fourteen hundred years ago.

Friedrich Julius Stahl, the political philosopher whom Frederick William IV appointed to a chair in the University of Berlin, tried in vain to rescue the solidarity of *all* conservative interests by denouncing as false that kind of conservatism that tried to rescue authority and property from the onslaught of revolution while sacrificing the Church and the sanctity of marriage. But he himself had created a conservative theory that, though preserving the monarchical principle, came much closer to constitutionalism and the national idea than Metternich would have thought permissible. It was becoming a feature of the time to abandon wholesale opposition to the revolution and to its ideas in order to make practical opposition to it more effective.

Such a trend is discernible especially in the 1850's, even in that wing of the Conservative party that leaned towards Catholicism and included the Halle historian, Heinrich Leo. Political circumstances had made these men doubt their own Protestant tradition, and Calvin's teachings of the democratic rule of the Church now appeared to them to be "the source and origin of all revolutionary elements . . . destroying Europe." It is easy to see how admiration for Catholic authoritarianism and for a priesthood independent of the congregation could readily be translated into secular terms. When, in 1860, on the initiative of Leo, Protestants and Catholics gathered in Erfurt to discuss the possibility of a rapprochement for concerted antirevolutionary action, their efforts met with no success. However, this attempt first demonstrated the possible anti-Christian implications of a conservatism whose veneration for "authority" was to be realized a few decades later in Germany, France, and Italy.

In the meantime developments had taken place which pointed to the more immediate future: inside the party, a younger and more activist wing criticized the inflexibility and the "governmental" position of men like Gerlach, Stahl, and Leo. Its central figure was Hermann Wagener, a parson's son, who, at an early date, had found his home in the party of the nobility and had made the *Kreuzzeitung* the aggressive organ that it became soon after 1848. Having left the newspaper, mainly because of constant friction with the government, he found a suitable forum for his ideas in the *Berliner Revue*, a weekly founded in 1855 for the express purpose of overcoming the "negative" character of conservatism. Wagener and his friends thought that the proletariat could furnish the decisive lever to do this and, in this way, a second Left element of far-reaching significance entered the Right.

It is not that conservatives had been unaware of the new world of industry. A decade before Marx, Franz von Baader had directed his attention to the *prolétaires*, and Joseph von Radowitz wanted to make the draining of the "swamps of the proletariat" a leading principle of Christian politics. Wagener was not the first to provide conservatism with a social element. But no one as yet had been so determined in proposing practical collaboration against liberalism as the common enemy. The basic note of demagogy was unmistakable when Wagener threatened the progressives with the "mass march of the workers' battalions." Obviously the proletariat, the latest product of bourgeois society, was to be pressed into the service of a prebourgeois ruling class on the basis of a purely negative community of interests. The *Berliner Revue* came close to accepting the iron law of wages and the theory of pauperization, and declared that the claims of the workers were morally justified. Yet the "social monarchy" for which it worked did not come into being. But the mere existence of the "Prussian feudal socialists à la Wagener" (as their opponents were to call them) changed the idea of the "extreme" Right. That wing of the conservatives that was farthest to the Left had now become the most resolute enemy of its immediate neighbor on the Left, the Liberal party, and was much more antigovernmental than the "old" extreme Right, whose representatives, known as Old or High Conservatives, were to oppose the younger element of the party.

The most important future developments were anticipated by the fact that the "broadening of the social basis," for which Wagener fought and which he made possible, was not finally brought about through an alliance with the proletariat but with other enemies of the capitalist order, the artisans and the petite bourgeoisie. There was a master craftsman in the presidium of the Preussischer Volksverein, founded on September 20, 1861. For quite a while the craft organizations were so much under conservative influence that even the hope of winning the rebellious capital back from the Liberals seemed justified.

A third and initially less obvious process must also be taken into consideration. Wagener, who edited the *Staats-und Gesellschafts-lexikon* as a conservative counterpart to the Welcker-Rotteck *Staatslexikon,* had acquired as principal collaborator no less a man than Bruno Bauer. Once a leader of the left Hegelians and a close friend of Marx, Bauer's disappointment with the outcome of the revolution had filled him with bitter hatred for the bourgeoisie and brought him ever closer to the Conservatives. In 1843 he had published an essay on the Jewish question, arguing that orthodox Judaism was an anachronistic phenomenon, rigidly opposed to "true humanism." Marx did not refute him but went beyond this in maintaining that the social emancipation of the Jew was society's emancipation from Jewry, that the end of usury and money would be the emancipation of our time. As a conservative, Bauer retained his anti-Semitism, but now stressed also the subversive character of the Jews. He transmitted this anti-Semitism to conservatism, and its success became evident in later anti-Semitic literature which counts Bruno Bauer among the greatest authorities.

This is, however, no reason to view anti-Semitism as still another Left element that conservatism took over: the Christlich-teutsche Tischgesellschaft had excluded Jews, and Metternich had made anti-Semitic remarks just as Marwitz had done. Yet when Marwitz spoke of the "newfangled Jew-state" he certainly did not believe that the Jews were the cause of change, any more than Metternich thought that the "Jew boys" who edited no less than seventeen German newspapers were responsible for the demagogy he abhorred. The conservatives of the first half of the century were too conscious of the deeply rooted character of the revolutionary changes taking place to ascribe them to such accidental causes. And they felt their social superiority to be so little challenged by the Jews that their anti-Semitism does not generally show the hardness and the bitterness of some liberal or socialist anti-Semites. These qualities were Bruno Bauer's contribution to the camp he joined, and to this extent conservative anti-Semitism (which was no longer the attitude of a ruling class and was most highly developed on the fringes of conservatism in the period before World War I) may be said to have been derived from the Left.

Thus, in the apparent calm of the decade from Olmütz (1850) to the constitutional crisis of 1859, a part of the Prussian Right took three important steps toward the Left by adopting certain socialist theories, by collaborating with the craftsmen, and by the new harshness of its anti-Semitism; in the process, it became a more extreme form of the Right.

Yet, in practice, the lines of division between the Young Conservatives around Wagener and the High Conservative group were not sharply drawn. The 1861 program of the Preussischer Volksverein attacked the unification of Italy wholly from an old-fashioned legitimist point of view, and rejected republican "muck," "crown robbery," and the "nationalistic swindle."

It is one of the most remarkable paradoxes of German history that it should be the most reactionary of the Old Conservatives who induced the Young Conservatives to surrender some of the positions of legitimism and to adopt an additional Left element, less radical than earlier adoptions but of incomparably greater political significance. Many of Bismarck's statements entitle us to call him the most reactionary of the Old Conservatives. In 1852, for example, we find him predicting the destruction of the rebellious cities by the rural population. As late as 1878, he calls "ease of communication" an "appeal to the common man and his most dangerous instincts." He was appointed envoy to the Federal Diet in Frankfurt because the camarilla trusted him. And yet, this reactionary founded what was in many respects the most modern state in Europe by using means that disturbed his old friends precisely because they were so modern. Bismarck was able to do this because he belonged to a younger generation than Metternich and the Gerlachs. He had not directly experienced the shock of the French Revolution and he had not been shaken by it to the depths of his being. Unlike his older friends, he had not seen Prussia wrecked by it and restored solely through "God's help" and the solidarity of all antirevolutionary states. He did not view the events of 1848 as the third eruption of an underground volcano—but, with the shrewd perception of one who was not dominated by old fears, he detected in them the weakness of an unplanned rising. He saw that it was only the weakness of the monarch that, in 1848, had given the revolution free play, and that liberal Germany had then offered itself to the Prussian monarchy as the dowry of union. For him, Prussia was not the passive object of revolution, capable of resistance only in concert with like-minded powers, but was rather a free agent that could use the revolutionary crises to "foster Prussia's growth" if only they were used "without fear and perhaps even without scruple."

Only in such a setting could the full force of Bismarck's nature unfold freely, and the history of this unfolding is at the same time the history of a far-reaching transformation of the German Right.

Bismarck did not, however, convince Leopold von Gerlach when he wrote to him that he completely subordinated the principle of legitimacy to his Prussian patriotism, and that hardly any phenomena existed at the present time which were not grounded in revolutionary soil. And he laid the basis for his worldwide reputation —while he was Minister-President of Prussia during the constitutional conflict—by conduct that was fully in line with the tenets of Prussian and European conservatism. But the weapon with which he won the bitter fight against liberalism for exclusive control of the army by the crown, namely the wars against Denmark and Austria, carried deep discord into conservative ranks. There the return to Frederick the Great's power politics found much sympathy, and Ludwig von Gerlach was almost alone in condemning it on moral grounds as Bismarck's "godless deed." But when, in the dispute with Austria preceding the war, Bismarck did not shrink from adopting the demands of the Deutscher Nationalverein, and stipulated a popularly elected national parliament, the interests of conservatives were much more tangibly threatened. It was no secret to them that Bismarck had once referred to the "God-damned fraud of the sovereignty of the German princes" because in some of their states parliament was the breeding ground of liberalism. They also knew that Bismarck expected universal suffrage to result in a conservative parliament because he thought the "people" loyal to the king and the middle class alone revolutionary. Nevertheless, it is questionable whether the Conservatives would have supported Bismarck in times of peace if the brilliant victory of Königgrätz had not dissipated their doubts and satisfied their instincts. Heinrich Leo was the first to surrender to Bismarck's "mystical power of personality" and the first to derive an unconditional glorification of war and its results from the premises of Haller's teachings. The bulk of the Conservatives did not object to the annexation of Hanover and the Electorate of Hesse, which constituted a truly revolutionary break with all legitimist principles; they also made their peace with universal suffrage which, at least in the Eastern provinces, would leave their strong position untouched. Von Gerlach's was a voice from the past when he called the annexations anachronistic and condemned Bismarck's wooing of the "liberal revolution." The Conservative party no longer heeded its old leader and no longer followed the old principles. By his military triumph, Bismarck had so firmly established Prussia's power, the position of the crown, the glory of the army, and the prestige of the nobility, that, in exchange, the Conservative party accepted another left element of great practical significance: thenceforth, without a privileged position, as one party among others, it would submit to the verdict of the voters. The fact that, as a consequence of an unequal three-class suffrage, the situation in Prussia remained different, and that the power of the national parliament was limited, made conservative acceptance of this step into the unknown easier.

This continued to be true, even though for a decade after 1866 the relationship of the Conservatives with Bismarck was in no way free of tension. Only one fraction accepted the new facts without qualification—the Freikonservative Partei (1867), which followed the tradition of the Wochenblattpartei and was in its makeup more West German and Silesian than old Prussian, more industrial than agrarian. Prussian particularism continued for some time to complain of the centralizing tendencies of the new state, and Heinrich Leo expressed the fear that "Prussianism would gradually be submerged by Germanism." Orthodox Protestants objected to the *Kulturkampf* and the great influence Bismarck had granted the Liberals after their turn to the right (the National Liberal Party had been founded in 1867). But before the conflicts of these groups with Bismarck and his policies could reach a crisis point they were resolved by the foundation in 1876 of the Deutsch-konservative Partei. There was now a wing of conservatism prepared to collaborate with Bismarck, especially when, soon afterward, the agrarian interests it largely represented were granted the protective tariffs they wanted. One consequence of this reconciliation was a split among the National Liberals whose extreme right wing, led by Heinrich von Treitschke, seceded from the party.

Bismarck had used his first two wars, against Denmark and Austria, to give new form to the country's "governmental" Right, and to turn a previously hostile opposition into a potential Right. His third war shattered the particularistic Right which, after 1866, barred the way to a German national state. Objectively, this was the meaning of the Franco-Prussian war—whatever Bismarck's subjective intentions might have been. After he had secured Italy as an ally against Austria, in 1866, the anti-Prussian feelings of the south Germans were the greatest remaining obstacle to the unification of north and south Germany. In Bavaria particularly, the newly founded Patriotenpartei (its most prominent speaker was the editor of the *Historisch-politische Blätter,* Joseph Edmund Jörg) found its raison d'etre in this opposition, and soon won over most of the kingdom. However, the national enthusiasm of the Franco-Prussian war gave the unity-minded Liberals the upper hand everywhere, and Bismarck founded the German empire on the defeat of one party of the Right, the betrayal of another's principles, and the turn to the Right of the liberal opposition represented mainly by the National Liberal party, for which, not long before, he had been the incarnation of all that was retrograde and obsolete. Was there ever a more revolutionary creation than Bismarck's Reich? Was Baron von Hodenberg, a Hanovarian legitimist, not right in calling him in the Reichstag "the greatest revolutionary of our time"? At least on one point friends and adversaries were agreed: Bismarck had brought to an end the era of politics based on principle and had opened, for all of Europe, a new era of power struggles between sovereign national states.

Yet this is not the whole story of Bismarck's relationship to conservatism and revolution. There is as little reason to suppose that Bismarck was ever guided by other than conservative intentions as to think that he ever ceased to be or to feel himself a Prussian Junker. He was certainly no less conservative than Ludwig von Gerlach, only in a different and, in fact, more limited way. He believed he could save a conservative Prussia but not the kind of conservative "world" Metternich had in mind. In his eyes Prussia's importance lay not primarily in the fact that she had preserved the unity of faith, ethos, and tradition, but in the secure rule of king and nobility over the army and hence over the state. He never expressed more convincingly the kind of conservative principles that ruled his life than in a letter of 1869: "The form in which the King exercises his rule in Germany has never been of special importance to me; I have devoted all the energies God gave me to strive for the substance of his rule."

Within the existing structure of German and European politics, the particularistic policies of conservative Prussia were in fact anything but conservative. But it was of great significance for the future of German politics that this revolutionary transformation was acclaimed by conservatives of all trends and countries. Whether it was the Emperor Franz Joseph, the publicist Jörg, the Russian czar, or the smaller German courts—all saw Bismarck as the conqueror of Liberalism and of its parliamentary claims.

But when Bismarck had completed his work, he also experienced the shock of revolution and prevailed upon the Reichstag to pass the anti-Socialist law of October, 1878. He said that his earlier sympathy for the beginnings of the workers' movement had changed when Socialist leaders in the Reichstag had held up the Paris commune as a model and openly professed the "gospel of these murderers and incendiaries." This had left him with "a powerful conviction of the danger that threatens us"; the reference to the commune had enlightened him and "from that moment on" he had recognized in Social Democracy an enemy toward whom state and society found themselves in a state of self-defense. Ludwig von Gerlach had died the previous year. Had he still been alive he would likely have replied that the international character of revolution had been clear for a long time, that Bismarck himself had caused the growth of Social Democracy by introducing universal suffrage, that he had repelled his most valuable allies, and that the anti-Socialist law would be of as little help as the Three Emperors' League. It is certain that the idea of society's defense against Socialism had preoccupied Bismarck since 1870, and presumably it was that preoccupation that gave his thoughts about Germany's future such a dark and pessimistic cast. But the only solution that came to his mind was the old conservative one, an updated version of the 1848 motto, *Gegen Demokraten helfen nur Soldaten* ("Only soldiers are of use against Democrats"). He now contemplated a coup d'etat or a "military action" against the Social Democrats. But the young emperor, William II, would not go along with his plans; the monarchical principle, the cornerstone of Bismarck's work, would not bear a war of extermination against the workers' party. Having lost his power in 1890, the most important creature and creator of the German Right became "antigovernmental" himself; for the first time in his life the man who had despised the sentimentalism of German politics came into close contact with a wave of mass sentiment. Possibly the idea occurred to him at times that he might have found other and more reliable allies than the emperor and the army, and that he might have done an injustice to Court Chaplain Stoecker.

Stoecker, like Bismarck, had wanted the annihilation of Social Democracy. Anti-Semitism was not his point of departure, but instead the question, "How can the working class be saved for the Protestant Church and through it for the Prussian monarchy?" Unlike Bismarck, Stoecker did not want to rely on soldiers but to win over the masses by working in their midst. For this, other weapons were needed than those which suited Bismarck, such as the demand for a progressive income tax which Ludwig von Gerlach had branded as communistic thirty years earlier, and which was introduced in Prussia only after Bismarck's fall. As a result, Bismarck simply lumped the Court Chaplain together with "the other Social Democrats," and, after a brief interval of tactical collaboration, Stoecker's final failure as a politician was owing largely to the Chancellor's antipathy, for Bismarck would not tolerate those Left elements that were indispensable for Stoecker.

Yet in conception and sociological structure, Stoecker's movement was an exact replica of Wagener's Preussischer Volksverein, with the difference that Socialism rather than "progress" was now the foremost foe. After Stoecker's appearance, Wagener, whom

Bismarck had removed from politics in 1866 by taking him into the Prussian Ministry of State, and Wagener's collaborators, found that their earlier work was not sufficiently recognized. Although the Court Chaplain lacked any theoretical originality, he distinguished himself from his predecessors by his personal energy and effectiveness.

The foundation, on January 3, 1878, of Stoecker's Christian Social Workers' party was a noteworthy event in the history of German parties. The German Right now entered an unfamiliar arena to fight for the masses which had slipped out of its control, for the descendants of those peasants and day laborers who, as a consequence of the Stein-Hardenberg reforms, had become not only free but also defenseless. In Stoecker, the Right found a popular leader of great talent. But it also became apparent that Social Democracy could not be vanquished in a direct attack. It was not Stoecker but the Social Democratic deputy Johann Most, speaking from the audience, who received the applause of the meeting—and half a year later the new party suffered a crushing electoral defeat. Only then did Stoecker begin his anti-Semitic agitation; and only then did his meetings fill with approving and cheering crowds. These were, however, made up not of workers but artisans and small tradesmen; Stoecker had learned, as Wagener had done before, that the social basis of the Right could best be broadened by recruiting the petite bourgeoisie, and that anti-Semitism was the most effective catalyst to bring this about. For this sort of anti-Semitism was a striking synthesis of Right and Left: it offered itself as the social protest of those who still had something to lose but neither dared nor desired a conflict with the state. Anti-Semitism would veil the great historical fissures in society and replace the class struggle with a "natural" difference. It appealed to the ruling class to save itself by sacrificing the Jews and held out to the masses the bait of a harmless revolution. Last but not least it promised compensation for the loss of truly human relationships in the anonymity of modern society by offering the negative compensations of collective hatred. Stoecker was hardly aware of what he was unleashing; he professed himself a Christian and he could credibly state that he loved the orthodox Jews—but did the masses who, on New Year's Eve of 1881, demonstrated in Berlin-Fried-richstadt and shouted "Juden raus" ("Out with the Jews") feel the same? Was the liberal Professor Virchow not right in assuming that "others would draw more extreme conclusions from his prem-ises than [Stoecker] himself?"

These extremists appeared while the Christian Social party, from which the word *Workers'* had now been dropped, was still in the ascendant and Stoecker was being called the uncrowned king of Berlin. In April, 1881, the so-called Anti-Semites' Petition was submitted to Bismarck. Initiated by the *gymnasium* teacher Bern-hard Förster (Nietzsche's brother-in-law) and a former officer, Max Liebermann von Sonnenberg, it bore at least 250,000 signa-tures. The petition did not demand the abolition of Jewish eman-cipation but, like Stoecker, it asked for greater stringency in the application of remaining anti-Jewish restrictions. The letter ac-companying the petition made unequivocal references to the Jews as a "race." With this petition, racial or populist (*völkisch*) anti-Semitism entered the public life of Germany. Though it was Stoecker who had unleashed it, it had its own roots. As early as 1873 the journalist Wilhelm Marr had published a pamphlet (*The Victory of Jewry over Germandom*) in which he promised to deal with this question from a nonreligious point of view. The connec-tion with the old conservatism is clear, and complaints about the preëminence of the Jews in Bismarck's "New Palestine" were un-doubtedly no more than especially sharp versions of conservative antipathy toward the "Laskerization" of federal legislation by the National Liberals. (Eduard Lasker, a distinguished Jewish lawyer, was a National Liberal deputy who had exposed the part played by a number of well-known aristocrats and high officials in dubious speculative enterprises.)

But it soon became manifest that the new parties of racial anti-Semitism were questionable allies for conservatism. In a widely circulated pamphlet, Hermann Ahlwardt, who had been dismissed as director of a Berlin school, attacked high society no less harshly than he attacked the Jews. In seeking election to the Reichstag he used demagogic methods of unprecedented crudeness and, once in the Reichstag, he called the Jews "cholera bacilli." Among the

Hessian rural population, which often did business with Jewish moneylenders and cattle dealers, a Marburg librarian, Dr. Otto Boeckel, founded an anti-Semitic peasants' movement and created "Jew-free" cattle markets where he was hailed as the "Hessian Peasants' King." But he violently attacked the Conservative party, too, calling for equal suffrage in Prussia, a demand the Conservatives most abhorred. These various anti-Semitic factions achieved their greatest success in the Reichstag elections of 1893, garnering 250,000 votes and sixteen seats, far more than Stoecker had ever been able to attain. Even though they soon fell out among themselves, torn by internal disputes and adversely affected by the prevailing political climate, a figure like that of Theodor Fritsch, owner of the "Hammer" publishing house in Leipzig, demonstrates the continuity of anti-Semitic nuclei from Ahlwardt to Hitler.

The question arises, however, whether Stoecker's Christian Social party and the parties of racial anti-Semitism can be considered as aspects of the Right, even of the extreme Right. In Stoecker's case the question is easily answered. He had always been an unyielding adherent of Protestant orthodoxy and, unlike Stahl and Wagener, who had dealt almost as equals with Prussian aristocrats, he had always had for that class the admiration of a bourgeois. Forced to choose between political agitation and his chaplaincy at court, he opted for the latter. But as late as 1896, when his future biographer, Dietrich von Oertzen, took over the editorship of Stoecker's newspaper, *Das Volk,* the maxim he gave to his successor was: *rechtser als rechts* ("more rightist than Right"). The turn toward the masses which he had accomplished for the Right was simply the practical realization of that Left element that had been prefigured by Wagener.

The problem is much more difficult with respect to the racist anti-Semites. In Bismarck's Germany, the battle cry "Against Junkers and Jews," if taken seriously, could not enlarge and transform the existing Right. Racist anti-Semitism joined with a bias against the upper classes was rather a revolutionary provocation of this Right, and therefore essentially Left. The same is true for the motto of Boeckel's newspaper (*Reichsherold*), "Everything for the People, Everything by the People." In a society that still retained strong feudal features, a *völkisch* movement inevitably had antiaristocratic implications. And until 1848 the national democratic movement had been *völkisch* in this sense. But the way in which the anti-Semites interpreted "race" meant in practice hostility to the Jews alone. And their basic statements leave no doubt that this anti-Semitism was a deviant kind of conservatism.

A program of 1889 describes Jewry as an unassimilable thorn in the nation's flesh which would devour and corrupt the German people. What in the case of a thoughtful aristocrat and landowner like Gerlach may have been a meaningful statement about the abstract power of money, becomes a piece of social mythology when used by half-educated teachers and subalterns.

In Theodor Fritsch's anti-Semitic catechism, *Handbuch der Judenfrage,* the most imperative demand is for purity of the blood. What is this but the primary postulate of European aristocracy adopted by the common people? And a program of 1899 states:

The development of modern means of communication will probably within the course of the 20th century make the Jewish question a world problem which will finally be solved by other nations through the complete segregation and, if required by the needs of self-defense, the eventual annihilation of the Jewish people. The true peace congress will be that which takes up the position of the Hebrews [*sic*] vis-à-vis the rest of humanity.

This is nothing less than the resumption of Metternich's international *Prinzipienpolitik,* but on the basis of such a mindless and narrow fanaticism as had never found expression in political literature before.

As an expression of plebeian would-be elitism and of antirevolutionary internationalism, anti-Semitism is therefore as far to the right as possible. But its ill-concealed resentment against the nobility of birth and its implicit hostility against the Christian churches are at the same time such pronounced leftist features that the fight between the extreme and moderate Right took on quite a different character than it had had in the controversies between Bismarck and Radowitz, Wagener and Gerlach, Stoecker and the Church authorities.

The Christian Social and the *völkische* anti-Semites were independent parties whose numbers and influence remained small during the reign of William II. Those tendencies of the extreme Right which did not form parties during this period were active as loosely constituted wings within the two big conservative parties. Bismarck's fall cleared the way for the Catholic conservatives of the Center party to come out of the opposition for good and to become a genuine party of the Right. With Bismarck gone, the abrogation of his anti-Socialist laws and Caprivi's gradual abandonment of a rigid tariff policy made it seem possible that the predominantly Protestant empire, ruled by a semifeudal monarch, was capable of being transformed into a nonconfessional, parliamentary state by new forces that would make its cause their own. In opposition to this tendency, both Agrarians and Pan-Germans strove to further that new German synthesis of the upper bourgeoisie and the less hidebound sections of the rural aristocracy which had imbued the nobility with bourgeois industriousness and the middle class with aristocratic values.

Until 1893 the German Conservative party took only a few hesitant steps toward becoming a firmly organized grouping of interests and beliefs which would have to contest its place in the political arena. In the eastern part of the country it could count on the support of the state, on a careful shielding of farm laborers from "subversive" agitation, and on the largely undiminished prestige of the manorial landlords. Here politics was conducted mainly *en comité* and there existed no real organizational center where reports could have been received and orders issued. The party's deputies were the confidants of the local dignitaries, and, for the most part, nobles. Only in Berlin did the party have a full-fledged political apparatus.

But Caprivi's commercial treaties with their lowered tariffs did not damage the interests of the manorial landlords alone. Founded in 1893, the Bund der Landwirte ("Agrarian League") appealed from its very beginnings to the entire rural population, rapidly established an extensive organization, and bluntly confronted the government as a pure-interest group. The German Conservative party, which had already taken a step in the direction of radicalism by adopting the anti-Semitic Tivoli program of 1892, was pushed more and more into becoming the parliamentary spokesman of a group whose antigovernmental position was virtually predetermined by the social and industrial development of the country. Conservatives who voiced the traditional idealistic complaints about the advance of materialism could now be silenced by opponents who called attention to their alliance with the agrarian lobby.

This kind of political realism was a basic feature of that age. The same is true of the demands of the Pan-German League. The impetus for its formation was supplied by the Helgoland Agreement between Germany and England, in which Germany exchanged a promising African colony for a strategic island nearer home. Four German citizens living in Zürich saw in this "an attempt to rob future generations of their share of the world" and they published a manifesto in the *Frankfurter Zeitung* which concluded with the cry: "Germany Awake!" An enthusiastic response made possible the foundation of what, after July, 1894, came to be called the Pan-German League (Alldeutscher Verband). Before World War I it had hardly more than twenty thousand members who came for the most part from the intellectual classes and were members of the National Liberal and German Conservative parties.

The cry for a German place in the sun was little more than the old National Liberal demand, and it was now reinforced by the conviction that German culture, as the "ideal essence of human thought," promised to render the greatest services to world civilization. The call for a great colonial empire and for a fleet to protect it was usually justified by references to English neoimperialistic literature. It would have been strange if the age of imperialism had not found its German champions, too.

But the Pan-German League was not just another expression of the imperialism of the time. Its peculiarity lay in its sharp domestic opposition to the "black and red Internationals" (i.e., Catholics and Socialists) and in its demands for *Lebensraum* in Continental Europe itself. The hostility to Catholics and Socialists was sparked by the domestic coalition of progovernment parties and obviously designed to deny the fact that the Catholic Center party and the revisionists among the Social Democrats were moving toward the right. The demand for territory was based on the belief that, within her existing borders, Germany could not in the long run maintain her absolute sovereignty nor remain the foremost military power of the world. The lack of raw materials would lead to growing international complications; the country's limited territory made it appear more vulnerable than the other great powers. Therefore, the pamphlet that Heinrich Class, the president of the League, published pseudonymously in 1912, went beyond a general imperialistic program; it rejected universal suffrage, demanded a stricter law against the Socialists, sought to deprive Jews of full citizenship by giving them the status of resident aliens, and proposed to solve the social question by the conquest of new *Lebensraum*. This program expressed the hostility and aggressions of the ruling class of the empire in which the national-minded liberal middle class was by this time included; and if this ruling class persisted in its course it was bound to try to impose its will on Europe just as Bismarck's Prussia had done in Germany.

But Bismarck, too, had had to make concessions to revolution which were incomprehensible to his friends, and he, too, had for a long time carried on his work to the applause of conservatives of all countries. If Class's neofeudal ruling class wanted to remain absolute master in Germany, against Social Democrats and Catholics, against Liberals and Jews, then the Germans had to become the master race of Europe against Frenchmen and Russians, Englishmen and Italians, and, to achieve this, they had to develop an extraordinary determination to "change the world." However, changing the world is tantamount to revolution, and both Metternich and Marx had looked upon change not as a mere feature of the Left but as its very essence. That even the central intentions of the Left were taken over by the Right is one of the great paradoxes of history. But in the realm of thought the change had already taken place, as can be seen in Nietzsche, or, on a lower level, in the various social Darwinists who, to combat the counterselective effects of modern civilization, would go very far to restore the processes of natural selection. We can see this clearly in Class. But since 1848 it had been evident that the Right had gained new strength only under the impact of revolution, and when led by a man who forced it to adopt the leftist elements for which the time was ripe. A major crisis was needed to make Class's program palatable. Neither the peaceable Social Democrats who paid purely verbal tributes to proletarian revolution, nor the moderate politicians of the middle class, could spark such a crisis. A world war and the Russian and German revolutions had first to supply the ingredients for a conflagration and then a unique personality to ignite them.

World War I very soon proved that Germany was the foremost military power in the world but that she had too many enemies to prevail in Europe as Bismarck had done in Germany. And there proved to be one fundamental defect in her structure: every German was equally expected to risk his life for his country, but the many Germans of Prussia, the largest state of the Reich, were denied equality of political rights. The masses were not whipped into unthinking obedience, but, though their opinions and interests could be freely expressed, they carried little weight with the makers of policy. It soon became evident that the war would leave intact neither the existing relation of forces in domestic affairs nor international position. In case of a "draw," the people would be the victors and Germany would become a state among others, incapable ever again of challenging the world and, in the long run, fated to be outpaced by the new world powers. To avoid this, and to maintain her traditional political structure as well as her international position, would require the most enormous efforts toward the total concentration of all authority in the hands of an integrated political-military leadership and the elimination of every hint of opposition. But the reward of victory would be the annexation of half of Europe. To do this meant risking Germany's very existence, for a country whose victory would bring ruin to its neighbors would itself perish if defeated. This was the position of the Vaterlandspartei, in which almost all the prewar Right met, though never quite sinking its differences, to work for "peace with victory."

On the other hand, to strive for a "peace of conciliation" and for greater parliamentary influence meant much unglamorous effort and the impossibility of exploiting the national passions which had seized large parts of the population, including the upper strata of the working class. It was no accident that the government had won all peacetime elections in which it had used nationalistic or militaristic slogans—and, significantly, the Free Workers' Committee for a Favorable Peace, from which the National Socialist German Workers' party (NSDAP) emerged, would be founded in 1918 by the workers of a Munich railroad repair shop.

Nevertheless, the victory of the Left which resulted from the collapse of the old order in 1918 had a solid chance for permanence. For this victory was not, after all, an accident but the outcome of a powerful trend which, time and again in the years since 1848, could be repressed by military action alone. But only from an obsolete perspective could 1918 be considered truly a victory of the Left. In reality what happened was the final inclusion of the Center party into the Right and the simultaneous transformation of the Social Democratic party into a nonrevolutionary Left and hence a potential Right. The old Right was thoroughly discredited and its reconstitution took place in great confusion. To save what could still be saved, German Conservatives, Free Conservatives, Christian Socialists, Deutsch-voelkische, and partisans of small anti-Semitic groups as well as Pan-Germans and National Liberals, gathered in the German National People's party (Deutschnationale Volkspartei). Its initial manifesto accepted the Weimar Republic, demanded freedom of person and of conscience, promised to promote public enterprise and equal rights for women. This leftist language was certainly only protective coloring and much of it was soon washed off, but the readiness to collaborate in a republic was an irreversible fact. When, in 1922, the *deutschvölkische* wing separated from the party, the way seemed clear for the People's party to become the third member of a governmental Right, while remaining in its propaganda the most vocal opponent of the Treaty of Versailles and the most unyielding champion of a policy of national restoration. The "goal" of that policy was to return to Germany the prestige and the power she had lost as a result of the war and the Treaty of Versailles. In principle, even the Social Democrats did not reject such a policy, but few among the People's party believed that it could be fully realized. There was, it is true, a good chance that a new extreme Right would do very

much better than its predecessors in wooing the masses by occupying revolutionary positions. It had, moreover, the advantage of
having words and intentions agree and it enjoyed powerful support, especially in Pan-German circles. Yet this Right was divided
on tactical questions and tended to splinter into small sects. Disunity and lack of realism were also characteristic of the writers of
the so-called national revolution. This included the whole of the
antigovernmental Right which often attacked Hitler for being a
Catholic or insufficiently radical. However, the strength of antidemocratic tendencies in leading intellectual circles was a sure sign
that Germany was not approaching a liberal and smoothly functioning parliamentary democracy. The best that could be expected
was a presidential government based on the moderate Right and
tolerated by the moderate Left under the pressure of the two extremes. This might have made possible Stresemann's moderate
policy of national restoration and the inauguration of a new policy
of international agreements.

If history took a different course it was owing to numerous
causes, of which the world economic crisis of the twenties was undoubtedly the most serious. But, long before that, an unprepared
and basically conservative population in one part of Germany had
been deeply affected by revolution and, once again, a particularistic
Right was to become important for the whole country. Without
the experience of a Soviet Republic (*Räterepublik,* from April
7 to May 1, 1919) in Munich, Bavaria would hardly have become
so quickly and so thoroughly a country of the Right, a "nucleus
of order"; and without the opposition of the Bavarian state authorities the central government in Berlin would probably have
suppressed the National Socialist movement without great difficulty. It was Hitler's mind that fused into a uniform *Weltan-
schauung* the horror of the Bavarian and the Russian revolutions,
the Austrian German's anxious concern for the survival of Germandom, and an infantile need to detect viruses of decay everywhere. There was nothing new in this, yet the old was presented
in a new way and, most important, in the context of a new and
revolutionary situation, so that the unsuccessful artist became the
most successful agitator of his time. In Germany, as in Italy and

some other European countries, the fear of Communist revolution, which had everywhere mobilized even hitherto apolitical strata of society, and the increasing moderation of Social Democracy, which had pushed some of its most active forces to the Right, had prepared the ground for the appearance of a mass party of an unknown—that is, fascist—structure. No matter how much Hitler had in common with Mussolini and Maurras, with Codreanu and Gömbös, there was one intuitive vision and one determination that only he as a German possessed: he combined the realization that the policy of national restoration pursued by the moderate Right would not really reëstablish Germany's prewar position with the commitment to a radical policy—that is, *Raumpolitik,* which is different from mere imperialism and vastly more ambitious. It is true that Hitler never ceased to use the formulae of the usual policy of recovery, and in some way he seems to have believed in them, but only the passion of antirevolutionary anti-Semitism gave him the strength for the incredible attempt to change the geographic and historical foundations of his country. The combination of anti-Semitism, nationalism, and *Raumpolitik* was the prerequisite for Hitler's success and he expressed it often and clearly. As it was a union of darkest fanaticism, of a hardly realizable concept, and of a generally accepted ethos, everybody chose what seemed credible to him and thus Hitler achieved what no one before him had even come close to achieving: he gave the Right a genuine mass basis, he paralyzed the moderate Right by the spell of his success and his consistency, he realized the old dream of annihilating Marxism, and, in the process, he undid the most important step toward acceptance of the existing state that had been taken by hitherto reluctant or revolutionary forces in the preceding hundred years.

This is certainly not the place to search out the causes or to discuss the psychological motivations of Hitler's success. Our only concern is to sketch the outlines of his place and that of his party in German political development. In this way it may be understood how in Germany, as in Italy, a party of the right used liberal institutions first to win total power, then to destroy those same institutions and, indeed, that very society that is the precondition for the existence of the Right as a political party. It has now to be demonstrated (1) that the NSDAP really was a party of the right, although it had many more striking features of the left than any comparable organization ever had; (2) that Hitler pursued a policy that was in accord with his premises; and (3) that his extremism brought the German Right to a turning point and, strictly speaking, to its end.

The hundreds of thousands who, on January 30th, 1933, and on later occasions marched through the streets to celebrate and demonstrate the power of the regime, were like brothers and sisters in the great national community—or so, at least, Hitler told them. Unity and solidarity of the nation—had not this been the war cry of the Left in 1848?

In 1932, before coming to power, Hitler had fumed against von Papen and his cabinet, calling its ministers "these right honorable gentlemen who as a consequence of their birth belong to a quite different race of men." The young Fichte had once used similar tones in trying to correct German views of the French Revolution. There was also an antireligious element—as there had been in the Enlightenment—in the anti-Semitic attacks on the "immoral" stories of the Old Testament, or in Hitler's many references to Voltaire. But, in fact, he and his party had already gone further to the left than that. The party's very name was a call for socialism, for that "socialist creativity" that would be realized by "the fourth estate, the workers." This is what the young Joseph Goebbels, as *Gauleiter* of Berlin, wanted to oppose to the "rotten" spirit of liberalism, and his posters showed "brownshirts, German proletarians . . . under the red storm banner" of what came to be called the national revolution. The method and style of the extreme Left had been taken over much more fully than Stoecker and Ahlwardt had been able to do, and Bismarck would certainly have counted the National Socialists among the Communists.

Such arguments fail to take proper account of the uniqueness of the historic moment and of the passage of time itself. In 1848 to invoke "the nation" meant to inveigh against the particularism of the individual states and the privileges of the nobility; to do so in 1930 was to take one's stand against international coöperation and for an elitist order. To attack the Old Testament in 1770 was to attack a ruling state Church, to do so in 1930 with the same arguments was either beating a dead horse or using the issue for other purposes. The socialists of 1880 wanted to raise the workers materially, morally, and socially, the National Socialists of 1930 wanted to crowd them out of the position of power they were said to have usurped.

The leftist elements in National Socialism are either historical anachronisms or sham acquisitions. It is quite otherwise with its rightist features. In *Mein Kampf,* Hitler had been extraordinarily frank in revealing his deep contempt for the masses and what he called their feminine nature; not even Ludwig von der Marwitz had been more scornful of the "big-city rabble." Hitler's enemies were the same ones who had already been denounced by the ex-Jesuits of Augsburg: Jews, Freemasons, and, though not explicitly, the Reformation, and also everything else that had been added to that list from the time of the romantics to that of anti-Christian radical conservatism—liberals and democrats, the parliamentary system and industrialism, Marxism and Christianity. What Hitler had to say about the origin of the state (Nordic invaders establishing their rule over an inferior population) might have been copied from Gobineau; but it is also compatible with Haller's teachings and would probably have met with Heinrich Leo's approval. In Hitler's case, "race" theory is in no way the final consequence of bourgeois nationalism; on the contrary, it corresponds exactly to the feudal concept of race which divided the nations into different strata related with each other across national boundaries. A hundred years earlier this notion had been part of Adam Müller's teachings; actually it originated in seventeenth- and eighteenth-century France.

Hitler's most original concept derives directly from his racial theory: Bolshevism is nothing but the appeal of the Jewish intellect to the racially inferior classes of every nation. It is a call for that great slave rising which, if not nipped in the bud, will inevitably annihilate the ruling classes.

There is perhaps no more convincing proof of the profoundly conservative character of Hitler's thinking than a casual remark recorded in his *Table Talk*. For five hundred years, he said, the price of bread in Venice had remained stable, until the Jews, with their rapacious slogan of "Free Trade," unsettled it. This remark makes clear what his anti-Semitism means: not just the usual complaint about decomposition and decay, but a rejection of historical change itself. Hitler's Reich, as he saw it, was but a consistently and thoroughly feudalized "iron-hard national organism" to be preserved from all "subversive," that is, historical, influences for thousands of years. It is true, of course, that this was not a genuine feudalism and that conservative arguments and realities had also changed meaning and position. But this observation does not negate the validity of the judgment that National Socialism was a genuine party of the Right, clearly identifiable as such because its ideas and attitudes are in the tradition of the Right.

Before 1933 not many were prepared to take seriously Hitler's fusing of three apparently heterogeneous motives. After 1945 everyone seemed convinced that, from the day he had seized power, he had pursued the goal of world conquest with inexorable tenacity. It therefore caused no little surprise when historical research showed how often in his course Hitler had wavered and doubted— although not even Bismarck had been as iron a chancellor as his people had liked to imagine. Hitler had fled ingloriously and collapsed completely after the failure of the 1923 *putsch;* even in later years a firm stand could bring him to make unexpected concessions. He was a monomaniac dreamer whose obsessions were often out of touch with reality. For this very reason he could be realistic in everyday life. This made him hesitate at times when he was faced with the need to make decisions, which, although logical as dreams, clashed with the facts of the waking world. If, "realistically," he failed to press the demand for South Tyrol and Alsace-Lorraine, it was only because goals of this magnitude seemed less important than the far vaster conquests in the East, of which he was dreaming. The consistency of his essential being is revealed not so much by the fact that eight years after taking power in a disarmed and impoverished country he had conquered almost all of Europe, as by the practical manner in which he planned to organize his conquests and to retain them forever. This was not, however, a purely personal trait but rather the new version of extreme Right attitudes adjusted to the necessities of a coming supranational epoch. In this respect, Hitler's conquest of Europe is a parallel to Bismarck's founding of the Reich—which was, however, governed by quite different conceptions of authority, liberty, and history.

Like Bismarck, Hitler could not even have begun the execution of his program without the sympathetic connivance of conservatives—particularly in those countries that were to become his victims. Bismarck had enjoyed this sympathy as the victor over liberalism; Hitler received it as the victor over Marxism. The history of profascist tendencies in the European middle class, in the armies and the churches, has yet to be written, but there will probably be more to it than to the history of antifascism.

Yet the man who knew how to exploit conservative sympathies for the extension of his power as coolly as Bismarck had done, nevertheless inclined toward a *Prinzipienpolitik* in Metternich's sense. This is shown by his intervention in Spain, represented as an anti-Communist measure, and is proved above all by his offer to guarantee the integrity of the British Empire. He saw it as his task to preserve the European ruling class in its traditional role of world dominion, except that he wanted to replace its racially decadent descendants by the healthy Nordic core of his SS. To the "Jewish" call for the unity of the proletariat he wanted to oppose the concept of the Jew as the universal enemy. And he did in fact defend certain basic features of the traditional structure of the European state: the preëminence of military values, the preservation of a clearly defined relationship between ruler and ruled, the full reality of sovereignty. Yet Metternich would doubtless have asked the Viennese drifter by what right he claimed to lead the fight against revolution when he himself was wholly the son of revolution. And Bismarck would certainly have told the demagogue that it would be absurd to preserve and shore up the foundations of the social order if the superstructure which alone gave them meaning were destroyed. Neither Metternich nor Bismarck would have recognized in Hitler the defender of their principles or their work. And it was no coincidence that long before the end of World War II so many German conservatives had become Hitler's opponents, nor did any war ever cause such havoc among the best names of the Prussian aristocracy as did this most radical champion of the elitist cause.

The thesis that the history of the German Right had run its course with Hitler's death must appear strange and in need of clarification. Because National Socialism was an aggregate combining all the features of the Right and almost all those of the Left in German political history, it fell apart after the war as easily as it had come into being without leaving more than diffuse sympathies for one or another of its "good sides." But apart from the top leadership itself, its younger cadres did better, as a rule, in the postwar period than did those of comparable movements in other European countries. It is true that they were hopelessly discredited, not least because of the very fact of their being alive and at liberty, and a great many withdrew from politics to participate in the economic revival. Yet a solid nucleus soon found an opportunity to present its cause in the press and in politics. In some parts of Germany the Sozialistische Reichspartei, and, after its prohibition, the Deutsche Reichspartei, achieved some disquieting successes around 1950. Their periodicals, like the *Deutsche Soldatenzeitung, Nation Europa, Wikingruf, Reichs-Ruf*, and the numerous pamphlets and books they publish, are often distributed privately through book clubs in order to circumvent the regular book trade. In general, these do not defend Hitler and National Socialism as a whole, but rather have recourse to concepts like "international law" and "self-determination" and tend to do little more than try to correct certain exaggerations of Allied war propaganda. Their strongest link with Hitler is their advocacy of an alliance of all white peoples against the threatening rise of the colored nations. But their best chance for a mass following lies in their reckless defense of German claims to the territories beyond the Oder and Neisse, a defense which brands any attempt at rational discussion of this issue as treason.

Paradoxically, the influx of many millions of expellees and refugees has helped to deprive the new extreme Right of its chances, so that at this time it represents at best only a latent political force in the Federal Republic. For, while the territories occupied by Western troops at the end of the war were protected not only from Soviet Russian invasion but also from Communist revolution, the influx of new citizens transformed traditional social divisions and neutralized them in the new atmosphere of economic competition. Only after World War II did Germany become fully a bourgeois society, a nation cut loose from its traditional moorings. The country survived on the basis of an industrial potential, vast even after its partial destruction, and its western portions enjoyed a freedom that offered the tense energies of each of its citizens a possibility of success denied in the Soviet zone. It was natural that only those parties should be successful which were both for freedom and against Communism. It was again the expellees and the refugees who helped bring about this success and the disappointment of the widespread hope for a socialist transformation that was the first and spontaneous result of Hitler's defeat. As a consequence, the Christian Democratic party (CDU), a union of all political forces to the right of the Social Democrats, realized the intentions of Radowitz and the Gerlachs under completely changed circumstances. The Social Democrats (SPD) drifted farther and farther away from the hopes and faith of the early postwar years. The Communists were ruined. The old Right was destroyed, for its main thesis had remained unchanged from the ex-Jesuits of the 1780's to Hitler—that it was only the liberty of liberalism that engendered revolution and communism, and that above all else discipline, hierarchy, and faith were necessary. It is true that a certain uneasiness about bourgeois society survived, and leftist writers helped to keep it alive. The negative aspects of bourgeois society were often deplored and still more often merely dimly sensed: the restlessness, the lack of community-mindedness, the weakness of surviving traditions, the absence of firm convictions. But its positive aspects were felt more strongly: the respect for the individual, the general and rapid growth of the standard of living, the unrestricted freedom of speech and the press, and the opening of the world beyond the borders.

The existence of one great liberal party became ever more clearly the central political fact of the Federal Republic. Differences within it concern only the degree to which either Marxist remnants or clericalism are regarded as dangers to freedom. Within this broad consensus the old Right not only disappears, but the very concept of "Right" loses its old meaning.

Traditionally, obedience, authority, and unity of belief had been considered as being of the Right; freedom, spontaneity, pluralism were Left. But divided Germany faces a paradoxical situation in which the German Democratic Republic, nominally a working-class state, has the characteristics of the Right, whereas the Right middle-class Federal Republic has more of the characteristics of the Left. This confusion shows clearly enough that something must be wrong with traditional political concepts. The Federal Republic and the German Democratic Republic seem to offer themselves as living experiments to test these concepts. It is to be hoped that in this confrontation liberal society will prove to be more than a particular form of regulating production and that more will be gained from it than a purely political triumph of one party over another.

For freedom is not, strictly speaking, a political principle; it does not demand breaking the will of others, but transforms it. It is precisely for this reason that a liberal society cannot set goals that aim at the destruction of the elementary political interests of an opponent. It is the weakness of the Liberal party in the Federal Republic that it has not absorbed this truth, though this is not equally true of all its factions. The possibility exists, therefore, that the disappearance of the traditional contrast between Right and Left in Federal Germany is based on an illusion, and that, as a consequence, the hour of the old Right could, one day, come again. But this Right could be victorious only in an international context, and its victory would then no longer be primarily a part of the history of the German Right.

SUGGESTED READING

BERGSTRAESSER, LUDWIG. *Geschichte der politischen Parteien in Deutschland.* 10th ed. Munich: 1960. (A standard work.)

BOWEN, RALPH. *German Theories of the Corporative State.* New York: 1947.

BULLOCK, ALAN. *Hitler: A Study in Tyranny.* London: 1952.

CONRAD-MARTIUS, HEDWIG. *Utopien der Menschenzüchtung. Der Sozial-darwinismus und seine Folgen.* Munich: 1955.

FRANK, WALTER. *Hofprediger Adolf Stoecker und die christlichsoziale Bewegung.* Berlin: 1928.

GERLACH, HELLMUT VON. *Von Rechts nach Links.* Zürich: 1937.

GOEBBELS, JOSEPH. *Wege ins Dritte Reich.* Munich: 1927.

GREBING, HELGA. *Geschichte der deutschen Parteien.* Wiesbaden: 1962. (An instructive general survey.)

HAHN, ADALBERT. *Die Berliner Revue. Ein Beitrag zur Geschichte der Konservativen Partei zwischen 1855 und 1875.* Berlin: 1934.

HAMEROW, THEODORE S. *Restoration, Revolution, Reaction. Economics and Politics in Germany, 1815–1871.* Princeton: 1958.

HITLER, ADOLF. *Hitler's Table Talk 1941–1944.* London: 1953.

HUBER, ERNST RUDOLF. *Deutsche Verfassungsgeschichte seit 1789.* Stuttgart: 1957, 1960. (Two volumes, dealing with the period before 1850, have been published so far.)

KAMPMANN, WANDA. "Stoecker und die Berliner Bewegung," *Geschichte in Wissenschaft und Unterricht.* XIII (1962).

KLEMPERER, KLEMENS VON. *Germany's New Conservatism.* Princeton: 1957.

KNUETTER, HANS-HELMUTH. *Ideologien des Rechtsradikalismus im Nachkriegsdeutschland.* Bonn: 1961.

KRUCK, ALFRED. *Geschichte des Alldeutschen Verbandes 1890–1939.* Wiesbaden: 1954.

LAQUEUR, WALTER Z. *Young Germany: A History of the German Youth Movement.* London: 1962.

MASSING, PAUL H. *Rehearsal for Destruction. A Study of Political Anti-Semitism in Imperial Germany.* New York: 1949.

MOHLER, ARMIN. *Die Konservative Revolution in Deutschland.* Stuttgart: 1950.

MOMMSEN, WILHELM. "Deutsche Parteiprogramme," *Deutsches Handbuch der Politik.* Vol. I. Munich: 1960.

MOSSE, GEORGE L. *The Crisis of German Ideology. Intellectual Origins of the Third Reich.* New York: 1964.

NEUMANN, FRANZ. *Behemoth: The Structure and Practice of National Socialism.* New York: 1944.

NOLTE, ERNST. *Der Faschismus in seiner Epoche. Action française, italienischer Faschismus, Nationalsozialismus.* Munich: 1963. (An American edition is in preparation.)

Parteien in der Bundesrepublik, Studien zur Entwicklung der deutschen Parteien bis zur Bundestagswahl 1953. Stuttgart-Düsseldorf: 1955.

PFLANZE, OTTO. *Bismarck and the Development of Germany.* Princeton: 1963.

RAUSCHNING, HERMANN. *The Revolution of Nihilism.* New York: 1939.

RITTER, GERHARD. *Die preussischen Konservativen und Bismarcks deutsche Politik 1858–1876.* Heidelberg: 1913.

SCHMAHL, EUGEN. "Die antisemitische Bauernbewegung in Hessen von der

Boeckelzeit bis zum Nationalsozialismus," Schmahl-Seipel, *Entwicklung der völkischen Bewegung.* Giessen: 1933.

SCHOEPS, HANS JOACHIM. *Das andere Preussen. Konservative Gestalten und Probleme im Zeitalter Friedrich Wilhelms IV.* Honnef: 1957.

STERN, FRITZ. *The Politics of Cultural Despair: A Study in the Rise of the Germanic Ideology.* Berkeley and Los Angeles: 1961.

VALJAVEC, FRITZ. *Die Entstehung der politischen Strömungen in Deutschland 1770–1815.* Munich: 1951.

VIERECK, PETER. *Metapolitics, from the Romantics to Hitler.* New York: 1941.

WAITE, ROBERT G. L. *Vanguard of Nazism. The Free Corps Movement in Postwar Germany, 1918–1923.* Cambridge, Mass.: 1952.

WERTHEIMER, MILDRED. *The Pan-German League, 1890–1914.* New York: 1924.

Austria

ANDREW WHITESIDE

The Right as a political category appeared in Austria in the decade
following the enactment of a liberal constitution in 1867. In this
last phase of the empire's existence, two separate, mutually hostile,
right-wing movements developed in protest against the political
and economic conditions ushered in by the establishment of parliamentary government, civil equality, and the laissez-faire economy.
Both movements reappeared in the Austrian republic after the dissolution of the monarchy in 1918, and the clash between them
led to the final act in the history of the republic—the German
Anschluss. This essay traces the history of the Right in the German-
speaking parts of the Austrian empire—that is, in the western half
of the dual monarchy—and in the first Austrian republic as the
successor of former "German Austria." An account of Austrian
Slav and Magyar right-wing movements before and after 1918
properly belongs to the history of the other succession states.

The transformation of Austria from a conservative monarchical
despotism into a constitutional and liberal entity can be briefly
summarized. The government after 1867 consisted of a bicameral
legislature called the Reichsrat, to which the emperor surrendered
nearly all power over internal affairs. The members of the lower
house were elected by a restricted three-class suffrage which returned a majority of urban middle-class liberals. As a result of
the peculiar historical development of the Austrian provinces these

liberals were almost entirely German-speaking and, in Austrian parlance, of "German nationality." The governing party, until 1879, was the Constitutional party (Verfassungspartei), usually known as the Liberal party. The German Liberals endorsed the principle of civic and national equality, and, although they were not democrats, they believed that the "reasonable will of all" should prevail. They held, like liberals everywhere, that wealth was the criterion of political responsibility and that in the long run the laissez-faire state would provide the maximum opportunities for every individual. They were not against religion but insisted that it was a private affair. In 1868–1869 and 1874 they passed laws regulating the relationship of church and state, and in 1870 terminated the old concordat. Public education was greatly expanded under the aegis of liberalism. Teaching was freed from Catholic control, and elementary schooling was made compulsory and free. The Jews emerged as an important section of Austrian society after 1867, and their prominence is a plain sign of the dissolution of the old preliberal, precapitalist order.

The period from 1867 to 1914 was one of great industrial expansion, accompanied by the rise of corporate business, large-scale finance, and the concentration of production in fewer and bigger firms. These economic changes had, as elsewhere, striking social consequences. The working population was drawn into the vortex of the Industrial Revolution: peasants left the land; artisans gave up their home shops; towns and cities rapidly expanded, creating great sprawling slums. It was a time of increasing material wealth, unevenly distributed.

After the introduction of constitutional government, the political scene was dominated by three camps: the Socialist, the German-nationalist, and the Christian Social-conservative. The Socialists were, of course, ideologically on the Left and socially consisted almost entirely of industrial workers. The other two camps were much less homogeneous. Neither was wholly Right or Left, and both showed a full spectrum of gradations from conservative to radical democratic.* Both also contained groups defying easy or

---

* The diversity represented by the two camps can be seen from the names by which their members were known. In the national camp these were *Grossdeutsche*,

conventional classification; today they would be called the radical Right. It is with these groups and their leaders that this paper is chiefly concerned.

The first evidence of a modern rightist movement in Austria did not come, surprisingly enough, from such logical opponents of liberalism and laissez-faire capitalism as Catholics and artisans but from the extreme German nationalists among the students at the universities of Vienna and Graz. They were the first to combine the defense of tradition with demands for revolutionary changes in the name of the people and to use a violent tone incompatible with the temperate, compromising spirit of classical conservatism. The original inspiration for nationalism was of course the "left" idea of popular sovereignty and national liberty.

In Austrian society at large most individuals of "German nationality" reconciled "German patriotism" and Austrian citizenship by combining loyalty to the Austrian state with support for German culture—and usually German political predominance—in the empire. Ambiguous as this may seem, until 1914 they managed it fairly well, and the German Austrians as a whole were among the strongest supporters of the Habsburg monarchy. The proportion of German and Austrian attachment varied from decade to decade and among classes and individuals, but a basic loyalty to

---

Kleindeutsche, Alldeutsche, Gross-Oesterreicher, Deutschnationale, Deutsch-Liberale, Betont-Nationale, Deutsch-Freiheitliche, Verfassungspartei, Linke, Junge, and *Nationalsozialisten*. The Christian Social-conservatives included *Konservative, Katholische Volkspartei, Christlich Soziale, Centrum, Vogelsang Schule, Oesterreichische Aktion,* and *Heimwehr*. The seating of deputies in the early imperial Reichsrat showed that the designations Right and Left were used more loosely than in other parliaments. On the far right sat the aristocratic Polish landowners and next to them other Slavs; toward the middle came various clerical parties; and on the far left were the wealthy laissez-faire German Liberals. In the mid-eighties the Pan-Germans sat on the far left. In the nineties, when the clerical Christian Socials and the Marxist Social Democrats entered parliament, they sat next to each other on the left, while the democratic Catholic People's Party sat on the right and the Pan-Germans found themselves in the center. After 1907 the Catholic People's Party sat on the left while the Social Democrats moved to the center. The successors of these groups in the republic were often confused as to where they belonged in the traditional Left-Right spectrum. The political category of the Right in Austria is therefore as elusive as it is anywhere in Europe.

Austria could always be counted on. A small minority took the opposite course, rejected the idea that the separation of Austria from Germany was permanent, and determined to achieve German unity by the *Anschluss* of German Austria—the Alpine provinces, Lower Austria, and Bohemia-Moravia-Silesia—to the Prussian Reich. This brand of nationalism was known in Austria somewhat confusingly as *Kleindeutsch* from its advocacy of Prussia as the inspiration and agent of German unity. In time it was more generally called *Alldeutsch* or Pan-German.

The university Burschenschaften, traditional nationalist social fraternities that had spread to Austria from Germany in the 1840's, were the earliest centers of Pan-German agitation. Vienna had, among others, the Olympia, Silesia, Alemannia, and Teutonia; Graz the Orion, Styria, and Arminia. Their members became fanatical proselytizers for an all-German Prussian Reich and set out to convert, dominate, or destroy the many other student organizations that were such a prominent feature of Austrian life in the constitutional era.

The young Pan-German fanatics gained control of these societies by electing their own men to offices and committees. They sponsored grandiose memorial ceremonies for heroes of German national history such as Richard Wagner and Bismarck and intimidated their opponents by their swaggering and physical violence. Duelling with sabers and the whole barbarous cult of the *Mensur* was exclusively a Pan-German practice in Austria. Vienna and Graz were the earliest and always remained the chief centers of Pan-Germanism. At Prague, Brünn, and Innsbruck, Pan-German influence was slight at first but acquired considerable strength after 1890.

The basic premise of the students' political ideology was that German national unity was the overriding consideration in every political question. After the battles of Königgrätz (1866) and Sedan (1870) it was obvious that this goal could be achieved only through the agency of Prussia and Bismarck. All political activity was therefore to be dedicated to destroying Austria so that its German-speaking provinces could return to the German Reich. "Home to the Reich" was a simple and powerful slogan.

As a result of the cult of Prussia, the Austrian Pan-Germans, like many once-liberal nationalists in Germany, came to admire as German virtues certain specifically Prussian attitudes and habits that repelled contemporary liberals and democrats. This Prusso-philia assumed an exaggerated, flamboyant, and uncritical form in Austria and appeared to Reich Germans who observed it as quite bizarre. The Pan-German students' speeches and broadside litera-ture of the seventies exalted service to the German state; they were full of the worship of force, contempt for humanitarian law and justice, and criticism of parliamentary government and capi-talism as selfish, "individualistic," antinational, and agents of "de-cay" (*Zersetzung*). The cult of Prussia as interpreted by the Aus-trian nationalist students in the age of "realism" and Social Darwin-ism encouraged inconsiderateness of every kind as proof of strength, as well as harsh behavior toward the weak, and summary, con-temptuous, and cynical acts.

The Pan-German students set out to destroy all "foreign influ-ences" in university life. They declared that only "Germans" could belong to German organizations and that in "German Aus-tria" only German organizations must exist. An almost inevitable next step was to define German nationality in terms of the well-known biological bias of the age. Pan-German societies first denied admission to Jews, and subsequently expelled those who were al-ready members—even if baptized—as representatives of an alien race who could never be assimilated. When exclusion became wide-spread it encountered considerable opposition, especially among the alumni or *alte Herren*, but by 1885 the racial anti-Semites were generally victorious at Vienna and Graz.

About 1876 the Vienna student fraternities began to have con-tacts with Georg von Schönerer, a left-wing Liberal member of parliament whose strident German nationalism appealed to them. By 1878 he was a frequent and honored guest of such Pan-German societies as the Teutonia, Libertia, and Oppavia. Schönerer and the students were temperamentally alike—both were firmly "un-compromising" or *radikal* in the German sense—and their affinity supplied a marked impetus to the birth of a right-wing political movement. Schönerer taught the students the importance of the social question in the political struggle, showed them how to appeal to the masses to defend German culture, and urged them to enter the political arena. By his bold attacks on the whole Austrian "establishment"—liberal, capitalist, wealthy, dynastic, and Catholic—he demonstrated that it was possible for ordinary men to attack the mighty enemy openly, and gave them the feeling that they would make history. On their part the students gradually converted Schönerer to their Prussophilia and anti-Semitism. Under their influence he moved, over a period of ten years, from radical leftist criticism of Austrian conditions to what may be described as a radical rightist position.

Two events in 1879 helped to close the ranks of the Pan-Germans and intensify their intransigence. The conclusion of the Dual Alliance between Austria and the German Reich detached from the Pan-Germans quite a number of students who reasoned that, since Bismarck now relied on Austria for the security of Germany, their duty was to give up their anti-Austrian position. Those who remained Pan-German, however, were now the toughest of the irreconcilables. The second event was the defeat of the German Liberals in the Reichsrat elections and the coming to power of a coalition of conservatives, clericals, and Slavs known as the Iron Ring, headed by Count Eduard Taaffe. By demonstrating the impotence of the German Liberals to block government action "against the Germans," the political struggles of the next thirteen years favored the growth of extremism.

As late as 1882 Schönerer worked with democrats and Jews like Viktor Adler (later a Marxist) and the reformist Liberals Heinrich Friedjung and Adolf Fischhof on a democratic program, the famous Linz Program, which advocated universal suffrage, advanced social legislation, and greater civil liberty. But he was soon to become obsessed with the central "evil" of Jewish influence. In 1884 in his fight against the iniquitous exploitation of the Austrian railroads by Rothschild interests, he mixed incongruous racial abuse with cogent patriotic arguments. During this period he fought for such disparate causes as economic justice for workers and peasants, protection against arbitrary police repression of strikers, and special legislation against Jews. His anti-Semitic proposal of 1887—that Jews be confined in ghettos and restricted to certain occupations—

may be regarded as a precursor of the Nazi Nuremberg laws. He was against military expansion in the Balkans but for the swollen German army, against privileged suffrage but in favor of gagging the Jewish-controlled press. He demanded civil liberty for Germans in Austria but countenanced authoritarian rule in Bismarck's Reich. In 1885 he broke all formal ties with the other German groups in parliament and formed his own party—consisting of himself and one other deputy—the German National Association (Deutschnationale Vereinigung), which in common parlance was called the Pan-German (Alldeutsch) party.

The most striking quality of Schönerer's ideology was its negativism. He was much more *against* Jews, Slavs, and Liberals than he was *for* social justice, popular sovereignty, or even German unity. His denunciations became so extreme that few of his contemporaries noticed how his position had shifted and only the Social Democrats, who claimed to be the exclusive champions of the Left, classed him in his day as a rightist. The common adjective used to describe Schönerer and his followers was *radikal,* the antithesis of conservative. His positive program, however, was conservative, even reactionary, insofar as it was designed to extend ad absurdum the existing privileges of all Germans, as such, and of certain classes, chiefly small peasants and artisans, whose livelihood was being undermined by the industrial transformation of the empire. In brief, he demanded revolutionary changes for conservative ends.

Schönerer's adoption of Pan-Germanism greatly aided the fanatically nationalist student leaders in their drive to make all the Burschenschaft fraternities and clubs (*Vereine*) openly Pan-German and anti-Semitic. Between 1880 and 1885 most of these groups at Vienna and Graz went extremist. In 1884 ten fraternities and two clubs signed a "German agreement" (*Deutscher Delegierten-Konvent*) to this effect. Few of them signed the "Aryan paragraph" without an internal struggle. The votes usually followed long periods of acrimonious dispute between an initial Pan-German minority and a more moderate but poorly led majority. In most instances the extremists drove their enemies into resignation or got them expelled.

Schönerer himself founded an extraordinary number of local, occupational, and general associations. In the eighties he extended these from Lower Austria and Vienna, where the Deutschnationaler Verein and the Oesterreichischer Reformverein were the most notable, to Styria, Bohemia, Tyrol, Upper Austria, Carinthia, and Carniola, and spent a good part of every year traveling up and down the country addressing the members. Without great physical vitality as well as fanatical conviction he could never have maintained this gruelling activity on which his influence outside Vienna was built.

A man of action and a brilliant phrase-maker on the stump, Schönerer was a poor theorist. He was not really interested in intellectual matters, and his conception of ideological unity and racial purity—proclaimed in his slogan "Through Purity to Unity"—meant simply unconditional conformity to Herr von Schönerer's ideas. The Pan-German movement produced no writers or theorists comparable to the exponents of integral nationalism in Germany and France. Its press featured petty squabbles and windy generalized abuse of Schönerer's enemies; his own journal, *Unverfälschte Deutsche Worte* (founded 1883), sold only between three and five thousand copies at its peak and was extremely dull.

In 1888 Schönerer made a bad mistake which nearly destroyed the whole Pan-German movement. At the head of a gang, he brutally assaulted the staff of a Vienna newspaper because of a trivial incident. Tried and sentenced to four months in prison, he lost his inherited knighthood, was deprived of the right to vote or to sit in any elected body for five years, and was compelled to resign from the Reichsrat. His party in parliament, now grown to five, fell apart amid recriminations. A number of Burschenschaften severed their long-standing close ties with him, and many of the local political clubs on which his influence with the voters depended either dissolved or, like the Reformverein, went over to his clerical rival, Karl Lueger. For nine years after Schönerer's sentencing the Pan-German movement was in confusion. Schönerer recovered his civil rights in 1893 and occasionally addressed loyal student societies or nationalist workers' associations but chiefly he sulked at Schloss Rosenau, his estate in Lower Austria.

The emergence of a number of new popular radical parties between 1890 and 1895 seemed to block Schönerer's chance of ever again putting himself at the head of the masses. The Social Democratic party, founded in 1888, soon established its claim as the representative of most union-organized and politically conscious industrial workers. The Christian Social party, inspired by notable Catholic social thinkers and led by Karl Lueger, the most gifted demagogue in Austria, was founded in 1890. In 1895 the democratic and nationalist radicals of the old Liberal party formed their own organization, the German People's party, and the more democratic conservatives formed the Catholic People's party. Both denounced surviving class privileges and the abuses of capitalism; and both called for a democratic suffrage, the preservation of German predominance in Austria, and legislation to protect the material interests of peasants, artisans, and the provincial intelligentsia. They also adopted anti-Semitism. These developments might have kept Schönerer in permanent oblivion had not an issue arisen in 1897 that gave him the opportunity of a lifetime.

The language question—that is, how far languages other than German would be permissible in courts and administration—had become by 1890 the most important political issue in Austria. In 1895, a scant two years after the fall of the Iron Ring, a new coalition of Slavs, conservatives, and clericals, headed by Count Kasimir Badeni, came to power. The Reichsrat election of 1897 returned an unprecedented number of radicals, among whom, almost as an unknown, was Georg Schönerer. After the years of virtual exile, the rising tension between Germans and Slavs returned him to the political arena. In April, 1897, Count Badeni issued his celebrated Speech Ordinances to meet the demands of his Slav —chiefly Czech—supporters, justifying them as a further step toward realizing the equality of Czechs and Germans which was guaranteed by the constitution.

Almost all German Austrians feared that the Speech Ordinances meant their submersion in a Slav state, while the great army of civil servants foresaw the loss of their jobs. For six months, therefore, the German parties obstructed the business of parliament by filibusters and noisy disorders. The whole country was aroused,

Amid this national excitement, Schönerer became the man of the hour. He dominated the berserk parliament, organized and led parades, addressed great crowds in Vienna and all the principal cities, and declaimed passionately about *Germania irredenta,* even hinting at revolution to be followed by *Anschluss* to Germany. The emperor and his advisers were intimidated by the "argument of the streets" and Badeni was removed. The mob credited Schönerer with having driven him from office.

The uproar incited by Schönerer had in fact done more than overthrow a minister; it had discredited parliamentary government. Thoroughly reasonable proposals had almost caused a revolution; the mood of a mob had prevailed over the government. The ordinances were modified, but neither the Germans nor the Slavs were satisfied, and the national hatred generated by their clash in 1897 was never allayed. It deadlocked the machinery of government till the end of the monarchy. The parliamentary stalemate compelled rule by decree, which led to increasing toleration of autocratic methods and to contempt for legal processes. Many German Austrians lost faith in liberal democracy, the difference between ethical and barbaric behavior was blurred, and the way was opened to dictatorship. If Schönerer cannot be held wholly responsible for this development, certainly no man contributed more to it than he.

Between 1898 and 1902 a large number of nationalist workers' associations were organized under Schönerer's aegis. In 1899 a congress of several hundred delegates, representing at least four thousand workers, met at Eger, Bohemia, and pledged allegiance to his person and program. A group of German workers' protective associations formed to combat the menace of Czech competition, known as the Mährisch-Trübaner Verband and counting over four thousand members by 1900, joined forces with him. Many other more or less formally organized nationalist-workers' groups enlisted under his banner. The Pan-German students, too, rallied once more to Schönerer with fanatical enthusiasm and apparently in a mood for revolution. In Vienna and Prague they fraternized ostentatiously with workers, in a way reminiscent of 1848. In Prague pitched battles took place when German students, parading with sabers, boots, and colors, met angry Czech mobs. Martial law had to be declared. Between 1897 and 1900 almost all German students at Prague, Brünn, and Innsbruck who were not Jews threw in their lot with the Pan-Germans.

After 1898, Schönerer, for purely nationalist reasons, became closely involved with the *Los von Rom* movement, which aimed to convert Austrians to Lutheranism, "the German religion." As early as the seventies some Pan-German students had left the Catholic Church. By 1897 a popular slogan at student gatherings was *Ein Volk—Ein Reich—Ein Gott* ("One People—One Country—One God"), and even nominally Catholic fraternities encouraged their members to become Lutherans. Schönerer announced that he himself would join the Lutheran Church when the ten-thousandth convert had declared himself. Among the converts was the mystic Jörg Lanz von Liebenfels, whose racist theory of high and low, blond and dark, heroic and cowardly, Germanic and non-Germanic "races" is thought to have had an important influence on Hitler.

Schönerer's central idea was the overwhelming importance of race in human destiny. He had acquired in the years since his first association with the Vienna students a fanatical belief in the existence and superiority of a pure undiluted German or Germanic-Nordic *Herrenvolk.* This was only an exaggerated form of theories widespread in Europe at the time. It was related to the romantic picture of freedom-loving German tribesmen, to Social Darwinism with its biological laws and notion of progress through struggle, to the racial theories of Gobineau and Lapouge, to Richard Wagner's Germanic cult and Nietzsche's exaltation of the "blond beast" and contempt for Christianity, to the economic theories of German anti-Marxist social reformers like Eugen Dühring and Adolf Wagner, and to the anti-Semitism of the Berlin court preacher Adolf Stöcker. For some of Schönerer's disciples this meant ultimately a rejection of Christianity, a new calendar with a Yule feast instead of Christmas, a condemnation of Charlemagne as the "Saxon killer" and of Roman law and latinate words as foreign, a preference for native dress (*Deutsche Tracht*) over foreign clothes and for German gymnastics (*Turnen*) over alien "sport." If Schönerer's worship of *Deutschtum* (Germanism) was a positive and in some ways constructive attitude, his hatred of Jews and later his unrestrained anti-Catholicism, amounting to a rejection of Christianity, were negative and sterile obsessions. They had, however, a powerful appeal when he proclaimed them in striking phrases. This was recognized with alarm by the Social Democrats and the moderate German bourgeois parties.

After the Badeni crisis, Schönerer might have become a great revolutionary leader of the Austrian Germans. For the better part of a generation he had been one of the most talked-about figures in political life. Vague though his notions of government were, he represented a complete break with the Austrian parliamentary tradition of trying to effect a compromise between Germans and Slavs, employers and workers, democracy and privilege. He promised to establish German rule, reduce Slavs and Jews to the status of helots, and drive the money-changers from the temple. The test of all legislation "was the good of the workers and peasants"; yet he would also strike down the Socialists, obnoxious to many for their heavily Jewish leadership and their insistence on proletarianization and national and racial equality. German workers were becoming dissatisfied with Marxist internationalism because it offered no immediate defense of their jobs against Czech scabs; many German artisans and shopkeepers, despite their clericalism, had concluded from the Taaffe and Badeni regimes that Catholic governments meant Slav rule. Schönerer addressed himself to the people's most pressing problems, and he had a gift for arousing mass passions. When the Reichsrat election of 1901 brought twenty-one Pan-Germans into parliament, he became a force to be reckoned with.

For the second time Schönerer destroyed his party through a succession of mistakes caused primarily by his own bad judgment and violent temperament. He quarreled in 1902 with his ablest lieutenant, Karl Hermann Wolf, over petty questions of authority. He lost much of his old imaginative sympathy with the aspirations, destructive as well as positive, of the common people. He actually became opposed to the idea of a mass movement because he feared that its program would be watered down as more people joined it. Hitler later wrote of Schönerer that to get real power he would have had to win the allegiance of the masses by a genuinely revolutionary social program couched in simple terms. Schönerer and the Pan-German party after 1901 lacked the essential democratic and revolutionary élan. As Hitler put it, they lacked the "desperation, courage, and toughness necessary to carry out a revolution."

Although Schönerer could not or would not fight for his program by leading a popular uprising, he worked for it in parliament. He wasted his energies, however, in sterile obstruction, and his measures were regularly defeated. In Hitler's words, "the Pan-German deputies could talk until their throats were hoarse, the effect was naught." The movement degenerated into little more than a middle-class club for academic discussion, mutedly radical. Its original, almost ecstatic cult of Germanism faded to futile sentiment.

A notable slackening of radicalism set in among the students after 1900. Schönerer's fiercest supporters in the Burschenschaften and Vereine began to question the wisdom of his policy. Many resented his dictatorial attitude and insistence on absolute obedience. After his quarrel with Wolf most of them followed the latter. They remained prussophile and anti-Semitic, but they wanted to get out of the "national ghetto" to which allegiance to Schönerer had confined them.

In the Reichsrat election of 1907, the first with universal and equal manhood suffrage, the Christian Socialists and Social Democrats emerged as the two largest parties. Schönerer, a thoroughgoing opponent of political democracy by now, refused to make common cause with anyone who would not swear fealty to himself —and the Pan-German party lost every one of its seats. Schönerer was defeated in his own constituency of Eger (Bohemia) by a crushing majority for the Socialist candidate. It was the end of his party in Austrian political life. The Austrian Germans had turned decisively against Schönerer's uncompromising position, recognizing at last that supporting him had cost them all real influence and participation in political life. The great majority accepted the Austrian state and urged German nationalists to take positive responsible political action. Schönerer again retired to Rosenau— where he lived, broken and aged, until his death in 1921—the fallen leader of a tiny beleaguered garrison in an enemy land.

Though decisively repudiated by the electorate, Schönerer was a figure of great and lasting consequence. He had almost single-handedly created a German national rightist movement and had given it the fundamental character and ideology it would have for at least a generation after his death. He was the first representative of the radical Right in Austrian political life. His work bore fruit only after 1918 when changed conditions revived the Pan-German movement in a new form and with redoubled force.

In *Mein Kampf* Hitler gave almost as much praise to Lueger as to Schönerer. This has helped to focus attention on the Christian Social party as the far Right of the Catholic conservative camp in Austrian society. The party and most of its leaders were indeed antiliberal, anticapitalist, anti-Marxist, and anti-Semitic. They were also committed to defend the Catholic character of the Austrian state, the integrity of the empire, and the honor of the dynasty. They exploited the techniques of democracy and occasionally used mob violence. The party, however, cannot justly be classified as simply a right-wing movement. Throughout the years, from its founding in 1890 to the end of the monarchy and down through the first republic, where it was the governing party par excellence, it represented a wide variety of views.

The starting point for the whole Christian Social movement was the attempt of Catholics in the 1870's to find positive ways of dealing with the problems confronting the Church and raised by the French and Industrial Revolutions. The accession to the papacy of Leo XIII (1878) and the assumption of the editorship of the Vienna Catholic journal *Das Vaterland* by Karl von Vogelsang (1875), a Protestant landowner from Mecklenburg who had been converted to Catholicism and had emigrated to Austria, mark the opening of an era in European and Austrian Catholic social thought.

In *Libertas Praestantissimum*, Leo XIII outlined a new program as a guide for Catholics in an age of expanding industrialism and democracy. His three fundamental political principles led to the ultimate emergence of a Catholic Right in Austria. Democracy, he declared, was not immoral in itself so long as it recognized the divine origin of civil authority and ensured the welfare of the people; the separation of Church and state might be tolerated but could never be accepted as ideal, and good Catholics were obligated to oppose it; the liberal bourgeois state led inevitably to Jacobin dictatorship. These statements were important to Austrians because the country was being rapidly transformed politically, economically, and socially, and Austrian Catholics were beginning to grapple with the problems thus created. The economic and social abuses of the *Gründerzeit* (1867–1874), together with the confessional legislation and repudiation of the concordat, had alarmed Vogelsang into thinking that the liberal state violated the basic principles of Catholic doctrine and social justice.

Vogelsang's ideal, expounded in *Das Vaterland* and a number of other journals he founded and edited, was a "social monarchy," corporative, highly centralized, and even dictatorial, but limited by its conservative *ständisch* (guild) basis. He traced the new problems of the times to the market economy and the rise of finance capitalism. In a society disorganized by the substitution of individual rights for *ständisch* rights (the corporate rights of occupational groups), he maintained that the workers would revolt and destroy everything unless wages were based on social needs rather than on the law of supply and demand. In his harsh polemical style he castigated the "false concept of equality and freedom" for destroying the family with its natural differentiation of functions necessary for a healthy life; liberalism for doing away with the guilds and estates that had mediated between employers and workers and had laid down socially valuable rules governing conditions of work; and the capitalists, who, freed from all restrictions on economic activity, used their freedom and power against the economically weak, to the detriment of society. "Gin and the Jewish press," he proclaimed, "that is to say, drunken stupor and obscenities, manage to kill the remaining memories of a Christian past in these unfortunate victims."

In Vogelsang's school of social theory, known as *Sozialreform*, the emphasis was on a complete break with liberal society and a restoration of what he believed to be the old organic order. He imparted to Austrian Catholic social thought, down to World War II, his strong medieval bias (acquired from his reading of Karl Adam Müller, Bishop Ketteler, Adolf Wagner, Johann Rodbertus, and Albert Schäffle), his conservative monarchism, and his concern for the industrial proletariat.

Several features of Austrian society help to explain why the monarchistic, romantic, utopian ideas of *Sozialreform* interested the general public and acquired lasting political importance. The peasantry and petite bourgeoisie were the chief supporters of Catholic political action; there had always been strong corporate organizations in the professions, agriculture, and trades; and until the end of the monarchy there was a very close tie between the dynasty and the Catholic Church.

Vogelsang was an energetic organizer of political action as well as a theorist. He gathered under his intellectual leadership a number of ambitious political leaders, such as Karl Lueger, hitherto a radical Liberal, Princes Alfred and Alois Liechtenstein, Franz Martin Schindler, and others. Out of this group, in 1890, came the Christian Social party, dedicated to reforming society on Catholic lines by winning the support of the masses.

The adherence of Karl Lueger made the Christian Social party an effective fighting force. Lueger saw that the newly enfranchised artisans and workers were likely to vote for the party least encumbered with doctrine, and he shrewdly guessed that for many of them the Liberals and Social Democrats had overstepped the mark with their highflown theoretical discussions. Both liberalism and Marxism were also, he reasoned, opposed to the economic interests of the petite bourgeoisie. Lueger accused the Liberals—who controlled the Vienna city administration until 1895 when he himself became the undisputed master of the city—of being freethinking in religion, and materialist and "Manchesterian" in ethics and economics, but he attacked them most effectively for representing the purse-proud, culturally snobbish upper bourgeoisie, in which Jews were prominent. The Social Democrats, he charged, were sterile preachers of class hatred, destroyers of property, levelers without respect for skills or training, who would grind everyone down to the drab faceless proletarian: Social Democracy was a consequence of liberalism and equally materialist, anti-Christian, and Jewish-dominated. Through the force of these utterances, derived partly from serious Catholic writers and partly from an opportunist appreciation of what would attract votes, he became the leader of the first modern mass party in Austria.

Lueger and many lesser leaders made anti-Semitism their principal theme. Though they tended to put it on a religious basis, not the racial one of Pan-Germanism, there was no noticeable distinction between their anti-Semitic vocabulary and Schönerer's. Both stressed the connection between Jews and pornography, prostitution, trickery, and cowardice, freely resorting to the language of the gutter in their speeches, newspapers, and broadsides. Lueger himself pandered to the anti-Semitic prejudices of the large artisan class in Austrian society, though in a famous phrase he reserved to himself the right to say "who is a Jew." Two extreme anti-Semitic artisan leaders, Ernst Schneider and Josef Buschenhagen, became influential in the party, and two editors, Ernst Vergani in the *Deutsches Volksblatt* and Karl von Zerboni in the *Oesterreichischer Volksfreund*, preached a vague jumble of antiliberalism, anticapitalism, and anti-Semitism that lacked any consistent legislative or social program but was popular with the Viennese masses.

Alarmed at the revolutionary implications of the Christian Social movement, the government refused four times between 1895 and 1897 to confirm Lueger as mayor of Vienna. In 1895 the government requested the pope to condemn the movement on the ground that it was exploiting and perverting patriotic and religious tenets under the cover of devotion to dynasty and Church. The Christian Social extremists, the government pointed out, attacked the whole social order with the very arguments used by the Social Democrats and, through their vehemence, fostered rebellious attitudes.

With successive extensions of the suffrage (in 1897 and 1907), the party rapidly increased its parliamentary strength. Represented in 1890 by only Lueger and Robert Pattai, a former associate of Schönerer's, it became in 1907 the second largest party in the Reichsrat, with 67 seats. It also captured the mayoralty and city council of Vienna and of many provincial capitals and industrial cities. By 1900 Christian Socialism had become an important factor in Austrian life.

Power brought a sense of responsibility, and in the last decade of the monarchy's existence the party became a supporter of parliamentary rule and statesmanlike compromise, the preëminent *Staats- und Reichspartei*. The accession of most of the former conservatives, along with contacts with members of the ruling class, high officials, and Archduke Franz Ferdinand, had a further moderating effect. The center of gravity inside the party shifted toward the conservatives; the peasantry and the haute bourgeoisie became more influential. The intellectual backbone of the Christian Social Right, the Vogelsang school of *Sozialreform,* lost influence after 1900. Vogelsang himself had died in 1890. *Rerum novarum* (1891) seemed to favor patient piecemeal reforms. The encyclical *Graves de communi* (1901) warned Catholics against the Church's too-enthusiastic radical supporters. The Vogelsang influence was also weakened by the prestige of Lueger, the supreme opportunist and skeptic of systems. When war broke out in 1914 and regular political life was suspended, the rightist role of the Christian Socialists faded away. Only in 1918, when the Habsburg empire disintegrated into the Succession States and the Social Democrats ruled Vienna, did a serious radical antidemocratic force appear again in the Christian Social-conservative camp.

The Pan-Germans and the Christian Social extremists were alike in being only pseudoconservative. They believed they were defending important institutions or values, but the primary interest of the Pan-Germans was German hegemony and the embodiment of the spiritual unity of all Germans in a political reality; that of the Christian Socialists was the destruction of capitalism and of Jewish business. Both were supported by certain specific precapitalist economic interests, yet they had little in common with true conservatism, demanding far-reaching changes that would have meant political and social revolution. Both sought total victory and suppression of all who disagreed with them: had Schönerer or the early Christian Social extremists come to power, representative government, civil equality, the rule of law, existing property relations, and many other institutions of the Austrian empire would certainly have been abolished. While both movements were ostensibly antiliberal, anticapitalist, anti-Marxist, and anti-Semitic, neither ever made clear whether or not these loudly trumpeted attitudes were its real raison d'etre. Both can be viewed as expressions of a fin de siècle vogue of violence as well as of serious ideological aims. Their followers were generally confused men who were more interested in action than in theories. Although the rise of the nationalist and Christian Social Right was a form of social and economic protest, deeply buried psychological motives were also operative: submissiveness to a leader was combined with anarchic impulses and chaotic destructiveness; defense of traditional values against real or imaginary dangers was combined with behavior consciously or unconsciously designed to destroy them.

Hitler, in *Mein Kampf*, paid tribute to Schönerer and Lueger as his teachers and justified his bloody uprising of November 9, 1923, to a Munich court by saying: "I came as a seventeen-year-old boy to Vienna. . . . I left Vienna as a 100 per cent anti-Semite, a deadly enemy of the whole Marxist movement, and a Pan-German in my political outlook."

The assassination of Archduke Franz Ferdinand and the outbreak of war in 1914 affected German Austrians with special force. The war was, for them, even more than for the Germans of the Reich, a struggle for survival as the "state people" of the multi-national empire. They actually welcomed the German chancellor's crude statement that the Central Powers were fighting a war of Teuton against Slav. The precarious position of the monarchy and the entirely defensive mentality of the Austrians militated against the appearance in Austria of rightist extremists advocating a "victory peace" and extensive annexations. Any possible annexations would have made the German Austrians an even smaller minority and weakened their political predominance further. The only expression of postwar plans in domestic German Austrian politics was the Easter Declaration of 1916 in which all German parties, including the "German" Christian Socialists, announced that their common postwar aim was a strong and healthy Austria under German-Austrian leadership.

The political situation of German Austria changed radically in early 1918 when appalling casualties, bad news from the fronts, food shortages, and rumors of mutiny, treason, and corruption caused a serious crisis in public confidence. By summer the Austro-Hungarian monarchy was in dissolution, national and social revolution threatened in the Slav lands, and strikes and sabotage by the workers of Vienna and Budapest showed that Bolshevik propaganda would find receptive ground. By October it was evident that an immense catastrophe was about to engulf the monarchy. The principal victim would be the German bourgeoisie, but the prospect for the emperor and the Catholic Church was equally dark. The Christian Social conservative and German national camps faced being ground between the stones of Slav nationalism and proletarian bolshevism. Only the Austrian Social Democrats could contemplate defeat with equanimity, since it would also destroy their enemies.

Amid these disasters the German deputies of the former Reichsrat met as the provisional National Assembly of "German Austria." Attended by 39 Social Democrats, 70 Christian Socialists, and 101 loosely allied German nationals, it represented the three camps that had dominated German-Austrian political life under the empire. On October 30, mobs of workmen and students led by Social Democrats began a series of demonstrations that became a revolution. Though in a minority in the Assembly, the Socialists seized executive authority; Emperor Karl abdicated at Schönbrunn on November 11. The following day, by agreement among the leaders of the three camps, "German Austria" was proclaimed a "democratic republic" and an "integral part" of the German Republic just established at Berlin.

The provisional (or revolutionary) government faced the almost insuperable task of settling seven basic questions in a way that would satisfy a majority of the population: it had to establish and defend the territorial boundaries of the state, draft a democratic constitution that would secure internal peace, decide on the relationship of German Austria to the Austrian Slav states and to the German Republic, rehabilitate the economy, find jobs for demobilized soldiers and thousands of now-redundant civil servants, stave off famine and civil war, and finally sign a tolerable peace treaty with the Allies. The Christian Social conservative camp would have preferred a monarchy and a federal union with the

Austrian Slav states, or, failing that, a federal union with Germany. It was willing, however, to accept a republic—Catholic theory was quite explicit on this point—because it was confident of protecting religion by persuading the electorate to return anti-Socialist majorities; the question of whether liberal democratic institutions were "appropriate to the time and circumstances of national life" could be reviewed later. The Socialists for their part insisted on a republic and hoped for a federal union with Germany; but they were ready to compromise doctrinal rigidity and accept a democratic republic, trusting that they, rather than the bourgeois parties, would convert the electorate and introduce socialism without force. The majority of German nationalists—who coalesced into two parties, the larger Grossdeutsche Volkspartei ("Great-German People's Party") and the Landbund ("Land League")—wanted, above all, *Anschluss* to Germany, but were prepared to wait until it could be accomplished peaceably. There was enough basis for compromise and common action to produce agreement on the fundamentals of the constitution.

In February, 1919, a constituent assembly was elected. The provisional republican government, headed by a Socialist, Karl Renner, and with a Christian Social leader as vice-chancellor, continued in office, and work proceeded on the constitutional document that would determine future domestic political arrangements. Meanwhile, the uneasy coalition, in which the Socialists were the ambitious and deeply distrusted senior partner, attempted to cope with the problems of famine, unemployment, epidemic disease, and Communist attempts to seize power in Vienna. The Socialist ministers suppressed the Communists, whose drive was spent by July. For a long time, however, many Austrians were terrified of Communism and could see little or no basic difference between Socialists and Communists. The Austrian Socialists' militant commitment to Marxist orthodoxy may have prevented the growth of a strong Communist party, but it heightened the bourgeoisie's dislike of Socialist rule.

Many of the Christian Social conservative rank and file had reservations about accepting their leaders' decision to collaborate with the Socialists in a democratic republic. They feared that life would become still further de-Christianized and that the republic was an instrument of Freemasons and Jews to destroy Christianity. Catholic social teaching had left in many members of the Christian Social camp a bias against liberal institutions and in favor of solving social questions by an autocratic state with an organic hierarchical society actuated by a single system of belief.

Despite the strong radical trends of 1918, the small extremist groups of the German-national camp, who carried on the Pan-German views of Schönerer, remained leaderless and politically unimportant. The moderates who dominated the Grossdeutsche Volkspartei represented German nationalist opinion. The extremists, however, continued to form a small hard nucleus of nationalist resentment against the republic and its institutions.

When the Socialist Chancellor signed the Treaty of St. Germain with the Allied Powers on September 10, 1919, popular resentment at the treaty's harsh terms and the way it was imposed turned against the Socialists and heightened the anti-Marxists' emotional conviction that socialism and democracy were responsible for all the country's woes. The rise of a new radical movement of the Right became almost inevitable.

The destruction of the polyglot Habsburg empire, in which the German Austrians had enjoyed many advantages, was perhaps the most spectacular of the many consequences of World War I. *Alt-Oesterreich* as a state and a state of mind was obliterated. "L'Autriche," Clemenceau observed cruelly, "c'est ce qui reste." Excessive nationalism prevented economic and political coöperation between Austria and the other Succession States. The peace treaty had expressly forbidden union with Germany; the famous principle of self-determination had succumbed to the Italian, Czechoslovak, and Yugoslav armies and, at Paris, to political expediency. The democratic Republic of Austria, at best second choice of all three camps, had been established under the spell of defeat and revolution. Many angry Austrians rejected the Vienna politicians' policy of collaboration with the Socialists and the idea of parliamentary government based on consensus. The return of soldiers hardened by their experience at the front and embittered by enemy prison camps added to the population several hundred thousand uprooted

and reckless men habituated to hatred and violence. In defiance
of the moderate Vienna leaders who favored a policy of compromise in the tradition of the old Reichsrat, these men wanted to take
things into their own hands. That they had no program and that
their problems were beyond solution by armed force made no
difference to them.

The first expressions of this mood of readiness for action appeared in the provinces and were directed against the threat of
foreign invasion. Gangs of men in the border provinces of Styria,
Carinthia, and Tyrol raided demobilization depots and armed
themselves with guns left from the war. Leaders formed these men
into military units and they became local "defense corps." Among
a variety of names by which they were known, two, Heimatschutz
and Heimwehr, both expressing the idea of a home guard, became
the usual designation for the whole movement. In Styria, Anton
Rintelen, a lawyer of Graz, raised an armed band to drive off
Hungarian Soviet marauders. In Carinthia, Heimwehr units fought
the Yugoslavs who were attempting to seize the Klagenfurt basin.
In Tyrol, Richard Steidle, an Innsbruck lawyer, raised a force to
combat both the Bavarian Soviet troops from Munich and the
Italians threatening the border at the Brenner Pass. His chief of
staff was a refugee from the collapsed rightist Kapp *putsch* in
Berlin, ex-Major Waldemar Pabst, a German citizen. Pabst was a
brilliant organizer and did much to weld the many disparate and
contentious defense corps into something like a single force. The
Heimwehr movement, however, always retained its local or provincial and personal character.

The provincial individuality of the units was a source of strength
as well as weakness. Their patriotism was stimulated by the use of
local insignia, colors, and costumes; they were often made up of
members of volunteer fire companies, veterans' associations, or
gymnastic clubs. A typical feature of their ceremonial was the field
mass at which flags were blessed by the parish priest. Some units
were clerical, others nationalist; some were inclined to serve a
political party as auxiliary police, others to form a Heimwehr party;
some wanted to take part in elections, others to seize power and
set up a dictatorship.

The men who joined the Heimwehr were chiefly urban middle-class tradesmen, professional men, civil servants, former army officers, small property owners, and rentiers. These were the groups that had been hardest hit by the collapse of the monarchy and had seen their situation deteriorating in the next few years as that of the workers and peasants improved.

Local conditions, social status, individual beliefs, and temperament determined whether a man became an active Heimwehr member or a supporter of the Vienna party leaders and the policy of compromise and coöperation. The provinces always remained the seat of Heimwehr strength; its activities furnished an outlet for the small-town inhabitants' jealousy of the capital's political power, of the cosmopolitan culture of the déraciné city dwellers, and of "Red Vienna."

The Heimwehr inevitably was drawn into the agitation for union with Germany. *Anschluss* sentiment was almost universal in Austria in the first years after the war, compounded as it was of economic misery, political helplessness, and despair over the imperial downfall. Many Catholics and conservatives felt that the Habsburg dynasty was finished and that only Germany could restore the lost provinces. Especially in Tyrol the amputation of South Tyrol rankled and people believed that only by *Anschluss* to Germany, followed by German pressure on Italy, could the area be recovered. Styria and Carinthia, old centers of racial fanaticism, resented the Yugoslav annexations. The *Anschluss* votes in Tyrol and Salzburg in 1921 were flaming protests against the peace treaty and the dismemberment of German Austria. When it became known that the French ambassador threatened to suspend all economic aid to Austria if the *Anschluss* movement were not suppressed, and that Italy, Czechoslovakia, and Yugoslavia supported French protests, a wave of xenophobia and hysterical anger at the country's impotence carried thousands into the Heimwehr.

In the face of a Christian Social–German national coalition, the Social Democrats, living up to their promise of legality, resigned the chancellorship in June, 1920, but at once began to organize their own armed force as a guarantee against a return of *Reaktion*. In October the new constitution was ratified, creating a federal state on the Swiss model, with eight provinces, one of which was Vienna. A legislature with two chambers was decreed, of which the lower, the Nationalrat, formed the principal agency of government. The Socialists then yielded to the anti-Marxist majority and left the government entirely.

Their resignation did not stop the drift toward the division of the country into two armed camps and a resulting civil war. The Socialists relied all the more heavily on the paramilitary Republikanischer Schutzbund ("League for the Protection of the Republic") because of the growing strength of the Heimwehr and the decision of the Central Federation of Industry to subsidize the anti-Marxist armed formations as a check on Socialist agitation, strikes, and advocates of red revolution. The anti-Marxists, for their part, were terrified by the Socialists' "possession of the streets," which was maintained by the big trade unions with the help of the armed and disciplined Schutzbund. The Heimwehr, to redress their numerical inferiority in Vienna, Wiener Neustadt, and other industrial centers, took to using their guns with increasing recklessness. Criminal and semicriminal elements, rootless adventurers, sadists, and every type of riffraff were attracted to the Heimwehr by these brawls and colored the character of the movement. Probably no one will ever be able to say what proportion of the rank and file consisted of despicable thugs, and what of timid, middle-class citizens concerned merely with "defense."

The Christian Social chancellors of the twenties—Mayr, Seipel, Ramek, and Streeruwitz—and their colleagues in the two anti-Marxist camps disliked and feared this unruly rightist army, but they feared the Schutzbund even more. They were willing to tolerate the Heimwehr as an auxiliary police to help maintain order, but this was a policy requiring great watchfulness. It worked reasonably well before 1929, when Monsignor Ignaz Seipel was (except for a brief interval) federal chancellor and European economic and political conditions were gradually improving. Unfortunately, the practice of private bloodletting became established in Austrian politics and lasted until the end of the republic.

A number of working-class groups that carried on the tradition of prewar Pan-German radicalism joined the political free-for-all of 1919–1920 via the German National Socialist Workers' party. The party was a descendant of the prewar German Workers' party (Deutsche Arbeiterpartei), but now began to appeal to a wider variety of interests and became really a new movement. In 1920 it federated with the Bohemian and Munich National Socialists, and a struggle began for control of the organization. In the Austrian party one faction favored legal politics and a degree of independence, though *Anschluss* and a National Socialist state were also its goal, and the other demanded unconditional obedience to the Munich leader, Adolf Hitler. The Hitler faction used physical assault, property damage, and character defamation against the "Austrian" faction and, after several years of struggle, won a complete victory; the "Austrians," like Walter Riehl, either resigned or submitted. By 1925–1926 the Austrian party was usually known simply as the Hitler movement or the Nazi party; it formed a provincial branch (*Landesverband*) of the National Socialist German Workers' party (NSDAP) under a directorate located first at Vienna and later at Linz. The provincial director (*Landesleiter*) was appointed by the party chiefs at Munich, and in 1926 all the Austrian leaders swore absolute obedience to Hitler as *Führer* and to the "immutable" Twenty-Five Points adopted as its program by the full party. (The Twenty-Five Points denounced the peace treaties, parliamentary institutions, Marxism, finance capitalism, "interest slavery," unearned income, bloated business profits, and, above all, Jews. They demanded that all citizens of the German Reich be of German blood and perform useful work, that income be equitably distributed, that the aspirations of the small shopkeepers and businessmen be satisfied, that land be given to the peasants, and that various reforms for better health and public education be carried out. Hitler emphasized that National Socialism was a radical rightist movement, not a form of the Left, by uncompromising anti-Bolshevism and assurances that he respected creative industrial capital [*schaffendes Kapital*] while seeking to seize Jewish international loan capital [*raffendes Kapital*].) The "province" of Austria was divided into eight regions, or *Gaue*, based on the Austrian federal provinces, and each was under a *Gauleiter*. In the years 1926–1928 the party structure was built up on the model of the German party with its hierarchy of *Kreis*, *Bezirk*, *Sprengel*, and *Block*, each under a *Leiter*, and with the special formations of SA, SS, Hitler Youth, and so forth. The Austrian party always had a greater predilection for violence than the German party. After the failure of the November, 1923, uprising in Munich, Hitler gave up the idea of seizing power by a *putsch* and decided to go into legal politics, but the Austrian party leaders continued to base their whole policy on terrorism and violence. Despite the inspiration of Hitler's leadership, the party remained an obscure *völkisch* group until 1930. The period 1926–1930 is important in the history of the Austrian movement only because the party then established a disciplined structure capable of withstanding all efforts of the Austrian government to destroy it.

The Heimwehr movement meanwhile spread to almost every locality in Austria. From time to time the extremists among its leaders precipitated incidents that nearly caused civil war, such as Rintelen's seizure of Judenburg, Styria, and his arrest of the local Socialist leaders. The example of the Italian Fascists' strong-arm methods against both workers and bourgeois parties, Mussolini's assumption of power (1922), and the widespread approval of the various rightist armed formations in Germany which was manifested in the border provinces, tended to induce the Heimwehr to assume gradually a more avowedly antidemocratic and dictatorial tone. The movement was too diverse, however, to support any comprehensive political philosophy or program other than anti-Marxism. Until a dramatic incident in 1927, the "July uprising" in Vienna, aroused new fears of a red revolution, it marked time, as much concerned with petty local questions and rivalries among the leaders as with what to do in Austrian national politics.

The July uprising occurred when three ex-soldiers accused of killing several workers in a street brawl at Schattendorf near Vienna were acquitted by a politically biased jury. The next day a mob of enraged Socialists surged through Vienna and burned the Palace of Justice in protest against "political justice." Ninety people were killed in the street fighting. The Socialist leaders then called a general strike which led to more clashes between the Heimwehr, trying to break the strike, and the Schutzbund. The Styrian Heimwehr leader, Walter Pfriemer, who later became a Nazi Reichstag deputy, first made his reputation by his brutality toward the striking workers in the Upper Styrian iron industry. The renewed specter of red revolution, real or imaginary, opened the way to the Heimwehr's greatest years of hope and glory.

The parade that the Styrian Heimwehr staged through the center of Wiener-Neustadt, reputedly the "reddest" city in Austria, on October 7, 1928, was an arrogant proclamation of its new power and confidence. When the Schutzbund announced a simultaneous demonstration, the Seipel government ordered police and soldiers to keep the two armed bodies apart. Again civil war was avoided by the narrowest margin, but the day was a great victory for the Heimwehr. The Socialists had lost their boasted "monopoly of the streets."

Chancellor Seipel's attitude toward defending the constitution was ambiguous enough to alarm the Socialists and to encourage the increasingly vociferous Heimwehr advocates of a rightist *putsch*. Although Seipel himself was probably for preserving the constitution in essential respects, many hitherto conservative Catholics were by 1929 abandoning their commitment to discussion as the essence of parliamentary government and beginning to favor the idea of an "ideal" organic social order as outlined by such Austrian theorists as Professor Othmar Spann. Catholic criticism of democracy became much stronger after 1927. Many Catholics asserted that the democratic system "perpetuated the dominant position of the Socialists," and the classes loyal to the Church associated the republic with a drastic decline in their own social and economic status. The deflationary measures demanded by Allied and League of Nations economists and carried out by Seipel were grist for the mill of Catholic rightism. Austrian Catholics understandably became interested in Catholic social theorists, past and present, who offered an alternative to democracy. Much of Catholic social criticism had always been directed against capitalist industry, but this did not dismay those who felt that they were already ruined; in any event there had always been a bias against capitalism and industrialism among the Christian Social *Kleinbürger*. Paradoxically, as Socialist militancy receded, Catholic rightism became once again an active political force.

In 1929 the Lower Austrian Bauernbund ("Peasant League"), one hundred thousand strong, joined the Heimwehr as a body. The Heimwehr parade became a regular weekend feature in many places, attracting cheers and recruits. Clashes with the Socialists continued. In June, Seipel resigned, chiefly for personal reasons, and the iron grip that had held the radical forces in check was withdrawn. When Seipel's successor, Ernst von Streeruwitz, resigned in September, the Heimwehr was popularly credited with driving him from office and naming his successor, Johann Schober.

The failure of the great Boden-Credit Anstalt bank in Vienna at the end of October, 1929, caused new economic misery and radical demonstrations by both the Socialists and the Heimwehr. Liberal democracy and capitalism were almost universally loathed now. While Chancellor Schober was working to strengthen the state's authority, reform the constitution, roll back Socialist influence, and get foreign economic and political backing, Major Waldemar Pabst, now Heimwehr chief of staff, was looking for ways to combat the movement's provincial and ideological disunity and bring it to power. After 1927 the Heimwehr had grown large and vociferous, but it was still an amorphous movement with no common bond or program except anti-Marxism, attracting an incongruous mixture of Christian Socialists, conservative monarchists, Grossdeutsche, National Socialists, anti-Semites, bourgeois Jews, big businessmen, artisans, veterans, students, and plain adventurers.

Fascist influence had been gaining ground in the movement for several years, and Mussolini and a few pro-Fascist Austrian industrialists like Fritz Mandel were supporting the trend with cash. Othmar Spann's neoromantic doctrine of the corporative "true state," however dimly understood, had aroused considerable interest. The *Stände* idea was quite nebulous, but its advocates in the movement felt the need of an intellectual system to combat Marxism. Steidle, the Federal Leader (*Bundesführer*), Starhemberg, Pfriemer, Rauter, and others, had frequently denounced, at least since 1929, the constitutional system as mere political jobbery and demanded its replacement by a Heimwehr dictatorship. Some lead-

ers urged that "the two revolutionary movements, National Socialism and the Heimwehr," should unite. At the meeting at Korneuburg, near Vienna, on May 18, 1930, several hundred Heimwehr
leaders, including Steidle, Pabst, Starhemberg, and Pfriemer, swore
allegiance to the principles of Fascism, denounced parliamentary
democracy, and declared that the Heimwehr would seek power for
itself.

Fascist ideology and the spectacular Korneuburg oath proved
more of a divisive than a unifying force. The corporative *Führer-
staat* described in the leaders' speeches was not favored by all
Heimwehr members and led to damaging quarrels. The attempt of
a few leaders to fasten a Fascist ideology and program on the movement deprived it of its character as a collecting point for all anti-
Marxists. The oath was a farce as well, for the Heimwehr leaders
were not the type of men to feel bound by any promise. Thus
ideological differences, provincial and personal rivalries, bickering,
and irresponsibility fatally weakened the Heimwehr movement at
what appeared the height of its power.

Chancellor Schober, far from knuckling under to Pabst's threat
of a *putsch,* had him arrested and deported as an undesirable alien.
The Chancellor had already provided for election of the president
by popular vote (replacing election by parliament), obtained
freedom from further reparations, laid the basis for French,
British, and American loans, and induced parliament to pass an
antiterrorism act which gave the government more power to defend
itself against a coup from either the Right or the Left. With these
measures he had accomplished legally most of the general objectives that the Heimwehr had claimed only a Heimwehr revolution
could achieve. Schober and most of the responsible leaders of the
two coalition parties in the government wanted to use the Heimwehr in support of the legally constituted authorities against a
Socialist seizure of power, but they would not tolerate a Heimwehr
putsch. The Heimwehr revealed its impotence by accepting the
deportation of Pabst without a rising, and Catholic conservatives
now openly expressed their alarm at the movement's radicalism.

Schober resigned the chancellorship in September, 1930, and was
succeeded by Karl Vaugoin, an old Christian Social politician who

formed a heavily clerical cabinet. Vaugoin took the measure of the divided and quarreling Heimwehr and concluded that it was not a serious threat to his regime and could continue to be of use to the republic. To attach the Heimwehr to his government, he offered Starhemberg, who had just ousted Steidle as *Bundesführer,* and Hüber, the Salzburg Heimwehr chief, the Ministries of Interior and Justice. To Starhemberg and many of the public this looked like capitulation by the government, Naïve observers concluded that the Heimwehr had arrived at last at real power. New parliamentary elections were scheduled for November, but Starhemberg boasted to his radical followers that he would seize power before they were held. When Vaugoin proved too watchful, Starhemberg formed a Heimwehr political party, the Heimatblock, and proclaimed that he would "conquer parliament and erect on its ruins the Heimwehr state."

In 1930 a red revolution was still dreaded by many people, and anti-Marxist programs received serious support. Fascist and other brands of strong men were either in power or were major figures in most of the surrounding states; a massive vote for a Heimwehr dictatorship as the only alternative to parliamentary fumbling was possible. Vaugoin proved to be correct, however, in his estimate of the movement's weakness. When the votes were counted, the Heimatblock had only eight seats. Major Emil Fey, the Vienna Heimwehr leader, hated Starhemberg and would not join the Heimatblock; many members deserted to the Christian Socialists or the Nazis, who benefited from Hitler's great Reichstag victory in September. The movement that had claimed to be the anti-Marxist organization par excellence had divided the anti-Marxist forces through lack of policy and political stupidity. For the first time since 1920 the Socialists were again the largest party in the Nationalrat with 72 seats (an increase of one); the Christian Socialists had 66 (a loss of seven); the Grossdeutsche had 19 (a gain of seven). The Nazis, despite their 110,000 votes, failed to secure a seat, but they had at last arrived on the political scene. Vaugoin resigned, and the new Ender-Schober government dropped the Heimwehr ministers. The imminent danger of a fascist *putsch* was over in Austria by December, 1930.

The government of the republic had maintained itself through the first year of the worldwide economic crisis, but the country's economic condition was deteriorating badly. In March, Schober, as vice-chancellor and foreign minister, negotiated a customs union with Germany designed to help the country economically and get popular backing for the government, but the project had to be canceled when France, England, Italy, and Czechoslovakia protested. The Credit Anstalt bank failed, owing in part to French withdrawal of short-term credits to force abandonment of the customs union with Germany. Only a British emergency loan saved the government's desperate financial situation, but relief was no more than temporary, and in June the Ender-Schober government resigned. Its successor, headed by a colorless Christian Socialist, Karl Buresch, was hardly more than a caretaker government while the country drifted.

At this point, Pfriemer decided to cut loose and seize power at the head of the Styrian Heimwehr, as he had been scheming to do for a year. At midnight of September 12 he led his men onto the streets of Graz and other Styrian towns and proclaimed that he had taken over the government. Heimwehr men broke into a few government offices in Graz in the early morning hours, while the confused officials waited for instructions from Vienna. As soon as the Socialists realized what was happening they called out the Schutzbund. Once more there was the prospect of civil war. Confronted by the disciplined strength of the Socialist battalions, Pfriemer lost his nerve. He telephoned Rintelen, the governor of Styria and a continual intriguer for the post of chancellor, who persuaded the government to let the *putschists* return to their homes. The rest of the Heimwehr failed to rise since Pfriemer had not coördinated his plans with the other leaders, and the uprising collapsed.

Though the failure of Pfriemer's coup had demonstrated the impotence and disunity of the Heimwehr movement, the prestige of the government had been damaged and the tension between Marxists and anti-Marxists heightened. The mood of the country swung still further toward extremism. The Nazi campaign of terrorism was stepped up as a new and more ruthless *Landesleiter,*

Alfred Proksch, formerly *Gauleiter* of Upper Austria, took over its direction. To tighten his control over the Austrian party, Hitler sent Theo Habicht, a former Communist, to Austria as his special agent and real head of the party. Most of the Styrian Heimwehr now went over to the Nazis as a group.

The *putsch* helped to clarify the confused relations between the Heimwehr and the Nazis. In some places their memberships partly overlapped and the leaders of the two movements had often discussed merging. The discussions had broken down in mid-1931 because of the Nazis' insistence on control and their refusal to pay the Heimwehr's debts, and because Mussolini, who had urged the Heimwehr to seize power on its own, opposed the merger. Italian support was attractive to a man like Starhemberg, who preferred becoming an Austrian *duce* to being Hitler's Austrian lieutenant; Mussolini was, after all, an established ruler while Hitler was only an opposition-party leader. After the *putsch* the two movements drew apart, and the Heimwehr became a more Catholic-oriented organization with Old Austrian sympathies. The Nazis absorbed the radical anti-Semites and uprooted opponents of democracy as well as most of those for whom *Anschluss* was the most important objective.

Austrian conditions favored the appeal of National Socialism, but the decisive factor in the growth of the movement was Hitler's series of victories in Germany from 1930 on. In 1930 the German Nazis suddenly became the second largest party in the Reichstag; in March, 1932, Hitler ran second in the presidential election, and in April his party won a great electoral victory in the provinces. During the German election campaign Austria held elections to the provincial diets (of which the Vienna city council was considered one), and to the municipal councils. Amid universal amazement the Nazis polled 16 per cent of the vote, sending fifteen men to the Vienna city council, where the Christian Socialists were cut down to half their former strength (19 seats) and the Grossdeutsche Volkspartei was erased. The Nazis' denunciation of the peace treaties and their vision of a Jewish conspiracy seemed plausible now to small businessmen, artisans, civil servants, and students who had lost their jobs and savings. Hitler suddenly appeared to many Austrians as a savior who would chastise Jews, foreigners, and contentious parliamentarians, unite all Germans in one powerful country, and put an end to economic misery and national humiliation.

The destruction of the Grossdeutsche—the moderate German national party which had helped through fourteen years to maintain the constitution—and the absorption of its members by the Nazis, revolutionized the political situation. Though the distribution of seats in parliament was not affected, the government was badly shaken. It was further weakened by the continuing strength of the Socialists and the internal disunity and lack of policy of the Heimwehr. Chancellor Buresch pessimistically scheduled new parliamentary elections for the fall and resigned his post. Economic conditions were rapidly becoming worse and it was evident that without outside help there would be national bankruptcy. In the midst of this crisis Dollfuss formed his first government.

The entry of Engelbert Dollfuss and Kurt von Schuschnigg into the government in 1931 had marked the arrival of young World War I reserve officers at the center of affairs. The older generation disappeared from the scene at about this time—Seipel and Schober died in 1932 and most of the old Christian Social leaders brought up in the traditions of imperial Austria, men like Vaugoin, Ender, and Buresch, were physically and politically worn out. The new generation seemed to be divided between intellectuals who wanted a corporative state modeled on Spann's ideas, and simpler men who saw in the appeal to force the only answer. The former looked to the government to carry out the changes they wanted, while the latter relied on the rival paramilitary battalions of the Heimwehr and the Nazi SA. The cabinet formed by Dollfuss commanded a majority of only one vote, and this depended on a coalition of the Christian Social party, the Heimatblock, in which Rintelen and other enemies of democracy were very powerful, and the Landbund, whose members were deserting to the Nazis. To obtain a League of Nations loan, Dollfuss reaffirmed for another twenty years the 1922 renunciation of *Anschluss*. He also suspended parliamentary elections for the duration of the crisis.

In January, 1933, Hitler became German Chancellor, and the

Nazi victory swept thousands into the party in Austria; all those who wanted *Anschluss* either had to give up the idea, as the Socialists had done, or join the Nazis. Dollfuss, with most of the country against him and unable to rely on his majority of one, suspended parliament, prohibited parades and assemblies, and curtailed the press. In reply the Nazis held a great demonstration that ended in a riot in Vienna. The Heimwehr threatened a *putsch*. Dollfuss ordered the Schutzbund to disband, while he kept his own Heimwehr supporters under arms. Socialist opposition forced him to rely more than he liked on the Heimwehr, and he now became, in Socialist and Nazi propaganda, "the prisoner of the Heimwehr." In the Innsbruck municipal elections of April the Nazis polled 40 per cent of the vote. Dollfuss suspended municipal elections.

Although the workers in the "free" trade unions were still largely immune to Nazi appeals, and the peasants, except for those associated with the Landbund, remained loyal to the Christian Social party, the Nazis saw that unless Dollfuss allied himself with the Socialists he would have most of the country against him—and he could not approach the Socialists because of his dependence on Mussolini and on extreme-rightist Heimwehr leaders like ex-Major Emil Fey of Vienna and Prince Starhemberg. Fey was a brawler and adventurer by temperament who made no secret of his belief in seizing power by violence. The Austrian Nazi leaders were convinced that a National Socialist regime could be established by a coup, and that the best means of preparing for it was to increase the use of terror. The party actually had two levels of appeal, one for the respectable Grossdeutsche, for whom the *Anschluss* was everything, and another for the radical brawlers to whom the chance for action was more important than any doctrine or specific goal. To the former group it raised the cry of "undemocratic and tyrannous government" as a pretext for openly committing illegal acts. Dollfuss met terror from below with force from above, but in doing so he lost moral and legal authority and alienated many conservatives who clung to the tradition of legality, the *Rechtsstaat*. Since the Nazis were now a clear threat to the independence of Austria, Dollfuss asked for the support of the French, the

British, and above all the Italian governments. The Nazis, in retaliation, accused him of being at the beck and call of the French, a friend of Czechs, servant of Jews. His policy of relying on Heimwehr bands, resembling the Nazi SA, made the outcome seem a question of brute force.

The Nazis, through Rintelen, suggested a joint attempt to "rebuild" the regime, and, when Dollfuss refused, braced themselves to make open war on the government. Believing they had the backing of the country and assured of massive German support by Hitler, they were confident of victory. In May, 1933, Dollfuss forbade the wearing of uniforms by members of any political party and harried some of the Nazi leaders into fleeing to Germany. He even expelled two ministers of the German Reich, Frank and Kerrl, for inciting the people of Vienna to violence. Hitler retaliated by levying a thousand-mark fee on Germans visiting Austria and at a stroke ruined the Austrian tourist industry. On June 19 a gang of Nazis killed a Christian Socialist gymnast in a brawl at Krems. Dollfuss immediately ordered the dissolution of the National Socialist party in Austria and outlawed all its formations. So many Nazis were arrested that eventually concentration camps had to be set up to hold them. Dollfuss also attempted to discharge Nazis from the civil service and even from posts in industry, and energetically prosecuted many front organizations. The next five years became known in Nazi annals as the "illegal period."

The difficulty of suppressing such an organization was great. The Nazis had a large number of fanatical followers; a considerably larger number of people were well inclined toward them or at least neutral; others were afraid of Nazi terrorists; and some assumed fatalistically that the Nazis would eventually triumph. Many of the police and officials whose duty it was to eliminate Nazi influence were either Nazis themselves or were for other reasons disinclined to do their duty. In countless instances Austrian officials connived at Nazi terrorism and frustrated the government's attempt to suppress it, attempts the Nazis called "the Dollfuss terror." The Nazis wished to prove that they were the only effective opposition. The mere existence of this highly disciplined and ruthless body did in fact make a strong impression on the Austrian people, especially the unemployed, in a state where order and legitimate government had practically disappeared.

One of the purposes of Nazi propaganda and obstruction throughout this period was to make the *Anschluss* appear not merely intrinsically desirable but the only alternative to chaos. In the first year of illegal activity the party terrorists and propagandists increased their attacks on railroads, telephone and telegraph lines, and government files, committed acts of ostentatious defiance such as painting swastikas on industrial chimneys and mountain crags, and showered leaflets on the streets and squares. The government was afraid that too great severity might provoke an uprising that would spread to the whole country, and the police were unable to break up the criminal gangs that were the basis of the party's strength.

It was impossible for the government, backed by only one-third of the people, to resist for long this pressure from the Austrian Nazis and Hitler. In hopes of gaining support for a form of government alternative to both National Socialism and Heimwehr rule, Dollfuss announced, in September, 1933, his plan for a "Christian corporative state" derived from the theories of Spann and Vogelsang. To replace both the Heimwehr and the Christian Social party by a catch-all organization unhampered by parliamentary tradition, he organized the Fatherland Front, and built a new paramilitary formation for protection against extremists of Right and Left. A decree dissolving all parties except the Fatherland Front was followed by clashes between police and Socialists and by serious Socialist uprisings at Linz, Graz, Steyr, Bruck on the Mur, Innsbruck, and Vienna. On February 12, 1934, government forces, aided by the Vienna Heimwehr, bombarded and captured the Socialists' citadel in Vienna, the famous Karl Marx Hof housing development; most of the Socialist leaders were jailed or forced to flee. This action slammed the door on all Dollfuss' hopes of getting working-class help against the Nazis. A single government trade union was substituted for the Socialist unions and, as a gesture to the Heimwehr, Starhemberg was appointed vice-chancellor (replacing Fey, who had held the office since 1933).

In April, 1934, Dollfuss set up his new constitution, designed to enable him to maintain the country's independence and to govern effectively. Its chief inspiration came from the Austrian Catholic theories of *Sozialreform*. The extremely complicated document contained a jumble of corporative, Catholic, authoritarian, romantic, liberal, and parliamentary elements; Spann scorned it as a perversion of his ideas. Catholic universalism appeared in the preamble: "God is recognized as the constituent authority." The forces and individuals favoring the new constitution had diverse motives. The pragmatic Heimwehr leaders regarded the *Stände* idea as a necessary intellectual weapon in their contest with Marxism and National Socialism. For industrialists in the Fatherland Front it was a façade behind which most of the capitalist practices that the corporative system aimed at abolishing could go on unhindered. The radical social and economic reforms envisaged by sincere believers in the new system were never carried out, and the constitution remained an empty victory of the proponents of *Sozialreform*. A list of the principal groups supporting Dollfuss points up the great diversity of the Christian Social conservative Right: Heimwehr, East Mark Storm Troops, Austrian Action, Spann school, Vogelsang school, Religious Socialists, Freedom League, and several cliques gathered around social-minded individuals. All these the Fatherland Front covered like a loose tent. Most of the higher Catholic hierarchy, who generally backed the government, were old-fashioned conservatives not completely at ease with Dollfuss and his rightist associates.

At the same time that he promulgated the corporative constitution, Dollfuss attempted out of bitter necessity to reach an understanding with the Nazis. Hitler insisted that he deal with the émigré leaders Proksch and Habicht. Their price was two ministries and new elections; this Dollfuss was unwilling to pay. The émigré Nazi leaders craftily induced the government to keep on negotiating with them, outlawed as they were, because the resulting confusion demoralized the government's supporters. In negotiating, the Nazis showed their "moderate" face, while the illegal activists continued plotting to seize power by violent means. The Nazis also negotiated with Fey and Starhemberg, partly with the knowledge of the government, partly behind its back. Each of the rival Heimwehr factions considered a *putsch* and saw that victory would go to the one with Nazi support. Arthur Seyss-Inquart, a lawyer, a Catholic, and a self-styled patriot of Vienna, who occupied a peculiar position partly in the Heimwehr and partly in the Nazi party, became active at this time as an intermediary, consulting with Dollfuss and the Heimwehr, the *Landesleitung* in Munich, and Goering and Hess in Berlin. The anomaly of the Austrian government negotiating with the enemies of its country's independence so as to prevent the Socialists, who were now completely against *Anschluss,* from coming to power, continued until the German invasion in 1938.

In July, 1934, the Nazi terrorists were ready to strike. A desperate frontal attack on the government appealed more strongly than did continued discussion to the illegal party leaders and fanatics in Munich. Convinced that only a good shove was needed to topple the Dollfuss regime, Habicht set out to neutralize the Austrian army by subversion and to win over a politically significant number of industrial workers. A nucleus for a Nazi following existed in mining and heavy industry in Upper Styria, notably at the great Donawitz works, and, on orders from the German government, the new German owners of the Upper Styrian Alpine Montan industrial combine helped the Nazis. The February bloodshed had also increased Nazi influence. It is hard to say how many workers were won over. The Nazis probably wanted only to make sure that the workers would not paralyze a Nazi revolutionary government by a dread general strike. Habicht's plan relied on the indifference of the masses, not on a national revolt against Dollfuss. He was confident that the population would accept the fait accompli of change brought about by a sudden blow.

The Nazis planned to install a pseudobourgeois cabinet headed by the crafty Rintelen, who had carefully cultivated a reputation for being "safe" among the provincial Catholic *Kleinbürger,* while keeping the key posts for themselves. Habicht had over a dozen meetings with Rintelen in and near Rome in March, 1934, and found him ready to coöperate. Ironically, the top-ranking Nazi within Austria was a "moderate" who disliked the hobnail-booted ruffians in the SA. The illegal party, however, was controlled by bombing, drinking, fighting desperados.

On June 6, 1934, Hitler met Habicht in Berlin. No written record was kept of the conversation, but apparently Habicht reported that chances for a successful coup were good and Hitler told him to go ahead. Habicht met the illegal Vienna Nazi leaders in Zurich, including SS Colonel Fridolin Glass, commander of the SS regiment that would carry out the *putsch*. Much remains suspicious and obscure about the affair. The *putsch* was certainly desired equally by the Munich party and the majority of the illegal leaders in Austria; each faction urged the other on. The Munich group seems to have left the details of time and place to the illegal leaders inside Austria, chiefly to the Vienna SS. Hitler was probably not optimistic about the result, but he was busy with other matters, such as rearmament and the disciplinary crisis in the SA, and left Austrian affairs in the hands of the émigré party leaders.

The Nazis thought that the best course would be for a small number of men to seize the whole government at a cabinet meeting. In July the right moment seemed to have arrived. The recent imposition of the death penalty for merely possessing explosives also threatened the whole illegal Nazi organization. Accordingly, the Vienna leaders planned to occupy the chancellery during a cabinet meeting on July 24, to broadcast that Rintenlen had formed a new government, and to arrest the President at his country place in Carinthia.

The *putsch* had to be put off a day and there was some confusion. On July 25, 1934, 154 men in army and police uniforms, all members of the Vienna SS Battalion No. 89, many of them former soldiers discharged for being Nazis, occupied the chancellery. Another group seized the radio station and broadcast the announcement that Dollfuss had resigned and Rintelen had succeeded him. Small risings also occurred in several towns in Styria, Carinthia, and Upper Austria. But then the only high officials in the chancellery at the time turned out to be Dollfuss, Major Fey, and State Secretary Karwinsky, so the plan to capture the whole government misfired at the start. The Nazis had intended to compel the cabinet at gunpoint to name Rintelen as chancellor. When Dollfuss tried to slip out by a side door into the state archives, former police sergeant Otto Planetta shot him down in cold blood. The dying man's requests for a doctor and a priest were refused, and three hours later he bled to death. Meanwhile Rintelen was waiting at the Hotel Imperial.

The other members of the government promptly struck back. The President by telephone named Kurt von Schuschnigg, then Minister of Education, acting chancellor; Starhemberg hastened back from Italy, and units of the police and army encircled the chancellery. Inside, the *putschists* waited in vain for Rintelen to arrive. After several hours and some parleying with representatives of the government, they emerged to give themselves up.

Planetta and five others were executed. The failure of the *putsch* was a heavy blow for the whole National Socialist movement. Recriminations between the moderates and the terrorists seriously disrupted the party. It should by now have been clear to all that a policy of arson and bombing was senseless and could not lead to power. Nonetheless, while the German party tended to produce conformity and the organization man got the top positions, the Austrian Nazis still behaved like characters in a Goebbels film script, sacrificing their careers and worldly goods, committing senseless acts of daring at every opportunity, and speaking and understanding only the slogans of the Führer's speeches. Their failure showed Hitler the folly of leaving the Austrian movement in the hands of Habicht and convinced him that the *Anschluss* would eventually have to be achieved by German power. The German ambassador at Vienna was replaced by Franz von Papen, who immediately insisted to Hitler that Habicht be removed, and then took over the task of achieving Nazi objectives in Austria by nonviolent means.

Whether or not the murder of Dollfuss was intended, the plot and the revelations that followed it, together with the particularly gruesome treatment the Nazi SS men had vengefully meted out to their principal enemy, greatly shocked the Austrian people and alienated large sections of opinion. Though the extreme activists— men prepared to accept murder as a political weapon—were very influential in the SA and SS, they were probably a minority of even the illegal party and certainly of the population at large.

On July 30, Schuschnigg was formally entrusted with the chancellorship by President Miklas. As Dollfuss' heir, he was plagued by all the problems with which his predecessor had struggled. In addition to continuing the suppression of the illegal Socialists and Nazis, he had to keep the Heimwehr on his side, yet guard against a Heimwehr *putsch*. The antagonism between the two anti-Nazi, antidemocratic partners in the government—the Heimwehr and the Catholic intellectual-conservatives—was a difficulty Schuschnigg set out to overcome as soon as possible. The Heimwehr leaders Fey and Starhemberg had a crushing superiority in physical power, but Schuschnigg intended, with the help of Mussolini, to destroy the military preponderance of his rivals. His need for reliable foreign political and military support against German pressure and internal opposition forced him to follow, in foreign affairs, the "Italian course" already set by Dollfuss. Collaboration with France and the Little Entente was out of the question, owing to the deeply rooted hostility of the population against the peace-treaty powers, and the fact that the Nazis would have made effective propaganda out of any pro-Czech or pro-French policy. Schuschnigg's reliance on Mussolini, however, involved Austria in the reckless foreign policies of Italy and Hungary and alienated the Western powers and the Little Entente. Since the economic situation remained serious, domestically Schuschnigg also had the problem of finding some means of making people's lives more bearable in terms of jobs, income, and hope for the future.

During the next fifteen months the government steadily extended the new corporative structure of private and public institutions. In private industry, voluntary associations were formed under government guidance to stimulate activity and negotiate with representatives of the single official trade union. Corporations of civil servants, artisans, and workers in banks, agriculture, forestry, trade, and communications, were established under a Statute of Corporations dated January 5, 1935. The provincial diets were reorganized on a corporative basis. These measures ensured that the younger generation of Christian Social conservative rightists would back the chancellor as the man who was seriously trying to realize their goal.

Schuschnigg reduced the military superiority of his Heimwehr allies by building his own counterforce. A law of December, 1934, ordered the army's complete political neutrality, with Schuschnigg assuming the post of commander-in-chief. In October, 1935, he felt strong enough to dismiss Major Fey from the Ministry of Security; in April, 1936, he introduced conscription, and in May he forced Starhemberg out of his offices of vice-chancellor and chief of the Fatherland Front. In October he disbanded the Heim-wehr and had its members absorbed into his own paramilitary formation, the so-called *Front-Miliz* of the Fatherland Front, of which he proclaimed himself *Front-Führer*. The Heimwehr leaders tried by every means to block these steps, but Mussolini had supported Schuschnigg against them, and they were too divided among themselves and too inept as politicians to overthrow Schuschnigg by arms or intrigue.

While overcoming the Heimwehr's monopoly of force, Schuschnigg was also working to secure the support of Catholic conservatives who were not entirely happy with the corporative system. In October, 1935, he repealed the anti-Habsburg laws and formally initiated a policy of encouraging the hopes of the monarchists and of all those who dreamed of the great days before 1914. By the end of 1936 Schuschnigg was master of the anti-Socialist and anti-Nazi camp.

The problem of what to do about the Nazis remained. The shock caused by the murder of Dollfuss made possible their more energetic suppression. Hitler, deeply embarrassed at the failure of the *putsch*, wanted to avoid arousing anxiety about his designs among the Western powers. The émigré *Landesleitung* was nominally dissolved, the German government disavowed all connection with the Austrian Nazis, whose moderate elements now also condemned Habicht's senseless violence and lamented the disaster it had brought on the party.

In late 1934 Schuschnigg and a committee of National Socialist "moderates" began discussions that went on for several months. The

Nazis demanded restoration of the seats they had won in the provincial diets in 1932 and that had been confiscated under Dollfuss; they demanded the dissolution of the Heimwehr (this was done in 1936), the admission of the National Socialists as a group into the Fatherland Front (to be renamed the German Front), new elections, and the release of all Nazis from jail. Schuschnigg was quite ready to promise a "German course" if that would satisfy the moderate Nazis—that is, the great number of old Grossdeutsche in their ranks—but the conversations broke up over his insistence that the National Socialist party pledge loyalty to Austria, drop the demand for *Anschluss,* and undertake not to organize outside the Fatherland Front. The opposition of Mussolini and Starhemberg added further weight to Schuschnigg's reservations. Though the negotiations failed, Schuschnigg never gave up wooing the moderate Nazis and trying to get them to join the Fatherland Front. As an inducement he regularly released groups of imprisoned Nazis.

The feeling between the Nazi moderates and the terrorists appeared to be very bitter, but their real relationship is obscure and their enmity may have been a ruse. Hitler certainly knew of the difference in their policies and may have played them off against each other for his own purposes, or to confuse the Austrian government. While the negotiations were going on, the government relaxed its severity toward the party and at Christmas (1934) released twenty-five hundred Nazis from the Wöllersdorf camp. Almost all the released men promptly fled to Germany and joined the ranks of the extremist émigrés in Bavaria. Concessions, in fact, almost always turned out to help the extremists, not the moderates. Outwardly the German government was "moderate," too, but Hitler probably intended in the last round of his Austrian policy to back the extremists with the German army. His apparent repudiation of Habicht diverted international attention from Austria and avoided arousing British, French, and Italian fears until the international situation was more favorable to Germany. Meanwhile, the extremists were restrained by both Schuschnigg's willingness to compromise and Hitler's need for peaceful international conditions.

Although the Nazi policy of seizing power by force was bankrupt, the government's inability to suppress the party was a major factor in the Austrian political situation after 1935. Effective suppression had proved impossible for four main reasons: the Nazi party had created an extraordinarily efficient organization in the "legal period" (1926–1933); it had penetrated into large and influential circles of Austrian life; the division of the people into sharply hostile camps enabled a well-disciplined minority to exercise a disproportionate influence; and German pressure and intrigue were too strong to be resisted by a small, economically stricken, and diplomatically almost isolated country. When it was outlawed, the party merely went underground and, with German help, reorganized as a subversive conspiracy. Funds and orders were transmitted at secret conferences on the Bavarian frontier, in Czechoslovakia and Hungary, or by the highly organized National Socialist courier service and German "visitors." Couriers often carried specie over the border in their rucksacks. Another way of transferring the money was through the bank account of an Austrian Nazi businessman, where it could be made to look like a normal transaction. A third channel was the German embassy. In 1936 the Austrian police estimated that about 200,000 marks a month (equivalent to about $200,000 today) were flowing into the illegal party's coffers from Germany, in addition to funds raised locally.

The organizational structure also remained largely intact. The SS, Hitler Youth, professional cells, and academic front organizations infiltrated their rivals—the army and the security services—and seemingly flourished under conditions of illegality.

The Nazis in Austria laid great emphasis on propaganda, from broadsides scattered in the streets to pseudolearned lectures on the ideology of the movement. Copies of suppressed newspapers were smuggled over the border from Germany or Czechoslovakia, with the aid of Konrad Henlein's Sudeten German party. There were also clandestine Nazi printing presses in Austria. Morawetz, the biggest Austrian press distributor, was in the Nazi system. When the party was declared illegal, in 1933, its propaganda director stayed on in Vienna and continued publication of the *Oesterreichischer Beobachter* in secret. The vulgar and violent *Deutsch-Oes-*

terreichische Nachrichten was edited under Habicht's supervision at Munich. The illegal papers were usually printed in miniature type on onionskin paper in the same format as presuppression issues. A multigraphed newsletter, *Illkor* (an abbreviation of *Illegale Korrespondenz*), specialized in high-level leaks of government plans. It was produced in Budapest by a fugitive Austrian Nazi journalist, financed from Germany, and distributed by mail or by courier to all representatives of the foreign press, important businessmen at their offices, foreign embassies, and legations. Nazi propaganda headquarters also started whispering campaigns designed to create public uncertainty and apprehension.

The success of the extremists in keeping the party alive, together with German victories in foreign affairs, discouraged the moderates and shifted the center of influence back to the advocates of violence. Habicht's reinstatement at émigré headquarters in Munich further encouraged the extremists. The Austrian Legion in Germany held threatening maneuvers on the border, and the German radio increased its attacks on the Austrian government. The Austrian police discovered a plan for a new *putsch* in February, 1935, and late that year the émigré *Landesleitung* ordered a resumption of terrorism. All during these months the German government was bombarding the Austrian government with demands that it stop persecuting the Nazis and grant proper representation in the government to the "national elements."

Mussolini's invasion of Ethiopia in October, 1935, was fateful for Austria because it laid the basis for Italy's dependence on Hitler. The Italian alliance cost Austria much respect among the Western powers and the Little Entente because it placed the country on the side of the Italian and Hungarian dictators. Italian defeats in Africa and Mussolini's commitments in the Spanish Civil War ultimately led to the formation of the Rome-Berlin Axis, which began actually with an agreement regarding Austria (October 26, 1936). The Alpine state was to become an early sacrifice to the "brutal friendship." Schuschnigg discovered with a shock in March, 1936, how much closer Mussolini was to Hitler than he had imagined, and saw that his own situation was critical when the Duce urged him to come to an agreement with Germany. In 1934 the Italians had marched to the Brenner to support Austria against Germany, but that time was past.

Schuschnigg signed the German-Austrian agreement of July 11, 1936, because it offered at least a temporary normalizing of relations. The German government engaged itself to respect Austria's independence, and Schuschnigg promised to pursue a policy befitting a "German state." Each agreed not to interfere in the other's internal affairs and to coöperate in maintaining peace in Central Europe.

The July agreement, far from strengthening Schuschnigg and the Fatherland Front, marked the dawn of a bright new day for the Austrian Nazis. They emerged everywhere as almost a privileged group, despite the continuing formal prohibition of the party. Hitler's promise not to interfere in Austrian internal affairs was more than balanced by the freedom of action obtained for the Austrian Nazis and the admission of German tourists, newspapers, and goods. Soon after Schuschnigg signed the agreement he took into the government two "pronounced nationalists" whom he trusted, General von Glaise-Horstenau and Dr. Guido Schmidt, and began the release of some fifteen thousand Nazi prisoners. By that time the illegal party had really completed its main work and the Nazi purpose was no longer to overthrow the Austrian government but to hinder it in its contest with the German government. A German SS officer and secretary of state in the Berlin foreign office, Wilhelm Keppler, took over the Austrian desk.

While Papen and the German government were working for *Anschluss* by gradualist methods and were putting pressure on the Austrian government to abandon one line of defense after another, the illegal party continued to follow its predilection for terrorism. The Germans, as before, backed both moderates and extremists, partly from policy, partly, it seems, because there was division in the Berlin hierarchy. Neurath and Keppler at the foreign office warned Seyss-Inquart to hold down illegal terrorism, Göring and Hess objected that the Seyss group was not getting enough concessions from Schuschnigg, and General Reinhard Heydrich of the SS high command declared that the Seyss moderates would take the steam out of the Austrian party's revolutionary drive and separate the Austrian from the German party.

For the history of the Right, the interest of the period 1936–1938 lies in the contest between the Nazi moderates and extremists for control of the party and in the relations of these two factions with the Austrian government. After the dissolution of the Heimwehr in October, 1936, and the distribution of its members between the Fatherland Front and the Nazis, Schuschnigg united in his camp practically the entire anti-Nazi Right. The personalities and abilities of the leaders of the various rightist groups— Schuschnigg, Fey, Starhemberg, Seyss-Inquart, Josef Leopold, Alfred Frauenfeld, and others—had much to do with the internal balance of power in Austria, but foreign affairs decided the important developments. In November, 1936, though he was officially backing the moderates, Hitler also encouraged the heirs of the 1934 *putsch* by making the notorious Leopold head of the party in Austria, with Leo Tavs, an advocate of terrorism, as his deputy, and by introducing the extremist Frauenfeld on the German radio as the "*Gauleiter* of Vienna."

Nazi infiltration of the Fatherland Front and the new economic and industrial guilds of the corporative state progressed rapidly in 1937. Since railroads, post and telegraph, rural electrification, salt, and tobacco were state monopolies, and urban transport, electricity, gas, and water were municipal concerns, employment in these fields channeled Nazis into public enterprises. A good percentage of the local judges supported Nazi aims, teachers and school administrators were active as illegal party members, and a Nazi Soldatenring was greatly enlarged with the help of two Austrian officers who later became *Wehrmacht* generals. The National Socialist Aid Association (NS Hilfsverein), a government agency for aiding Austrian refugees in Germany, was allowed, in late 1936, to open an office in Vienna, where it became yet another center for Nazi propaganda and subsidies. This was one more example of what German pressure could accomplish.

The party began to make inroads into the Christian Social peasantry by early 1937, especially in the Styrian mountains and parts of Upper and Lower Austria, where its appeal seems to have been the expectation that it would bring economic prosperity. Austria's dependence on German markets enabled the Nazis to extend their hold on both agriculture and industry. By 1937 the Austrian film industry was German-owned, and it was professionally injurious to an actor or actress to speak against the Nazis. Much of the Austrian publishing industry was in German—which meant Nazi— hands by 1936, and German influence in banking and insurance was so great that the Austrian government felt compelled to appoint special officers to guard against treasonable activity. By 1937, the process of infiltration had been extended to virtually every large factory in Austria. When the government seized or closed plants as a countermeasure, its actions only provided grist for Nazi propaganda mills—which could make it appear that Austrian independence was chiefly responsible for the country's economic difficulties. As a result of the easing of restrictions after the German-Austrian agreement, the illegal party was considerably better entrenched a year later.

The international situation also improved rapidly, from the Nazi point of view. The Rome-Berlin Axis had been formed in October, 1936, and in November the German-Japanese pact was concluded to counterbalance the Franco-Russian alliance. The League of Nations had suffered mortal wounds, and the Western powers were evidently not prepared to fight for Austrian independence.

Schuschnigg's reach for more effective conservative support in February, 1937, by hinting at a possible Habsburg restoration, was of course highly objectionable to Hitler and reinforced the Austrian Nazi extremists' demand in Berlin to be allowed a free hand for more terrorism. When the German Foreign Minister von Neurath visited Vienna in February he was greeted with gigantic Nazi demonstrations. Schuschnigg finally dismissed his pro-Nazi Minister of Public Security, Neustädter-Stürmer, in March, but a few months later he had to knuckle under to Hitler's anger and admit two Nazis, Seyss-Inquart and Eduard Pembauer, to the cabinet, the latter as "Minister for Political Pacification," a title that in fact meant Nazification. A number of Nazi underground organizations, such as the Ostmärkischer Volksverein ("East Mark People's Society"), now emerged under new names. The government's relaxation of suppression in the interest of reaching an agreement with the moderates was exploited by Leopold to establish an open Nazi party at Linz and Vienna which collected money without official interference. Innocuously called the Provisional National Party, it became an organ of terrorism. The confusion prevailing at this time is evident from the fact that the trial for terrorism of thirty-one SS men in Vienna opened on the same day that Seyss-Inquart was admitted to the cabinet. Massive Nazi demonstrations, clearly directed from Germany but supported by a network of illegal local cells, rocked Upper Austria. The only way the governor could maintain order was by imposing martial law.

The Munich party headquarters pretended to support Papen in its orders to the illegal *Gauleiter* in Austria, but secretly it encouraged Leopold. Goering reprimanded Leopold in October for having overplayed his hand, but Leopold continued to receive subsidies and orders for acts of terrorism from Munich. In the fall of 1937 he began to prepare for an armed *putsch* by the illegal Vienna SA and SS.

In the spring of 1937 Schuschnigg had allowed a group of Nazis in Vienna to form what became known as the Committee of Seven to promote political coöperation between the Fatherland Front and the "national opposition." Leopold, Tavs, and the extremists infiltrated the committee and made it a center of a radical group to whom the gradualist policy was anathema. In January, 1938, the police finally descended on the committee's offices and found a plan for a new armed uprising, the so-called Tavs plan. As the group's followers could not by themselves have brought off an effective coup it seems likely that the Tavs plan was an expression of terrorist dissatisfaction with Hitler's evolutionary policy, and an attempt to provoke Schuschnigg to reprisals that would force Hitler to act. (The murder of Papen in his legation by Nazi thugs dressed as Austrian monarchists was part of the plan, the idea being to exploit Hitler's phobia about a restoration. Papen's death would provide the provocation for intervention and simultaneously remove the advocate of gradualism.) Such a bold scheme must have had the backing of someone in the highest echelon of the German Nazi party, and although the name of the individual has never been discovered, there is evidence pointing to Rudolf Hess.

During 1937, the beginnings of an ultimately radical shake-up of the German army high command and of the foreign office, in which Hitler assumed command of the army and Joachim von Ribbentrop became Foreign Minister, were signs that Hitler would soon be ready for a new round of important moves, and that the liquidation of Austria would probably be carried out in early 1938. When Ribbentrop returned from Rome in November he brought the assurance that Germany had a free hand to deal with Austria whenever the conjunction of Hitler's western European policy and his eastern plans made it necessary. Schuschnigg was now isolated and helpless.

It was evident by Christmas of 1937 that new negotiations with Berlin would soon be necessary. In January, Schuschnigg was invited to meet Hitler at Berchtesgaden in February. Meanwhile, Schuschnigg continued to negotiate with the Nazi "moderates" and their "pronounced nationalist" allies in the belief that they were really good Austrians and could be won over to support the Fatherland Front. On the day he told Hitler's envoy that he could make no further concession he ordered his colleague, Guido Zernatto, to speed up "domestic truce talks" with Seyss-Inquart. It was typical of the strange alliances in the Austrian Right that Schuschnigg felt almost as close to Seyss, his most dangerous Austrian enemy, as to Zernatto, his most loyal supporter. The sympathy was partly emotional, but it was also based on similar convictions in the minds of the two men: both thought of themselves as Austrian patriots, both aimed in the last analysis at *Zusammenschluss* rather than *Anschluss*,* and both believed that settling Hitler's lesser grievances would be enough. Seyss as much as Schuschnigg misunderstood the character of the Austrian National Socialist party, but he finally bowed to the realities of power and in February became simply an agent of Hitler, while Schuschnigg never gave in. The ultimate divergence between the originally parallel views of these two men is an example of the confusing course of the Austrian Right.

---

* The distinction is hard to express in English. *Zusammenschluss* may be considered a growing together of two equals; *Anschluss*, a joining of a subordinate organism to a superior one by a single act.

The final decisions on the fate of Austria were made in Berlin, not by any of the Austrian factions. On February 12, 1938, Schuschnigg promised Hitler at Berchtesgaden to release all Nazis imprisoned for illegal party activities, to admit certain Nazis to the cabinet, and to open the Fatherland Front to members of the party. In a stirring radio address to the Austrian people he reaffirmed the country's independence. The Austrian Nazis, however, were now confident of success and took the offensive, instigating serious disorders at Graz and many other places in Styria. The government could not deal with the spreading Nazi defiance of the law without inviting German intervention. Belated efforts to arrange a reconciliation with the Socialist workers came to nothing.

As a last resort Schuschnigg suddenly announced on March 9 that a plebiscite would be held on the following Sunday on the question of Austrian independence. *Yes* ballots would be distributed; those who wished to vote *no* would have to supply their own ballots of specified form. The Nazis raised a tremendous uproar. Hitler, forced to act perhaps before he wished to, delivered an ultimatum on March 11 demanding postponement of the plebiscite and the resignation of Schuschnigg; German troops began concentrating on the Austrian frontier. Unable to resist, Schuschnigg resigned, and Seyss-Inquart became chancellor. On March 12 the German army invaded Austria. On the following day Seyss-Inquart proclaimed the country's union with Germany, and on March 14 Hitler arrived in Vienna to take possession of the *Ostmark*. With the end of Austrian independence the Austrian Right ceased to exist as a political movement.

A few general conclusions may be offered concerning the nature of the Austrian Right. As a political category the term is especially elusive and unmanageable because of the complexity, overlapping, and inconsistency of Austrian political parties. The political spectrum in the Austrian empire was perhaps the most complicated in Europe, and the consequent difficulty of understanding Austrian politics before 1918 was carried over into the Republic. Even the continuity of the three "camps" from the mid-nineteenth century to the *Anschluss* is as much a cause of confusion as it is a guidepost to understanding the Austrian Right.

The more striking characteristics of the Right are not in dispute —the pseudoconservative revolutionary program, extreme rancor, and predilection for violence—but its essence is likely to be debated. It was obviously more than a preference for a certain form of government, and attempts to identify it with authoritarianism, reaction, racism, or fascism do not penetrate its complexity. The abundant ideological literature of the Austrian Right may be regarded as a theoretically sound promise of intentions, as barefaced fraud, or as a rationalization of deep-seated emotional needs. Its component groups were concerned with ideas about the nature of society but were also the prey of mass emotion.

The relationship between the doctrines of intellectuals and the programs and behavior of popular, essentially pragmatic, power-seeking movements, will always pose a question for historians. Catholic social theorists provided an arsenal of arguments against capitalist democracy and fostered a bias against it in the minds of the Christian Social masses, but it is hard to say how much this contributed to the weakness of Austrian liberalism and parliamentary rule. Nationalist tenets and Prussian influence pose a similar problem. The historian of the Right hesitates to decide whether the Burschenschaft students and the illegal SA, for example, believed and behaved as they did because they were converted to hatred and violence by the logic of the doctrines of German integral nationalism or became integral nationalists and radical rightists because for psychological reasons they required a life of violence. The high proportion of youths and uprooted individuals in the various rightist groups and the opportunist tactics of the leaders suggest that principles were less important to the Right than action for action's sake.

The two rightist movements before 1918—the Christian Social and the Pan-German—established a tradition of rejecting political tolerance in favor of crusading for total victory and belief in violence. Their ideological origins were quite different; those of one lay in Catholic and Christian Social thought, of the other ultimately in the doctrine of popular sovereignty and the heritage of the French Revolution. They were alike, however, in social composition: the rank and file of both contained a high proportion of the dispossessed and embittered. Their similarity in composition was reflected in their denunciations; the difference in their ideologies in their opposed attitudes toward the role of the state in religion and the imperial and Habsburg tradition.

The Catholic Right then and later was somewhat sentimental about *Alt-Oesterreich;* the German-national Right was always more for radical, even revolutionary changes. Both were ambivalent about violence and order, cynicism and idealism, masses and elites. Their notions of the legislation they would pass if they came to power were equally vague. Their leaders were much alike in character and capacity. Schönerer and the Christian Social roughnecks of the early nineties, the illegal National Socialist leadership, and the Heimwehr commanders were all from the same cloth. Their specialty was physical courage and action; their political skill was of a very low order. On balance the similarities were probably more significant than the differences—yet their members fought each other in the streets, and in the end the victorious German-national Right shipped the leaders of the Catholic Right to concentration camps in Germany.

Foreign aid was a decisive factor in the power of both wings of the Right after 1933. The Heimwehr came to depend upon Italian financial subsidies and Italian Fascist ideological backing, while the Austrian Nazis were tied to Hitler.

The power of the Right to alarm the authorities stemmed not so much from its numbers as from its recklessness and from the failure of the three political camps—Christian Social conservative, Socialist, and German national—to achieve a consensus, so that most Austrian governments either had a majority of the population against them or secured popular support through unstable coalitions. By themselves the rightists were never able to get power. Before 1918 they were completely impotent; after 1918 the Heimwehr failed again and again to come to power and only shared in power as the combined Socialist and Nazi danger forced the government, temporarily, to rely on it. The illegal Nazi party proved unable to enlist the bulk of the population or to overthrow the Austrian government without German help. Only in the technique of propaganda did the Right show real talent, though it

paid a heavy price for its effective self-advertisement in the re-
vulsion aroused in most people against its ideas and acts.

The Right helped to discredit parliamentary government under
the empire as well as the republic, but the decadence of Austrian
parliamentarism was a complex phenomenon and the blame for it
cannot be assigned entirely to the Right. Whether the Right was
a cause or a symptom of the increasing rejection of many traditional values of Western civilization in Austria after 1890, its
authoritarian and intolerant forms of socialism and equality, its
dependence on the fanatical intervention of the masses, and its
substitution of opportunism for principle, gave sinister warning
of what could be expected from a totalitarian regime.

SUGGESTED READING

ALMAYER-BECK, JOHANN C. *Vogelsang.* Vienna: 1952.
Beiträge zur Geschichte und Vorgeschichte der Julirevolte. Vienna: 1934.
BENEDIKT, HEINRICH, ed. *Geschichte der Republik Oesterreich.* Vienna:
1954.
BILGER, FERDINAND. *Die Wiener Burschenschaft Silesia von 1860 bis 1870:
Ihre Bedeutung für die Anfänge der deutschnationalen Bewegung in Oester-
reich.* Heidelberg: 1911.
DIAMANT, ALFRED. *Austrian Catholics and the First Republic. Democracy,
Capitalism, and the Social Order, 1918–1934.* Princeton, N. J.: 1960.
EDER, KARL. *Der Liberalismus in Oesterreich.* Vienna: 1952.
EICHSTÄDT, ULRICH. *Von Dollfuss zu Hitler.* Wiesbaden: 1955.
FRANZ, GEORG. *Der Liberalismus. Die Deutsch-Liberale Bewegung in der
Habsburgischen Monarchie.* Munich: 1955.
FUCHS, ALBERT. *Geistige Strömungen in Oesterreich.* Vienna: 1949.
FUNDER, FRIEDRICH. *Als Oesterreich den Sturm Bestand.* Vienna: 1955.
———. *Vom Gestern ins Heute.* Vienna: 1954.
GEHL, JURGEN. *Austria, Germany and the Anschluss, 1931–1938.* London:
1963.
GULICK, CHARLES A. *Austria from Habsburg to Hitler.* Berkeley: 1948. 2
vols.
HANTSCH, HUGO. *Die Nationalitätenfrage im alten Oesterreich.* Vienna: 1953.
HITLER, ADOLF. *Mein Kampf.* Munich: 1925.
Hochverratsprozess gegen Dr. Guido Schmidt, Der. Vienna: 1947.
JEDLICKA, LUDWIG. *Ein Heer im Schatten der Parteien.* Graz: 1955.
JENKS, WILLIAM A. *Vienna and the Young Hitler.* New York: 1959.
KANN, ROBERT A. *The Multinational Empire, Nationalism and Reform in the
Habsburg Monarchy.* New York: 1951. 2 vols.

KUPPE, RUDOLF. *Dr. Karl Lueger. Persönlichkeit und Wirken.* Vienna: 1947.
LANGOTH, FRANZ. *Kampf um Oesterreich.* Wels: 1951.
MAYER-LOEWENSCHWERDT, ERWIN. *Schönerer der Vorkämpfer. Eine politische Biographie.* Vienna-Leipzig: 1939.
MOLISCH, PAUL. *Die Deutschen Hochschulen in Oesterreich und die Politisch-Nationale Entwicklung nach dem Jahre 1848.* Vienna: 1939.
————. *Geschichte der Deutschnationalen Bewegung in Oesterreich von ihren Anfängen bis zum Verfall der Monarchie.* Jena: 1926.
PICHL, EDUARD (pseud. Herwig). *Georg Schönerer und die Entwicklung des Alldeutschtums in der Ostmark.* Vienna: 1912; Berlin: 1938. 6 vols.
SCHUSCHNIGG, KURT. *Dreimal Oesterreich.* Vienna: 1937.
————. *Ein Requiem in Rot-Weiss-Rot.* Zurich: 1946.
SHEPHERD, GORDON BROOK. *The Anschluss.* Philadelphia, New York: 1963
————. *Engelbert Dollfuss.* London: 1960.
WHITESIDE, ANDREW G. *Austrian National Socialism before 1918.* The Hague: 1962.

Hungary

ISTVÁN DEÁK

The history of the Right in Hungary between the two world wars is the whole chronicle of Hungary at that time, for between 1919 and 1944 Hungary was a rightist country. Forged out of a counter-revolutionary heritage, its governments advocated a "nationalist, Christian" policy: they extolled heroism, faith, and unity; they despised the French revolution, and they spurned the liberal and socialist ideologies of the nineteenth century. These governments saw Hungary as a bulwark against bolshevism and bolshevism's instruments: socialism, cosmopolitanism, and Freemasonry. They perpetrated the rule of a small clique of aristocrats, civil servants, and army officers, and surrounded with adulation the head of the state, the counterrevolutionary Admiral Horthy.

Yet, these governments' rightist orientation cloaked wide political variations. Indeed, Horthy Hungary tolerated some genuine liberal practices as well as occasional terror; she brought to the fore not only ruthless Fascists but some decent and honorable men. A basic trait of the Horthy era was political inconsistency, a trait that was often to the advantage of the country. Not without reason was this rightist regime attacked by a rightist opposition, which criticized exactly these contradictions between ideology and practice.

Between 1919 and 1944 there were two Rights in Hungary. One may be called the Horthy Right, and the other, the Right of the

National Socialist movement. While the Horthy Right tolerated the existence of a multiparty parliament, suffered and occasionally fostered a Social Democratic party and socialist trade unions, and, though anti-Semitic, almost succeeded in saving the lives of the country's considerable Jewish population, it was the aim of the National Socialist Right to destroy all of this.

Nothing shows better the dominance of the Right in Hungarian politics than the fact that Admiral Horthy's regime was never even remotely threatened by a popular movement of the Left. On the contrary, in the decisive years 1938–1944 the few leftist parties proved to be Horthy's loyal supporters against Germany and the National Socialists. Even the underground Communist movement in the 1940's saw its only chance of success in temporary co-operation with the Horthy government. It is no less indicative that most of the accumulated social discontent—and there was infinite reason for complaint—was expressed not so much through the leftist movements as through the regime's radical rightist opposition.

The opposition between the Horthy Right and the National Socialists was something of a class struggle. The final victory of the National Socialists in October, 1944, also meant the beginning of a still unfinished social revolution.

The stability of the Horthy regime (it was overthrown in October, 1944, not so much by the Hungarian Nazis as by German troops) was owing to the skill of the Hungarian police, of course, but also to the genuine loyalty of large segments of society and to the rather hopeless imbecility of the Radical Right, especially its leader, Ferenc Szálasi. But, perhaps even more, the Horthy regime owed its stability to the fanatical patriotism that characterized most Hungarians, rich and poor, Christian and Jew alike. Indeed, no greater accusation could be raised against a person in Hungary than that he was "un-Hungarian," a term that implied cowardice, treason, cunning, and lack of chivalry; in short, it implied Swabian (German), Czech, or Romanian, but not Hungarian, behavior. Judged by these standards, Hungary's Radical Right often came dangerously close to being un-Hungarian, and ultimately deprived itself of an overwhelming popularity.

And finally it must be borne in mind that the Hungarian political scene between 1918 and 1944, despite some newly acquired harshness, still reflected something of the casual temperament of the era of Franz Josef. In Hungarian politics, where anybody who was anybody knew everybody, personal friendships often warded off political clashes. Here, even the wildest anti-Semite had his Jewish friends, and the most persecuted revolutionary seemed to have useful connections. Indeed, the whole story is permeated by a certain lightheartedness and by a sense of humor that characterized Hungarian, and particularly Budapest, society— qualities that often gave these great political and social conflicts the aspect of a musical comedy.

The establishment of a rightist regime in 1919 was the last political triumph of Hungary's "historic classes." The aristocracy and the gentry, these two separate, often mutually hostile but never completely alienated classes, had been for centuries Hungary's undisputed masters. They alone had formed the political nation; the struggle for Hungarian sovereignty against Habsburg centralization had been their privilege, and so had patriotism. The linguistic and cultural revival of the 1830's was their doing, and in 1848 they were the leaders of the war for independence. True, "classless" intellectuals and the land-owning peasantry took part in the revolution, but when the ensuing period of Austrian oppression was over it was the nobles alone who concluded the compromise agreement with Vienna. In 1867, Hungary was guaranteed an equal position in the Dual Monarchy, and the Magyar nobles regained their position of authority over Hungary's population.

Since the treaty of 1867 was a compromise agreement, it called for constant watchfulness toward Austrian, but also Romanian and Slav, aspirations. The national minorities, who formed more than half of Hungary's total population, were clamoring for the same consideration that Hungary had received from the Habsburgs. A suspicious attitude toward Vienna and an attempt at Magyarization at home became the main themes of Hungarian politics in the compromise era, but although the Hungarians managed to maintain and even to strengthen their position in the Dual Monarchy, Magyarization was only partly successful. Occasional brutality, bribery, and constant propaganda did not change the ethnic setup of the Hungarian villages. Only in the cities did the Magyar middle class grow fast between 1867 and 1914, owing to the influx and assimilation of non-Magyar elements who often exhibited the newcomer's rabid nationalism.

Urban development took a strange turn during the compromise era. Between 1867 and 1914 Hungary experienced a genuine industrial revolution (in 1910, industry employed more than a million people: 5.8 per cent of the total population), but this was not the achievement of the historic classes. The Hungarian nobleman, who knew how to spend money with an inimitable gesture, remained forever unwilling to learn the secrets of money-making. His attention was absorbed by the constitutional struggle with Vienna (it required an unwieldy army of jurists), by politics, and by the constantly swelling civil service. Commerce and industry were left to the established inhabitants of the towns (mainly Germans), to the German and Slovak newcomers from the villages, and especially to the Jewish population.

Until the nineteenth century the number of Jews in Hungary was small: 83,000 (1.0 per cent) in 1787; but then their numbers grew rapidly as a result of immigration from Eastern Europe, particularly from Galicia. In 1848 there were 336,000 Jews, and in 1910 there were 909,500, or roughly 5.0 per cent of the population. The liberal-conservative government of the compromise era encouraged the immigration, as it rightfully expected from it both economic and political benefits. Indeed, the Jews showed their gratitude by eager assimilation, ardent patriotism, and financial support of the government and the party in power. As, in all statistics, Jews were counted as Magyars, Jewish immigration constituted the greatest Magyar ethnic gain; and, as an increasing number of Jews flocked into the cities, they came to constitute the bulk of the educated class. In Budapest alone there were over 200,000 Jews in 1910, that is to say, more than 20.0 per cent of the city's population. (In so-called Jew-ridden Berlin in 1920, only 5.0 per cent of the population was Jewish.) In 1910, 21.8 per cent of the salaried employees in industry, 54.0 per cent of the self-employed traders, and 85.0 per cent of the self-employed persons in banking and finance were Jews. Mining and heavy industry were almost entirely in their hands. In the free professions, their proportion was very high: in 1910 every second Hungarian lawyer and physician was a Jew. Even by 1907 all the better-known Budapest newspapers were owned by Jews, and in Budapest 70.0 per cent of all journalists were Jewish. They figured among the prominent scientists, writers, poets, and artists of the country.

True, both wealth and influence were the privilege of a few hundred families. The great majority of the Jews, particularly the immigrants who settled in Carpatho-Ukraine, in the northeast of Hungary, lived in poverty, often in abject misery. Yet upon the privileged few, some of whom converted to Christianity, the government heaped its favors. Franz Josef elevated twenty-five families to baronial rank and two hundred and ninety other families were ennobled. There was considerable intermarriage between the old aristocratic families and the new Jewish nobility. Jews began to own land, and, in the Austro-Hungarian army, some Hungarian Jews rose to the rank of general.

Anti-Semitism, although not unknown, was no serious matter before 1918. The government and the intellectuals combated its first signs vigorously; it developed into nothing comparable with prewar Vienna's anti-Semitism. "In growing Hungary, there is a place for everybody," ran the popular slogan. As stated by an observer of the Hungarian scene: "In Hungary, pre-Hitlerian anti-Semitism was . . . a concomitant of the semi-feudalistic mentality of the landed gentry, a feeling of antipathy toward an ethnic group of alien origin and dissimilar religion engaged in pursuits unbecoming a gentleman." * While the writer should have drawn the boundary not at pre-Hitlerian but at pre-1918 Hungary, it was true that rabid anti-Semitism was unknown in Hungary. Even the Catholic Church, which had not looked kindly on hurried Jewish assimilation, suffered a defeat when, in 1896, a liberal law on marriages obliterated the last traces of religious discrimination. However, after 1900 there was a decline in the influence, and

---

* János Kovács, "Neo-Antisemitism in Hungary," in *Jewish Social Studies,* VIII (July, 1946), 147.

numerical strength, of the Jews, a fact that later anti-Semites carefully overlooked. Hit by emigration from Hungary, by conversions, and by a declining birth rate, the Jewish community did not grow between 1910 and 1920, and declined by about thirty thousand between 1920 and 1930.

"Jewish predominance," or rather the unwillingness of Magyar nobles to go into business, was but one of the problems inherited by the post-1918 generation. No less serious, yet even less noticed, was the misery of Hungary's agrarian population. The revolution of 1848 had won the emancipation of the peasants but failed to bring about division of the large estates. After 1867, nothing was done to improve the situation. The distribution of landed property was highly inequitable, perhaps the worst in Europe outside of Romania and Russia. In 1900, agriculture employed 66.5 per cent of the population, but about one-third of the country's entire area was owned by fewer than four thousand proprietors. A great many holdings were too small to provide their owners with a living, yet these "dwarf holders," together with the landless peasants and farmhands, constituted a rural proletariat encompassing two-thirds of the agricultural population.

It was inevitable that World War I should emphasize Hungary's grave problems. Once the initial enthusiasm for war had faded, the Magyar nationalists agitated for complete independence from Austria, the national minorities for autonomy within Hungary, the Budapest democratic press for peace, the Social Democrats for universal suffrage, and, finally, the left radicals for a socialist revolution. On October 31, 1918, a bloodless revolution swept away king and government; about two weeks later, Hungary was proclaimed a republic with Count Mihály Károlyi as its provisional President. Károlyi had been the leader of the radical wing of the nationalist Independence party. He was also a convinced democrat and proposed a sweeping land reform, universal suffrage, and reconconciliation with the national minorities. His proposals came to nothing. The national minorities went their own ways; the Entente refused to consider even the most modest Hungarian proposals. When Hungary's dismemberment by Czechoslovaks, Romanians, and South Slavs became a fact, Károlyi resigned, and on March 21,

1919, handed power over to a coalition of left-wing Social Democrats and Communists. As the Communists held out the promise of Russian aid (which was never given) for the defense of Hungarian territorial integrity, and were the only ones willing to assume power, Károlyi's step could hardly have been avoided. Yet it served in the public mind to associate Hungary's brief "Weimar period" with Bolshevism and the country's shameful degradation.

The Council of People's Commissars, headed by Béla Kun, an until-then unknown journalist and former prisoner of war in Russia, destroyed whatever enthusiasm remained for a leftist regime in Hungary. Its doctrinal experiments, including the nationalization of the large estates—but not their distribution among the peasants—and its terrorist detachments turned the peasants into fierce anti-Communists, and provided popular backing for the ensuing counterrevolution. In the summer of 1919, Romanian troops invaded rump-Hungary, acting on Entente orders. The Communist regime collapsed and, on August 1, 1919, the Communist leaders fled abroad. Not until 1945 were they or the workers again to play a significant political role in Hungary.

The brief Bolshevik reign was crucial. The historic classes could not forget their humiliation, and as it was inconceivable that peasants and workers—true Hungarians—could have been responsible for these revolutions, the dark designs of a foreign hand emerged. The Jews were responsible, the Jews who had eluded their share in the war effort, who had stabbed the army in the back through their agitation, who had comprised the majority of war profiteers, and—worse—had furnished the great majority of Communists in power. From that time on, these beliefs, widely shared, became one of the determining factors in Hungarian policy.

The Communists seemed still firmly in the saddle in Budapest when the first counterrevolutionary forces began to organize at a safe distance. In Vienna and in southeast Hungary, in the French-occupied cities of Arad and Szeged, anti-Bolshevik committees were formed. These were strictly family affairs, formed by aristocrats, army officers, and civil servants. The Vienna committee was led by Count István Bethlen; the Szeged committee was led by the

Austro-Hungarian Admiral Miklós Horthy. When Romanian forces occupied Budapest and the Communists fled abroad, Horthy transferred his headquarters to unoccupied western Hungary, where his small officers' detachments established their own regime of terror. Communists were hanged and hundreds of Jews killed, the latter regardless of any complicity. In November, 1919, after the Romanians had finally withdrawn from the nation's capital, Horthy marched into the city at the head of his small national army. In a public address, he promised well-deserved punishment to Budapest, the "sinful city." The White detachments of Horthy began to operate in Budapest; pogroms were organized, and special courts sent Bolsheviks and workers to the gallows, into prisons, or to specially constructed internment camps.

The newly formed counterrevolutionary government received quick Allied recognition. The Entente, which had not hesitated to wreck Károlyi's democratic government, now—enlightened by the experience with Communism—eagerly accepted the only available force of order. But, as the Entente wanted the whole country to accept the coming peace treaty, it insisted on an early end to the White Terror, on universal, secret elections, and on a representative government. The counterrevolutionaries partially obeyed these demands. Within a year, order was more or less reëstablished, but, as Horthy himself had been involved in the terror, no serious measures were taken against the White terrorists. In January, 1920, elections were held throughout Hungary and with secret balloting. The Social Democrats, whose leaders and many members were in prison or internment, boycotted the election. As for the Communist party, it remained outlawed throughout the Horthy era. Two principal parties emerged from the elections: the conservative Christian National Union and the Smallholders' party. The latter represented the farmers and advocated a land reform. Judging by the temper of the majority of the deputies, the country wanted order, but it was not averse to social reform—a concession, however, that Horthy and the ruling nobles were not willing to grant. In any event, reconstruction could begin, and, indeed, the new regime was inaugurated under favorable domestic auspices. It felt free from all responsibility for the defeat of Hungary and the revolutions. It had to sign the peace treaty, but its very existence seemed to be Hungary's most efficient protest against the treaty's humiliating conditions. More than that, standing on anti-Bolshevist and antidemocratic principles, the Horthy regime foreshadowed European developments. When the fascist wave swept over Europe, the respectability the Horthy Right had by then acquired secured its continuance.

As for Hungary's international status and economy, the situation was almost hopeless. Hungary was completely isolated, her economy was barely viable, there was widespread unemployment, prices rose rapidly, stocks were exhausted, machinery had deteriorated, and the withdrawing Romanian troops had taken with them all that was movable. The Treaty of Peace signed at Trianon on June 4, 1920, deprived Hungary of 71.4 per cent of her prewar territory, and 63.5 per cent of her population. (Of the 325,411 square kilometers that had comprised the lands of the Holy Crown, Hungary was left with only 92,963. Of the population of 20,886,-486 [1910 census], Hungary was left with only 7,615,117.) Of the persons of Magyar tongue, no less than 3,200,000 became the subjects of Romania, Czechoslovakia, Yugoslavia, and Austria, in complete defiance of the principle of self-determination.

The Treaty exasperated everyone and created a sense of common suffering that the Horthy regime knew well how to exploit. The slogan *Nem, Nem, Soha* ("No, No, Never") became the outcry of Hungary's determination never to accept the terms of the dictated Treaty. It was repeated tirelessly at every political meeting and in every schoolroom for over two decades. Although Hungary's policy was one of peaceful revision, no one doubted that she would eventually attempt to recover her lost territories by force of arms.

Beyond this commonly shared irredentism, there was little unity in the ranks of the counterrevolution. There were, of course, the binding slogans: anti-Bolshevism, historical values, positive Christianity, struggle against Jewish influence, order, authority. But there was no governmental policy. For Roman Catholic Bishop Ottokár Proházka, one of the spiritual leaders of the counterrevolution, the new rightist course meant primarily moral restoration: a struggle against Jewish and liberal cultural and moral influence. It also meant "justice for the poor." For others, the future spelled the decline of urban civilization and the country's return to the "blessed, eternal Hungarian soil." For still others, the counter-revolution was to bring a return to the old: to undisputed rule of the historic classes. For some it promised a return to Habsburg rule.

What form of state was Hungary to adopt? This problem proved insoluble. Since a republican form of government was associated with Károlyi's experiment, that was unthinkable. The Entente would not permit a return of the Habsburgs, nor would the younger, extremist wing of the counterrevolutionaries hear of a monarchist restoration. These extremists, who came mainly from the gentry class, associated the Habsburg monarchy with liberalism and with aristocratic hegemony, both of which they loathed. Finally, Hungary was proclaimed a kingdom and on March 1, 1920, Admiral Horthy was made regent by parliamentary acclamation. The much bemused era of the "kingdom without a king, and the admiral without a fleet" began. In 1921, the Habsburg King Charles IV (Charles I of Austria) made two attempts to claim his throne, each time making a personal appearance in Hungary. Immediately, the counterrevolutionary front split into a conservative, "legitimist," and an extremist, nationalist camp. The latter enjoyed the support of the Entente, and Charles was made to withdraw, on the second occasion not without bloodshed. Parliament thereupon ratified the dethronement of the House of Habsburg, but the antagonism between the two camps remained. The "legitimists," actually a small group of aristocrats and ecclesiastical dignitaries, never forgave Horthy. This did not prevent them from supporting him whenever the regent leaned in a conservative direction. In any event, Horthy now reigned undisturbed. He was Supreme War Lord; he had the right to convene, to prorogue, and to dissolve parliament, and although he did not have the power to veto, he did have the right of initiative and could return a bill twice for consideration. His person was inviolable and, after 1937, he could no longer be called to account by parliament. It must be stated that the Regent never transgressed his rights. Indeed, he usually refrained from using his privileges to the full. Yet his power was very great. The army was directly under his orders; the prime minister—always a man of his choice—was responsible, in fact if not in law, to him alone. A man of mediocre intelligence, Horthy enjoyed great prestige and genuine popularity. Not until the last year of World War II did anyone in Hungary, or for that matter in Germany, conceive of a Hungarian government constituted without his assent. Altogether, the regency proved a great asset in the stability of the counter-revolution. Under Horthy's reign the country underwent several political changes, but he was able to head off an increasingly radical rightist tendency in government by the simple exercise of his authority.

Horthy was surrounded by adulation. An official publication of the Budapest municipality summed up the regent's role in Hungary in the following words:

Our gloriously ruling Great Lord, the Regent, His Serene Highness, the Hero Miklós Horthy of Nagybánya, came among us as if hurrying into our midst from the ranks of heroes eternally galloping along with Prince Csaba [the Hun Attila's favorite son and legendary ancestor of Hungarians] on the path of the Warriors high up in the sky to lead his forlorn race in the most terrible hours of its downtroddenness and inhuman trials.

Such servility, which, incidentally, blinded Horthy to the fact that not all members of his officer corps or of the civil service were loyal to him, pervaded the whole society. Unless he was a proletarian or a peasant, a person was addressed by one of four titles: "Excellency," "Dignity," "Greatness," or "Authority," the latter being used for members of the upper sector of the lower middle class. According to some estimates, one out of ten persons in Hungary in 1914 was a noble (of course, many titles were doubtful and many genuine nobles were little better than peasants). There was a complex system of hereditary and nonhereditary ranks and titles which were either granted or acknowledged by the state.

In July, 1921, the Regent appointed the former leader of the Vienna Anti-Bolshevik Committee, Count István Bethlen, as prime minister. In the following "Bethlen era," the counterrevolution took a definitely conservative turn.

Bethlen was a scion of an old Transylvanian family of ruling princes. He was clever, intelligent, cultivated, averse to demagogy, and unmindful of the lower classes. He was interested only in the restoration of order and of "historic" Hungary; in this he succeeded amazingly. When he was appointed, the Smallholders' party had already been neutralized, together with its clamor for land reform, in the traditional Hungarian aristocratic manner. Flooded by large-estate owners and middle-class politicians, the Smallholders merged in July, 1920, with the Christian National Union to form the Unified party, which, under various names, was to be the party of the government for the next twenty-four years. Bethlen then settled with the socialists. In a secret agreement, the government returned to the Social Democratic and trade-union leaders the right to organize and the right of collective bargaining. It also undertook to restore the freedom of the press and to decree a general amnesty. In return, the Social Democrats pledged to restrict their activity to the cities, and the trade unions to refrain from organizing public employees, railway and postal employees, or the agricultural laborers. This agreement both sides respected, not only under Bethlen, but—freedom of the press excepted— until the end of the Horthy regime.

As a next step, Bethlen abolished the wide suffrage introduced early in 1920 under Entente pressure. The new franchise gave the vote to only 27.0 per cent of the population (uneducated and unsettled people being excluded), and reintroduced the open ballot in country districts and the smaller towns. What this meant in practice can be learned from the account of the peasant politician, Ferenc Nagy, who, after World War II, was for a time democratic Hungary's prime minister. His *Struggle Behind the Iron Curtain* tells a tale of bribery, blackmail, and physical violence, generously applied by the administration at the time of elections. When necessary, the dead were made to vote in the open ballot areas, and the living were kept away from the polls by gendarmes. That country districts were nevertheless generally able to send a few dozen opposition party deputies to the parliament was owing not to some administrative oversight, but rather to deliberate governmental policy.

In 1926, Bethlen reorganized the House of Lords, calling it the Upper House. In it sat all resident members of the Habsburg dynasty; representatives of the higher nobility; the highest church dignitaries, including the chief rabbi; representatives of rural and municipal councils, of the universities, of trade, industry, agriculture, and the professions; and, finally, forty-four members whom the regent had the right to nominate. This reactionary chamber of the vested interests was to become, during the Hitler years, the bulwark of humanism, opponent of anti-Semitism, National Socialism, and German aspirations.

The elections of May, 1922, held under the new franchise, gave the government's Party of Unity its absolute majority. (The parties of the opposition were the Legitimists, some radical rightist splinter groups, and, on the left, bourgeois Liberals and Social Democrats.) Never again were "unruly elements" to challenge the supremacy of this governmental party. Membership in the Party of Unity became the key to a political career. Of course, such an unwieldy grouping was not without its internal dissensions, and, particularly after 1936, a strong rightist faction was to grow up within it. Yet discipline or cowardice were forever binding; on only two occasions did the Party of Unity revolt against the prime minister who was also its leader. But, when the Regent refused to dismiss him, he was promptly voted confidence.

Having now provided for domestic order and discipline, Bethlen scored a number of foreign successes. In September, 1922, Hungary was admitted to the League of Nations and in the following year a "reconstruction loan" was granted through the good offices of the League, permitting Hungary to put an end to inflation. To reassure international financial interests, the Prime Minister cloaked the counterrevolution's anti-Semitic past. In 1920, a "numerus clausus" law—the first anti-Jewish measure of post-1918 Europe —had restricted the proportion of Jewish students at Hungarian universities. Without revoking the law, Bethlen let it fall into oblivion. In addition, a number of prominent Jewish personalities were rewarded with titles for their services and were given seats in the Upper House.

Reinforced by foreign capital, Hungary became relatively prosperous. This happy age, however, ended as it did everywhere with the great depression. Then, under the impact of declining industrial production, the collapse of wheat prices, the growing despair of the land-owning class, and the unemployed young intelligentsia, the Bethlen system collapsed. After an unsuccessful experiment with another conservative politician, the Regent, in September, 1932, appointed General Gyula Gömbös as prime minister. This marked the return to power of the counterrevolution's radical wing.

Gyula Gömbös of Jákfa was considerably younger than Bethlen (thirty-three at the time of the counterrevolution), and, unlike him, without any political experience in 1919. Nor was he an aristocrat, but the son of well-to-do Swabian peasants, who simply usurped a title of nobility. He had been a captain on the General Staff of the Austro-Hungarian army, from which he emerged a fierce Hungarian chauvinist. During the counterrevolution Gömbös had been one of Horthy's loyal supporters and the spokesman of the younger officers. Unlike Bethlen, he hated the Habsburgs and, in 1921, had organized the armed defense against troops loyal to King Charles. Later, resigning his army commission, he entered politics, first in the Party of Unity then at the head of the small Party of Racial Defense, dedicated to anti-Semitism. (One of the members of this party was Endre Bajcsy-Zsilinszky, who, in the 1940's, became the head of the anti-German resistance movement and was executed by the Hungarian Nazis.)

In 1928, having acquired sufficient nuisance value, Gömbös was taken back into the Government Party and, a year later, became Minister of Defense. He celebrated this appointment by promoting himself from captain to lieutenant-general. Vain and aggressive, Gömbös was not without a certain charm and talent; he was also hopelessly sentimental. Discovering the glories of Italian fascism, he groomed himself for the position of dictator—under the regent, of course—and imitated the *duce* in his outward appearance. Once a dictator, he was confident he would rid Hungary of the Jews and Freemasons; he would spread happiness by providing the workers with jobs and the peasants with land.

Gömbös's appointment by the regent was owing to the pressure of a large group of younger counterrevolutionaries and some businessmen who had been extremely dissatisfied with Bethlen's fulfillment of the peace treaty with the Allies, his "philo-Semitism," and with the whole parliamentary system. Gathered in scores of secret and semisecret patriotic associations (as far as any secret could be kept in Hungary, where journalists had keen ears and where everyone was privy to everyone else's moves), these people cultivated the spirit of "national revival." The patriotic organizations, such as the Awakening Hungarians or the more mysterious EKSZ (Etelköz Association), were generally constructed along a supposedly ancestral tribal pattern. New members took fearful oaths of unconditional obedience to their "chieftains," and swore to die rather than to divulge the associations' secrets or to abandon the pursuit of a "great, Christian and racially pure Hungary." Actually, as the pogroms ended in 1920, these groups became mere political clubs, with membership advisable for all who aspired to a civil service career. On the fringes of these associations officiated the Turanians, priests of a new Hungarian mystical creed; they worshipped, with various degrees of conviction, a certain Hadúr, or War Lord, supposed god of the ancient Hungarians. For good measure, this brotherhood of the Turanians (that is, of the Turkish and Ural-Altaic "races") attempted to prove that such ancient peoples as the Persians, Hittites, Egyptians, and particularly the Sumerians, were the Magyars' direct ancestors, and that Jesus himself must have been Turanian. From this deep fount of wisdom, many a Hungarian National Socialist was later to drink.

Although usually harmless, some of these patriots, Gömbös included, flirted with the idea of a coup d'etat whenever they saw the "ideas of Szeged," that is, of the counterrevolution, downtrodden by Bethlen and his Jewish-liberal-aristocrat cohorts. In 1923, for instance, some of Gömbös's friends, if not Gömbös himself, negotiated with Hitler for *putsches* to be carried out simultaneously in Bavaria, Hungary, and perhaps in Russia as well. The execution of the plan was thwarted by the police, who from the outset had been privy to it. In the words of police president Hetényi, his intervention became necessary only after "the gentlemen had ignored repeated warnings to stop this nonsense." The conspirators received light sentences of honorary confinement and were immediately released; Gömbös was not even indicted. This official leniency was in line with the government's habitual policy toward "patriotic" offenders, especially if they happened to be gentlemen. Only later, when lower-class National Socialists were engaged in subversive action, were harsher measures applied against the radical Right.

Once in power, Gömbös proved surprisingly weak. He was undoubtedly restrained by the now thoroughly conservative regent, by all the forces of the old, by Hungary's economic and military weakness, but his own weakness must have been no less a factor. In any event, he did not abolish parliament, did not set himself up as a dictator, and toward the Jews he "extended his friendly hand." The proudly announced ninety-five-point program of his government was even made available in an English version (*The National Programme of the Hungarian Government* [Budapest: 1932]). It reads like a curious litany of promises and their simultaneous denials. It envisaged, for example, a "reform of the electoral law on the basis of the secret ballot," but with the proviso "that at the same time the great national ideals of the Hungarian people must be safeguarded"; and it promised freedom of the press "as long as the press faithfully serves the interests of the nation."

The four years of the Gömbös government (1932–1936) brought no major reforms. What they did bring was a change in political atmosphere. The aristocratic restraint of Bethlen gave way to the demagogy of Gömbös. In his first address as prime minister he said: "I stand here before you as your Leader. I might lead you on a new path, but do not fool yourselves by expecting miracles. Our path will be a steep, rocky, thorny one, but I feel, I know, that it will lead us to the goal. Hungarians! My brothers! Ignite the candle of trust at the life-fire of my soul that burns for you, my nation! Spread this illumination!"

Under Gömbös the state became more authoritarian. A form of press censorship was introduced; heavily subsidized newspapers were created to present the government's point of view; a system of informants was built up; the secrecy of mail was violated. There was also a changing of the guard in the civil service and the army, especially in the General Staff, with a great number of "Gömbös boys," partly of Swabian origin, taking over the key posts. This process was speeded up after May, 1935, when Gömbös was in a position to "make" the elections and thus bring into parliament a strong contingent of his own followers. In foreign policy, Gömbös took a fatal step by committing the country to a German-Italian orientation. In his enthusiasm, he saw Central Europe divided among Germany, Italy, and Hungary, and pressed Hungary's friendship upon the two great powers.

Gömbös died in 1936, but the dangers of this step to the Right were clearly recognized by the saner segment of Hungarian society. Slowly and hesitantly, the conservative wing of the Government Party established a working agreement with the Left-opposition. Though never publicly acknowledged, a new front came into being, of the Bethlen wing of the Government party, the Christian party (with royalist tendencies), the resurrected Smallholders' party, the Social Democrats, and various liberal, democratic elements. A strange conglomerate indeed, but a durable one. It lasted as long as the Regency. These aristocrats, nationalists— like Endre Bajcsy-Zsilinszky—Jewish financiers, democratic intellectuals, politically educated peasants, and representatives of the organized workers, included the country's most reactionary as well as its most enlightened and progressive groups. They were united by fear of German expansion, and of domestic dictatorship. In the puzzling Hungarian pronaos, from then on determined by the country's relationship with Germany, this front definitely constituted the Left. Against them were lined up the rightist elements in the Government Party, the National Socialists, many civil servants, the unemployed and unemployable young "diploma holders," almost the entire officer corps, a great part of the petite bourgeoisie, and many of the workers and agricultural laborers. And while this "Left" talked of domestic peace, order, and historical values, the Right argued social reform, an end to feudalism and capitalism, and the necessity of a close alliance with a triumphant Germany.

Of the seven prime ministers Horthy appointed after the death of Gömbös in 1936, only one, Sztójay, was at the time of his appointment a known pro-German, a rightist, and an anti-Semite. His appointment, however, was the direct consequence of the German invasion of Hungary on March 19 1944. The others were appointed because of their expected "leftist" sympathies. That two of these prime ministers (Imrédy and Bárdossy) did not fulfill these expectations, but proved to be Germany's best allies, was owing not to Horthy's intentions, but to personal ambition with Imrédy, and to a miscalculation of Germany's chances of success with Bárdossy. But even these two men, while in office, were staunch anti-Nazis in domestic policy. When they were dismissed, it was because they had disappointed the regent in their foreign policy.

This is not the place to analyze in detail Horthy Hungary's foreign policy and the reason she became Germany's satellite. Foreign policy was determined by Hungary's territorial claims and, later, during World War II, by her determination for once to avoid the losing side. As to who would win the war, the Hungarian military experts did not at first entertain the slightest doubts; when there was reason to worry, after 1942, it was fear of Russian bolshevism that led them to advise a firm, pro-German stand. No less important for Hungary was the Germans' skillful handling of national antagonisms in the Danubian basin, which they exploited in the period from 1939 to 1944 as the Habsburgs had done in 1848 and the French in the 1920's. Indeed, as far as Hungary was concerned, the Little Entente of the 1920's changed but in name—pro-French Czechoslovakia, Romania, and Yugoslavia being replaced by fascist and pro-German Slovakia, Croatia, and Antonescu's Romania. As a result, everybody in Hungary looked to the country to rearm, some against Russia, others against the new Little Entente, still others against Germany, or against all of these powers combined. But arms could be obtained only from Germany and, to obtain arms, Hungary had to make concessions.

Once these were made, and more arms had been demanded, anxious Hungarians pressed for further rearmament so as to protect Hungarian sovereignty. But arms could be obtained only from Germany. . . . And so the vicious spiral wound around until it brought Hungary's destruction.

In November, 1938, through the good offices of Italy and Germany, Hungary reannexed the Magyar-inhabited areas of Czechoslovakia. In August, 1940, she reacquired from Romania the northern part of Transylvania, again through the good offices of Italy and Germany. In November of the same year she entered the Three-Powers Pact of Italy, Germany, and Japan. In April, 1941, in the wake of the German army, Hungarian troops entered Yugoslavia to reoccupy another territory that had belonged to Hungary and, finally, in June, 1941, submitting to German pressure, Hungary entered the war against the Soviet Union.

Horthy, the old sailor, was convinced from the outset that "sea-power will defeat land-power," and that the British would win the war. To this belief he held obstinately. But he was, at least for a while, unable to resist his "land-locked" generals, who pressed for an even closer alliance with Germany. It must be said also that public opinion generally approved of the territorial reannexations at whatever price; and it was precisely the Left, especially the spokesmen of the Jewish community, who begged the regent to make concessions to Germany in order to avoid, or at least to delay, a German invasion of Hungary.

As Hungary became increasingly dependent on German foreign policy, her domestic policy followed, limping, the German example. There was more talk of the glories of the military, of Hungary's right to a place in the sun, of the necessity of a strictly nationalist, Christian policy. And these slogans were so much a part of counter-revolutionary Hungary that the Left had to use the same vocabulary to urge resistance against Germany. Finally, ever stricter laws were adopted against the Jews. The first law, of 1938, was clearly meant to undercut the anti-Semites; it imposed some restrictions on Jewish economic activity but exempted—among others—almost all baptized Jews from adherence to this law. The second law, ratified in 1939, restricted the proportion of Jews in the professions to 6 per cent, and was more drastic both in its definition of "Jew" and in all other measures. By then anti-Jewish legislation benefited so many Christians that a ferocious agitation began, mainly in the rightist press, for further, more efficient measures. Hungary, very much against the intentions of her legislators, found herself on the road to drastic social changes. Although the hierarchical structure of society remained unchanged, the anti-Jewish measures brought rapid advance to many members of the lower bourgeoisie and weakened the old respect for private property.

The Left saw the danger clearly, and it was primarily in the Upper House that the Jewish laws found their opponents. But, as usual in Hungary, the government's proposals became law without difficulty. In subsequent measures, Jewish religious leaders were banned from the Upper House; all Jews, even former officers, were excluded from the armed services and obliged to perform labor service instead, and, finally, Law XV of 1941 forbade both marriage and sexual intercourse between Jews and Christians. These were cruel laws, indeed, but until March, 1944, the Hungarian government declined the German demand for a "final solution" (extermination) to the Jewish problem. And while the Jewish lower classes suffered from unemployment, the wealthy continued to live very much as they had before. In the great Jewish enterprises it was common practice to employ a few Christians to improve the "ratio," but management was left in the hands of the old employers. A select group of Jewish manufacturers and financiers remained Horthy's personal friends and trusted advisers until the very day of the German invasion.

Clearly, these half-measures could not satisfy the rabid anti-Semites and it was mainly in protest against the government's unwillingness to "solve" the Jewish problem, that a National Socialist movement arose in Hungary.

The Gömbös conspiracy of 1923 was by no means the only extreme rightist undertaking of the Bethlen period. It has been mentioned here only because it was characteristic of the "gentleman era" of the radical Right, with its secret, conspiratorial activities and its lack of popular appeal—for the *putschist* of the 1920's was just as reluctant to appeal to the masses and thus stir up dangerous waters as was Bethlen himself. The first popular agitator, Zoltán Böszörmény, emerged during the great depression. His political party, although awkward and helpless, was also National Socialism's most original, most characteristically Hungarian version.

Böszörmény, born in 1893, was the son of a bankrupt landowner. His youth was a succession of odd jobs that turned him, successively, into an apprentice, a messenger, a worker, and a porter. In 1919 he joined the counterrevolution; later he dabbled in journalism and managed to enter the University of Budapest, where he was elected leader of the patriotic student fraternities. Böszörmény was also a poet, and to peddle his patriotic verses he employed a couple of agents who later became his party's organizers.

In 1931, if his confessions are to be believed, Böszörmény visited Germany, where he met Hitler and was instantly converted by him. On his return, he published a manifesto and announced the birth of the Hungarian National Socialist Workers' party, the first of a great many undertakings bearing the same or similar names. As his party's emblem, Böszörmény chose the crossed scythes. He never doubted his destiny. In 1932, he wrote:

Even among the giants of intellect I am a giant, a great Hungarian poet with a prophetic mission. . . . My heart shudders at the cry of pain of Hungarian mothers. . . . I have listened to the call of the sweetest mother of all, Mother Hungary, and—answering it—I started off on the road, abandoning all worldly goods and happiness. . . . I knew well that my fight, begun without arms, would be ruthless: a fight to the teeth-gnawing bitter end.

To this, he later added: "This is the fullness of time, and the lonely poet, the Man, who always stood alone, departs to oppose the destructive forces of Money. . . . One Man against the whole world."

For the time being, the "tribune," who—in his own words—was ready "to caress but also to have hundreds of thousands executed without batting an eyelash," became the favorite target of the Budapest satirical newspapers. Yet, among the peasants of Eastern

Hungary, his message spread fast. In these arid regions beyond the Tisza River, where villages were strangled by large estates, the "agrarian proletariat escaped into sectarianism to get away from misery," wrote Imre Kovács, one of the famed "village explorers" who in 1937, in his book *A néma forradalom* ("The Mute Revolution"), recorded the plight of the Hungarian peasants. Kovács describes how the hopeless life of these peasants forced them to seek salvation in religious ecstasies and in pursuit of fanatical "ideas." When the Scythe Cross movement became their savior, he writes, they inscribed on their banners: "We have had enough!" Kovács met some members of the Scythe Cross in 1934: "It was on a large estate beyond the Tisza; they were seasonal workers and very poor. They all wore the Scythe Cross armband and a badge: two crossed scythes on green background, in a red circle, with a skull in the center. 'We fight for the Idea'—they repeated when I questioned them, but were unable to tell what the 'Idea' was about. They hated the Communists and the Gentlemen."

In Gömbös' Hungary, the Scythe Cross did not have a chance. By the end of 1932, Böszörmény boasted of twenty thousand party members and, supported by some boisterous storm troopers, he made several attempts to run as candidate at parliamentary by-elections, but the customary vigilance of the local authorities prevented him from collecting the necessary number of "recommendations" for candidacy. Only once did he manage to stand for election and then he won only a few hundred votes. The party's weekly was occasionally suppressed and the Leader himself condemned to short prison terms which, however, he never served.

Böszörmény's ideology is not easy to define. He was against Jews, Bolsheviks, and liberals, and for his own dictatorship, land reform, and "justice for the poor." In the "Ten Commandments of the Storm Troopers," published in 1935, he exhorted his followers to violence, in language enriched by Hitlerite slogans and magic Turanian terms. He described his comrades as "Gardeners of the Hungarian race, fateful Death Reapers of the Jewish swine and their hirelings . . . opponents of all Habsburg aspirations," but history records no serious evidence of Scythe Cross violence, and its one attempt to act failed miserably.

A regular peasant rebellion was planned for May 1, 1936, when three million peasants were to march on "sinful" Budapest and raze it to the ground. In one peasant town of the great Hungarian plains a few thousand peasants actually met on the appointed day, but they were easily dispersed by the ubiquitous gendarmes. Several trials ensued. Böszörmény and his principal codefendants were given relatively light sentences, varying from a few months to two and a half years in prison; none of them was placed in custody, and Böszörmény was allowed to escape to Germany in the spring of 1938. He was the first of many Hungarian National Socialists to seek asylum from the Horthy authorities in Hitler's Germany.

The mass trial of the Scythe Cross rank and file presented a disheartening spectacle. Altogether 700 peasants were arrested, and 113 of them judged at a single trial. All declared themselves ready to die for the "Idea," but were unable to provide the judge with further elucidation. "Out of a hundred defendants," wrote Kovács, "98 owned neither house nor land. . . . They wore torn trousers, miserable short overcoats or old sheepskin vests; none of them wore a shirt." The judge permitted most of the defendants to return to their poverty.

By the time Böszörmény's movement was suppressed, he was no longer in the forefront. National Socialism had shifted to the cities, especially to Budapest, where socially acceptable leaders turned it into a more consequential political force.

It was during the premiership of Gömbös that Zoltán Meskó, an independent deputy, announced in parliament on June 16, 1932, that he had formed a "Hungarian Hitlerite movement." As the *Budapesti Hírlap* reported on June 17, 1932, Meskó, whose appearance in parliament in a brown shirt caused great hilarity on both sides of the House, expounded the demands of his National Socialist Peasants' and Workers' Party as follows:

Emphasis on public, rather than on private interest; prevention of religious persecution; restoration of Hungary's historic frontiers; safeguarding of Hungary's independence; universal, secret suffrage. . . . Naturalization restricted to people of clearly established Turanian descent. . . . Forced labor sentence or death for profiteers, embezzlers, perjurers and swindlers.

. . . Abolition of all entailed estates; universal military service; compulsory premarital medical examination. . . .

At the close of his oration, Meskó "attached the Swastika to his jacket." His National Socialism brought little that was new to the parliamentarians. The demands he voiced were those of all rightist splinter groups. A year later brown shirt and swastika were forbidden by the Minister of Interior as "official emblems of a foreign power." Meskó then exchanged his brown shirt for a green one, adopted the *nyilaskereszt* (arrow cross) as his party's emblem, and trimmed his Hitler-type moustache in the Hungarian style. The green shirt and the Arrow Cross subsequently became the symbols of most Hungarian National Socialist movements.

Now that the ice was broken, scores of new National Socialist parties sprang up. Their programs repeated that of Meskó, or rather of the German Nazi party, with more or less servility. Some were brutally anti-Semitic, others were more precise on the issue of land reform; still others were more generous than Meskó in defining membership in the Magyar race. Thus Aryans were added to Turanians, presumably to the relief of Meskó himself who was of pure Slovak descent. By 1933, several Hungarian aristocrats had each founded his own Arrow Cross movement. This made National Socialism somewhat more palatable to good society, and provided the Arrow Cross with desperately needed cash. Count Sándor Festetics—Leader of the Hungarian National Socialist party and a candidate, in 1935, for parliament, in one of the rural open-ballot districts which he practically owned—simply ordered his employees to vote for him rather than for the government's candidate. Faced with the agonizing dilemma of disappointing either the gendarmes or the count's stewards, the electors voted their lord into parliament with a comfortable majority.

At this time the National Socialists had two representatives in parliament, a fact which annoyed Gömbös. For the moment, however, there was little to worry about, as the National Socialist parties were engaged in the complex strife so characteristic of this movement outside of Germany. Leaders negotiated, amalgamated their parties, expelled each other, or proceeded to tearful reconciliations, all to the great delight of the satirical press. Not until the emergence of the Prophet, Ferenc Szálasi, did the Arrow Cross achieve at least spiritual unity, and then only because Szálasi elevated himself to such philosophic heights as to remain undisturbed by mean factional quarrels or practical political considerations.

In Hungary's troubled history, perhaps no politician was subjected to such extremes of abuse and of idolatry as Ferenc Szálasi. In C. A. Macartney's *History of Hungary, 1929–1945*, the author describes Szálasi as one of the strangest and most interesting characters of contemporary Hungarian history. While his many enemies spared no invective in denouncing him, Macartney writes that he inspired a personal devotion among his followers "such as no other Hungarian of his age could equal, and after his death they carried on the cult of him, passing his words from hand to hand, speaking of him as early Christians spoke of the Messiah."

As for Szálasi's personality, Professor Macartney provides us with the following description:

. . . an original, for whose mental processes the word eccentric would be a strong meiosis; but not . . . a brute, a traitor or a stupid man. . . . Incidentally, had he been a brute, and above all had he been a traitor, he could have achieved power before he did. It was precisely his refusal to compromise on matters of principle which kept the Germans from giving him support and led time and again to less scrupulous followers deserting him. His responsibility for the many sins committed under the aegis of his name lies in his unwillingness or inability even to see, much less to guard against, the dangers of the spirits which he conjured up. For himself, he was a man of the most unyielding principles, on which he insisted with a maddening monotony and a rigidity which rejected the slightest compromise.

Although this is too tolerant a judgment, it is certain that Szálasi was no hireling of Hitler. In his childish conceit, he considered Hungary Germany's equal partner in a new Europe. He was convinced that the Hungarians, "this little people," could reorganize Europe if only they would follow him. "I have been selected by a higher Divine authority to redeem the Magyar people—he who does not understand me or loses confidence—let him go! At most

I shall remain alone, but even alone I shall create the Hungarist State with the help of the secret force that is within me." Szálasi coined the word "Hungarist" (*Hungarista*) to designate his principles and program. It indicated that his National Socialism was different from that of the Germans. It also made Szálasi's movement invincible for, while his Arrow Cross party could be and often was suppressed, the "Hungarist Movement" would continue to live in the hearts of his followers.

It must come as no surprise that this superpatriot was also of foreign descent. Szálasi's father was of Armenian, and his mother of mixed Slovak-Magyar, stock. His father was an NCO in the Austro-Hungarian army. Like so many other sons of noncommissioned officers, Szálasi chose an officer's career. He served on the front during the late years of World War I; in postwar Hungary he was permitted to enter the General Staff College from which he graduated with highest honors. It was in the General Staff College, where such activity was encouraged, that Szálasi began to write on political and economic subjects. But he was already a major on the General Staff when, in 1933, he published, without permission of his superiors, his "Plan for the Construction of the Hungarian State." As the plan seemed to do injustice to Magyar aspirations, he was severely reprimanded for insubordination. He then addressed a memorandum to Prime Minister Gömbös, criticizing the government's policy. This angered Gömbös, who had no use for officers—besides himself—in politics. Apparently, the Prime Minister nevertheless attempted to win Szálasi over, offering him a mandate in the coming elections, but Szálasi put forward impossible conditions. In March, 1935, he resigned his army commission and founded his first political movement, the Party of National Will. He was then thirty-eight years of age. He stood twice for election, but was handsomely defeated. He then decided (1936) never again to run as a candidate.

On April 16, 1937, he was for the first time arrested and the party headquarters, comprising two rooms, were sealed. The police found a total of 420 *pengös* ($84) in the party treasury. The court sentenced him to three months in honorable confinement for anti-Semitic agitation, but he was never called to serve the sentence, although it did bring his name before the public. The nebulous statements on social reform he made at the trial won him many sympathizers. Soon after that he visited Germany, which caused the Budapest liberal press to credit him with Germany's favor. Membership in his party, renamed the Arrow Cross Party–Hungarist Movement, grew rapidly to twenty thousand by the summer of 1937. In October of the same year, he effected a merger of most National Socialist parties in an impressive demonstration held in Budapest. The merger lasted only a few weeks, but no one now doubted Szálasi's political importance. Yet his sudden popularity was hard to explain. He was neither a good speaker, nor a good organizer; but his sincerity and undoubted honesty kindled admiration, perhaps because such qualities were rare in contemporary Hungarian politics. He was fond of visiting, à la Hitler, in every corner of the country, where he amazed and charmed his followers by remembering their names. His popularity among women was one of his great assets. More important were his connections in the officer corps. Indeed, the younger officers who formed the bulk of the General Staff were impatient for political and social reform, which, they felt, was mandatory in view of the coming war. They besieged the regent with warnings against the leftist and Jewish agitation, and insisted that he implement a "new, determined, uncompromisingly Christian, national and popular policy." This meant in essence that the regent should curtail parliament and impose further restrictions on socialists and Jews. The officers negotiated with Szálasi and counted on him, but most of them were still reluctant to entrust him with political power.

The regent himself was aware of Szálasi's activity and, although he consistently refused to give an audience to his factious officer, he allowed the chief of his military cabinet to seek out Szálasi and inquire into his intentions. Szálasi made his views clear: the regent should "take charge of the country," that is, he should stage a *putsch* with the help of the army, and nominate Szálasi prime minister. But the regent refused to listen.

The year 1938 promised to be stormy. Rumors of a coming rightist coup were circulating and were played up enormously by a near-hysterical liberal press; the Arrow Cross flooded the streets of

Budapest with leaflets, announcing Szálasi's impending triumph. The regent himself was booed by students and officers at a gala performance in the Budapest Opera. At parliamentary by-elections, some of Szálasi's younger lieutenants ran successfully against the candidates of the Government Party and half a dozen Smallholder deputies left their party to join the National Socialist movement. In addition, the Arrow Cross now seemed to have almost unlimited funds. Through some Hungarian agents and through the German minority in Hungary, German money flowed into the coffers of the radical Right. Some influential Budapest newspapers changed hands and endorsed a National Socialist program. Szálasi knew nothing of these transactions, but then he was above such petty considerations.

Finally, the regent took matters in hand. In May, 1938, he dismissed the hesitant Darányi, Gömbös' immediate successor, and appointed Béla Imrédy prime minister. Imrédy was a financial expert and had the reputation of being a liberal and an Anglophile. He subsequently disappointed the regent because of his violent anti-Semitism and his aspirations to dictatorship, but for the Arrow Cross his appointment was a great blow. Imrédy, like Gömbös, had no use for other leaders and least of all for the unruly Arrow Cross. A week after his appointment he forbade all employees of the state to be members of political parties; as there were very few civil servants with leftist sympathies, this was designed as a measure against the Right.

Next, Szálasi was arrested. This time the government meant business; he was indicted for subversive activity, and sentenced to three years' hard labor. On August 27, 1938, he was taken to Szeged prison from where he was not to emerge for over two years. From then on, until the German occupation in March, 1944, the Arrow Cross was subjected to almost continual harassment. Its newspapers were suspended, its meetings forbidden, some of its leaders imprisoned, hundreds put in internment camps, there to outnumber by far the Communist prisoners. The German press reacted with violence to such persecution and hailed Szálasi as a martyr. At home, the Arrow Cross went into the new elections with his name on its banner. The parliamentary elections of May,

1939 (the first since 1935), were held with secret balloting in accordance with a law adopted a year earlier. The National Socialists scored a great success. Out of 259 seats the Government Party won a comfortable 183, but the National Socialists increased the number of their mandates to 49 (Szálasi's Arrow Cross alone received 31 mandates). The Social Democrats and the Smallholders were defeated. They won 5 and 14 seats respectively. Worse still, the majority of the Government Party had clearly rightist sympathies.

The popular vote was even more favorable to the Arrow Cross: out of a total of approximately 2,000,000 votes, they scored 750,-000. In Budapest the National Socialists obtained 72,385 votes, as opposed to 95,468 for the Government Party and 34,500 for the Socialists. "Red" Csepel, Budapest's most industrialized suburb, elected two National Socialist deputies.

In the new parliament the Arrow Cross deputies became the government's first true opposition. They remained, of course, completely impotent but they posed as the people's champions; between 1939 and 1944 their parliamentary speeches repeatedly harped on the plight of Hungary's poor. The extreme Right spoke with fire and conviction. No longer did it have to parrot the Horthy Right's slogans; it had its own ideology, formulated by Ferenc Szálasi.

Judging by the exhilarating effect of Szálasi's ideas upon the mass of his followers, one would expect some rational or emotional appeal in his many speeches and writings. Nothing could be further from the fact. Not only do these pieces of wisdom make dull reading, they are also infuriatingly garbled. Szálasi was fond of the newly coined word, of the juxtaposed phrase, and the involuted sentence. His magnum opus, Ut és Cél ("Road and Goal"), was published in 1936 and is as incomprehensible in the original as it is in translation:

. . . Social Nationalism is life's only genuine physics and biology. The true individual forms matter with his soul; his hand is but an instrument. And since this is so, the formed matter is a value and not a ware. Social Nationalism is therefore the nation's biological physics and not its historical materialism. Its biology: the nation; its physics: socialism fulfilled in the nation. It is life-community and matter-community in partner-community and fate-community, with a basis in the nation and Fatherland, pure and true in its moral and its spirit.

Or again from the same chapter:

The ideological foundation of Hungarism's national economy and work-order is Social Nationalism and its conscious practice. Only through the ideology and practice of Social Nationalism can the individual become a true national socialist. . . . National Socialism means nationalist order in socialism, Social Nationalism means socialist order in nationalism, therefore: spiritual order in matter, material order in the spirit. The soul's order in the body, the body's order in the soul.

Although these and similar pronouncements make the reader wonder about the intellectual climate of a General Staff College from which such a writer could emerge with distinction, it must be admitted that not all Szálasi's writings betray equal depth and confusion. On the question of Hungary's territorial aspirations, his major field of interest, Szálasi is almost precise. His aim was to restore Hungary's historic boundaries. That he gave to his resurrected Great Hungary the name Carpatho-Danubian Great Fatherland, or The United Lands and the March of Hungaria, was not without its justification. For Szálasi was intent upon establishing a happy community of nationalities in the Carpathian basin. The national minorities were to have their autonomy, while submitting, of course, to the authority of the Hungarian state. To the Magyars, he allotted the plains, to the Germans the hills, to the Romanians the "Alpine" regions, and to the Slavs the rest of the mountain areas.

It is true that on his maps Magyar autonomy far exceeded the limits of the plains and incorporated a good many areas inhabited by Slavs and Romanians, but then he was certain that such favoritism would meet with the approval of those concerned. Indeed, the Magyars alone had been able in the past to form an "organic state system" and it was therefore natural that they should occupy the largest areas and assume a commanding position in the new Hungarist state.

The unity of the Carpatho-Danubian Great Fatherland was to

be created by the Hungarian army. To this army would belong a commanding position in the state, and to its needs all the material and moral resources of the nation would have to be surrendered. "When the Army sees that in the nation the three pillars of Religion, Patriotism and Discipline have been shaken"—wrote Szálasi in his party daily—"then it is the Army's duty to force the nation back on these pillars."

This time, he said, the "stab in the back" tragedy of 1918 would not be repeated: "The war of the future will be total; from it only those nations will emerge successfully where the masses stand united behind the fighting army." Thus the army needed the domestic peace that neither Marxism nor liberalism could secure. The solution was "national capitalism." In that system, labor peace would reign; there would be no privileged classes; work would be both a right and a duty. Strikes and idleness would be outlawed, the tyranny of money abolished, the National Bank expropriated, and a General Council of Corporations formed to direct the national economy. As for agriculture, the agricultural proletariat would be transformed into a smallholders' class, a system of cooperatives set up, and the "planning of agricultural production" introduced. He failed, however, to announce which lands he intended for distribution or where, in his view, the upper limits of land ownership lay.

Szálasi was a devout Catholic; his vaguely Turanian Christ was the King of all Hungarians. The Hungarist state was to be based on a "Christian moral order" where atheism and nondenominationalism would not be tolerated. On the other hand, Church and state would be separated, and education taken out of the hands of the religious orders. A "political Church" had no place in the "Hungarist order." His religious orthodoxy was not necessarily shared by his followers. The party intellectual, Dr. Pál Vágo, for instance, was violently anticlerical; he accused the Church of propagating a Jewish version of Christianity. Dr. Vágo considered himself an expert in biblical studies and was able to prove that Christ was a Scythian (and thus a Turanian), and so were all the early Christians.

In Szálasi's opinion women and children were two of the "seven pillars of the nation." The concept of illegitimate birth was to be abolished, and divorces restricted to cases of "national interest." Church weddings were to constitute the only legal act of marriage, civil marriages were to be forbidden. Women were to remain at the hearth. "The basis of Hungarism is the family . . . the head of the family is its warrior, the mother its soul, the child its weapon, and the youth its symbol." As for the Jews, alien to Hungarians in both spirit and physique, they were to find themselves a new home. Szálasi insisted he was no anti-Semite, but an "a-Semite," a fact that did not prevent him from publicly referring to the Jews as a pestilence, and believing in the existence of an anti-Christian Jewish world conspiracy as formulated in the "Protocols of the Elders of Zion."

Macartney maintains that Szálasi was no brute. Indeed, very few of his speeches or writings contain expressions of hatred. He loved his people and had no such low opinion of the credulous masses as Hitler did. He did not attempt to coërce, but rather to persuade. But in his obsession with ideology and with his utopia, he allowed his subordinates to bring human sacrifices to the altar of his "Idea."

There are no studies or reliable statistics concerning the organization or membership of the Arrow Cross party. Sources of information are limited to contemporary reports, newspaper accounts, or interviews with former Arrow Cross leaders now in exile. The task is not made easier by the fact that the Arrow Cross, many times suspended, established a secret network alongside its regular organization, nor by its mania for archaic terminology in designating its officers and subdivisions. A few facts, however, can be cited.

At the top of the Arrow Cross pyramid, authority was divided: Szálasi, the National Leader, reserved for himself the party's spiritual direction and left a Party President, the young journalist Kálmán Hubay, in charge of politics and organization. Below the national leadership functioned a set of various central departments, among them the Councils for Land-Building, Party-Building, Recruitment, Industrial Recruitment, Propaganda, Social Problems, and Ideology. The different social classes and sectors were represented in headquarters by so-called Grand Councils, and congresses of these groups were held at regular intervals. Parallel to these organizations functioned several secret groups to which this writer's informants attach a great deal of importance. Thus, the Land-Building Council, in addition to its officially recognizable members, gathered about fifteen hundred or two thousand non-party intellectuals, professionals, engineers, army officers, and so on, allegedly engaged in drafting bills and planning social, political, and economic reforms for the period after Szálasi's assumption of power. Another secret group consisted of civil servants and employees of large private enterprises whom Imrédy's decree had excluded from official membership. These secret members formed the so-called Clan Organizations where they were registered by number rather than by name. Membership in these groups seems to have reached fifty-eight thousand by April, 1944.

As for storm troops or a National Socialist militia, these could not exist as long as Horthy was in power. Although there were some incidents, like beatings of Jews and isolated acts of terror, on the whole the Minister of Interior, Keresztes-Fischer, kept order, and the street scenes of the Weimar era had no parallel in Horthy Hungary.

Regarding membership, the data are contradictory but, according to one source, it rose from an original 8,000 in September, 1935 (Party of National Will), to approximately 19,000 in April, 1937, 116,000 at the end of 1940, and, finally, 500,000 in September, 1944. These figures, however, cannot be guaranteed. Membership fluctuated wildly. In December, 1943, for example, Szálasi noted in his diary that membership sank well below 100,000. Apparently he himself could not keep up with the changes. If these calculations, furnished mainly by former National Socialists, are correct, national membership rose from 0.3 per cent in the summer of 1938 to 4.0 per cent of the total population by September, 1944, not counting about another hundred thousand members of National Socialist groups not under Szálasi's authority.

The former President of the Supreme Audit Office in the Szálasi government provided me with information on the occupational distribution of Arrow Cross party members. According to him, industrial workers made up one-half of the party's membership in April, 1937, and even at the end of 1940 their proportion was as high as 41 per cent. During the same time, the proportion of peasant members rose from 8 to 13 per cent, and that of professionals, self-employed people, and so on, from 12 to 19 per cent. Army officers in 1937 constituted 17 per cent of the membership! This was at a time when over 52 per cent of the working population was engaged in agriculture and only 23 per cent in industry and mining. The reasons for the preponderance of workers are not far to seek. The Socialist trade unions included only skilled workers, and those chiefly from heavy industry and the large plants; the Christian unions, or the government-sponsored yellow unions, had never achieved serious proportions. For unskilled or unemployed workers, and for small artisans and their journeymen, the Arrow Cross was their first friend. Contemporary Arrow Cross newspapers are crowded with reports of convivial dinners, excursions, varied social contacts of workers' groups, requests for mutual help, and announcements begging aid for some unfortunate, unemployed "Brother." The Arrow Cross performed a function that the socialists were unable to fulfill.

The release of Szálasi from prison in September, 1940, did not mean the beginning of a triumphant rise to power. On the contrary, his party's strength appeared to have passed its zenith. Factional struggle became more violent and several of Szálasi's lieutenants deserted him, charging him with insanity or embezzlement of party funds. Furthermore, the government was more firmly in the saddle than ever. The territorial gains made between 1938 and 1941, and Hungary's involvement in the war, commanded national unity and order; this the government was resolved to enforce.

Hungary took up arms on Germany's side in June, 1941. But although she intended to profit from this alliance, she was also intent upon making few sacrifices, and it was not before late 1942 that substantial numbers of Hungarian troops were sent to the Russian front. These units were all but annihilated in the Russian offensive in the winter of 1942–1943; the remaining soldiers were thereupon ordered back to Hungary and only some light units were left in the Ukraine, well behind the front lines. By this time, Hungary was engaged in an ambiguous policy. Horthy, who never surrendered his belief in an Allied victory, dismissed the over-eager Bárdossy and in March, 1942, appointed Miklós Kállay prime minister. Kállay was a country gentleman of pure Magyar stock with relatively little political experience and a great deal of hatred for everything Russian or German. He and Horthy planned a "purely Magyar" policy. Convinced that the Western Allies would never permit the Red army to penetrate into the heart of Europe, they decided to defend the eastern borders of Hungary against the inevitable Russian onslaught and, meanwhile, to make Hungary ready for an eventual surrender to the Anglo-Saxons.

Under Kállay's premiership, between March, 1942, and March, 1944, Hungary underwent a remarkable transformation. She became a safe haven for many victims of German National Socialism, harboring close to a million Hungarian and foreign Jews, refugee Polish soldiers, and French, English, and American prisoners of war who had escaped from German camps. Contacts were established with the Western Allies who were given repeated assurances of Hungary's friendly intentions. Government-sponsored newspapers were ordered to comment with moderation on German triumphs; the Arrow Cross was kept under strict control, and the "Left" was advised to attack the government. Indeed, Kállay encouraged the formation of an "Independence Front," composed mainly of Smallholders, Social Democrats, and bourgeois Democrats, and their leaders were asked to demand an "independent Hungarian policy" in parliament. By 1943 Hungary was, for all practical purposes, a neutral country. English, American, or Russian planes flying overhead were not fired upon; contacts were established with Tito; enemy agents were received and some hidden in, of all places, the regent's residence. On December 31, 1943, the semiofficial *Magyarország* ("Hungary") published a government-inspired editorial that said in essence that Hungary would gladly surrender but could not, in the absence of an enemy.

The Germans, well aware of what was going on, finally lost patience when, in the spring of 1944, the Russian front moved dangerously close to Hungary. In March, Horthy was ordered to visit the Führer in Germany, where he was blackmailed into cooperation by the threat of a joint German-Romanian-Croatian-

Slovak attack on Hungary. On March 19, German troops entered the country and Horthy was forced to appoint the pro-German General Döme Sztójay, former Hungarian minister to Berlin, as prime minister.

The cabinet of Sztójay, at least in appearance, did not differ greatly from previous counterrevolutionary governments. While Kállay hid from the Gestapo in the Turkish legation, and Minister of Interior Keresztes-Fischer was imprisoned, other more coöperative members of the Kállay government remained in office where they were joined by rightist members of the Party of Government. Later in the spring, Béla Imrédy, now head of the Party of National Renewal, joined the cabinet. A few non-Arrow Cross National Socialists were also given important positions but not on the ministerial level.

Under Sztójay, the essential duality of the Horthy Right was once again proven. Wavering constantly between the old aristocracy's parliamentary traditions and the fascist ideology of the "young" counterrevolution, most of the deputies and the nationalist press eagerly accepted the latest turn of events. The new government was feted as Hungary's savior by the same deputies of the Party of Government who, a few days earlier, had celebrated Kállay for similar endeavors. The government announced a "new, rightist, Christian and national" policy, the same announced by all governments in the past but, this time, with determination to put at least part of it into practice. Of course, there could be no question of social reforms—the war would have made these impossible anyway—but at least Hungary could rid itself once and for all of Jews and of their hirelings. A flood of restrictive measures descended on the Jews. First "Jewish" telephones were cut and "Jewish" horses confiscated; eventually distinctive badges were made compulsory, Jews were excluded from all skilled employment, and their rations were greatly reduced. Finally, they were concentrated in ghettos and deported to extermination camps. This was achieved in negotiations between Eichmann and two National Socialist secretaries of state in the Hungarian Ministry of Interior, and carried out by the SS with the enthusiastic coöperation of the notoriously brutal Hungarian gendarmes. The deportations began on May 14, 1944, and, as far as the Jews in the provinces were concerned, they were completed within two months. In this short interval, 434,000 Jews were taken to Auschwitz, there to be gassed or—a minority—to be transferred to concentration camps.

Yet, as usual during the Horthy regime, the Left was far from silenced. The deportations and even the gassings remained no secret, and, for the first time in Nazi Europe, a storm of protests arose. The leaders of the Budapest Jewish community and conservative politicians in hiding addressed Horthy, and so did the Hungarian churches. When the papal nuncio, neutral governments, and President Roosevelt added their protests, Horthy finally roused himself and, in July, 1944, decided to put an end to the deportations. In the provinces not a single Jew remained, but in Budapest there were still at least 200,000. Fearing a coup against his person, Horthy stopped the gendarmes from coming to Budapest and deporting the Budapest Jews. The last two or three trainloads of deportees had to be literally smuggled out of the country by Eichmann and his SS. Further, on August 27, 1944, Horthy dismissed Sztójay and appointed General Géza Lakatos as prime minister. The latter was ordered to make preparations for Hungary's surrender to the Russians who now, after Romania's volte-face, entered Hungarian territory.

In all these events, Szálasi and his Arrow Cross played no part. In May, 1944, Szálasi had had his much-sought-for audience with the regent, but there had been no agreement between them. Upon the appointment of Lakatos, the Arrow Cross had finally decided on action. Abandoning his previous loyalty to the regent, Szálasi began negotiations with the Germans, offering his services and warning them of Horthy's surrender plans. Veesenmayer, the German plenipotentiary, who had a very low opinion of Szálasi, was slow to come around to the Arrow Cross point of view; but even he gave in when the SS Command in Hungary decided that Szálasi alone, of all Hungarians, remained a true friend of Germany. Clearly, the surrender of the Hungarian troops, now fully involved in operations against the Russians, would have caused the collapse of German defenses. Szálasi was therefore groomed for a take-over, and preparations were made for the day when Horthy would announce his surrender. This came when Horthy, following an agreement concluded in Moscow, made the armistice public in a radio address on October 15.

Perhaps no political turnabout was more poorly prepared. There were no troops in Budapest to defend the regent; the Hungarian generals were taken by surprise; the socialist workers and the resistance movement had not been given the promised arms. The armistice was literally the undertaking of Horthy and his immediate family with the help of a few trusted officers and a few conservative politicians. (The latter, like Bethlen, emerged from their hiding places for that occasion.) The exclusiveness of Horthy's undertaking was motivated not only by a very justified fear of betrayal, but by the clique character of the whole Horthy system. The true Left, particularly the Social Democrats, had always been regarded as instruments, never as serious partners. On the decisive day, Horthy remained isolated. The great majority of the officers disobeyed Horthy's orders; commanders loyal to the regent were arrested. The Germans acted rapidly: the radio station and the royal palace were seized by a few tanks; Horthy was placed in custody and forced to withdraw his orders. German arms were distributed to the Arrow Cross and, before the people of Budapest could recover from their surprise, the formation of an Arrow Cross government under Szálasi was announced. In his first order of the day, Szálasi exhorted the nation to a final effort against the Russian invaders.

Szálasi's reign was a sad epilogue to a tragic story. Insisting on legal sanctification of his coup, and using his enforced appointment by the regent, Szálasi had himself accepted as prime minister by a rump parliament, and, subsequently, proclaimed himself National Leader. On November 3 he took a solemn oath to the Holy Crown in the Royal Palace.

Szálasi was not entirely without support among the "historic classes." Although liberals, conservatives, socialists, and royalists were sent to German concentration camps, he was enthusiastically accepted by some members of the Upper House—including the

head of the House of Habsburg in Hungary—and by the right
wing of the former Government Party, which had formed a "National Alliance" with the National Socialist deputies in the parliament. The majority of the civil servants and the army officers took
their oath to Szálasi, and so did the National Socialist splinter
groups, now finally united with Szálasi's party.

The social composition of Szálasi's cabinet did not completely
differ from that of the Horthy governments. It contained, beside
Szálasi, other pensioned officers, two generals in active service, and
a former White terrorist officer who had spent the war years in
German exile as a member of the SS. There were also some aristocrats and three civil servants; the latter had served in Horthy's
cabinets. But there was also a journalist, a physician, a pharmacist,
and finally, a former left socialist who liked to boast that he had
known Lenin. Arrow Cross appointees took over the important
positions in the ministries and in private business. They were
almost without exception of lower-middle-class origin.

Elated, Szálasi published a working program that announced,
among other things, the transformation of Hungary into a
Hungarist state, and the creation of a prosperous peasant class before January 1, 1945. Szálasi's subordinates proceeded with equal
enthusiasm. Total mobilization of the nation's human and material
resources was again and again proclaimed; the formation of representative corporations was announced, and parliament drew up
plans for the coming years. But as the Russians approached and
reached the outskirts of Budapest in November, contradictory
orders were issued. Workers who had been ordered to stay put and
work hard were now asked to pack and leave with their dismantled
factories. Several classes of recruits were mobilized and then sent
home, as they could be provided neither uniforms nor arms. These
orders were generally disregarded; in some factories the workers
engaged in sabotage; the underground movement, now largely
Communist, began to make life difficult for the Nazis. Nevertheless, in the final days of their reign, the Germans and the Arrow
Cross managed to transport to Germany practically all the movable goods of Hungary.

Meanwhile, Eichmann reappeared in Hungary, and, following an agreement concluded with Szálasi, about 50,000 Jews were driven, during the winter, from Budapest to the Austrian border, there to build fortifications and to perish in the process. The rest of the Jews (unless they were in hiding, or under the more or less effective protection of neutral legations) lived in a ghetto in misery and starvation. The Red army found 124,000 Jews in Budapest. Altogether 200,000 Jews survived within the boundaries of pre-1938 Hungary.

By December, the situation was completely out of hand. The wholesale disposal of stocks of former Jewish stores turned into regular looting. National Socialist terror commandos hunted down army deserters and Jews. On December 24, 1944, the Red army surrounded Budapest. By that time, the government, the ministries, and the high army command had abandoned the capital for western Hungary. The city was left in charge of the SS and of self-appointed Arrow Cross commanders. The latter sent policemen, mailmen, streetcar conductors, and children to the front, which usually lay only a few blocks away. There, German and Hungarian troops resisted until February 13, when the 800,000 civilians of Budapest were finally liberated from the horrors of the siege.

The fighting in western Hungary, bolstered by some powerful German Panzer attacks, continued for two more months. A few Hungarian divisions were engaged in this struggle. This, however, was no longer the work of the Arrow Cross but of Hungarian officers who wanted to save themselves and their soldiers from Russian captivity. Arrow Cross activity was restricted to the execution of underground leaders captured in Budapest, and to some propaganda speeches. Szálasi was busy writing his copious memoirs and could seldom be disturbed. On January 20, 1945, he made his last speech in a small village near the Austrian border. He promised the liberation of the country within a year, threatened death to those who would doubt his words, and assured his peasant audience that "everyone in Hungary will be compensated down to the last red farthing for his losses."

On April 4, 1945, the last German and Hungarian troops left Hungary, preceded by the two houses of parliament and Szálasi's cabinet. These institutions continued to meet in German exile until they were picked up by the Americans and sent back to Hungary at the request of the new Hungarian government. There was not one among the Arrow Cross leaders who obeyed Szálasi's orders: "Better be a hero for a moment than a slave for life." None of them died a hero's death.

After December, 1944, Hungary had a new government. Appointed by the Russians, it was composed of such members of the "Left" as could be found in eastern Hungary and was headed by a former Horthy general. It concluded an armistice with the Russians and declared war on the German Reich.

The trials of the Horthyite and Arrow Cross war criminals were conducted during 1945 and 1946 in Budapest by a People's Court composed of a professional judge and delegates of the four parties assembled in the National Independence Front (Smallholders, Peasants, Social Democrats, and Communists). This was avowedly a political court, acting under revolutionary conditions. Capital sentences were passed in 264 cases, and 122 of these were carried out. Among the executed were five former prime ministers (Imrédy, Bárdossy, Sztójay, Szálasi, and Szöllösi, Szálasi's later prime minister), several army commanders, all the members of the Arrow Cross cabinet, and those accused of the deportation or murder of Jews and of resistants. Szálasi faced his trial with equanimity; he denied all knowledge of the Jewish persecutions, refused to admit that his acts on October 15 had constituted treason, but upheld his Hungarist ideas with unflinching conviction. He marched quietly to his execution.

The majority of the "small Nazis" were permitted—after a brief period of internment—to join the democratic parties. Most of them seemed to favor the Communist Party. As for the more important National Socialists whose lives were spared by the courts, they were, after 1948, joined in prison by their former democratic opponents. Indeed, it was a common sight to see, in the concentration camps of the Stalinist Rákosi era, the torturer working alongside his former victim, and both watched by a Communist political police officer who was himself often a former member of the Arrow Cross movement.

The political history of Horthy Hungary was characterized by a conflict between different segments of a counterrevolutionary movement. Its moderate element constituted a "Left" in contemporary Hungarian parlance but not in its political practices. The Left was conservative; it thrived on noble Hungary's parliamentary tradition, and had neither democratic nor socialist aspirations. Yet, inevitably, it came to enjoy the support of the country's weak liberal and socialist forces. Curiously enough, it was the Right that opened the way to social upheaval.

In the final reckoning, the Horthy regime represented the successful extension of a traditional system, while the Szálasi experiment was both an epilogue to the history of traditional Hungary and the beginning of the emancipation of Hungary's lower classes.

SUGGESTED READING

There are no published studies on the Right in Hungary that are known to this writer. C. A. MACARTNEY'S *A History of Hungary, 1929–1945* is an exhaustive study of Horthy Hungary's political history, with less emphasis on social and cultural matters. Professor Macartney, now a Fellow of All Souls College, Oxford, is a former Corresponding Member of the Hungarian Academy of Sciences. He knows Hungary very well and speaks Hungarian fluently. His work is based on long research, unique documents (the manuscript diary of Ferenc Szálasi among them), and extensive correspondence with almost all Hungarian political personalities now in exile. To a degree, it reflects the views of Professor Macartney's conservative informants, and, because of its monumentality, it is difficult reading.

Aside from this authoritative work, there are but few studies of modern Hungarian history published in languages other than Hungarian.

General Histories

MACARTNEY, C. A. *Hungary: A Short History*. Edinburgh: 1962. (The best summary of one thousand years of historical development.)
SINOR, DENIS. *History of Hungary*. London: 1959.

Recent Studies of the Horthy Era

BEREND, IVÁN, and GYÖRGY RÁNKI. "German-Hungarian Relations Following Hitler's Rise to Power (1933–1934)," *Acta Historica*. VIII (Budapest; 1961), 313–346. (Marxist.)
BOLDIZSÁR, IVÁN. *The Other Hungary*. Budapest: 1946. (On the anti-German resistance.)

CZEBE, JENÖ, and TIBOR PETHÖ. *Hungary in World War II: A Military History of the Years of War.* Budapest: 1946. (Short but reliable.)

HILLGRUBER, ANDREAS. "Deutschland und Ungarn, 1933–1934," *Wehrwissenschaftliche Rundschau.* IX (1959), 651–676.

————. "Das deutsch-ungarische Verhältnis im letzten Kriegsjahr. Vom Unternehmen 'Margarethe I' /19.III.1944/ bis zur Räumung Ungarns durch die deutschen Truppen /4.IV.1945/," *Wehrwissenschaftliche Rundschau.* X (1960), 78–104.

KERTESZ, STEPHEN D. *Diplomacy in a Whirlpool: Hungary Between Nazi Germany and Soviet Russia.* Notre Dame, Indiana: 1953.

MACARTNEY, C. A. *A History of Hungary, 1929–1945.* New York: 1956. 2 vols.

ROZSNYÓI, A. "October Fifteenth, 1944 (History of Szálasi's Putsch)," *Acta Historica.* VIII (Budapest: 1961), 57–105. (Marxist.)

ULLEIN-REVICZKY, ANTAL. *Guerre allemande paix russe: le drame hongrois.* Neuchâtel: 1947. (By a former diplomat of Horthy.)

Memoirs and Autobiographies

HORTHY, ADMIRAL NICHOLAS. *Memoirs.* New York: 1957. (More anecdotal than informative.)

KÁLLAY, NICHOLAS. *Hungarian Premier: A Personal Account of a Nation's Struggle in the Second World War.* New York: 1954. (Frankly conservative but detailed and reliable.)

KÁROLYI, MICHAEL. *Memoirs: Faith Without Illusion.* New York: 1957. (Contains little on the period 1919–1944.)

KOVÁCS, IMRE. *Im Schatten der Sowiets.* Zurich: 1948. (By the former secretary-general of the Hungarian Peasant party.)

NAGY, FERENC. *The Struggle Behind the Iron Curtain.* New York: 1948. (The sections dealing with pre-World War II Hungary are short but picturesque.)

Jewish Persecution

BRAHAM, RANDOLPH L. "Hungarian Jewry: An Historical Retrospect," *Journal of Central European Affairs.* XX (April, 1960), 3–23.

————. *The Destruction of Hungarian Jewry: A Documentary Account.* New York: 1963. 2 vols.

Gutachten des Instituts für Zeitgeschichte. Munich: 1958. (Contains two valuable chapters on the persecution of the Hungarian Jews.)

KOVÁCS, JÁNOS. "Neo-Antisemitism in Hungary," *Jewish Social Studies.* VIII (July, 1946), 146–160.

LÉVAI, JENÖ. *Black Book on the Martyrdom of Hungarian Jewry.* Zurich: 1948. (Comprehensive, trustworthy account. Many documentary photographs and reproductions.)

————, ed. *Eichmann in Ungarn.* Budapest: 1961. (Consists mostly of documents.)

REITLINGER, GERALD. *The Final Solution: The Attempt to Exterminate the Jews of Europe, 1939–1945*. New York: 1953. (Valuable chapter on the fate of the Hungarian Jews. Some factual errors, however.)

Documentary Collections

Documents secrets du Ministère des Affaires Étrangères de l'Allemagne. Traduit du russe par Madeleine et Michel Eristore. Hongrie: la politique allemande (1937–1943). Paris: 1946.

Finland

MARVIN RINTALA

The chief concern of this essay is with the political thought, action, and organization of the extreme Right in Finland during the years from 1917 to 1939. The choice of thought, action, and organization follows the conviction that these are the three basic aspects of politics. Men as political creatures perceive in one way or another existing and ideal political systems, act to defend the former or to create the latter, and in this action relate themselves to other men, either as leaders or as followers. At any given time, of course, all three aspects are present. This essay traces the development in the political thought of the Finnish extreme Right from a purely negative reaction toward parliamentary government to the eventual construction of an explicitly totalitarian world view encompassing all aspects of human existence; in action from political inactivity to direct extralegal action (and unsuccessful revolt), to advocacy within parliament of an ideal political system; in organization from a loosely knit aggregation of like-thinking individuals to an antiparty movement, an integral party in which each member was assigned a specific role.

The choice of time limits is inevitably a matter of judgment. The period under consideration is, however, characterized by a certain internal consistency. The February Revolution in Russia brought a burst of political activity to Finland, which had, since 1809, enjoyed a substantial degree of autonomy within the Russian empire, although the years of Russification since 1899 had pre-vented political parties from participating significantly in the deci-sion-making process. Events within Russia and Finland brought parliamentary government and national independence to the latter in 1917, and civil war in 1918. A new complex of Finnish political parties, representing conflicting interpretations of the Finnish Civil War, soon emerged. After adoption of the republican constitution in 1919, the structure of the Finnish political system remained fundamentally unchanged for two decades. The record of extreme Right thought during these decades is voluminous. That of its actions during these years is also known, at least in most important instances. Until the eve of World War II, it did not need to hide the nature of its leader-follower relationships.

Although the People's Patriotic Movement, the totalitarian party formed in 1932, continued to exist until 1944 (when it was dis-solved under terms of the armistice agreement between Finland, on the one hand, and the Soviet Union and United Kingdom, on the other), the year 1939 represents a distinct break with the previous two decades. Because of wartime censorship, the published record was no longer a faithful reproduction of political thought. Political differences tended to disappear under the overriding threat to na-tional survival. Wartime needs and wartime losses decimated the party organization of the People's Patriotic Movement, and espe-cially its zealous young district leaders. Since 1944, the extreme Right has been illegal in Finnish politics, and there is every reason to assume that it has been forever shattered by the bankruptcy of Finnish foreign policy in 1944.

Only during the period 1917–1939 was the extreme Right a significant independent force in Finnish politics. It was—to use Sigmund Neumann's telling distinction—postdemocratic rather than predemocratic. It represented, among other things, a negative response to the democratization of Finnish politics which took place in the first two decades of the twentieth century. This democ-ratization involved the achievement of executive responsibility to a unicameral Parliament elected by universal suffrage. Finnish pop-ular support of the Russian Revolution of 1905 resulted in the creation of a unicameral parliament elected by universal suffrage, replacing the antiquated Four Estates elected by restricted suffrage, but until the February Revolution in Russia this parliament seldom met and never exercised real power. It was not until 1917, when Social Democrats had a parliamentary majority, that the principle of executive responsibility to parliament was implemented. Until that time, therefore, no pressing reason spurred opponents of parliamentary government to organize for political action.

Those few Finns who can legitimately be characterized as belonging to the extreme Right before 1917 were non-Socialist activists who favored armed opposition to Russification measures. Many of this tiny minority were in exile, and those who remained in Finland were politically isolated. Because political realities never entirely match ideal types, the precise extent of the extreme Right in Finland after 1917 is difficult to define. There can be no doubt, however, that the crucial element in this definition is provided by the events of 1919. All those Finns who, in that year, and for whatever reason, favored military intervention against the Bolsheviks in the Russian Civil War are classified in this essay as belonging to the extreme Right. Since many of the persons discussed below were not yet politically active in 1919, this definition must also include all those whose formative years fell in the interwar period and who accepted the proposition that Finland should have intervened in Russia against the Bolsheviks in 1919. During most of the interwar years, therefore, the extreme Right consisted of three distinct groups: the older generation of conservatives, who came to maturity before the beginning of Russification in 1899 and therefore looked forward to the resumption of peaceful relations between Finland and a reconstructed Russia; the war generation of 1918, which found the meaning of its life in militant opposition to everything Russian; and a new generation of educated youth which, as university students after 1922, accepted the world view of the Academic Karelia Society. During the interwar decades the extreme Right at no time presented an integrated whole. Its internal conflicts were a major factor in preventing its rise to power; these conflicts were dictated by differences in formative experiences and outlook between the three distinct generations of which it was composed.

It was in World War I that the major extreme right-wing movements of interwar Europe were born. This was true in Finland as well. In 1914 the attempt to Russify Finland was already fifteen years old. Although Finland remained free of direct military involvement in the war, the conflict encouraged attempts by the Russian government to reduce the practical significance of Finnish autonomy. A development of the Russo-Finnish relationship favorable to autonomy seemed increasingly improbable, and this became apparent to a small group of young Finns, primarily university students and recent university graduates. They saw in Russian military defeat the only opportunity to gain Finnish independence, or even to regain autonomy. Therefore, with the help of some older activists, they formed an illegal movement, financially supported by Germany, to send young Finns to train with the German army. Their actions were to serve as an indication to the Central Powers that Finland expected something concrete for itself at war's end. This hope was not unrequited, for the German government privately declared Finnish independence to be in accordance with German interests.

For the Russian government, at war with Germany, it was difficult to see this recruitment as anything but treasonable. Many Finnish activists were arrested and sent to Russian prisons. From the point of view of most older Finns, including almost all party leaders, the recruiting of troops to serve in the German army could only harm Finland. Many conservatives, especially of the Old Finnish Party, felt that such activities would only result in extreme retaliatory measures by Russia. Not even the leaders of the Young Finnish Party, which had previously taken a more vigorous stand against Russification measures than the Old Finns, supported this recruitment to any substantial degree. (The differences between the Old Finns and the Young Finns reflected generational differences to a considerable degree, but in this instance they were united in opposition to the war generation.) Even between the older and younger activist leaderships there arose serious conflicts during these years of secret activity. In a real sense, this disagreement between older and younger nationalists over the degree of caution or boldness to be exercised in sending recruits to Germany for military training was the beginning of the larger conflict between parliamentarism and extraparliamentary action, between constitutionalism and direct action, which would characterize the development of the extreme Right during the interwar decades.

For the young Finns who shared the experiences of the German army during World War I, these years were to prove decisive. The Finnish volunteers were organized into a *Jäger* battalion. They became German soldiers, and they were drilled and treated as such. The degree to which they accommodated themselves to a measure of discipline they had never before encountered—the Finnish army having been abolished early in the Russification period—surprised even German officers. The eagerness of this battalion for actual participation in battle against Russian troops was satisfied in 1916 on the Eastern Front. Iron Crosses and mention in Orders of the Day became the visible symbols of success. Alternating with periods at the front were training sessions in which the officers of the future Finnish army were indoctrinated with the values of the German military establishment. During these years the *Jägers* became alienated from politics, even those of their homeland. Isolated from news of the world at large, knowing almost nothing of what was happening in Finland, they developed an intense sense of comradeship which made the battalion a real community (*Gemeinschaft*) in the sense of Ferdinand Tönnies. These shared experiences were the historical origin of that sense of comradeship-in-arms (*asevelihenki*, or *Waffenbrüderschaft*) that bound the *Jägers* together throughout their lives, until in 1941–1944 it culminated in a renewal of the German-Finnish *Waffenbrüderschaft*. Not only did surprising numbers of the *Jäger* battalion members choose to become professional soldiers after 1918 (forming the core of the Finnish officer corps before and during 1939–1944), even though they had prepared themselves in the university for other, unrelated careers, but the conception of war which many of them retained was similar to that of the German front generation. A decade later, Arne Somersalo, a Finn who had fought in the German ranks, and who was by then an important leader of the extreme Right, expressed his reaction to World War I:

I acknowledge that I am one of those who sees good as well as evil in the war. It was a storm over the old Europe, that violently shook its nations, which were sinking into the softness of excessive culture. That which was weak or rotten disintegrated or perished. But a healthy tree, even when bruised, rises again out of the turmoil of the storm. With a broken top and with branches stripped bare it sinks its roots twice as deep and again pushes forth new buds. Soon it stands more erect than before, spreading a new, stronger crown of leafy branches. . . . Even though millions fell and one generation sank into misery, it means no more in the thousand-years' life of nations than a floating cloud in the summer sky. Every manly act and every gladly borne sacrifice that purely rose to the surface from amidst torrents of blood and crimes is immortal, for it unites all who confess the obligation of the past, to build the future of their race. —And, finally, even if no other good had emanated from the World War, it nevertheless rescued *our* nation from the deadly, slimy embrace of a loathsome cuttlefish.

After the October Revolution in Russia and widespread violent clashes between Reds and Whites in Finland, P. E. Svinhufvud, an intensely nationalist and conservative jurist, became prime minister of Finland. In the months to come, he was to prove the chief figure in the partial realization of the political goal of Finnish activists: an independent but pro-German Finland ruled by a German-born monarch. The degree to which Svinhufvud accommodated himself to German policy both as prime minister and as regent (the latter after the end of the Civil War in May, 1918) was very high. One instance of the intimate relationship of German and Finnish policy was the Finnish decision formally to proclaim complete independence from Russia. In late November, 1917, the German military command insisted that Finland proclaim its independence as a precondition for German support of the Finnish position at possible Russo-German peace negotiations. Svinhufvud decided that the Cabinet would, on November 30, notify parliament that independence had been proclaimed. In fact, however, it was on December 6 that parliament, rather than the Cabinet, proclaimed the independence of the Republic of Finland. During the week's delay it became apparent that, although all parties accepted independence in principle, there were deep disagreements over the procedure to be followed in attaining it. Social Democrats held that independence ought to be achieved by means of negotiations with the Bolshevik government in Russia. Many bourgeois party leaders considered that a proclamation should be issued only after all Russian troops had been withdrawn from Finland. There was basic disagreement over whether the country should orient itself toward the Central Powers, as activists and the Cabinet argued, whether Finland should be neutral in World War I, as many Center party leaders wished, or whether the country should turn toward Bolshevik Russia as the Social Democrats demanded. The cleavage between the Social Democratic and bourgeois parties was crucial in inducing the center parties to support Svinhufvud's decision to proclaim independence immediately. In this instance, class consciousness proved more important for Center party leaders than did considerations of foreign policy.

In connection with the proclamation of independence, the Finnish government asked the German government to secure the withdrawal of Russian troops from Finland at the Brest Litovsk negotiations. Though this request was not acted upon by the German delegates, the extreme Right believed throughout the interwar decades that, at Brest Litovsk, Lenin had not dared to oppose German support of Finland. In private conversations with Joffe, the Soviet representative, the German delegation did learn that the Russians were willing to recognize Finnish independence if the Finnish government approached Petrograd directly. Such a direct approach had previously been ruled out by Svinhufvud, but now he was forced to journey to Canossa. On New Year's Eve, 1918, he met with Lenin to request Russian recognition of Finland. On January 4 this recognition was granted. But Russian troops were not immediately withdrawn from Finnish territory.

At this critical juncture it became apparent to Svinhufvud's cabinet and to the activists supporting it that they lacked an outstanding military leader who could serve as Commander-in-Chief of the bourgeois Civil Guards if war should break out between Reds and Whites in Finland. Within older activist circles there were many men of organizational ability and experience, but they had insufficient military training. As the Finnish army had been abolished in 1901, those who had held high posts within it were already advanced in years or had been inactive since then. The members of the *Jäger* battalion were still in Germany, and they were too young to fill the highest military positions. The remaining possibility was that Finnish-born officers of high rank in the Russian army would return to the land of their birth to assume these posts. With the collapse of military discipline in the Russian army during 1917, and the personal risks that commanding officers encountered in those chaotic months, many of these older Finnish-born officers did return to Finland. Several of them had served with distinction in the Russo-Japanese War and World War I, but by far the outstanding member of this group was Gustaf Mannerheim, whose last command had been the Sixth Cavalry Corps in Transylvania, and who had served for thirty illustrious years in the Russian imperial army.

Mannerheim accepted the position of Commander-in-Chief of the Civil Guards, and initiated the Finnish Civil War on January 28, 1918. His Civil Guards fought against Finnish Red Guards as well as against some (but not all) of those Russian troops still in Finland. The spirit in which the war was waged on both sides is only suggested in an Order of the Day issued by Mannerheim on March 14, 1918:

The hour has come, the hour for which the whole nation is waiting. Your starving and martyred brothers and sisters in southern Finland [largely in the hands of the Red guards] fix their last hope on you. The mutilated bodies of the murdered citizens and the ruins of the burnt-down villages call to heaven: vengeance upon the traitors. Break down all obstacles! Advance, White army of White Finland!

It was in this atmosphere that young Finns who fought on both sides spent their formative years. The heritage of 1918 was to prove the major element in the appeal of both the extreme Left and the extreme Right throughout the interwar decades. The ranks of the non-Marxist war generation were greatly expanded by the Finnish Civil War, since there were far more Civil Guards than there had been *Jägers*.

During this war there were fundamental disagreements between the Finnish political and military commands, emerging out of entirely different conceptions of the purpose of the war. Svinhufvud's cabinet was concerned with the achievement of Finnish independence in reality as well as in proclamation. Paradoxically, German military intervention was seen as the only way in which this could be accomplished. The presence of German troops in Finland would not only force withdrawal of the remaining Russian troops, but would also silence the Red Guards forever. The developments of the Civil War proved at least the partial validity of Svinhufvud's assumptions. Mannerheim's aims were much broader in scope. He conceived of a "Finnish War of Independence" as one aspect of military action on a much wider scale to overthrow the Bolshevik government in Russia. Mannerheim's large policy was destined to remain largely unfulfilled. After the signing of the Treaty of Brest Litovsk on March 3, 1918, an advance upon Petrograd by Finnish troops was incompatible with the desire of the German political and military commands to prevent a recurrence of hostilities on the eastern front. Svinhufvud's cabinet, anticipating the victory of the Central Powers, could ill afford to risk German displeasure, even though the prospect of Finnish territorial expansion to the east was by no means undesirable.

After the military collapse of Germany in November, 1918, Mannerheim's large policy met larger obstacles. He was elected regent of Finland to succeed Svinhufvud, after the need for a foreign policy based upon coöperation with the Allied and associated powers had finally become apparent to most Finnish bourgeois party leaders. As regent, Mannerheim, with the enthusiastic support of other members of the older generation of conservatives, engaged in extensive negotiations with counterrevolutionary Russian generals. The older conservatives felt that the reconstruction of a non-Bolshevik Russia was a task in which Finland should participate. Major General Hannes Ignatius of the Finnish army expressed this point of view when he remarked: "It would have been glorious, deserving of world fame, two hundred years after the Treaty of Nystadt, to have captured Petrograd and restored order to Russia." These older conservatives explicitly assumed that a White Russian government would not be imperialistic, and that within the framework of a reconstructed Russia there would be ample territory for Finland, too, to expand. If, in the end, the

Finns did not participate in a march on Petrograd, it was because the White Russian leaders insisted that Finland was within the historic boundaries of the Russian empire and therefore refused to recognize Finnish independence.

The fact that the extreme Right, including both older conservatives and members of the war generation, not only insisted upon White Russian recognition of Finnish independence, but also anticipated the acquisition of large areas that were an integral part of Russian territory, greatly decreased the chances of Mannerheim's interventionist policy. The war generation supported Finnish military action against the Bolsheviks, but not to restore the old order in Russia. Throughout the interwar decades the ideal of the Greater Finland (*Suur-Suomi*) served as the organizing principle of the war generation. This goal included uniting all Finnish-speaking peoples, with the possible exception of the Estonians, under one government. It seemed clear to the war generation that the Finnish nation, in fulfilling its historic mission as the easternmost guardian of Western civilization, was entitled to live, act, and develop within the boundaries the Guardian of nations had granted it and which He had clearly defined. Both His law and His promise to the Finnish-speaking peoples entitled them to live in one political system. Union with the Finnish-speaking peoples still outside Finland's boundaries was seen as the sacred task of the war generation, acting as the special instrument of God.

The territorial extent of this divinely ordained goal was indeed substantial. The Greater Finland included, in addition to interwar Finnish territory, East Karelia, Kola, Ingria, and (in a special sense) Estonia. Finland would thus stretch from the Gulf of Bothnia to the White Sea and from the plains of Estonia to the Arctic Ocean. The easternmost extent of Finnish territory would be the dividing line between Finnish-speaking and Slavic-speaking peoples. Since there was no clear-cut spatial break between Finnish-speaking and Slavic-speaking peoples in northwestern Russia, and many assumed kinsmen of the Finns lived in the Volga-Ural region, the Greater Finland, in its most inclusive sense, implied the extension of Finnish power to the Urals.

Although the precise territorial extent of the Greater Finland was uncertain, the hard core of the policy it inspired was at all times the acquisition by Finland of East Karelia; this territory, at least, was clearly defined. The eastern border of East Karelia ran from the southernmost point of the Bay of Onega to the eastern shore of Lake Onega, along the Svir River to Lake Ladoga, and finally to the Gulf of Finland. East Karelia was held to be inseparably connected with Finland by an imposing list of geographical, geological, botanical, hydrographic, ethnographic, colonial, economic, transportation, and strategic ties. On the basis of similar reasoning, the vast Kola Peninsula was claimed as part of Finnish territory. The acquisiton of East Karelia and Kola would have doubled the territory of the Finnish state.

Sweeping as was the geographical scope of the Greater Finland, its ideological content was even more inclusive. Its adherents saw the course of world history as a regular northward movement of the center of world power. From the fertile soils of Egypt and Babylonia this center had moved consistently toward less and less productive areas in which existence was more and more of a struggle against a harsh nature—first to the shores of the Mediterranean, then to the Iberian Peninsula and Northern Italy, then to the centers of continental Europe and England. During the interwar decades, the struggle for the mastery of Europe was already taking place at the latitudes of northern Germany and Moscow. There, where nature and life were severe, the soil barren and miserly, where joy and bread did not come free, in the north, in the mountains, on the shores and islands of great oceans, there the people were tough and strong, loving danger and adventure, free, warlike, spirited, and ascetic—all at the same time. By the basic law of world history, the hegemony of Europe would fall to one of its northernmost races: the Scandinavians, the Finns, or the Russians.

The identity of the final victor in Europe was also to be sought in the philosophy of history. The fundamental fact of life was, in the experience of the war generation, struggle. The conflict of competing forces laid the basis for everything of value in history. The concept of perpetual progress, once so popular, was meaningless. There was only the search of struggling species of men for ever harsher environments. It was this search that was the essential meaning of world history. In this struggle it was not the racially pure nations that would take the final prize of world mastery, but rather those nations in whose blood two or more races were united in internal struggle. The Finns, in whose blood the Scandinavian and East Baltic "races," as well as Cro-Magnon man, were engaged in serious but balanced struggle, were racially dynamic. Their long history, especially the events of 1918, indicated that they were the healthiest and strongest of the northern nations. The Finns belonged to the healthy core of Europe. The Scandinavians and the Russians were both relatively pure racially, hence less likely to win control of the north, and thus of Europe. As militant Finns, the members of the war generation pledged themselves to do everything possible to ensure that Northern Europe would, during its large future, speak Finnish rather than Swedish or Russian. Insofar as the decadent nations of the rest of Europe had any future at all, this future would depend on the Finns as the young peoples of the North.

The ideal of a Greater Finland was by no means new. "Karelianism" had long been an important aspect of romantic Finnish nationalism. For many decades, however, this ideal had remained completely in the realm of artistic creation and scholarly speculation. Before World War I it had no political significance. It was not until this war had indelibly impressed itself upon the members of the *Jäger* battalion serving on the eastern front that the Greater Finland became a conscious political goal. It was these warlike young irregulars who first seized upon the ideal of Greater Finland as a life's mission; it was these men who attempted to establish it by force of arms between 1918 and 1922; it was they who were the most eloquent spokesmen for the greater Finland during the interwar decades; and it was they who marched triumphantly as high-ranking army officers and administrators into Petrozavodsk, the capital of Soviet Karelia, on October 1, 1941. Earlier romantic nationalists had been content wistfully to contemplate white-haired, *kantele*-plucking Karelians; the war generation rushed into battle, even without governmental support, to give its life, if need be, for the dream of the Greater Finland. Many members of the war generation lie buried in the wild terrain of East Karelia, the spiritual locus of their life as well as of their death. Their devotion to their cause was complete, and it was to this devotion that the Greater Finland owed its central position in the politics of the extreme Right during the interwar decades.

That the large majority of Finnish political leaders was unwilling to go to war with Bolshevik Russia to create the Greater Finland, at a time when Russia was torn by civil war, alienated the war generation from the party system. This tergiversation was considered a betrayal of those who had fallen in 1918. Even after 1918, advocates of the Greater Finland recognized that military action would be necessary for the attainment of their goal. The war generation, having abandoned all halfway measures, constantly looked toward the east, prepared for military action. Its members assumed that, after adequate preparation, the matter should be left to the Finnish military leadership, and they were certain that the last word concerning the fate of the Finnish-speaking peoples had not yet been spoken.

The areas included in the Greater Finland were not Finnish irredenta in the strict sense of that term, since they had never been part of the Finnish state, and thus could not be redeemed by it. Just as the goal of National Socialism was not restoration of the pre-1914 order in either world or German politics, even though many conservatives mistakenly thought it was, but was rather construction of totally new world and German orders (or, more precisely, the collapse of the distinction between these), the goal of Finland's war generation was not a return to any historic past in either world or Finnish politics. Its goal was instead a boldly conceived, radically new order. It was the future rather than the past on whose behalf its members acted. Finnish romantic nationalists had worshipped at the altar of East Karelia because it represented the beauty of the past; the war generation dreamt of heroic action aimed at conquest of the centuries to come.

The conception of the Greater Finland did not exist merely in the political thought of the war generation; it led directly to political action as well as to new forms of political organization. During the Civil War, it was accepted as a war aim by no less a personage than the Comander-in-Chief of the Civil Guards. Mannerheim repeatedly expressed his desire to conquer East Karelia, and he acted toward this end insofar as the subservience to German policy of Svinhufvud's cabinet and the perilous military situation of the Civil Guards within Finland permitted. Elaborate plans were drawn up by Mannerheim's headquarters for the invasion of East Karelia, but they had been only partly executed before Mannerheim resigned as Commander-in-Chief in late May, 1918, in opposition to the government's pro-German orientation. Later, as regent, Mannerheim sent Finnish "volunteers" into East Karelia. More effective military action was precluded in 1919 by the need to maintain the approval of the Allied and associated powers, who supported the White Russian position on East Karelia.

The final blow to Finnish military intervention in the Russian Civil War came with the election, on July 25, 1919, by a large majority of parliament, of K. J. Ståhlberg as first president of the Republic. Ståhlberg was the leading Finnish liberal and chief author of the republican constitution adopted a month earlier. The defeated candidate was Gustaf Mannerheim. The outcome of the presidential election was correctly interpreted by the extreme Right as removing the possibility of official military action either in East Karelia or against Petrograd. Soon after his election, Ståhlberg began to gather Finnish support for resumption of peaceful relations with the Russian government. The administration of the first president produced what both the older and the younger proponents of a vigorous foreign policy had most feared: a peace treaty with Bolshevik Russia, in which the Greater Finland was not achieved. The Treaty of Dorpat preserved the boundaries existing in 1917, which were the historic boundaries as well, with one exception: Finland gained Petsamo.

The war generation never accepted the Treaty of Dorpat. Its impact on the development of the Finnish extreme Right was approximately comparable to the impact of the Treaty of Versailles on the development of National Socialism. This does not mean that the Treaty of Dorpat shared the faults attributed to Versailles. There was no question of an imposed peace. Not only were the Finnish negotiators highly successful in the economic discussions at Dorpat, but in the eyes of the extreme Right the treaty was the result of Russia's military defeat by Finland. Finns, not the Soviet government, were blamed for its shortcomings. What blame was later attached to the Soviet government derived from its failure to carry out even those promises actually made at Dorpat concerning the autonomy of East Karelia. The treaty's most shameful aspect was the withdrawal of Finnish troops from two parishes— Repola and Porajärvi, which had been occupied by Finland since 1918—in obvious exchange for Finnish acquisition of Petsamo. This withdrawal was seen (quite incorrectly) by the extreme Right as an intentional betrayal of the local inhabitants by President Ståhlberg.

Members of the war generation had already fought in the German army, in the Finnish Civil War, and as volunteers in Estonia and East Karelia. One more such armed struggle remained before this generation began another, much more demanding kind of warfare: that for the political soul of the Finnish nation. During the winter of 1921–1922 Finnish volunteers crossed secretly into East Karelia to join their kinsmen for the last time but one in battle against the barbarian East. From the military point of view, the effort was obviously hopeless. The short but spirited warfare was over by February 16, 1922. The participants were viewed coldly by both the Soviet and Finnish governments. A more than temporary political consequence of this otherwise minor and unsuccessful expedition into East Karelia was the founding of the Academic Karelia Society.

Immediately after their return to Helsinki from East Karelia, three members of the war generation, Elias Simojoki, Reino Vähäkallio, and Erkki Räikkönen, decided to found a political organization of university students and graduates devoted to the cause of the Greater Finland. They met in the spirit of dejection occasioned by the military defeats of the previous months, determined, nevertheless, that the goal of a Greater Finland would not die. Their society was, at the time of its birth, unique in the annals of Finnish politics. Its members knew they had no chance of reaching the heights of political power—indeed, they did not even wish to do so—unless the Finnish nation were converted to activism in foreign policy. This conversion, and nothing less, was a corollary of the ultimate goal of the Academic Karelia Society. No fact is more remarkable in all Finnish politics than that, during World War II, this conversion took place, and that the Finnish flag was raised over large areas of the Soviet Union; later, of course, it was lowered over even larger areas.

The small group that was primarily responsible for this conversion (and thus at least partly for its consequences) began its life as a brazen voice declaring war on the indifference of Finnish university students toward East Karelia. Other members of the war generation, many of them still finishing their studies, interrupted so many times by battle, responded enthusiastically to this trumpet call. Among the academic youth of Finland the Academic Karelia Society rapidly became the dominant political organization, a position it maintained until 1944, when it was banned under the terms of the Armistice. During these decades the society collaborated with the Lapua Movement and especially closely with the People's Patriotic Movement.

To its members, the Academic Karelia Society was more than a mere organization. It was a world view, dominated by one idea: the Greater Finland. In everything its members experienced during the following two decades, the basic standard of value was the extent to which the cause of the Greater Finland was advanced or retarded. The oath taken by all new members, at initiation ceremonies resembling entrance into a religious order, was an expression of this total commitment to territorial expansion:

Under our [society's] flag, and to our flag, I swear, in the name of all that which is sacred and dear to me, to sacrifice my work and my life to my fatherland, on behalf of the national awakening of Finland, Karelia, and Ingria, the Greater Finland. For as surely as I believe in one great God, so I believe in one Greater Finland and in its great future.

In view of the origins and goals of the Academic Karelia Society, it is hardly surprising that its political thought was bitterly anti-Russian. There was always contempt in the voices of its members when speaking of Russians. Even the Finnish term used to signify a Russian (*ryssä*) was unflattering, to say the least. The correct

Finnish term (*venäläinen*) was seldom used by the leaders and followers of the society, even in publications and speeches. Active love of the fatherland and hatred of the Russian were equated. The pervasive loathing of everything Russian was not left to suffer a possible natural demise. The society considered one of its main tasks to be propagation of this emotion. Members greeted each other as "brothers in the hatred of the Russians," and considered reconciliation impossible. For them the antagonism between Finland and Russia did not depend, as it did for the older generation of conservatives, upon the nature of a particular Russian political system. Elias Simojoki, a clergyman, in dedicating the new flag of the society, explained its black color: "Black is our hatred toward that nation, mention of whose name must not disturb our moment of worship. Our hatred is as black as this flag, but our hatred has the right to victory, for it is controlled by the [Finnish flag's] blue and white colors of our love."

Strong as it was, this negative reaction to Russia was not the only element in the political thought of the Academic Karelia Society. The basic goal of the Greater Finland, involving, as it did, one political system for all Finnish-speaking peoples, led directly to an image of a new order within Finland itself. Given this emphasis upon nationality (language) as the organizing principle of politics, the position of the Swedish-speaking minority in Finland was likely to come under serious attack by the society. The latter's members, all either university students or graduates, particularly resented what they considered excessive educational facilities granted to a minority comprising only one-tenth of the population. During the first two years of the society's existence, a number of Swedish-speaking Finns had joined it. In 1924, the increased emphasis the majority of members began to place upon the desirability of a unilingual state caused a number of influential members of both language groups to resign. These dissidents formed an organization of their own, the Independence League, also aimed at achievement of the Greater Finland, but without stressing the role of the Finnish language within Finland itself. The internal inconsistency of this new program, together with the relative inertia of its leaders, made of the Independence League an innocuous stepchild which often gave the appearance of having been stillborn.

Significantly, many of those members of the Academic Karelia Society who resigned in 1924 because of disagreement over the language question belonged to the Society's Seniors' Division, a special section including leading professors and other older academicians. The majority of these seniors could not approve the language program of the society, and led the exodus of that year. The result was that the Seniors' Division collapsed. The attitude of this division was typical of the stand taken by the older generation of conservatives toward the language question within Finland. As the language policy of the society became more extreme, the position of its remaining Swedish-speaking members became less tenable. The common experience of the war generation became inadequate as an organizing principle when conceptions of nationality differed basically. By the second decade of the society's life, all members (with very rigidly defined exceptions) were required to bear Finnish surnames. This meant, in practice, besides the departure of remaining Swedish-speaking members, that many Finnish-speaking students, whose families still retained Swedish surnames, were forced, as actual or prospective members, legally to change their names. Much of the society's time was taken up with agitation for reduction in the number of Swedish-speaking professorships at Helsinki University, in the number of state-supported Swedish-language secondary schools, and in state subsidies to Swedish-language cultural institutions.

Inside the society—although not necessarily outside of it—it was recognized that this increased emphasis upon the language question within Finland was not an end in itself, but rather a means to the highest end. The Academic Karelia Society always remained faithful to the primacy of its foreign policy goal over domestic political considerations. It saw the totality of Finnish politics in the light of the Greater Finland, and thus adhered to Ranke's interpretation of the relationship between foreign policy and domestic politics. The achievement of the Greater Finland was regarded as impossible without the creation of a far more powerful sense of national consciousness than existed among the majority of Finns. National disunity, it was held, had prevented successful resolution of the question of East Karelia immediately after the Russian Revolution. So that internal disagreements would not again prevent realization of the Greater Finland, a completely Finnish-speaking internal political order was considered necessary. Agitation for this internal order was undertaken only as a preparatory step toward the ultimate victory: territorial expansion. The possibility that such agitation tended to increase rather than decrease national disunity within Finland, and thus to lessen the possibility of ultimate victory, did not present itself to the majority of the extreme Right.

The impact of the political thought of the Academic Karelia Society upon Finnish politics during the interwar decades was substantial and its influence upon the development of Finnish nationalism decisive. It rapidly gained control of all major organizations of university students, including their governing bodies and publications. This hegemony was no minor matter, for these organs of student life have traditionally been of considerable significance in Finnish politics. The dominant position of the society among Finnish-speaking students was further strengthened by special branches for female militants, and numerous branches in secondary schools.

Not all university students who wished to join the Academic Karelia Society were permitted to do so. The society at all times attempted to bar new members whose devotion was less than absolute. Joining it was, therefore, no easy task. Prospective members trained for one academic term by attending an extensive course of lectures explaining the thought, activity, and organization of the society, and by serving prescribed long work hours. If, after this period of indoctrination, the responses of the candidate were deemed satisfactory, he could become an apprentice member, in which capacity he served by working and learning to follow orders for another academic term. Only after this second period had been successfully completed could the apprentice member take the oath of the society and become a full member. The result of this intensive selection and indoctrination process was that the full members of the society represented only the most devoted of those university students and graduates who accepted its program. The maximum number of full members was maintained at between two and three thousand.

The society was not an organization to which members belonged only during their student days. It was more in the nature of a religious order, to which members were intended to belong all their lives, than of a political club. It was because of this that a shift in its composition inevitably took place. After several years of the society's existence, it became necessary to form district branches throughout Finland for those members who had left the university and were now gainfully employed. It was not long before these district branches accounted for more than half the total membership of the society. It was these members who carried the message of the Greater Finland to the rest of Finnish society. They served as civil servants, teachers, lawyers, physicians, and clergymen—in other words, they were in positions of extensive responsibility and public influence. Although their ambition was no smaller than that of the Russian Populists, their position within the milieu they wished to convert was much stronger. Fifteen years after the first trumpet call was sounded, the society could proudly count among its members cabinet ministers, bishops, judges, and professors. Its distinction among interwar European student organizations was undeniable. Few others were so well organized, so completely in control of their immediate surroundings, and so well on their way to capturing their whole national culture.

One reason for the effectiveness of the society in its war against Finnish political passivity was the nature of its organizational framework. The structure of the society was completely military in character. This fact was an expression both of that historical reality its founders had experienced and of that they hoped to construct. The leader of the society was called its commander. Subordinate officers, including those at district levels, also bore military titles. Members were ordered to carry out the decisions of the leadership; their obligation to obey was absolute. They were not permitted to absent themselves from meetings. According to an official history of the society, iron discipline was the basis of its success. Its military organization helped to inculcate younger members with the conception of war resulting from the formative experiences of the society's founders.

The Academic Karelia Society's image of the ideal man, developed in part out of the historical experience of the war generation, was widely accepted among the younger Finnish educated class. After 1922, by molding the world view of Finnish-speaking secondary-school and university students during their formative years, the war generation succeeded in transferring its conception of man to new political generations as well. But the vast majority of Finns, bourgeois as well as Marxist, who had matured politically before the Finnish Civil War, were not converted. Even more damaging to the society's intention of radically transforming the values of Finnish society was the fact that the inroads made among young Finns outside the narrow circles of secondary-school and university life were relatively insignificant. Within these narrow circles, nevertheless, the new image of man found overwhelming acceptance.

The themes of previous student generations had been created by brilliant and caustic debaters, atheistic law students full of intellectual paradoxes, esthetic gentlemen, and dedicated uplifters of those in need. All this was part of the past and had no place in the values of the Academic Karelia Society. The new ideal was the active, masculine preacher, able passionately to gain public support for the Greater Finland, and spending large portions of each day in physical exercise to keep fit for the time when fitness would be needed. The new man was militant, acting directly and powerfully, without compromise. As Reino Ala-Kulju, a leading member of the society, put it: "The program of the Academic Karelia Society is the program of the future: it is the nationalist program for life. It will not triumph through negotiations and compromises." The values of traditional Western rationalism and individualism were not the values of the society's members. They required faith rather than thought, but, as Ala-Kulju wrote, in the Society's 1937 yearbook, their faith was not in the past:

The spirit of the Academic Karelia Society also has not adjusted itself to that conservatism which in our country has sought to preserve conditions and forms even when they are antiquated and foreign and degrading to the nation. That youthful spirit of independence, full of faith in the future, that forward-rushing and forward-looking will of a new state, which has given birth to the Academic Karelia Society, has led it many times *into a position of conflict with the older generation*. This has not been caused by an inclination to underestimate the heritage of the fathers and the experiences of the older generation. It has been caused by that difference in ideals and goals, that difference in spirit, which exists between the generations of the period of autonomy and the period of independence.

The war generation and the younger believers in the Greater Finland were not alone in rejecting the politics of compromise. The older conservatives, especially their leaders—Mannerheim, Svinhufvud, and J. K. Paasikivi—also resented the attempt of Finnish center party leaders after 1918 to bridge the gap between Red and White with social and economic reforms. The testament the conservative trinity left to the victors of the Finnish Civil War received its definitive statement in Mannerheim's speech to Svinhufvud's cabinet on May 16, 1918. The Commander-in-Chief recalled—in his own interpretation—the events of late 1917 and early 1918, and added:

Determined that such a state of things shall never recur, the army regards it as its right to express openly its firm hope, that through the creation of a social order and an executive power of the State, safeguards will be created to protect us forever against new months of terror such as those through which our country has passed. The army regards it as the only possible guarantee of this, that the helm of the ship of the Finnish State is placed in a strong hand, which is not affected by party strife, and not forced, through compromises, to whittle down the power of the Government.

It was Mannerheim also who, shortly after his defeat in the presidential election of 1919, called for the creation of one great party which would be clearly conscious of the importance of its actions. He meant by this the creation of a united bourgeois front against Marxism. With many others of his generation, Mannerheim never accepted the unicameral parliament elected by universal suffrage. The fact that parliament was the fruit of opposition to Russification did not sanctify this institution in the eyes of Mannerheim and other older conservatives, but it did tend to have precisely such an effect upon the political generation created by the years of intensive Russification, from 1899 to 1914. In contrast to the older conservatives, this generation, intermediate between the older conservatives and the war generation, was vigorously and lastingly anti-Russian. Its members, nevertheless, felt less need than did the war generation to combine anti-Russian with antiparliamentary sentiments, as parliament was the concrete embodiment of what Finland had gained as the result of its own general strike in 1905. Furthermore, during the first decade of its existence, the Finnish parliament was the chief forum of opposition to Russification. There was thus, after 1918, no outstanding barrier to loyal and effective participation in parliamentary government by this generation whose political roots were in the Russification period. Indeed, it became the Finnish parliamentary generation par excellence. Many of its members, upon being elected to parliament, made lifetime careers of political leadership.

In contrast to the members of this intermediate generation of parliamentarians, the political vocabulary of all three generations of the interwar extreme Right was dominated by the Finnish term *kompromissi*. This inelegant loanword was used to signify precisely the meaning in German politics of the term *Kompromiss*, rather than the meaning in British politics of the term compromise. The extreme Right meant by it betrayal of one's principles, rather than necessary adjustment to the views of others with the aim of common action. The meaning the term was given by the extreme Right symbolized the basic divergence between its world view and that of Finnish parliamentarians. A parliamentary compromise leading to formation of a cabinet or to passage of legislation was termed a *lehmäkauppa*. This derogatory word was used in the same sense as the German term *Kuhhandel*, of which it was a literal translation. Such unjustified compromises were seen by the extreme Right as the essential element of Finnish parliamentarism.

From late 1929 to early 1932, dissatisfaction with the politics of compromise practiced by Finnish parliamentarians found expression in the Lapua Movement. All three generations of the extreme Right were able to unite in support of a mass movement that announced its goal to be the extinction of Communism in Finland. The first spark flew at an anti-Communist riot in the southern Ostrobothnian village of Lapua. This spark, in itself insignificant, set fire to the tinderbox that was the potential appeal of the extreme Right, thus initiating a series of events which almost proved fatal to parliamentary government in Finland. The central concept of the new movement was expressed by what was called the Law of Lapua. The existence was assumed of a law higher than the written statutes that had failed to prevent Communist activity in Finland. This supreme law was the continued existence of an independent White Finland. Direct popular action had to be taken to guarantee its survival even though such action might violate written statutes. It was argued that there are moments in history when the written law must be by-passed, when the healthy, patriotic instinct of popular self-preservation should be followed, without stopping to study legal clauses. Above the statutes stood the movement of history and the destiny of the nation, both under divine guidance. The Law of Lapua was defended in parliament on the basis of the legal theories of Hippel, Kohlrausch, and Bieberstein, but such sophistication had no political significance. The failure of erudite arguments to influence the course of political action did not mean that there was no political thought motivating members of the Lapua Movement, but that their conception of the Law of Lapua was relatively simple and uncomplicated by the intellectual efforts of juridical theorists. Much greater in its political significance was the clear proposition that all means were permissible to eradicate communism in Finland.

The Lapua Movement demanded, and obtained, legislation which would effectively outlaw all communist activity. Between 1930 and 1944 communism was illegal in Finland. This legislation did not satisfy advocates of the Law of Lapua, however, and they continued to engage in the politics of violence. A reign of terror was the dominant feature of Finnish politics during the summer of 1930. Only late 1917 could rival mid-1930 in the number of unpunished illegal acts. Finland's leading law enforcement official argued that any police attempt to prevent or punish these crimes would "absolutely" lead to open conflict between the state and the

Lapua Movement, and added: "There is no right to provoke the risk of civil war when the controversy is not over the matter itself, but merely over methods and tactics."

Although there were numerous political murders, the most common way of enforcing the Law of Lapua was to kidnap opponents and drive them toward or across the Soviet border. Many, but by no means all, of the victims were Communists. Väinö Hakkila, the Social Democratic First Vice-Speaker of parliament, was kidnapped, as was the retired first President of the Republic, K. J. Ståhlberg, who had strongly attacked the Law of Lapua in a series of speeches and newspaper articles. This last crime was planned by no less a personage than Major General K. M. Wallenius, Chief of the General Staff of the Finnish army, and a leading member of the war generation. In repayment for his services, Wallenius, now unemployed, was appointed secretary-general of the Lapua Movement. The approval his deed encountered among advocates of the Law of Lapua was unqualified:

Everyone certainly agreed that Professor Ståhlberg was rightly and deservedly kidnapped, since it was precisely he who was one of those most guilty for the decline of our country's domestic and foreign policy position into the existing misuse of democracy. In addition, there were many bitter memories of his presidency, even though they could not be expressed so long as he remained *the country's former President.* Now, when he again came on the scene as the very same standard-bearer of that liberalism, leading to disaster, of which there were already bitter enough experiences, he too could be judged according to his deeds. He could no longer be the former President and, in that capacity, inviolable.

The gratitude the Lapua Movement expressed to Ståhlberg's kidnappers was quite undeserved. The response of the vast majority of Finns to this political crime was fatal to the movement's chances for coming to power on the basis of popular support, for they considered the kidnapping one of the most shameful events in Finnish history. Even most newspapers and political leaders who had been opposed to Ståhlberg's vigorous liberalism shared this negative reaction. The loss of popular support did not, however, result in the immediate demise of the Lapua Movement. As its leaders could no longer depend upon popular support to bring them to power, they chose the logical alternative: armed revolt. For more than a year after Ståhlberg's kidnapping they postponed the execution of plans for an armed rising. A crucial factor in this delay was the need to create an integrated organization down to the local level. The form this organization would take was clear. Already in 1930 the movement conceived of itself as an army, whose general staff was at Lapua. Like those of the Academic Karelia Society, members of the movement were "ordered" to act by their leaders. In spite of passage of the anti-Communist bills of 1930, it was considered necessary to create a "regular army," composed of the nation's finest, to replace the "volunteers" of that year. District organizations were formed on the basis of the same territorial divisions as Civil Guards districts. The goal was creation of the largest and most powerful national organization, which would compare favorably with the largest Finnish party organization. Soon a well-organized movement, with little of the spontaneity that had characterized its first few months, was in existence. The movement could now go forward into new offensive positions, ending a period of positional warfare.

The final days of February, 1932, seemed to provide the long-expected revolutionary situation. The Agrarian prime minister was ill. Several members of the cabinet were outside Helsinki. The femme fatale of the movement, Minna Craucher, was in the process of informing police officials and the press of the movement's innermost secrets—thus, so its members believed, threatening them with prison terms and fines. In the judgment of Vihtori Kosola, its leader, the appropriate moment had arrived. Members had been alerted by a speech of his informing them that the existing government was spellbound by Marxism, and he warned his followers that the forthcoming struggle might involve the sacrifice of many before the final victory. The chief newspaper of the movement sent out a call for a "Finnish Hitler."

Kosola commanded that the revolt begin with interruption of a speech which a Social Democratic Member of Parliament was to deliver in Mäntsälä, a small community in southern Finland. Lapua forces took over the community, and sent a message to the president of the Republic, P. E. Svinhufvud, demanding the removal of the Minister of the Interior and of the provincial governor, both firmly opposed to the Law of Lapua. The rebels promised to destroy Social Democracy in Finland even "if we must first destroy the power of the State which, with its representatives, supports and protects it. . . . The power of the State may possibly crush our group, but it will not be able to defeat the avalanche of patriots which will storm over our bodies." This message passed through the hands of the Conservative First Vice-Speaker of parliament before reaching the president. The following day the movement demanded the resignation of the entire cabinet and the naming of a new cabinet obedient to its will. To add emphasis to this demand all members were ordered to mobilize in key cities. Many powerful groups, including the League of War Veterans, the Civil Guards, and the Academic Karelia Society, supported the demand that the cabinet resign. The Commanding General of the Finnish army was informed that many of his officers, former *Jägers,* would not obey orders to advance upon Lapua Movement forces. Two Conservative cabinet members, both prominent in the movement, resigned, and were supported by their parliamentary bloc. Even the Liberal Minister of Justice agreed that the cabinet should resign.

The final decision concerning the policy of the government toward this revolt rested with Svinhufvud. The Lapua Movement assumed that he would prove himself their man, as he had been elected president in 1931 with their strong support. This assumption proved a serious mistake. Throughout his long political career, Svinhufvud believed in the rule of law. Two decades earlier he had suffered exile in Siberia rather than enforce, as a judge, Russification policies which violated Finnish law. Now that he was the guardian of the constitution, even though he did not care for all its aspects, there was little reason to assume that he esteemed legality any less. Any revolt against the existing political system was inevitably a reflection on its center of power, and that focal position certainly belonged to Svinhufvud during his presidency. The final element in Svinhufvud's decision to crush the revolt, with armed force if necessary, came from the demand of the Lapua Movement's prospective prime minister, Rudolf Walden, that

Gustaf Mannerheim become president. That Walden's demand was made on his own initiative is unlikely, for he was Mannerheim's chief lieutenant.

Although Svinhufvud in a few days succeeded in crushing the revolt, its impact upon Finnish politics was very great. The Lapua Movement was soon outlawed. Public support for the Civil Guards was substantially weakened. The revolt provided the last bit of evidence needed to convince center party leaders that the most serious single threat to parliamentary government in Finland came from the extreme Right. It was finally recognized (but not by much of the extreme Right) that the Law of Lapua was in fundamental contradiction to those assumptions of order and stability upon which Finnish bourgeois society was built. The way was finally cleared for closer coöperation between all the democratic parties. Parliamentary government was eulogized by many who had been sympathetic to the anti-Communist emphasis of the Lapua Movement. Only the Conservative party remained aloof from these affirmations of faith in the strength and vitality of Finnish parliamentary government.

The outlawing of the Lapua Movement left the extreme Right without an inclusive organizational home. Such organizations as the Academic Karelia Society and the League of War Veterans included only clearly defined segments of the extreme Right. Steps to remedy this situation were soon taken by Erkki Räikkönen, member of the war generation, Svinhufvud's lieutenant, and chairman of the Independence League. Räikkönen had left the Academic Karelia Society to help found the Independence League because of the society's growing antagonism to Swedish-speaking Finns. Leaders of the extreme Right met privately with Svinhufvud and Räikkönen less than three weeks after the revolt to discuss measures to continue the fight against Marxism begun by the Lapua Movement. They agreed that the sacred flame of Lapua would not be permitted to die and that a new organization would be created. In accordance with this decision, the People's Patriotic Movement was founded on April 10, 1932. The intention of Svinhufvud, as the moving force in the creation of the new organization, was to establish a nonparty bourgeois front which would legally oppose Social Democracy as well as communism. Svinhufvud and his lieutenants soon found themselves outnumbered in the inner circles of the new organization, however, and the People's Patriotic Movement became a militant new party. With the departure of supporters of a conciliatory language position, the new party was free to attack Swedish-speaking Finns and to label Swedish as a foreign language, thereby alienating those Swedish-speaking Finns who were otherwise sympathetic to the People's Patriotic Movement.

The new party's leaders recognized that, in a much more significant sense, they spoke a political language that was not understood even by most Finnish-speaking Finns. The vocabulary they used was unique within its national milieu. The most important single concept introduced into Finnish politics by the People's Patriotic Movement was expressed by the Finnish term *kansakokonaisuus* ("national community"), a direct translation of the German *Volksgemeinschaft*, which played a major role in the political thought of National Socialism. The Finnish term was used by its advocates to mean precisely the same as its German original. *Kansakokonaisuus* became the battle cry of the new movement, which saw itself living in one of the great crises of history. It proclaimed that selfish liberalism was dying and a new political ideal rising in its stead, in which the obligations of citizens to society preceded their rights. Conflict characterizing the regime of parties would be replaced by a genuine sense of national community. The individual meant nothing, the fatherland everything. Except as a member of the nation the individual was like a rootless tree, lacking the strength to live. This conception of the insignificance of the individual was opposed to the view of earlier Finnish romantic nationalists, who had seen individualism as the basis of everything worthwhile in human life.

According to the People's Patriotic Movement, Finland would be recreated. This would necessitate abandonment of that conception of individual rights which had thus far prevented the achievement of a powerful and logical state authority. In the future Finnish political system, the executive would have the greatest responsibility for the success of the nation. An executive forced to listen constantly to parliament would fail to guarantee this success. It was therefore of prime importance that parliament not have a decisive voice in the political system of the future. The birth of this system would be opposed, but it could not be prevented, by the party regime characteristic of parliamentary government.

The new state would no longer be simply a nightwatchman, guarding the lives and property of its citizens. It would, instead, establish a world view of national solidarity among them. This would mean placing certain values above discussion: the creation of a powerful unilingual Finland, the preservation of the Lutheran religion, and the necessity of national defense. Conformity to these values would be enforced. The People's Patriotic Movement also embraced an organic conception of the state which has often provided a logical basis for acceptance of a corporate state structure. Elaborate plans describing in detail the structure of the corporate state, decisively influenced by Italian Fascism, were drawn up.

This was, of course, a radical program. The People's Patriotic Movement proudly proclaimed that it was not conservative, nor reactionary, nor dependent upon capital. It saw itself as closer to communism than to the regime of parties, for communism at least promised reforms, while no candid person expected anything new of the regime of parties. Since Marxism was destructive, however, the only creative radicalism in Finnish politics was to be found in the ranks of the People's Patriotic Movement. The world view of the latter involved a new way of thinking about politics: "We cry: down with parties, down with Socialists and bourgeoisie! There is only one Finnish nation." The meaning of *Volksgemeinschaft* for the new party, and the complex mixture of dream and reality it introduced into Finnish politics, appeared in a statement by Martti Tertti, one of the noblest members of the war generation:

The People's Patriotic Movement represents not only new colors; it represents a new conception of the world, it heralds the new in place of the old. . . . *Blue-Black is something other than White. It is more than White.* White has a glorious past, the most glorious to be found in Finland's history. An even more glorious future belongs to Blue-Black. Namely, *Blue-Black will finish that which was left half finished in 1918.*

We believe that, just as White raised half of our nation from a state of humiliation sixteen years ago, Blue-Black will yet raise our entire nation, with the exception of those few who have sold their souls to Marx. *The breach between White and Red will be filled by Blue-Black,* and it has already been partially filled. Namely, many former battlefront enemies have already met as friends on the Blue-Black front, have found each other as Finns, have extended a brother's hand to each other. . . . The People's Patriotic Movement is just as much a movement of the working class as of other honest citizens. The People's Patriotic Movement is thus not a bourgeois movement. It is a people's movement. . . . In the future there cannot be in this land bourgeoisie or Marxists, a right wing or a left wing in political positions, but simply Finns working honestly for the good of one common fatherland and nation.

This appeal for support from Finnish workers failed to arouse a significant favorable response. Whatever the party's professions of brotherhood, it was unlikely that those whose communism was rooted in the events of 1918 would now join their former enemies, nor was it likely that Social Democrats who had remained faithful to parliamentary government even after those events would now join an anti-Marxist totalitarian group. Bitter denunciations of capitalism in general and Finnish capitalists in particular did, however, alienate almost all Finnish industrialists, even those who had been prominent in the Lapua Movement, from the People's Patriotic Movement.

Even more serious for the new party was the alienation of most of the older generation of conservatives. Strikingly few older conservatives joined the party. All three major leaders of this generation were soon disenchanted with it. Mannerheim and Svinhufvud were driven off by its extreme language position, and the response of Paasikivi proved of special significance, to his own political future, to the new party, and, above all, to the strength of parliamentary government in Finland. After an initially favorable response, Paasikivi soon recognized that the People's Patriotic Movement was basically different from the bourgeois parties. The new party, in his judgment, aimed at nothing less than a fascist dictatorship. It was therefore a revolutionary movement, and as such had to be vigorously opposed. Whatever the defects of political parties, it was childish fancy to assume that a democratic society could exist without them. The end of the party system would be the end of democracy, which was, in spite of its short-comings, the highest political system men had yet attained. Enforcement of conformity had to be rejected. Conservatism did not involve destruction of parliamentary government, overthrow of the state machinery, or destruction of personal freedom, all of which characterized the totalitarian political systems. Conservatism involved, instead, the principle of English conservatism, proved valid by the experience of many generations, that all change must suit the habits and traditions of the nation involved. Evolution, not destruction, was the basis of conservatism.

As is generally true with political thought, these reflections by Paasikivi resulted from a concrete political situation. The essence of this situation was that the Conservative party organization had been captured by the People's Patriotic Movement. The latter, upon its formation, had asserted that it was above parties. Its members, and even its leaders, could therefore be members of another party as well. This meant that the Conservative party was used, in a type of Jekyll-Hyde relationship, to provide a cover of bourgeois respectability for the radical activities of the new party. The People's Patriotic Movement claimed that it had conquered the Conservative party just as the National Socialist party had conquered the bourgeois nationalists in Germany. This claim was entirely justified. Paasikivi returned to active political life after a retirement of fifteen years to drive members of the People's Patriotic Movement out of the Conservative party. As the retired director of one of the two largest Finnish banks, his intimate connection with the major financial contributors to the Conservative party enabled him to be elected chairman of its Executive Committee. Through an overwhelming display of organizational skill, Paasikivi had by late 1936 achieved his goal, and retired as Chairman.

Paasikivi's success drove the *Gesellschaft* out of the People's Patriotic Movement, and left it a pure *Gemeinschaft*. The sense of community within the new party did not obscure for its members their larger goal of a national community, however. This national community was, in turn, not an end in itself, but merely the precondition for fulfillment of the historical mission of the Finnish nation. The achievement of national unity would make Finland invincible. Breaking down all barriers within Finland would lead to breaking down all barriers dividing the Finnish-speaking peoples. This would mean, of course, the achievement of the Greater Finland. The first point in the program of the People's Patriotic Movement proclaimed: "The entire Finnish race must be united into one Greater Finland on the basis of national self-determination." The leaders of the party left no doubt as to the primacy of this goal. The hearts of party members did not beat for the West, but rather for expansion into the East. Confidence in the future of the Greater Finland seemed especially justified after Munich, when the outlines of the new world order, which would bring justice even to East Karelia, were becoming increasingly clear.

The new party's acceptance of the Greater Finland as its ultimate goal led to close coöperation with the Academic Karelia Society. The society supported the party's parliamentary candidates. Members of the society who had previously refused to join any party, and who had not entirely approved of the conciliatory language position of the Lapua Movement, found themselves completely at home in the People's Patriotic Movement, and the overwhelming majority of Finnish-speaking university students supported it. There was extensive interlocking of directorates between the People's Patriotic Movement and the Academic Karelia Society. The society was particularly prominent in the youth organization of the party. Leaders of this youth organization openly compared it to the Balilla and the Hitlerjugend, with which they developed personal contacts. It was often difficult to tell just where the society ended and the party began.

A fundamental similarity between the society and the party was the military structure of both. The party accepted as its basic organizational principle the concept expressed by the Finnish term *johtajaperiaate* ("leadership principle"), a direct translation of the German *Führerprinzip*. Whatever the weaknesses of this leadership principle, it was at least free from the duplicity of the Communist organizational principle of democratic centralism. The leadership principle was accepted by the People's Patriotic Movement because of deep admiration for Mussolini and Hitler, both of whom were regarded as fulfilling the highest standards of leadership. Within the new party, democracy was as little favored as it was to be within the new political system. Farsighted policies could not be followed if party leaders were forced to depend on popular support. Each level of leadership within the party organization was chosen by the level immediately above it. Some of the subordinate party organs on the national level did not even meet. If democracy was considered unjustified within the party, it was doubly so among the Finnish people at large, who were considered totally incompetent to judge public affairs.

The Finnish people were, nevertheless, competent enough to reject the political thought, action, and organization of the People's Patriotic Movement, whose popular support was never very large. In 1936, its best year, its parliamentary candidates received 8.3 per cent of total votes cast, and by 1939 this support had clearly diminished. It was this year, however, that saw the achievement of a national unity unprecedented in Finnish politics. The beginning of World War II saw the Finnish nation attain *Volksgemeinschaft* in the most fundamental sense of that term, although not under the leadership of the extreme Right. The tragedy that engulfed Europe, and with it Finland, led the People's Patriotic Movement to declare that it had nothing unfavorable to say about the Social Democratic party. In the dark night that was the Winter War, Red could not be distinguished from White. Just as the Civil War of 1918 had divided the Finnish nation, the Winter War united it—temporarily. Among the casualties of World War II were the Academic Karelia Society and the People's Patriotic Movement. With Creon, their members learned that proud men pay the price for their proud words. Like Creon, the price they had to pay was higher than they deserved.

SUGGESTED READING

GRAHAM, MALBONE W. *The Diplomatic Recognition of the Border States: Part I: Finland*. Berkeley: 1935.
———. "Finland," in his *New Governments of Eastern Europe*. New York: 1927. Pp. 169–245, 621–645.

————. "Stability in the Baltic States: Finland," in Vera Micheles Dean, and others, *New Governments in Europe: The Trend Toward Dictatorship.* New York: 1934. Pp. 261–279.

HARMAJA, LEO. *Effects of the War on Economic and Social Life in Finland.* New Haven: 1933.

HODGSON, JOHN H. "Finland's Position in the Russian Empire, 1905–1910," *Journal of Central European Affairs.* July, 1960, pp. 158–173.

————. "The Paasikivi Line," *The American Slavic and East European Review.* April, 1959, pp. 145–173.

KNOELLINGER, CARL ERIK. *Labor in Finland.* Cambridge, Mass.: 1960.

KUUSISTO, ALLAN A. "The Paasikivi Line in Finland's Foreign Policy," *The Western Political Quarterly.* March, 1959, pp. 37–49.

LUNDIN, C. LEONARD. *Finland in the Second World War.* Bloomington, Ind.: 1957.

RINTALA, MARVIN. "A Generation in Politics: A Definition," *The Review of Politics.* October, 1963, pp. 509–522.

————. "An Image of European Politics: The People's Patriotic Movement," *Journal of Central European Affairs.* October, 1962, pp. 308–316.

————. "The Politics of Gustaf Mannerheim," *Journal of Central European Affairs.* April, 1961, pp. 67–83.

————. "The Problem of Generations in Finnish Communism," *The American Slavic and East European Review.* April, 1958, pp. 190–202.

————. "Short List of English-Language Studies of Finnish Politics," *Journal of Central European Affairs.* April, 1963, pp. 77–80.

————. *Three Generations: The Extreme Right Wing in Finnish Politics.* Bloomington, Ind.: 1962.

————. "Väinö Tanner in Finnish Politics," *The American Slavic and East European Review.* February, 1961, pp. 84–98.

SMITH, C. JAY, JR. *Finland and the Russian Revolution 1917–1922.* Athens: 1958.

WUORINEN, JOHN H. *Nationalism in Modern Finland.* New York: 1931.

Russia[*]

HANS ROGGER

"The Russian Right"? The very linking of the words appears an
incongruity, a contradiction in terms. What soil was there for the
growth of an intellectual or political Right in the oldest of Europe's
old regimes, where autocracy and a hidebound bureaucracy held
out longest against representative government, against political and
civil liberty, against civic equality and public rights? Indeed, what
need was there for autonomous, public forces to defend inherited
principles of social and political life when state and monarchy regarded this task as their eternal and sacred obligation and sacrificed
to it their very existence? There was no obvious failure here of the
old order to defend its birthright and the privileges of its beneficiaries, although elsewhere such a failure had been cause and
beginning of the emergence of the Right as a movement and attitude distinct from, and at times opposed to, a defensive conservatism. Old regimes are barren ground for rightist movements and
ideologies, which need the open air of political challenge and
combat as much as, if not more than, their adversaries on the
Left, and it was only with the government's retreat in the stormy
days of the 1905 Revolution that the Russian Right as a political

* I am grateful to the Russian Research Center, Harvard University, and
to the Research Committee, University of California, Los Angeles, for their
support of studies of which the present essay is a by-product.

movement was born, to decline again in strength and importance as authority recovered confidence and control.

Yet, even before the changes of 1905 made possible and necessary the entry of the Right into the political arena in order to save the country from political liberalization, and the monarchy from itself, the outlines and elements of a Russian Right were discernible. There existed a potential Right, a complex of attitudes and principles found in varying degrees in individuals or small groups convinced that there were better and more imaginative answers than those given by the government or the possessors of wealth and station to the threat of liberal reform, democratic aspirations, or revolutionary upheaval. Even before they became patently violent, vocal, and aggressive in 1905, frightening friends and enemies alike by the radicalism of their techniques and their demagogic appeals to the masses, Russian rightists were recognizably different from conservative supporters of the status quo and reactionary advocates of repression. They shared with these certain basic assumptions about the nature of the Russian state and society: the uniqueness of Russia's historical experience and the rejection of Europe as a model; the need for Russian dominance in a multinational state; the belief that the autocrat alone must wield political power. But, in addition, the men of the potential Right insisted that the government's preoccupation with its own security was cowardly and would finally paralyze its will to resist the onslaught of liberalism and revolution. These men felt that an exclusive reliance on the bureaucracy, a failure to respond to national needs and to seek a broader and firmer basis for authority than the privileged classes, made doubtful the regime's ability to preserve the nation's political traditions or to assure its welfare and greatness.

It would, however, be a distortion of Russian political reality to maintain too sharp a distinction between the Right and traditional conservatism. In practice such a distinction is less clearly visible than it is in the historian's pattern, and a broader perspective reveals the Russian Right as rooted, though often unhappily, in the conservative part of the political spectrum. The narrow limits within which, particularly before 1905, all but illegal or private political debate had to be conducted, prevented the development and statement of such sharply defined positions as elsewhere marked off the Right from conservatism and reaction. It proved impossible, for example, for the Russian Right to dissociate itself entirely from the bureaucracy or to admit publicly what might be conceded in private—that in view of the limitations, the weakness, and the indecision of its chief representative, the monarchy was a liability for those who spoke most loudly on its behalf. In czarist Russia it was difficult to be decisively or radically rightist without seeming to stand with the revolutionaries and inviting persecution, a risk none seemed willing to run. To appeal to the masses as the only part of the population preserving healthy national and political sentiments also proved difficult, for there was no entirely satisfactory way to put these sentiments to political use without seeming to advocate a representative system or staging mass demonstrations and pogroms with all their unpredictable consequences to public order and private property.

The difficulty of describing Russian political topography in terms borrowed from Western Europe and making a clear distinction between conservative and rightist positions stems not alone from the poverty and limitations of political life under an autocracy. It derives also from the character of the Russian state which played the dual role of protector as well as dissolver of the past and could, by turns or even simultaneously, be both conservative and revolutionary. M. N. Katkov, who has the reputation of being Russia's most influential reactionary journalist in the period from 1863 until his death in 1887, maintained that in Russia it was the people and society that were the conservative elements, whereas the state had always been a force making for change and the disruption of custom and inherited rights.

The modernizing role of the state and its imposition of certain social and economic reforms—from Peter the Great's universal service state to the emancipation of the serfs, from industrialization to the dissolution of the village commune—the state's impatience with privilege and tradition where these interfered with its purposes, and the impartial arbitrariness of its bureaucrats, led many Russians of conservative views to look upon their government as almost revolutionary and brought some of them to political positions and techniques that belied their conservative origin and purpose. An opposition to liberalism, democracy, and socialism which was not only independent of the state but also profoundly critical of it must surely be regarded as being of the Right. This was especially true when the Great Reforms of the 1860's and the granting of a representative assembly in 1905 made it appear that the fortress of government itself had been infiltrated by the liberal enemy. In such a situation it was possible for conservatives to believe that a weak or ill-informed czar needed help from outside the government to preserve the autocracy and that a more active, more broadly based fight against the enemies of Russia was needed than had so far been waged.

To act on that belief and to engage in that fight meant, in fact, to challenge the state's monopoly of political activity, and to provoke its deep distrust of any independent or unsupervised action on the part of even its most loyal supporters. It meant leaving the shelter of the government, risking its disapproval, abandoning safe conservative ground and plunging into the sea of politics. To the extent that they were willing to do this, Russian conservatives moved toward the Right, but there were few who completed the journey. Most of the history of the Russian Right, therefore, is that of a would-be Right, a record of constant wavering between caution and boldness, between past and future, between the restrictions imposed by what was, after all, an old regime, and the opportunities its modification or removal would have created. The Right was never to find a lasting basis of popular support and remained a minor, though not unimportant, phenomenon of the Russian scene. Among the politically sophisticated it was suspect either because of its conservatism or the lack of it; among the masses, its temporary successes could never be translated into sustained political pressure because the Right could match neither the political nor the social and economic radicalism of the Left, and because, ultimately, it recoiled from a consistent exploitation of mass passions and grievances.

Czarist Russia was not an Oriental despotism—stagnant, self-contained, brutally efficient in the stifling of dissent. If, therefore, some of the basic conditions for the existence of a Right were met, others were not. The absence of politics as an open contest over the distribution and employment of power, the fear of mass anarchy among all but the most disaffected, the strength of dynastic loyalties or the inability to conceive of a feasible alternative to personal autocracy—these factors kept the Russian Right from achieving the drive and stature of some of its Western counterparts. Although the protean character of the Russian state made possible the appearance of a Russian Right, or at least of rightist elements in Russian conservatism, the country's political backwardness kept them from developing fully.

The case of the Russian Right, like that of the country as a whole, is one of uneven development. Yet its history is important; it offers insights into the character of Russian politics, and supplies bench marks for measuring the ebb and flow of rightist ideas and movements between conservatism and radicalism in a variety of settings. Our concern in the following pages is to describe these ideas and movements and to distinguish them within the larger context of conservative thought and politics in Russia.

The most influential formulation of Russian conservatism, the background against which a potential Right would have to define itself, came from the pen of the writer and historian Nicholas Karamzin (1766–1826). His "Memoir on the Old and the New Russia" of 1811 was a stern warning against any change in the foundations of the state—the tacit agreement between the monarch and the *dvorianstvo* (the land-owning nobility or gentry) by which the former was limited in the exercise of his power only by Christian precepts and a strict respect for the social and economic privileges of the latter. Karamzin held that without such respect monarchy would turn into despotism and break the covenant by which the gentry, the only class capable of so doing, would faithfully serve and support the state. As a member of that class and as its spokesman, Karamzin recalled how the Emperor Paul (1796–1801), in a reign of terror which equaled that of the Jacobins, had reduced all his subjects, even the most exalted, to the insecurity of slaves, endangering the state, subverting its principles, and bringing about his own ruin. If now there was renewed grumbling in palaces and huts, where one would expect only joy at being freed of a capricious tyrant, the cause was once again the specter of a one-sided infringement of the harmonious relationship between the czar and his foremost subjects. This time the danger had its source not in the tyrannous disposition of one man, but in intellectual conceit, ignorance of Russia, and an infatuation with foreign theories.

These vices, Karamzin felt, were all too common in the present emperor's entourage. In the first years of Alexander I's reign, they dominated his Unofficial Committee of young aristocrats, which contemporaries jestingly or fearfully called the Russian Committee of Public Safety. One of its members had, in fact, attended meetings of the Paris Jacobins, and others were Anglophile admirers of constitutional monarchy. But they were also convinced that in backward Russia, where a selfish upper class confronted a brutish peasantry, reform had to be imposed by the crown and carried out by an enlightened and obedient bureaucracy. In this they were agreed with Michael Speransky, the priest's son who, by dint of personal ability, had risen in the civil service to become, in the second period of Alexander's reforming activity, his trusted counselor and friend. Working in secrecy or outside normal channels of government, the bureaucratic upstart and the young aristocrats addressed themselves to the task of reordering the administration of their country, streamlining its machinery, and reforming its abuses. To safeguard citizens from arbitrary acts, they sought the rule of law rather than the protection of corporate privileges. In retrospect it is clear that most of the remedies they proposed were cautious rather than bold and far from being revolutionary or even liberal in any doctrinaire sense of the word; but they did question long-cherished assumptions as well as established practices and institutions.

Their preference for innovation, their institutional bias, their wish to bring logic and symmetry to the archaic confusion of Russia's government and laws, convicted Speransky and the members of the Unofficial Committee of doctrinaire radicalism in the eyes of their opponents, whose worst fears were confirmed by the measures promulgated in the first decade of Alexander's reign.

Conservatives thought these not merely bad in themselves, but still more ominous in what they seemed to reveal of the ultimate intentions of the monarch and his counselors. Even members of Alexander's family began to worry, and it was his sister, the Grand Duchess Catherine, who introduced Karamzin to her brother and prevailed upon the respected historian to draft the "Memoir" as a document to be used against the innovators.

Surveying the years from 1801 to 1810, Karamzin first addressed himself to questions of foreign policy, where he doubted that "the counselors of the Emperor had followed the principles of a sincere and wise patriotism." The French alliance concluded in 1807 was unpopular on ideological as well as economic grounds. It had not only led Russia to the side of Napoleon, the usurper and heir of revolution; it had also closed English markets to the products of Russia's fields and forests. The main conclusion Karamzin drew from Russia's unhappy relations with France was not that patriotism required the provocation of an uncomfortable and distasteful ally, but that the country look strictly to its own interests. These demanded neither a crusade for Europe's liberation from tyranny nor a craven seeking for Napoleon's goodwill, but a proper regard for the welfare and stability of Russia which had not been advanced by either the ill-conducted campaigns against Napoleon or by the ill-considered alliance with him. Karamzin was an isolationist as, for a century afterward, were most conservative Russians who saw in a dynamic or expansionist foreign policy a threat to their interests as well as to their principles.

The most serious danger signals Karamzin perceived were on the domestic horizon, where, instead of existing institutions being perfected, new ones which bore unmistakable traces of their foreign and revolutionary origin were being created. There were rumors that serfdom and the autocracy were about to be abolished, that a charter of rights was being prepared in the Unofficial Committee, that Speransky would impose a constitution curbing crown and nobility. Alexander had indeed received something very much like a constitutional project from the hands of Speransky, but, lacking the determination to defy the rising conservative opposition that was brought about by alarm at the reforms already carried out, he had not acted upon it. The collegiate administration of government departments had been replaced by that of single ministers; the departments themselves were soon reorganized. A Council of State, its very name reminiscent of the French model, was established. The first parts of a new civil code, patterned after the Napoleonic one, appeared. Court appointments became purely honorary distinctions, without right of title or preferment in the civil service where promotions to the higher grades were, in the future, to depend at least partly on educational qualifications and examinations; seniority and birth no longer carried their former weight. The expansion of educational opportunity, the right given nonnobles to acquire land without serfs (buttressed by references to Adam Smith), then extended to wealthy merchants with rights of serf ownership—all these measures spelled the growing bureaucratization of the state and its eventual break with the gentry.

Against this trend, Karamzin warned that distinctions gained in state service must not take precedence over the inalienable rights of the nobility or lead to the dilution of its privileges. Noble status should not derive from rank, but rank from noble status. To undermine the rights of the nobility would destroy the very basis of monarchy and transform it into an arbitrary despotism, placing the first estate at the mercy of men who had only ambition, particularly the lust of power, to motivate them in the performance of their duties. If, as appeared possible, serfdom were also to be attacked, then none of the gentry's prerogatives would remain and it would sink into a nondescript mass of subjects without the rights or property to defend itself against an all-powerful state. The law of 1803, allowing owners to free their serfs, along with some land, was far-reaching neither in its effects nor in its conscious intentions, but it betrayed the attitude of its authors toward the institution of serfdom and appeared to the gentry to be another portent of things to come. The consequences of freeing the serfs would not, however, be ruinous to their masters alone. The state, Karamzin warned, would then be faced with a task beyond its resources—replacing the gentry in its economic and administrative role among an uncivilized peasantry not yet ready to live without the tutelage of its betters. It was to be an oft-repeated argument against serf-emancipation and, after 1861, against peasant self-government and the legal equality of social classes.

Karamzin's conception of the role of government was a negative one, and is best summarized in his observation that Russia needed not new institutions or new laws but fifty good governors. Change was to be looked for in the human heart. Not abstract principles but capable and honest men would insure justice, order, the safety of property, and the security of the country and its citizens. To hope for more was dangerous frivolity, a hankering after novelty for its own sake, a trait which had come into the national character with the changes imposed by Peter. The process of Europeanization was irreversible and probably unavoidable, but it had gone too far and its excesses had caused Russians to lose their bearings and their native good sense. The slavish imitation of Europe, personified by Speransky, had finally to be stopped. Russia had need of neither new universities nor a constitution, and no czar had the right to share or surrender the power he had sworn to uphold. Autocracy had created the Russian state; its inviolability was the necessary condition of national greatness and its head the final and only source of authority. But it could not survive without the nobility which had helped to make it strong, and which must not be debased by being subjected to a classless, faceless army of civil servants, or by being impoverished by emancipation.

The historian carried the day over the bureaucrat and Speransky was dismissed in 1812. Until the fall of czarism, Karamzin's prescription for the stability of the state and its social structure remained the only one advanced by gentry spokesmen against the lowering of class barriers and the granting of political liberties. It was echoed in 1874 by General Rostislav Fadeev ("Russian Society in Present and Future"), and in 1885 by A. M. Pazukhin ("The Contemporary Situation of Russia and the Class Question"). The latter asked also for a reversal of the "leveling" course initiated by the Great Reforms of the 1860's and for assurances of gentry primacy in local government, in the central administration, and in state service, as the only salvation of autocracy and the surest protection against the spread of alien ideas by a classless intelligentsia. A. I. Elishev warned in "The Gentry Cause" (1898) that to deprive the gentry of its special position would rob the peasants of their natural leaders and drive both classes into the ranks of the opposition, and Alexander Polovtsev, a member of the state council, advised Nicholas II in 1901 that only by abandoning a purely centralist-bureaucratic approach to rural administration and restoring the broken link between the peasant masses and their "elder brothers," the great landowners, could order and material progress in the countryside be achieved. All those who took Karamzin as their guide assumed an intimate community of interests between monarch and gentry, asserted the absence in Russia of political and social conflict, and consequently denied the need for any formal devices to adjust such conflict. They wished to be protected in their possessions and prerogatives; in exchange they were fully prepared to leave political power in the hands of the autocrat, provided, of course, that they shared in its administration and that its demands be not too onerous.

Karamzin's mixture of Montesquieu and Muscovite traditions stood revealed as an absurdity almost from the moment of its formulation, for the good understanding it presumed between crown and nobility was wish rather than fact. The Russian gentry was not a deeply rooted estate with strong corporate traditions and consciousness, but monarchy's creature or client, at best an uneasy partner, alternately feared, coddled, or ignored. Nor, as soon became evident, was the state as dependent upon this class as the proponents of gentry conservatism liked to believe. When liberal ideas found a home among the upper classes and exploded in the Decembrist rising of noble officers in 1825, the monarch began increasingly to place reliance on a professional bureaucracy, though still proclaiming himself the first noble of the land. Even the grandson of Nicholas I, the reactionary Alexander III, while paying generous tribute to the gentry, realized that the restoration of its economic well-being and administrative role, attempted in his reign, was less important to the country's power than the strength of industry, sound finances, and an efficient police. Although Karamzin's conservatism had moral as well as economic roots, it became after him a more selfish defense of gentry prerogatives at the expense of economic development and an active foreign policy. A state wishing to play the role of major power was not always willing to pay this price, nor were those who cherished larger views of Russia's destiny.

The frequent divergence between gentry interests and state needs made Karamzin's conservatism an inadequate statement of the interests of even his own class. As a result some of the gentry were eventually led to liberalism and to the wish for formal, institutional restraints on absolute power. Others, though unwilling, like Karamzin, to follow this "un-Russian" road, were fearful that autocracy could not survive as the anxious guardian of privileges alone and wished to place it on a more popular basis, to make it not responsible to the nation but more responsive to it. This would mean inevitably the broadening of nonpolitical rights and the development of a populism of the Right, which Karamzin's conservative heirs rejected. But how could such a populism of the Right become articulated and distinguish itself from the main body of conservatism without leaving the common ground of national traditions in political and social life? It was Slavophilism that supplied the ideological devices by which opponents of political liberalization and representative government could claim to represent the true needs and feelings of the nation more fully than could parliaments and political parties.

By no stretch of the imagination can the founders of Slavophilism be considered as belonging to the Right. Yet they are part of its prehistory, they contributed significantly to its stock of ideas and vocabulary, and prepared the ground for men who gave a sharper and harsher turn to their cultural and social ideals.

The starting point for the Slavophiles was the need and the wish to see their country as something more than a benighted backwater of civilization ruled by a Germanized court and bureaucracy. But although they were repelled by the official Russia of Nicholas I, they did not seek salvation in a liberal or socialist West. All they abhorred in the empire created by Peter the Great—from its capital with its non-Russian name and aspect and its Prussianized army and civil service to the injustices a Europeanized upper class inflicted on an enserfed people—seemed to them to be of Western origin. And with that West of one-sided rationalism, of purely formal rights and sharp class divisions, the Slavophiles contrasted an ideal Russia that was whole in soul and character, truly free and spontaneous. To the West's self-interested individualism, they opposed the spirit and practice of communal solidarity as preserved in the Orthodox Church and in the peasant village.

Although Slavophilism, as formulated in the 1840's and 1850's, had no political program or intentions, it did have political implications. The government as well as many conservatives sensed that the nationalism of the Slavophiles and their rejection of Western doctrines had quite different sources than simply the official defense of established institutions. The fears that revolutions in Europe and rebellion in Poland had induced in Nicholas had led him to an ever greater emphasis on those repressive features of the state that the Slavophiles regarded as alien to national traditions. And though they would agree with Karamzin and Nicholas that Russia had to be preserved from revolution and constitutional illusions, they did not place their trust in the power of the state or the protection of privileges. Bureaucratic despotism, doctrinaire liberalism, and revolution were equally the children of an abstract, ahistorical rationalism; to oppose them successfully required the resurrection of national traditions which waited only to be called back to life by love and respect.

Pre-Petrine Muscovy was the ideal, the natural, the national, and the organic period of Russia's history in which an unforced harmony had reigned between a patriarchal monarch and the national family. Peter's reforms had by the forcible imposition of Western ways disturbed this harmony and given rise to a non-national elite with selfish appetites and un-Russian political pretensions. But Russians had never wished for political rights and they shunned power as at best a necessary evil, a burden to be borne by the monarch as a Christian duty. All that the people asked of the state was to be left free in the pursuit of their "inner," nonpolitical life—their social rights, their consciences, and their opinions. In Russia there could be no basis for a constitutional movement, for a democratic or a socialist revolution. These were all contests for power, possible only in states that had grown out of conquest and represented the rule of one part of the nation over the rest. Such was the case in Europe. The Russian people, renouncing power, nonetheless recognized its necessity for external defense and the safeguarding of their religious and social life, their customs and economic pursuits. This was the sacred obligation of their chosen protector, the absolute monarch. Absolutism was the only conceivable form of government; any other would require the participation of the people in politics, lead to struggles for power and disagreements over its limits, thus introducing legalism and formalism into a relationship that should be based on mutual trust and respect.

The historical idyll the Slavophiles painted was not, however, a portrait in which the family and its relationships served as the only model for the larger society. There had been a number of institutions intermediate between the czar-father and his children even in Muscovite Russia; only if these were allowed to function freely could Russia hope to be immune from the Western disease of political and social strife and economic envy.

The most important of these institutions was the Orthodox Church. Freed of the Babylonian captivity of governmental control, it could restore a national community of custom and belief. The Slavophiles wanted neither the synodal administration of the church as an arm of government nor the compulsory maintenance of its supremacy over other religions and sects, and though far from proposing the formula of a free church in a free state, they stood for religious toleration and freedom of conscience. Of nearly equal importance in their retrospective Utopia was the *zemskii sobor* ("the Assembly of the Land"), which had in the past assured the people of access to their ruler and would in future make unnecessary a representation of Western type. Its purpose was not to limit autocracy or to establish a parliamentary regime, but to act as an organ of free expression for all classes, which the monarch would consult on issues of paramount importance, as had been the custom before Peter. Only by returning full freedom of opinion to all the people, represented in the *zemskii sobor,* could the breach between state and nation be healed and the pressure for a parliament and a constitution resisted. Finally, there was the village commune, the most popular institution the national genius had created, the nucleus of a more just social order, Russia's chance to escape the horrors of capitalism and class war, of revolution and socialism, of the dry rot of bourgeois selfishness.

But what could the gentle and humane Slavophiles contribute to the Right, besides a suspicion of politics and a horror of industry and capital and of the social conflicts they generated? Nationalism and the rejection of Western ways, the stress on the uniqueness of Russian culture and the central importance of absolutism and Orthodoxy, became integral elements of rightist thought and programs, yet they did not save the Slavophiles from conservative distrust or governmental persecution. For they were also against serfdom and the exploitation of the masses by a self-indulgent minority; they were against censorship, religious persecution, and the self-willed abuses of power by a bureaucracy that had stepped between the monarch and his people. And it was among the people, the *narod,* the mass of simple men that the Russian faith and way of life were best preserved. The expression of such beliefs made the Slavophiles suspect in the eyes of the guardians of authority; they were summoned by the political police to explain themselves; their publications were harried or closed down.

In truth, the Slavophiles were so far from being admirers of the Russia of their day that anarchists and socialists could hail them as precursors and comrades in the battle against an all-powerful and all-devouring state. The Slavophiles had been the first to pillory that state as doing violence to the national character, its government as being removed from the majority of the people and deaf to their needs, and although they wanted to keep state and nation, government and people restricted to separate spheres of power and opinion, politics and social life, they wanted also to narrow the gulf between them through the Assembly of the Land. This narrowing, when carried to the point of wishing to create a monolithic national community, free of class conflict and political contention, became one of the key demands of the Right, which saw the near-mystic communion between ruler and ruled as Russia's answer to the convulsions of the modern age. But too many elements of that answer were drawn from a fanciful interpretation of the past and based on assumptions difficult to maintain as the century wore on.

Rightist views of Russian history, society, and government, insofar as these were articulate, were much influenced by the teachings of the Slavophiles, though the Slavophiles can hardly be taxed with the intellectual and moral impoverishment of their ideas by others. The Slavophile notion that Russians were not interested in politics and power became a favorite rightist axiom, for it made the denial of the need for parties and parliaments rest not on the continued dominance of one class, but on the experiences and traditions of the people. Slavophilism's stress on Orthodoxy as the core element of Russian nationalism degenerated into religious exclusiveness and eventually into anti-Semitism with racial and anticapitalist overtones; its indictment of the upper class for a thoughtless Westernism and neglect of their lesser brothers would be crudely applied to "alien" exploiters, the liberal intelligentsia, or "disloyal" servants of the czar, while the words "the people" became in time little more than a magic spell intoned to ward off real examination of their needs and thoughts.

In an impersonal, historic sense, the Slavophiles must bear a degree of responsibility for the coarse uses to which some of their most generous ideas and sentiments were put. Utopians and romantic nationalists, their preoccupation with the realms of history and the spirit made easier the evasion of many troublesome problems of Russian reality, and favored passion over the more painful processes of reason. Such reluctance to grapple with specific and concrete tasks, a readiness to decry attempts at practical though partial solutions as formalistic, un-Russian, and heartless also characterized rightists who managed to derive from Slavophilism a measure of intellectual respectability. Above all, Slavophilism bequeathed to them an irreconcilable tension between the spacious vistas of political romanticism and the pedestrian and pragmatic requirements of the battle against social revolt and political revolution. In the eyes of those who conducted it, this battle demanded not the transposition of political and social issues into a philosophical and historical key, but a far-reaching acceptance of the status quo and of the men and methods employed in its defense. Even

among those unquestionably loyal contemporaries of the Slavophiles, the standard bearers of what is aptly called "Official Nationality," there were men afflicted with this tension—notably the
historian and publicist Michael Pogodin (1800–1875), and the
poet and diplomat Fedor Tiutchev (1803–1873), who, in the very
act of eulogizing the Russia of Nicholas I, also became its critics.

Profoundly influenced by Karamzin, whose memory he revered
without sharing his idol's noble prejudices, Pogodin was equally
attracted by the Slavophile vision of Russia's history and character.
He had, however, more exalted and dynamic views of the character and duty of monarchy than either Karamzin or his Slavophile
friends. The very intensity of his nationalism, the very beauty
and grandeur he envisioned for Russia, carried Pogodin beyond official definitions of the content and direction of national life. He
wished to bring Russia to the starry firmament of glory; Nicholas
was more concerned with order, stability, and unquestioning obedience to a narrower interpretation of the triune formula—Orthodoxy, Autocracy, Nationality—that was the guiding maxim of
his reign. In Pogodin's and Tiutchev's Pan-Slav sentiments, in
their hope that Russia would lead mankind to a new dawn, were
sounded the first notes of a national messianism of which the state
was to become the bearer. Nicholas, as well as his successors, found
such a role unacceptable, for they were guardians of the legitimacy
and the integrity of thrones and governments. Calls for a Slavic
federal union, for the liberation of Russia's Slavic brothers from
Austrian and Turkish rule, smacked too much of revolution to
find favor in the eyes of Nicholas. He might perhaps be flattered
by Pogodin's judgment that he had come closer to the ideal of a
universal monarchy than Charles V or Napoleon, or by the suggestion that Russia should step forward as the champion of all
humanity, but neither rhetoric nor flattery betrayed the Czar into
abandoning the cautious, conservative course he had marked out
for himself and his country.

Both the Czar and conservatives in general sensed only danger
in the release of national energies envisioned in the broad vistas
sketched by Tiutchev and Pogodin. In numerous letters written to
Nicholas at the time of the Crimean War, some of which circu-

lated in thousands of copies, Pogodin made no secret of his conviction that the state's power and respect were being undermined by the cupidity, the mediocrity, the arbitrariness of its administrators; that the Czar was kept from learning the true feelings and condition of his people by selfish bureaucrats, and that the common people, shedding their blood for czar and country on the battlefield, were objects of exploitation and contempt in time of peace. Only by becoming the Czar of all the people, by listening to their voice in the *zemskii sobor* and granting them full freedom of opinion could Nicholas close the rift in the national family and strengthen it during a time of trial. Of humble origin —his serf father was freed when Pogodin was six years old— Pogodin displayed an almost democratic pathos, proclaiming that the voice of the people was the voice of God. He urged the abolition of serfdom and a better fate than knout and prison for the unfortunate peasants whose holy deeds of bravery and self-sacrifice were saving Russia's honor at Sebastopol and would also assure her future. In Tiutchev's mind, too, when the convulsions of 1848 divided the world into two hostile camps—Russia and Revolution —the issue was very much larger than the protection of one dynasty or state. In this struggle between two principles, Russia represented more than herself; on her victory would hang the political and religious fate of mankind for centuries to come. The content of that future Tiutchev did not set forth in detail, except to indicate that Russia's victory would lead not only to the defeat of Revolution but to her own transformation, to an epiphany in which she would make manifest to the world the last word on the besetting problems of mankind.

Distress over the obtuseness of official Russia, which would not heed the call to greatness, drove even Tiutchev, whose emphasis was, on the whole, religious and metaphysical rather than political, to castigate the Czar's ministers for their lack of faith in the nation's destiny. Their timidity paralyzed Russia abroad, and at home prevented that union of government and people which alone could make the autocracy national and enable it to carry out its mission. "For that purpose the public need not be taken into legislative councils, but there must be an intimate communication between government and people to arouse its spontaneous and unanimous collaboration." Pogodin, for his part, believed that in no other country was such collaboration easier of attainment. Spared conquest, feudalism, and aristocracy, which were the causes of dissension and division, Russians enjoyed more freedom, social justice, and equality than any Western people and therefore a degree of unity that made them invincible. Pogodin desired Russia's power as much as the welfare of her people and therefore felt that, where unity and power were threatened by special interests of class or region, they must submit to the majestic machinery of the state; for it alone could give full weight to the elements of Russia's physical and moral greatness. Guided by the hand of one man, the "Russian Czar," animated by the confidence and devotion of his subjects, that machine could move in any direction and at any speed willed by its master.

The Moscow historian's ideal image of an irresistible, all-embracing mechanism that would, when necessary, subordinate the claims of individuals and groups to the demands of power was not echoed by his contemporaries. It was too modern, too monolithic, too comprehensive to be acceptable to a traditionalist monarch, and although it had much in common with the Slavophiles' ideal of patriarchal monarchy, neither they nor the conservative heirs of Karamzin were prepared to go as far as Pogodin in identifying the spiritual and material well-being of the masses or the classes with those of the state. Indeed, though he was the first to set forth the elements of a rightist political doctrine, Pogodin himself did not develop or fuse them into a consistent and coherent theory or program. The reign of Nicholas I, when the heavy hand of the state was felt by all, was not a propitious time to extol or magnify its authority. Many Russians, the Slavophiles among them, wished not for victory but for defeat in the Crimean war, so that their country might turn inward and pursue other goals than glory or power. After the death of Nicholas and the end of the Crimean War, in 1855, a new epoch began in which, for a few brief years, it appeared possible that government and society might be reconciled in a grand program of reform and renovation, and might find through it the strength and unity for which Tiutchev and Pogodin had hoped and pleaded.

The disappearance of the stern and unbending figure who, for thirty years, had controlled the levers of power, created vast and varied yearnings for changes in almost every sphere of life on the part of almost every sector of society, and these yearnings were all the more ambitious, diverse, and ill-defined for having been repressed so long. Alexander II, despite a strong commitment to his father's principles, encouraged these hopes. He did so not by the adoption of liberal doctrines but by a more tolerant treatment of public opinion, a more humane conduct of the administration, and, above all, by concrete demonstrations of his belief that only a reformed autocracy could survive. The emancipation of the serfs with land, in 1861, followed by the introduction of a significant degree of self-government in town and country, by an enlightened judicial reform, by a more equitable sharing of the burdens of military service by all classes, and by an easing of the censorship, seemed to signal a steady evolution toward an equality of rights and duties for all citizens and their eventual participation in government.

Yet the political currents released during Alexander's first years led to no unanimity in welcoming such a possibility. Democrats and socialists asked for much more than concessions granted from on high and it was their influence and propaganda—loosely called "nihilism"—that was blamed for the peasant risings, student disorders, and mysterious fires of 1861 and 1862. The Slavophiles worked loyally in the preparation and execution of the reforms, hoping in this way to lay the basis for the popular national monarchy of their dreams and to prevent the advance of doctrinaire liberalism or gentry constitutionalism. Many of the former serfowners, hoping to be compensated for their losses by extensive political rights, toyed with the idea of a constitutional system. Even those of the nobility who did not, were fearful that the revolution they sensed could not be stopped because of drift and indecision. Conservatives who opposed the reforms or feared they had gone too far said that destructive ideas had found shelter in the salons, the editorial offices, and chancelleries of St. Petersburg; that weakness and indifference at the top caused doubt and cynicism below; that an unprincipled readiness to experiment undermined domestic tranquillity and the security of the state. It was for this reason that a man like Michael Katkov (1818–1887) was brought to seek support outside of government, hoping to mobilize opinion and in that way stiffen resistance to the liberal flood.

To demonstrate what want of courage and firmness would lead to, conservatives could point not only to disorders and mounting discontent among peasants and students, but also to the Polish rebellion of January, 1863. The proximity of the threat, the bitterness of its suppression, and the sympathy of Europe's governments and peoples for the Poles deeply affected public opinion and raised doubts of the wisdom of further loosening the bonds of strict authority. The waves radiating from this shock (deepened in 1866 by the first of many attempts on the life of Alexander II) bore Katkov, who became editor and publisher of the daily *Moscow News* in 1863, to a height of influence and popularity never attained by any other private figure and journalist in Russia. Though his views changed with bewildering rapidity, they ultimately revolved about one central point: the preservation and heightening of state power at home and abroad. In pursuit of that goal he displayed an almost revolutionary zeal and vehemence, feeling himself called to rouse society to an intensity of nationalist and patriotic spirit that would make it impossible for the country's leaders ever again to lose sight of Russia's dominant interests as he perceived them. "For those who are active in our public life, there is only one binding principle . . . Russia itself . . . and that comprises our faith as well as our autocracy. Russian policy cannot lose its way if it pursues only the interests and grandeur of Russia." If this meant giving second place to doctrine, even monarchical doctrine (late in life Katkov became the foremost proponent of an alliance with republican France), it did not mean isolation or a defensive nationalism. And in that very heightening of national sentiment, in its activation for state purposes which Katkov regarded as the best bulwark against revolution, many a conservative saw the exploitation of a revolutionary principle.

"National fervor," warned Count Peter Shuvalov, a diplomat and former chief of the gendarmerie, "is being mixed with democratic tendencies."

In the Polish question, Katkov had taken issue with the moderate policy favored by liberal opinion, by "liberalizing" statesmen, and by the Slavophiles. After the first signs of Polish unrest, in 1861, there had been a good deal of sentiment for reconciliation and concession. In the case of the Slavophiles, who would not deny to fellow Slavs—that is, the Polish people, not their Latinized ruling class—what they demanded for themselves, this went as far as a willingness to concede complete Polish autonomy in domestic affairs. Enjoying home rule and full civil and cultural liberty in an area whose eastern boundaries were to be drawn along ethnic and linguistic lines, Poland would have a chance to rediscover her Slavic identity, the necessary basis for amity with Russia. To Katkov this seemed shameful resignation, and he rejected as a sign of collective weakness the notion that the area of full Russian sovereignty should be reduced by "dictionary and grammar." A nation possessed of the will to assert itself could never make a voluntary surrender of rule or territory; to do so would be the symptom of a fatal illness afflicting the entire political organism. The loss of Poland, inevitable consequence of what was being prepared, would mean Russia's renunciation of her status as a great power and reversion to the half-Asian isolation of Muscovy before Peter had dragged her by main force onto the stage of a larger world. No country conscious of its greatness could countenance such a retreat, and when unrest exploded into revolt and war, Katkov began to urge its ruthless suppression. Even the Slavophiles came to be convinced of the necessity of firmness; they also joined Katkov in urging upon the government a policy of economic benefits to Polish peasants designed to isolate the upper-class leaders of the rebellion. For this the journal *Vest'* ("News"), which represented the interests of the large Russian landowners, called both Katkov and the Slavophiles "reds" and "democrats."

In the Polish question the Slavophiles' partial withdrawal from their philosophical and cultural nationalism showed how close their nationalism had moved to the statist, political variety Katkov represented, foreshadowing the emergence of a Pan-Slavism that would make up in political militancy what it lost in moral and intellectual attractiveness. In their effect, the vituperations of Iurii Samarin against "Polonism," Jesuit machinations, and the feudal rights of Baltic-German towns and nobles, were hardly distinguishable from the cruder chauvinism of Katkov—even if Samarin and other Slavophiles, who had proved their dedication to the *narod* by opposing the Russian gentry's political and economic claims, maintained that they were only protecting Polish and Baltic peasants against their masters. Katkov, for his part, embraced certain Slavophile positions, called upon Russia in 1867 to unite the Slavs as Prussia had united the Germans, and in 1876 urged his government to go to war against Turkey to free "our enslaved Slavic brothers." Though his brand of "Slavism" reflected calculations of power and prestige and his invocation of national traditions against Western theories and institutions was free of any deep-seated, Slavophile anti-Westernism, Katkov demonstrated that even a statist nationalism could no longer do without the terms the Slavophiles had contributed to the debate over Russia's destiny and character.

In time, Poland became Katkov's Carthage and Cuba, a threat to Russia's standing among the powers and to her internal security, the fixed idea and chief villain of his demonology. His obsessive certainty that Polish rebels were but the advance guard of universal revolution, that they and the "nihilists" at home were making common cause, led him to see evidences of "Polish intrigue" everywhere. The wavering of the government in 1863; its liberal course in education before 1866; its wooing of the moderates in the search for public support against the revolutionaries (from 1878); the attempts on the life of Alexander II and his assassination in 1881—all this the Moscow editor came to view as the treacherous work of Polish conspiracy. The true source of sedition, however, lay not in Paris or Warsaw, but in St. Petersburg, where indifference and cosmopolitanism were endemic among the upper classes and officialdom. The people alone had remained sound and kept the bases of national life free of infection. While simple and pious folk were praying for the victims of Polish treachery, the capital on the banks of the Neva continued to shelter the enemies of Russia. The ministers of Education, Justice, and Foreign Affairs, the Council of State, and the Senate became at one time or another the objects of Katkov's anger for insufficient zeal in the battle against the ever present enemy.

Katkov remained always an uncomfortable ally but, as both Alexander II and his son believed, an indispensable one, for his very independence and intractability assured for him an audience that "safer" writers and their journals never commanded. A contemporary called Katkov a "Camille Desmoulins *à rebours*," who, on occasion, was not above arranging or encouraging demonstrations of popular wrath or popular loyalty, much to the distress of the guardians of public order who felt constrained to warn him to moderate his tone, to avoid extremes, and not to appeal to the base instincts of the crowd. Emperor Alexander III himself, whose special favor Katkov enjoyed, lost patience with him, at one point called him a rebel for urging a bolder foreign policy, and asked that he be curbed.

Alexander's outburst showed an awareness that the ultimate target of Katkov's attacks on the government must, in an autocracy, be the autocrat himself. For all his protestations that the "supreme power" alone, not the changing views and personnel of its agencies, embodied the interests of the state and the welfare of its people, Katkov had really no more confidence in the occupant of the throne than in his servants. Even when his influence at court and in the government reached its height, in the years after 1881, he had little hope of the future. "I have completely lost heart," he confided to a friend; "I have seen the representatives of all strata of Russian society pass before me, and nowhere is . . . a promise of strength to be seen." The gentry was clamoring for political rights; the bureaucrats, products of the universities, were fashionably toying with liberal and radical notions; an appeal to the masses was too hazardous. Even Pobedonostsev, Procurator of the Holy Synod, gray eminence of the government of Alexander III, the mainstay and philosopher of reaction, disappointed Katkov. He tried vainly to prod Pobedonostsev into more decisive action to undo completely the harmful innovations of the previous reign, to repress even more severely all stirrings of dissent. "Pobedonos-tsev," a friend of Katkov's recalled, "remained true to himself, shrugged his shoulders, lamented and raised his hands to heaven. . . ."

From this intrinsic immobility of Russian conservatism Katkov could not escape, and therefore his legacy was one of failure and frustration. He left to future generations the specter of Polish intrigue, a superficial and fantastic explanation of the country's difficulties which could conveniently be extended to include Jews, Armenians, and others. He conjured up the perils to the unity and might of Russia which decentralization of authority and any grant of autonomy to the czar's non-Russian subjects would entail. But these perils were employed as tactical, defensive weapons, by government and rightists alike; they provided no positive solution for the dilemma of Katkov's simultaneous opposition to bureaucracy *and* representative government. He had once admitted the need "for introducing the living forces of society into the organism of state," but the reality of such a step frightened him. Within the framework of the Russian monarchy, Katkov's problem was insoluble, and it left him with no more heartening advice to give to his countrymen than absolute submission to their anointed leader. Yet he himself was not convinced of the validity and efficacy of his conception of a power above classes and parties guiding Russia along a road, "the czarist road," which was neither liberal nor conservative. Without a commanding vision to point out a direction in which to travel, all his considerable energy remained essentially unproductive.

Such a vision dominated Ivan Aksakov (1823–1886), the youngest of the original Slavophiles and in later life the principal spokesman of Pan-Slavism, who illustrated in his own person the progression of the doctrine from the cultural and religious into the political sphere. Unlike Katkov, however, Aksakov was not a political realist unwilling to risk the certainty of the known in the gamble for a more glorious future. His utopianism, the heritage of his Slavophile youth, helped to protect him from the complete pessimism that afflicted and finally paralyzed Katkov, Pobedonostsev, and other conservatives who saw no anchor of salvation for their world. Aksakov looked beyond this world, beyond Russia, and so sustained hope in the possibility of its redemption. In the fervor of this belief and his unwillingness to compromise it— which for many years led the government to deny him access to the public he wanted to serve and educate—he was truly of the Right, at one and the same time "extremely conservative, even reactionary and in the highest degree radical" (Kornilov).

Pan-Slavism—Russia's headship of the Slavic peoples in their fight for freedom from Turks and Germans, and Aksakov's dream of Slavic unity and greatness—this was the cause that gave to those Russians who embraced it something of the exaltation and nobility of the Risorgimento, and something similar to the taste for the might of united Germany. Even a man like Pobedonostsev was touched by it, though only for a moment, fearful that such enthusiasm could not be contained and that it harbored revolutionary instincts. Dostoevsky, too, was carried along by it and as a journalist helped to sustain it to a point where his Christian universalism was momentarily in danger of being submerged by jingoistic sentiments. Yet there were millenarian expectations in Dostoevsky's call for war against the Turks, and these gave testimony that Pan-Slavism was more than a heightened form of nationalism: this war would be fought not merely for Russia's salvation from stifling "rottenness and spiritual narrowness," nor for her Slav brothers only; it would be a crusade for the regeneration of all Europe, for her liberation from bourgeois selfishness, from liberal and pacifist illusions, and from the threat of revolutionary materialism. "We need war and victories. With them, the new word will come and the new life begin." In this, Aksakov was at one with Dostoevsky, though his new word and life bore more Slavic than Christian traits. More than a decade earlier Aksakov had welcomed the prospect of war with Austria over Poland as Russia's "baptism to a new profession of faith." Now he hoped that Russia's battle for Slavic freedom and unity, this "people's war," would mean her spiritual and social rebirth. Yet nothing could have been farther from the minds of the men in charge of Russian policy who were pursuing limited military, political, and diplomatic goals. It is the explosive burden of social and spiritual regeneration born by Aksakov's Pan-Slavism that made him appear a radical in their eyes even while he protested his devotion to Orthodoxy, Autocracy, and Nationality and his hostility to liberalism and socialism.

Pan-Slavism is a phenomenon of the Right because it is in large part an attempt to transcend social and political conflict by merging it in the larger issue of Slavic unity. Since the formulators and tribunes of Pan-Slavism chose not to take the revolutionary or liberal road to the solution of these problems, they had no other choice but to hope that the fires of war would fuse the nation into unity, purify it of class narrowness, reveal and light the new road to be followed. At the least, war would open a sphere of dynamism and action that was denied at home. This was the radical component of Pan-Slavism, not merely in the sense that an appeal to peoples rather than to governments was a revolutionary form of nationalism and therefore subversive of the conservative and cautious course the Russian foreign ministry pursued, but also in its hope of finding answers to the vast questions of Russian life.

The imperial government was keenly aware of the dangers posed by the revolutionary implications of Pan-Slavism and tried to check them and the movement that had given them birth. It was disturbed by the notes of social and Slavophile idealism expressed by the Pan-Slavists: by Aksakov who opposed "Slavic democracy" —the "Russian ideal" which would assure political harmony and the national character of the monarchy through the *zemskii sobor* and resist the evils of capitalism and social injustice by the communal organization of agriculture and artisan coöperatives—to the despotism of selfish minorities or numerical majorities; by Danilevsky (the author of "Russia and Europe," the "Bible" of Pan-Slavism and, like Dostoevsky, attracted to socialism in his youth) who foresaw Russia's headship of the Slavic world guaranteeing not only her political supremacy but the birth of a "social-economic system which would satisfy the masses in a just way" and at last bring about real and concrete equality among men; and by General Skobelev, the "Red Pan-Slavist," who believed in a "Russian democracy" secured by the supreme will of the autocrat. Even the future Alexander III, who was sympathetic to the Slavic cause, said in 1876 that it was time for the authorities to take into their hands all the Slavic committees, collections, "and all that popular movement, otherwise God only knows what may come of it or how it will end."

The Grand Duke's chief target was the Moscow Slavic Benevolent Committee of which Aksakov was treasurer and secretary from 1858 to 1875, and president until its dissolution in 1878. During the twelve years of his enforced silence as a publicist, which ended in 1880, the Committee provided a forum for the propagation of his views; when insurrection and war broke out in the Balkans, Aksakov became chief fund-raiser and organizer for the five thousand volunteers that his and similar committees helped send to Serbia. But however generous the response to his appeals, it did not and could not fulfill his expectations of an outpouring of generosity, of a common sacrifice that would unite the state and Russians of all classes in a new-found dedication to their common heritage. Both the government and the upper classes disappointed Aksakov. He complained that most of the donations came from the poor and lowly who were least able to pay. The wealthy, and he named a number of prominent families, had only grudgingly opened their hearts and pocketbooks; the contribution of the imperial family had been shockingly modest. On the state level, the situation was much the same. The Minister of Finance, speaking for several colleagues and many conservatives who had remained unmoved by what was derisively called the "Montenegrin ecstasy," warned that war would set Russia's development back fifty years.

Such considerations carried little weight with Aksakov or other Pan-Slavists, and he went so far as to hold the threat of a popular rising over the government and the upper classes should they fail to go to the aid of the Slavs. The country's diplomats, Aksakov charged in a public speech, were spineless in their devotion to peace and, worse than the nihilists, destitute of all historical consciousness, of every spark of living national feeling. Among the upper classes there was ignorance, stupidity, and moral rot, he claimed, but the will of the people would prove strong enough to tear the web of treason spun at home. That Aksakov remained at liberty despite such recklessness is something of a tribute to the old-fashioned forms of authoritarianism, the more so since he had just been reproved for the "democratic insinuations" of an address composed for the town council of Moscow.

When the Czar finally committed Russia to war against Turkey, the conflict brought victory in the field, but defeat at the council table by the combined forces of European diplomacy, and the inevitable dashing of Aksakov's hopes. Once again he railed at the cowardice of diplomats, called up the people's rage, and implied that the emperor had not kept his vow to fight the sacred cause to the end—bold words for which, this time, he was banished to his estate. But the deepest reason for his despair was that war had brought no lasting regeneration of those who had fought it; that it had not reconciled the classes and the masses, slowed the growth of the bourgeoisie and the revolutionary movement, or stilled the clamor for a constitutional regime such as Alexander II had, alas, granted the Bulgarians. Aksakov continued to speak and to write— just a few days before his death he was again censured for attacking the government's foreign policy—but he no longer commanded much of an audience. The war he had so fervently preached had not solved their problems and Russians were disposed to turn inward once more, to work for more modest and attainable goals—except for the revolutionaries whose bombs ended the life of the Czar-Liberator on the very day, March 1, 1881, that he had approved the advisory participation of elected representatives of the public in the work of administrative and fiscal reform.

Under the stern regime of Alexander III there was little likelihood that the tribunes of Pan-Slavism would find much scope for the preaching, and even less for the realization, of any bold schemes. There was little tolerance for independent thought or action. "Misunderstanding and distrust," Aksakov complained in late 1881, "have spread like a blight over Russia. . . . Between the nobility and the people, the government and society, the educated and the ignorant, even between members of the same classes of society, there exist distrust . . . misunderstanding. Everything is out of joint, everything has lost its foundation, discontent is everywhere." Yet within weeks he would make one more attempt to remove distrust and to restore the foundations by enlisting the help of the new Minister of the Interior, Ignatiev.

A man of uncertain views and unsteady temperament, Ignatiev had, as a diplomat, gone far in identifying the goals of Pan-Slavism with those of official policy; association with the cause and its advocates had led to his absorbing a large, though diluted, dose of a Slavophile brand of populist nationalism. Since the accession manifesto had announced no definite program beyond the repression of disloyal elements and the strengthening of autocracy, while at the same time incongruously promising to continue the great reforms of the previous reign, Ignatiev felt justified in adopting a superficially Slavophile course that would heal the breach between state and people. To that end, he promised to allow the participation of "local men" in the affairs of the administration and within a month summoned informed representatives of the public to discuss with him a number of questions concerning peasant life and economy. The gesture could hardly satisfy the demands of constitutionalists or remove the bad taste left by the harsh police measures instituted at almost the same time, but the new minister yearned for popularity and a place in the history books. This made him receptive when Aksakov, early in 1882, promised a way out of the impasse created by an undesirable reliance on repression and an impossible surrender to liberalism, a way that would put all the constitutions of the world in the shade without doing violence to national traditions: there would be a *zemskii sobor*, elected directly by the estates that history had sanctioned—peasants, merchants, gentry, and clergy. The presence in such an assembly of some thousand peasants would so clearly affirm the national and popular character of the autocracy and the devotion in which it was held that it would put an end to liberal, aristocratic, or revolutionary illusions without recourse to coërcion.

Ignatiev was delighted. He adopted Aksakov's proposal and presented, for the Czar's signature, a manifesto calling the assembly of three thousand deputies to meet in the old capital at the time of the coronation. Its wording gave rise to suspicions that Ignatiev and his inspirers were thinking of more than just a decorative addition to the coronation festivities, that they had in mind a permanent body to advise the czar on all important questions of state, including legislation. When Pobedonostsev got wind of what was going on, he sensed "revolution, the end of government and of Russia," mobilized all his influence, and, with the help of Katkov, succeeded in having the Aksakov-Ignatiev project defeated in the Council of Ministers and its ostensible author dismissed.

One other bond—anti-Semitism—linked these two men. The appearance of a virulent, largely nonreligious anti-Semitism among educated Russians was new and rather startling. That a man like Aksakov could accept the naïve and primitive notion of an international Jewish conspiracy aiming at world domination (he published an early version of the *Protocols of the Elders of Zion* in his paper *Rus*); that a Dostoevsky could believe that the Jew and his bank were the real, even the only power behind the facade of European politics—such things can only be signs of a perplexity that overwhelmed these and lesser men when new and incomprehensible social forces threatened all they held dear. They wished to believe that their ideal world of human dignity and honor, a stable and preindustrial way of life, could be saved from the cash nexus and the satanic mills and refused to see that even the elimination of the Jew would fail to hold up or reverse processes whose roots lay deeper than any perfidy of the Israelites. It was this failure of intellectual courage that showed the anti-Semitism of Aksakov in its true light, as another aspect of his political and social romanticism, a Utopia in which there were no Jews, no bourgeois, no bureaucrats or socialists to disturb the familial solidarity of the people and its natural leaders. In its delusion that such a state of harmony and well-being could be attained by further curtailing Jewish participation in the social and economic sphere, Russian anti-Semitism revealed itself as a variant of romantic populism which could, with Aksakov, look upon pogroms as acts of popular resistance against predatory exploiters, as an instinctive reaching out for social justice. The Jews, said Aksakov, had no one to blame but themselves, and for these prime exponents of capitalism to pose as victims of anarchy and socialism would gain them little sympathy.

But conservatives in and out of government were keenly aware of the risks to property and order from such primitive forms of social turbulence and wished to avoid all signs of official indulgence. When Ignatiev, in the Committee of Ministers, proposed far-reaching measures against Jews because they were "leeches who suck the blood of honest folk," two of his colleagues protested. The first major pogroms took place during Ignatiev's administration, and what was known of his attitude to Jews undoubtedly encouraged these and accounted for their less than prompt repression. The Minister of Finance, the same who had warned against the Turkish war, now raised his voice against encouraging or tolerating the plunder of Jews, for next it could turn against *kulaks*, then merchants and landowners. The end result would be the "most devastating socialism." Pogroms were not tolerated by Ignatiev's successor, Dmitry Tolstoy, though he had little liking for the "Hebrew leprosy" and harsh discrimination against Jews remained official policy. It was the major concession the government made to latter-day Slavophilism and the foremost legacy of the last third of the century to the militant Right.

The Russian government in the two decades after 1881, which straddle the reigns of Alexander III and Nicholas II, must surely be regarded as an extraordinary phenomenon in the history of modern Europe. Although its reputation for blackest reaction is well deserved, its conduct was guided by no overall conceptions and it represented no clearly discernible interests other than its own. If it reacted against the recent past by curbing local self-government, the press, the universities, and national and religious minorities, it neither could nor would completely undo the reforms of Alexander II. It also undermined its own efforts at securing stability by fostering the growth of industry and business, introducing the ferment of change into one sector of national life while trying to exclude it from others. The government behaved often in the fashion of a military occupation solely concerned with the maintenance of tranquillity and order. Indeed, from 1881 until the end of the old regime, much of the country was subjected to so-called temporary regulations (initially for three years) which suspended normal administrative and judicial processes in many areas and imposed conditions not far removed from martial law.

The two chief figures of reaction during this period, Tolstoy and Pobedonostsev, far from pursuing a positive political program, doubted that any course they chose would significantly affect the general drift of things. Pobedonostsev was not the Torquemada the foreign press painted. He was not a fanatic—if he had been, he might have found a cause and a following—but a skeptic, and his skepticism extended to allies and opponents alike. He was fearful of change, whatever its direction, and wished to reduce the activities of government to a minimum. A friend said of him that in the course of twenty years Pobedonostsev had not once given an indication of what he would put in place of the institutions and practices he anathemized. Konstantin Leontiev, the most consistently reactionary thinker of the period, who wanted to preserve Russia by freezing her in a Byzantine mold, denied that Pobedonostsev was genuinely reactionary, calling him "a watchman, an unventilated tomb, an 'innocent' old maid and nothing more." Tolstoy, also, lacked confidence that "nihilism" or the "Hebrew leprosy" could be stamped out; at best they could be contained, and although he was known as a champion of Orthodoxy and nationality, he had no intention of giving free rein either to the Church or to nationalist passions. "My entire program," he said, "can be summed up in one word: 'Order.'" The measures taken to restore the gentry to its position of buttress of the state were stillborn; they were incapable of returning to that class either its economic power or its social prestige, or of insuring the political reliability of all its strata. To have satisfied the agrarians would have meant a full retreat from the striving for financial solvency and industrial power associated with the name of Sergei Witte, Minister of Finance from 1892 to 1903, and a further mounting of discontent among industrialists and businessmen. The monarchy could make partial concessions to one or another interest group, but it was barred from following a program that would allow it to appear as the impartial arbiter of conflict and the embodiment of the national will.

All that remained was a policy of naked force which, although successful for almost two decades in preventing the resurgence of organized revolutionary opposition, also silenced the potential Right and prevented its further development as a distinct movement or ideology. The conspiratorial "Holy Brotherhood," formed in 1881 to protect the life of the czar and to infiltrate the revolutionary camp, was soon closed down by Tolstoy as a seat of "noxious liberalism" and a dangerous nuisance that interfered with the organs of the regular police and, by its very existence, implied the incompetence of the state machinery. A later attempt to found a "patriotic" society failed for want of police permission, and, in 1897, a journal of similar patriotic persuasion, the *Russkoe Oboz-renie* ("Russian Review"), ended a precarious existence of seven years. "At that time," wrote one of their number, "those who represented conservative thought in Russia found it very difficult to express their thoughts and sentiments." Radicals and liberals, forming illegal parties in the years 1898–1903, had no such difficulty and were finding a sympathetic response even among the respectable elements of the population. Apprehension rose that the cumbersome and inflexible apparatus of government was not equipped to deal with a reviving opposition.

But it was not until late 1900 that well-placed members of St. Petersburg society founded the *Russkoe Sobranie* ("Russian Assembly") for the avowedly nonpolitical purpose of counteracting the "spreading cosmopolitanism of the upper classes" by liberating and awakening national feelings; yet even such an unimpeachable aim made V. K. Plehve, an official of the Ministry of the Interior and its future head, hesitate as to whether he should close down the group or join its ranks. He chose the latter course, and while his presence and that of many officers and officials guaranteed the Assembly's "safe" character, it also raised doubts about its independence. One of its members, the Slavophile editor Sergei Shara-pov, accused the Assembly of being "the essence of St. Petersburg police patriotism." Though it was the first public organization to speak out in defense of autocracy, it could hardly fill the need for a popular answer to the movement of protest rising in the country. The predominantly conservative and quasi-official complexion of the Assembly was never to change very much, despite the fact that a number of patriots of radical temperament, anti-Semitic rabble-rousers and journalists like P. A. Krushevan (one of the instigators of the Kishinev pogrom of 1903), P. F. Bulatsel, and A. I. Dubrovin and V. M. Purishkevich (future leaders of the Right) began to grace the membership lists along with archbishops, generals, members of the Council of State, and senior civil servants. Poorly attended evenings of Russian culture—lectures, dramatic readings, poetry and song recitals—could hardly convince sophisticated devotees of alien ways that their tastes were a form of disloyalty or compete with radical agitators and their more immediate appeals to the concrete grievances of workers and peasants.

The inadequacy of such a program was self-evident, and consequently the range of the Assembly's activities expanded somewhat in 1902–1903 with the publication of popular brochures, the opening of provincial branches, and a student circle. But the governing council in St. Petersburg was so concerned over the possible infiltration of hostile elements that it limited the admission of new members and the chartering of additional branches. Most meetings were closed and there was apparently more fear of infection by untrustworthy outsiders than hope of influencing the public mood. If the assumption was correct that dedication to Orthodoxy, Autocracy, and Nationality was strongest among the masses of town and country and that the seeds of doubt and rebellion were planted in their minds by upper-class renegades, then the restricted approach of the Assembly had at least the merit of consistency. To attack the infection at its source, to educate the bureaucracy, to lend moral support to the disheartened advocates of firmness, to provide a rallying point for them and demonstrate that the intellectual domination of the opposition was not unchallenged—these were logical as well as realistic goals for such an organization. For efforts toward these ends, the *Moscow News* hailed the Assembly as a welcome note of dissent in the liberal chorus of the period, but its three thousand members, although they may have taken comfort and courage from each other, preached mainly to the converted.

Only after the general strike of October, 1905, and the creation of entirely new conditions of political contest by the October Manifesto did the Assembly abandon its self-imposed restraints without, however, being able to adjust to the new style of politics. It failed in its attempt to weld the many like-minded groups, which had sprung up in the course of that year, into a solid front in time for the elections to the first Duma, and it had to make way for more militant successors, especially the Union of Russian People, the most successful of the parties of the Right in attracting mass support. As the Assembly had, before 1905, performed the task of identifying and preparing the leaders of the new Right, so it continued afterward to serve as a link between them and their more conservative and respectable well-wishers. The latter had come to realize the need for allies and, for a time, were willing to countenance methods that in an earlier period would have been considered little short of revolutionary.

The adoption of such methods by men who embodied authority in their persons and functions is a measure of the perplexity felt in the face of new dangers and forces with which experience had not equipped them to deal. To the sporadic and violent outbursts of peasant discontent, student riots, and liberal petitions for civil and political rights, a growing wave of labor unrest was added in the late nineties. Nicholas II might try to minimize this new source of disturbance by describing strikes as the invention of educated Europe, but educated Europe, as he was resentfully aware, had so deeply penetrated his realm in the form of factories, ideas, and techniques that the working class was bound to increase rather than decrease in numbers, organized strength, and political consciousness. Industrialization, fostered by the state, had called this new antagonist into being; there was no wishing him away. In this indisputable fact the chief of the Moscow Okhrana, the secret police colonel and erstwhile radical, Zubatov, saw a unique opportunity not only to take the wind out of the sails of socialist agitators, but also to build a bridge between the monarchy and the people. To this end he organized, in 1901, a union of industrial workers in Moscow, and subsequently in other cities, with the approval of the Czar, the hesitant assent of the Ministry of the Interior, the wholehearted coöperation of the Governor-General of Moscow, the Grand Duke Sergei, and over the violent objections of Witte and other members of the government.

The Minister of Finance, who for many years had been trying to win the confidence of the Russian business community and foreign investors, was appalled by the Grand Duke's and Zubatov's "police socialism" and complained to the Czar that even Millerand and Jaurès would not have dared such an open defiance of common sense and public order. Neither of the two chief sponsors of this elaborate and rather unusual form of company unionism aimed at the socialist transformation of Russia, but even their more modest aims were far-reaching by the standards of the time and place, and, more important, seemed to place the seal of official approval upon the activities of Zubatovists and Marxists alike. To employers it could be little comfort that they were struck under such high auspices; they would probably have preferred to deal with an opponent, even if he were Marxist, whose meetings and organization were not protected and managed by the secret police who also printed the strikers' leaflets and allowed them to defy their bosses with impunity.

At the initiation of the experiment there had, of course, been no mention of the possibility of industrial warfare; the Zubatov unions were simply to set forth the workers' needs, take only peaceful and legal steps for their satisfaction through voluntary agreement with employers—avoiding harm to property or production—and help the government in its efforts to meet the just aspirations of the workers. There were also to be libraries and reading rooms, adult education classes, social and cultural evenings. But as its enemies predicted, the movement developed larger aims and stimulated appetites for such things as the eight-hour day, wage determination by law, profit-sharing, mutual aid funds, labor exchanges, and consumer coöperatives. Zubatov, a man of intellectual pretensions, may have dreamt even greater dreams; in later years he claimed that he had envisioned a social monarchy, based on the progressive "self-organization of the people" into professional and other corporate entities, as the only alternative to the already discredited idea of representative government.

The Grand Duke's thoughts, if he had any ideas beyond the preservation of order and a military man's dislike for moneybags, must have harked back to 1861 when a czar had taken the side of the people against the privileged orders. In Moscow, one of his subordinates had told him, the oppression of the workers by their masters was worse than the fate of the former serfs. It was in keeping with such notions that, on the anniversary of the emancipation in February, 1902, his Imperial Highness sponsored and took part in a demonstration and memorial meeting of fifty thousand workers at the monument of Alexander II and ordered their employers to pay the day's wages. It was a truly grand-ducal gesture, but it was both illegal and ill advised.

Among those who did not share the Grand Duke's confidence in the magical and pacifying effect of imperial patronage there was worried talk of anarchy in the Moscow factories and dire warnings that mass meetings arranged from above would only train workers for the real thing and increase ferment among them. In the summer of 1903 these predictions were borne out when Odessa police had to put down strikers organized by a Zubatov assistant who had lost control over his creation. After that, Zubatov was disgraced and his movement declined rapidly—to give only one more ghastly reminder of its existence on "Bloody Sunday," January 22, 1905, the opening act of the Revolution. On that day, an enormous procession of workers, having marched to the palace of their czar to protest their devotion and their faith that he would help and protect them, was fired upon by troops. The marchers were led by one Father Gapon, a priest who had headed one of the "police unions" and seems still, until that fateful moment, to have been animated by the ideal of a popular monarchism.

"In Moscow," the chief organ of the liberals, published abroad, had stated in 1903, "socialist measures are being carried out by the Chief of Police and the 'Moscow News' is proclaiming as official policy that the autocracy will . . . by-pass the bourgeois era and usher in the epoch of socialism." The *Zubatovshchina* was neither socialism nor, as one of its sympathizers asserted some twenty years later, fascism. Yet it was a form of rightism, a tacit admission by its originators that the government of which they were a part was very nearly isolated; theirs was a confused groping for a way out of that isolation. Like the leaders of the opposition, they were reaching out for contact with the masses who were becoming a factor in Russian political life. Yet the advocates of such an "opening to the Right" were never able to carry the whole of the administration with them in a consistent line of policy and, as a result, relations between the government and the Right in the years after 1905 were troubled by ambivalence on both sides.

The closing down of the Zubatov unions did not end strikes or still the clamor for reform. Pressed on all sides, involved in a disastrous war with Japan, and made aware of the general contempt felt for it in the aftermath of "Bloody Sunday," the government next tried the road of concessions. An imperial rescript of February 18, 1905, to Minister of the Interior Bulygin, provided that elected representatives participate, in a purely advisory capacity, in the drafting of legislation. A simultaneous decree to the senate assured every subject of his right to be heard by the crown and invited suggestions for the improvement of the public welfare. Still another imperial proclamation of the same date condemned the attacks that had been launched against the legal and religious bases of the state and asked for public aid in the battle against disorder and disloyalty. The limited and contradictory nature of these pronouncements left liberals and radicals dissatisfied, but their enemies at last felt sanctioned to bestir themselves. "Only after the rescript to Bulygin," a member of the Russian Assembly noted in his memoirs, "did the conservative elements of the Russian public realize that in order to apply their ideas and to preserve Russia from forced and untimely experiments . . . they would have to take a stand for their opinions and . . . unite into political organizations."

But what ideas and opinions could conservatives agree on and still hope to find a hearing beyond their own very restricted circles? It might be true that the broad masses, especially the peasantry, retained their devotion to the czar and had no wish to trade his

rule for that of an impersonal parliament dominated by professional politicians. Yet popular indifference to the political goals of
radicals and liberals implied no willingness to forego basic social
and economic demands, and these the conservatives could hardly
satisfy. It is for this reason that such organizations as the Ote-
chestvennyi Soiuz ("Fatherland Union"), formed in April, 1905,
by a group of highly placed officials, failed to attract much of a
following. Indeed, during most of its year-long existence the Union
did not even try to step before the public with a political program,
but confined itself to private discussions, to delegations assuring
the czar of their loyalty, and to demands that the franchise for
the proposed consultative assembly be restricted, unequal, and indirect. This advocacy of an extreme application of the class principle was largely ignored by the government in favor of a system of
voting (still by estates) that gave the presumably loyal peasantry
a wider representation than the Fatherland Union was willing to
concede. The peasants were also forgiven state debts and taxes,
and the disabilities of certain religious minorities were eased. But
such mild remedies were no longer adequate to break the fever
that seemed to have the country in its grip.

The predicament in which the authorities and conservatives in
general found themselves was seen most clearly by the publisher
and editor of the *Moscow News*, V. A. Gringmut: it was impossible
to outbid radicals and constitutionalists; no amount of piecemeal
reform would be satisfactory but would only whet appetites
further. Moreover, whatever reforms might actually be justified
could not be carefully considered and prepared under existing
conditions; above all, no changes must be conceded as a result of
revolutionary pressure. The conclusion was that victory over Japan
and the full restoration of law and order must precede any reforms.
Even then, the main goal must be the still greater strengthening
of the unlimited autocratic power.

Such a formula, put forward three days after the Bulygin rescript, had at least the merit of consistency and firmness. For it
proposed to a government divided in its counsels a decisive course
of action which might for the moment take the place of a program
and give heart to the administration's sympathizers. Gringmut

must have been the first to realize that neither the Czar nor Bulygin would readily adopt his formula. A government capable of rousing itself to firmness needed no exhortation to do so; nor, while the Japanese war lasted, did it have the means for firmness. Awareness of this fact colored Gringmut's conduct as it did that of the Monarchist party for which he was laying the foundations in March, 1905. The function of this party was to be less a political movement competing with others for public support than a pressure group designed to prevent weakness and passivity in the state apparatus. Yet the only way this could now be done was to shape public opinion, to become a political party in the true sense of the word, to descend into the political arena and run all the risks of a broadened public awareness and participation.

This dilemma was never resolved by the Monarchist party, which was rigorously logical in the acceptance of autocracy and all that implied—the czar as the nation's only law-giver and representative, and a strong and efficient bureaucracy as the executor of his will. This admitted of no invocation of vague Slavophile principles—such as the fullness of power to the czar, the freedom of opinion to the people—for they would have conflicted with the party's opposition to any kind of representative body, even the most innocuous, such as a *zemskii sobor*. Nor could the great landowners and prominent grandees in the party's leadership have embraced the Slavophile denunciation of the fissures in Russian society. Gringmut, much more of an activist than his conservative colleagues, chafed under the restraints to which his party's program condemned him, but all he could do was to ask for a dictatorship exercised in the name of the czar, in the hope, presumably, of freeing the administration for decisive action of some kind. Lacking that, he was reduced for a time to calling in a general way for demonstrations of patriotism on the part of the czar's loyal subjects, with the aim of stiffening the government's determination and warning its enemies. On February 24, the *Moscow News* appealed to all true Russians to close ranks, to heed their sovereign's call, and to rally for the fight against rebellion, treason, and folly. More practically, they were asked to make public declaration of their loyalty to the monarch, to establish contact with like-minded men in all parts of the country, and to unite in the name of nation, czar, and Church.

The veritable mushroom growth of right-wing groups in dozens of towns all over the country in spring and summer, 1905, was less a response to Gringmut's appeal than a confused outburst of popular resentment against change as well as on behalf of change; it was at one and the same time a sign of resistance against the liberalization of the political order and an instinctive reaching out for social justice and economic relief by artisans, peasants, and small traders who believed that their class enemies were fighting the autocracy for selfish motives. Here the guardians of absolutism, having at last come to accept the inadequacy of their own resources, saw the foot soldiers who might be mobilized to come to their aid. Clergy, local police, and other agencies of government supported, encouraged, or tolerated street demonstrations and pogroms against Jews, liberals, socialists, students, and other "traitors." They also helped in the preparation and distribution of leaflets, especially in the countryside, hoping in this fashion to deflect discontent into these safer channels. But these People's Unions, Leagues of Struggle against Sedition, and patriotic brotherhoods and societies were almost without exception ephemeral and, in the absence of a common program and positive purpose, disintegrated quickly. Even now, the central authorities were wary of driving out the devil by using Beelzebub in any sustained manner, though they might give him occasional employment. However, these bands reappeared briefly and violently after the issuance of the October Manifesto, which granted civil liberties and an elected assembly with legislative rights, and they then became known as Black Hundreds, a term later extended to the more permanent organizations of the militant Right.

Although a liberal journal asked whether the Black Hundreds were not perhaps a revival of the horrors of the Pugachev rebellion, and the majority of conservatives remained fearful of directing mass hostility against the well-to-do, the educated, and the powerful, whatever their politics or religion, Gringmut took hope from these manifestations of popular passion. There had been the hint of a summons to direct action in the February appeal of his newspaper, and although, as a proponent of "order first," he should have disavowed violence, he, like Katkov before him, greeted it in July as the awakening of Russia, as a sign that the healthy forces of national life were finally looking to their own defense. The Monarchist party, in its program of October 15, 1905, called for the application of lawful means to repress revolution. Gringmut, however, both before and after that date, called on the people to rise in defense of order, organized demonstrations, and wanted to wrest control of the Moscow streets from the socialists with the help of draymen, porters, and toughs. Temperamentally, perhaps ideologically as well, Gringmut was prepared to leave behind the caution and reserve characteristic of Russian conservatives and reactionaries. Not deeply rooted in the upper class himself, this rightist of the extreme Right (as the conservative *New Times*, with some exaggeration, called him), seemed ready to turn demagogue, willing and able to stir the masses with his considerable oratorical talent. By the time of his death in September, 1907, he had moved quite far in that direction. He collaborated with the radical Right (the Union of Russian People), addressing peasants in the provinces and workers in the towns, and in their joint meetings hailed Katkov, Aksakov, and even the older Slavophiles as apostles of the national cause. But he did not carry his party with him. Its leaders cautioned him against further fanning popular passions; its program took no account of the cry for political reform, but defended the bureaucracy along with the czar, and stood for the preservation of privilege, keeping the party weak and Gringmut ineffective. The formula through which the inchoate forces of the Right could coalesce and make their weight felt had yet to be found.

The Soiuz russkikh liudei ("Union of Russian Men"), founded in Moscow in April, 1905, came much closer to the discovery of such a formula than had the Monarchist party or its predecessors. Although no more successful than these in building an organizational network, and equally burdened with ranks and titles in its leadership, it did offer a program and a style of political discourse more likely to attract a wide following than the stand-pat phrases of the monarchists. Those who formulated the program of the Union, in particular the editor and publisher of *Russkoe Delo* ("The Russian Cause") and *Pakhar* ("The Plowman"), Sergei Sharapov, assumed an identity of interests on the part of the agrarian majority of the population, landlords and peasants alike, that made them willing and eager to give organized expression to that majority. They welcomed the imperial rescript of February 18 and saw it as an opportunity for the most truly Russian strata of Russian society to circumvent arrogant bureaucrats recruited from a cosmopolitan intelligentsia or upper bourgeoisie. They exhorted the gentry, clergy, merchants, and peasants to organize in their guilds, assemblies, or parishes and to unite on a nationwide basis, without regard to social differences.

The goals of the Union of Russian Men may be described as a kind of Tory democracy in Slavophile dress. Although as much opposed as the Monarchists to fundamental changes in the Russian polity, which was to be preserved from further alien innovations and cleansed of those that already had crept in, the Union viewed the historical principles on which state and monarchy rested in a different light. Where the Monarchist party looked back to the reign of Alexander III, the Russian Men took their inspiration from an idealized Muscovy. Russia and autocracy were indeed synonymous and indivisible, but to accept and even to affirm this identity implied no automatic endorsement of the present bureaucratic regime which fostered a competitive, industrial, money-ridden, Westernized society in which the precapitalist classes found it increasingly difficult to maintain their social and economic life. It was to these classes that the Union's appeals were primarily addressed.

Debt-ridden peasants and gentry, small property owners and provincial businessmen, petty traders, unemployed artisans and others unable to find a niche for themselves in industry, government, or the professions were expected to respond to the Union's attacks on the causes of the country's ills. These were, the Union said, the *chinovniks,* ostensibly the czar's servants but actually the wall between people and czar which had kept him from learning of the nation's needs; the domination of the country's economy by international capital and the "stock exchange," personified by

Witte, high industrial tariffs, and the gold standard; the loss of the people's right to run their own affairs in parish and village in the face of an overweening concentration of power in the hands of St. Petersburg officialdom; and, as a source and symptom of all this, the pernicious Jewish influence in every sphere of Russian life, but especially in education, banking, and the press. The remedies suggested were as simple as the analysis. Restoration of the close communion between ruler and ruled through an advisory Assembly of the Land would also return a true Russian autocracy and do away with the bureaucratic, imperial absolutism that had grown in its place since Peter's day. The present financial system, favoring industry and tied to the international money market, would be replaced by one based on national *assignats* and the availability of cheap credit. Local self-government would be freed from excessive tutelage by the central administration, and state influence over the Orthodox Church would be reduced by abolition of the Holy Synod (an arm of the government), reëstablishment of the patriarchate, and, locally, introduction of the elective principle by the laity. Church reform would be prepared and carried out by a council (*sobor*), which would play in the religious life of the nation the role assigned to the Assembly of the Land in the political sphere, and which would bring Church and people closer together. Jews, and the non-Russian peoples of the borderland, would be forever excluded from the public life of the national community.

Such a combination of antibureaucratic, anticosmopolitan, antiurban, anti-Semitic, anticapitalist, and antiliberal notes had never yet been sounded quite so openly and consistently. When, in addition, Sharapov's newspapers kept referring to "the people," to the "80 million plowmen" who wanted neither political power nor alien constitutions and parliaments, the impression was created of a right-wing populism that seemed to some observers to be holding out a hand to the Social Revolutionaries.

It is questionable whether the populism of the Union of Russian Men was genuine; but that this was the most radical voice yet heard on the Right is shown by the fact that even Gringmut's *Moscow News*, though finding the Union more to its liking than any other political group, took fright at its "radicalism" and deplored the "liberalism" of its program. Nor did the Moscow newspaper and the Monarchist party match the Union's rabid anti-Semitism, and the Union remained for the time being the only rightist movement that tried to reach the lower levels of society by assuming a militantly popular aspect. There were leaflets, public meetings (even one especially for workers in St. Petersburg), and, at the time of the October general strike, appeals to all loyal citizens of Moscow to assemble in their parish churches and form themselves into committees and bands (*druzhiny*) for the restoration of order. In November, the Union of Russian Men also made the first attempt to consolidate the forces of the Right at a conference attended by some three hundred delegates, including those of the newly founded Union of Landowners and the Monarchist party, who had been driven closer to the "plebeian" or "democratic" rightists by the fear of revolution. The conferees agreed to petition the czar for a *zemskii sobor*, rather than the promised legislative Duma, called on the people to take the place of striking postal workers, and set up a council to coördinate the activities of the participating organizations.

None of these steps had lasting or concrete results. They came too late, when the government, now headed by Witte, had already determined to move in the opposite direction. There were, of course, men at court and in the administration who disapproved of the October Manifesto and of Witte, soon to be accused of having extorted it from a reluctant czar; but though these men might look with favor upon the continued rowdyism of the Black Hundreds, they were forced to realize that pogroms and street violence were poor preparation for the political contests ahead. In this fundamentally changed situation, the existing formations of the Right were ill-equipped to function. Their great problem and their great opportunity was to make contact with the masses who were soon going to be an electorate; for this, new techniques, new men, and new organizations were needed.

The founding of the Union of Russian People (Soiuz russkogo naroda, or URP) in a meeting hall provided by the Russian Assembly in St. Petersburg on October 22, 1905, was an attempt to respond to these needs by forming an "all-class" party of the Right.

A broadly based, million-voiced front of all true Russian folk, free of an aristocratic or bureaucratic taint, independent of the government and of vested interests—such was the image the propagandists of the new movement wished to project. It is hardly surprising that their claims were met with skepticism and that there were those who regarded the URP as little more than a refurbished version of Zubatovism. But although the head of the political section of the department of police appears to have given his blessing to this enterprise initiated by a Petersburg physician, A. I. Dubrovin, there is no evidence to suggest that it was in any meaningful sense of the word "created" by the police or any other agency of government. If certain officials aided the URP in the early months of its existence, they expressed individual sympathies rather than governmental policy. Even the Czar's acceptance of the URP badge from one of its deputations, aside from conferring a measure of respectability upon its donors, was without immediate concrete benefit. It was only when the elections to the first Duma in the spring of 1906 returned a solid antigovernmental majority and not a single unmistakable rightist that Witte's policy of governmental abstention from party politics was abandoned. Aid from "the higher spheres" would soon constitute the Union's major source of funds. After the dismissal of Witte in April, 1906, Stolypin, first as Minister of the Interior and then as prime minister, began reluctantly to subsidize the Right, along with the more moderate Octobrists. Nonetheless, ministerial support was never to be reliable or adequate, never the expression of a definite commitment, and although it helped eventually to moderate the extremism of the Right, it did not tame it fully.

Whatever the exact circumstances surrounding its origin may have been—and, like much of its history, they remain obscure—friend and foe agreed that the URP represented a novel phenomenon on the political scene which could not be dismissed as simply a hired auxiliary of reaction. It had, it is true, inscribed the traditional devices of Orthodoxy, Autocracy, and Nationality on its banners, and it spoke sternly of discipline and order, but it developed a momentum of its own which brought it into conflict with its supposed employers. The very existence of the URP betrayed a belief that the state was no longer a healthy organism and that its guardians could not be trusted to save it. This was now the task of the truly Russian elements of the population, and these, it was implied, were not to be found near the top of the social ladder. Whether by accident or design, rank, title, and aristocratic lineage were inconspicuous in the leadership roster of the URP, and none of its prominent figures belonged to the country's social or political elite.

Dr. Dubrovin, the Union's founder, was a shadowy figure of unknown antecedents, a physician who was said to have given up a poor (or rich) medical practice to devote himself to politics. He proved in the end to be the most intransigent of the party's leaders, in spite of his initial links with the police, and when other Unionists arrived at some kind of accommodation with the powers, he refused to concede that the government's recovery of firm control eliminated the need for his special brand of violence and vigilance. The revolution, he insisted, had merely fled from the streets into the palaces and mansions. It is likely that more generous handouts would have made him more tractable. His associate and rival-to-be, Vladimir Purishkevich, had a more subtle intelligence and a degree of tactical flexibility which allowed him, in 1908, to accept the changes brought by the October Manifesto and to use the Duma as a sounding board for his own views. The grandson of a Bessarabian village priest, Purishkevich was a landowner by social category; a former civil servant by profession; a novelist and author of patriotic and scurrilous verse by avocation; and a scandalist by preference. Wherever he appeared, on the floor of the Duma or in a German spa, he created an uproar by his vulgar and hysterical outbursts, most often against the Jews. Besides these two there were lawyers, journalists, an engineer, a part-time university lecturer, an occasional priest or merchant, and even an impecunious prince to make up the chief staff of the URP, and all of them were types, according to Witte, whose company decent people would shun.

The success of the Union of Russian People, as compared with the older organizations of the Right, was attributable, however, less to the character of its leadership than to that of its following.

The social composition of its membership is impossible to determine accurately from the available data, but even its Marxist enemies agreed that, besides the *Lumpenproletariat*, disgruntled bourgeois, and backward provincials, it was for a time able to attract genuine peasant and proletarian elements. It never made any lasting nation-wide inroads among these two classes, yet it did manage for much of its life to retain a popular aspect by the studied coarseness of its language and conduct, by its anti-intellectualism, and its willingness to employ social demagogy. In politics, too, the URP showed that it was sensitive to the mood of the country. Though it warned against viewing the October Manifesto as a constitutional document that in any way diminished or limited the sovereign's power or sanctioned a parliamentary regime, it welcomed the promise of popular participation in politics and in the work of legislation. Autocracy, as its past history had demonstrated, was fully compatible with an assembly of elected people's representatives and could only draw strength from their concern for the general welfare. In loyal union with the supreme power, such an assembly would facilitate the closer supervision of a bureaucracy that was equally distrusted by czar and people for its liberal leanings, its arbitrary disregard for the interests of state and nation, and its links with big business.

A frontal attack on the Manifesto would, in any event, have been fatal to the URP, not only stamping it as irrevocably re-actionary but also isolating it from the stirrings of hope and the high expectations that followed the Czar's promises. Anyway, the Union declared, it was not the civil liberties the sovereign had so graciously bestowed, but their misuse by subversive elements that threatened Russia's dissolution and her enslavement to the dark powers of Jews and Freemasons. To combat the perversion of Russian freedoms into parliamentary license, the Union declared that it wished to unite all true Russians devoted to czar and fatherland, whatever their rank or station, on the following principles: Russia one and indivisible; the union of czar and nation through elected people's representatives; a Duma enjoying direct access to the sovereign and the right to interpellate ministers and control their official conduct; legal accountability of public officials for abuses of authority; strict limitation of Jewish representation in the Duma to three deputies; the fullest application of the civil liberties granted and their safeguarding from administrative as well as revolutionary violation; firm protection of all private and public property, and the avoidance of all violent means of political struggle. The URP also promised to work for an increase in the holdings of land-poor peasants, expressed concern for the laboring classes in general, deplored the hard plight of industrial workers, and suggested the legal determination of wages and working conditions.

Although later events made it appear that Union acceptance of the October Manifesto might have been only a tactical maneuver, at the time its leaders gave no sign of regarding it as anything but an expression of the imperial will to which they gladly submitted. They conceded the need for certain basic reforms to make the voice of the people heard in the councils of government; they acquiesced in the Duma, believed that the broad franchise would work in their favor, and paid some regard to the grievances of workers and peasants. Such a platform was hardly striking for its radicalism, but it was in rather sharp contrast with the more inflexible positions of most of the Right. It is this fact that allowed the URP to become the strongest, the best organized, and the largest of the right-wing parties, with more than two hundred branches and, according to a most cautious estimate, as many as twenty thousand members. Many who felt condemned to impotence by the negativism or narrowness of other groups, such as the Monarchist party or the Union of Landowners, gravitated to the URP. By the spring of 1907 its preëminence was recognized when a national congress of some five hundred delegates of right-wing organizations designated the URP's governing council as the agent for unifying and, in fact, leading their joint forces. URP had for all practical purposes become synonymous with Right, a force to be reckoned with, the only one, besides the army and the police, to have taken the field against liberals and revolutionaries.

It was largely the strengthening of the left wing in the second Duma (April to June, 1907), bringing it from 124 to 216 deputies, and the fears this inspired, rather than URP successes in the electoral arena (this time the entire Right sent only 10 deputies), that led to its acceptance as head of the counterrevolutionary camp. Neither the conduct nor the language of the URP could have inspired much confidence in the reliability of such a rambunctious ally. "To be a conservative at this time," wrote Boris Nikolskii, one of the few intellectuals in the Union's leadership, "means to be at least a radical or, rather, a revolutionary." Unionist speakers, newspapers, and pamphlets now denounced the Duma as a would-be parliament and the October Manifesto as the work of the diabolical Count Witte. Though URP backers welcomed these attacks, even its less fastidious supporters must have been given pause by simultaneous Black Hundred violence in the streets, by the murder of political opponents by URP agents and their attempted assassination of Witte, by pogroms, and by yellow-shirted bands that terrorized the entire city of Odessa for three days. Big business, banks, and syndicates came under verbal fire. There were demands to equalize the peasants' legal status with that of other classes, promises to facilitate their purchase of additional land, and, for the workers, the prospect of a shorter workday, state insurance, and coöperative workshops. It all made a senior official of the Ministry of the Interior, which helped to pay for such activities, wonder whether there was much to choose from between Right and Left. He recalled in his memoirs that both had promised the distribution of private property to the masses, with the Right wishing it to be done in the name of the autocrat as the representative of the nation and the defender of the poor.

These recollections were not entirely accurate—at least not as far as the Union's stated goals were concerned—but there were URP branches and members, especially in the provinces, who arrived at similar conclusions. Even if the social and economic radicalism of the URP did not need to be taken entirely at face value, its warning to Stolypin that the fate of Russia would be decided either by the extreme Left or the extreme Right—"there can be no middle ground"—offered little reassurance to the prime minister, who wished to steer a course that would keep him somewhat to the right of center and also gain him the support of moderates on selected issues.

The contradictions and difficulties in which the radical stance and the genuinely popular complexion of its membership landed the URP, became painfully obvious at the very Congress which, in April, 1907, formally sanctioned its primacy of the Right. When the delegates of the Union and allied organizations, of student clubs and workingmen's guilds, turned to the discussion of the program to be adopted, the congress was barely kept from disintegrating. The peasant members, spurred on by the fanatic monk Iliodor, demanded the compulsory alienation of private lands and proposed a delegation to the czar to submit this demand. Worker delegates succeeded in having their demands and grievances incorporated in a resolution that had to be carefully edited behind the scenes to cleanse it of its socialist overtones. It became evident that most of the rightist leaders were not prepared to go that far and they avoided a direct confrontation of the agrarian question only by a compromise which admitted the need for more land but reserved a final solution to the monarch and a *zemskii sobor*. In the meantime, the administration was asked to keep peasant lands from passing into the possession of other classes, ethnic non-Russians, and Jews, and to assist resettlement and extend liberal agrarian credits. Respect was duly paid to the village commune, the only safeguard against the growth of a landless proletariat, but this position was soon to be abandoned in favor of Stolypin's "wager on the strong and the sober"—the breakup of the commune for the purpose of creating a prosperous class of smallholders. Only Dubrovin and a few rightist deputies of the third Duma clung to the communal village, claiming that Jews and Freemasons alone could take any joy in seeing this buttress of autocracy and historical embodiment of social justice destroyed.

The resolution adopted on the working class acknowledged the workers' situation as being especially difficult, deplored unemployment as well as poor conditions in shops and factories, and stressed the need for old-age pensions, factory legislation, and inspection. In the unequal battle between capital and labor, big business and small, the state and the URP were to assist the Russian worker and craftsman by the organization of marketing coöperatives, the provision of credit, mutual aid societies, and remedial legislation. Russian entrepreneurs were to be protected from the competition of foreigners and Jews, the state bank made independent of the international money market, and its directorate expanded to include representatives of small as well as large firms. How precisely these goals were to be attained or what the content of the proposed legislation would be were not indicated. Certainly, the setting up of "true Russian" consumer shops and the economic boycott of Jews would have little effect in protecting the victims of a burgeoning capitalism or in bringing about its transformation.

When the second Duma was dissolved by Stolypin and an electoral law imposed by decree, which drastically reduced the franchise among workers, peasants, and national minorities, the Right was relieved of having to respond to the social and economic grievances of the masses. If the URP still spoke of the peasant need for land and the plight of workers and employees (especially in the western and southwestern provinces where landlords were Poles and shopkeepers Jews), it was equally insistent that the rights of other classes and "the unshakable rights of property" be respected. From then on, the vague anticapitalism of the Union was more and more exclusively directed against the Jews, and anti-Semitism, that "socialism of fools" (Bebel), became its major stock-in-trade. Its increasing conservatism was also reflected in the conduct of the 51 deputies of the extreme Right who made up 11.5 per cent of the third Duma's (1907-1912) membership. These deputies were still capable of shrill denunciations of Jewish or liberal infiltration of the schools and the press, of "liberal" or "constitutional" ministers—the Duma, after all, retained the right of legislation which Stolypin vowed to uphold if it proved coöperative—but most of them tired of being always in the opposition and found it possible to coöperate on many domestic issues with the government and the so-called moderate Right and Center of the Duma.

Irritants there remained, and the deputies of the URP continued to parade their uncompromising extremism—"To the right of me there is only the wall" (Purishkevich)—and their contempt for the deliberative process by catcalls and interruptions. But their main targets were now the Jews, the national minorities, the detractors of the army and the monarchy and all those who wanted to convert the Duma into a genuine parliament and Russia into a country where all enjoyed equal rights of citizenship. These were not issues that would lead to serious conflict with the government, and rightist criticism was shifted largely to questions of foreign policy. Here, fears of unrest in the event of war, and ideological distaste for Russia's Western allies, coincided with resentment over Britain's hostility to Russian expansion in Central Asia and the Near East to make the Right wish for closer ties with Germany— or at least the avoidance of risks in the Balkans incurred in the name of an emotional Pan-Slavism. In an ironic reversal of roles, liberals and moderates were now more likely to be the heirs of Aksakov's Pan-Slavism and the successful advocates of an active Russian role in Europe than were the rightists who invoked his name.

In the years after 1908, the URP gradually lost the dynamism, the unity, and the mass appeal it had briefly shown before the government recovered strength and nerve under the firm guidance of Stolypin. Its leaders had come to realize that politics could no longer be conducted in the old way, but their recognition of the need for new tactics was not matched by the insight that these would be fruitless without a new content of ideas. The rightists were debarred by their very successes from building upon the foundations laid in the years after 1905, the more so as these successes were achieved by other hands. If the virtual coup d'etat by which Stolypin illegally changed the electoral law had not made the last two Dumas nearly as coöperative as the first two had been recalcitrant, if the revolutionary forces had not been beaten back, or if the Czar had become a genuinely constitutional monarch, the Right's freedom of action would have been greatly enlarged. It would then have been able to reëxamine—indeed, it would have been forced to reëxamine—many of its basic positions, particularly the commitment to autocracy, its intimate identification with Orthodoxy, and, at least for tactical purposes, its rejection of a genuinely representative government. The URP, since it wished to draw adherents from all sectors of society and gave expression to this wish in its social and economic program, was especially hampered by these commitments. Its prospects might have been better if the revolution it fought so bitterly had gained a more conclusive

victory. In a full-fledged parliamentary regime, with all its probable confusion, contention, and almost inevitable crises, and freed
of the necessity of defending the autocracy (which meant, unhappily, defending Nicholas II), the Union's call for order, social
discipline, and national unity might have been more readily heeded.

In spite of the show of intransigence that the URP made, it
never broke completely or decisively with the government of
Nicholas II and its essential conservatism, thus revealing a fundamental uncertainty about its role and nature. Its willingness to embrace street violence, individual terror, and social demagogy had
frightened conservatives, though it did not lead to a cutting of
all ties with the administration. The latter's aid helped the URP
and, after the URP split in 1909, helped its successor organizations
to remain in being when support in the country dwindled, to make
certain gains in the fourth Duma elections (1912), and to continue to play a role in localities of mixed population where national and religious conflicts embittered existing political differences. But this assistance also imposed restraints and a stigma
that played a part in keeping the movement from recovering its
independent strength and vitality. The government, divided in itself, especially after the assassination of Stolypin in 1911, assisted
the URP but accepted its support only intermittently and halfheartedly, almost furtively, so that it had neither the full benefit
of that support nor credit among the opposition for an unequivocal
repudiation of the Right. The Czar in particular continued to lend
his favor to the URP because it allowed him to cherish the illusion,
reinforced by occasional deputations of peasants and loyal addresses, that the "real" people continued to look to him as their
guardian and guide. He was never happier than when he could
walk down a line of men in kneeboots and Russian blouses, feeling
close to his people who, he was convinced, would never turn
against him after having shaken his hand. The maintenance of that
illusion, which Nicholas retained to the last, was perhaps the greatest disservice the Right could have rendered its monarch. Unable
to become a genuine mass movement that could impose its will
on the directors of Russian policy, the URP in its declining years
was reduced to the staging of such charades, local pogroms, the

noisy celebration of patriotic festivals, and the strict enforcement of restrictions on the Jewish population.

The paucity of its intellectual resources and its remaining capacity for monstrous mischief were both highlighted by the tragicomedy of the Beilis case, Russia's Dreyfus affair, which was the URP's last triumph and also the sign of its nearly complete retreat into a world where the manipulation of myths and fantasies took the place of politics. When, in 1911, the body of a thirteen-year-old Christian schoolboy was found in a cave outside Kiev—murdered, as was almost universally agreed, by a gang of thieves who feared that their young helper would betray them—the URP and its allies launched a charge of ritual murder into an astounded world, found a putative killer in the person of a pitiful and bewildered Jewish clerk, Beilis, and succeeded in having the judicial authorities arrest and charge him for the crime. From the tribune of the Duma, in broadsides and in the columns of its publications, the leaders and agitators of the URP tried for more than two years to make acceptance or rejection of their version of the Kiev atrocity a touchstone of political reliability for an entire country, the agent to catalyze and fix its allegiances. They tried, incongruously, by reviving a hoary legend they did not themselves believe, and they failed. The only victory gained was over the monarchy and the state, which, in the persons of the Czar, his Ministers of Justice and Interior, let the case come to trial in 1913 before a jury and more than two hundred newspapermen—a witch-trial conducted in full view of the twentieth century. The jury acquitted Beilis, but by prosecuting him the state and its head diminished what respect and affection they still retained.

In the choice of a medieval legend on which to build a case against the Jews and stage a political comeback, the URP revealed its inability to free itself of the burden of the past. Its final failure, which was that of the entire Right, was not so much the inadequate radicalism of its social or economic program as it was a lack of universality and breadth, either of denunciation or ideal, with which to sweep along the young, the disoriented, and the disgruntled on a wave of vague hope and expectation. It is not necessary that the shape of the future be clearly outlined, but it is essential to create the impression of movement toward that future. Pan-Slavism, if it could have operated under similar conditions as the URP, might have succeeded in creating such an impression, but after defeat at the hands of Japan and the shocks of the 1905 Revolution, rightists recoiled from the dangers of an external dynamism as conservatives had done a generation earlier. The year 1905 had thoroughly frightened them; it had roused them briefly to develop new techniques and an unwonted activism, but neither the revolution of that year nor the war and the greater revolutions that followed it dissolved old loyalties and certainties sufficiently to allow the shedding of worn formulas.

Some men of the Right dimly perceived the fact and the character of their captivity; just as many leftists thought to leap straight from backwardness to an egalitarian socialism, many rightists wanted to pass directly from a bureaucratic, traditional absolutism to a national dictatorship acclaimed by all the people. But though they were willing to dispense with Nicholas II, they did not think they could dispense with the monarchy and risk arousing the political interests and energies of the masses. Their dilemma was put succinctly and pointedly by Lev Tikhomirov, the repentant revolutionary and originator of a rightist corporatism who was the only social theorist the movements of the Right could claim. Despite his abhorrence of violence, whether of the Left or Right, and his refusal to declare his formal adherence, he addressed rightist meetings and wrote for rightist papers and pamphlet series, hoping against hope that an initiative from below would meet with a positive response from above and reëstablish confidence and intimate communion between the supreme power and the nation, the Russian autocracy and the Russian people, doing away at last with the bureaucratic absolutism of Western inspiration established by Peter. But:

The government is not only non-existent, it appears not to be capable of existing. Thus, since the nation is perishing, the government must arise from below . . . but this is difficult to imagine without slaughter. It will result in something like revolution. A *zemskii sobor*, of course, could be a savior, if it could arise as a national assembly. But this is still harder to do than create a tsarist government [i.e., a true autocracy], and again, only one probable outcome will result—revolution.

A national dictatorship, like a national revolution, was impossible in a country that had not yet experienced its liberal revolution; where the middle classes were not yet sufficiently disenchanted with liberalism or fearful enough of the Left to turn to the Right; where conservatives, after 1907, again looked to the state for their defense and where the Right itself was denied the chance—by law, by history, or by its own timidity—to develop and maintain a distinct identity and existence. For these reasons the history of the Russian Right is largely the record of a frustrated potential that was never realized but that held valuable lessons for others, particularly in Germany where many Russian rightists fled after the Bolshevik revolution, transmitting the instructive experience of their brief success and their larger failure to a budding National Socialism.

SUGGESTED READING

In Russian historical literature neither the Right, as here defined, nor traditional conservatism have received much attention, and some of the best work has been done only very recently by non-Russian scholars. The best general survey of social and political thought is still THOMAS G. MASARYK's *Spirit of Russia* (London: 1915; New York: 1955), 2 vols. S. V. UTECHIN, *Russian Political Thought* (New York: 1964), is too sketchy and only occasionally helpful for present purposes. *Karamzin's Memoir on Ancient and Modern Russia* is available in an English translation (Cambridge, Mass.: 1959) by PROFESSOR RICHARD PIPES who has also supplied it with a splendid introduction to both Karamzin and Russian conservatism. NICHOLAS RIASANOVSKY's *Russia and the West in the Teaching of the Slavophiles* (Cambridge, Mass.: 1952) is an excellent survey of Slavophilism which also raises the question of its influence on the Right. There are in addition special studies of two major figures of the movement: PETER CHRISTOFF, *A. S. Xomjakov* (The Hague: 1961) and EDWARD CHMILIEWSKI, *Tribune of the Slavophiles: Konstantin Aksakov* (Gainesville, Fla.: 1962). Pogodin and Tiutchev are given their due in RIASANOVSKY's *Nicholas I and Official Nationality in Russia* (Berkeley and Los Angeles: 1959). The difficulties of classifying Katkov are tellingly illustrated by the title of MARC RAEFF's article, "A Reactionary Liberal, M. N. Katkov," *The Russian Review*, XI (1952). There is a not very satisfactory biography of him in French: G. LIWOFF, *Michel Katkoff et son époque* (Paris: 1897). On Ivan Aksakov there is, in English, only Stephen Lukashevich's unpublished doctoral dissertation (Berkeley: 1962), soon to appear as a book (Harvard University Press). For Pan-Slavism in general, see HANS KOHN, *Pan-Slavism; Its History and Ideology* (Notre Dame: 1953), and MICHAEL B. PETROVICH, *The Emergence of Russian Panslavism, 1856–1870* (New York: 1956). The characterization of

Skobelev as a Red Pan-Slavist comes from WALTER GÖRLITZ, *Russische Gestalten* (Heidelberg: 1940). PROFESSOR KOHN'S *The Mind of Modern Russia* (New Brunswick: 1955) contains excerpts from the writings of Slavophiles and Pan-Slavists.

The conservative distrust of dynamic nationalism is made abundantly clear in REINHOLD WITTRAM'S "Die russisch-nationalen Tendenzen der achtziger Jahre," in his *Das Nationale als europäisches Problem* (Göttingen: 1954). Nationalism as a factor of internal politics is also dealt with in EDWARD C. THADEN'S *Conservative Nationalism in 19th-Century Russia* (University of Washington Press: 1964).

Though neither Pobedonostsev nor Konstantin Leontiev are, in our terms, part of the Right, they do belong to what is normally regarded as the right part of the political spectrum and they help to mark off its subdivisions. They have both received a good deal of attention, POBEDONOSTSEV speaking for himself in *Reflections of a Russian Statesman* (London: 1898), an uncompromising indictment of liberalism and modernism. Of secondary works the following are most relevant: A. E. ADAMS, "Pobedonostsev and the Rule of Firmness," *Slavonic and East European Review*, XXXII (1953), and "Pobedonostsev's Religious Politics," *Church History*, XXII (1953); R. F. BYRNES, "Pobedonostsev's Conception of the Good Society," *Review of Politics*, XIII (1951); and W. B. WALSH, "Pobedonostsev and Panslavism," *Russian Review*, VIII (1949). There is a German biography of Leontiev: IWAN KOLOGRIWOFF'S *Von Hellas zum Mönchtum* (Regensburg: 1948), and an English article: H. H. CLOUTIER'S "Leontiev on Nationalism," *Review of Politics*, XVII (1955).

The *Zubatovshchina* was described as an attempt to create a Russian fascism by General A. I. Spiridovich in a Paris émigré newspaper of fascist sympathies, *Mladorosskaia Iskra*, Nov. 15, 1933; Feb. 25, 1934; April 22, 1935. For other views of Zubatov and his experiment see KARL STAEHLIN, *Geschichte Russlands*, IV (Berlin: 1939; Graz: 1961); KIRIL TIDMARSH, "The Zubatov Idea," *American Slavic and East European Review*, XIX (1960); and S. D. BAILEY, " 'Police Socialism' in Tsarist Russia." *Review of Politics*, XIX (1957).

Developments after 1900 and the emergence of rightist political movements are described in my "The Formation of the Russian Right: 1900–1906," *California Slavic Studies*, III (1964), and "Was there a Russian Fascism?—The Union of Russian People," *Journal of Modern History*, XXXVI (1964), both of which contain full references to the literature in Russian. A very brief survey of right-wing parties, their programs, and strength, is given by HORST JABLONOWSKI, "Die russischen Rechtsparteien, 1905–1917," *Russland Studien, Schriftenreihe Osteuropa*, no. 3 (Stuttgart: 1957), who describes rightist appraisals of Russian foreign policy after 1905 in "Die Stellungnahme der russischen Parteien zur Aussenpolitik der Regierung," *Forschungen zur Osteuropäischen Geschichte*, V (Berlin: 1957). ALFRED LEVIN, *The Reactionary Tradition in the Election Campaign to the Third Duma*, Oklahoma State University Publication, vol. 59 (1962), though proceeding from somewhat different assumptions than does the present essay, contains most valuable material on the conduct and appeals of the Right in 1907.

Romania

EUGEN WEBER

Political activity in the modern sense of the term developed in the
Romanian lands quite differently from the countries of the west.
At the crossroads of secular invasion routes, in the path of the
expansionist ambitions of great empires, the regions destined to
form the Romania of today lived for centuries divided and under
foreign domination. Some, like Transylvania, were under the direct
rule of Habsburg emperors; others, like Moldavia and Wallachia,
were subject states of Turkey and, later, of Russia—buffer regions
at best, which armies marched across, camped on, fought over, occupied, or which alien masters exploited for timber, grain, and
taxes.

As the nineteenth century opened, the two principalities of
Moldavia in the north and Wallachia in the south, from which a
united kingdom was to grow, were Turkish satellites. For a century
they had been ruled by Fanariot despots (Greeks of the Fanar, a
suburb of Constantinople), who had bought this dangerous privilege from the Sublime Porte and who spent the brief spell of their
reign recovering their investment from their subjects.

The vast majority of these subjects consisted of peasants, squeezed
dry by taxes and forced labor, and ruled over by the *boierime*—
landed gentry, of which the greatest families were mostly of Greek
extraction, the older Romanian nobility having perished or declined. There was no middle class to speak of; the towns were only

greater village markets, and the historic merchant class was rural or semiurban. These merchants' activities, sometimes far-flung and somewhat reminiscent of the fifteenth- and sixteenth-century west, were destined to decay under modern conditions.

At the end of the eighteenth century, representatives of foreign powers—Russia and Austria first, Britain, France, and Prussia later —were established in the principalities. Their presence encouraged an influx of foreign traders—Jews, Greeks, Armenians, Bulgarians —who prospered under their protection. By 1830, the removal of trade restrictions had gone far in destroying the old exclusive artisan and trade guilds. The foreigner, relieved of certain duties and taxes, supported by his consul, benefiting in many instances from a more enterprising mentality and more up-to-date methods, enjoyed such advantages that some Romanians sought foreign nationality as a key to commercial success. The foreign governments were not to abandon the privileges of their protected persons until 1882.

The disintegration of ancient forms and structures which accompanied these developments did not, as one might expect, accelerate the growth of a new Romanian middle class. Between the rural masses, whose position tended to deteriorate under the impact of freer trade, and the *boieri*, high and low, the role of middle class was filled largely by Jewish immigrants from Galitia and by other foreign traders and small entrepreneurs. The bourgeoisie, which played such an important part in western politics and thought, was absent here. The initial revolutionary movements were led by Greeks or started under Greek influence, as echoes of the early nineteenth-century Greek fight for independence. The first really Romanian revolutions were led by the *boieri*, and, if their immediate object was always to rid the country of foreign domination, it did not take long before their nationalism turned also against foreign exploitation, whose obvious and irritating representatives lived in their midst.

Romanian nationalists had to affirm themselves not only against their Turkish masters but also against the Greeks, who tried to involve them along with other Balkan peoples in their own struggles, and against the Russians, whose solicitude for fellow Christians

seemed likely to end in annexation. In the century before independence was won, Russian troops occupied the principalities for
over twenty-one years, and a Russian protectorate held sway over
them for longer than that. It was an enlightened Russian governor
with Voltairean ideas, Count Kiseleff, who gave Moldavia and
Wallachia their first constitutional instrument: the *Réglement
Organique* of 1830. But if power threatened from east and south,
hope lay in the west where young *boieri* went to study and whence
they brought back the ideas of the liberal century.

"You who lie asleep, unfeeling," wrote Vasile Alecsandri in 1848,
"Don't you sense from depths of healing / This triumphant voice
that calls?" It was the voice of Paris, rattling the shackles and
twisting the innards of the continent again, announcing the coming of a new order, of—or so the forty-eighters thought—a new
and better world. Romantic traditionalism and nationalism came
to Romania not from Germany, but from France, and it was
French liberal and nationalist doctrines that inspired the generation
of '48, the men who united the principalities, freed the serfs,
sought and won independence, and placed a western prince upon
the new nation's throne. National folklore would thenceforth provide the basis of Romanian self-consciousness, and the peasant
would furnish the basic figure of the Romanian national myth as
he did of Romanian society and economy.

But the reality was different from the lore. Giving the peasant
his due in literature seemed to absolve the cultivated ruling classes
from giving him his chance in fact. And the liberalism that spurred
and inspired the movement to political independence also sanctioned the movement to despoil and exploit the peasant, by letting
those who could *faire* and *passer* make the most of their opportunities and of the people's ignorant helplessness.

In Romania, as elsewhere at that time, liberalism subordinated
ideas of social justice to principles of economic and political freedom. Liberals accepted reform when it favored their interests, state
interference when it brought grist (or contracts) to their mills.
They were ready to use the state as an instrument of Westernization, much as in Russia. But they operated from outside, upon
masses unwillingly affected by processes that others manipulated.

To the peasant in his bucolic hovel, full of misery and proverbs, rights and duties under the new state "added up to tax-payment and sending his son off as a soldier." [1] To the ex-peasant enlisted in the service of modernization—railroads, gas works, factories, and port installations—the new techniques appeared as alien and alienating forces. The proletariat of western countries participated in the industrial revolution not only by their efforts but by their inventions. They shared the cultural background, skills, and language of their masters. In Romania, as in Algeria or Peru, master and worker belonged figuratively and sometimes literally to different nations, with the worker seeming always the manipulated, never the participant in the industrialization process.

Modernization brought the trappings of Western-style institutions, but they were grafted on native stock and the grafts would give strange fruit.

Some of the fruits of political and economic reform were bitter. Modernization seemed to mean colonization. The *Romanian Encyclopedia* (Vol. III, Bucharest: 1938) writes bitterly: "All manufactured articles sold in the principalities came from Austria and Prussia. . . . Our goods were taken at very low prices, as from any other colony. . . ." Soon, French and British firms appeared, to compete with the Germans, and quickly gained ground. But this in no way changed the fact "of being permanently a colony, open or disguised, of the foreigners. [This calamity] not only keeps the whole national life in a situation of poverty, exploitation and slavery, but brings also gradual political serfdom, stifling any attempt to conquer one's rightful place in the world."

Foreign travelers, too, wrote about the country in tones similar to those used for "any other colony." In 1876, an Austrian expert showed little faith in the Romanians' capacity to develop an industry of their own:

The Romanian of the lower class, despite his natural intelligence and ability, is little apt for persistent industrial labor, because he lacks perse-

---

[1] Quoted by Leften S. Stavrianos, "The Influence of the West on the Balkans," in *The Balkans in Transition,* edited by Charles and Barbara Jelavich, Berkeley and Los Angeles: 1963. The whole essay is well worth reading, and so is the symposium which will be frequently referred to in this chapter.

verance, love of work and spirit of enterprise, and because his physique, conditioned by climatic conditions, cannot bear it. A further proof that the Romanian has no talent or inclination for any other occupation than agriculture is also that trades of every sort, the urban professions, and even ordinary domestic service, are filled mostly by foreigners who immigrate in great numbers from neighboring countries. . . .

Economic development will be difficult, said the foreign expert, because only foreigners really work. Economic development will be possible, said the Romanians, only when the country has been rid of foreigners. "Foreigners at the head of the state," wrote the historian and economist B. P. Haşdeu in 1871, "foreigners in the ministries, foreigners in parliament, foreigners in the magistracy, foreigners at the bar, foreigners in medicine, foreigners in finances, foreigners in trade, foreigners in publicism, foreigners in public works, foreigners up, foreigners down and yet—*Romanism is on the move.*"

First and most obvious among the hated foreigners, because of both speech and garb, were the Jews, particularly numerous in Moldavia. Religious intolerance is not particularly evident in the Romanian past, nor anti-Semitism as such, with its ghettos and its massacres. Articulate anti-Semitism first appeared in the nineteenth century out of a combination of nationalism and economic analysis. One of its first proponents, D. Pop Marţian, the son of a Transylvanian priest, had studied in Vienna and there been influenced by the ideas of Hegel and Lorenz von Stein. Settling in Bucharest, he had in 1859 become the first director of the Statistical Office. Haşdeu, quoted above, had also taught statistics in the Moldavian capital of Iaşi. Both opposed economic dependence on foreign capital, arguing that it was no better than the political dependence against which the country struggled, and attacked the Jews not on religious but on socioeconomic grounds.

As early as 1822, an abortive, liberal constitution project had already sketched out certain measures against Jews. In the decades that followed, Jewish migration increased. Unlike other immigrants whose Orthodox faith made integration easy, the Jews remained a nation apart, their prejudices reinforcing those of their hosts, their repeated appeals for Western support stressing their alien connections. In *Les Juifs de Moldavie* (Paris: 1867), Ernest Desjardins explains that Jews remained alien to the life of the nation, avoided Romanian schools, eluded military service, and bent their steps toward usury. "The Jewish invasion" was on all the lips: "The Jewish question!" we find Alecsandri, the poet, writing to a friend: "This question of life and death for us. . . ."

Some disagreed. What people called the Jewish problem, declared a politician in 1879, was a Romanian problem: "Romanians are ignorant and lazy. Getting rid of Jews will not change that. Jewish numbers are the symptom of a Romanian evil—lack of education and economic activity." A conservative statesman agreed: "There is only one way to rid yourselves of Jews: work and become civilized." But even such men as these disapproved of the campaigns of the Alliance Israélite Universelle, which, by appealing to foreign powers to secure constitutional rights for Romania's Jews, forfeited the sympathies of their Romanian friends.[2]

Jews, in any event, were only one facet of the problem. Though anti-Semitic, the poet Mihail Eminescu attacked Greeks even more bitterly than he did Jews (as being "as cunning but more corrupt. . . . Jews are ten times more honest, more moral, more human than these men"). Everywhere Eminescu looked, as the nineteenth century drew to an end, he saw foreigners and cryptoforeigners: the intelligentsia, recruited from men who had inherited their character and ideas from Greek or Bulgarian forebears; the ruling Liberals, who drew their manners and policies from the Seine, the Spree, and the Bosphorus, not from a land and people whose language they hardly spoke; the whole Establishment, heavily colonized by *Venetics*—demagogic, unproductive, patriotic only when there was something in it for them, lacking culture and character,

---

[2] Jewish observers had a pretty good understanding of the situation. In a letter to the Liberal leader, Ion Brătianu, quoted in I. C. Codrescu, *Cotropirea Judovească în România* (Bucharest: 1870), the Romanian representative of the Alliance Israélite Universelle argued that, in the absence of a native bourgeoisie in eastern Europe, the Jews had carried out that social role. As long as they did not compete with anyone, they were not persecuted as they were in the west. But "today, when a middle-class is in process of formation on the Danube's shores, you will soon find yourself faced with the same [anti-Semitic] exigencies."

exploiting the people's labor, looking abroad for their support, altogether one vast xenocracy.

To save the country from them, a new social organization was needed, one that would encourage and honor work and the worker. And to make way for this, the dominant class had to be eliminated, suppressed if need be by poison, rope, or steel.

> He who takes strangers to heart
> May the dogs eat his part
> May the waste eat his home
> May ill-fame eat his name!

wrote Eminescu in verses later to be engraved on his statue, piously cleaned by Codreanu, fervently quoted by twentieth-century nationalists. The nation had to be saved from the alien rot, albeit at the expense of humanitarian principles. No truth, no principle could hold against the life of the state and of society. The supreme law, wrote Eminescu, was "the conservation of nation and country by every means and in every way, even if the means and the way do not conform to civilization and humanitarianism." Humanitarian concepts were, in any case, only masks behind which the West fought and exploited backward societies.

Romantic, pessimistic, sentimental, nationalistic, and religious, fascinated by history and folklore, Eminescu was both an inspiration for the post-World War I generation and a focus of Romanian nationalism. His anti-Semitism was to be taken up by A. C. Cuza, his antidemocratism by Aurel Popovici,[3] his populism by Iorga, his racial theories by Iorga's student, Vasile Pârvan. He remains, as Stefan Zeletin has written (*Neoliberalismul*, Bucharest: 1927), the greatest figure of Romanian reaction against the middle class.

But if Eminescu now appears as the greatest nationalist of his time, he was far from being alone. A cohort of intellectual nationalists, poets, politicians, and publicists, sang the same song. Their cultural campaigns were political ones. "I had the joy of fighting

---

[3] "Let us drop the cliché of popular sovereignty," wrote Aurel C. Popovici, "and accept only the sovereignty of the fatherland. From the tombs of the land more votes are cast than from our voting booths."

old and ridiculous prejudices, of setting the Romanian theater on the true national way and of proving that the Romanian language lends itself perfectly to comedy and music too," one of them was to boast. "But, I confess, my greatest satisfaction has been that, through the theater, I contributed to making Greeks impossible in my land. I rendered them so ridiculous that, in town, no man would have his daughter marry one." The claim was exaggerated, but the intention was characteristic of the aspirations of Romanian nationalism, and so was the specification "in town." For the revolution of the nineteenth century was an urban revolution and the ideas and manners of the West were acclimated only in the slowly growing cities. Moreover, the young revolutionaries of the time, deeply inspired by populist ideas, deeply concerned with the *people* as depositor of the profound realities of *romanism*, tended to keep their enthusiasms on a literary and artistic plane. In their more concrete aspects, the changes they sparked, like all changes in a long-established way of life, were rather uncomfortable for the peasant mass.

The population of the principalities, 4,500,000 in 1880, numbered 7,300,000 by 1913. The increase was largely on the land. As the rural population grew, cultivable land became scarce; farming trusts, expropriations, enclosure, and foreclosure created what socialist commentators called a neoserfdom. Between 1885 and 1913, per-capita taxation more than doubled. The peasant paid for railroads, cities and streets, canals and port installations, all of which seemed to profit others, and sent his sons into the army—an even more grievous kind of tax. In February, 1907, the peasants rose in northern Moldavia, on lands farmed out to a Jewish trust, and their revolt, which spread throughout the country like wildfire, across the sorry fields and hungry villages, was not put down without much bloodshed until March. One gets a sense of the peasants' state and of contemporary circumstances in novels like Panait Istrati's *Thistles of the Baragan,* or Petru Dumitriu's *Family Jewels.* When massive army intervention had restored order, scores of country houses smoldered in ruins and over ten thousand peasants had died.

It was inevitable that men, especially young men, should be concerned with the social problems that beset the country. A socialist movement arose in the 1880's, led by Romanians who had lived or studied in Russia and by Jewish immigrants. Between 1885 and 1900, most country schoolteachers seem to have been socialists. The Socialist group, however, joined the ruling Liberal party in 1899, and their failure to give a radical lead opened the way to the idealistic and simili-social nationalism of men whose solutions to social problems lay in nationalistic measures. Here, the two leading figures were university professors: a political economist, A. C. Cuza, and a historian, Nicolae Iorga.

Educated in French and German schools, Cuza had started out as an atheist and a socialist. He soon shifted toward conservative nationalism, populistic, traditionalistic, and hostile to economic liberalism and democracy. Cuza followed in the tradition of nineteenth-century economic nationalists like Pop Marțian (1829–1865), Petre Aurelian (1833–1909), who edited the Romanian edition of Friedrich List, Hașdeu and D. Xenopol (1847–1920), for whom the solution of the country's economic problems lay in fostering popular enterprise, expelling the foreigners who stifled it, fighting alcoholism, and educating the people. For Cuza, whose writings show him to be a sort of sub-Drumont, all this came down to anti-Semitism, rabid, repetitive and sterile. Appointed in 1901 to the chair of political economy at the University of Iași, he preached his doctrine for thirty years to receptive audiences to whom all politics and economics thenceforth resolved themselves into the Jewish question. By dint of longevity and persistence his influence grew and spread. The swastika, which he adopted as a symbol several years before World War I, was flaunted in Romania long before it had become a German party symbol. Cuza's whole career reflects the paradoxes of superficial social nationalism, rejecting the parliament in which he sat for half a century, the democracy he courted, the bourgeois values he incarnated, the God and Church to which he turned, à la Maurras, because they served a traditionalism itself at war with the radical views he had begun by professing.

In 1906, Cuza began writing for a periodical, *The Romanian People* (*Neamul Românesc*), just founded by the professor of history at the University of Bucharest, Nicolae Iorga. Like others of his generation, Iorga's political views were sparked by a social conscience—and a historian's social consciousness. "Divine literature is a social product and a social factor," he wrote in 1912, "and the most natural human society is the nation." A manuscript sketch for a novel he had planned shows him sharing the feelings of other romantic nationalists: love and pity for exploited peasants, hatred for their (Greek) exploiters, sympathy for the Romanian gentry whom the alien had displaced. But Iorga was a greater man than Cuza, a scholar of real stature, of gargantuan intellectual appetite and capacity, of immense energy and erudition. His published works number hundreds of volumes and several thousand articles in half a dozen languages. At the beginning of the century he had already established an international reputation.

Early in the 1900's Iorga began to contribute articles to conservative publications which apparently hoped to use his nationalism and his talents to spur a conservative rejuvenation—as the Liberals had done shortly before, when absorbing the Socialists. His Romanism, however, like that of his predecessors, had a hard row to hoe. At the beginning of the twentieth century, Romanians of good family spoke French, not only in company but in the privacy of the home. Cultivated society looked to France, whence it got its fashions, its manners, its reading, and its children's governesses. Speaking French was a mark of quality, of belonging to the elite which cut itself off from the uncultivated masses.

In March, 1906, a ladies' committee organized a benefit performance at the National Theater, in Bucharest, to be attended by the cream of the capital's society, headed by the heir to the throne and his wife. With one exception, the program of the show consisted of plays in French. Iorga saw this as a provocation. He was well aware (says Pamfil Șeicaru revealingly in the account he gives in *Nicolae Iorga,* Madrid: 1957) that the Establishment ignored Romanian literature, "as an English colonialist ignores the literature of the blacks." The benefit program, however, wounded him to the quick and prompted an article appealing to the public to boycott the show. His call found unexpected echoes in student quarters and had unexpected repercussions when student demonstrations on the night of the show flared into widespread riots which had to be dispersed by the army.

Parturiunt montes; nascetur ridiculus mus. The crowds and the army had battled only to produce a new review, the *Romanian People*, over the next decade the most widely noted and influential of nationalist publications. But the *Romanian People* was subsidized by great Conservative landowners and also by certain leading Liberals, and, although this was in part owing to its patrons' personal admiration for a great historian, it must have been, too, because his nationalism could be reconciled with their interests. Like other conservatives, Iorga refused to envisage any radical solution of the peasant problem, any real land reform, and limited the agrarian question to the peasant's economic difficulties, attributed to alcoholism, lack of organization, and lack of education. The *Romanian People* campaigned vigorously against Jews and concessionaires. The latter were mostly Jewish in Moldavia, mostly Greek in Wallachia. Jews as such were also attacked for their numbers and their activities as usurers and tavern-keepers, leading poor peasants to ruin. None of this threatened the Establishment. On the contrary, it gave them good conscience and a feeling of security by suggesting that others than themselves were to blame for the obvious failings and injustices of the society they ran.

The style and the simili-social nationalism of Iorga won over the young, substituting in the political thought of pre-1914 students a romantic and traditionalistic nationalism for the socialist ideology previously so popular in university circles. In 1909, Iorga and Cuza founded the Nationalist-Democratic party, the essence of whose program lay in manhood suffrage and restrictive measures against Jews. One of the party's first militants was a high school teacher in a small town of northern Moldavia, one Ion Zelea Codreanu, a name we shall hear again. In 1909, too, Iorga opened his summer courses at Vălenii-de-Munte, which were to become the seminar of the new populist and patriotic intelligentsia. One of the students was a country schoolteacher, Ion Mihalache, who founded the Peasant party after World War I. Another was to be the heir to the throne, Prince Carol.

Romania came out of World War I with double its former population, territory, and industrial capacity. The 7,300,000 Romanians had by 1919 become 16,200,000, but they still lived mostly on the land.

The country's economy, like that of its neighbors, was characterized by agricultural overpopulation and by low productivity per acre—about half the productivity of western Europe. Four-fifths of the population was engaged in agriculture or in connex activities, but, although the area devoted to gain-production increased all the time, poor crops and poor techniques actually caused output to fall. Fewer crops were exported and fewer were available for domestic consumption. Economically, the interwar years were worse than the prewar years, much worse for the population of the new western provinces (Transylvania, Bucovina, and Banat) which had fared better under the Habsburgs.

The increase in population, which was relative as well as real, also meant increased pressure on arable land, a pressure only temporarily relieved by the land reforms that followed the war. Many holdings, divided and subdivided among numerous progeny, were too small to support a family. Half the country's agricultural population was surplus to the needs of agricultural production, a burden on their fellows and on the national economy which industrialization expanded too slowly to assimilate them. Industrial growth lagged far behind population growth; the number of potential workers grew much faster than the number of industrial workers. As late as 1939, only one-tenth of the population worked in industry or mines. There was no urban safety valve for rural overpopulation, or, rather, the valve was much too narrow and it became more so in the depression years.

At the beginning of the twentieth century, over three-quarters of the country's population was illiterate. Between the wars, less than 1 per cent of peasant youths pursued any studies above the elementary level. Around 40 per cent of the population over seven was still illiterate, most of them micro-landowners who made ends meet by hiring themselves out as laborers or domestic servants. Until 1920, many still owed villein labor to the local landowner to whom (along with the local shopkeeper) they were usually in debt. The landowner, meanwhile, cared more for social prestige and sumptuary expenses than for the modernization or rational exploitation of his lands, still often farmed out or run by a steward. Those landowners who did care were hampered, like the peasants, by a paucity of credit, low prices, and government indifference to their needs.

The agricultural reform of 1921 divided half the country's arable land between a million and a half beneficiaries, who got an average of ten acres each. But it failed to provide the equipment, the credits, the agronomic investments, and advice which would help make the reform effective. More than half the peasants could not read or write, half of them lacked a plow or oxen. Without a viable public credit structure, they fell into the hands of usurers or of their rich neighbors. By the time of World War II, the 0.7 per cent of farms over 125 acres covered 32 per cent of the arable land.

Meanwhile, the expense of modernizing the state and endowing it with a large army, bureaucracy, and all sorts of public facilities increased the tax burden, the national debt, and the nation's dependence on foreign creditors. During the ten years following 1913 the foreign debt more than doubled. "A gigantic backlog of backwardness," writes Nicholas Spulber in *The Balkans in Transition,* "increasing demographic pressures, consistently erroneous economic policies, insuperable nationalist barriers to fruitful cooperation in the area, all but arrested the progress of economic growth." In the third volume of the *Romanian Encyclopedia,* the country's foremost statistician describes the resulting professional structure: "an overwhelmingly agricultural population with a primitive familial exploitation system, a modest and insufficient level of industrialization, a rather important administrative structure," which resulted in "low revenue of the peasant population, high cost of industrial products, slow rhythm of circulation and commerce in general—permitting the accumulation of profits in the hands of a restricted minority, and lastly the modest living standard of the bureaucratic and white collar class."

It is worth noting in this connection that the country's interwar economic policies were dominated by a small group of middle-class economists, all trained at German universities. Whatever the party in which these men chose to make their career, they all shared similar ideas of industrialization and protection which inclined them to sacrifice the peasant to industrial and commercial interests. But peasant poverty excluded the possibility of an expanding internal market; lack of planning prevented the rational development of national resources and let industry grow or stagnate according to luck, not need. Expansion there was but it was anarchic, costly, wasteful, and it lagged far behind that of comparable economies. Between 1926 and 1939, per-capita income grew 35 per cent in Bulgaria, 11 per cent in Greece, but only 8 per cent in Romania.

The trained manpower for the industrial development envisaged was also far away. Education, as we have seen, was largely of and for the cities. In secondary schools, Stephen Fischer-Galati tells us in his useful book on *Romania* (New York: 1957), there were eight city boys to every country lad. Few of them went on to universities, and fewer in the poor depression years. In the decade 1929–1938, there were 283,583 students in all who attended institutions of higher learning, and less than 10 per cent of them got out with a degree. Even those few were hard to place. The bureaucracy, overexpanded as it was, could take only so many. Teaching, ill-paid though it was, could not absorb enough. Romanian students and graduates, facing the problems inherent in the growth of an educated class in an undereducated society, formed a chronically dissatisfied, disgruntled, revendicatory body of socially displaced and ambitious persons, constantly ready to express ambient frustrations in violent word and action. Between the wars, they provided the troops of every radical and nationalist movement. To accomplish anything, however, political opportunism was more important than political ideals. The choice, writes Leften Stavrianos in *The Balkans in Transition,* lay "between joining a party machine and forswearing their political principles or maintaining their principles and forswearing a career."

In the early 1920's, the possibilities of choice between political parties were anyhow rather limited. "If you look at the two major parties," wrote an observer of the political scene, "you see that their membership is interchangeable, with the Conservatives based on the big landowners and their clientèle and the Liberals founded by young men of the same class who had been touched by western democratic and liberal ideas." The contenders for political power changed, their labels changed, their slogans changed but, *mutatis mutandis*, the essentials remained the same and so did the opportunistic and time serving elements of politics.

The Conservative party passed out of the hands of the great landowners who loved Romania like a prey into those of neo-Conservative nationalists, and soon disappeared after the war. The new conservative party of the interwar years was the Liberal party, recruited from the upper bourgeoisie, with little or no popular following, but economically dominant, controlling the country's credit flow by its hold on the National Bank. Liberal governments ruled for ten of the sixteen years between 1922 and 1938, and there is no evidence that Liberal bankers were out of power during any of this time.

All this is only a specific illustration of the general fact that the identification of government and people, so characteristic of Western political theory and (sometimes) structure, was not respected in Romania even in the breach, let alone in the observance. The characteristic political attitude here, as in all Balkan lands, was that expressed by the editors of *The Balkans in Transition*: "distrust towards authority and indifference to the concept of civil responsibility, acceptance of corruption and deception in political life as normal and natural." The poet, George Coşbuc, had written of the *haiduci,* popular outlaws whose historical outline has become lost in Robin-Hoodlike legends:

> The haiduc in the forest
> You take him for a friend
> You show him hidden by-ways
> And aid him to the end.
> When he jumps in the saddle
> You're glad to hold his rein.
> When he lifts up his rifle
> You're glad with him again.
> And when he sights a-smiling
> You laugh, because his lead
> Is aimed at your despoiler
> And hits him in the head.

The haiduc's methods were the only ones recognized for dealing with despoilers. But few had the heart to try them.

For a while after the war, populist (and popular) hopes focused on the war hero, General Averescu, who founded his People's party in 1918 to oppose the corruption and inefficiency of the old parties, even engaging in abortive negotiations with the extreme left. Peasants and veterans idolized the old soldier who had promised land for everybody, until his turn in power disabused them. Averescu was the first of a series of self-professed saviors, reformers, and men of destiny who, once in power, dropped their radical verbiage and concentrated on patching up the ruling order they had until then abused. The same proved true of the Peasant party, on which, during most of the 1920's, were focused the hopes of the best among peasants and young reformers. The Peasants' fusion in 1926 with the Transylvanian National party moderated their populism and the National-Peasant tenure of power after 1928 proved little different from that of other parties. Whoever held it, power seemed an opportunity for personal spoils. Whoever governed, governed for himself and his clique. Politics were resolved in terms of personalities and electoral manipulation. In 1926, an electoral law voted by a Liberal majority introduced a bonus for any party securing 40 per cent of the electoral vote and ensured a secure majority to any party "making" the elections. The measure, inspired by the recent Fascist electoral law passed in Italy, was bitterly opposed by the Nationals and the Peasants. Once in power, however, Nationals and Peasants found it convenient to use and made no attempt to reform it or other iniquities they had opposed.

"Everything begins in mystique and ends in politics," has written Charles Péguy. The faith in peasant reform, briefly placed in Averescu, thereafter embodied in the beginnings of the Peasant party, trickled away in the sordid politics of ministerial antechambers and electoral committees. The gap this left would be filled by the mystique of other movements and other men.

The most fascinating—though not for some time the best known —of these men was Corneliu Zelea Codreanu, son of one of Cuza's most faithful supporters. Codreanu's mother, Elisa Brauner, was the granddaughter of a Bavarian immigrant. Codreanu's father came from Austrian-ruled Bucovina. Whether of Polish descent, as the original surname of Zelinski suggests, or of Romanian stock as he always maintained, the foreign resonance of his name recalls the frequent phenomenon of nationalist leaders stemming from border regions, like Hitler and Degrelle, or from assimilated national groups, like Szalasi, Gömbös, and Iorga.

Leaving Austrian territory in 1898, Ion Zelinski had secured a teaching post at the lycée of Huşi, a small north Moldavian town, where his son would be born on September 13, 1899, the day of St. Cornelius, the Roman centurion of Caesarea, the first gentile to receive the word of God, and the first of Christian soldiers—all facts which Codreanu's admirers never failed to stress. It was only three years later that little Cornelius Zelinski became Corneliu Zelea Codreanu, as his father officially changed his name, romanizing the Polish surname and adding to it a new one in memory, he explained, of his forester ancestors (*Codru* = forest).

Eldest son in a family of seven, the boy was brought up in the cult of the fatherland (one of his brothers was named after the last Dacian king, Decebal; another after the Transylvanian hero, Horia) and of the provinces awaiting reunion to it (one of his sisters was rather confusingly named Iredenta). From the ages of eleven to sixteen he attended a famous military school, Mânăstirea Dealului—the Cloister on the Hill—established, like many schools and prisons, in a sometime cloister. When war broke out in 1916 the boy was unable to enlist because of his age, but he trailed his father's regiment for several weeks of hostilities. Finally admitted to the Infantry Officers' School, he graduated only when the war was over.

One cannot overrate the importance of the military schools, and especially the formative years at Mânăstirea Dealului, in the life of Codreanu; there he learned respect for order and discipline, hierarchy and honor, "fear of God and only of God," and a great sense of national oneness without regard for social provenance. There also he picked up certain ideas characteristic of his later movement's ethos: an appreciation of physical hardship, marching, and the outdoor life, the habit of singing on the march, the fascination with the symbolic values of crosses and skulls (the skull of a Romanian hero rested in the college chapel which the boys attended daily). He never forgot the words of a visiting conservative states-man: "Scholars and bookmen we have a-plenty on the Dâmbovița's shores; what we need in the great Romania of tomorrow is men of character!" nor those of one of his teachers killed in the war: "In the forward march of a nation, the essential role belongs to the elites and elites mean men of character."

These were the lessons Codreanu retained. "A nation is not led by itself but by its elite," he would write in his memoirs a quarter of a century later. "The idea of an elite is connected with sacrifice, poverty, a hard, severe way of life; where self-sacrifice ends there ends the legionary elite." The new elite he sought to form would be "an aristocracy of virtue."

At the war's end, the danger of red revolution loomed large. Bolshevik regimes ruled on east and west, Bolshevik ideas were rife among workers and intellectuals. Codreanu's first battles would be fought in Iași, in 1919–1920, against striking workers, where he distinguished himself in the van of a short-lived strike-breaking league called the Guard of the National Conscience. With Con-stantin Pancu, leader of the Guard, Codreanu tried to set up a new party—National-Christian Socialism. "It is not enough to defeat communism," they argued. "We must also fight for the rights of the workers. They have a right to bread and a right to honor. We must fight against the oligarchic party, creating national workers' organizations which can gain their rights within the framework of the state and not against the state." He already realized that "in the shelter of tricolor formulas an oligarchic and tyrannous class could install itself on the backs of the workers . . . and literally skin them, while continually appealing to the Fatherland which they do not love, the God in whom they do not believe, the Church in which they never set foot, the Army which they send to war with empty hands." For the moment, however, there was little he could do about it.

National-Christian Socialism got nowhere. Averescu had come to power and anti-Bolshevism could dispense with the services of amateurs. Codreanu went back to his studies, his political activity for the next few years limited to student politics.

The strikes of 1919–1920 had presented Codreanu with a picture of Romanian working men led astray by Jewish leaders of the Communist party. Cuza's lectures at Iaşi University put his experience in the broader context of a Jewish conspiracy against humanity in general and Romania in particular. Codreanu's nationalism would henceforth focus on three objectives: Communism, Jews, and irreligion, all abhorrent to his profound religious and patriotic faith. Against liberals and leftists, Codreanu and his friends proceeded to take over the student movement, first at Iaşi, then at the other Romanian universities. Their brutal and irreverent methods proved effective. Militant nationalism was established in the universities and held them until World War II. By 1923, student strikes could keep the country's universities closed for a whole semester, even against the intervention of the army. It was all in a good cause. "We cause disorders, certainly," Codreanu declared, "but only to prevent the great, irreparable disorder which the apprentices of Communist revolution were preparing." Preventing Communist revolution involved keeping Jews out of student clubs and hostels, breaking up Jewish theatrical performances, beating up leftists and Jews, and rioting to ensure that the academic year opened with a religious service. Expelled by the University Senate for his extracurricular activities, Codreanu was reinstated in an unheard-of action by the Cuza-dominated Faculty of Law which broke with the Senate on this issue. Codreanu graduated from the Faculty of Law in 1922 but never from the University of Iaşi. Admitted to the bar on the basis of his law diploma, he continued to be simply an expelled student of the university whose rebel faculty had enabled him to graduate.

In 1923, out of the student agitation of the few years past, the LANC was born, the League of National-Christian Defense, with an anti-semitic program calling for the *numerus clausus* to be applied to Jews in secondary schools, universities, and liberal professions according to their proportion of the total population. Several small groups of the extreme right joined the LANC, including the National Romanian Fascio, whose inspiration is evident, and a

Transylvanian group of Maurrassian leanings, Acţiunea Româ-
nească (Romanian Action). Headed by Professor Cuza, but sparked
mostly by Codreanu and his friends, the league inherited many
sympathizers of the prewar Nationalist-Democratic party and some
of Averescu's followers.

In the elections of 1926 the LANC was to win 120,000 votes
and elect ten deputies, including Codreanu's father. Its agitation,
however, had not prevented the modification, in spring of 1923, of
the country's constitution to grant citizenship and political right
to resident Jews, a measure demanded by Romania's allies on the
basis of commitments reluctantly accepted in 1919. Most nationalists opposed the constitutional amendment. None, however, had
gone beyond words. With a few close friends, Codreanu decided to
punish those who had betrayed national interests by voting the
measure. A list was drawn up of those to be shot *pour encourager
les autres*. At the last moment, the conspirators were denounced by
one of their number, arrested, imprisoned, tried, and acquitted.
"What we did, we did for our country and our faith," declared
the accused. All were released except one, Ion Moţa, who had shot
their denouncer on the very day of the trial and had to await a
second acquittal at a later date.

Back in Iaşi, Codreanu and his companions apparently gave up
the thought of further murders. Violence was not the way: faith
and labor was. In the prison church, awaiting trial, Codreanu had
been struck by the image of the Archangel Michael, the warrior
saint under whose patronage he would henceforth place himself
and his activities. Out of prison, he set up in Iaşi the first of the
FDC's—Brotherhoods of the Cross, to enlist students, schoolboys,
and village youths in nationalist action. The Brotherhoods referred
to the Orthodox custom of calling children baptized in the same
water "Brothers of the Cross," and to the historical tradition of
Balkan cross brotherhood, another name for blood brotherhood.

The day after Moţa was acquitted of having shot the man who
had revealed their plot, Codreanu named him to head the Brotherhoods. Son and grandson of Transylvanian village priests, Ion
Moţa (1902–1937) had sucked his nationalism with his mother's
milk. His father had been a leading figure of Transylvanian na-

tionalism, and in Transylvania, as the old man later explained, "everyone was a right extremist, and we could not be anything else if we wanted to keep our nationality." After the war, the son had gone to Paris to study law and political science but, lacking the means to continue, had returned to the Transylvanian university of Cluj where he became president of the student association, helped found the Romanian Action group, and, active in nationalist agitation, learned to know and admire Codreanu. In 1923 he had just finished translating the *Protocols of the Elders of Zion* from the French, which he dedicated to the Romanian Student Body.

Moța's articles have a scent of Péguy's style but are particularly marked by a wild anti-Semitism which makes him dub as Jews all those he dislikes (e.g., Lord Rothermere) and see the Jewish spirit at work in every situation he deplores (e.g., the de-Christianization of Transylvanian Saxons). Moța's Jews were everything Romanians should have been—united, powerful, and dangerous to cross —a sort of transferred wish-fulfillment fantasy, and devious besides. No wonder they obsessed him!

Better than most, the articles Moța contributed to the movement's publications reflect the reactionary romanticism, the violent wistfulness, the monomaniac logic of the young and passionate group of friends who felt themselves (as others had done in many other places, at many other times) lost in an alien world, who suffered for their country and enjoyed the pangs, who offered themselves up for the public good and found the excitement and the tension of it a drug of which ever greater doses would be needed. "Our soul," he wrote in *Cranii de Lemn* ("Wooden Skulls," Bucharest: 1937), "still tied to another [older, better] world, wanders today in a life which is not ours. When we face the world of today, we feel alien, we find no sense in it other than the possibility of harnessing it to revive the days of old and to increase their beauty—their beauty and the right Romanian order." He was to die in January, 1937, at 34, fighting for the right Spanish order on the Madrid front.

This was the Byronic leader Codreanu had assigned to his Brotherhoods, and for many young men the combination of Moța and

Codreanu proved a heady brew. The indoctrination of a novice into the Brotherhood stressed a sense of mystery enhanced by allusiveness, ritual, secret meetings in forests or ruins, and special readings. Great stress was laid on inspiring adventure stories like the *Three Musketeers* and something called the *Samurai's Treasure*, carrying edifying examples of comradeship, bravery, loyalty, and enterprise. Initiation came at nightfall, in a secret place, complete with torches, songs, oaths, and the invocation of the dead. "The chosen one," recollects a member, "told that he was entering a world apart, was promised that by following the teaching and practice of this new world he would become a man of special essence." Thereafter, "there grew in him, out of the excesses of so-called religious practices, mystic exaltation and the wish to perform some resounding deed."

The rigmarole included the essentials of later legionary practices, especially songs and the cult of the dead. "Through song man participates in the cosmic rhythm," one of Codreanu's friends explained, "fills himself with the secrets of the world, shares in the unknown. . . . Through song man reaches the kernel of truth, the essence of things. . . . The legionary style is directly bound to song." Many are the refrains that sing of death or of dead comrades:

> Legionary do not fear
> That you will die too young
> For you die to be reborn
> And are born to die.

And:

> With a smile on our lips
> We look death in the eye
> For we are the death team
> That must win or die.

Or, the last stanza of the movement's hymn:

> The wind blows over the waters
> And the willows weep
> We do not forget you, brother,
> But you go on, asleep.

"The finest aspect of legionary life is death," one of the movement's publications asserted somewhat perplexingly (*Dacia*, December 15, 1940). "Legionary death has nothing in common with ordinary death. By legionary death the legionary becomes engaged to eternity . . . is translated into legend." And it quoted the song:

> Death, only legionary death
> Is a gladsome wedding for us
> The legionary dies singing
> The legionary sings dying.

All this sounds like gibberish and it probably is. It did, however, serve the essential purpose of impressing an impressionable public, of inspiring young men in search of a faith, of frightening some and putting starch in others. An Italian journalist recently reminiscing on a distant encounter with Codreanu refers to his movement's special *mistica dei morti:* "The rite of calling out the names of the dead and answering 'Present!', taken over from Fascist practice, was used in forms some of which seemed close to magic evocation," writes Julius Evola in *Il Secolo d'Italia* (January 24, 1964). No form of magic, no kind of incantation can be ignored which has proved effective. Codreanu's magic often worked. Dismissing its childish trappings and its theatricals out of hand would be to miss an important point.

The romantic ritual of the Brotherhoods and, later, of the Legion, the messianism or what would soon become the messianism of Codreanu, were effective and subversive means of revolutionary action, liberating some men from the constraints of an exceptionally unsatisfactory society. Students of African history have long noted the rise of novel revivalist churches, "creations of an ignorant but self-conscious [common] people, striking against crushing injustice and against benefactors whose sympathy for tyrants irritate it." But these movements and their leaders also try as a rule to restore cohesion and order in disintegrated or disintegrating societies. The messiah of the Ba-Kongo, for instance, Simon Kimbangu, comes to restore confidence and order, to mend broken social and religious bonds, and canalize propitious social "forces." As Georges Balandier describes him in his *Sociologie actuelle de l'Afrique noire* (Paris: 1963), Kimbangu insists above all on the ancestor cult, and on the permanence and stability this implies. Imprisoned, condemned to death, pardoned, but exiled, Kimbangu becomes a Martyr and a Savior, eventually assimilated to Christ and Mahomet. The analogy between his martyrdom and Christ's passion is insistently drawn by his followers:

He whom God had sent as Savior of the Blacks was handed over to the Authorities who sent him to Elisabethville where he was imprisoned and enslaved for years. Then the Authorities decided to have him executed. But as soon as they made him stand up and shot at him, he *appeared* in our country. He came to Kinzwana and to Kituenge, where he made himself known. . . . That is when he himself designated his apostles and ordered that places of prayer be created. . . .

In a sense, and especially in eastern Europe, movements like Codreanu's are closer to cargo cults than they are to fascism. We must remember that a cult such as developed around him, insisting on a fresh relation between man and God, invests man with responsibilities of a terribly subversive nature. It picks him out of an irresponsible world, insists on his direct and responsible relationship with God, makes him an active agent theoretically free to choose, rather than the passive, submissive subject of the established order. Once he feared the police. Now he fears God more. That may mean that he will obey God or God's interpreter rather than the police. The change is an important one. The transfer of authority from society to the leader can thus be highly subversive (or liberating)—as the followers of Christ found long ago. They also knew about the liberating and *dynamic* effects of sacrifice—another thing on which Codreanu always insisted.

In some introductory remarks to his play *Iphigenia* (Valle Hermoso: 1951), Professor Mircea Eliade explains how *jertfa,* the sacrifice, is an archaic conception which he had already discussed in a wartime work, *Commentaries to the Legend of Master Manole* (Bucharest: 1943). Iphigenia gives her life to open the way to an army; Manole, the master builder of an old Romanian legend, sacrifices his wife so that the church he builds shall stand. The human sacrifice carried out to make something like a building last or endure is equivalent to a mystical transfer of the soul from the

mortal human body into the new building: not only is the building given a soul, but the victim is endowed with a new, glorious,
and more lasting body. For Manole, this body would be the monas-
tery he builds. For Iphigenia, it would be her father Agamemnon's
war and victory against Asia and Troy.

Codreanu and his followers really believed in the constructive
and saving value of sacrifice, a point of view not surprising in
Christians but which they held with exceptional fervor. Ion Moţa
would go to fight in Spain quite determined to die there and to
offer his death as a sacrifice. When he did die, at Majadahonda,
Professor Nae Ionescu expressed his belief that "for the salvation
of our nation, God had to accept Moţa's sacrifice, as for the salvation of the human race he accepted that of the lamb." Again, all
this may be moonshine. It was potent enough, however, to carry a
small and quite unknown group of young men very close to success and to leave its mark on the history of a country.

The first task which Codreanu set himself and the members of
his Brotherhoods was to build their own student center with bricks
they made themselves and money raised by working in a market
garden. But the authorities suspected that their intentions were less
pacific than they seemed, and the prefect of Iasi himself led police
and gendarmes to break up the group with great brutality. Arrested without apparent reason, while at their work, they were tied
up with ropes, dragged through the streets, spat on, beaten, humiliated, and released only on the intervention of Cuza and other
leading citizens. Arbitrary beatings and arrests were hardly unusual
in Romania, but this was Codreanu's first experience of sheer injustice. An official inquiry which established the unwarranted
arrests, beating, and torture of the schoolboys led only to the
decoration of the prefect, Manciu, and the promotion of his principal assistants. A series of actions brought by the injured in the
courts also came to nothing.

Denied a hearing for his griefs, let alone any sanctions against
the guilty, Codreanu now took the law into his own hands and
shot Manciu down. Public opinion was on his side. Aware of this,
the authorities decided to hold the trial away from Iaşi: first, in

another Moldavian town, then at the other end of the country, at Turnu-Severin, where the emperor Trajan had thrown his bridge across the Danube. Everywhere the townspeople and especially the young demonstrated in the prisoner's favor, schoolchildren came to cheer him outside the prison yard, thousands of tracts and letters from the FDC Brotherhoods alerted the citizenry to prevent the compounding of one injustice by another. The trial turned into a triumph for Codreanu, with trainloads of sympathizers pouring into town and the tribunal abandoning its courtroom for the local theater, itself hardly sufficient to hold the public. The jury stayed out for only a few minutes and returned sporting on their lapels the LANC emblem—the red, yellow, and blue national colors with a swastika on top. Codreanu was not only acquitted but vindicated. On the way back to Iași, the peasants gathered to cheer him as he passed, priests blessed him, and in the cities great crowds filled the railroad stations with flowers and songs.

But things in the LANC were not going well. The plot of 1923 and even more the murder of Manciu had strained relations between the older nationalists who, like Cuza, disapproved of illegality and violence, and the angry young prophets of national revolution at all costs, be it in- or outside the limits of legality. Even when they defended the young rebels, the older men disliked their methods and hoped they would soon learn to fit into the existing pattern. The younger men, on the other hand, led by Codreanu and by Moța, wanted a disciplined movement, organized and uniformed on semimilitary lines, to carry on their earlier student agitation. To avoid an open break, Codreanu and Moța now left for Grenoble, to continue their studies there. By 1927, when Codreanu returned, the movement had disintegrated in internal struggles. Its parliamentary delegation, split into rival groups, was to vanish in the next elections.

Refusing to ally themselves with either camp, Codreanu and his friends now moved to found their own movement on the lines Cuza had rejected and which his rump-LANC would shortly try to copy even to the uniforms. Expectably, it proved impossible for rival groups of anti-Semitic zealots to compete amicably. As a rule the anti-Semite sees his opponents, if not as Jews, then as sold to

Jews. Since he alone is fighting the good fight against Jews, anyone who disagrees is "objectively" the tool of the Jewish conspiracy, no matter whether bought by Jewish gold or quite unconscious of serving Jewish interests. Thus, when the LANC split, in 1927, the resulting splinter groups accused each other in perfect good faith of having sold out to the Jewish foe. From then on, relations between Codreanu and his former mentor, between green-shirted legionaries and blue-shirted Cuzists, deteriorated fast.

In June, 1927, after ceremoniously taking their leave from Cuza, Codreanu and four prison friends founded their own organization, the Legion of the Archangel Michael, whose basic characteristics Codreanu listed in his memoirs : (1) faith in God, (2) faith in our mission, (3) love for each other, and (4) songs as the chief manifestation of our state of mind. The legion had no program: "The country is dying for lack of *men,* not programs." Its task was to devise not programs, but new men. "Let him of boundless faith come join us. Let him who doubts stay out," read the first order of the day.

Most of those who did not ignore the new micro-movement altogether took him at his word and stayed out. Enough joined, however, to give the movement's new bi-monthly, *Pământul Stramosesc* ("Ancestral Land"), 2,568 subscribers within two months, thus making it self-supporting.

Beginnings were modest. The friends were young and unknown: in 1927, for instance, Codreanu was twenty-eight, Moța twenty-six. Older nationalist leaders in the government, the universities, the established press and parties, had a better start. But their challengers were to make this a virtue of their own, directing their first appeals to the young in high schools, normal schools, trade and commercial academies, theological seminaries, and the villages that city intellectuals and politicians ignored. The legion deliberately looked to the younger generation, that of its own leaders. One interesting aspect of this was that, unlike most contemporary movements of its kind, it appealed less to the veterans of the war than to those who had been too young to fight and who found themselves spiritually divorced from predecessors who did not see things their way. Codreanu's movement was a crusade of adolescents, sheering away from their elders' line of march. In the struggle to reshape the nation, wrote one of its doctrinaires,

> . . . the essential condition of victory is for us to be as alone as possible, as much by ourselves as possible, with our soul and our thoughts as they are [i.e., uncorrupted]. We must beware of trying to accommodate our thoughts, action and judgment to the model of our elders. . . . Other ideas guided them, our ideal is different. . . . With the older generation an era ends, with us another one begins. We are the pioneers that head the column of the future.

The message that the Legion brought was misunderstood, rejected by "the elderly majority that lives for stomach, entertainment and democracy," wrote Ion Banea. The young, however, hearkened to it.

What was this message?

Its roots lay in the widespread disillusion with existing conditions and the unwillingness or inability of the country's leaders to improve them.

> Gold lies in our mountains' core
> But we beg from door to door

runs a Romanian proverb. The middle and upper classes lived well. One can paraphrase Talleyrand's remark to say that those who have not known Romanian life before the war have not known *douceur de vivre*. The country was potentially rich. Food was cheap, if only because the government had taxed its export to keep prices down and, with them, salaries. Industrial wages were certainly kept down and so was the income of the working population as a whole; Colin Clark (*Conditions of Economic Progress*, London: 1940) estimated it to be the lowest in all east European states and well below the pre-1914 level. The Romanian peasant ate enough, but the quality of his diet was reflected in the high prevalence of pellagra and other nutritional diseases. Yet statistics cannot reproduce the variations of reality, the beauty of the countryside, the joy of life to be found in so many places even by the poorest. Nevertheless, one must conclude with Henry Roberts (*Rumania*, p. 81) that "the flat picture of widespread poverty and squalor presented by the statistics is not far from the truth. The colorful costumes and picturesque folk dances of the Rumanian peasantry should not obscure the fact that . . . in 1938 one child in five died before it was a year old."

The poverty of the masses was emphasized by the wealth of the few, the luxury of the upper classes, with their gambling clubs, their American cars, and their Paris fashions. The extravagant and unproductive way of life they affected contrasted strikingly with the surrounding poverty. It was easy to see them, as Eminescu had done half a century before, as foreign to the real life and problems of the people—*Venetic* parasites, sterile and corrupting, sucking the country dry.

> You've come with foreign laws
> To steal my stock, my song, my poverty;
> Out of my sweat you've built your property,
> And taken from our children for your whores

wrote a legionary poet. And a song put it more forcibly:

> A herd of foreign bastards
> Hard-hearted heathen band
> Have come to be our masters.
> There's wailing in the land.

Between five- and six-sevenths of industrial capital investment was owned or made available by foreigners. Foreign capital owned two-thirds of the oil industry, dominated the insurance business, controlled the banks. On June 19, 1937, the official *Bulletin périodique de la presse roumaine* published figures showing that in the textile industry 80 per cent of the engineers were Jews; in the Army Medical Corps 1,960 doctors were Jewish, 460 belonged to other minority groups, and only 1,400 were Romanian; 70 per cent of journalists were Jews; and in the universities, where, in 1925, 27 per cent of the student body had been of foreign origin, the proportion in 1934 had risen to 43 per cent. According to anti-Semitic sources, to be used *cum grano salis*, of 258,000 white-collar workers, over 173,000 were Jewish, 39,000 Romanian, and the rest belonged to other minority groups; in Bucharest, of 14,300 employees of banks and commercial enterprises, 11,200 were Jewish, and 1,964 Romanian. Of 10,481 lawyers, 3,066 were Jewish (in Bucharest: 1,390 Jews, 3,475 Romanian). Of 120 drug stores in the province of Bessarabia, 117 were kept by Jews. On the Bucharest stock exchange, 139 of the 142 brokers were said to be Jewish.

Whatever the accuracy of such figures, they did not fail to impress, and the impression seemed confirmed by the concentration of the Jewish community in urban areas where their numbers appeared more strikingly. Nor could it be denied that, although Jews counted for 4 or 5 per cent of the country's population, their participation in the economy, the schools, and the professions was immensely greater. That this should be attributed to enterprise, sobriety, and hard work did not appease their foes. The foreign grip, said these, had to be broken at all costs; and Jews, unassimilated and unassimilable, were the prototype of foreignness. Unlike their fellows elsewhere, Romanian anti-Semites blamed Jews not for infiltrating the nation but for failing to integrate in it. Legally, of course, most Jews were Romanian citizens. This did not prevent them from appearing—to themselves and to others—a separate group, set apart by their religion, their names, their communal solidarity and institutions, the Yiddish they often spoke, and sometimes by their dress. They were like other national minorities, but with two differences: their lack of a national home, and their crucial economic role.

To Codreanu, as to other anti-Semites, Jewish influence was a threat to his nation's being. He visualized a highly organized Jewish state-within-the-state, part of a vaster world organization above and beyond the state, a Jewish conspiracy to corrupt and take over his country. All this, however, was the result of prior causes, the Jewish problem merely a symptom of more serious illness. Democracy, liberalism, the parliamentary structure, were all foreign, all alien to native development, traditions, and needs. Codreanu's successor, Horia Sima, still insists that democracy did not develop organically in Romania, but was superimposed on a quite different tradition as a gimmick imported from the West. "The imported state, the state of today," wrote the legionary review *Axa* on February 5, 1933, "was invented for us by the economic and political interests of the European powers. . . . The invention-state continued as their state, the state of the foreign protectors . . . and of their tools." This had to be changed, the state purged, the nation purified, regenerated, and set back on the right road. Romania should be great, happy, and united, but "only when all its sons carry in their souls the same faith, the same hopes and desires, when in a word the national soul appears as one *unit*." A new-model state had to be forged, but, said the *Legionary Manual*, "the new state presupposes . . . a new type of man. A new state with men with old sins is inconceivable."

Here lay Codreanu's task and that of the movement he created as a school, first for its members, then for the whole nation. "To create a movement," we read in his memoirs, "means *in the first place* to create, *to generate a state of mind*, which does not rest in reason but in the soul of the masses. This is the *essence* of the legionary movement." That being so, the only program for Codreanu was that of spiritual regeneration. "You want programs?" writes the *Manual*: "They are on everybody's lips. Better look for men. Anyone can turn out a program in one night: that is not what the country needs. It needs men, and wills to do what is needed."

The legion's task was not to seize power but to train men. To do this, Codreanu devised a highly structured organization whose activities were regulated in great detail from the basic unit called the nest, numbering from three to thirteen members, up through village, commune, city, county, and regional groups.

The nest was, in the *Manual*'s words, a chapel, binding together men who *felt* the same and who had to be taught the discipline of acting in a common purpose. Discipline and initiative were stressed in the same breath. From top to bottom of the movement, a higher responsibility was invoked. "The leader is not a master or dictator who does what he wants," noted Codreanu, "but the expression of an invisible consensus, doing not what he wants but what he must, led neither by individual nor collective interests but by the interests of the *eternal nation*. . . ." Capacity of leadership had to be proved by every chief—who was not appointed from the center but forced to establish himself, showing by achievement and activity that he could build his own following. This policy made for a tight, effective network, bound by ties of personal loyalty, constantly purged by harsh trials and deliberate policy, harnessed and trained by the detailed instructions of the *Manual* which has been fairly compared to Loyola's *Institutes.*

As the *Manual* symbolically presents it, the legionary's progress up the mountain of suffering, through the forest with wild beasts, across the slough of despond, is a pilgrim's progress full of trials, deeply committed and profoundly Christian. Christian symbolism and mysticism played an important part in arming the champion of a great struggle between good and evil, presented in chiliastic, increasingly apocalyptic accents. Leadership in the struggle fell, of course, to Codreanu himself, a man of fine presence, striking personality, and evidently charismatic gifts. If magic is the possibility of producing certain effects without the obvious intervention of contact or agent, then Codreanu's was a magic power of attraction, affecting not only his immediate followers but many bystanders, too. To his followers he was the providential man, "fated to be our Captain, the man without whom our generation could not carry out its mission." "In this giant of our generation . . . *we all found ourselves,*" wrote one. "We all believe in *him*. . . . Him we love. To him we listen. We are at his orders. He is our hope and the hope of the Romania of tomorrow. We are strong through him. We are feared through him. *We shall win through him.*"

This was powerful medicine. The cult that surrounded Codreanu would grow after his death, the faithful falling back on capitals when referring to Him, his martyrdom enveloped by an aura of sanctity. This he seems to have sought, consciously or not, from the very first. Humiliated by Manciu, whom he would shortly shoot, he had retired for six weeks into a mountain wilderness, where peasants brought him food. He fasted and prayed regularly and often, tried to lead a life of exemplary poverty, never setting foot in cinema or tavern, insisted that legionaries must become a byword of correctness and sobriety. His last prison notes show him comparing his passion with that of Christ, the injustice wrought against him with that which the other messiah suffered.

In his *Afrique ambigue* (Paris: 1957), Georges Balandier describes Congolese messianic cults, not unreminiscent of this. Here are some statements he has noted: "We have a man who wanted to work for our future—André Matswa. He suffered and then died in prison. The villagers continue to say that he is our Savior. They vote for him at election time. They consider him to be our black Christ. . . ." "We have Saviors who can speak for us, since they are at the side of God. They are André Matswa and Simon Kimbangu. They have suffered for the blacks. Jesus Christ suffered only for the whites. . . ."

In Romania, too, the native savior seemed at times closer and more potent, not a contender but an intercessor in the harshness of days. Like every savior, Codreanu insisted on the importance of utter faith and unquestioning obedience, the corrupting effects of doubt, the essential value of sacrifice, martyrdom, and expiation. Legionary leaders had to swear to lead a life of poverty—"Poor ourselves," his father later explained, "that the nation and the land should be rich." Another fundamental law was that the legionary should answer for his actions, albeit with his life. In theory, legionary violence was justified only when expiated, and many legionaries gave themselves up after a crime, when they could easily have escaped, some even when they had begun by escaping.

The Christian law of forgiveness was transcended by the higher necessity of defending and avenging the nation, and this could necessitate un-Christian acts. Such acts, however, had to be paid for here on earth and it was recognized that they probably excluded their performers from eternal salvation, too, a supreme sacrifice accepted for the sake of their fellows and the nation's good. Legionary doctrine recognized that ends could be soiled by means. "Even if he should win," Codreanu insisted, "he will remain defeated because he has used devilish weapons. His breast must be of iron, but lily-white his soul." The argument by which such a dilemma was resolved ran in a curious way, and may be found in works of exegesis published since the war, particularly by Constantin Papanace, a Macedonian who was for years one of Codreanu's close advisers. Since the enemy uses all the arms of darkness, runs the argument, the Legion as a *political* movement cannot insist on the absolute purity that it stresses in its indoctrination. It has to maintain the moral essence of its values, but it also has to fight. The only way to do this without giving way to general moral corruption is for those who are fighting with the enemy's own arms never to forget their sin and always to suffer for it in their hearts. "This expiation by suffering constitutes the sacrifice which can reëstablish the balance of absolute legionary purity," Papanace explains. He tells the parable of several legionary companies which, while the main body of their movement crosses a narrow pass, detach themselves to engage the enemy ensconced in caves and caverns along the way, where they must fight with weapons suited to such dark recesses. "But their weapons are not the weapons of light. They have lost their candor and their purity. They have had to fight with the arms of darkness. Thanks to them, the mass of legionaries has crossed the pass unharmed. They have not known the struggle in the gloom. . . . The others [who have known it] will have to expiate. . . . Their suffering will uplift both them and the Movement."

Such religious accents were both peculiar and important. As the major means of political identification under Ottoman rule, religion had been a major factor of national self-assertion. It might be expected to bulk large in a nationalism directed even more against internal alien elements than against neighbors of the same faith, and directed above all in this instance against "atheistic Communists" and Jews.

Here we might note the difference between the Romanian situation and that in the West. Most western societies are lay societies, religion playing either a private role or an essentially secular social function. The churches are rivaled and partly replaced by "secular religions," embodied sometimes in the fatherland, sometimes in a party or a cause. In Romania, this situation did not yet exist. Codreanu appealed to a religious tradition that was still very much alive and, to the extent that he revived it in certain sections of the intelligentsia or the middle class, the memories he stirred were very near the surface. Where Western fascist movements were generally a-religious or antireligious, his was a religious revival, or, perhaps more correctly, a revivalist movement with strong religious overtones.

This movement benefited, incidentally, from the antimaterialistic trend which, starting in the west at the beginning of the twentieth century, had reached Romania after World War I. The new anti-materialism had suggested among other things an "idealistic" or "philosophical" anti-Semitism, in which the Semitic spirit stood for utilitarianism and materialism, for the cult of quantity and the science of numbers. Several influential teachers participated in the neoidealistic revival. Some of them and many of their students showed interest in or sympathy for the Legion. The most influential of these seems to have been Nae Ionescu who, after studying in Munich from 1913 to 1919, returned to become Professor of Logic and Metaphysics at the University of Bucharest, and to edit a news-paper—*Cuvântul* ("The Word")—which enjoyed much credit in intellectual circles.

The theories of Einstein and Max Planck, which moved many philosophers toward forms of relativism, were to Ionescu arguments in favor of a new mystical transcendentalism which rediscovered security, authority, and discipline in God and religion. The magic of physics had failed. It was time for the magic of metaphysics—pending the appearance of the metaphysics of magic. Early in the 1920's, Ionescu began a campaign for Christian and Orthodox revival, insisting on the importance of love, tradition, and the popular, organic nature of Christian Orthodoxy. In his foreword to Ionescu's *Conversations* (Freiburg: 1951), Mircea Eliade presents him as "the first professor who, at a time when positivism and agnosticism still dominated Romanian universities, showed the va-lidity of metaphysics, spoke with understanding of mysticism and religious experience." Since Ionescu himself defined the metaphy-sician as "a man who does not care how the world is in reality, but only in its *possibilities*," one wonders whether his insistence on this realm of experience could have been an attempt to escape from the other and less satisfactory realm of everyday life. Transferring this to a somewhat broader plane, one might consider whether Ionescu's orientation may not have been an attempt to free Ro-manian philosophy from its long vassalage to the west. Eliade credits Ionescu with the fact that for the first time Romanian philosophy overcame the inferiority complex that "held it in com-plete dependence towards western philosophical schools." "Before any interest for religious experience made itself felt in western culture, Nae Ionescu lectured on religious philosophy. . . . for him, the creations and the values of the spirit were, above all, *real*."

Without wishing to question the significance of all this (and it did, at any rate, help to inspire the valuable and suggestive studies of Professor Eliade himself), we might consider whether Ionescu's attitude was not designed to compensate for a paucity of other creations and ideas, whether in effect it did not operate as a compensation mechanism typical of dependent or underdeveloped societies: eager to show some original creation of their own and to prove that their material and technological backwardness is irrelevant in the light of other, higher, values; that, far from being a sign of inferiority, such "backwardness" is indeed an advantage and the counterpart of superiority on a much more relevant plane.

In such societies, religion can play a twofold role. The attribution of ultimate power and decision to God can shift the responsibility of objective evils from the shoulders of the rulers to an immanent and distant destiny, encouraging the masses to acceptance and fatalism. Fatalism, however, can also work the other way, by suggesting that everyday reality is irrelevant and the exploiter, the oppressor himself, unfree and insignificant. The individual who accepts the will of God then becomes ready to ignore or reject that of men, especially as what matters in his perspective is not the everyday reality of political and economic forces but the superior and far more terrifying reality of supernatural forces. The return to religion might thus have been, more than the mere reaffirmation of national entity in its historical tradition, a compensation for the insulted and the injured. In prison, Codreanu had turned to the Archangel Michael for defense and support. But the confidence this gave him could have been based on a consequent dissociation from everyday reality, and the movement it inspired did move in effect from one alienation (political) to another (religious), right to the verge of madness.

With Codreanu dead, the brief legionary tenure of power during the winter of 1940–1941 saw a hallucinatory development of this messianic tendency, the Captain and his successor Horia Sima being exalted in the most extravagant terms. "The Captain," wrote a provincial periodical, "is the Mastery, the Elect of God, with right of life and death over his subjects. He is the one fated to take our destiny and replace it in history. . . ." "The Horia of our days," wrote another, "is greater than the mountains. He has the looks of an angel, the sword of an archangel. . . . He comes to fulfill the Captain's will. . . . Horia is the thought, Horia is the feeling, Horia is the light, the will, and our strong right arm. In Horia we have fanatically believed and in him we believe unto death. . . ."

In the meantime, it should be observed, Codreanu's mysticism did not exclude a very hard-headed appreciation of the situation. From a mendacious people he demanded honesty, in a lazy country he demanded work, in an easy-going society he demanded self-discipline and persistence, from an exuberant and windy folk he demanded brevity and self-control. Over and over he insisted on the importance of these things, again and again he noted successes and failures, tested the militants, praised the valiant, punished backsliders, bewailed his incapacity "to impress on these men the necessary legionary education. . . . I greatly regret that in so many years, these men have not been able to understand me," he noted on March 10, 1933.

What most retained best were the simple, obvious parts of the doctrine: rejection of the hollow ideals of liberty and equality scouted for too long by those who professed them, and affirmation of the new commandments—faith, work, order, discipline, hierarchy, and, above all, action. "We know only one ideology, the Deed," affirmed Vasile Marin, who would die in Spain with Moţa. "We believe in the ethical value of force. . . ."

We come here to a problem inherent in the judgment of every extremist movement, and particularly important in this one. Between 1924 and 1939, a superficial count, probably incomplete, shows eleven murders and attempted murders by legionaries, and 501 legionaries killed in various ways by the authorities. The report of a special commission appointed to investigate persecutions suffered by the Legion, and published by General Antonescu after his elimination of legionaries from power, shows 292 of them killed without trial in the eleven-month period between November, 1938, and October, 1939. The official German news agency, DNB, on the other hand, reported on September 11, 1940, that 1,221 legionaries had been killed between April and December, 1938, alone. Presumably, all such figures are at best approximate. Later, between September, 1940, and January, 1941, several hundred persons were killed by legionaries or their henchmen and several hundred legionaries died fighting or were executed in their turn. Murder and countermurder seemed to escalate until they exploded in a sort of Götterdämmerung in the wintry Bucharest of the January rising.

The accountancy of violence is a useless pastime; but it does seem at first glance as if the forces of the established order defended themselves more ruthlessly and bloodily than their assailants did. This may have been a question of superior means, though it is well to remember that Codreanu always insisted (after 1924) that dedication and sacrifice, not violence, would secure victory, that guns were less important than propaganda, and that he had no intention of trying to gain power by force.

The essence of this question of violence lies in the fact that what Edward Shils calls the politics of civility were as unknown in Romania as in Algeria or Viet Nam. Lenin's description of the bourgeois state as a monopoly of violence and oppression in the service of the economically dominant class aptly portrays the Romanian situation, a fact confirmed by evidence from many quarters. Already, in 1886, Vasile Alecsandri had described the regime as "a stupid comedy played by stupid actors before a naïve public." What the poet wrote privately was expressed publicly in 1897 by a well-known politician, G. E. Lahovary, in his *Histoire d'une fiction: le gouvernement des partis*. Yet, as a respectable patriot wrote a friend, "it would be very hard to change the country's situation *legally*, because the Constitution is so made that no one but the men of disorder can govern." In the words of a more detached observer (Traian Stoianovich, writing in *The Balkans in Transition*), "the reactionary forces were too potent to be eliminated without the threat or use of force."

To any real threat against the established order, its beneficiaries reacted by all the means at their command, however violent, however illegal: army, police, gendarmerie, the courts—both military and civil, the administrative apparatus with all its possibilities of intimidation and chicanery, were mobilized against those who challenged the system. "The greatest and most fruitful revolution which could be accomplished in Romania," wrote a liberal paper, *Adevărul* ("Truth") on February 25, 1937, "would be simply to apply the existing laws." That the laws were not applied, the Left had long testified. A small pamphlet of 1922, *The Black Book of Elections Held in 1922 in the County of Argeş*, is full of typical details of brutal beatings, intimidation, and fraud. Another, with an introduction by Panait Istrati (*Au pays du dernier des Hohenzollern*, Paris: 1926), explains that "in Romania, murder has been the very basis of the regime for centuries," and, in discussing the police murder of a Communist student (the Communist party had been out-lawed two years before), notes "tortures, vile insults, violences, brutalities and ferocities," adding that cases of arrested persons committing suicide were becoming more frequent.

"Romania, which likes to claim itself part of civilized Europe . . . is at present the most Balkanized country in Europe," wrote H. Hessell Tiltman, in a book called *The Terror in Europe* (London: 1931). "Balkanization . . . meaning violence and corruption. . . . In Romania suppression and distortion of news . . . have been carried to a fine art. Graft and petty tyranny rule, while men sentenced for their opinions twelve years ago remain in prison." With every election bringing its tale of killed, wounded, and arrested, electoral abstentions sometimes equaled and even passed the number of those voting.

The liberal (not Liberal) opposition had long drawn the conclusions of this state of affairs: "We consider ourselves faced with an armed gang which sets itself outside the laws and uses brutal force," *Adevărul* had written on October 5, 1919. "If we knew that incitement to rebellion against the so-called legal order could be effective, which is unfortunately not the case, we should not hesitate for a moment to do it, for against a dictatorial and terroristic regime there is no other way of fighting."

This is the context of our story, this is the background against which the Legion operated, its violent methods reflecting the encompassing violence of the society in which it moved, the brutality of its methods reflecting the brutality with which the men in power sought to meet its calls for change. Shame, as Marx said, is a revolutionary sentiment. It is often the best in man which revolts against humiliation. Codreanu shot Manciu when he believed that all redress had been refused him. We need not sympathize with the ideas or the motives of men who fulfilled their dreams in blood, but it is well to understand the circumstances that drove them to it, the frequent impossibility to act any way but violently, even murderously.

"A political crime," Mihail Eminescu had written, "committed by a private person, ceases to be a crime when it is based on higher views and dictated by the clean notion, even if it be mistaken, of saving the state."

This kind of reasoning justifies every kind of barbarism, murder, and injustice; and this was the reasoning behind most legionary crimes. But, in effect, the cause of their crimes was both deeper and more obvious, lying in the nature of the regime they challenged. "The violence of colonial regimes and the counterviolence of the colonized," says Frantz Fanon in *Les Damnés de la terre* (Paris: 1961),

balance and answer each other in an extraordinary reciprocal homogeneity. . . . The development of violence in the colonized people will be proportional to the violence exercized by the contested colonial regime. . . . From the moment when the colonized chooses [the way of] counterviolence, police reprisals automatically bring about the reprisals of nationalist forces. There is, however, no equivalence in results, since official actions surpass in consequence and horror the response of the colonized.

Founded in 1927, the Legion started slowly, encouraging early sympathizers to set up nests in their localities, which were chiefly in Moldavia, Bucovina, and central and eastern Transylvania. Its first "battles" (Codreanu's vocabulary was full of warlike terms: fronts, struggles, offensives, trenches, ranks, camps, and campaigns, reappear constantly) consisted of raising money, buying a little truck, selling vegetables, and organizing summer training and propaganda marches in the back country of Transylvania. By the end of 1929 Codreanu felt strong enough to begin public meetings.

His account of his first campaign, among the villagers of south-eastern Moldavia, provides a perfect illustration of his methods and of their success.

The first meeting had been announced for December 15, 1929, in the market town of Bereşti.

On the evening of December 14 I was at Bereşti. Lefter, Potolea, Tânase Antohi and others met me at the station. The town is a real wasps' nest of Jewry: house squeezed to house and booth to booth. The only street runs through the middle of town. Mud to the ankles. On the sides, some wooden sidewalks. We put up at Potolea's house.

The next morning, early, I am greeted at the door by the major of gendarmes and the public prosecutor who had come up from Galaţi [the county town] to tell me that I am not allowed to hold my meeting. I told them: "What you affirm is neither right nor legal. In this country everybody has the right to hold meetings: Germans, Hungarians, Turks, Tatars, Bulgarians, Jews. And I alone should be denied this right? Your measure is unjust. It is outside the law and I shall not obey. I shall hold the meeting at any cost."

At last, after a lot of argument, they let me hold the meeting, but I must cause no disorders. What was I going to do? What disorders? Break down people's houses? It was my first public meeting. Didn't I have every interest for it to take place in perfect order, so as not to lose my right of holding the others?

At the hour set for the meeting, a very small number of people had gathered. Just about a hundred. I found out from them that many more people would have come, but were stopped by the gendarmes in the villages.

All the meeting lasted five minutes. Lefter spoke for one minute, Potolea for one, and I for the rest. I said:—I have come to hold a meeting. But the authorities are using force to keep people from attending. Against all orders, I am going to hold ten meetings. Bring me a horse and I shall ride over the whole region.

As a matter of fact, a horse was the only way of getting through the local mud. After a couple of hours, they brought me a horse and I left. After me, on foot, came Lefter with four other legionaries. I got to the first village, to Meria. There, in the churchyard, in a few minutes, everybody had gathered: men, women, and children. I spoke few words to them and did not unfold a political program:—Let us all unite, men and women, and fashion another fate for our nation and for ourselves. The hour of Romanian revival and salvation is drawing nigh. He who believes, he who will fight and suffer, will be rewarded and blessed by this nation. New times are knocking at our doors. A world with a sterile, dried-up soul is dying and another is being born: the world of those whose souls are full of faith. In this new world, everybody will have his place, not according to his schooling, not according to his cleverness or learning, but above all according to his character and his faith.

I left and went on. After about four kilometers I got to another village, to Slivna. The people, however, had been waiting on the road with lighted candles. As we entered the village, a legionary nest came to meet me. On ways I'd never trod. And here, too, people awaited me with lights and candles, and the lads singing.

Folk greeted me gladly, with no difference of political parties. We did not know each other, but it was as if we had been friends forever. Enmities had melted away. We were one water, one soul, one people.

The next morning we went on. This time I was no longer alone. Three horsemen had asked if they could accompany me and we set out together. At the edge of the next village, Gănești, we stopped at Dumitru Cristian's. About forty years old, with the face of a *haiduc* and a glance that shot out under his eyebrows. A nationalist and a fighter from the days of the student movements, he unharnessed the horses from his cart, put his saddle on one of them and set out with us. Soon our numbers grew still more, with Dumitru and Vasile Popa, with Hasan and Chiculiță.

So, going from village to village, the number of the riders got to twenty. We were mostly young men between twenty-five and thirty. Only a few were between thirty-five and forty, and the oldest was uncle Chiculiță from Cavadinești, about forty-five.

As we got more numerous, I felt the need of a uniform, of some distinctive sign. But because we had no other possibility, we all put turkey feathers in our fur caps. And so we would enter the villages, singing. Passing in song and the gallop of our horses along the hilltops by the river Prut, where our forefathers had so often marched and fought, it seemed that we were the shades of those who had defended Moldavia's land once upon a time. The live men of today, the dead of yesterday, we were the same soul, the same great unity carried by the winds over the crest of hills: that of romanism.

The news of my coming spread, from man to man, through all the villages. The people awaited us everywhere. Whoever we passed on the road greeted us with the question:—When will you come to our village, young Sir? They were waiting for you yesterday, till late in the night.

In the villages, when we sang or spoke to the men, I felt that I penetrated into undefined depths of their souls, where the politicians with their borrowed programs had been unable to descend. Here, in these depths, I struck the roots of the legionary movement. No one will be able to pull them out again. Thursday was market day at Berești. At ten in the morning we appeared, fifty riders, on the crest above the town. From there, in a column, singing, we rode down into town.

There, people greeted us with great enthusiasm. The Christians came out of their houses and poured buckets of water in our path, after the old custom, so that we should have success and plenty in our way. We went back to Nicu Bălan's yard where the first meeting had been scheduled. Now we were over three thousand. I did not hold a meeting. I gave the riders, some of them, a keepsake of me.

To Nicu Bogatu I gave my cigarette case, whittled in prison; to uncle Chiculiță I gave a swastika. Lefter and Potolea I appointed to the supreme council of the Legion and Nicu Bălan to the staff of the county. Dumitru Cristian became legionary leader for the region. (*Pentru Legionari*, Bucharest: 1936.)

This passage shows us everything—or almost: the ill-will of the authorities, the determination to get the better of them, the imagery and the talent that could turn the worst conditions to advantage, the charismatic leader who finds the words to touch the listening crowds, whom men follow on horseback or on foot through miles of winter mud, whom villagers await and greet like a savior, whose reputation precedes him, whose gestures are surrounded by dreams of identification with the blood and the soil and the heroes of the past in a confused but inspiring medley in which it is hard to tell how much is acting and how much is real.

Everything he does is simple but effective: not speeches, but songs. "The village lads knew little of what we were or what we wanted," the foreword of the *Legionary Song Book* tells us. "But they sang our songs." Not words, but gestures: the villagers heard what he said, but what they retained was the vision of the apparition on horseback with turkey feathers fluttering from the black fur cap.

Codreanu never disregarded the peasants whom the city politicians so persistently ignored. To them and to the young he ceaselessly appealed and they responded tenfold. As one of his early admirers wrote to him when love had turned to hate: "And we the young, seeing you on a white or black horse, cross in hand, thought we saw realized the legends and the tales we had read in books, and followed you out of romanticism."

Active in the northern parts of the country, the Legion was little known in the southern regions, especially in the capital, Bucharest. It was soon going to recruit an important group of supporters among the Macedo-Romanian students there, and this partly by coincidence.

Macedo-Romanian immigrants had been settled in Dobrogea after World War I. Their sons who came to study in the capital introduced a sober and passionate note into the rather easy-going world of Romanian students, with a nationalism more violent than that of their replete countrymen and more strongly oriented against Bulgarians and Greeks. In 1927, disappointed by the poor showing of the LANC and threatened by policies that seemed to favor Bulgarians over Macedo-Romanians in Dobrogean land settlement, this group began an agitation which, for a while, was the focus of most of the energies of nationalistic students. In 1930, one of their number, Gheorghe Beza, tried to kill the National Peasant minister they held responsible for legislation unfavorable to the colonists. His attempt, though unsuccessful, understandably created a certain stir, and those Macedo-Romanian student leaders who declared their solidarity with Beza were arrested.

Codreanu's agitation, in the meantime, had kept him in constant hot water. In the spring of 1930, marches and meetings had marked the Legion's appearance in Bessarabia, where the peasants had greeted Codreanu as enthusiastically as they had at Bereşti. Soon after this, the so-called Iron Guard was founded, to be the militant political section of the Legion in its struggle against Communism ("for me Communism = Judaism," said Codreanu). Codreanu had refused to encourage Beza, whom he knew but who was not a member of the Legion; but, though he disapproved of the attempted murder, he eventually endorsed it. A nationalist extremist could hardly blame extreme nationalistic acts. Arrested and imprisoned for alleged involvement in the crime, Codreanu was now thrown in with the imprisoned Macedonians, and befriended them. Soon the Macedo-Romanian group joined the Iron Guard, to provide some of its most active elements.

Early in 1931 both Iron Guard and Legion were dissolved by a decree of the National Peasant government. This did not prevent them from fighting the elections of that summer as the "C. Z. Codreanu Group," winning a paltry 34,183 votes. With less than 2 per cent of the total vote, the movement elected nobody to parliament. But one month later, in a by-election in the county of Neamṭ, Codreanu himself was returned with 11,176 votes as against the 7,124 of his Liberal runner-up. The dissolution of the Iron Guard had been quashed by friendly courts, and the movement was reactivated only to be dissolved again in 1932 by the right-wing government of Iorga. The officially nonexistent movement nevertheless went on to win a second by-election at Tutova, in south Moldavia, sending Professor Ion Codreanu to join his son in parliament. In fresh general elections held shortly thereafter, in July, 1932, the Iron Guard was to win 73,135 votes and five seats in the Chamber. The Legion was on its way.

Codreanu's insistence on organization and on going to the people were beginning to pay off. Legionaries campaigned by walking from village to village and from man to man. When Codreanu had run at Neamṭ, his teams had gone out to give a hand in the fields and had stayed on in the villages, gathering round the fires in the evening to tell the peasants what they had to offer. The following winter, in the Tutova by-election, they were mostly on foot once more. "Neither money nor means of transport, and a terrible winter all over the land. The election date fixed for March had to be put off until April because the automobiles of the politicians could not get past the snowdrifts." Where cars could not go, however, legionary teams got through on foot, playing hide-and-seek with the gendarmes, once hijacking a train, sometimes crossing frozen rivers, sometimes even falling into them, but carrying the word. These methods they never abandoned, partly from necessity (they were poor), partly because they proved effective. In every election, general or partial, legionaries stayed in the villages, gave a hand in the fields, played with the children, handed out small icons of the Captain, talked little, and sang much. It seemed to work.

Organization and devotion were not all the story. Depression had come to Romania, bringing hard times for everybody, most of all for peasants and civil servants. Using 1929 as a base year, Fischer-Galaṭi shows that money wages (100 in 1929) declined to 61 in 1933 and rose to 69 in 1939, while real wages which had risen to 116 in 1931 had by 1939 declined to 92. The wages of state employees were pared to the bone and, even so, sometimes remained unpaid for months. The commander of a provincial garrison got into trouble for appropriating credits—designed to pay the regiment's local suppliers—to give three months' back pay to his officers, who had been unpaid for half a year.

Hopes placed in the National Peasant party had vanished during its tenure of power. Despite its good intentions and the sincerity of two or three leading figures, it had turned out to be like all the others—incapable, greedy, and corrupt, its good elements powerless against the time-serving majority. In counties where the Peasant party was strong, the Iron Guard with its grill symbol made little headway. Outside these, however, the peasants were turning to the radical nationalist alternative it offered. The Guard, meanwhile, adjusting its propaganda to the new situation, insisted less on the anti-Semitism inherited from Cuza and more on concrete economic needs. In Transylvania, Muntenia, and especially Oltenia, Jews were few and anti-Semitic slogans fell rather flat. After 1932 legionarism tried to address all Romanians. Over half the country's four-score counties had been organized, seventeen legionary publications turned out some 35,000 copies a month, and membership was claimed to stand around 15,000. Shun programs though they did, an economic policy was found in the corporatist doctrines of an economist who had been governor of the National Bank, and held several ministerial posts: Mihail Manoilescu. Manoilescu argued that economic principles suited to economically advanced societies did not apply to more backward ones, like Romania. Free trade, which favors industrialized countries against agricultural ones, should be abandoned. The country needed a protected economy planned to foster those activities most productive in the national context. And this itself had to be based on a society in which an authoritarian government and a corporatist structure had eliminated the social conflicts inevitable in a liberal economy. The doctrine appealed to the peasants (those few who cared for such), to students and intellectuals fascinated by corporatist ideas current further west, and to enemies of the parliamentary system who envisaged a structure harking back to traditional guilds and trades.

But it was no monopoly of the Legion and never played a major part in its thinking or propaganda.

Trouble continued. There were clashes with the authorities, shootings or attempted shootings of ideological enemies, official reprisals against legionary militants. A frequent cause of friction was Codreanu's policy of propaganda by work. Local leaders were advised to initiate small projects for the public good: mending a bridge or a road, digging a culvert, clearing a ditch, draining a pond in their villages—without accepting any payment. There were churches to be restored or improved, dikes to build; all sorts of things needed doing. When the authorities, who recognized the propaganda value of such enterprises, forbade them, Codreanu made political capital out of that, too.

On December 10, 1933, at the height of yet one more electoral campaign, the ruling Liberal government, responding to its western allies' fears of fascist agitation, again dissolved the Guard. In the ensuing persecution, half a dozen legionaries were killed and hundreds were imprisoned until the elections had been held and the Liberals had secured the desired majority. On December 29, three legionaries "punished" I. G. Duca, the premier responsible for this, by shooting him down at point-blank range on a railroad station platform, and then gave themselves up.

When Duca had signed the decree that dissolved the Legion and kept it from the polls, General Gheorghe Cantacuzino (1869–1937), an old follower of Averescu's Popular Party who had since joined Codreanu, had written him, "You have signed your will." Although Duca's murderers seem to have planned their coup alone, they were encouraged to do it—if not put up to it—by the General. Codreanu, though he endorsed their act post facto, always claimed he had no knowledge of it. Even if that were true, the moral responsibility for this and other acts of murder and mayhem must be placed at his door. In any event, the hunt for him and his legionaries was now on in real earnest and those who could went into hiding for several months. Meanwhile, the murderers themselves seem to have been well treated. Guardians were friendly and facilitated movement and visits. They had cigars, sweets, and wine in the cell they shared, and their trial in spring, 1934, before a military court martial for which Codreanu emerged from hiding to take his place in the dock, turned into an indictment of Duca and the Liberal administration. The murderers were condemned to life imprisonment, but Codreanu and the Legion, vindicated, were cleared of guilt and free to take up their activities where they had left off.

The years that followed were years of success. Scores of work camps sprang up on land lent or donated by wealthy supporters (among them the king's own brother) or friendly communes; legionary restaurants, coöperatives, and stores were founded; the legionary organization spread. The political party was now known as Totul Pentru Ţară or TPT ("All for the Fatherland") and presided over by General Cantacuzino, a fierce, bemonocled, hirsute old soldier, much decorated for his war service in command of the Frontier Guards Brigade. Political opponents seemed cowed by the Legion's determination to strike back, no longer at underlings, but at the highest quarters. To stress this point, special death teams were set up "to punish traitors and scoundrels who sought to exterminate the Captain and his movement." Political personalities were warned that they would pay in person should anything happen to Codreanu, and teams of potential avengers were individually assigned. That these so-called death teams meant business became clear when, in 1936, a group of ten killed a sometime legionary leader, Mihail Stelescu, who had turned against Codreanu. They entered the Bucharest hospital where Stelescu lay recovering from an appendectomy, fired 120 shots into him, then (according to an official account) "they chopped up his body with an axe, danced around the pieces of flesh, prayed, kissed each other and cried with joy." These murderers also gave themselves up, to be sentenced to life imprisonment; and this time, too, the party hierarchy was cleared of any implication in the act.

Before the end of 1936, the foundation of a Legionary Workers' Corps reflected the movement's growing influence among artisans and industrial workers. The failure of the strikes of the 1920's had left workers disorganized and largely leaderless. The moderate parties ignored them. The Communist party was suppressed and practically nonexistent. The so-called Socialists were a small urban group drawing fewer votes (0.8 per cent of the total vote in 1937) than even the Jewish party. Codreanu's appeal, his hostility to capital, to the bourgeoisie, to the banks, to the system; his gospel of work and revalorification of labor, attracted the workers and, even more, the urban poor. Neither violence nor anti-Semitism put these off. Many of their bosses were Jewish, after all, and as to violence, enough had been used against them for them to be unmoved when their enemies were paid back in their own coin. After Duca's murder, many industrial workers turned to the Legion as the only movement willing to back its words with action. Soon after the Legionary Workers' Corps was founded, it boasted six thousand in Bucharest alone.

The growing exasperation of political passions was reflected in foreign as well as domestic policy and led to violent polemics in the press, which were resolved only by blows, attacks on newspaper staffs, and armed raids against the plants, newsstands, and vendors of rival publications. The Legion did not hide its admiration for Hitler and Mussolini. Much of its propaganda focused on the necessity for Romania to switch allies, following its true interests into the fascist camp. When civil war broke out in Spain, a symbolic group of seven legionaries (including a priest) went to fight for Franco. Two were killed: Ion Moța, by then vice-president of the All for the Fatherland party, and Vasile Marin. With unerring showmanship, their funeral in Bucharest, in February, 1937, was turned into a legionary triumph. It was attended by the Ministers of Germany, Italy, and Franco Spain, representatives of Portugal and Japan, delegates of the Polish Patriotic Youth, and a number of native personalities. The immense and orderly procession (by agreement with the police, order was kept by the Legion's own guards) demonstrated legionary popularity and power. Embarrassing questions were asked in parliament and the press when it was revealed that the Legion possessed its own police and its own judiciary.[4] The Ministers of Justice and of the Interior resigned, to

---

[4] In January, 1937, this legionary police had arrested the president of the Liberal Students' organization and tortured him. Tried before a Legion "court," he had been condemned to twenty-five lashes with a whip and released after execution

be replaced by more determined figures. Magistrates were instructed to proceed more vigorously against an organization whose growing influence now seemed to threaten not just the peace but the security of the state.

"The Legionary Movement will never have recourse to conspiracy or coup d'etat," Codreanu had announced in February, 1937. "Such things are foolish." But subversion could also proceed by legal means, at least as the Establishment saw it, and the 1937 election proved it. Unwilling to let the ruling Liberals manage the elections so as to secure the 40 per cent of the total vote needed to give them another ruling majority, TPT joined the National Peasant party and the right-wing Neo-Liberals in an ad hoc coalition against the Liberals who had allied themselves to a number of older nationalist groups. The strange coalition served its purpose. For the first time in a decade, relatively free elections produced a relatively faithful expression of the voters' will. With nearly 16 per cent of the votes and sixty-six deputies, TPT emerged as the third strongest party in the land, running close behind the National Peasants.

With Liberals discredited by years of ineffective rule and National Peasants out of the running through the King's disfavor, which had long kept them in the wilderness, Codreanu's hour seemed to have come. The King, who objected to his last-minute alliance with the Peasant party, nevertheless regarded Codreanu's criticism of democracy, parliament, and political parties with sympathy. He had reason to remember the Legion's support at the time of his return to the country in 1930 and to appreciate its monarchist sentiments. But the King's mistress was Jewish and his closest advisers and friends had long been the chief target of the Legion's hatred. King Carol liked to deal with pliable men, and this Codreanu was not. It is said that, invited to pay a discreet visit to the royal palace, Codreanu refused. It had to be the front door or nothing. And nothing it was. The King fell back on Co-

---

of the sentence with strict injunctions to keep his mouth shut. It took police a month to get to the bottom of the affair, and they might never have done so had it not been for the changes in the government and governmental policies that occurred after the February funeral.

dreanu's worst enemies, the National Christian party of old Professor Cuza who now shared its leadership with an agrarian nationalist, the Transylvanian poet Octavian Goga.

In the elections of December, 1937, the Goga-Cuza ticket had garnered 9.7 per cent of the vote and thirty-nine deputies out of 387. But the new chamber was dissolved before it ever met and Goga was entitled to hope that, at the levers of power, he would reap the usual governmental benefits. Coalitions were declared illegal, the National Peasants were split by attracting some of Codreanu's tougher opponents into the cabinet, all paramilitary formations were suppressed, and heavy censorship silenced or suspended the hostile press, especially that of the moderate left.

In honor of his peasantist adherents and the four Peasant ministers of his cabinet (one of them, Armand Călinescu, a particular foe of the Legion), Goga changed the name of his formation to the National Christian Peasant party; but the measures he introduced were typical of Cuzist anti-Semitism. The citizenship of Romanian Jews was to be subject to unfriendly revision and the country purged of alien elements. "Romanization" of education and the professions began, excluding Jewish lawyers, teachers, and state employees, prohibiting Jewish ownership of certain enterprises, applying the *numerus clausus* in fact if not in name. Frightened and resentful, Jewish and foreign interests withdrew from the market place, bringing business to a standstill, and threatening the country's economy with collapse. Meanwhile, a fresh electoral campaign produced a situation akin to civil war, with nationalist fighting nationalist under the sly gaze of the King.

Intervention from various quarters—including the Germans, who were heavily backing Goga, and from General Antonescu, then a minister in Goga's cabinet—led to negotiations between Codreanu and Goga, as a result of which, on February 8, 1938, Codreanu announced that his party would abandon all further electoral activity. It would run but, henceforth, keep out of the campaign. This evidence of a nationalist entente did not suit Carol. Within forty-eight hours Goga had been ousted by royal fiat (he retired quietly and died soon after); within two more days the constitution had been abolished, the elections indefinitely adjourned, the activities of political parties suppressed, a puppet national government set up under the Orthodox Patriarch but run in practice by Codreanu's foe, Călinescu, who was soon to succeed to the premiership. Unwilling or unable to come to terms with the nationalist revolutionaries, the King was going to sponsor a similar national revolution of his own, based on his own one-man rule in his own one-party state.

Codreanu's reaction to all this was to combine formal protest with a call for fasting and prayers, the self-liquidation of his party with the affirmation that he would wait and see. Events abroad were running in his favor, as German predominance in eastern Europe became clearer every day. When Romania, in its turn, entered the German orbit, the King would have to change his tune. The Legion, announced a circular of February 21, would refuse to answer violence with violence, but would bear whatever was done to it. "Our time has not yet come. It is still their time. If the generation of our elders thinks that what it did is best, we have no lessons to give them. Before God and History, they bear the responsibility."

But if Codreanu thought he could afford to wait, his enemies could not. Within a few weeks, having refused his friends' advice to leave the country, he was arrested. Condemned first on a charge of insulting a minister in office—Iorga—by castigating his share in the King's coup, he was retried on charges of conspiring to take over the state. The prosecution argued that the Legion was a pure terrorist organization, with a widespread espionage network and close connections with foreign powers, was involved in the murder of Duca and others, possessed hidden arms, and planned an armed rising. Most of these allegations were founded, but they were never proved in court. The trial was a hurried, put-up job, the military court as prejudiced against Codreanu as others had been in his favor on past occasions, and the verdict came as a foregone conclusion. Codreanu was condemned to ten years' hard labor and six years' further loss of his civil rights. The alleged conspiracy against the state was never demonstrated. Codreanu had repeatedly insisted on keeping within the bounds of legality, respecting the constitution and avoiding provocation. Legionary terrorism was a fact, but actual terroristic acts had never been brought home to Codreanu himself. In any event, charges of subversion ill became the men who had just subverted the country's constitution. The most interesting charge was never clearly formulated: that of Codreanu's connections with foreign powers, a matter which remains imprecise even today.

What are the ascertainable facts in this connection?

In a memoir submitted to the King on November 5, 1936, Codreanu assured Carol that legionaries would refuse to fight alongside "Bolshevik powers" and pressed for alliance with "the states of national revolution, fighting in defense of the cross [*sic*] and of a millenary civilization against bolshevism and its satellites, fighting for the destruction of nations and the downfall of Christian civilization." A year later (November 30, 1937) he made a resounding declaration to the press: "Forty-eight hours after the victory of the legionary movement, Romania will be allied to Rome and Berlin, thus entering the line of its historical world mission: the defense of the cross, of Christian culture and civilization."

Legionaries looked for allies and supporters abroad, as all Romanians did, and they were encouraged by Fascist and Nazi successes, as their opponents were by those of the Western democracies. In the 1930's, all the Romanian Right sought German support, and Codreanu's competitors were far less discreet about this than he seems to have been. Invited to Germany, Cuza and Goga had been received by Hitler and Goering. So had the Neo-Liberal leader, George Brătianu. Yet, complained a legionary in a letter to Charles Maurras, it was the legionaries, who had refused the German invitations, who were accused of being Nazi tools.

All the evidence leads one to believe that serious German support went largely to Goga and Cuza, whose coalition itself seems to have been spurred by German intervention. The Germans, of course, kept their irons in several fires and their documents show that they were in a position to intervene in all nationalist quarters, including legionary ones. The documents also indicate that, contrary to legionary claims at the time and since, the Legion received support from Germany at least in 1937 and early 1938, although probably not nearly as much as did Goga. A certain amount of confusion always existed in the public mind concerning different national groups, and this was perhaps deliberately maintained, as when the *Bulletin périodique* (September 9, 1936) referred to "the Iron Guards of Mr. Cuza" and the Hitlerite subventions they received. But Sir Reginald Hoare, who had been British Minister to Bucharest, could still declare (in *La Roumanie indépendante* of December 25, 1947) that, in 1937, "the Iron Guard was not directed by Germany and remained a pre-Nazi formation."

Until 1938, the Legion seems to have derived the bulk of its funds from the contributions of members, dignitaries, and deputies, from donations, and at times perhaps from subsidies provided by sympathetic government officials. It has been affirmed that certain industrialists contributed what might have been protection money, and although some of these were Jewish, it is possible that they did indeed contribute as they also contributed to Franco at the time of his rebellion. Subsidies may also have come through Spanish channels, as Henri Prost affirms in his well-informed *Destin de la Roumanie* (Paris: 1954), though the legionaries deny it. In any event, subsidies or no, while Codreanu lived the Legion was no conscious agent of Nazism. The Captain always insisted on the peculiar Romanian national tradition, on the Legion's own peculiar style, and on those matters—especially spiritual—that separated it from other kindred movements. One might add that this state of things changed after Codreanu's imprisonment and even more after his death. Then, deprived of its popular base, of local support and local resources, the surviving leaders of the Legion fell back more on German support and paid for it by letting themselves be used increasingly, though often unconsciously, as catspaws, less of "Germany" than of Nazi party policies. The fact that they were driven to this by necessity does not alter the seeming but not uncommon paradox of nationalists serving the ends of alien nations.

It is hard to tell whether, with Codreanu once put away, the King and his premier, Călinescu, really intended his death. Certainly they meant to steal his thunder. Their new regime had all the verbiage and the trappings of the new order in Europe. To fill the gap left by abolition of the parties, a new party—the

Front of National Revival—was set up, complete with uniforms and military hierarchy. For the nation's youth, which Carol hoped to wrest from the Legion's influence, another uniformed organization was developed, the Străjeri ("Watch"), many of whose instructors were secretly devoted legionaries. Călinescu's speeches are fascinating for their imitation of legionary themes and style. Labor, patriotism, probity, correctness, youth, sacrifice, ridding the country of foreign elements, Christianity, nationalism, pride and dignity, family and tradition, were all given their due, while the old regime, divisive and corrupt, was scornfully set at nought. Clearly, the old regime had found a man determined enough, and sufficiently imaginative and opportunistic, to defend its essentials while replacing some of the surface trappings with others more up to date. And Călinescu was able; with time, he might even have realized some of his reforming plans. But time he would not have.

The Legion, meanwhile, though broken, was hardly supine. Hundreds of its leaders lay in concentration camps; others were in hiding. From his prison, Codreanu, convinced that time worked for him, urged resignation and calm. Those legionary leaders who had escaped arrest, however, began to doubt the rightness of his views. An unsuccessful attempt seems to have been made to detach these men from him and persuade them to follow Carol. But, if they disregarded Codreanu, they were more inclined to rationalize their action in going the other way: toward the violence from which Codreanu sought to dissuade them. The depleted legionary leadership had been taken over by provincial militants among whom one of the most active was a high-school teacher called Horia Sima, regional chief of the Banat and sometime student of Nae Ionescu. Unknown to the Bucharest police, he and his friends could get about more easily than the older activists.

Sima's underground teams began by distributing incendiary flysheets and threatening letters, but soon went on to more positive action: a Jewish lawyer was shot down, Jewish shops and taverns were sacked, Jews were beaten, bombs were thrown in provincial synagogues, timber yards were set on fire. Codreanu felt increasingly that the terrorists outside were playing with his life and those of their imprisoned comrades. A letter smuggled out to this effect seems to have fallen flat. At last, on November 24, a student murder group ambushed the Rector of the University of Cluj, a relative and friend of Călinescu, gravely wounded him, and killed the policeman who accompanied him. Sima, apparently, had tried to stop the attempt, but had been ignored. The sorcerer's apprentice had sown the wind; it was his comrades who reaped the whirlwind.

Whatever Carol's and Călinescu's intentions may have been, the Cluj murder attempt coming on top of the long terrorist campaign settled Codreanu's fate. On the night of November 29–30,[5] Codreanu, the three murderers of Duca, and the ten murderers of Stelescu, were taken from their prison, tied with ropes, and sat on benches in two military trucks. Behind each prisoner sat a gendarme. The trucks drove off and stopped on a deserted stretch, the gendarmes slipped cords over the prisoners' heads and pulled, strangling them to death. The fourteen bodies were then laid by the roadside, shot in the back, reloaded in the trucks, and buried in a common grave within the precincts of the military prison at Jilava, not far from Bucharest. On December 1, 1938, a brief communiqué announced that they had been shot while trying to escape. Out of their corpses, dragons' teeth would grow.

In February, 1939, *Paris Soir* quoted an interview with Călinescu: "The Iron Guard is already an old story. . . . The Iron Guard no longer exists." The premier's words were somewhat premature. Only a month before, the explosion of a hidden laboratory in a Bucharest back street had exposed a plot for a rising on Malapartian lines (Curzio Malaparte's *Technique du Coup d'Etat* was no less popular with legionaries than with *Cagoulards*) and a large cache of homemade flame-throwers destined to provide the clinching argument on that occasion. Groups of legionaries had taken refuge

---

[5] On November 28, King Carol had returned to Bucharest from a foreign tour during which he had had an interview with Hitler on the very day of the attack against the Rector of Cluj. The German Minister, Fabricius, expressed the view that legionary violence always broke out when other Romanian political figures tried to reach an understanding with Germany. See A. Hillgruber, *Hitler, König Carol und Marschall Antonescu* (Wiesbaden: 1954), pp. 26–28, 276.

in Germany and Poland, but there was a lot of coming and going and police were constantly discovering plots focused on avenging the dead leader. Rumors circulated that Codreanu was not dead but had escaped and hidden to await the moment for his return. The government seems at first to have encouraged these, expecting to disorient Codreanu's followers and use hope to soften their vindictiveness. This was a game at which two could play, and surviving legionary leaders in turn helped fan the rumor to keep their followers' faith alive and confuse the public.

Still, they knew better. Codreanu was dead. Even had he not asked explicitly for revenge (as he had done in a circular of February, 1938), his murderers would have been pursued with unrelenting rancor. The exiles in Berlin thought only of revenge. But there was one problem: the legionary hostages in Călinescu's camps. Codreanu had to be avenged. But his avengers had in advance to accept their own death, too, because their act was likely to precipitate the execution of many imprisoned comrades. On the basis of this equation, several teams of terrorists began to lay their plans. But the police were on the alert and the legionary rump at home was infiltrated with police informers. One after the other the conspirators were captured, men and women were tortured, strangled, beaten or shot to death, their bodies quietly cremated. At last, on September 21, 1939, a group of six succeeded in ambushing the premier and shooting him dead. Then, driving to the offices of the broadcasting station, they took them over for long enough to announce over the air that Codreanu's murderer had been "punished"—after which they surrendered to the police.

Within a few hours, their corpses and those of three accomplices lay on the spot where Călinescu had been shot. Nor did retribution cease there. In every county, prefects were ordered to designate three local legionaries for immediate execution. Their bodies, hung on telegraph poles or spread-eagled in the market place, were for days, like those in Bucharest, on public exhibition. In the concentration camps, meanwhile, selected groups were being shot—sixty-eight say some reports, ninety-two say others. The government was in a position to exact retribution two and three hundredfold. The years of overbidding had come to a hideous end. But those responsible apparently regretted nothing. The public had come to think that the Legion had been broken, the faithful had been losing faith and drifting away. The bloodletting of September, 1939, was a terrible thing, explained one of the men who had planned it in Berlin, but it got the Legion out of a critical situation [sic] and restored its faith. It was a fine epitaph upon a hecatomb.

The mass reprisals over, both sides stopped to draw breath and take stock of the situation. Călinescu's murder had come three weeks after the beginning of a war that threatened the country's very being, and his death deprived Carol of the only man sufficiently strong and able to hold the country together for him. German successes seemed to show how right the advocates of a German alliance had been. With Poland gone, the threat of Russian expansion further corroborated the arguments of those who had never believed the Western democracies could or would afford effective help. Ill-led, ill-armed, and ill-prepared to face external pressures, the government now sought to restore a precarious internal unity. In January, 1940, it began to free those legionaries who had survived the purges. By spring, it was pressing them to accept the thaw and sending emissaries to Berlin, hoping to coax back those who had taken refuge there. Sima, arrested while trying to reënter the country, was treated with special consideration. German victory in the west turned the terrorist leader into a useful partner. On June 23, a Sima manifesto called legionaries to join Carol's new Party of the Nation. On June 26, a Russian ultimatum forced Romania to abandon Bessarabia and northern Bucovina. On June 28, as Russian troops entered these provinces amid scenes of humiliation and chaos, Sima and two of his henchmen entered the government of the man he had for so long opposed. Although he resigned his portfolio shortly thereafter, representatives of the Legion continued in office for the remaining days of Carol's reign.

Consistently antirevisionist and cool to Germany heretofore, Romania now hurried to curry German favor by anti-Semitic and anti-British measures, and to assert its German sympathies by promoting those known to have been Germany's friends. The legionary hierarchy briefly split, one group insisting on Carol's abdication, another arguing that the foreign dangers demanded a suspension of internal feuds. By the end of August, however, the opponents of compromise were gaining. Unable to resist German pressure, Romania was forced to give up southern Dobrogea to Bulgaria and northern Transylvania to Hungary. It was the cost of ill-preparedness and of a steadfast and honorable adherence to the Anglo-French camp, but the responsibility fell on Carol. The evidence of the Vienna Award was obvious. The King and his henchmen had failed, and now they had to go. A new state could not be forged by men with old sins.

On September 3 the legionaries rose in Bucharest and in two big provincial cities—Braşov in the Carpathians and Constanţa on the Black Sea. They tried to occupy strategic points—broadcasting stations, telephone exchanges, police barracks. The *putsch*, which seems to have succeeded in the provincial towns, failed in Bucharest and would soon have been scotched by army intervention. But the disturbances and the mass demonstrations they sparked made Carol turn to the one man he had till now avoided: General Ion Antonescu. Sometime chief of the General Staff, Antonescu was the ablest and most awkward of Romanian soldiers, a redhead of strong convictions and strong will who had served in several cabinets, including Goga's. The General had incurred royal disgrace as much for his refusal to compromise on vital defense issues as for his associations with Codreanu. Now he was the only man who might control the army and, with the army by him, Carol need not despair. But the King clutched at logs destined to crush him. Antonescu pressed for abdication and, finally, the King gave in. On September 6, 1940, while Antonescu announced the accession of a new king, Carol's son Mihai, a special train heavily laden with royal possessions carried Carol, his mistress Helena Lupescu, and his retinue out of the land. The abortive *putsch* had attained its object.

To the "Dear Legionaries," Antonescu now appealed in solemn tones: "The powers of evil have been broken forever. With the aid of destiny, the Fatherland's day of rebirth has come and with it your victory and mine." On September 14, a royal decree established the National Legionary State, with Antonescu as its Leader, and Sima, Commander of the Legionary Movement, as vice-premier.

The Legion was in power at last. But for how long? The tandem was less viable than it seemed. Nationalism is an equivocal means of plastering over divergencies between men of different minds. It does not work very well when temporary allies are placed in a situation where incantations must give way to policies. Antonescu was no doctrinaire. On September 6 he had declared that his program would "stem wholly from integral nationalism." The first laws of his regime, like those of any soldier, were discipline and order. He was less interested in social reform than in fostering agriculture, if need be at the expense of "artificially created industries." Conservative, paternalistic, authoritarian, he sought honesty, efficiency, and unity on traditionalistic lines.

Sima and his friends, on the contrary, wanted a totalitarian legionary state and wanted it at once. An end should be put to the last vestiges of liberalism and corruption. "A legionary regime cannot last in a liberal economic structure," Sima wrote to Antonescu. "Those of the old world, even when sincere, can do no good, for they cannot think in the spirit of a state-directed economy. Here is the nevralgic center of the problem, nowhere else." The country's economy, its press, and its cultural activities directed, the leftovers of the old regime suppressed, the Legion's monopoly should be established once and for all. "In legionary Romania there is no longer room for any other party," wrote Sima to Antonescu again. . . . "Who dares, must be punished. This is a fundamental attribute of totalitarian states. But in Romania, exactly the contrary happens. Not only are the old parties, murderers of our youth . . . not placed on the index, but they are encouraged and quietly advised to reorganize."

In the conflict between the two men, Antonescu represented the old order, Sima something else. That something else, however, was not very like Codreanu's dreams. As Harald Laeuen observes in his book on *Marschall Antonescu* (Essen: 1943), Sima's Legion was no longer the Legion of Codreanu. That had gone down in the persecutions of 1938–1939 and in the blood bath in which they culminated. The new legionary leadership was made up of men of the second rank. Worse, the new legionary membership was a looser, more heterogeneous collection, less dedicated, less disciplined, less well trained.

In 1936, one of Codreanu's circulars had warned against admission "of weak or bad elements. It is a known fact: whenever a current runs more strongly in favor of an organization, all sorts of inferior elements . . . rush to get into it." A year later, another circular had shown how easily a certain kind of success could threaten failure of the movement's aims:

How horrible it would be if upon the holy sacrifice of our comrades a victorious caste should set up shop, the sacrifices of their predecessors opening the doors to business, to coups, to thefts, to the exploitation of others. . . . In such a case, the miserable mass of Romanians would, by our victory, change only the firm of its exploiters and the squeezed-out country would waste its energy supporting a new category of vampires out to suck its blood: ourselves.

Now what Codreanu had envisaged came to pass. Opportunists, time-servers, men on the make, seeking profit or simply excitement and the cheap glory of a crossbelt and a colored shirt, rushed to the support of victory. With prefectures, police, and most ministries in legionary hands, opportunities for profitable patriotic activity were not lacking. The "romanization" policy provided plenty of occasions to take over, buy cheaply, or simply annex businesses and real estate owned by Jews and foreigners. State-appointed Romanization Commissars, all of them legionaries or friends of legionaries, proved as greedy and dishonest as the profiteers of the old regime, but ruder and more rapacious. The Legionary Workers' Corps suddenly boasted over 13,000 members, who contributed vast sums to party funds, some through dues, some through donations, most of them through unwilling exaction. The party treasury thrived on the unscrupulous activities of its members, whose crookedness it condoned because they served its needs.

Fish begins to smell from the head, runs a Romanian proverb; and the legionary state smelled worse with every week that passed. With the enthusiastic support of many faculty members, an official commission charged with "the adaptation of higher education

to the structure of the National Legionary State," set up its inquisition in schools and universities. Antonescu had frequent reason to complain of legionary campaigns to rid the schools of their
political enemies. "You're all going to fall under Bolshevik rule,"
he warned his cabinet. "At the School of Agronomy, legionary
students are expelling the best students on the pretext that they
are not legionaries." "The teachers must be reëducated by their
own students," the legionary Minister of Education had declared;
and thousands of students took up his words against their non-
conforming mentors. Boys and girls of high-school age were the
keenest partisans, encouraged by their elders to turn pranks into
effective and sometimes murderous action. Members of rival nationalist groups were the special object of legionary persecution.
The Cuzists had never been forgiven for spurning Codreanu and
adding to his woes. Now they received their deserts. The records
teem with cases of Cuzists, their families, even their widows, being
attacked, molested, having their homes searched, their swastikas
broken, their literature confiscated.

More disquieting, however, were the reforming glances the
Legion cast toward the army. "The officer must no longer belong
to a separate caste," wrote one reformer ominously. "He must pre-
occupy himself with all the social, political, economic, cultural
problems that affect the nation's soul. The army must belong to the
people. The officer must no longer be a chief imposed by orders and
regulations. He must be elected, or considered as elected by the
soldiers under his command."

Antonescu suspected the Legion was preparing another rising,
one of its own, which to him would be no better than a Bolshevik
revolution. He knew that all nests, and especially the Workers'
Corps, were being armed and that they made much ado about
training in weapon-handling, street-fighting, target practice, and
night marches. Insistent rumors heralded a night of the long knives,
in which the movement would take revenge on past persecutors,
but also perhaps grasp the total power it coveted.

At the end of November, sixty-four prisoners accused of crimes
against the Legion and held in Jilava jail, where the remains of
Codreanu and his thirteen fellow victims were being exhumated,

were murdered in one bloody night. On the following day legionary teams attempted to kidnap several leading political figures and succeeded in murdering two—one of them the old conservative nationalist, Professor Iorga. More would probably have died but for Antonescu's intervention and that of the horrified and embarrassed Sima. The murderous spree at Jilava, the butchery of political enemies, precipitated the first serious crisis of the alliance, which was patched up by the intervention of a German envoy who argued (according to Sima's recollections) "that things should not be taken tragically, that revenge is the order of the day when radical changes of regime take place, and that Antonescu should understand the situation."

Antonescu did. The decisive factor in it were the Germans, and the Germans cared less for their ideological allies than for an orderly regime which would ensure internal peace and prove a reliable satellite, delivering the oil, grain, and manpower they needed. The Germans had to be convinced that legionary enthusiasm did not excuse instability, lack of experience, incapacity in running things, and the chaos and dissensions they created. This, the legionaries themselves would do in time. The question was how long that time would be and whether the general could outlast his foes. Both sides jockeyed for power and for German support. And in that game the legionaries were hopelessly outmatched.

As far as one can tell, the November murders affected legionary popularity little. Sima declares that, far from proving harmful, this evidence of determination and of power (for the criminals received no punishment) brought such an influx of adherents that admissions to the movement had to be temporarily suspended. Far from apologizing for having his followers run amuck, Sima was moved to complain of the "extreme susceptibility of the representatives of the old order, whenever the slightest infringement of the law takes place. But this," he told a crowd of Bucharest students on December 10, "is a very new sentiment, never evident when legionary corpses were left to rot in the street. The men of a thousand illegalities and crimes ask the legionaries to be saints and gods, after killing our Leader who alone could forgive them and after humiliating and crucifying our youth for the last twenty years."

Cabinet meetings had to deal with endless crimes, confiscations, and thefts committed by legionaries or by persons masquerading as such. Antonescu was shocked by their easy way with private property:

Some day you will have to account for it. . . . Public opinion holds with humanity, with legality, with respect for right and law. It does not approve this sort of thing: going into people's houses and taking their money and their shares. These are gangsters' habits. . . . I cannot endorse them. I cannot even take the fortunes of the Jews, because they belong to them. General Antonescu has said [*sic*] that he guarantees everybody's fortune and property. And then comes a man in a green shirt and takes everything.

Soon Antonescu was accusing Sima and his Minister of the Interior of bolshevizing the country—"Terrible things are happening . . . the Bolsheviks have got into the Legionary Movement"—and that is how it must have seemed to him. But it was also a convenient line to take against the anarchic social revolutionary velleities of his rivals.

Tension mounted. There was serious talk of a legionary plan to murder their political enemies on New Year's Eve so that Romania could enter the new year "purified of the leprosy of the past." Loyal police and army units were warned to stand by. Nothing happened, and perhaps nothing was meant to happen; but the scare reflected the strain of unrelenting legionary excesses. Official figures, perhaps inflated, published by Antonescu in his account of these days, give a partial list of legionary exploits committed before the final rising of January, 1941, and exclusive of the Jilava murders: people maltreated, 450; people kidnapped and illegally held, 323; people killed, 9; houses broken into (mostly Romanian), 88; cases of confiscatory "sales," 1,162; goods illegally "confiscated," 1,081; houses forcibly taken over and occupied, 260; cases of pillage, 65. Antonescu's New Year Message appealed to legionaries as to riotous children:

The country needs quiet, work, and brotherhood. Remember that the fall of others came from greedy pursuit of worldly goods and interests. . . . Do not inflict on others the sufferings you suffered. . . . Eliminate from your ranks those who do such deeds. . . . Peoples are not led by destructive thunderclaps. . . . The enemies of the Legion and of the land rejoice over the excesses some of you perpetrate. . . .

As Antonescu probably expected, such warnings went unheeded. January, 1941, saw an intensification of legionary campaigns to discredit the General as protector of the corrupt old order. Wild attacks against the bourgeoisie, the British (Antonescu was known as an anglophile), and the Masons, succeeded each other in the extremist press. Police raids on masonic lodges preceded a communique promising sensational revelations and an attempt to implicate Antonescu's friends in the Judeo-Masonic conspiracy. "The Revolution is not finished," warned the front page of the legionary *Buna Vestire* ("Good News") on January 16.

Antonescu had just returned from Germany, where Sima had declined to accompany him. The General had convinced Hitler that further coöperation with Sima was impossible and that one of the two men would have to go. He seems to have returned to Bucharest assured of Hitler's favor and at once signed a decree abolishing the Romanization Commissars, a direct blow at the Legion's prestige and income. Within forty-eight hours the murder of a German officer in the capital gave him the opening he needed to displace the legionary Minister of the Interior and his chief of police, replacing them with reliable soldiers. The new Minister of the Interior then took steps to remove legionary prefects and chiefs of police and to replace them with army officers. In most places this was achieved by calling the incumbents to "conferences" in Bucharest or in the regional capital and then moving in while they were away.

Meanwhile, in Bucharest, vast legionary demonstrations protesting the removal of the Interior Minister soon turned to something more. Demonstrators clashed with troops, weapons were brought out, legionaries barricaded themselves at key points throughout the capital, and wild rioting and looting broke out in certain districts, in which about two hundred people were killed, mostly Jews, and some with dreadful brutality. Dozens were hung on butcher's hooks in the slaughterhouse. Soldiers caught by the crowds were doused with oil and set on fire. Nor did the participants' patriotic fervor obscure more concrete interests. After the fighting was over, 144 truckloads of stolen wares were recovered from legionary centers alone.

For two days the issue of the struggle remained uncertain. The head of the German secret services in Bucharest, eventually removed in disgrace, seems to have backed the Legion. But German official circles stood by the General and made it clear that Sima could expect no German support. Hitler's telephoned advice to Antonescu had been radical: "After the bloodletting, attack and make a clean sweep. . . ." The advice was followed and the Legion collapsed for the last time. Its rule had lasted from September 14, 1940, to January 23, 1941. The National Legionary State was officially abolished a few weeks later, on February 15. Like all who take the sword it had perished by the sword. According to official figures, on January 21, 22, and 23, 370 persons had died and 44 been wounded in Bucharest; 46 were dead and 78 wounded in other parts of the country. During the month that followed, while scores of legionaries were smuggled out under the German aegis, some eight thousand people were imprisoned, some of whom still linger in jail today.

The Legion's "rebellion" was actually its resistance to a coup by its governmental partner to eliminate it from power. There is every reason to suppose that legionaries had considered a coup of their own, but Antonescu beat them to it. Once again, in the game of illegality, the forces of "order" proved more enterprising, more expeditive, and more ruthless than those of revolution. Every government with which the Legion had tangled had shown more ability in breaking the law or using it against them. The legionary story is one long tragicomedy of errors. At no time does Hitler, who thought well of Codreanu, seem to have given a damn for the Legion. Those who were smuggled out, probably in German uniforms, owed their escape to the private enterprise of the secret services and of a few German friends.

In March, 1941, a plebiscite approved Antonescu's new "national and social state" by 99.9 per cent of the votes cast. The exaggerated figures nevertheless reflected the widespread support enjoyed by Antonescu, whose fight against the Legion had increased his popularity. The Legion itself was dissolved, but many of its older members, Codreanu's father among them, who had disapproved of the younger firebrands and their cruder ways, pledged the new dictator their support. Antonescu himself became the object of public adulation similar to that which Codreanu and Sima once enjoyed. In the introduction to a volume of his speeches we find him variously described as leader, visionary, philosopher, apostle, father, savior, synthesis of Latin genius, personification of Daco-Roman tradition, and superman of dizzying simplicity.

Despite the trappings of fascism and the politics of anti-Semitism which it took over, Antonescu's regime remained resolutely conservative. His invasion of Russia at Germany's side in the summer of 1941 provided all the required slogans from the cornucopia of the anti-Bolshevik crusade. Vague suggestions of a "Romanian imperialism" from the Tisa to the Bug, put forward by crackpot Cuzists, never got anywhere. Romanians wanted their lost provinces but coveted no empire, only a peace which neither their German masters nor their Russian enemies would permit. Held in gentle confinement by the Germans, several hundred legionaries hung, like a sword of Damocles, over Antonescu's head. And when Romania finally left the war, on August 24, 1944, the legionaries who had been interned in German camps were dusted off once more and set up in Vienna as a government-in-exile under Sima's premiership. This puppet government helped recruit new forces from Romanian prisoners and workers on German-held territory, and some units thus formed saw action before the end of war. In April, 1945, as Russian troops approached Vienna, Sima's group moved to Alt-Aussee and, shortly thereafter, went underground to await better days (Sima himself used papers in the name of Iosef Weber). They have long since resurfaced and are busily engaged in the post-mortems, hagiography, and factional strife that mark the annals of all émigré politics.

What can we note, what can we learn from this superficial account of the legionary movement? The first thing is that in a country where everybody is nationalistic, nationalism does not set a movement apart either as extremist or as especially right-wing.

Nationalism had helped to win Romania's independence and its vast accessions of territory, but it implied no specific line of conduct. Slogans it had a-plenty but no program as such. Chauvinism had to make up for a defective economic policy, xenophobia atone for poverty and stagnation, leader cults promise to remedy all ills and answer all questions. The Legion was not the first to introduce unreality in Romanian politics. Codreanu merely sensed a need and devised a more powerful magic than did other prestidigitators around him. His answers to Romanian problems were "religious" because in effect Romania's problems—those she was in a position to tackle herself—were spiritual ones first. In other words, Romania's economic problems could be approached only through an ideological revolution, and after it. The Communists have proceeded no differently.

But Romania's freedom to act at all was limited—limited on one level by the interests and decisions of greater powers, and on another, more immediate one, by her economic, technological, and cultural dependence on others. Dominant in nineteenth-century Romania, these remained factors of consequence in the greater Romania of the twentieth century, creating conditions not dissimilar to those we can observe today in Latin America or certain new African and Asian nations: the use of the state as an instrument of westernization; the growth of a bureaucracy that becomes almost a social class, and the quasi-structural corruption of this class; the vital role of foreign minority groups, increasingly resented by the natives, and its counterpart—the laborious development of a native middle class and intelligentsia, and its conflict with those foreign elements that had begun by developing commerce, industry, and the professions; the upper classes and the politicians behaving like potential migrants, salting funds away in foreign banks, brandishing the national banner the more vigorously for their lack of faith in the country's future; the educated classes' dream of escape toward the cultivated and social centers of the west, with a concomitant aping of Western fashions and manners; the fascination of bright young men with foreign policy and foreign affairs, which offer escape from the insoluble difficulties at home; last but not least, the tendency to react against foreign threats too vast to face by attacking local targets weak enough to be destroyed (e.g., not Russians, but Jews), the hunt for internal conspirators consoling the fearful but impotent victims of external pressure and providing attractive derivatives for popular discontent.

On all these counts, Romanian conditions were similar to those in other postcolonial societies, with the vast mass of the population slow to shift from its traditional agricultural pursuits and feeling Western technology an alien thing, causing an industrial and economic revolution in which the masses appear not as actors but as objects. It is not surprising that most Romanian nationalists were populists and traditionalists, opposing modernity sometimes even more than they did Communism. The greater part of the liberal left and the Peasant party seem to have agreed on this with the radical right. And here is another obvious peculiarity of the Romanian situation: the formation and the spirit of the Romanian intelligentsia were rural. All loved the peasantry, all saw in it the reservoir of national energies, the source of possible renewal for the state. "We are a country of peasants," Eminescu had written, "and must run our house in peasant fashion." When the Legion echoed his words it was not as different from other parties as movements in other countries might be, with a different sociocultural structure. In Romania, as in Algeria or Egypt, to lean on the peasants was to lean on the masses.

But Legionary leaders were of the middle class, more specifically of the lower-middle classes, the sons of wealthier peasants, of priests, of teachers, already removed from the toiling poor. This, it might be remarked, is the class that seems to have furnished the leaders of most postcolonial nations today. More important, though, is the fact that middle-class origin provides little proof of anything. Most socialist and labor leaders belonged to the middle classes, as many communists have done. Lenin and Trotsky did, not only by birth but by education and occupation; and neither Stalin's background as a seminarist nor Zinoviev's as a teacher kept them from revolutionary leadership.

Not social origins but social values decide a man's orientation. Codreanu was not committed to the values of the society in which he moved, but to their radical change. That made him a radical

revolutionary. True, many of his ideals were those we associate
with the traditional Western bourgeoisie: work, family, the fatherland, honesty, and justice. But the musketeer ideal which he proposed ignored security, the romantic ideal neglected thrift, the
youthful spirit emphasized adventure and risk. Besides, Western
bourgeois ideals themselves had not become acclimated in Romania.
Had they done so, there would not have been such need for the
very homely but essential aspects of Codreanu's reformism. In the
circumstances, even bourgeois ideals could play a radical role, as
they had done in the French Revolution he so much disliked.

In their revendications and their criticism, Codreanu and his
friends did not go far beyond the existing Romanian tradition. It
was in the conclusions they drew from observations they shared
with many others that they stood out. It was by acting on these
conclusions that they became dangerous radicals rather than ordinary tavern critics. And it is perhaps by their readiness to act on
ideas many others express that all extremists are identified.

The common identification of extremism and alienation ("An
extremist group is an alienated group," writes Edward Shils in *The
Torments of Secrecy* [Glencoe: 1956]), does not apply to them—
or only applies post facto. It was not alienation that made extremists of the Iron Guard, but commitment. In Romania, the
concept of alienation is better applied to the ruling group and to
the urban, commercial, and professional classes. Their ideas and
their ways, in many ways commendable, were foreign to the local
tradition and to the local conditions they sought to change. The
Legion, on the contrary, operated like a fish in water—to borrow
a figure of speech from the other extreme. Their references to tradition were references to a reality corrupted but still very much
alive for them and their supporters, who were recruited largely
from the peasantry and from a lower-middle class just one remove
from the land.

The legionaries remind one, rather, of the fundamentalist mentality described by Alan F. Westin in his essay on the John Birch
Society (in *The Radical Right,* edited by Daniel Bell [Garden
City: 1964]). Both assume the existence of total conspiracies and
total solutions, both "refuse to believe in the integrity and patri-

otism of those who lead the dominant social groups"; both "reject the political system [and] lash out at 'politicians,' the major parties, and the give and take of political compromise"; both despise existing recipes for solving current problems and favor "drastic panaceas requiring major social change"; both advocate direct action, even to the point of calculated violence.

Yet the social makeup of the two groups is entirely different, their motivations appear quite different, and the problems they set out to solve and the circumstances in which they set out to solve them are different. The conspiratorial view of events was not dominant in legionary policy or propaganda; their low estimate of the integrity and patriotism of the nation's leaders was largely justified; the system, the parties, and the politicians they attacked were rotten; existing conditions did call for drastic remedies; the direct action on which they fell back reflected that which the Establishment used against all challengers; and the mystical imagery of persecution and martyrdom not only provided an intoxicant but was borne out by events.

Of course, much of the contrast may be ascribed to differences between haves and have-nots, between a movement of relatively prosperous people in a prosperous society and an angry, hungry one in an underdeveloped society. In the end, however, we come back to the fact that Romanian nationalists in general and the Legion in particular, far from being alienated like their Western counterparts, voiced popular aspirations and reflected (though they never solved) popular needs.

In Romania the language of politics differed so obviously from the reality, the pretense of freedom and democracy departed so blatantly from the truth, that an immense gap yawned between the constitutional means of securing power and the existing practice which effectively kept nonconformists out of range. The frustration of the idealistic, the young, and the ambitious was the harsher because few alternatives were offered to their ambitions and their energies. Economic stagnation and eventually depression set stringent limits to consolation prizes. Meanwhile, the incompetence and insuccess of ruling groups discredited the ruling order and its tenants far more than mere corruption ever did. The rebels despised the Establishment as much as they hated it. And as the Establishment was weakened by continued failure, even when it tried some of the rebels' recipes, the politically active public, swollen by recruits from the indifferent and apathetic masses, swung against it. The country was ripe for revolution. Ripe, but not ready as long as the army and police remained loyal to the King. Only foreign intervention could change that; and in 1940 it did.

That was when the Legion got its chance and also its comeuppance. It may be that Codreanu could have managed things differently; and there were those in the Legion's councils who wanted to keep out of power until men had been trained who were capable of shouldering the responsibilities of office. But Codreanu was dead and the more prudent temporizers went unheeded. The Legion in power was a miserable and bloody failure. A great capital of popularity was squandered in a few months. Performance never measured up to the ideals.

This may be because so many of the ideals had been negative and wrong-headed. Yet neither wickedness nor waste suffice to condemn a regime in practice, whatever the judgment of history may be. Other regimes, not least those of the French Revolution, have squandered effort and resources on scapegoats; other regimes have excommunicated racial and social groups and have survived. If the legionaries did not, this was owing first and foremost to the personal incapacity and muddle-headedness of their leaders. In a private letter to Codreanu, Ion Moța once criticized his "lack of attachment for certain formalities and accounts, which often brings great shortages of funds." This lack of attention to details and routines, against which Codreanu fought all his life, both in himself and in others, this lackadaisical *schlämperei* so characteristic of Romania, contributed to his followers' doom.

More important still for political men was the legionaries' blurred vision of reality, their lack of perspective, their way of treading in everyday life as if it were myth. The qualities that gave them some of the strength to act like heroes and martyrs also prevented them from acting in the long run like sensible men. The Legion had called not for programs, but men. In power, when positive action was needed, it had neither the program nor the men capable of devising one. Whether in office or out, Aléxandre Dumas *père* wrote their scenarios; and, although the code of a samurai or a musketeer may serve a street-fighter well, it does not help much with government. In office, the radical extremist must become, if not more moderate, at least more constructive, or else get out. The legionaries chose the latter alternative, less out of principle than out of necessity. That was how they were. Had they been different, they would not have got there in the first place, done what they did, endured what they endured. But, once in power, with very few exceptions, they lacked the qualities needed to handle it usefully. They failed. And they lost.

SUGGESTED READING

Material for a thorough study of the Legionary movement is woefully scarce. Runs of Romanian newspapers and periodicals in western collections are few and incomplete. Authors who have approached the subject have usually done so as partisans or publicists. Legionaries who have taken refuge in the west have published or republished many accounts of their doings and works of doctrine and analysis, but the case against the Legion has never been presented in detail. The Antonescu regime has provided the fullest documentation in this sense, with *Asasinatele dela Jilava* (Bucharest: 1942) and *Pe Marginea Prăpastiei* (Bucharest: 1942), 2 vols., both naturally weighted against the legionaries but offering a mass of information on the period of the National Legionary State.

Good accounts of Romania between the wars, in which the Legion features prominently, may be found in HENRY ROBERTS, *Rumania: Political Problems of an Agrarian State* (New Haven: 1951), and HENRI PROST, *Destin de la Roumanie* (Paris: 1954), and there is a heavily biased history by a legionary priest, ȘTEFAN PALAGHIȚĂ, *Garda de Fier* (Buenos Aires: 1951). Books on Codreanu and his movement have been published in several languages: KLAUS CHARLE, *Die Eiserne Garde* (Berlin: 1939), TOMAS ESCOLAR, *Vida y doctrina de C. Z. Codreanu* (Barcelona: 1941), ALFONSO P. FINOTTI, *La Guardia di Ferro* (Florence: 1938), G. ROSSI DELL' ARNO, *C. Codreanu. Pensieri e massime di vita* (Rome: 1940), EMINARDO SALEO, *Mussolini e Codreanu* (Palermo: 1942), JÉROME and JEAN THARAUD, *L'Envoyé de l'Archange* (Paris: 1939), and LORENZO B. TUA, *La Guardia di Ferro* (Florence: 1938). In 1942, a doctoral dissertation at the University of Leipzig dealt with the movement's spell in power: KLAUS G. HEUTZEN, *Die Verfassung des rumänischen national-legionären Staates.*

Codreanu's memoirs, *Pentru Legionari* (Bucharest: 1936), of which German and Italian translations exist, his collected circulars and manifestos, *Circulări și Manifeste* (Omul Nou: 1951), the manuals he edited, *Cârticica Șefului de Cuib* (Bucharest: 1933) and *Îndreptarul Frățiilor de Cruce* (Bucharest: 1935), his prison notes, *Însemnări dela Jilava* (Omul Nou: 1951), and the account of his last trial, *Adevărul în Procesul lui Corneliu Z. Codreanu* (Bucharest: 1938), remain excellent evidence, along with the works of his closest collaborators—ION MOŢA, *Cranii de Lemn* (Sibiu: 1936), VASILE MARIN, *Crez de Generaţie* (Bucharest: 1937), VICTOR P. GĂRCINEANU, *Din Lumea Legionară* (Omul Nou: 1951), and ION BANEA, *Capitanul* (Bucharest: 1936).

The best documented aspect of the subject is that of legionary doctrine, which can be studied in two major series of publications: "Biblioteca Verde," published in Rome by Constantin Papanace, and "Omul Nou," published in Germany by friends of Horia Sima. Of Sima's own writings, the most interesting are *Mişcarea Legionară şi Democraţia* (Omul Nou: 1955), *Dos Movimientos Nacionales. Jose Antonio Primo de Rivera y Corneliu Zelea Codreanu* (Madrid: 1960), and *Cazul Iorga-Madgearu* (Madrid: 1961).

The works of N. Iorga are generally available, those of A. C. Cuza almost unobtainable in the west. In the absence of other accounts one can consult PAMFIL ŞEICARU, *Un Junimist Antisemit: A. C. Cuza* (Madrid: 1956). Şeicaru, who was, between the wars, the editor-publisher of a right-wing newspaper hostile to the Legion but who is now reconciled with it, has given us a history of interwar politics in his two-volume *Istoria Partidelor Naţional, Ţărănist, şi Naţional Ţărănist* (Madrid: 1963). The speeches of Armand Călinescu have been published in *Noul Regim* (Bucharest: 1939), those of Ion Antonescu in *Câtre Români* (Bucharest: 1941). On the Antonescu period and its preliminaries one may consult G. BARBUL, *Mémorial Antonescu* (Paris: 1950), A. L. EASTERMAN, *King Carol, Hitler and Lupescu* (London: 1942), ION GHEORGHE, *Rumäniens Weg zum Satellitenstaat* (Heidelberg: 1952), A. HILLGRUBER, *Hitler, König Carol und Marschall Antonescu* (Wiesbaden: 1954), H. LAEUEN, *Marschall Antonescu* (Essen: 1943), and, also, in a more general sense, MARTIN BROSZAT's useful monograph, *Das Dritte Reich und die Rumänische Judenpolitik* (Munich: 1958). Broszat and Hillgruber indicate in their notes the relevant German documents made public since the war.

Reference to the Legion may also be found in occasional articles by repentant survivors in the Romanian Communist periodical, *Glasul Patriei*. Runs of the legionary *Buna Vestire*, the Cuzist *Porunca Vremii*, and Şeicaru's *Curentul* may be found in the Austrian National Library in Vienna. The Biblioteca Universitaria Alessandrina in Rome holds files of Nae Ionescu's *Cuvântul* and of another periodical sympathetic to the Legion's cause, *Gândirea* (Thought). But any attempt at a fuller study must await the opening of Romanian collections.

Afterthoughts

HANS ROGGER

In view of one reader's comment that the authors of the preceding pages had dealt not so much with a distinct phenomenon called the Right as with varieties of conservatism, it seems appropriate once more to state what the editors had in mind when first planning the volume. "Without wishing to impose our views and preferences," we wrote to our contributors, "we have yet had to make certain assumptions in order to delimit the meaning of 'Right' for present purposes, and hope that these assumptions will be shared. They are that the Right is a phenomenon of fairly recent history (i.e., the last sixty to eighty years), that it is characteristically a postliberal (or postdemocratic) and postindustrial phenomenon, that as a reaction to the liberalization of political life it was more violent or radical than the conservative wish to preserve privilege or the status quo, and that it implied a readiness to conduct politics with some or all of the techniques and appeals introduced by the mass parties of democracy and the Left, as well as some novel ones." We meant, in other words, to speak about a novel phenomenon in European thought and politics which, though having many features in common with other occupants of the right end of the political spectrum, wished to be and was, in fact, distinct from them in important ways. Our purpose was to trace the emergence of this New Right and to describe how it came to distinguish itself from conservatism, traditional authoritarianism, and reaction.

The contributors accepted our definition, though not necessarily our terminology, and continued to designate as belonging to the Right men and movements that our more rigid classification would have excluded as conservative or reactionary. In practice, however, the distinction was maintained and the new phenomenon characterized as radical, violent, intransigent, extremist, modern, or totalitarian—the antithesis, in short, of classical conservatism which was most often described as temperate, compromising, and opportunistic, dedicated to inherited institutions and values, to privilege (or at the least to social and economic stability), and fearful of mass politics and mass passions.

Yet some of the contributors (including the editors themselves) did not limit themselves to a discussion of the Right so defined. They evidently felt constrained to go back to earlier forms of opposition to political and economic liberalization, social and economic reform. They were led to do so, presumably, because as historians they saw no other way of illustrating the differences and divergences between the old and the new Right. But in the process they also demonstrated, perhaps unwittingly, a certain continuity of themes and attitudes between the old and the new, such as the Right itself was wont to assume between liberals and socialists in the opposite camp. On such matters as nationality and "race," the relations between leaders and led, the burdens and the benefits of wealth or power, the new Right spoke often in tones that were reminiscent of a preindustrial, predemocratic, traditionalist vocabulary and outlook.

Does this then suggest a continuity of essence, an intrinsic sameness; does it mean that the Right remained rooted in conservative soil and retained the marks of its provenance? Yes, but only partially and to a different degree in different settings. Nowhere does the Right divest itself fully of traditionalist trappings and appeals; everywhere its radicalism, its willingness to strike out in new directions, is roughly proportionate to the degree to which the environment in which it has to operate had been radicalized or traumatized by startling changes and severe strains in the social, political, and economic order.

At the extremities of the continent, though for profoundly different reasons, England and czarist Russia proved to be the least favorable climates for the growth of right-wing radicalism, just as both had remained least touched by the revolutionary waves of 1848—in the one instance, because established institutions (parliament, the party system, the class structure) had proved themselves resilient in absorbing the shocks of modernity and change, and had a longer time in which to do so than was granted any other country; in the other because absolutism rigidly resisted political modernization and was, until almost the very end, successful in retaining a monopoly of political activity, making an independent movement of the Right impossible and seemingly unnecessary.

It was in those countries where the tensions created by industrialization, by social protest, by the novelty of political combat, or by defeat in war had not yet been mastered, practically or psychologically, that the Right found its characteristic expression. Where the maturity of England and the backwardness of Russia were lacking, where the old and the new, parliamentary politics and a paternalistic social structure, a modern industry and a feudal or near-feudal agriculture, lived uneasily side by side, there the Right arose to furnish answers to problems that new institutions and processes were not yet, and old ones no longer, able to handle effectively. There, also, the Right was most rightist, as conservatism and reaction had either given way before the onslaught of liberalism and socialism or had compromised and, as a result, undermined belief in their own validity and viability. When old loyalties were gone and new ones did not yet command general assent, when the bonds of traditional authority and obedience had been dissolved and new ones of agreement and consent not yet been forged, then the Right could be most universal in its appeal, claiming to be a superior legatee of the heritage of the past (of national greatness, unity, discipline, order and pride) without being its prisoner.

Reds *and* Reaction, in the words of the Nazi anthem, were the enemies, and although Hitler might be pictured a thousand times over with Frederick the Great and Bismarck as the third member of an authoritarian, national trinity, his movement was even more emphatic in stressing its novelty. It was, its very name proclaimed, both national and socialist; it believed in the leadership principle (whose tenets are often strikingly similar to the ideal of Germanic kingship) yet called itself a workers' party; if it damned Weimar and the parliamentary republic, it did not, however, suggest a return to a form of political life from which the masses would be excluded. Fascism, Mosley said in England, is modern, it is in accord with the needs of the time, a claim Russian rightists could not, dared not, make because for them the incubus of the past (the autocratic monarch, an illiberal political system, the unen-franchised and discontented mass and a minority clinging to their privileges) had not yet been removed by revolution or reform. And although, where this has been the case, the Right will usually come to some kind of accommodation with interests and insti-tutions it once denounced as backward and selfish (big business, industry, the churches, the monarchy), it never becomes simply their servant. True, the radicalism and populism of the Right, even when genuine, are rarely sustained into the period of power; its radicalism is more likely to be one of language, style, and conduct than of social and economic program; the instincts and motivations of its followers are often conservative, born of anxiety and fear of change. All this may make it appear that a radical Right is a contradiction in terms, that the Right does, after all, have more in common with conservatives than with leftists, and that it is an extension of conservatism.

It can easily be conceded that, in spite of certain similarities (particularly in forms of political control and organization), the extreme Right almost never approaches its counterparts of the ex-treme Left in social and economic radicalism. In that respect, *les extrêmes se touchent* is a striking but not very accurate aphorism. The extremes resemble each other in their very extremism but only if one is prepared to overlook questions of content. Yet its remote-ness from the Left does not automatically move the Right closer to conservatism. Precisely because of its eclectic blending of diverse strains, the Right represented something new and unprecedented on the European political scene. Where it was most deeply divided from the Left over economic and social issues it also differed most radically from classical conservatism in political style and practice, and to a point where differences in degree turned into differences in kind. The authoritarianisms of Fascism or Nazism were not simply heightened forms of an older authoritarianism. In their ruthlessness, their exaltation of limitless power, their criminality, their willingness to employ the basest instincts of men on a vast scale, their intrusions into every sphere of public and private life, the extremists of the Right were truly radical and equally far removed from conservatives, liberals, and socialists. Abjuring the restrictions of conventional morality as well as the restrictions of doctrine (even its own) in the name of an affirmation of life, vitality, and action, the extreme Right recognized few loyalties, principles, or obligations that would interfere with its dynamic march to a vaguely defined or unspecified goal.

Whatever features rightist movements and regimes may have in common, it becomes clear, however, from a reading of these essays that differences on the Right are even more pronounced than those on the Left, and it is this that makes it so difficult to generalize about the Right, to arrive at universally valid definitions. But the difficulty of constructing an "ideal" or typical Right also reveals something of the character of what we have been trying to describe. Thus, nationalism apart, and nationalism is no monopoly of any camp, the Right lacks the shared doctrinal commitment of liberalism or socialism. It avoids ideological formulations and is, in almost all instances, intellectually inferior to its opponents, making a virtue of necessity. It has no consistent world view, which is both an element of strength and a source of weakness. The gain comes in the form of great tactical flexibility, the ability to attract support from all points of the political compass; the disadvantages are all too visible in the many power struggles, personal disagreements, and great internal strife that so often rob the Right of disciplined effectiveness even when it is greater numerically than its enemies. The Bolshevik belief that, to be unified and effective, a revolutionary movement had to have and be guided by a revolutionary doctrine, had no counterpart on the Right where, as a result, the single and literal-minded dedication to a complex and elaborate view of history and society was also lacking. With very few exceptions, Maurras being perhaps the most important, there were no Lenins or Trotskys on the Right, few Jaurès or Bebels, and certainly no Marx or Engels. Instead of philosophical profundity or even mere studiousness, in place of revolutionary puritanism and self-denial, there was an inordinate amount of vanity, selfishness, display, and greed, and the symbolic simplicity of Hitler's soldier's tunic was more than made up for by the brilliance and variety of Goering's uniforms and the private and public antics of Mussolini and his hierarchs. To pass in review, before the mind's eye, most of the rightist leaders who have figured in these pages is to become aware of how little nobility and grandeur of mind or character there was among them, how much banality and pettiness (even in the monumental evil that some achieved together with power). These flaws of character, though not sufficient explanation, also help to account for the Right's many failures and the brevity of its successes.

The diversity of the rightist phenomenon is also magnified by the militant nationalism which is its ubiquitous component and accompaniment. Each rightist movement proclaimed the nation, its character, history, and future to be the highest good and, in stressing the uniqueness of the national experience, affirmed its own. The mechanisms of each movement may have been the same, the purposes similar, but the differences of content and emphasis were significant. One does not need to accept the notion of a biologically fixed national character to recognize that the German Right, for example, by virtue of its Germanness (viewed as the reflection of historical experience and the expression of historical aspirations), was different in style and goal from the Maurrassian or Italian Right, and that there could be no true and lasting harmony between them. If Mussolini, on the other hand, failed to convert his Italians into lions, the failure was in large measure attributable to the very qualities of the Italian character—a wise skepticism born of the knowledge of many rules—which he deluded himself into seeing as imperial boldness. That racism and anti-Semitism were not universal companions of right-wing nationalism is further testimony to the national specificity of the Right.

Although nationalism ("national socialism") at times made possible the building of bridges across gulfs of class and party and the creation of an image of a harmonious national community, it also deprived the Right of an international dimension. Proletarian internationalism may be an utter impossibility, a generous dream, or a shameless deception, but the summons to the workers of the world to unite has had a real emotional impact and a certain political effectiveness. Even as a slogan, "Nationalists of all countries unite" is nonsensical, and Hitler's racism, the vision of a new Europe governed by an international elite of blood and race, must be viewed as an attempt to overcome the limitations of nationalism and find an equivalent for international working class solidarity. It failed, and there was not a genuine internationalism of the Right (though Professor Nolte sees evidence of it in Spain). Mussolini furnished a model for many rightists, but substantial support to only a few (the Austrian Heimwehr leaders, Degrelle), and assistance from the Nazis was most often the prelude to German infiltration and conquest, leading even Belgian, Hungarian, and Romanian rightists to view German Nazis as national enemies rather than as ideological allies.

The Right, as a political movement, also lacks the relative uniformity of a common class basis, contributing further to the difficulties of generalization. Almost everywhere the Right proclaims its intention of being above classes and parties, of representing not a part but all of a nation. It disavows the narrowness of particular and sectional interests, though it may energize and exploit their grievances, and claims to speak in the name of larger and more generous ideals—state, nation, or race. And although the invocation of a larger community than that of material or class interests may be no more than the rhetoric of political propaganda, it is also a recognition of the realities of European politics. The novelty of the Right consists precisely in this, that it sees the futility of trying to fit into a sociopolitical structure in which the upper, middle, and working classes had habitually and traditionally given their loyalties to conservative, liberal, and socialist parties. Their nearly total domination of the political arena had been challenged, but not conclusively, by only confessional, regional, and agrarian parties. That form of challenge, from a limited basis, was not open to the Right, and the new rightist groupings therefore called themselves by names intended to stress their comprehensive and inclusive character, avoiding the very designation of party or explaining that they were something other than conventional parties. They were and called themselves movements, leagues, or unions of patriots and nationalists of all classes and if, like the court preacher Stoecker in Germany, they included the workers in their title and appeals, this was soon changed because the proletariat failed to turn its back on the trades unions and parties that had fought for the economic and political rights of the working class.

The strong attachments formed by custom, interest, and emotion that prevailed for so long in the political life of Europe were not, however, the only reasons for the Right's inability to become firmly identified with a clearly defined segment of the social structure, or for its failure even to make the attempt. The realization that competing with existing parties on their own terms presented few opportunities was combined in some instances with a genuine wish not to exacerbate social conflict; and to this was added the awareness that economic interest or class were no longer sure guides to political behavior or preferences. The complexities of modern society had, after all, made old categories of social classification inadequate in the more advanced countries, with the result that increasing numbers of men were inaccessible to appeals addressed to classes with which they did not clearly identify. World War I, with the dislocations it brought, intensified this process where it had already begun and extended it to countries so far untouched by it, with the result that political allegiances more and more cut across class lines. Clerical workers and employees, hard-pressed artisans and shopkeepers, officers, bureaucrats and intellectuals (ex, present, and would-be), pensioners and impoverished aristocrats, debt-ridden peasants and disgruntled domestic servants, as well as manual workers, could all be found, at one or another time or place and in differing proportions, to be members of, or voters for, the Right.

This is not to say that the class analysis of political behavior is either impossible or without value; Professor S. M. Lipset has demonstrated the opposite in his investigations of " 'Fascism'—Left, Right and Center" (*Political Man,* New York, 1960 and 1963). But the correlations between class and politics, in the movements described by our contributors, were not uniform, stable, or clear. It is significant that the rightist leaders explicitly disavowed identification with a given class and if, according to Lipset, one variant of the Right, fascism, is a movement of the once-liberal propertied middle classes, it is largely because the middle class had become so diverse, numerous, and inclusive a category as to have lost the clearly discernible features by which it could be recognized for most of the nineteenth century. Middle-class votes helped fascist parties into power; they did not make them middle-class parties in any conventional sense of the term. A great deal of work certainly remains to be done by historians and sociologists (as well as political scientists and psychologists) in examining the social bases of the political movements of the radical Right. Only in that way can their specific and characteristic features be fixed.

It seems clear, in any event, that the new Right did not put forth class parties as Europe had come to know them in the nineteenth century, notwithstanding the fact, pointed out by a number of our authors, that it may have found a wider echo in one social stratum than another, usually where individuals were cut loose from their class moorings or threatened in their class identity, most often in the middle class. The very problem of class in politics was stated by the Right in terms that represent a groping for new formulas to express the new and shifting complexities of social structure as well as the fact that in an age of intense international competition the state could ill afford to alienate any substantial portion of its subjects. Among the liberal and democratic parties this realization led, during and after World War II, to the concept of the welfare state. Half a century earlier, the Italian Nationalists had indicted the "ruling clique" (not "class") of the kingdom for its ineptness and greed. The Nationalist remedy was not class war, but economic and political competition with other nations. For this, and for the greater well-being of all Italians, class solidarity was a necessary prerequisite, and the means for achieving it was the formula of Italy as a nation of proletarians, or a proletarian nation, in conflict with the plutocracies for her rightful place in the world.

Rightists in Italy as elsewhere thus tried to transcend, or to submerge, the problem of class by translating it to the international sphere; yet this was more than mere evasion. It was an attempt to utilize the divisive energies of social conflict for what were believed to be constructive national purposes. If often the call for unity and solidarity was specious, designed to block the legitimate aspirations of workers or peasants, the Right's vague corporatism, its concern with national welfare, its insistence on justice for the poor and attacks on the forces of money, were part of the search for a way to reconcile the classes and concentrate national energies. When Austrian, German, or Hungarian National Socialists organized themselves into "workers'" parties, they did so not to narrow but to broaden the basis of their movements; they were not giving expression to a restricted view of politics or economics or embracing conventional, doctrinaire definitions of the working class. They were passing moral judgment, not stating economic or sociological doctrine, and were prepared to welcome as a worker anyone who contributed productively to the national welfare as defined by them and ready to accept their definition. "Workers of all classes, unite!" was the slogan of the Belgian Rexists, and while they were competing in the political arena, rightists wished to appear as, and to be, all-class parties. If, once in power, Italian Fascists and German National Socialists relied extensively on the police power of the state to "reconcile" the classes, and in the process favored management more often than workers, they were guided by an interest in continued and efficient productivity rather than by any love for capitalism as such.

The Right's failure to identify itself decisively and intimately with a given class had consequences which were as important as the lack of a binding doctrine. It made a broad electoral appeal both possible and necessary in order to capitalize on the grievances to be found in all segments of society. But though protean appeals to diverse audiences and their varied resentments might be effective in garnering votes, they were not similarly successful in creating such solid, cohesive, stable, and disciplined movements (or even electorates) as socialists and Communists were capable of putting into the field with their organized strength coming mainly from one class. This helps to account for the impermanence of so many rightist groupings, for their marginal and volatile character, for their internal differences and divisions, for the breakup of coalitions when the conditions which had brought them into being had disappeared. Nor, under these circumstances, could the Right afford to be and to remain a conspiratorial sect. It had to operate publicly and openly in order to attract votes and adherents from all sectors of society in that very political arena whose rules and customs it abhorred and condemned. Here is the source of that often observed incongruity of rightists seeking election to the very parliamentary assemblies they condemned as ineffectual talking shops, and then serving in them.

The absence of the cohesive factor of class or interest, added to the absence of doctrine, also placed extraordinary burdens on leadership, making demands of character and ability which few could meet. For want of personal magnetism or determination, ruthlessness or flexibility, a rightist movement might be condemned to impotence, ridicule, or disintegration much more readily than organizations held together by the cement of a commonly perceived interest. The rigor or the elaborateness of formal structure could never substitute for the gifted leader who was the dramatic embodiment of deep-seated resentments and imperfectly articulated aspirations.

Yet the wide range of social and political background, of personality and ability among successful as well as unsuccessful leaders of the Right, presents the historian with still another baffling problem. What combination of talents and achievements, gifts and acquisitions, tricks and techniques, would serve to convert a mere human being into an adored leader and commander of thousands or millions? Patient, painstaking effort on behalf of cause or organization played little or no role, nor did the mastery of doctrine, while a smattering of poorly digested political philosophy helped to identify the new movements as vehicles of history rather than of avarice or ambition. A radical or liberal past, though common, was far from universal and did not necessarily confer the advantage of political experience or the common touch. Hitler, the drifter, who hated all parties and parliaments, had been inspired by Lueger's German Workers in his lonely Viennese youth, but had never joined them; and Szalasi, the son of a noncommissioned officer in the Austro-Hungarian army, had acquired his political education while serving as an officer of the General Staff, from which he resigned, to form, within a year, his party of the National Will. Like Mosley, Déat, Doriot, De Man, and others, Mussolini had been a radical of the Left, an intransigent socialist repelled by the moderation and conservatism of his comrades, yet he was far less radical, far less revolutionary in remaking Italy than was Hitler in Germany. The erstwhile socialist militant proved to be more of an opportunist and pragmatist than the Germanic dreamer or the practicing Catholic Degrelle.

Nor does social origin furnish a reliable criterion for success or failure in building a movement and leading it to victory, except in the negative sense that too visible or pronounced traces of class (or region) would be a hindrance in the wooing of popular favor. What appears to be essential is the dimming of the clear outlines of personal history, the creation of a new heroic personality out of the travail of war, revolution, and social dissolution. In the hero journey of many a rightist, the fires of war burned away old restraints and prejudices and revealed the road to be followed. Hitler's loss of his eyesight at the front, his recovery of it in a military hospital, his rebirth to a new life and vocation ("I then decided to enter politics"), was merely the most dramatic example of war as the central experience for many, leaders as well as followers. Finnish Jägers, German shock troops and Free Corps men, Italian arditi, French, Hungarian, Austrian, and Belgian veterans, began to think of themselves as the generation of the war fronts, as having been reborn in the "bath of steel" where they had recovered their faith in the vitality of the national community and discovered the camaraderie of battle-hardened youths. The old men, meanwhile, who had not shared in this experience, were said by them to be squabbling over profits and wondering how to restore a world irretrievably lost. Youth was the indispensable quality of the rightist leader, for it promised vitality and dynamism and created the expectation of a brighter tomorrow which was bound to be an improvement over the dreary present. It is surely no accident that in 1933, when most of the directors of Europe's political destinies were in their sixties or older, the men who were prominent on the Right ranged in age from twenty-four (Degrelle) to forty-four (Hitler and Mussolini). Even before World War I the first manifestations of the new Right appeared among students (the Austrian Burschenschaften), "Young" Tories who rebelled against their stodgy elders, and Italian Nationalists too young to have participated in the stirring drama of unification.

Although it would be going too far to see the appeal of the Right primarily in its stress on youth—electoral statistics do not bear out such an assumption—the claims of youth versus age, vitality versus exhaustion, freshness versus corruption made on behalf of the Right were decisive in building the hard core of loyalty from which the leader could be launched into a larger prominence.

The trouble with the attractions of youth is, of course, their impermanence, and when the balance sheet is drawn up of the Right's achievements and failures, it is the latter that predominate. The affirmations of youthful boldness, of action for action's sake, the displays of strenuous energy, of drive and violence, do not conceal what is the fatal flaw of even those rightist parties and leaders who attained power and set up regimes planned to last millennia: an ultimate pessimism, a despair of the modern world with neither patience nor confidence enough to try and set it aright or to adjust to it. There are many concrete and specific reasons for the defeats and failures of the Right: the lack of organizational unity; the excessive dependence on one man; the suppleness of old parties and politicians; the inadequate or intermittent support from any organized group or class; the vagueness of program or doctrine; a failure of nerve or an excess of brute force which at last solidified the opposition. In the final reckoning, however, and in spite of some shrewd appreciations of the needs of the contemporary world, the Right represents not the wave of the future but a nihilistic hostility to modernity, a fear of the unfamiliar, and an infantile yearning for protection (through nation, race, boundless power, or aimless activism) against dark and only dimly comprehended forces that lurk and threaten on all sides.

In this very important respect, the radical Left and the radical Right, however great and striking the similarities between them, are profoundly different. For all its sweeping endorsement of the future and emphatic renunciation of feudal past and capitalist present, the Right had neither understanding nor sympathy for a world on which industrialism and urbanism were irrevocably placing a rationalist, egalitarian, and internationalist stamp. At its very origins and through its Marxist heritage the Left had affirmed that world, and, while wishing to soften its impact and equalize its benefits, had recognized its inevitability and predicted its worldwide victory. It is hard to conceive how the Right would have survived into the second half of the twentieth century and met the challenges posed by the continuation and intensification of processes that preceded and survived it. How, for example, would it have dealt with the emergence of new peoples, states, and continents? The Right had no understanding of the larger world beyond Europe's borders and could view its relations to it only in terms of dominance and submission. In fact, where Right regimes would have brought about and maintained a genuine national socialism they could have done so only by the exploitation of alien peoples and races from which, in all other ways, they would be rigidly isolated. And such a relationship would have been reactionary or retrograde in the most fundamental sense of the word, a reversion to practices and values that civilized communities cannot tolerate, and that would be, therefore, destructive and anarchic. It is these tendencies of the Right—particularly the cult of action and of force (rather than its rational employment for limited goals) and the elitism which, even if it was collective, was restrictive, since it derived from nonrational criteria (such as blood or birth) rather than from talent or ability—which seem to justify its characterization as ultimately reactionary and pessimistic. Though such a characterization does not apply with equal force to all rightist movements and regimes, they all bore within themselves the seed of their own destruction, which was a sickness unto death, not merely of liberalism, their greatest enemy, but of the world that liberalism had helped to bring about and to shape. Is it too much to say that the whole history of the new or radical Right is one of failure, and that it failed most where it succeeded best?

The preceding essays have supplied only some of the materials for a better understanding of the phenomenon of the Right. If they have yielded the profile of our title, they will have gone a long way in fulfilling our hopes for this volume. But we also realize that, more than a profile, a full-scale portrait is still needed.

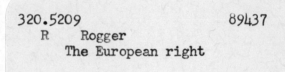